CW01019621

alan colquhoun

collected essays in architectural criticism

introduction by
kenneth frampton

black dog
publishing

london uk

Contents

Introduction

Kenneth Frampton

Alan Colquhoun first emerged as a critic of stature in 1960 with his review of Reyner Banham's *Theory and Design in the First Machine Age*; an occasion that was auspicious on two counts: first because of Banham's unprecedented historiographic approach which cited the protagonists of the time in order to reveal how their intentions had a direct bearing on the works under consideration and second for Colquhoun's critical posture which subjected architectural culture, be it written or built, to a more rigorous examination than that to which it had hitherto been exposed. While *Theory and Design in the First Machine Age* raised the standard of historiography in the field, subverting, as it did, both the functionalist rhetoric of the Modern Movement and the neo-Hegelian exegesis with which it had been proselytised, Colquhoun challenged Banham's position of deprecating the finest achievements of the pre-war avant-garde while asserting Buckminster Fuller as the ultimate prophet of a techno-scientific approach to the culture of building. As Colquhoun wrote towards the end of his critique, "It is a curious fact that, having admitted that certain buildings are masterpieces, Dr Banham should reject those mystiques without which they could not have come into existence. One wonders by what criterion he judges a masterpiece and by what casuistry he would be able to demonstrate that a building was simultaneously a masterpiece and a failure."

Colquhoun's writings falls into three distinct periods, reflecting not only the development of his sensibility but also changes in the focus of the contemporary debate. With the exception of his seminal "Typology and Design Method" of 1967 Colquhoun's texts of the 60s and the early 70s were largely devoted to a re-evaluation of Le Corbusier. In the 70s, however, beginning with his penetrating essay, "The Superblock", 1971, he turned his attention to the failure of contemporary building form to generate coherent urban space. This shift, accompanied by his short but sympathetic appraisal of Alvar Aalto, led to an initial philosophical overview, entitled, "Rules, Realism, and History". In the third and last phase of his writing, thematically overlapping with the second, Colquhoun turned his attention to semiological issues and more generally to typology and the impact of semantics on the generation and interpretation of architectural form. The common strand in all this was the way in which Colquhoun consistently opposed the various forms of reductivism which stemmed not only from Banham's technocratic proclivities but also from the cybernetic behaviorism of Christopher Alexander, and the method-idolatry of the HfG, Ulm. Following the art historian EH Gombrich, by whom he was profoundly influenced, Colquhoun was initially more of a neo-Hegelian than the influential, scientifically empirical Karl Popper, as is evident from his attempts to salvage Hegel's synchronic view of history and culture while rejecting his metaphysical teleology.

As touched by British moral empiricism as Banham, and as influenced by Popperian skepticism as Rowe, Colquhoun for his part gravitated towards the categorical distinctions favoured by French Structuralism, in particular the distinction between synchronic and diachronic conceptions of both history and culture. Colquhoun's capacity to reveal the utopian socio-cultural rationalisations that frequently underlay the work of the rising generation of the early 70s, came to the fore with his critical appraisals treating two of the most seminal works of that era; Centre Pompidou and the Centraal Beheer. This is at once evident from his 1976 essay on the Centre Pompidou, Paris, where he digresses on the different meanings accorded to the word "culture" by different nations at various moments in their history. Where the English favoured sociological empiricism as a way of rationalising the egalitarian welfare state of the post-war world century, the French embraced the idea of culture as part of a decisive effort to liberalise their state institutions. Of this shift as manifest in the populist cultural policy of the Centre Pompidou, Colquhoun wrote:

> What is new in the Gaullist position is that the respect usual among conservatives for the traditional values of the 'organic' society has been replaced by an enthusiasm for the 'modern' and the avant-garde. This enthusiasm compounds the contradictions inherent in their attitude since avant-gardism itself suffered from similar contradictions. On the one hand, it wished to abolish the academic (elitist) culture in the name of free creation (the artistic equivalent of pure liberalism). On the other, it proposed a severe functionalism and a pure formalism which was unacceptable to the 'average man' because it excluded all those conventions and habits of feeling to which he is attached (and to which the commercialism of the liberal state attaches him more and more firmly).

While Colquhoun's critique of a technocratic modernity came into its own with his essay on the Centre Pompidou he had already addressed himself to the elusive ideal of flexible space some two years before, when writing a sympathetic evaluation of Herman Hertzberger's Centraal Beheer which had then just been completed at Apeldoorn in The Netherlands. It is typical of Colquhoun's discrimination that subtly perceptive distinctions are made in his respective evaluations of these works. What is at stake for him in both instances is the attitude adopted by both architect and client toward the spontaneous appropriation of open-ended, orthogonal volumes and the then currently accepted wisdom that a new organic culture could be brought into being by contemporary social forces realising themselves in undesignated space. In the Centre Pompidou we encounter the belief on the part of both the architect and the client that the museum/machine is a liberative instrument in itself; whereas in the Centraal Beheer we are confronted with the building as a labyrinth which will acquire its intimate and dynamic significance through the spontaneous appropriation of its interstitial spaces. Thus we are brought to see how the stratagem of open-endedness is handled in a distinctly different way in each building and Colquhoun comments on the way in which each responds to a totally different socio-cultural preconception. In the case of the Centre Pompidou we find him writing that:

> ... this principle of flexibility seems to have led to an overschematic solution which does not take into account the size of the building. It seems to have been conceived on a much smaller scale, with the result that both its spaces and its elements appear to belong to an order of magnitude quite different from that originally imagined.... The introduction of a intermediary group of 'programmers' between the architect and the user makes it an open question of whether a 'flexible space' is any more flexible in reality than spaces of a more conventional type. One sense in which it is obvious that a new tyranny has merely been substituted for an old is that the 'furniture' of the spaces has to be 'designed'.... Otherwise the space would lose all its visual coherence. We therefore arrive at the apparently paradoxical situation where as a result of making a building more 'democratic', and more sensitive to 'feedback', we impose on it an even greater inflexibility and turn it into a *Gesamtkunstwerk* of bureaucracy, infinitely more unpleasant that the *Gesamtkunstwerk* of the artist which Adolf Loos opposed which such vehemence.

This common strategy of adapting a technologically inflected form to achieve a spatially liberative result was formulated in Apeldoorn in an entirely different manner and generated from a totally different set of social values. As Colquhoun's remarks of the Centraal Beheer:

> Walking through the interconnected spaces of this building, enjoying the *enfilade* of diagonal views, sensing areas of relative quiet and relative movement, or looking into voids flooded with daylight from above, one can believe it is indeed 'a place where everyone would feel at home'. This feeling seems to have been created by increasing the sense of total community while at the same time suggesting islands of semi-privacy with which individuals and groups can identify.... The fundamental achievement of this building is that it puts into practice on a large scale a certain principle of publicly shared working space... the principle that it is equally important to provide for an awareness of the whole building (in contrast to a building that is subdivided into self-contained office rooms) and for a sense of identity on a small scale (in contrast to the *Bürolandschaft* type of office plan).

What is equally problematic about both buildings for Colquhoun is that neither responds adequately to the urban context in which it is situated. His main reservation about the former is that it is a free-standing, megastructure, brutally isolated within the Parisian city fabric. He holds a similar view with regard to the Centraal Beheer in that its castellated mass contributes nothing to the potential coherence of the urban fabric surrounding its pyramidal form. Here, as in Moshe Safdie's Habitat realised, in Montreal, in 1967, one is confronted with a situation in which an interstitial labyrinthic assembly fails to yield a corporeal form capable of shaping the contingent space by which it is surrounded.

This lack of civic presence corresponds to the thesis advanced in Colquhoun's "The Superblock" essay in which he emphasised how neither the singular, free-standing modern office building nor an aggregation of dwelling units into a continuous block, as in Ralph Erskine's Byker Wall, Newcastle upon Tyne, of 1970, are able to generate urban fabric through establishing the counterform of the street. As he put it:

> The superblock and with it the concepts of the 'designed whole', is a fact of the modern capitalist state. It has evolved from the representational building and has gradually superseded the system according to which small plots were designed within a metonymic set. It is not simply a new type to be added to the repertoire of the city but a type of types, whose presence is rapidly destroying the traditional city.

In "Historicism and the Limits of Semiology", 1972, Colquhoun begins to trace the evolution of his own evaluative principles, that is to say the development of the operative method which he will employ as a critical fulcrum in all his subsequent writing. Herein he endeavours to establish the essential difference between linguistic and aesthetic discourses, arguing that where linguistic systems are open, conventional, and "natural", aesthetic signs are closed, "artificial" and symbolically motivated and that where language is synchronically structured by combinatorial rules and only gradually transformed by happenstance, aesthetic systems are diachronically determined by historical and ideological forces lying outside the field of architecture. Elsewhere, in a later essay, Colquhoun goes on to argue that aesthetic rules are normative inasmuch as they reflect the attitudes, values and ideology of a particular society.

It is one of the paradoxes of nineteenth century eclecticism that prior to its dismissal as a kitsch historicism by modernist historians like Nikolaus Pevsner, the battle of styles was regarded by post-Hegelian intellectuals, such as Gottfried

Semper, as a cultural legacy in transformation. Historical style was viewed by nineteenth century eclectics as a synchronic repertoire of partially extinct metaphors, available for appropriation in much the same way as the Renaissance had appropriated antique types and elements for its own ends. The historicist elements embodied in this repertoire were just as much an aesthetic code as they were the constituents of an eclectic typology. As Colquhoun suggests this eclecticism eventually came to be discredited, partly because the uprooted urban populace was unable to situate itself within the framework of the bourgeois city, and partly because the historical styles were incapable of accommodating the new technological reality. In anticipation of this impasse the Enlightenment adopted a number of evasive strategies. In the first instance it attempted to adduce a universal lexicon of sensational form (Burke, Boullée); in the second it speculated with the essential arbitrariness of the sign as in the work of CN Ledoux. Finally, at the end of the last century, it sought to reconstruct architectural culture on the basis of organic form. This involved having recourse to the psycho-physiological empathetic theories of Lipps and Worringer. It was just this psycho-socialist ethos that engendered Henri Van der Velde's *Jugendstil* "literature without an alphabet". This also made itself manifest in the elaborate arabesques of his fellow Belgium architect and socialist Victor Horta. Working exclusively in iron and steel, after the French neo-Gothicist Eugene Viollet-le-Duc, Horta sought through the exuberance of his talent to accommodate and represent the new technology of the *fin de siècle*. As Colquhoun argues, Modern architecture had sufficient vestigial meaning to assert itself, first as a universal culture and then as a radically elite aesthetic. At the same time, it lacked popular support because of its limited capacity to function as a representational art. Its expressive scope was always compromised by the necessity of having to solve new building tasks, as efficiently as possible, within the technical capacity of the epoch.

The unexpected neo-rationalist postmodern return to classical typologies, coming to the fore in the mid-70s, had the seeming virtue of not only recovering the representational capacity of architecture but also of hypothetically establishing a normative aesthetic code. However the flaw, as Colquhoun cautions us, lay in the fundamental atrophy that arose from its polemical emphasis on preindustrial building. This neo-classical dead end necessarily entailed the projection of architectural phantoms as we find in the retro-guard visions of Aldo Rossi and Leon Krier.

In "Historicism and the Limits of Semiology" Colquhoun insists that semiology in itself cannot be regarded as a generative method, first because no system of logic can contain its own explanations (Gödel), and second, because structural linguistics is a descriptive method. It is concerned with the formal structures underlying language, not with meaning and value. Of this last Colquhoun argues that the architect, like the poet cannot escape the modern impulse to reconstruct an expressive language on the basis of an aesthetic range that society inherits from the past. In this regard, Roland Barthes' concept of a *répétition differente* appears as an inescapable destiny, presaging the future prospect of a culture *bricolée*. But, as Colquhoun reminds us, if this is so, how can such forms be regarded as normative?

The author pursues this question further in his essay "Form and Figure", 1978, wherein he argues that while form may be said to possess some of the attributes of "natural" meaning attributed to language, figure is to be seen as deriving its significance from culture. By introducing the rhetorical category of the figure, the distinctions made in the earlier essays between linguistic and aesthetic discourse become paradoxically compounded, for traditional architectural figures such as the Vitruvian order or the Gothic vault are exactly those elements which were once symbolically motivated and culturally embedded and mutually recognisable as such by society. On the other hand, the modern triumph of form over figure—that is to say the rise of universal geometry as the abstract underpining of architectural order, as in Le Corbusier's Purism, produced a formal structure which was open and recombinable. As Colquhoun puts it:

> While the notion of figure assumes that architecture is a language with a limited set of elements which already exist in their historical specificity, that of form holds that architectural forms can be reduced to an a-historical 'degree zero'; architecture as a historical phenomenon is [thereafter] not determined by what has existed before but by emergent social and technological facts operating on a minimum number of constant physiological and psychological laws.

While acknowledging the degeneracy of modern architecture over the last 30 years—above all through spectacular commodification—Colquhoun develops the conceptual paradigm of form and figure in order to establish a critical *parti pris* from which to assess the relative value of two reformist drives that came to the fore in the second half of the twentieth century; the neo-realist school of Charles Moore and Robert Venturi and the neo-rationalist school having its origin in the radically subversive work of Aldo Rossi. Where the first exploited the Anglo-Saxon culturally empirical tradition as a means for positing architectural signs as though they were fragments of some generally received semiotic system open to inflection by personal taste and private circumstance, the second, inspired by Marxist negative thought, sought to establish a figural metalanguage with which architecture could be brought to refer analogically to an implicit "space of public appearance". If the former cynically exploited the technological informality of the American balloon frame to play with figural fragments of a lost private vernacular, the latter, committed to the rationalism of the late Enlightenment, rejected the super-technology of the twentieth century in favour of such implicitly civic/tectonic figures as the pediment, the pierced window, the courtyard, and the arcade, as these had been determined and refined over time by the techno-ideological capacity of a pre-industrial epoch. As Colquhoun notes, "In the age of architectural rhetoric the [rational] demands of pragmatics were not in opposition to the demands of symbolic form; today they often are."

While remaining critical of the pragmatic limits of neo-rationalism in a technological age, Colquhoun was equally unable to condone the theatrical dissolution of the civic which suffused the work of the American neo-realists. Thus in "Sign and Substance", 1978, he remarks that Venturi and Rauch chose to interpret the Memorial Art Museum in Oberlin as a decorated shed, in order to avoid being contaminated by the aura of high art emanating from the classical form of the original building. Colquhoun reveals that the idea of the decorated shed was not restricted solely to commercial programmes but could be readily applied to all cases except those in which an intimate, vernacular symbolism was deemed to be appropriate.

In his essay "From *Bricolage* to Myth, or How to Put Humpty-Dumpty Together Again", Colquhoun perceptively locates the work of Michael Graves in an ideological no-man's-land, somewhere between the opportunistic empiricism of the American neo-realists and the critical refusal of contemporary European neo-rationalism. The elements of Graves' middle position were brought into being through a conscious return to a kind of Jeffersonian deism which opened itself to "a belief that architecture is a perennial symbolic language, whose origins lie in nature.... The frequent use in his [Graves'] writings of the words 'sacred' and 'profane' shows that he regards architecture as a secular religion which is in some sense revelatory." In this light Colquhoun contrasts the vicissitudes of contemporary neo-classicism with the rather hermetic trajectory of Graves' achievement:

> This system of representation is the exact opposite of the 'classical' process by which the ephemeral was translated into the durable, according to which durability as such was a value and materiality a symbol of the

transcendental. With the instrumentalisation of structure, the mythic is rechanneled and, in the Modern Movement, takes up its abode in instrumentality itself. In the architecture of Michael Graves, the alternative route is taken. The myth becomes pure myth, recognised as such, and the architectural sign floats in the dematerialised world of *Gestalt* and the dehistoricised world of memory and association.

As far as contemporary practice is concerned, Colquhoun's criticism has been at its most revealing in his interpretation of Le Corbusier, above all in those pieces in which he has been able to demonstrate the full complexity of the Corbusian semiotics which continues to display a level of intercultural resonance that is largely absent in a great deal of current architecture. It is as if Le Corbusier's exceptional talent was such that he alone, among the modern pioneers, was able to impart a multi-levelled/semantic layering to any given building. This was never more so than in the case of two buildings which form the subject matter of one of Colquhoun's finest early essays, entitled "Formal and Functional Interactions: A Study of Two Late Buildings by Le Corbusier". What is fascinating about this study is the way in which the projects in question, namely the French Embassy, Brasilia, 1964–1965 and the Venice Hospital, 1964–1965, both involve discriminating between *architecture* as public representation and *building* as cultural process while acknowledging that these two conditions are never entirely split apart even where the one takes, momentarily, precedence over the other. Colquhoun argues that where the Embassy refers directly to the concept of simple volumes intended to "release constant sensations" and to the related idea of the 'surface' which form the basis of Le Corbusier's classicising tendencies, the Hospital, derives from an active opposition between the two concerns which emerge as a dialectic from his investigations into patterns of growth, along with his long-standing concern for the irregular and spontaneous forms of folk architecture, and the necessary direct transformation of a dynamic organism into a resolved form. And yet, as Colquhoun argues "if we look more closely, we can see that the polarity of these attitudes is present in both projects and that each owes more to its complementary principle than first seems the case". By discriminating between the Dutch Structuralist school of thought, as represented by the work of Aldo van Eyck and Herman Hertzberger, and the superficially similar structural pattern adopted by Le Corbusier in his proposal for Venice, Colquhoun shows how the isomorphic repetitions that constitute van Eyck's Amsterdam orphanage of 1960 are quite different to the structural cluster system adopted by Le Corbusier:

> Here the basic unit is itself hierarchically arranged, with biological rather than mineral analogies, and capable of local modification without the destruction of its principle. It is obviously related to such matrix schemes as the Candilis, Josic and Woods project for the Free University in Berlin, 1963, ... The concept of the top floor plan is reminiscent of the Islamic *medresehs* of North Africa, where subcommunities of students' cells are grouped around small courtyards, forming satellite systems around a central court.

Colquhoun goes on to note how the additive pattern of the Venice Hospital is subject, like the *medreseh* typology, to an overarching harmonically proportional control, and it is this, above all else, that distinguishes Le Corbusier's labyrinthine approach from the repetitive modularity of Dutch Structuralism. While the Venice Hospital, like Centraal Beheer, would have been a building without a facade in the traditional sense, it would nonetheless have been integrated into the interstitial fabric of the city. It was at the same time a city in miniature in itself, one which reflected in the vaulted monitor roofs of its wards and interstitial corridors the Medieval street/canal/campo morphology of the Cannareggio district within which it would have been inserted. Le Corbusier's Venice Hospital was possessed of a poetic complexity which is invariably absent from the general run of twentieth century building. At once prehistorical lake dwelling, *medreseh*, labyrinth, phalanstery, hospital, necropolis, the work seems to have been endowed, as Colquhoun prophetically observed, with a set of readings "wholly at variance with a society whose values are based on the likely opinions of the 'average man', and it is possible that such a *machine à guérir* may not commend itself to the committee in whose hands the fate of the building resides".

This observation confronts the dilemma of modern architecture's reception with a directness that is largely absent in contemporary criticism. It is a measure of Colquhoun's discretion that he is able to sustain an ethical front without succumbing to moralism. As he himself puts it in writing of Michael Graves, "Criticism occupies the no-man's land between enthusiasm and doubt, between poetic sympathy and analysis. Its purpose is not, except in unique cases, either to eulogise or to condemn." And yet, as he proceeds to argue, the ludic, in itself, is insufficient cause for art; architecture must instead arise out of a subtly informed but nonetheless disjunctive reconciliation of those diverse values of which the modern world is compounded.

By way of demonstrating such a synthesis, Colquhoun provides the reader with an exemplary essay, which, as its title would suggest, deals directly with the "Displacement of Meaning in Le Corbusier". Colquhoun adumbrates the "deconstructive/reconstructive" compositional method adopted by Le Corbusier and the way in which this method was used to reconcile certain cultural contradictions lying at the very core of the modern world, namely the antimony between traditional classical typology and the necessity of assimilating the instrumental into the body of modern forms. This was the essential synthetic project of Purism, irrespective of whether it was applied to painting, architecture or industrial design. At the same time it attempted to respond to the egalitarian predicament of modern architecture: namely; how to combine heterogeneous elements with such skill and conviction as to gain broad societal acceptance. As far as the mature Le Corbusier was concerned this translated into how to combine the authority of classical *ordonnance* with the accessibility of referents drawn from the vernacular. As Colquhoun shows, it was Le Corbusier's strategy of inversion that enabled him to reinterpret classical paradigms in such a way as to open them towards the assimilation of industrial and vernacular elements. Sometimes this entailed the literal displacement of classical form, as when the classical peristyle reappears in Le Corbusier's architecture in the form of *pilotis*; the columnar now being situated *under* rather than in front of the building. That the intention here, as Colquhoun insists, was first to subvert and then to repropose the traditional format of "bottom, middle and top". This hypothesis tends to be borne out by the fact that the "Five Points" of a New Architecture had originally included a sixth point, namely, "the elimination of the cornice". As Colquhoun demonstrates (citing the Villa Stein and the Pavillon Suisse as the most striking examples), the plastic energy of the cornice was to become dispersed in the form of a deep parapet, whose vestigial capacity for consolidation of the composition was reinforced through the location of a central window or cyclopean oculus at the top of the main facade. Thus the apparent displacement of the peristyle and the cornice was to be paralleled at a more detailed level by Le Corbusier's transformation of classical fenestration. Thus the French window, so beloved by Auguste Perret, was to find itself eclipsed by the *fenêtre en longueur,* which as a horizontally sliding industrial window subverted not only the form of the traditional *la porte fenêtre* but also its manual operation. As Colquhoun remarks, how this radical move did not entirely eliminate the aedicular window, since pierced openings were also often used by Le Corbusier as compositional accents. He notes their appearance along the access corridors of the Pavillon Suisse, where, as he puts it, "the introduction of strip windows would have been incompatible".

After remarking how Le Corbusier restricts the use of his free plan to the traditionally hierarchic first floor, Colquhoun goes on to show how the "Five Points" enabled him to combine a strictly classical envelope with the empirical convenience of a vernacular interior. In this articulate manner Le Corbusier addressed the Loosian project of reconciling the rival values of classical culture, vernacular form, and modern technology through the poetics of metaphor and the strategy of metonymic displacement. In retrospect this reconciliation should surely be assessed not only in terms of the moment of its ingenious inception but also in relation to the confusions of the present. As to the creative potential of this conjunction Colquhoun writes:

> Architectural theory has been dominated for the last decade or so by various forms of determinism or populism, neither of which recognises architecture as constituting a cultural entity in its own right. But the raw material of architecture is to a large extent, the architectural culture at any moment in history. Unless those aspects of architectural creation... aspects which involve the transformation of an existing culture—are understood, we are not going to achieve an architecture by which cultural meanings can be carried.

Colquhoun's re-reading of the work of Le Corbusier persists well into the 1980s as we may judge from three essays written in the first half of that decade, successively entitled "The Significance of Le Corbusier", "Architecture and Engineering: Le Corbusier and the Paradox of Reason" and, finally, "The Strategies of the Grand Travaux". In retrospect these essays appear as a triad in which the author re-approaches the heterogeneous body of Le Corbusier's architecture in light of the constantly changing tropes and elements from which it was compounded, along with the ideological implications that were ambiguously attached to certain forms. Colquhoun attempts to deconstruct this material in relation to the legacy of the Enlightenment. He shows how Le Corbusier's world view was caught between the skeptical Cartesianism of the seventeenth century, corresponding to Claude Perrault's distinction between *positive* and *arbitrary* beauty, and the social utopianism of the nineteenth. Herein we encounter not only Le Corbusier's conflation of the mathematical norms of classicism with the empiricism of engineering—his famous conjunction of the engineer's aesthetic with architecture—but also the presence of the spirit of the age, the *Zeitgeist*, that is, emerging from the dialectical idealism of the German historical tradition. In his third essay dealing with Le Corbusier's civic projects of the late 20s and the early 30s, Colquhoun demonstrates how prior to the constructivism of his proposal for the Palais des Soviets of 1931, Le Corbusier invariably posited a subtle opposition between the one-off, free-standing symbolic building and the adjunct continuity of such cellular elements, such as offices. This juxtaposition, first posited by Le Corbusier's League of Nations project of 1927, would reappear as a series of variations in his Centrosoyus Proposal for Moscow of 1929. Colquhoun sums up the shifting synthesis achieved by these projects in the following terms:

> In thus interpreting the complex as a series of heterogeneous objects in space, Le Corbusier turned it into a constructivist icon whose tumultuous silhouette complements that of the domes of Saint Basil and the Kremlin.... The structural and circulatory demands of the complex are used to give expressive form to each element. The desire to create a building of appropriate character led Le Corbusier to interpret the Palais des Nations in terms of what we might call 'an architecture of humanism'; the same desire led him to make the Palais des Soviets into a symbol of mass culture and the work of art in the age of the machine.

The exegetical trajectory uniting these essays is the emphasis that Colquhoun places on the fact that, unlike all the other architects of the Modern Movement, Le Corbusier sustained a parallel career as both an architect and a painter, practised on a daily basis throughout his adult life; with the mornings dedicated to painting and the afternoons to architecture and, later, vice versa. Through this assiduous cultivation of his own dichotomous persona,

> … Le Corbusier justifies the work of the artist/architect in an industrial society and establishes the work of architecture as simultaneously a work of technology and a work of art. Although the architect and the engineer employ different means and have different intentions, they are both working to the same historical ends; architecture cannot ignore technology as it did in the nineteenth century. We therefore find in Le Corbusier a double assertion. On the one hand he invokes historical destiny and demands a total commitment to technology and, ultimately, the technocratic state. On the other, he clings to the idea of the architect as a creative subject who transforms technology into art, material production into ideology.

Colquhoun's focus on Le Corbusier as the magus of the Modern Movement is brought to some kind of summation with his critical overview of a whole series of studies, books, essays, and exhibitions, devoted to his work on the occasion of his centenary in 1987.

Within this compendium there is possibly no essay that so exemplifies the historical tenor of European thought than the piece entitled "Three Kinds of Historicism", 1980. This essay once again suggests that there are few architectural critics of the past half century who have so consistently displayed such a pertinent juxtaposition of erudition and discursive logic. This singular text discriminates between the historical construction of the eighteenth century, oriented towards the universality of nature and reason and the teleological projection of the nineteenth century in which both subject and circumstance were supposedly impelled by an implacable historical will in which the individual was little more than an unconscious agent of the *Zeitgeist*. Against this closure Colquhoun posits a third kind of historicism addressed to the self-conscious cultivation of tradition. While accepting the view that socio-cultural phenomena are indeed influenced by their historical contexts, he nonetheless contends that any kind of unitary world view is bound to lead to a system of thought, which presupposes the unproven hypothesis, namely that the history of mankind is an evolutionary process leading inevitably to the progress of the species.

Much of Colquhoun's later criticism is elaborated from the standpoint of suspicion rather than from any kind of ideological conviction. Herein, once again, one detects the shade of Karl Popper, the insistence that is, that all verification must be able to withstand the test of "falsification" and that this standard should be applied as much to cultural discourse as to scientific fact. Under this rubric Colquhoun's critical posture brings him to reexamine a whole series of layered late modern antinomies, not only classicism vs. vernacular and regional expression vs. universal technology, but also composition vs. project, axonometry vs. perspective and, lastly, the still enduring avant-gardist belief in the possibility of the transforming of the human condition vs. the postmodern acceptance of an endlessly reiterative *répétition different*.

All of this serves to return Colquhoun to his point of departure as a critic; namely his review of Reyner Banham's *Theory and Design in the First Machine Age* and his subsequent relationship with Banham's rather different view of the modernist destiny, as this evolved over the two decades separating *Theory and Design* from Banham's last book, *The Concrete Atlantis* of 1982. Colquhoun's take on all this is set forth with characteristic lucidity in an essay entitled "Reyner Banham: A Reading for the 1980s". What Colquhoun appreciates about the later Banham is the way in which his repudiation of High Modernism and his championship of popular mediatic culture in general would bring him close to the value-free pluralism of Jean-François Lyotard's *The Postmodern Condition*. For Colquhoun, that which remained oddly unresolved in this prospect was the fact that Banham would never quite relinquish his ideal of *une architecture autre*, that is to say an invisible architecture, as this was narcissistically represented through reiterated images of Banham himself, sitting around a Brion-Vega player in a totally transparent plastic bubble; an updated version of the New Man talking to himself in a totally dematerialised primitive hut. This virtual otherness, transcending Mies van der Rohe's spiritually redemptive concept of *almost nothing* was to come closest to the realisation, as far as Banham was concerned, in the High-Tech architecture of Foster Associates. However, as Colquhoun points out:

> Like all historians who are concerned with projecting the future, Banham had to arbitrate between two equally important aspects of history: that which manifests itself as material cause, without which the future cannot exist, and that which manifests itself as individual freedom, without which it can have no purpose. What was the guarantee that the growth of the mass media would develop in the way Banham and the Pop Art movement hoped? In other words, did their idea coincide with "the forces of history", or were they, rather, the reaction to these "forces" of a group of artists who wanted to create works of art (in the traditional sense) out of a certain raw material, and whose work would therefore only affect a limited subculture? Banham's own historiography had done much to discredit the kind of crude determinism that underlay the theory and history of the Modern Movement, by showing the necessary over-determination of all artistic movements. Nonetheless, and contrary to the empirical precepts which he followed as an art historian, he continued to believe in a future which would be expression of a general *Kunstwollen* in which the individual artist would be fully integrated in society, on the model of apparently "organic" examples of Medieval history. In his faith in technology and the mass media his position echoes to some extent that of Walter Benjamin in his famous essay "The Work of Art in the Age of Mechanical Reproduction". It was a faith that dissimulated the fact that it was based on a moral preconception of how the mass media could be managed by an intellectual elite. Technology and the mass media were reified as quasi-natural phenomena with certain cultural consequences—consequences that were in fact assumed in the premise. But such an apocalyptic view was hardly compatible with Banham's enthusiasm for certain expressions of popular taste, which was based on their supplementary value and their redundancy—on the pure pleasure that they provided, and on the further pleasure, mixed with irony, resulting from their assimilation to the purpose of high art. This suggests not the application of technology and the mass media to society as it 'ought' to be the moral dimension that Banham so often invokes but rather the free play of semiosis within society as it is....

Nowhere does Colquhoun distance himself so decisively from Banham than in his long disquisition on architectural rationalism entitled: "A Philosophical Concept in Architecture", of 1987. Herein he follows Le Corbusier in advocating the adoption of a systematically abstract formal language which remains open to technological inflection; one that is not overdetermined neither technologically nor ideologically. In much the same vein, Colquhoun aspires to a relatively autonomous, architecture in which the abstract rationale of form will be culturally mediated through the technical and programmatic discipline of the type. However this juxtaposition of formal with empirical reason does nothing to dispel the persistence of an irresolvable doubt, for as Colquhoun asks at the end of his essay "... can we still use the word rationalism in architecture in the sense that it has always been used despite all the change in meaning; as the attempt to provide the sensuous analogue, the emblematic presence, of that reason which was once supposed to permeate the universe?" In leaving this rhetorical question unanswered, Colquhoun testifies to an enduring skepticism that has driven all of his essays forward in a continuous cascade of thought.

PART I 1962–1980

The Modern Movement
in Architecture

First published in *The British Journal of Aesthetics*, January 1962.

A re-evaluation of the significance of artistic expression in a world revolutionised by the machine has been, consciously or unconsciously, at the root of all avant-garde movements of the last 50 years. But whereas in literature, music, and painting, the machine, as a direct protagonist, has played an intermittent and often purely picturesque role, in architecture it has been fundamental to the development of new forms and the evolution of aesthetic theory. This fact has tended to obscure the equally important subjective factors which lie behind man's need to give expression to symbolic forms and which are as relevant to architecture as they are to the other arts. Critical histories of the Modern Movement in architecture (eg. Nikolaus Pevsner's *Pioneers of Modern Design)* have tended to concentrate on its social and technical influences or on those movements immediately preceding it, such as Art Nouveau and the English Free Style. In stressing its active and craftsman-like aspects at the expense of its theoretical background, they have given the impression that the forms of modern architecture were a spontaneous outgrowth from an immediate and radical past.

In *Theory and Design in the First Machine Age* Reyner Banham has shifted this emphasis and has investigated precisely those sources which were taboo to an earlier generation of writers on the Modern Movement. In his opening chapter he gives the following summary of the causes of the architectural revolution which occurred during the first decade of the century:

> These predisposing causes were... first, the sense of an architect's responsibility to the society in which he finds himself...; secondly, the Rationalist, or structural approach to architecture... codified in Auguste Choisy's magisterial *Histoire*...; and, thirdly, the tradition of academic instruction... owing most of its energy and authority to the *Ecole des Beaux-Arts* in Paris.[1]

It is clear that in giving this entirely new weight to the influence of the Beaux-Arts, Dr Banham intends to establish some thesis on the Modern Movement, though what this is to be is not immediately apparent.

The Beaux-Arts, which came in for the most virulent attacks from the first Modern architects, taught certain principles of plan organisation and form composition whose foundations went back to eighteenth century theories of psychological response and to that recurrence of neo-Platonic doctrine which had been enshrined in the academies. The idea that art contained certain principles independent of its craft or technical aspect was as strong at the end of the nineteenth century as it was at the time of Etienne-Louis Boullée; it was the mental atmosphere which produced at once an academic like Charles Blanc and a revolutionary like Paul Cézanne.[2] It needed very little to strip these ideas of stylistic clothing and to conceive of an architecture or an art based on principles of abstract form, owing allegiance to universal values. Modern architecture crystallised when this movement collided and partly merged with those rationalist and moral theories which embraced the new structural techniques and the new social consciousness emerging toward the end of the last century.

Dr Banham shows how the academic tradition, especially as summed up in the writings of Julien Guadet at the end of the century, continued to have an influence even on those Modern architects who were loudest in their vituperations against the Beaux-Arts. This is, in fact, one of the main themes of his book and the conclusions that he draws from the effect of this influence would seem to make Dr Banham vulnerable to criticism. Although he postpones the disclosure of his critical position until the end of the book, his general attitude begins to make itself clear at a fairly early stage. That he evidently does not look upon the facts that he has uncovered with detachment shows itself in his constantly pejorative use of the term "academic" as if the presence of academic features constituted a self-evident condemnation of works which otherwise might pass the test of modernity. His final thesis is that by their persistence in believing in certain 'constant' architectural values Modern architects like Le Corbusier were led to a misunderstanding of the Machine Age with which they were trying to come to terms. It is undeniable that Le Corbusier made simultaneous claims for his architecture which were incompatible, but Dr Banham is concerned not only with the theories by which the architects rationalised their work but with this work itself. He accepts the general theory that modern architecture is a branch of techniques and condemns the buildings of the 1920s because they failed to live up to this theory. According to him, in seeking to arrive at perfected and final forms, especially those based on the Phileban solids which they took to result logically from machine technology, they closed the door to the natural evolution of mechanical forms and arrived at a premature academicism.

This argument seems to rest on the assumption that the evolution of architectonic forms is a constant flow and that the technical processes out of which it emerges are capable of only a single and literal interpretation at any one moment. It may be true that in evaluating history a certain interpretation seems to have been inevitable; but this would presumably be the interpretation that actually did take place, not one that *should* have taken place. This seems to be a very different thing from claiming that the interpretation should have been determined solely by the objective facts of the technical process.

Whatever the contradictions in the rationale of the avant-garde movement, it would appear that Dr Banham has oversimplified, and so falsified, the essential ideas behind those theories which led to functionalism. In their pure form they seem to represent a position at the opposite extreme from the traditional notions of the nature of art and the role of the artist. In the latter the architect, as artist, is seen as the manipulator of tangible and visual form according to laws belonging to architecture itself, and deriving its ultimate justification from psychological facts which govern man's apprehension of the world. In the former, architectural form is seen to derive from causes which lie within the matrix of the world and which are outside the architect, whose own thought is a part of that matrix. According to this view the architect acts as midwife, as it were, to the forces of nature and bears witness to its hidden laws. He performs no specifically 'artistic' acts, since he is merely the medium through which the technique becomes substantiated. The object which results is a 'created' thing only insofar as it partakes of the creative forces latent in the universe and has absorbed just so many of those forces as are appropriate to the problem to be solved. It is not an artefact apart from other artefacts and emits no special kind of effulgence.

This would seem to be fundamentally an idealist view, and it is to this view that functionalism adheres. Far from being utilitarian and pragmatic, functionalism sought to spiritualise the mechanical process and to destroy the dichotomy of the mechanical and the spiritual, of determinism and free will. Le Corbusier's constant use of biomorphic parallels to mechanical forms is indicative of this and reveals a type of thought analogous to that of Theodule Armand Ribot in his discovery of the role of motor forces in the creation of emotional states.[3] At this generalised level of thinking, one can see a curious inversion if one compares Piet Mondrian's philosophy with that of functionalism. Superficially they would seem to be at opposite poles of thought, yet in both there is a rejection of mediate steps between man and the absolute. The rejection of natural forms as a subject for painting is equivalent to the rejection of derivative and subjective forms in architecture. Art for art's sake and the architecture of complete engagement are one and the same thing.

It would seem that this attitude differs from the 'traditional' one rather in its perfectionism than in its adherence to a more demonstrable truth. If, as Dr Banham shows, academic systems of thought persisted even in those works which laid claim to the most extreme functionalism, it would seem, to indicate that they were a necessary ingredient of practice which could not be assimilated into the rationale. In the writings of Le Corbusier we see the two attitudes lying side by side—on the one hand, the unitary view in which form and function are presented as identical; on the other, the idealist view that function is preceded by form. But Le Corbusier made no claims to be writing a systematic treatise, and it could be that the contradictions in the argument represent a necessary conflict of ideas which can only be resolved in the works themselves—a dialectical sequence the third term of which can only be introduced at the level of symbolic representation. It would seem just as reasonable to assume that we come into the world with certain paraphernalia with which to fashion the world in our likeness as it is to assume that we make our debut naked except for our techniques—that we are historical animals, in the sense that we carry history in our mental attitudes as well as in our accomplishments.

Although Dr Banham is too scrupulous a historian to commit himself exclusively to certain movements or personalities, it is to the Futurists and to Buckminster Fuller that he evidently feels most strongly drawn. The Futurists were undoubtedly an important germinating influence on the Modern Movement, even if in the excitement of discovering new and hitherto neglected material he probably exaggerates this influence. Yet the precise degree of influence is unimportant, since the Futurists represent only one aspect of the complex cross-fertilisation of ideas which took place at the time. Dr Banham deplores the absence, in Le Corbusier's plans, of those Futurist qualities which he detects in his sectional organisation. Yet the same "impure" qualities exist in the Futurists themselves, and it can hardly be denied that a reconstruction of Antonio Sant'Elia's Central Station in the *Citta Nuova* would reveal a thoroughly Beaux-Arts *parti*. If the Futurists are to be taken as the fountainhead of an architecture of revolution, then the presence of academic features would seem to be a necessary component of this revolution. To extract from Le Corbusier the academic and from a Futurist the dynamic aspects in order to show that the former is *retardataire* and the latter progressive would appear to be a procedure of dubious historical validity.

The case of Buckminster Fuller is rather different, and in introducing him as the *deus ex machina* of his argument, Dr Banham is raising the fundamental question of the validity of architecture itself in any sense that we understand that term. Fuller represents an extreme form of the functionalist dogma. He criticised the European moderns just at the time when all avant-garde opinion was on their side and at the same time produced a series of projects which owed nothing to any preconceived notion of formal organisation. Yet if Fuller's philosophy rests on the idea of an "unhaltable trend to constantly accelerating change", he nonetheless, in the Dymaxion House project as in the domes, presents a final form—the image of a technique which has reached an optimum of undifferentiation. Nor could it be denied that Fuller's attitude toward mathematics conceals a certain mysticism; and if this differs considerably from the Platonism of Le Corbusier, it is no more rational and should therefore equally be condemned by Banham on the grounds of its not representing a truly positive and pragmatic attitude toward technology. The difference between Fuller and Le Corbusier lies not in the ideal importance which they attach to mathematics but in the symbolic role it plays. In Fuller's domes the forms are identified by their lines of force, resembling those High Gothic structures where a framework alone defines the volumes which it encloses and seeming to exemplify Fuller's philosophy of the forms of art being absorbed back into the technical process. In Le Corbusier, the plastic act is hypostatised. His forms are, as it were, congealed in space, as in a solid graph. In both, the Phileban solids play an essential part; in both, the aesthetic and the discipline are identified. But whereas in the case of Fuller the formulation and the identification take place on a supersensuous level and the aesthetic is transmuted into the act, in the case of Le Corbusier the act becomes solidified in the sensuous object. With Fuller the idea explains the form; with Le Corbusier the form explains the idea. To argue, as Dr Banham does, that mathematics is a discipline of a negative kind which is totally absorbed in the end product would reduce the constructive principle to a purely empirical level. Yet Fuller's domes, which are pure structure, are conceived and presented as objects of aesthetic value and are charged with a meaning surpassing that of particular occasion or use. In fact, Fuller's domes are 'ideal' structures every bit as much as is a building by Mies van der Rohe or Le Corbusier. Their difference is that they constitute an idea on such a general level that no articulation of activity is expressed.

It seems, indeed, that man has an ineradicable urge to extract from the flow of events a token of stasis, a fixed point against which to measure himself. And indeed, although a state of constant flux may be the nature of the world as it is presented to us, the concept of continuous change, considered as an object of factual experience such as technical development, is itself an abstraction. We must set it against the palpable tendency of the senses and intellect to see the world in the form of recognisable and nameable wholes.

In spite of the weight he gives to the opinions of Fuller in the last chapter of the book, Dr Banham's final view of the Modern Movement remains ambivalent. If Fuller were right, the whole oeuvre of the European architects of the 1920s would be invalid, since its impact clearly lies in formal patterns which are not solely dictated by techniques. If it is true, on the other hand, that these architects were concerned not with the literal but with the symbolic interpretation of the machine, then Fuller's criticisms are invalid, and the meaning attributed to the role of the machine in architecture is more important than the degree to which structures reflect the course of machine technology as such. And Dr Banham seems to confirm this view when he analyses the works themselves and allows his sensibility free play. He discusses at length Walter Gropius' Werkbund Pavilion from a purely aesthetic point of view and devotes several pages of analysis to the two buildings which he has chosen to represent the movement at its point of climax, Mies van der Rohe's Barcelona Pavilion and Le Corbusier's Villa Savoye at Poissy-sur-Seine. Of these he says: "Their status as masterpieces rests, as it does with most other masterpieces of architecture, upon the authority and felicity with which they give expression to a view of men in relation to their environment."[5] This sentence clearly implies an acceptance of the symbolic role of architecture and of other than purely technical values.

It is curious that, having admitted that certain buildings of the period are masterpieces, Dr Banham should reject those mystiques without which they could not have come into existence. One wonders by what criterion he judges a masterpiece and by what casuistry he would be able to demonstrate that a building was simultaneously a masterpiece and a failure. The ambiguity that existed in the Modern Movement, and which Dr Banham wants to tidy away from the face of history, lies in the fact that the functionalist theory was, in a profound sense, the outcome of attitudes prevalent in the nineteenth century, although in conflict with them on a superficial level. The breaking apart of the ancient and Medieval traditions, in which idealism and pragmatism, the creative act and the craft discipline, were inseparable, did not finally occur until the mid-eighteenth century, and it ushered in a period of history in which the conscious search for the unity of the architectural act became the main preoccupation. What is known as the academic tradition was, in fact, the beginning of a revolution rather than the end of a period of decline, and the final distinction which it drew between the crafts and the liberal arts was prophetic of the rise of an architecture produced on the drawing board and in the workshop, owing nothing to manual sensibility and habit. It is this fractured condition of architecture that the whole Modern Movement reflects.

Dr Banham's book commands our admiration in its method of analysis and its presentation of a comprehensive picture of the Modern Movement. But it would have been more objective if the author had drawn his conclusions more exclusively from the historical evidence which he himself has adduced. He has demonstrated that many of the overt aims of the Movement were not achieved; but it may well be that these aims themselves were often of doubtful value, and that the true meaning of the Movement lies in the unconscious substratum of the theory and is to be recognised in the works themselves. That a personal point of view should enter into a historical judgment is inevitable and even desirable; yet one is left with the feeling that the last word on the Modern Movement has not been said—and will not be said for a very long time to come.

1   Banham, Reyner, *Theory and Design in the First Machine Age*, New York: Praeger, 1960, p. 14.
2   Blanc, Charles, 1813–1882 was the author of *Grammaire des Arts du Dessin*, Paris: Vve J Renouard, 1870.
3   Theodule Armand Ribot, 1839–1916, was the author of several popular books on psychology written from a positivist and mechanistic point of view.
4   Banham, *Theory and Design,* p. 327.
5   Banham, *Theory and Design,* p. 325.

Symbolic and Literal Aspects of Technology

First published in *Architectural Design*, November 1962.

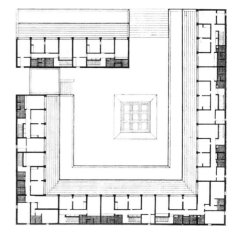

One of the remarkable facts about the architecture of the mid-twentieth century is that so many of its buildings exploit heavy and traditional methods of construction. From the point of view of building technique this would seem to be a regression from the ideals of the early period of the Modern Movement, which aimed at an expression of the lightness inherent in tensile structure and synthetic materials.

It is true that architects for the majority of buildings put up today make use of the simple principle of a concrete or steel frame sheathed in some form of curtain wall and in doing so appear to be putting into practice the theories formulated by Le Corbusier in the 1920s. Yet the architectural qualities of most of these buildings are so meagre that one is forced to ask whether, in the mere application of an apparently logical system, the essential features of good architecture are not being overlooked. And indeed, there is a tendency among architects, whenever the programme allows, to break away from the simple frame structure with panel infill to some form of structure that allows the building a greater plastic flexibility and gives to its forms a greater density.

Both the Caius College hostel and the Royal College of Art building, by Sir Leslie Martin and HT Cadbury-Brown respectively, aim at and achieve an effect of mass which is not a necessary product of the programme and its structural interpretation. In the case of the Royal College of Art building the reinforced concrete frame is partly covered by brick panels which, together with the studios at roof level, emphasise the vertical axis and create an impression of ambiguity as to whether the structure consists of a frame or of solid load-bearing walls. In the case of Caius College a brick structure is used in such a way as to exaggerate the massiveness of this kind of construction and to create a feeling of enclosure and protection reminiscent of a walled town or a Roman amphitheatre.

A layman might conclude that such buildings were a reaction against the 'glass box' architecture rising in our cities, and that there must be a split in the architectural profession reflecting the sort of chasm that seems to him to exist between what is proper to 'office' architecture on the one hand and private houses on the other. But if there is such a split, it is probably in the mind of each architect. Every architect today is torn between two concepts of architecture. On the one hand, architecture is seen to consist of unique works of art, the creation of individual sensibility. On

Top: Caius College hostel, Cambridge, England. Sir Leslie Martin and Colin St John Wilson, 1962. Third floor plan.

Bottom: Caius College hostel.

Royal College of Art, London.
HT Cadbury-Brown, Hugh Casson,
and RY Gooden.

the other, it is seen as belonging to the public sphere, where private sensibility is under the control of "techniques" in the broadest sense of that word.

In spite of its theory, the Modern Movement failed to establish a substantial relationship between these two concepts. To see why this is so, it is necessary to look more closely at the real conditions that sustained it. It has become a truism to say that the buildings of the Rationalist Movement were, whatever their mystique, built largely of traditional materials. The only real innovation brought into use in the early twentieth century was tensile structure. The other changes that were brought about in the organisation and appearance of buildings were the result of *a priori* theories about the nature of the Machine Age and the social purpose of architecture. Together they formed a 'functionalist' architecture of enormous power, whose image was created largely out of Expressionist, Cubist, or neo-classical aesthetic theory. This architecture formed the active wing of the avant-garde movement as a whole and was concerned as much with the salvation of society through art as through technology. The functionalist building was, in fact, a pure work of art, freed from the arbitrary rules of craft and of individual fantasy and raised to the level of Platonic form by means of the machine—a work of pure exactitude.

We cannot grasp the meaning of the Modern Movement unless we understand that the role which symbolic expression played in it was fundamentally the same as it had been in previous architecture. There is a tendency in criticism to distinguish between utilitarian and moral criteria, on the one hand, and aesthetic criteria, on the other. According to this conception, aesthetics is concerned with 'form', while the logical, technical, and sociological problems of building belong to the world of empirical action. This distinction is false, because it ignores the fact that architecture belongs to a world of symbolic forms in which every aspect of building is presented metaphorically, not literally. There is a logic of forms, but it is not identical with the logic which comes into play in the solution of the empirical problems of construction. The two systems of thought are not consecutive but parallel.

This was as true of the Modern Movement as it was of any other period of architecture. In it the new technology was an idea rather than a fact. It became part of its content as a work of art and not merely or principally a means to its construction. Our admiration of the buildings it created is due more to their success as symbolic representations than to the extent to which they solved practical problems. However much the materials they used were conceived to be the products of machine techniques, these architects never regarded them as 'ready-mades' but adapted them to a preconceived plastic form, even though, of course, this form itself was triggered by a notion of machine technology. One might quote as an example Le Corbusier's unique use of the curtain wall, in which the glazing bars are so profiled and proportioned as to preserve the integrity of the plane and to create the feeling of a tight skin stretched over the entire surface of the building.

The fact that the technico-social revolution assumed by the Modern Movement did not take place brought to the surface the extent to which its work was the result of a private will to form—and the extent to which *all* architecture must be so based. Once this was admitted, the ontological link between art and technique was broken, and the architect was free to enlarge the theoretical context within which he designed. This link had been forged from a utopian and eschatological view of society, art, and technique which was no longer tenable. What inevitably followed was a more flexible attitude toward construction and new researches into form.

To some extent this has been forced on designers by economic necessity, but there is no doubt that the feeling of mass and permanence which traditional or semi-traditional materials give has been sought after for its own sake, and that the technical and public aspects of building have fallen progressively outside the field of private symbolic expression. It is as if the urge to create the world anew by means of structures which had the lightness and tenuousness of pure thought had given way to the desire to create solid hideouts of the human spirit in a world of uncertainty and change.

And here we come to the dilemma which was at the root of the Modern Movement and which is still present today. If buildings are to retain their quality of uniqueness as symbols, how can they also be the end products of an industrial system whose purpose is to find general solutions? In the 1920s a series of unique solutions stood as symbols for a universal idea which could not be put into practice. But today we are faced with an imminent revolution in building technique, the very existence of which may make the unique solution impossible.

All forms of symbolic expression emerge from and feed on the world of fact. Architecture can exist only in the context of its sociological, technical, and economic conditions, and as soon as it ceases to do this it dies. But up till now the means of construction at the disposal of society, out of which it has created its symbolic forms, has always been malleable to the will of the designer. This condition can exist whether the method of manufacture is manual or mechanical, but to make this possible the designer must participate at the beginning of the process.

When we are discussing architecture, we are discussing whole buildings or building complexes. Therefore any element which is being designed must be thought of in the context of the whole of which it is to be a part. A simple system of components based on an additive module, which are interchangeable to suit any situation, does not give this essential condition, since the character of the form of a building alters according to its size, situation, and programme. A building is not the mere sum of its parts.

Yet it is just such a system that would recommend itself to an organisation concerned with the economic carrying out of a large and complex building programme. A number of such systems have, in fact, been operating, and while they satisfy more or less the needs of flexibility of assembly, they do not satisfy the need of flexibility in design. They are only capable of solving the simplest arrangement of all the possible arrangements to which they apply. Thus, a structural grid with infill panels becomes inexpressive to the extent that these panels are simply additive. It is true that a building which is an agglomeration of units can achieve great intensity and unity, but this can only be achieved if the design of each unit anticipates the complex as a whole. This will require modifications which are neither economical nor logical from the point of view of the simple operation of joining one unit to another in an additive series. We have here a confusion between technology as a means to construction and technology as the content of the building form itself. Such systems render a building incapable of symbolising plastically the utopian ideals which undoubtedly inspire them.

Le Corbusier, in discussing the design of a series of metal houses at Lagny, says, "The problem here is utterly commonplace." Yet these houses have a charm which derives from their uniqueness. They are designed for repetition, but the components have been subject to a control which has always kept a certain plastic and expressive end in view and which does not allow for extension or diminution. Similarly, in the design of cars a particular model is unique however many times it is repeated. Whether or not such examples are relevant to the problem, say, of mass produced housing or schools, there is no doubt that serious thought will have to be given to the question of component design in relation to a particular architectural intention if architecture is not to lose all possibility of symbolic expression.

In a fluid situation where the decisions on fundamental questions seem to be outside the control of the architect, there is a tendency for him to flee into escapist backwaters of irrelevant symbolism. But it is not the urge to symbolism itself which is wrong, for without it architecture would cease to exist. However much society needs an architecture which expresses its ideals and which provides for

Project for Metal Houses, Lagney, France,
Le Corbusier, 1958, model.
© FLC/ADAGP, Paris and DACS, London 2009

the human spirit, there is a danger that its economic mechanisms may make such an architecture impossible. This is particularly so because many architects considering themselves to be the heirs of the Modern Movement fundamentally misinterpret its aims and its virtues. The science of building, the rationalisation of construction and assembly, however vital in themselves, remain in the world of literal action. It is only when the architect, seizing this world, organises it according to the logic of symbolic forms that architecture results.

Formal and Functional Interactions: a Study of Two Late Buildings by Le Corbusier

First published in *Architectural Design*, vol. 36, May 1966.

The projects for the French Embassy in Brasilia and the Hospital in Venice seem to represent two extremes in the work of Le Corbusier. The Embassy refers directly to the concept of simple volumes intended to "release constant sensations" and to the related idea of the "surface", which form the basis of Le Corbusier's classicising tendencies.[1] The Hospital, on the other hand, seems to derive from opposing tendencies which are typified in his investigations into patterns of growth, his interest in the irregular and spontaneous forms of folk architecture, and the direct transformation of a functional organism into its appropriate form.

Yet if we look more closely, we can see that the polarity of these attitudes is present in both projects and that each owes more to its complementary principle than at first seems the case. The most immediately striking fact in the Embassy project is its division into two buildings of simple but contrasting volumes. An architect wishing to express the functional interaction between the residence and the chancellery might have developed his scheme in a single complex. But in such a solution it would have been difficult to avoid the administration overpowering the residence. Le Corbusier's solution avoids this danger.

The residence has the low cubic form of a villa, placed across the lower half of the site and looking toward the lake, dominating the site from the east and screening its upper half. The chancellery is situated near the western site boundary, where it has a more direct relation to the centre of the city—a cylindrical seven-storey

Project for the French Embassy, Brasilia, Le Corbusier, 1964–1965. Model viewed from the north.
© FLC/ADAGP, Paris and DACS, London 2009

tower, its height giving it views over the residence toward the lake, its cylindrical form enabling it to act as the complement of the smaller, rectangular mass of the residence. A driveway links the two buildings and the opposite ends of the site, switching across the site between one building and the other and underlining their complementarity by giving the site a chiasmatic symmetry—a frequent device of Le Corbusier's plans.

The chancellery is the only example in Le Corbusier's oeuvre of a fully worked out cylindrical building (no plans of the housing cylinders at Strasbourg and Meux have, as far as I know, been published), but his early studies of simple solids, the photographs of grain silos in *Vers une architecture,* and his drawings of Pisa indicate a lifelong interest in this problem. In this solution, a circular *brise-soleil* screen encloses an irregular orthogonal building, whose walls and floors extend only to the inner face of the screen at certain points. The impression of an object within an object which this gives is enhanced by the fact that the enclosing arc only extends for about three-fifths of a circle, allowing the corner of the enclosed building to emerge sharply from its sheath at the point of the elevator shaft and staircase. The effect of this is to slice off the circle in response to the driveway and to divide the building into an entrance and movement zone and a quiet working zone. Balconies prolong the *brise-soleil* on the driveway side, and their random spacing allows the lowest one to detach itself and to be read as a canopy over the entrance. A central hall on each floor, offset slightly from the centre of the circle, opens into rows of offices facing north and east. These offices and their private balconies vary from floor to floor giving constantly new relations with the inner surface of the *brise-soleil*. The cylinder is therefore hollowed out, and its interior surface is always felt as independent of the enclosed structure. The Platonic form of the circle acts as a field within which a functional rectangular arrangement is established.

The same ambiguities exist in the Ambassador's House, working within a different set of functional and formal determinants. The problem has been reduced to three elements: a main body consisting of the reception rooms and their offices, an 'attic' containing the ambassador's private apartments, and a vast porch-vestibule linking the two and containing the main staircase. The entrance and reception rooms are on the second floor, and two broad ramps connect this level with the ground—one leading to the entrance porch from the west, and the other leading from the reception rooms on the east to a *parterre* surrounding a pool, creating a chiasmatic pattern similar to that of the site plan.

The motif of a porch at one end of a block is another favourite motif of Le Corbusier. It first appears at the Villa Stein in Garches (though this itself is a derivative of the Pavillon de l'Esprit Nouveau) and reappears, greatly modified, in the High Court at Chandigarh. In the French Embassy it acts as a lens through which the chancellery is related to the ambassador's house and the lower end of the site (the two buildings are sited so that the chancellery can be seen through the porch from the east boundary and so that the offices on the east face of the chancellery look through it toward the lake). It is the eye of the building, the aedicule through which one enters its inner spaces and by means of which one also enters into relationship with the public space of site or city.

The classical overtones of this porch are obviously intentional, and its position implies a rejection of classical symmetry and gives it a curious, rhetorical independence. Equally subversive is the way in which it breaks through the solid wall of the attic and in doing so allows one to attribute to this floor an importance equal to that of the reception rooms—an importance which is reinforced by the 'domestic' scale of their *brise-soleil.*

The apartment floor is similar to the director's apartment in the Pavillon Suisse. Here, however, the walls are not penetrated as they are in that building, partly because the linking action of the porch makes this semantically unnecessary and partly because at the Pavillon Suisse the *pilotis* necessitate the visual hollowing out and lightening of the top floor. Here the absolute privacy of the ambassador's residence is established, and roof patios form private open spaces which repeat, on a more intimate scale, the public open spaces related to the reception rooms.

Both in this building and in the chancellery the *brise-soleil* belongs to the type first used in India, consisting of deep reveals supported independently of the main structure. The earlier *brise-soleil* structures were conceived of as projections from the glass wall. Their use as independent structures is one of the major developments in Le Corbusier's later style (although he continued to use them in their original form in certain late buildings). When used in this way they become perforated walls, which establish a transitional space between outside and inside. The continuous penetrability of this element at ground level made it possible to dispense with *pilotis* without implications of massiveness and, in this way, also made it possible to put the principal rooms on the first floor. The ground floor can be read as either open or solid, thus permitting it to be partially concealed by solid ramps, which give the impression of the ground floor rising to meet the first floor. Where rooms occur on the ground floor, the *brise-soleil* carries right down to the ground, but where the space is void the spacing is doubled to suggest vestigial *pilotis* without, however, destroying the surface value of the *brise-soleil*.

While the organisational problems in the Brasilia buildings are relatively simple, those in the Hospital at Venice are complex and specialised. It is possible (even within the height restrictions imposed by the site) to imagine a solution in which vertically organised blocks of different classes of accommodation would be related horizontally, but Le Corbusier has decided to separate the different classes vertically, so that each level serves a different purpose, and a cross-section at any one point is, in principle, typical of the whole organisation. This has obvious advantages both from the point of view of administration and that of extensibility. But it also repeats the pattern of the city with its overall texture—a solid mass of building penetrated by canals and courts. In Venice, the city itself is the building, and the Hospital is an extension of this building spreading tentacle-like over the water.

The Hospital is sited near the northwest end of the Grand Canal and extends over the lagoon separating Venice from Mestre. The decision to contain the wards in a solid wall and to light them from the roof would seem to be justified by the proximity of the railway terminal and the industrial squalor of Mestre. The building covers a large area and is comparable in its mass and public importance to such groups as the Piazza San Marco, the Ospedale Civile, and the monastery of San Giorgio Maggiore. It therefore forms an important addition to that small but significant collection of buildings symbolising the public life of Venice. The solution combines the monumentality suggested by this role with an intimacy and textural quality in harmony with the city's Medieval scale. If built, it would go a long way toward revitalising the 'kitchen sink' end of a city which needs more than the tourist trade to keep it alive.

The ground level accommodation occupies an L, with an isolated block contained within the arms of the L. The reception, the administration, and the kitchen occupy the L, and the nurses' hostel the isolated block. A straight access system breaks through the L where gondola and car entries converge onto a common entrance lobby thrown across the gap. The gondola approach route is bridged by a route linking religious and recreational centres at its extremities. There is an entresol containing extensions of the ground level accommodation.

The analytical and treatment departments are on level 2a and are arranged freely around the cores. They include the operating theatres, which are organised around the cores in an analogous way to the wards above. Level 2b consists of a horizontal interchange system between all elevator points—patients using the central, and staff the peripheral, corridors. The ward block, which occupies the

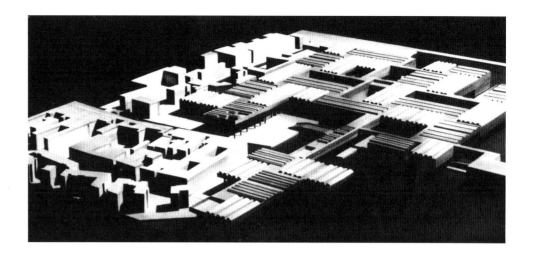

entire top floor, is both the largest department of the building and represents its typical element, and the organisation allows this element to extend to the limits of the building with which it becomes identified by the observer, whatever position he may be in.

The basic unit of the plan and its generator is a square group of wards rotating around a central elevator core—which Le Corbusier calls a *campiello*. These units are added together in such a way that wards next to each other in adjacent units merge, thus 'correcting' the rotation and making the independent systems interlock. An agglomerate of units creates a square grid with a *campiello* at each intersection.

The plan differs from those isomorphic schemes where the unit of addition is elementary (as implied, for instance, in the roof of Aldo van Eyck's school at Amsterdam). Here the basic unit is itself hierarchically arranged, with biological rather than mineral analogies, and capable of local modification without the destruction of its principle. It is obviously related to such matrix schemes as the Candilis, Josic and Woods project for the Free University of Berlin. The concept of the top floor plan is reminiscent of the Islamic *medresehs* of North Africa, where sub-communities of students' cells are grouped around small courtyards, forming satellite systems around a central court. As in the *medreseh*, the whole dominates the parts, and the additive nature of the schema is overlaid with a strong controlling geometry.

The geometric, as opposed to the additive, schema consists of a system of overlaid squares and golden section rectangles. The smaller of the two squares establishes a centre of gravity asymmetrical in relation to the scheme as a whole and related to it diagonally. This centre is also on the intersection of the rectangles formed by dividing the total square according to geometrical proportion. The additive grid consists of eight units, which allows for division of the Fibonacci series into 8, 5, 3, 2. The centre of the small square is the centre of gravity of the treatment department and the main vertical circulation point for patients around which there is an opening in the top floor giving light to a ground floor court which wraps around the central core. As at the monastery of La Tourette, the traditional court with circulation around it is modified by a cruciform circulation system on its axes—a typical Corbusian superimposition of functional and mythic orders.

The central core (which from another point of view is merely one of a number of equidistant elevator cores) assumes a fixed relationship with the southeast and southwest faces of the building only. Conceptually, the building can extend on the northwest and northeast faces, and these are developed in a freer way over the lagoon to the northwest and the Canale di Cannareggio to the northeast,

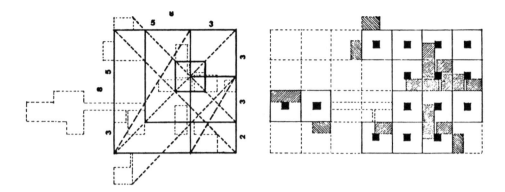

where one assumes further extension could take place. (Between the first and second project a new site has, in fact, become available, and it is possible to see how extension has been achieved without detriment to the overall schema). The wards are grouped around the central lightwell, extending in a wing over the lagoon, and form a U-shape over the gondola entrance to provide the echo of an *avant-cour*. From this 'soft' side a bridge extends over the canal to an isolated ward complex on the opposite side.

Despite the uniqueness of this building in the work of Le Corbusier—a uniqueness that perhaps can be explained by the complexities of the problem and by the peculiarities of the site—a number of prototypes exist in his earlier work. At the Villa Savoye in Poissy the flat cube, projected into the air and open to the sky, was first established as a 'type' solution. It seems clear that this sort of type solution cannot be equated with the *objet-type* discussed by Reyner Banham in his *Theory and Design in the First Machine Age,* since Le Corbusier

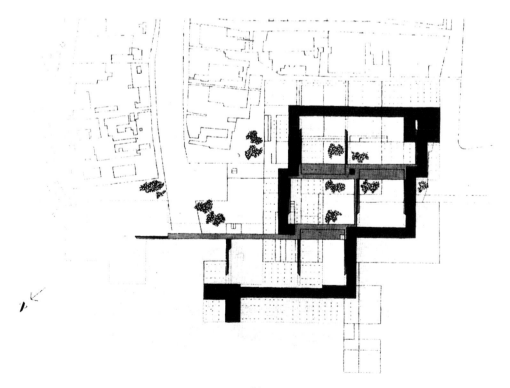

Opposite: The Venice Hospital, Le Corbusier, 1965. Model of the second project.

Top: The Venice Hospital, Le Corbusier, 1965. geometrical schema (left), additive schema (right).

Bottom: The Venice Hospital, first project, 1964. Level 2b plan.

© FLC/ADAGP, Paris and DACS, London 2009

frequently uses the same type in different contexts. We must assume that his concept of "type" relates to a mythic form rather than to a means of solving particular problems, and that, as with physiognomic forms or musical modes, a number of different contents can be attached to the same form. A similar idea is apparent in the project for the Museum of Endless Growth of 1930–1939, also connected with the problem of extensibility as at Venice, though solving it in a different way. In the 1925 *Cité Universitaire* project a solid single-storey block of studios was proposed, where the rooms were lit entirely from the roof.

There are also a number of projects where a building on *pilotis* extends over water, possibly stemming from Le Corbusier's early interest in reconstructions of prehistoric lake dwellings in central Europe. The monastery of La Tourette resembles such schemes through the way in which the building is projected over rough sloping ground which, like water, offers no foothold for the inhabitants of the constructed world suspended above it.

But in the Hospital scheme the potential symbolism of these forms has been harnessed to a new and unique problem. The space of the *pilotis* forms a shaded region in which the reflections of sunlight on water would create continuous movement. Over this space, which is articulated by numerous columns whose grouping would alter with the movement of the observer, floats a vast roof, punctured in places to let in the sunlight and give a view of the sky. This roof is, in fact, an inhabited top storey, whose deep fascia conceals the wards behind. It is the realm of the sky in whose calm regions the process of physical renewal can take place remote from the world of water, trees, and men which it overshadows. But apart from its suggestions of sunlight and healing, it has more sombre overtones. The cave-like section of the wards, the drawn representation of the sick almost as heroic corpses laid out on cool slabs, the paraphernalia of ablution, suggest more personal obsessions and give the impression of a place of masonic solemnity, a necropolis in the manner of Claude-Nicolas Ledoux or John Soane.

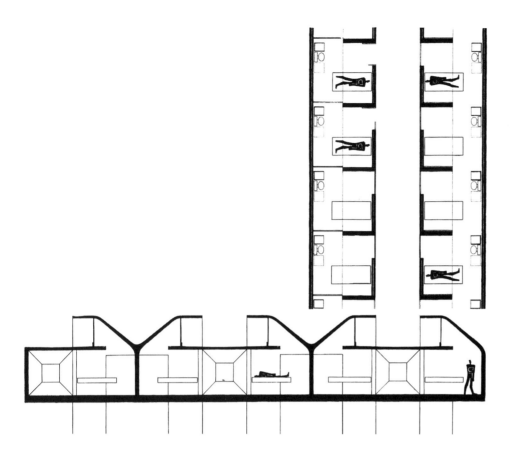

Typical of Le Corbusier's office is the way in which the logic of a total conception has been relentlessly applied to the organisation of the wards and has resulted in a solution which stands the accepted idea of "convenience" on its head. There is a civic *gravitas,* a ritualistic seriousness, about this scheme wholly at variance with a society whose values are based on the likely opinions of the 'average man', and it is possible that such a *machine a guerir* may not commend itself to the committee in whose hands the fate of the building lies.

In spite of its different purposes and the different organisational patterns which these produce, the Venice Hospital resembles the Brasilia scheme in the way in which it evokes complex and overlapping responses. The analytical way in which the constituent functions are separated allows them to develop pragmatically around and within fixed patterns. The form is not conceived of as developing in a one-to-one relation with the functions but is based on ideal schemata with which the freely deployed functions engage in a dialogue. The building is both an agglomeration of basic cells, capable of growth and development, *and* a solid which has been cut into and carved out to reveal a constant interaction of inside and outside space.

The impression of complexity is the result of a number of subsystems impinging on schemata which, in themselves, are extremely simple.

1   Le Corbusier, *Vers une architecture*, Paris: G Crès et Cie., 1923, and Le Corbusier and Pierre Jeanneret, *Oeuvre Complete 1910–1929*, Zurich: Edition Girsberger, 1937.

Opposite: The Venice Hospital, first project, 1964. Level 3.

Above: The Venice Hospital. Le Corbusier, 1965. Plan of ward (top) and section (bottom).

© FLC/ADAGP, Paris and DACS, London 2009

Displacement of Concepts
in Le Corbusier

First published in *Architectural Design*, vol. 43, April 1972.

The work of Le Corbusier differs from that of the majority of his fellow Modern architects in the extent to which it makes reference to the architectural tradition or to examples of existing buildings. Most of the theoretical statements by the Modern architects of the 1920s, including those of Le Corbusier himself, stress the need to reject tradition in favour of an architecture derived from a new technology or destined for new functions. Yet in his work Le Corbusier refers constantly to the architectural tradition either by invoking its principles and adapting them to new solutions or by overtly contradicting them in such a way that some knowledge of the tradition is necessary in order to understand his architectural message. The modification or contradiction of traditional works is the constant *leitmotiv* in his work.

Le Corbusier was the only Modern architect to prescribe architectural rules for the new architecture.[1] It was possible for him to do this because he took as his starting point the rule system of the academic tradition (in contrast to the majority of Modern architectural theorists who based their arguments on matters of content rather than form, or on physiognomic, expressionist aesthetics). This is demonstrated by the rules which Le Corbusier prescribed in his "Five Points", each of which takes its departure from an existing practice and proceeds to reverse it. The use of *pilotis,* for example, is a reversal of the classical podium; it accepts the classical separation of the *piano nobile* from the ground but interprets this separation in terms of void rather than mass. The *fenêtre en longueur* is a contradiction of the classical window aedicule. The roof terrace contradicts the pitched roof and replaces the attic storey with an open-air room. The free facade replaces the regular arrangement of window openings with a freely composed surface. The free plan contradicts the principle by which distribution was constrained by the need for vertically continuous structural walls and replaces it with a free arrangement of non-structural partitions determined by functional convenience.

It might be argued that any innovation is bound to contradict previous practice and that therefore it is redundant to include within the concept of innovation the practice which has been replaced. But the fact that each new set of rules in the "Five Points" takes as its basis the traditional articulation of building elements seems to indicate that, in the case of Le Corbusier, the original practice and the new prescription constitute a paradigmatic or metaphoric set, and that the new can only be fully understood with reference to the old, *in absentia*.

It is therefore legitimate, when discussing Le Corbusier's creative process, to speak of the "displacement of concepts" and by this to indicate a process of reinterpretation, rather than one of creation in a cultural void. The change in the arrangement and interpretation of existing elements found in Le Corbusier's work takes several forms, two of which seem to be of particular importance. The first occurs when elements of the 'high' tradition are radically transformed under conditions alien to their normal use. The second occurs when elements belonging to a tradition outside that of 'high' architecture are assimilated into architecture and given a symbolic significance which they have not hitherto possessed.

I have already mentioned, in connection with the "Five Points", the reversals involved in the invention of *pilotis* and the roof garden. Both these transformations belong to a larger problem: the gradation of the multi-storey building. In the Pavillon Suisse the *pilotis* and the roof garden/penthouse are the two outside elements of a tripartite division, whose middle term (corresponding to the *piano nobile* in a classical building) consists of *all* the repeating floors of student rooms. These floors are enveloped by a curtain wall whose purpose is to suppress the succession of individual floors. Le Corbusier's procedure here is identical in overall conception to Louis Sullivan's principle of tripartite division in the skyscraper office block. But Sullivan interprets this tradition more literally. The podium, though pierced with large windows, still provides a massive base for the superstructure, while the superstructure itself is provided with a colossal order of pilasters embracing the repeating floors of offices. Similarly the attic is simply an additional floor pierced by smaller windows and topped by a cornice whose size is adjusted to the great height of the building.

In the case of the Pavillon Suisse, the central section does not have pilasters but is conceived of as a cube, which, due to its lack of architectural articulation and its suspension over a void, seems to defy gravity. It is like an element in a painting rather than an element of architecture—a pure form, devoid of weight, and not suggestive of any particular scale. The scale has to be inferred from its relation to the *pilotis* and the attic floor and from the subdivision of delicate window mullions—the only elements of the facade that relate directly to the scale of the human being. Thus, while Le Corbusier's general scheme is the same as Sullivan, the 'cues' by which the observer can relate it to his normal architectural experience are fewer and less certain, and to some extent deliberately ambiguous or contradictory.

In the case of the *fenêtre en longueur,* the replacement of the repetitive, vertical window and the elimination of any static element threatened to remove all coherence from the facade. But Le Corbusier, unlike many other architects of the Modern Movement, retained the traditional isolated window, at the same time transforming it from a repetitive to a unique element. The presence of windows (or quasi-windows) in Le Corbusier's facades has the double effect of intensifying the generalised surface created by the *fenêtre en longueur* or the curtain wall and of referring to especially important episodes in the building. In the Cartesian Skyscraper, a large recessed aedicule is placed at the centre; and in the Secretariat at Chandigarh and the Algerian Skyscraper, this becomes a series of large openings. In all three cases these openings refer to the 'brain' of the building—the directors' rooms or the council rooms. In the Cartesian Skyscraper the effect is schematic and surreal because of the lack of support which the element has in the total facade. But in the other two schemes the previous introduction of *brise-soleil* allowed Le Corbusier to construct the large openings out of the elements forming the general facade system and therefore to give them a more concrete meaning. (A similar organisational feature had already been incorporated by the Vesnin brothers in their 1923 competition project for the Palace of Labour, in this case related to the expressed structural frame—for which, in one sense, Le Corbusier's later *brise-soleil* configurations are a substitute.)

In the Villa Stein in Garches there are two 'windows'—one placed centrally on the attic floor of the entrance facade, the other placed at one end of the first and second floors of the garden facade. One of the effects which both these openings have is to provide the same kind of human referent as is provided by the classical

Top: Wainwright Building, St Louis, Missouri. Adler and Sullivan, 1890–1891.

Middle: Cartesian Skyscraper. Le Corbusier, 1935. Model.
© FLC/ADAGP, Paris and DACS, London 2009

Bottom: Secritariat, Chandigarh. Le Corbusier, 1958. Southeast facade.
© FLC/ADAGP, Paris and DACS, London 2009

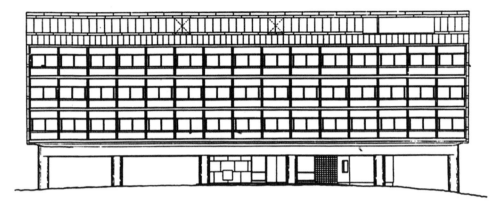

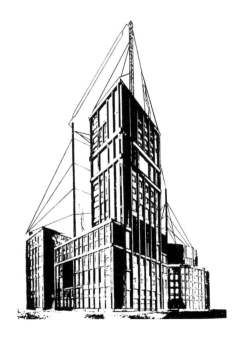

window aedicule. But at the same time, there has been a transformation: each 'window' is unique in its own facade, and its function has been altered. In the entrance facade the opening has become completely detached from any literal denotation; its purpose is simply to bring the facade to rest, to create a focal point, and to indicate the penetrability of the thin surface and its expression as volume rather than mass. In the garden facade its function is that of a loggia, which is both 'inside' and 'outside' the building, and it serves to link the building and the garden. By being placed asymmetrically, it establishes the 'free' and diagonal organisation of the internal spaces on the facade. In spite of the new meanings attached to these openings, it is legitimate to speak of them as "windows", if we extend this term to mean any discrete opening which, by its proportions and position, indicates a volume behind it that is not part of the spatial continuum but is a special point of rest.

An example of a much more literal use of windows, which seems to escape the definition given above, is seen in the corridor facade of the Pavillon Suisse. Here the window has a different function. Its small size and repetition indicates some secondary and anonymous use (in this case "walking down an access corridor"), since the more obvious solution of the continuous strip (as in La Tourette, for example) would, in its suppression of horizontals, be inconsistent with the way in which the curtain wall suppresses the floors on the front facade. However, with the exception of these repeating windows, Le Corbusier's use of the window is usually anthropomorphic. The unique, over-scaled aedicule acts as an 'eye' and animates the facade by giving it a suggestion of the human face.

The window in Le Corbusier's ideolect plays a special part in relation to all the other elements in the facade, a part which is different from that played by the traditional window. It therefore constitutes a radical transformation. But a displacement has occurred, which, in order for its full significance to be grasped, depends on the residual semantics of the traditional window.

An aspect of the survival and transformation of tradition in Le Corbusier, which belongs less to the organisation of the facade than to the very conditions of its existence, is the problem of frontality. Other writers have drawn attention to the fact that Le Corbusier tends to organise his internal and external surfaces so that they form a series of planes (actual or phenomenal) at right angles to the line of movement of the observer. Colin Rowe, Robert Slutzky, and Kenneth Frampton cite the Bauhaus at Dessau and Hannes Meyer's project for the League of Nations as counter-examples in which the buildings, far from being organised frontally, are consciously treated as three-dimensional 'machines', for the understanding of which it is necessary to move around and within the building.[2] This 'space-time' aspect was widely taken as one of the primary attributes of Modern architecture and was linked by Sigfried Giedion to Albert Einstein's theory of relativity, thus demonstrating Modern architecture's participation in the *Zeitgeist*. But there is no connection, in fact, between Einstein's mathematical model and the phenomenal experience of architecture, whether this is assumed to take place instantaneously or through

Opposite top: Pavillon Suisse, Paris.
Le Corbusier, 1930–1932. South elevation.
© FLC/ADAGP, Paris and DACS, London 2009

Opposite middle: Cité d'Affaires, Algiers.
Le Corbusier, 1938–1942. East elevation.
© FLC/ADAGP, Paris and DACS, London 2009

Opposite bottom: Project for the Palace of Labour, Moscow. Alexander and Leonid Vesnin, 1922–1923. Perspective drawing.

Top: Villa Stein in Garches. Le Corbusier, 1927. Entrance facade.
Photograph by FR Yerbury.

Bottom: Villa Stein. Garden facade.
Photograph by FR Yerbury.

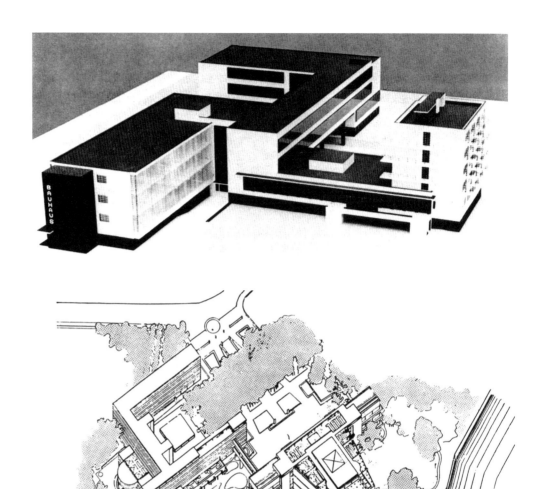

CU 2797 FACADE NORD

Top: Model of the Bauhaus, Dessau.
Walter Gropius, 1926.

Middle: Project for the League of Nations,
Geneva. Le Corbusier, 1927–1928.
Axonometric view.
© FLC/ADAGP, Paris and DACS, London 2009

Bottom: Pavillon Suisse, Paris. Le Corbusier,
1930–1932. North elevation.
© FLC/ADAGP, Paris and DACS, London 2009

the passage of time—a fact which was well understood by El Lissitzky.[3] The notion of space-time was quite alien to Le Corbusier's concept of the *promenade architecturale,* which is the temporal experience within a building that has already imprinted itself on the mind as a conceptual and spatial unity, and which seems to be connected with Le Corbusier's parallel conception of the dialectical relationship between Platonic form and empirical content, to which reference will be made later.

The notion of frontality is at the root of the concept of the facade. The non-frontalised building was for other exponents of the Modern Movement a logical extension of the fact that in modern buildings the surface should be conceived as merely the edge condition of an internally organised volume. In Le Corbusier the facade of a building is the critical boundary which one has to cross in order to pass between two types of space which are phenomenologically distinct. The fact that he created ambiguous spaces of which it is impossible to say whether they are 'inside' or 'outside', far from contradicting this basic difference, depends on it, since before an ambiguity can be set up, it is necessary to establish the two terms in relation to which the ambiguity is being created.

Both the organisation of the facade (including the 'window') and the frontalised composition are elements in which we see the tradition of architecture being transformed by Le Corbusier—the displacement of concepts already in existence—which constitute part of the buildings' meaning.

The second kind of displacement which I wish to discuss in Le Corbusier consists not of transformations of the 'high' tradition of architecture but of the assimilation into architecture of elements outside this tradition. Little can be said here about assimilations from vernacular building, which ought to be the subject of a separate study. One might list, among other numerous examples: the Catalan vault; the use of rubble walls and rough-cut timber; the use of parallel brick walls and short spans; the grouping of houses in sympathy with the configuration of the ground, a notion derived from the vernacular traditions of Greece and Italy—as in the Cap Martin project of 1949. It is not so much the case that these vernacular elements are added to the high tradition, as that the tradition itself is modified to include them. The process is not peculiar to Le Corbusier; it is a general feature of the Modern Movement in its second (1930s) phase, though in Le Corbusier it gave rise to an inventiveness which was perhaps only rivalled in the work of Alvar Aalto. We can see in this an echo of Le Corbusier's own 'National Romantic' phase and an attempt to reintegrate into Modern architecture ideas which stem from the *Lebensphilosophie* of the late nineteenth century.

One should also mention in this context Le Corbusier's assimilations of monastic architecture, particularly Carthusian, which date from his visit to the Monastery of Ema near Florence. Architecture as the symbol of, and vehicle for, the collective life was a recurrent theme in Le Corbusier, as it was in Aalto. The difference between their two interpretations lies in the fact that whereas Aalto was inspired by its secular forms—especially as found in the late Medieval hill towns of Italy—Le Corbusier was more attracted to its religious forms, to organised and hierarchical communities whose regularity and economy implied an ascetic and disciplined life dedicated to a coherent system of beliefs. The monastic organisation of the Carthusians, which provided each monk with an apartment set in a walled garden, became a model for the "Immeubles Villas", 1922, and later, after considerable modification, for the various Unités d'habitation—though in both of these cases other typological influences were at work.

Influences on Le Corbusier from outside the mainstream tradition can also be discovered in the urban traditions of Paris. I do not refer to the well-known examples of the small cafe and artist's studio but to eighteenth century *hôtels particuliers.* In the plans of these houses there were specific spaces which were

not part of the 'architecture' but which were necessary to the practical functioning of the building. This planning by means of *poché,* which became codified in the teaching of the Beaux-Arts, is noticeable in many eighteenth century Parisian *hôtels* where the needs of comfort and privacy demanded a sometimes quite elaborate series of service corridors and stores tucked away behind the main rooms (which are arranged according to the Baroque tradition, *en echelon*). Whether or not Le Corbusier was consciously influenced by this, the plans for the grand houses designed by him in the 1920s had similarly complex secondary spaces, a characteristic which clearly differentiates his planning from that of other Modern architects. But there is a crucial displacement of concepts. According to the theory of the free plan, these spaces are no longer concealed but become an integral part of the architectural experience. Inherent in the idea of the free plan, though never explicitly mentioned by Le Corbusier, is the principle that every kind of space has a right to architectural expression and that no part of the building should be concealed. If a wall creates a convex surface in one space, there must be a corresponding concave curve in the adjacent space; in this way the structure of the space is entirely explained and there is no 'space left over'.

This principle is closely related to the procedures of Cubism, in which a representation must include all the space within the pictorial volume, and not merely the space between objects. Just as a Cubist painting is a description of the structure of the pictorial space, so Le Corbusier's houses are descriptions of the structure of the architectural space.

Thus Le Corbusier's transformation of *poché* spatial planning not only facilitates the pragmatics of the free plan and the attribution of equal status to different spaces; it also makes the house a complete representation of its own spatial structure. Nonetheless, this transparent 'exhibition' of space retains, while it inverts, the traditional distinction between service areas and living areas, giving to the first positive and to the second negative spatial characteristics.

In certain ways this procedure is similar to that of Mies van der Rohe, in his articulation of space by independent planes. But there is an important difference. Even when service spaces are implied by a crowding together of the planes, as in Mies' Brick House project, the spaces differ only in degree. In Le Corbusier the traditional difference between the main and service spaces is maintained, just as the Beaux-Arts principles of distribution are never entirely abandoned. However 'free' a plan of Le Corbusier's may be, not only does it

Opposite top: Weekend House, Paris. Le Corbusier, 1935. Axonometric. © FLC/ADAGP, Paris and DACS, London 2009

Opposite middle: Roq et Rob housing, Cap Martin. Le Corbusier, 1948. © FLC/ADAGP, Paris and DACS, London 2009

Opposite bottom: Anticoli Corrado village in the Sabine Mountains, Italy.

Top: Errazuris House, Chile. Le Corbusier, 1930. Perspective sketch. © FLC/ADAGP, Paris and DACS, London 2009

Bottom: "Immeubles Villas". Le Corbusier, 1922. Perspective drawing. © FLC/ADAGP, Paris and DACS, London 2009

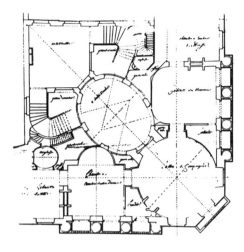

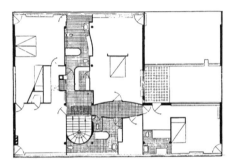

consist, in large part, of quite traditional 'rooms', but a certain axial magnetism persists which has the effect of emphasising the process of expansion and distortion to which the plan has been subjected. Such a spatial 'discourse' does not exist in De Stijl plans, where the blowing apart of the 'box' and the assertion of crystalline structure are never met with any resistance, and where the intensity of the plan regularly diminishes from the centre toward the infinity of outside space. With Le Corbusier the semantic connotations *of poché* planning are maintained, only to be contradicted by the fact that now these spaces are felt to contribute to the total architectural experience, nudging and distorting the major spaces. This interaction is no more than a special case of the general tendency in Le Corbusier's work toward the setting up and artistic reconciliation of opposites. The main elements of this opposition are traditional 'high' architecture and the characteristic 'equipment' of the modern industrial world, the one asserting an idealist world of expected order (as enshrined in a particular cultural tradition), the other responding to new behaviour patterns and their equivalent forms. Throughout his writings, Le Corbusier constantly refers to this dichotomy, without ever attempting to resolve it on a theoretical level. 'Reason' and the 'heart' are seen as complementary faculties, but sometimes reason is used to support a positivist position, and sometimes, as in the *satisfaction de l'esprit*, it is associated with experiences of a higher order to which matters both of sentiment and of practical convenience are subjected.

The resolution of this conflict takes place on the plane of the building as a work of art. It can do so because the work of art is not limited *a priori* to a set of forms but is able (and indeed compelled) to absorb raw elements from the 'real' world, although these are apparently in opposition to its idealistic essence. It is in the assimilation of objects of technology in architecture that we can obtain the clearest insight into this process of absorption and reconciliation in the work of Le Corbusier. The presence of elements of technology in his work might be thought to be no more surprising than their presence in the Modern Movement as a whole. Technology provided the means of rescuing architecture from the false rhetoric into which it had degenerated in the nineteenth century and of re-establishing that identity between technique and representation which existed in the periods still dominated by a craft tradition—an identity by virtue of which the essence of a building consisted of the objectification of the building process. But in Le Corbusier, more than in any other Modern architect, technology had a metaphorical role, in which complete machines became paradigms for the new architecture. One of the most important of these paradigms was the ocean liner. Not only was the ocean liner designed according to scientific principles, it provided, for the limited period of its use, all the requisites of communal life. It was a symbol not only of objective design, in which the arbitrary choice of the designer was reduced to the minimum, but also of a human society organised according to rational principles.

In the Unité d'Habitation not only are the rational principles underlying the ocean liner involved but also the poetry of its forms. The building is poised on its *pilotis* like a ship afloat; its inhabitants have the same relation to the surrounding countryside as the passengers of a liner have to the sea. It reproduces the liner's communal promenade decks and its private cabins; its plant is arranged on the roof like the liner's funnels and superstructure. But this is not just a picturesque evocation. Every visual analogy is tied to a functional correspondence. The liner is not just a romantic image of the Modern age; it is an example of its very principles at work and is thus a valid model for architecture.

But the liner is dumb. It is the result of imperative but limited demands. Not until these demands have been deepened to satisfy the needs of a rational society and have become a conscious object of the social will can such a structure achieve the status of architecture. Thus, in Le Corbusier, the reverse process to that proposed by Hannes Meyer takes place. According to Meyer, architecture should become like

machinery, unconsciously following the dictates of an implacable economic destiny. According to Le Corbusier machinery has to be raised to a conscious level—in fact, to become architecture—before it can truly serve and represent man.

The final type of displacement which I will discuss here concerns industrial buildings. In *Vers une architecture* Le Corbusier followed other propagandists of the Modern Movement in giving examples of warehouses, silos, and factories to illustrate the pure formal qualities of industrial buildings. Such buildings not only made use of advanced structural techniques but, because of their economic and utilitarian criteria, they expressed this construction in a way which resulted in a repertoire of basic plastic forms. The relationship of these forms was based on a new, if unconscious, compositional principle, according to which the elements were distributed purely on the basis of practical necessity. This type of building suggested to Le Corbusier a new kind of conscious architecture; it was not, itself, this architecture. It suggested a method which might supersede the "rules of Vignola", but it remained latent until its pragmatism could be converted into ideal architectural forms.

This conversion involves an apparent contradiction. The organisation of the parts, which has merely been suggested by unconscious, naïve design, has to be the result of aesthetic 'ordering', but the very freedom on the basis of which this ordering must now take place (without academic rules) is dependent on the laws of practical distribution, and the more stringent they are, the more they deny to the designer any freedom of manipulation. This contradiction can be resolved only if it is assumed that a consciousness of the reasons for practical organisation in some way becomes a part of the aesthetic experience of the building. The 'designed' building thus becomes something in which the elements of order and the elements of disorder (or chance) achieve a momentary equilibrium.

That this is what Le Corbusier achieves in the transformation of industrial buildings into architecture can be seen by comparing his factory at St-Dié with a factory illustrated in *Vers une architecture* and noting the remarkable parallels between them.[4] The fact that this example is a case of transformation from one industrial building to another does not weaken the argument for displacement in the broader sense, since we are less concerned here with displacements between different building types than with those between processes outside and those inside the realm of architecture. Moreover, this example illustrates very clearly the way in which Le Corbusier worked. With him it is not a question of establishing general and abstract principles before becoming involved with a particular design; the concrete vision and the general principles always seem to appear simultaneously.

The architectural solution already exists in embryo in the factory which Le Corbusier uses as a model. The shop floors consist of a repeating grid into which an office with a different scale of window is inserted on the ground floor. On the roof further random elements occur, completing the suggestion of the tripartite division we have seen in the Pavillon Suisse—a ground floor and a roof where the particular incidents can occur, and a middle section which is completely regular.

In the factory of St-Dié this implied separation of parts is made more distinct. The office is now inserted within the space of the *pilotis,* and the mechanical plant on the roof is joined by a range of penthouse offices. The ground floor and the roof are no longer tentative and accidental events but precise and important ones, which give life and meaning to the regular middle section.

Nothing could illustrate more clearly the way in which Le Corbusier 'architectures' the given elements of a practical building programme. The form of the building is not—as with Mies—reduced to an overall simple order in which the random elements of life are invisible. These elements become part of the architectural message and are aesthetically integrated with the building as a whole.

Opposite top: Hôtel de Montmorency, Paris. Claude–Nicolas Ledoux, 1770. Plan of original design.

Opposite bottom: Villa Stein in Garches. Le Corbusier, 1927. Third floor plan.

Above: Project for a Brick Country House. Ludwig Mies van der Rohe, 1922. Plan. Collection, Mies van der Rohe Archive, The Museum of Modern Art.

The phenomena analysed here no doubt represent only one aspect of the work of Le Corbusier. But it is, I believe, an important aspect, and one which has not received sufficient attention. Architectural theory has been dominated for the last decade or so by various forms of determinism or populism, neither of which recognises architecture as constituting a cultural entity in its own right. But the raw material of architecture is, to a large extent, the architectural culture at any one moment in history. Unless those aspects of architectural creation which have been discussed—aspects which involve the transformation of an existing culture—are understood, we will not achieve an architecture by which cultural meanings can be sustained.

1   This point was noted by Leonardo Benevolo in *History of Modern Architecture*, Cambridge, MA: MIT Press, 1971.
2   Rowe, Colin, and Robert Slutzky, "Transparency: Literal and Phenomenal, Part II, "*Perspecta*, nos. 13–14, 1971, pp. 287–301; Frampton, Kenneth, "The Humanist vs. the Utilitarian Ideal", *Architectural Design*, no. 38, March 1968, pp. 134–136.
3   "A number of modern artists... believe that they can build up multi-dimensional real spaces.... Lobachevsky and Gauss were the first to prove that Euclidean space represents only one case among an infinite number of other spaces. However, our senses are incapable of visualising these spaces.... We can only change the form of our physical space but not its structure." El Lissitzky, *Russia: An Architecture for World Revolution*, Cambridge, MA: MIT Press, 1970, pp. 145–146.
4   I am indebted to Robert Maxwell for this observation.

Top: Factory, St-Dié, France. Le Corbusier, 1946–1951. Southeast elevation.

Bottom: Factory illustrated in *Vers une architecture*, 1923.

© FLC/ADAGP, Paris and DACS, London 2009

Typology and Design Method

First published in *Arena*, vol. 83, June 1967.

During the last few years a great deal of attention has been given to the problem of design methodology and to the process of design as a branch of the wider process of problem-solving. Many people believe—not without reason—that the intuitive methods of design traditionally used by architects are incapable of dealing with the complexity of the problems to be solved and that without sharper tools of analysis and classification the designer tends to fall back on previous examples for the solution of new problems—on type-solutions.

One of the designers and educators who has been consistently preoccupied with this matter is Tomás Maldonado. At a seminar at Princeton University in the fall of 1966, Maldonado admitted that in cases where it was not possible to classify every observable activity in an architectural programme, it might be necessary to use a typology of architectural forms in order to arrive at a solution. But he added that these forms were like a cancer in the body of the solution and that as our techniques of classification become more systematic, it should be possible to eliminate them altogether.

Now, it is my belief that beneath the apparently practical and hard-headed aspect of these ideas lies an aesthetic doctrine. It will be my purpose to show this to be the case and, further, to try to show that it is untenable without considerable modification.

One of the most frequent arguments used against typological procedures in architecture has been that they are a vestige of an age of craft. It is held that the use of models by craftsmen became less necessary as the development of scientific techniques enabled man to discover the general laws underlying the technical solutions of the pre-industrial age.

The vicissitudes of the words "art" and "science" certainly indicate that there is a valid distinction to be drawn between artefacts that are the result of the application of the laws of physical science and those that are the result of mimesis and intuition. Before the rise of modern science, tradition, habit, and imitation were the methods by which all artefacts were made, whether these artefacts were mainly utilitarian or mainly religious. The word "art" was used to describe the skill necessary to produce all such artefacts. With the development of modern science, the word "art" was progressively restricted to the case of artefacts which did not depend on the general laws of physical science but continued to be based on tradition and the idea of the final form of the work as a fixed ideal.

But this distinction ignores the extent to which artefacts have not only a 'use' value in the crudest sense but also an 'exchange' value. The craftsman had an image of the object in his mind's eye when starting to make it. Whether this object was a cult image (say, a sculpture) or a kitchen utensil, it was an object of cultural exchange, and it formed part of a system of communication within society. Its 'message' value was precisely the image of the final form which the craftsman held in his mind's eye as he was making it and to which his artefact corresponded as closely as possible. In spite of the development of the scientific method, we must still attribute such social or iconic values to the products of technology and recognise that they play an essential role in the generation and development of the physical tools of our environment. It is easy to see that the class of artefacts which continue to be made according to the traditional methods (for example, paintings or musical compositions) has a predominantly iconic purpose, but such a purpose is not so often recognised in the creation of the environment as a whole. This fact is concealed from us because the intentions of the design process are 'hidden' in the overt details of the performance specifications.

The idolisation of 'primitive' man and the fundamentalist attitude which this generates have also discouraged the acceptance of such iconic values. There has been a tendency since the eighteenth century to regard the age of primitive man as a golden age in which man lived close to nature. For many years, for instance, the primitive hut or one of its derivatives has been taken as the starting point for architectural evolution and has been the subject of first year design programmes in the schools, and it would not be an exaggeration to say that frequently a direct line of descent is presumed to exist from the noble savage through the utilitarian crafts to modern science and technology. Insofar as it is based on the idea of the noble savage, this idea is quite baseless. The cosmological systems of primitive man were very intellectual and very artificial. To take only kinship systems, the following quotation from the French anthropologist Claude Lévi-Strauss will make the point clear: "Certainly", he says, "the biological family is present and persists in human society. But what gives to kinship its character as a social fact is not what it must conserve of nature; it is the essential step by which it separates itself from nature. A system of kinship does not consist of objective blood ties; it exists only in the consciousness of men; it is an arbitrary system of representations, not the spontaneous development of a situation of fact."[1]

There still seems to be a close parallel between such systems and the way modern man approaches the world. And what was true of primitive man in all the ramifications of his practical and emotional life—namely, the need to *represent* the phenomenal world in such a way that it becomes a coherent and logical system—persists in our own organisations and more particularly in our attitude toward the man-made objects of our environment. An example of the way this applies to contemporary man is in the creation of what are called "socio-spatial schemata". Our senses of place and relationship in, say, an urban environment, or in a building, are not dependent on any objective fact that is measurable; they are phenomenal. The purpose of the aesthetic organisation of our environment is to capitalise on this subjective schematisation and make it socially available. The resulting organisation does not correspond in a one-to-one relationship with the objective facts but is an artificial construct which *represents* these facts in a socially recognisable way. It follows that the representational systems which are developed are, in a real sense, independent of the quantifiable facts of the environment, and this is particularly true if the environment is changing very rapidly.

However, no system of representation, is totally independent of the facts which constitute the objective world. The Modern Movement in architecture was an attempt to modify the representational systems which had been inherited from the pre-industrial past and which no longer seemed meaningful within the context of a rapidly changing technology. One of the main doctrines at the root of this transformation was based essentially on a return to nature, deriving from the Romantic Movement but ostensibly changed from a desire to imitate the surface of natural forms, or to operate at a craft level, to a belief in the ability of science to reveal the essence of nature's mode of operation.

Underlying this doctrine was an implied belief in biotechnical determinism. And it is from this theory that the current belief in the supreme importance of scientific methods of analysis and classification derives. The essence of the functional doctrine of the Modern Movement was not that beauty or order or meaning was unnecessary, but that it could no longer be found in the deliberate search for final forms. The path by which the artefact affected the observer aesthetically was seen as short-circuiting the process of formalisation. Form was merely the result of a logical process by which the operational needs and the operational techniques were brought together. Ultimately these would fuse in a kind of biological extension of life, and function and technology would become totally transparent. The theory of Buckminster Fuller is an extreme example of this doctrine.

The relation of this notion to Spencerian evolutionary theory is very striking. According to this theory the purpose of prolonging life and the species must be attributed to the process as a whole, but at no particular moment in the process is it possible to see this purpose as a conscious one. The process is therefore unconscious and teleological. In the same way, the biotechnical determinism of the Modern Movement was teleological, because it saw the aesthetic of architectural form as something which was achieved without the conscious interference of the designer but as something which nonetheless was postulated as his ultimate purpose.

It is clear that this doctrine contradicts any theory which would give priority to an intentional iconic form, and it attempts to absorb the process by which man tries to make a representation of the world of phenomena back into a process of unconscious evolution. To what extent has it been successful, and to what extent can it be shown to be possible?

It seems evident, in the first place, that the theory begs the whole question of the iconic significance of forms. Those in the field of design who were—and are—preaching pure technology and so-called objective design method as a necessary and sufficient means of producing environmental devices persistently attribute iconic power to the creations of technology, which they worship to a degree inconceivable in a scientist. I said earlier that it was in the power of all artefacts to become icons, no matter whether or not they were specifically created for this purpose. Perhaps I might mention certain objects of the nineteenth century world of technology which had power of this kind—steamships and locomotives, to give only two examples. Even though these objects were made ostensibly with utilitarian purposes in mind, they quickly became *Gestalt* entities, which were difficult to disassemble in the mind's eye into their component parts. The same is true of later technical devices such as cars and airplanes. The fact that these objects have been imbued with aesthetic unity and have become carriers of so much meaning indicates that a process of selection and isolation has taken place which is quite redundant from the point of view of their particular functions. We must therefore look upon the aesthetic and iconic qualities of artefacts as being due, not so much to an inherent property, but to a sort of availability or redundancy in them in relation to human feeling.

The literature of Modern architecture is full of statements which indicate that after all the known operational needs have been satisfied, there is still a wide area of choice in the final configuration. I should like to cite two designers who have used mathematical methods to arrive at architectural solutions. The first is Yona Friedman, who uses these methods to arrive at a hierarchy of organisation in the programme. Friedman, in describing methods of computing the relative positions of functions within a three-dimensional city grid, has acknowledged that the designer is always faced, after computation, with a choice of alternatives, all of which are equally good from an operational point of view.[2]

The second is Yannis Xenakis, who, in designing the Philips Pavilion while he was in the office of Le Corbusier, used mathematical procedures to determine the form of the enclosing structure. In the book which Philips published to describe this building, Xenakis says that calculation provided the characteristic form of the structure but that after this, logic no longer operated, and the compositional arrangement had to be decided on the basis of intuition.

From these statements it would appear that a purely teleological doctrine of technico-aesthetic forms is not tenable. At whatever stage in the design process it may occur, it seems that the designer is always faced with making voluntary decisions and that the configurations which he arrives at must be the result of an *intention* and not merely the result of a deterministic process. The following statement of Le Corbusier tends to reinforce this point of view. "My intellect", he says, "does not accept the adoption of the modules of Vignola in the matter of building. I claim that harmony exists between the objects one is dealing with. The chapel at Ronchamp perhaps shows that architecture is not an affair of columns but an affair of plastic events. Plastic events are not regulated by scholastic or academic formulae; they are free and innumerable." Although this statement is a defence of functionalism against the academic imitation of past forms and the determinism it denies is academic rather than scientific, it nonetheless stresses the release that follows from functional considerations rather than their power of determining the solution.

One of the most uninhibited statements of this kind comes from László Moholy-Nagy. In his description of the design course at the Institute of Design in Chicago, he makes the following defence of the free operation of intuition. "The training", he says, "is directed toward imagination, fantasy, and inventiveness, a basic conditioning to the ever-changing industrial scene, to the technology-in-flux. [...] The last step in this technique is the emphasis on integration through a conscious search for relationships. [...] The intuitive working mechanics of the genius gives a clue to this process. The unique ability of the genius can be approximated by everyone if only its essential feature be apprehended: the flash-like act of connecting elements not obviously belonging together. [...] If the same methodology were used generally in all fields we would have *the* key to our age—seeing everything in relationship."[3]

We can now begin to build up a picture of the general body of doctrine embedded in the Modern Movement. It consists of a tension between two apparently contradictory ideas—biotechnical determinism on the one hand and free expression on the other. What seems to have happened is that, in the act of giving a new validity to the demands of function as an extension of nature's mode of operation, a vacuum has been left where previously there was a body of traditional practice. The whole field of aesthetics, with its ideological foundations and its belief in ideal beauty, has been swept aside. All that is left in its place is permissive expression, the total freedom of the genius which, if we but knew it, resides in us all. What appears on the surface as a hard, rational discipline of design turns out rather paradoxically to be a mystical belief in the intuitional process.

I would like now to turn back to the statement by Maldonado which I mentioned earlier. He said that so long as our classification techniques were unable to establish all the parameters of a problem, it might be necessary to use a typology of forms to fill the gap. From the examples of the statements made by modern designers, it would seem that it is indeed never possible to state all the parameters of a problem. Truly quantifiable criteria always leave a choice for the designer to make. In modern architectural theory this choice has been generally conceived of as based on intuition working in a cultural vacuum. In mentioning typology, Maldonado is suggesting something quite new and something which has been rejected again and again by modern theorists. He is suggesting that the area of pure intuition must be based on a knowledge of past solutions applied to related problems, and that creation is a process of adapting forms derived either from past needs or from past aesthetic ideologies to the needs of the present. Although he regards this as a provisional solution—"a cancer in the body of the solution"—he nonetheless recognises that this is the actual procedure which designers follow.

I suggest that this is true and, moreover, that it is true in all fields of design and not only that of architecture. I have referred to the argument that the more rigorously the general physical or mathematical laws are applied to the solution of design problems the less it is necessary to have a mental picture of the final form. But, although we may postulate an ideal state in which these laws correspond exactly to the objective world, in fact this is not the case. Laws are not found in nature. They are constructs of the human mind; they are models which are valid so long as events do not prove them to be wrong. They are models, as it were, at one remove from pictorial models. Not only this. Technology is frequently faced with different problems which are not logically consistent. All the problems of aircraft configuration, for example, could not be solved unless there was give-and-take in the application of physical laws. The position of the power unit is a variable; so is the configuration of the wings and tail plane. The position of one affects the shape of the other. The application of general laws is a necessary ingredient of the form. But it is not a sufficient one for determining the actual configuration. And in a world of pure technology this area of free choice is invariably dealt with by adapting previous solutions.

In the world of architecture this problem becomes even more crucial, because general laws of physics and the empirical facts are even less capable of fixing a final configuration than in the case of an airplane or a bridge. Recourse to some kind of typological model is even more necessary.

It may be argued that, in spite of the fact that there is an area of free choice beyond that of operation, this freedom lies in the details (where, for instance, personal 'taste' might legitimately operate). This could probably be shown to be true of such technically complex objects as airplanes, where the topological relationships are largely determined by the application of physical laws. But it does not seem to apply to architecture. On the contrary, because of the comparatively simple environmental pressures that operate on buildings, the topological relationships are hardly at all determined by physical laws. In the case of the Philips Pavilion, for example, it was not only the acoustic requirements which established the basic configuration but also the need for a building which would convey a certain impression of vertigo and fantasy. It is in the details that these laws become stringent and not in the general arrangement. Where the designer decides to be governed by operational factors, he works in terms of a thoroughly nineteenth century rationalism, for example in the case of the office buildings of Mies van der Rohe and Skidmore, Owings and Merrill, where purely pragmatic planning and cost considerations converge on a received neo-classical aesthetic to create simple cubes, regular frames, and cores. It is interesting that in most of the projects where form determinants are held to be technical or operational in an avant-garde sense, rationalism and cost are discarded for forms of a fantastic or expressionist kind. Frequently, as in the case of Archigram, forms are borrowed from other disciplines, such as space engineering or Pop Art. Valid as these iconographic procedures may be—and before dismissing them one would have to investigate them in relation to the work of Le Corbusier and the Russian Constructivists, who borrowed the forms of ships and engineering structures—they can hardly be compatible with a doctrine of determinism, if we are to regard this as a *modus operandi*, rather than a remote and utopian ideal.

The exclusion by Modern architectural theory of typologies and its belief in the freedom of intuition can at any rate be partially explained by the more general theory of expression which was current at the turn of the century. This theory applies most clearly to the work of certain painters—notably Wassily Kandinsky, in his book *Point and Line to Plane,* when he outlines the theory on which his paintings are based. Expressionist theory rejected all historical manifestations of art, just as Modern architectural theory rejected all historical forms of architecture. To it these manifestations were an ossification of technical and cultural attitudes whose *raison d'etre* had ceased to exist. The theory was based on the belief that shapes have physiognomic or expressive content which communicates itself to us directly. This view has been subjected to a great deal of criticism, and one of its most convincing refutations occurs in EH Gombrich's book *Meditations on a Hobby Horse.* Gombrich demonstrates that an arrangement of forms such as is found in a painting by Kandinsky is, in fact, very low in content, unless we attribute to these forms some system of conventional meanings not inherent in the forms themselves. His thesis is that physiognomic forms are ambiguous, though not wholly without expressive value, and that they can only be interpreted within a particular cultural ambience. One of the ways he illustrates this is by reference to the supposed affective qualities of colours. Gombrich points out in the now famous example of traffic signals that we are dealing with a conventional and not a physiognomic meaning, and he maintains that it would be equally logical to reverse the meaning system so that red indicated action and forward movement, and green inaction, quietness, and caution.[4]

Expressionist theory probably had a very strong influence on the Modern Movement in architecture. Its application to architecture would be even more obvious than to painting because of the absence, in architecture, of any forms which are overtly representational. Architecture has usually, with music, been considered an abstract, non-mimetic art, so that the theory of physiognomic forms could be applied to it without having to overcome the hurdle of natural representation, as in painting. But if the objections to Expressionist theory are valid, then they apply to architecture as much as to painting.

If, as Gombrich suggests, forms by themselves are relatively empty of meaning, it follows that the forms which we intuit will, in the unconscious mind, tend to attract to themselves certain associations of meaning. This could mean not only that we are *not* free from the forms of the past and from the availability of these forms as typological models but that, if we assume we are free, we have lost control over a very active sector of our imagination and of our power to communicate with others. It would seem that we ought to try to establish a value system which takes account of the forms and solutions of the past if we are to gain control over concepts which will obtrude themselves into the creative process, whether we like it or not.

There is, in fact, a close relationship between the pure functionalist or teleological theory that I have described and Expressionism, as defined by Gombrich. By insisting on the use of analytical and inductive methods of design, functionalism leaves a vacuum in the form-making process. This it fills with its own reductionist aesthetic—the aesthetic that claims that "intuition", with no historical dimension, can arrive spontaneously at forms that are the equivalent of fundamental operations. This procedure postulates a kind of onomatopoeic relationship between forms and their content. In the case of a biotechnico-determinist theory, the content is the set of relevant functions—functions which themselves are a reduction of all the socially meaningful operations within a building—and it is assumed that the functional complex is translated into forms whose iconographic significance is nothing more than the rational structure of the functional complex itself. Put another way, the existent facts of the objective functional situation are the equivalent of the existent facts of the subjective emotional situation. But traditionally in the work of art, the existent facts, whether subjective or objective, are less significant than the values we attribute to these facts or to the system of representation which embodies these values. The work of art, in this respect, resembles language. A language which was simply the expression of emotions would be a series of single-word exclamations; in fact, language is a complex system of representation in which the basic emotions are structured into an intellectually coherent system.[5] It would be impossible to conceive of constructing a language *a priori*. The ability to construct such a language would have to presuppose the language itself. Similarly a plastic system of representation such as architecture has to presuppose the existence of a given system of representation. In neither case can the problem of formal representation be reduced to some pre-existent essence outside the formal system itself, of which the form is merely a reflection. In both cases it is necessary to postulate a conventional system embodied in typological problem-solution complexes.

My purpose in stressing this fact is not to advocate a reversion to an architecture which accepts tradition unthinkingly. This would imply that there was a fixed and immutable relation between forms and meaning. The characteristic of our age is constant change, and it is precisely because of this that it is necessary to investigate the part which modifications of type-solutions play in relation to problems and solutions which are without precedent in any received tradition.

I have tried to show that a theory according to which the problem-solution process can be reduced to some sort of essence is untenable. I would like to conclude by postulating that the process of change is carried out, not by a process of reduction, but rather by a process of exclusion. It would seem that the history of the Modern Movement in all the arts lends support to such an idea. If we look at the allied fields of painting and music, we can see that, in the work of a Kandinsky or a Schoenberg, traditional formal devices were not completely abandoned but were transformed and given a new emphasis by the exclusion of ideologically repulsive iconic elements. In the case of Kandinsky it is the representational element which is excluded; in the case of Schoenberg it is the diatonic system of harmony.

The value of such a process of exclusion enables us to see the potentiality of forms as if for the first time and with naiveté. This is the justification for the radical change in the iconic system of representation, and it is a process which we have to adopt if we are to keep and renew our awareness of the meanings which can be carried by forms. The bare bones of our culture—a culture with its own characteristic technologies—must become visible to us. For this to happen a certain scientific detachment toward our problems is essential and with it the application of the mathematical tools proper to our culture. But these tools are unable to give us a ready-made solution to our problems. They only provide the framework, the context within which we operate.

1 *Structural Anthropology*, trans Claire Jacobson and Brooke Grundfest Schoepf, New York: Basic Books, 1963, p. 50.
2 Friedman discussed this issue at a lecture given at the Architectural Association in 1966.
3 *Vision in Motion*, Chicago: Paul Theobald, 1947, p. 68.
4 It is interesting that since his book came out it has been reported that the Chinese have, in fact, reversed the meanings of their traffic signals.
5 For the study of language as a system of symbolic representation, see Ernst Cassirer, *The Philosophy of Symbolic Forms,* trans Ralph Manheim, New Haven: Yale University Press, 1957. For a discussion of language in relation to literature (metalanguage), see Roland Barthes, *Essais Critiques*, Paris: Editions du Seuil, 1964.

Rules, Realism and History

First published as *"Regeln, Realismus und Geschicte"*, in the *"Realismus in Architektur"* issue of *Archithèse*, no. 19, 1976.

Perhaps the most crucial problem in architecture today is that of its relationship with the culture of society as a whole. Is architecture to be considered as a self-referential system, with its own traditions and its own system of values, or is it rather a social product which only becomes an entity once it has been reconstituted by forces external to it?

There is undoubtedly today a strong current of opinion which tends toward the first of these alternatives. These ideas seem to have appeared as a reaction against the weak theoretical position forced on architecture during the last 15 years or so, during which its defenses have been attacked by successive waves of operationalism, systems methodology, poetic technology, social realism, and even certain semiological discussions, all of which have had as their chief aim the dismantling of 'architectural values'—what Reyner Banham has called the "cultural baggage". On the one hand, architectural creation has been postponed until an apparently endless process of induction and analysis (whether technical or social) has been completed; on the other, aesthetic fervour has been encouraged, provided that its roots were either expressionistic or populist, and the existence of any valid system of rules or norms belonging to the tradition of 'high architecture' has been denied. If it has been admitted that architecture is a 'language', then it is a language which springs from intuition, unhampered by any previous knowledge of the subject—a language more natural than natural language itself, since it does not have to be learned.

These tendencies—which are still very strong—are, in one sense, the result of one of the most powerful motives of avant-garde art since the mid-nineteenth century—the drive toward 'realism' or 'naturalism'. The successive artistic revolutions of the last 150 years have all been attempts to 'get behind' 'stylistic' conventions, to destroy the artificial rules which not only mediate between reality and its representation but also give this representation a particular ideological colouring. It is true that this search for a primordial language with which to express man's relation to reality eventually took a form which seems almost the antithesis of realism, when, instead of imitating structures which were immediately given, it attempted to discover hidden and underlying structures. This turn toward formalism, which sought to create analogues of the real world, not only affected painting and literature as 'mimetic' arts but also architecture and music, where the humanising and reassuring elements of style belonging to the 'classical' tradition were rejected in favour of more open structures. But if the aim of this revolutionary force was to eliminate style and to discover essences, it was in the end bound to come up against the fact that our mode of understanding 'reality' and our mode of 'representing' reality artistically are separate things.

Already in the 1920s, the critic Boris Tomashevsky drew attention to the infinite regress in which the avant-garde found itself in literature:

> In general, the nineteenth century abounded in schools whose very names hint at realistic techniques of motivation—'Realism', 'Naturalism', 'the Nature School', 'Populism', and so on. In our time the Symbolists replaced the Realists in the name of some kind of transnaturalism... a fact which did not prevent the appearance of Acmeism... and Futurism.... From school to school we hear the call to 'Naturalism'. Why, then, has a 'completely naturalistic school' not been founded...? Because the name 'Realist' is attached to each school (and to none).... This explains the

ever present antagonism of the new school for the old—that is, the exchange of old and obvious conventions for new, less obvious ones within the literary pattern. On the other hand, this also shows that realistic material in itself does not have artistic structure and that the formation of an artistic structure requires that reality be reconstructed according to aesthetic laws. Such laws are always, considered in relation to reality, conventional.[1]

The facts stated here, though clearly admissible in the case of the fine arts, might be questioned in relation to architecture, which has to embrace both the real and the representational—the work of architecture being part of the real, 'usable' world, as well as a representation of that world. It could be argued that the Modern Movement radically confused these two aspects, attributing to the need for practical buildings a representational function or, conversely, burdening the representational function with the responsibility for solving practical building problems. But if it did this, the reason must lie in the fact that these two aspects of architecture, which are independent from a logical point of view, are never independent experientially, and that the search for the 'essence' of the building has an aesthetic motivation, embracing a certain idea of utility and its representation—one in which the transparency of the form was symbolic of a reality which could be totally described and manifested.

Thus the 'materialism' of modern architecture was just as 'metaphysical' as architecture had ever been, and this seems to show that when we are talking of architecture, we are referring to a system of representation of essentially the same kind as that found in the other arts. It is no more possible in architecture than any other system of representation to arrive at the *ne plus ultra* in which the representation and the represented coincide; the need for aesthetic laws of construction must be admitted. Such laws are not like the laws established on the basis of hypothesis and experiment in the physical sciences—laws which, according to Karl Popper, have to be capable of falsification. If we are to make a scientific analogy, we should rather say that they are like the 'paradigms' which, in Thomas Kuhn's analysis, determine the area of scientific discourse. They are norms, and a complete description of the phenomenon of architecture could no more neglect to include them than could a description, say, of football omit to include those rules which alone render the game intelligible. In Tomashevsky's terms, they are "conventional".[2]

But however much the necessary existence of such laws may justify a view of architecture as a self-referential system, it does not support a view which would regard such a system as dependent on laws which are absolute and unchanging. The laws regulating aesthetic construction are subject to change, and this change comes about not from inside the aesthetic system but from outside.

That this is true can be seen even in a system so apparently independent of technical and economic conditions as music. The change in musical language which came about in the eighteenth century, when a contrapuntal gave way to a linear method, can only be explained by a change in the social function of music. What took place was, of course, a purely *musical* change, and it can be completely explained in terms of rules which belong to music alone. Nonetheless, the motivation of the change was external to music.

Up until the nineteenth century, the external pressures on architecture were no more than on the other arts, but since the Industrial Revolution, and with increasing intensity in the twentieth century, architecture has been subject to social and technological pressures of a more direct kind than in the other arts. Changes in patterns of settlement and work, technical changes involving the use of new materials, economic changes due to a vast increase in the profitability of land development, changes in the method of distributing information, people and goods, have radically altered the architectural infrastructure. None of these

changes has originated from inside architecture; all of them have necessitated a change in architectural rules.

Such a process, involving two variables—the socio-economic system and the aesthetic rule system—can only be accounted for dialectically. As an example of this process in operation, let us look at what might be called the "facade problem" in modern architecture. In the early days of the Modern Movement this problem was widely held to be non-existent. According to the organic analogy, the external form of a building was supposed to be the result of its internal organisation; 'facadism' was identified with an architecture of false rhetoric. Yet certain architects, notably Le Corbusier, retained the facade and the related function of frontality as part of their architectural language. The problem of frontality is not simply the problem of the outside appearance of the building, though this in itself is bound up with the whole problem of the building as a representation in the public realm and cannot be attributed to superficial rhetorical needs. It is also connected with the problem of the interface between 'public' and 'private' and the transition from 'outside' to 'inside'. In these terms it is a purely architectural problem—a problem that will not dissolve however much the conditions external to architecture change.

But the problem cannot be solved by recourse to any unalterable system of architectural rules. It can only come from taking the existing rule system, adapting it to the new conditions, and laying down a revised set of rules. In all his major buildings, we see Le Corbusier facing this problem with unrivaled inventiveness: the turning of the staircase through 90 degrees at the Villa in Vaucresson, the system of virtual frontal planes in the League of Nations building, the elaborate entrance system in the Salvation Army Hostel, the invention of the *brise-soleil*, to mention only a few cases. As a counter-example we might take one of Herman Hertzberger's projects. In his attempt to generate the plan as a system, Hertzberger has ignored the problem of the facade. His buildings can only be comprehended as internally generated, and no reference is made to the problem of the building as a representation or to the approach to the building from outside. The building is seen as a fragment of 'real' space, whose laws of extension lie in the building's internal organisation, and the space between buildings as a specifically architectural problem is ignored. These criticisms are objective. The faults which they expose are the result of the belief that architecture can be created without the establishment of aesthetic conventions.

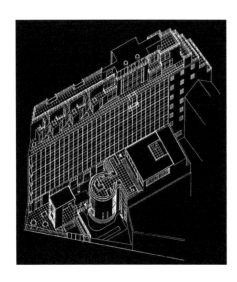

It is also to Le Corbusier that one must turn for an example of new architectural rules. The most obvious of these are the "Five Points", and with this example one notices a characteristic of the modern situation which differs from the past; rule systems tend to be invented by individual architects and tend to attain only a limited degree of acceptance. To borrow a term from linguistics, what in previous epochs was part of the *langue* has become a function of the *parole*. Mies' invention of a network of virtual structure superimposed on the curtain wall is another such rule system. The rule system can even extend to

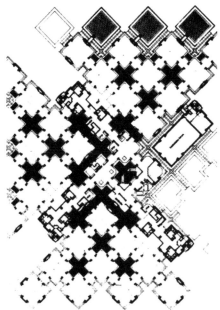

the behaviour of people within a building—as can be seen in Le Corbusier's drawings—thus annexing to the architectural sphere something which, in earlier periods, belonged to an external rule system (rules of social behaviour).

The invention of rule systems by individual architects has often resulted in the transformation of buildings in accordance with a contradictory rule system. One of the most striking examples of this is the modification of Pessac, where the organisation of homes according to the principles laid down in the "Five Points" has been altered to conform to petit-bourgeois norms requiring small windows, shutters, pitched roofs, and so on.

The proposition that architecture is a self-referential system has been accompanied by a 'softening' of the rule system which was developed during the 1920s and which, albeit with important developments and shifts in viewpoint, governs architectural practice today. Owing to the fact, mentioned above, that the rule systems of Modern architecture were made by individual architects, or, at most, by small groups claiming to stand in some special rapport with the *Zeitgeist*, there cannot be said to exist, within the framework of the Modern Movement, any firm basis for excluding alternative rule systems.

The norms of Modern architecture have no 'right of exclusion', and the very fervour with which the Modern Movement insisted on the inextricable links between architecture and the approaching 'world culture' meant that, once that great ideological vision had faded, the rules of architectural form supporting it would also tend to weaken.

It is therefore possible to see the modern tendencies toward historicism, not as constituting an alternative to a monolithic Modern Movement but simply as acting out a centrifugal tendency which was never far beneath the surface. But this development nonetheless has its paradoxical side. However much architecture derives its historicity from its own internalised tradition, it still depends for its realisation on the 'occasion'. And the occasions which are provided by modern social life for the kind of symbolism inherent in the rule systems of classical architecture are very rare. In this way we seem to see a separation taking place,

Opposite top: Project for the League of Nations, Geneva. Le Corbusier, 1927–1928. View from the lake.
© FLC/ADAGP, Paris and DACS, London 2009

Opposite middle: Villa in Vaucresson. Le Corbusier, 1922. Street facade.
© FLC/ADAGP, Paris and DACS, London 2009

Opposite bottom: Salvation Army Hostel, Paris. Le Corbusier. Axonometric view. Redrawn from original plans with verification by H Lapprand.
© FLC/ADAGP, Paris and DACS, London 2009

Left: Millowners' Association Building, Ahmedabad. Le Corbusier, 1954. West facade.
© FLC/ADAGP, Paris and DACS, London 2009

Right: Centraal Beheer, Apeldoorn, The Netherlands. Herman Hertzberger, 1974. Plan.

not only between architecture and the broader ideological patterns, but also between architecture and those very occasions which a 'realistic' architecture should accept. From a situation in which 'style' was finally to be superseded, we find ourselves in a situation in which everything is 'style'—including the forms of the Modern Movement itself—a type of eclecticism more arbitrary than that of the nineteenth century, since at that time the choice of a style was based on its ability to represent certain political, philosophical, or religious ideas.

An example of this can perhaps be seen in Aldo Rossi's Gallaratese, where the 'virtual' elements—giant *pilotis*, a 'classical' arrangement of windows—refer less to the programme than to some kind of 'absent' architecture. The function of the rule system seems less to establish an architecture of meaning than to bring architecture back from the verge of an empty garrulousness, where reality is reflected in endless functional episodes each more banal than the last—those stair towers and service shafts which so often form the lexicon of modern buildings. Whatever one may say in defense of such an architecture of polemic, there is a danger that the belief in an architecture which is purely self-reflective might lead to a devaluation of the building programme and to an architecture which would no longer need to be built. The dichotomy posed earlier (architecture as an internally or externally referential system) should be replaced by a less simplistic concept—that of a dialectical process in which aesthetic norms are modified by external forces to achieve a provisional synthesis.

The kind of realism according to whose tenets a fundamental language can be disclosed, and which rejects the mediation of style, should be replaced by a new realism which would gain its validity both from existing aesthetic structures and from a reality which would affect and alter these structures—a realism which accepts the fact that it is no longer possible to foresee a society whose unity is fully reflected in the forms of its art.

Top left: Pessac workers' housing. Le Corbusier, 1926. Street facades. Photograph by FR Yerbury.

Top right: Pessac workers' housing transformed by its inhabitants.

Middle: Wanner Project, Geneva. Le Corbusier, 1928–1929. Sketch of a "*jardin suspendu*".
© FLC/ADAGP, Paris and DACS, London 2009

Bottom: Residential Units in the Gallaratese district, Milan. Aldo Rossi, 1970. Elevation.

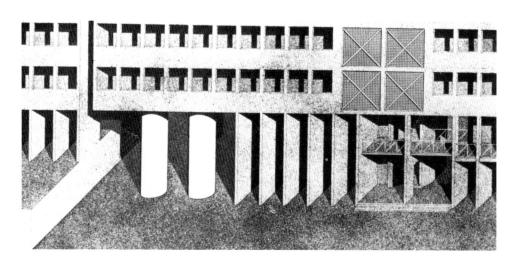

1   "Thematics", *Russia?! Formalist Criticism: Four Essays,* Lee T Lemon and Marion J Reis trans., Lincoln: University of Nebraska, 1965, pp. 82–83.
2   I am not concerned here with the question of whether the norms of art have any basis in nature. This problem, which belongs to epistemology, has a long and complex history, and, as a problem, it appears in different guises at different historical periods. In the Renaissance the laws of art were considered to be divinely ordained. With the rise of the bourgeoisie and the development of empiricism, artistic norms began to be considered as residing in the link between sensation and mind (that is to say, in the subject rather than in the object) and their universality as being due to social customs. But from the eighteenth century, and increasingly with the development of mass culture and consumerism, social customs lost their *de jure* force, and the resulting incoherence (expressed in eclecticism) was certainly one of the reasons for the attempt by avant-garde art to rediscover archetypes and to reduce the subject to psychological, and even physiological, laws. At the same time an opposite tendency emerged—the study of the sign as a social function. The sign was not studied, as it had been in the eighteenth century, as the natural reflection of normative social customs but, in the generalised form in which it appears in any society whatsoever, as constituting a *de facto* rather than a *de jure* system, and as being essentially arbitrary and conventional. This essay, by stressing the *de facto,* conventional, and ludic aspects of the architectural sign, creates, perhaps, an unbalanced picture. It leaves out the extent to which the sign is always, in an ideological sense, motivated and therefore the extent to which meanings are historically limited.

Alvar Aalto:
Type versus Function

First published in *L'Architecture d'Aujourd'hui*, 1976.

Although his first major projects—the Paimio Sanatorium and the Viipuri Library—belong to the canon of the 1920s, from the start Alvar Aalto's work diverged from that of the main Dutch, German, and French architects of the period. What was lacking in Aalto's work was the equation of functionalism and rationalism. Although Leonardo Mosso is no doubt right to deny any direct influence from Frank Lloyd Wright, it is easy to see how this idea arose. Aalto's work has many features in common with the romantic and expressionist wing of the Modern Movement—the wing which was descended from the Arts and Crafts Movement through Henry van de Velde, as opposed to Hermann Muthesius. Aalto interprets function in terms of a Heraclitean, rather than a Platonic, view of nature. What interests him in nature is its emergent and phenomenal forms, rather than the rational order to which it may be reduced. The Modern Movement in its early phase was concerned with the general schemata by which both society and architecture could be reconstructed according to rational principles. Apparently Aalto never concerned himself with such a universalism. He was content to remain "close to the ground" and to follow where his instinct for form led him.

But it would be an error to associate his work too closely to that of Expressionists such as Hugo Häring and Hans Scharoun. He was as remote from their formalism as he was from the schematisation of their opponents. His forms always pick up meanings from the context and are not based on *a priori* categories. Thus, the complexity and variety in Villa Mairea are the result of a response to particular features of the programme. Neither the main living area nor the bedrooms face the concave space of the garden, as a simple binary classification (open/closed) might have suggested. Instead, this initial implication is contradicted, and the space of the house expands on both entrance and garden sides, permitting a variety of views and lighting and a generosity of lifestyle that would have been denied by a more obvious *parti*. Each zone of the house is allowed its own individual character without being dominated by a strong unitary concept: the bedroom windows lean toward the sun, the studio introduces an entirely new formal theme, the cluster of poles which screens the staircase introduces a theme that echoes the forest outside. All these statements and counterstatements come about because the causes of things are seen to be multiple; the greater order aimed at must not be so elementary as to stifle the life of the parts. Aalto's strength lay in his ability to maintain artistic control over many contradictory elements and an apparent excess of ideas, which he was able to synthesise into a rich metonymy of architectural forms.

There are many analogies between Aalto's work of the late 1920s and 30s and the work of other schools within the Modern Movement. But Aalto gives to these common themes an entirely new interpretation. For example, his use of repetition, reminiscent of Constructivism and of certain works of Laszlo Moholy-Nagy, is less concerned with mechanical reproduction as such than with establishing an analogy between mechanical reproduction and biological or geological processes.

Aalto's relationship with Le Corbusier is more complex. At first sight one could not imagine two architects with more contradictory sensibilities. Aalto seems to have had no interest either in Le Corbusier's *esprit du système* or in the spirit of French classicism, which was so important a feature in Le Corbusier's work. This is demonstrated in their differing attitudes toward the plan. For Le Corbusier

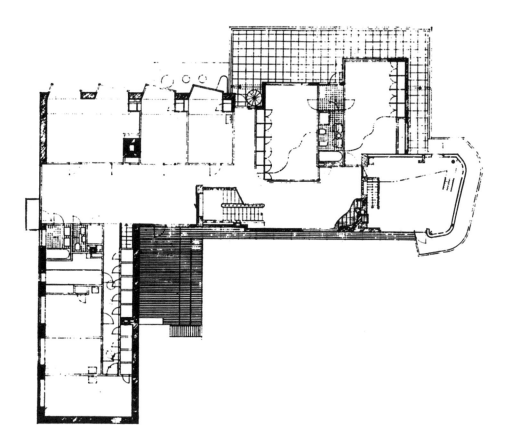

the plan gives order and intelligibility to the whole building. In Aalto's early work the plan is dealt with pragmatically, and at Viipuri, for example, there is a clumsiness in the entry system which comes from trying to create an axis across the stratified volumes, leading to the projecting porch and large window terminating the block—both of whose relationships to the main masses seem unresolved. In Aalto's later work the plan becomes more closely integrated with the principle of overlapping and ambiguous volumes, but in doing so it seems to diverge even further from Le Corbusier. However, in Aalto's work there is, together with a sensitivity to contingency, a typological drive which relates him to Le Corbusier.[1] The difference between them is that for Le Corbusier the emphasis is on the creation of new types established on rigorously rational principles, while for Aalto the type is something which already exists as a historical and social reality. As such it is not reflected in his work as formally complete but as an underlying idea susceptible to paraphrase and variation.

Aalto is reported to have admired Le Corbusier more than any other Modern architect. This may perhaps be partially explained by his recognition of powers of intellectual formulation which he himself lacked. But it may also be due to certain preoccupations which they had in common. These preoccupations included an admiration of both the architecture of peasant societies, particularly around the Mediterranean (which dates back to their early involvements in National Romantic movements), and the architecture of neo-classicism, which they saw as providing a core of traditional doctrine outside the confines of modernist doctrine.

Perhaps the most outstanding feature of Aalto's work, and one which seems related to his study of Italian towns, is the way in which he strives to make each building into a social microcosm. The majority of Aalto's projects were of a type to encourage this interpretation—libraries, cultural centres, theatre complexes and

Opposite top: Villa Mairea, Noormarkku, Finland. Alvar Aalto, 1938–1939. View from the entrance into the hall.

Opposite bottom: Municipal Library, Viipuri. Alvar Aalto, 1939–1935. Aerial view.

Left: Villa Mairea. Upper level plan.

Right: Bentwood stools for the Library, Viipuri. Alvar Aalto, 1938.

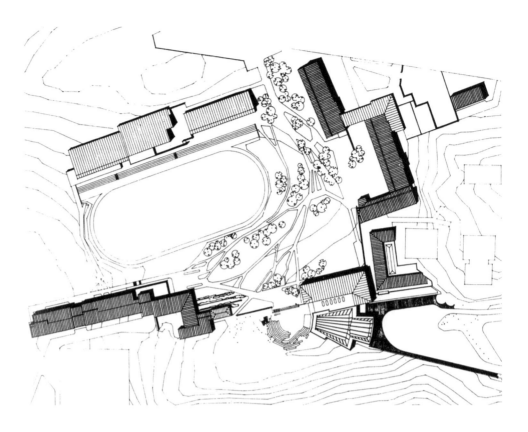

churches—but he even aims at the same spatial hierarchy in individual apartments, as in the Hansaviertel apartment block in West Berlin. But whereas in Le Corbusier a clear external form establishes precise limits to the universe of the building, in Aalto the subsidiary elements are freely grouped around the central core. The building becomes a kind of town, whose outer elements take up their positions as if through a tropism. A number of functions are classified into a closed set, each of which is partially opened up again into the neighbouring set or into the core itself. This 'peeling away' of forms is an important ingredient of Aalto's work: the *subtraction* of forms is as important as their addition or juxtaposition.

This characteristic leads to the extraordinary impression that parts of Aalto's buildings are, in fact, ruins. Thus in the library of the Institute of Technology at Otaniemi the form of the auditorium roof creates the impression of an archaic fragment. Fragmentation, in Aalto, has a metaphoric, picturesque dimension, unlike in De Stijl, where it is formal and systematic.

In the conflict in Aalto's work between a typological approach and a reliance on contingency and function to generate architectural form, certain general problems related to functionalism make themselves felt. There are two levels in the notion of function. At the first level a function exists as a generalised type bringing together many dimensions of meaning. At the second level it exists as the solution to a specific operational problem. Aalto sometimes starts from this specific level, as in the Baker House dormitory at the Massachusetts Institute of Technology, where the undulating wall is intended to reduce traffic noise or to provide views up the river, or in the Church at Imatra, where the volumetric articulation satisfies the need for multiple uses. In neither of these cases is the form-determining function really fundamental to the idea of the programme, and yet it establishes the overall configuration of the building. The fact that the forms have 'poetic' contents which reverberate far beyond the original functions does not bring them any nearer the central meaning of the programme. In some of his late work Aalto seems to depend on minor and accidental aspects of the programme to produce

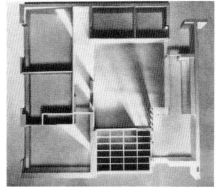

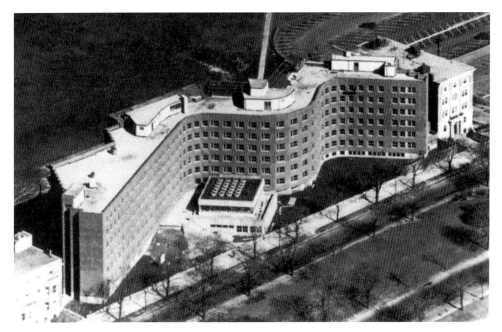

Opposite top: Pedagogical University, site plan.

Opposite bottom: Pedagogical University, Jyväskylä. Alvar Aalto, 1953. View of teachers' and students' dining halls.

Top left: Institute of Technology, Otaniemi, Finland. Alvar Aalto, 1964. View of the auditorium.

Top right: Hansaviertel apartment block, West Berlin. Alvar Aalto, 1955–1957. Model of the "patio-apartment".

Bottom: Baker House dormitory, Massachusetts Institute of Technology, Cambridge, Massachusetts. Alvar Aalto, 1947–1948.

Church, Vuoksenniska, Imatra, Finland.
Alvar Aalto, 1957–1959. Exterior view.

ever-varying solutions to basically similar problems. In his late churches the relations between altar, spatial axis, and light source are always being modified according to criteria which are not altogether clear, it is as if the idea of a church was no longer able to provide him with a typical solution.

For Aalto to have submitted to external norms—to the idea of "type" advocated by Muthesius and Le Corbusier, for instance—would have meant an artificial restraint on spontaneous invention and a denial of architecture as the expression of the richness and complexity of life. But it is here, in the idea of "architecture as expression", that we may find the clue to weaknesses in certain projects of Aalto, to some of which I have alluded. It is doubtful if the undulating walls at the Massachusetts Institute of Technology or the billowing masses at Imatra actually 'express' anything, for the simple reason that the functions they represent do not correspond to any expectations which users or observers of the buildings would be likely to have. They therefore become pure forms, meaningful perhaps in terms of a nominalism which would consider all functions as of equal importance, but meaningless in terms of the architectural programme and its cultural context.

That Aalto himself was aware of this problem can be seen from one of his articles in which he discusses the different meanings of towers in the landscape and differentiates between towers with potentially cultural meanings, such as church spires, and those whose meaning is restricted to their utilitarian function, such as water towers.[2] Here he seems to be implicitly admitting that the meaning of forms is due less to their innate expressive power than to their semiotic and conventional meaning. To act according to this admission would not necessarily entail a rigid conservatism, but it would entail an awareness of pre-existent forms which form part of the architectural vocabulary.

The uniqueness of the best work of Aalto lies in the fact that it does show such an awareness, and a consideration of the work of the greatest exponent of 'expressive function' in the Modern Movement inevitably leads us to question some of the basic tenets of the functionalism to which he was committed.

Protestant Parish Centre, Zurich-Alstetten, Switzerland. Alvar Aalto, 1967. Interior model of the church.

1   "The Burst of Memory: An Essay on Alvar Aalto's Typological Conception of Design", *Architectural Design* 49, nos. 5–6, 1979, pp. 143–148.
2   See Karl Fleig, ed, Henry N Frey, trans, "Water-Towers as Landmarks of Towns", conversation between Karl Fleig and Alvar Aalto, Summer 1969, Alvar Aalto, 1963–1970, New York: Praeger, 1971, p. 13.

The Superblock

First published in *Arquitectura moderna y cambio histórico: Ensayos 1962–1976*, 1978.

I

If one looks at any modern city, one cannot help being struck by the fact that much of it consists of large pieces of real estate, each of which is financed and organised as a single entity. The size of each unit—or superblock, as I choose to call it—is not determined by any single physical factor. It may be limited by the existing street pattern; it may encroach on one or more adjacent blocks by virtue of roads having been closed off; it may consist of a single building or a group of buildings. But however individual cases may differ, there is always one common factor: the enormous reserves of capital that exist in the modern economy which enable either private or public agencies, or a combination of both, to gain control over, and make a profit from, ever larger areas of urban land. In practice the area of control is limited by the constraints of competitive interests. But this does not prevent large areas coming under single control for the simple reason that each of these interests—a corporation, a speculator, a local authority—is in itself a very large unit. Bylaw legislation keeps pace with this process. The regulations covering light angles, zoning laws, and laws relating to plot ratio and building height all tend to reinforce the tendency toward breaking up the city fabric into large discrete lumps, each of which is under unified financial control.

These facts are obvious enough in themselves, but they have architectural consequences which are often neglected. The financing of a piece of land by a single agency usually results in the buildings on this piece of land being consciously designed as a single entity. The larger the area of land, the larger the volume of building that is subject to a single architectural concept.

There are two important problems connected with this fact that I wish to discuss. The first is, what is the relation of the individual dwelling to the superblock of which it may be a part? The second is, what are implications of the superblock as a representational element in the city? These two problems in turn related to the concepts of the private and the public realm.

II

Whatever general attitude may be adopted as to the relevance of tradition to modern life, it cannot be denied that of all institutions it is the city in which the past is most tangible. Ancient laws and customs still persist beneath the surface of our social life, but it is in the city that these laws take on a physical form in which implements made under social, economic and technical conditions different from our own are still in use. To a large extent, our ideas about pleasant and meaningful city environments are based on our actual experience of living and working among the buildings and city structures of the past. The incredible time lag in architecture is the chief factor which conditions our response to the city environment. This time lag has two causes: first, the durability of architecture, which is related to the amount of capital it represents, and second, what Aldo Rossi has called its "indifference to function". What is specific about a building is less its exclusive adaption to particular functions than its capacity for representing ideas.

The ancient structure of our cities is so strong that we are continually reminded of a distinction which has always been fundamental to the economy and mythology of the city, the distinction between the public and the private realm. The public realm was representational; it not only housed activities of public and collective nature but it symbolised these activities. The aesthetic of public architecture consisted of a second-order language organised, to use a linguistic analogy, into syntagmata and constituting a complete text. The private realm, on the contrary, though still comprised of aesthetic formulae common to the whole of society, was not representational in a public sense and was the property of individuals who were free to use them much as one uses everyday language, as a personal possession.

In the Middle Ages the city belonged to the merchants and artisans. The representational elements were the church, the market square, the buildings of the guilds, and the city gates. All these elements constituted a collective investment. Individual houses, on the other hand, were seldom financed as whole groups. Even in the planned *bastide* towns in the southwest of France, the separate lots were under individual control. Although the town was laid out on a regular grid and all the plots were identical, the housing consisted of a kind of connective tissue. The public realm of the town consisted of the principal roads, the market square which occurred at their crossing and which converted them into covered arcades, and the church, always related diagonally to the market square.

During the Middle Ages and in the Renaissance, a number of critical changes occurred which were to revolutionise the public realm and, though somewhat belatedly, the private realm as well. GC Argan has noted three fundamental characteristics of the Renaissance city: First, a new historical awareness which transforms the city from a commercial to a political entity; second, the revival of the Platonic doctrine that the nature of the universe was geometrical; third, a change in design method, which was virtually the invention of a single man, Filippo Brunelleschi.[1] In the design of the dome of Florence Cathedral, Brunelleschi revolutionised existing building procedures by proposing that a building was something that should be conceived as a total project and carried out according to a preconceived plan. A building was an act of the mind; its construction was the work of builders who merely carried out the instructions of this mind. It is true that, already in the later Middle Ages, the cathedral was a conscious political and aesthetic object, but the traditional crafts made a greater contribution to its total semantic elaboration than in the case of the Duomo or any subsequent church, and the role of the immediate tradition was correspondingly greater. With Brunelleschi we arrive at the moment when architecture is transformed from a craft to a 'liberal art' and its practice is raised, in the Renaissance mind, from the realm of *doxa,* or opinion, to that of *episteme,* or certain knowledge.

Not only buildings but also entire cities were projected in this manner and reflected the triple values of the Renaissance: political meaning, geometrical construction, and conscious totality. (The latter value, particularly, has persisted to the present day, despite the demise of so many Renaissance ideas.) If we look at any Renaissance city plan, we see the image of a community whose organic unity is metaphorically expressed in terms of geometric forms and by the geometrical dominance of the castle or public square. The Medieval marketplace has become the geometrical as well as the topological centre, symbol of the *logos,* and ideally the actual centre of political power. The city is conceived as a solid, carved up by streets, hollowed out by squares, and articulated by public buildings. The individual house does not contribute to this imagery. The prolongation of the public realm that took place in the Baroque and neo-classical city, by means of unified street facades and residential squares, did not radically alter the status of the private dwelling. Behind the regular facades, the design of individual houses behind facades was often left to the individual owner, as in the Place Vendôme or Berkeley Square.

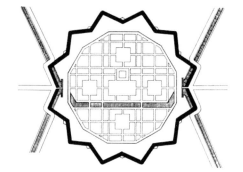

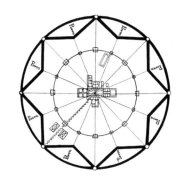

Top: Plan of an ideal city. Vincenzo Scamozzi (from *Dell'Idea dell'Architettura Universale*, 1615).

Bottom: Plan of the ideal city, Sforzinda. Antonio Averlino Filarete, 1464.

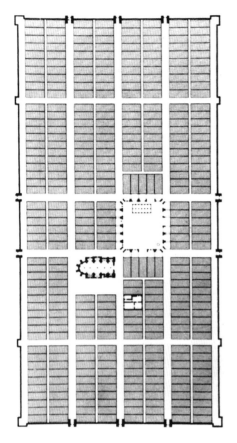

It is true that sometimes, as in the Strada Nuova in Genoa the street is made up of individual mansions. But here each house is thought of as a palace, and a whole class of inhabitants takes on a representational role—the class of aristocrat or man of wealth, whose representational function corresponds to its instrumental position in society.

In the Medieval and Renaissance city there were two types of structures: representational buildings and ordinary habitations. There is admittedly a fundamental difference between the Medieval and Renaissance city. In the former both representational and private buildings were constructed according to craft tradition, upheld by the guilds, and transmitted, like an aural literary tradition, by rules of thumb. In the Renaissance both the aesthetic and the constructional codes became subject to systematic theory, and art and science were harmonised through the epistemology of a geometric universe. So radical is this difference that it is often asserted that it reflects a new split between ruler and ruled. The public square becomes the symbolic representation of the *logos,* rather than the natural forum of the masses. But both the Medieval and Renaissance city consisted of an undifferentiated mass of houses or tenements out of which emerged the buildings which represented the mythos of collective life—social, political, and intellectual.

In early representations of the city, representational buildings become a synecdoche for the whole city. In reconstructions of Jerusalem or Rome, the city is depicted as nothing but a collection of public monuments. If any residential buildings are shown at all, single houses stand for whole groups to provide the minimum context for the monuments. The monuments themselves consist of a typology of elementary forms: cylinders, obelisks, ziggurats, pyramids, and coliseums—metaphors of collective or ceremonial functions.

In many of these pictorial representations, the monuments appear to be in competition with each other, and they thus ignore an important ingredient common to the Medieval and Renaissance city—the principle of hierarchy and subordination. In these depictions we have a strange foreshadowing of the modern city, in which this principle is also lacking. The proliferation of important public buildings in a pictorial representation of Rome resembles the proliferation of superblocks found in the post-industrial city. But this analogy is superficial. The Rome which is depicted is intended as a paradigm of the historical city, prodigal in significant public monuments; whereas the modern

city, if it can be said to provide a mental image at all, merely represents an inventory of objects of material wealth. This difference is of vital importance and can only be explained by epistemological and economic changes which took place in the seventeenth and eighteenth centuries. It was then that a political and philosophical watershed occurred which radically changed the course of European culture and also, if more slowly, the nature of the European city and the concept of the public realm which had hitherto been an integral part of it.

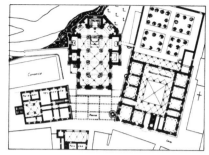

Opposite top left: Montpazier, Dordogne. Thirteenth century plan.

Opposite top right: Santa Maria del Fiore, Florence. Dome by Filippo Brunelleschi, 1420–1436.

Opposite bottom: Engraving of the city of Aachen.

Top: Pienza, schematic plan of the monumental centre of the city.

Middle: Circus at Bath, England. John Wood the elder, 1754.

Bottom: Strada Nuova, Genoa (from an eighteenth century print).

III

Until the scientific and philosophical revolutions of the seventeenth century, the state was able to be represented by the city in terms of a figural metaphor. Alberti's analogy between the house and the city was supported by the further metaphor of the city as a human body with its head and its members in hierarchical subordination. The philosophical justification of the baroque state formulated by Thomas Hobbes was based on a similar analogy.

With the development of mercantilism in Holland and England in the seventeenth century and the corresponding scientific discoveries, a new political concept emerged. The theory of John Locke introduced a new model of political organisation, to which the American and French revolutions were eventually to give constitutional form.

For present purposes, the crucial fact about these new liberal-empiricist ideas is that they introduced an era in which society was seen to be in a 'lower' state of organisation than before. The period of *laissez-faire* commercialism which followed was not subject to the same visual analogues as the previous centralist system.

But this fact is complemented by another. If the concept of the State becomes vague, and if society as a whole is seen to cohere by means of a system of checks and balances and to consist of a series of autonomous subgroups whose mutual conflicts cancel each other out, the forces controlled by each subgroup becomes, in itself, much more highly organised, complex, and powerful. We have only to compare a Medieval town to a nineteenth century residential quarter to see that, at the level of the individual, the earlier centralist system allowed greater randomness to occur than did the later liberal system. In the liberal system the freedom of the whole was achieved at the expense of an increasing rigidity in the parts.

One of the results of the new structure is that there is an increase in the number of independent institutions, each of which has an equal importance within the organisation of society as a whole. A society based on a strict hierarchy gives way to one based on anarchy, but at the same time each institution is itself organised hierarchically. To each of these institutions corresponds a new building type, and so, to the old repertoire of church, palace, and city hall, there are gradually added such new types of public buildings as law courts, parliaments, schools, hospitals, prisons, factories, hotels, railway stations, department stores, galleries, and other places of amusement and consumption.

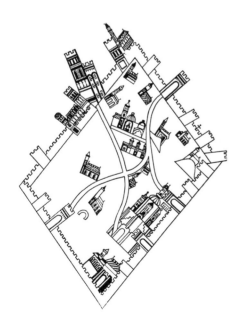

Though this evolution can be traced in actual cities, it is in the parallel development of discourse—including the delineation of utopias attempting to create a new hierarchy and a new unified concept to replace that which has been lost—that we have the clearest notion of eighteenth and nineteenth century developments. In Ledoux's plan for Chaux an entire community is related to its place of work. The city in its traditional capacity as marketplace and political centre is abandoned. In the words of Francjois-Noel Babeuf there should be "no more capitals, no more large cities… the magnificence of architecture… will be reserved for public stores, for amphitheatres, for circuses, for aqueducts, for bridges, for canals, for squares, for archives, for libraries, and above all for the places which dedicated to the deliberations of magistrates and the exercise of the popular will".[2]

In such programmes there is the same emphasis on public buildings as before but their content has changed. The magnificence of Rome is identified with the popular will, just as in Jean-Jacques Rousseau the sovereign state of a baroque king becomes the sovereign state of the collective will of the people who must sign a voluntary contract by which they give up part of their individual freedom for the good of the collective. In the eighteenth century, the building as a symbol cannot be clearly separated from the building as an instrument of the good life. We seem to be witnessing the progressive secularisation of the Platonic concept of architecture, rather than its destruction, just as in social

Opposite top: Bendetto Buonfigli, Translation of the Remains of Herculanus, late fifteenth century, fresco.

Opposite bottom: Jerusalem (after the plan in the Library, Cambrai).

Top: Ancient Rome. A reconstruction from *Theatrum Urbium Italicarium*, Pietro Bertelli, 1599.

Bottom: Chicago, view from Fifth Avenue westward.

theory republican and democratic contents are grafted onto the centralised institutions of the baroque state. In the *architecture parlante* of Boullée and Ledoux the metaphor of the state as symbol of the cosmos becomes a social metaphor, seeming to echo that grand secularisation of religion announced by Immanuel Kant when he spoke of the moral law below, initiated by human

reason, and the starry heavens above, revealed by Newton's discovery of the laws of mechanics.

Ledoux, Fourier, and Owen proposed substituting for the existing cities new towns that were related to the workplace in order to rediscover the primordial social group. As a result, they suggested very large 'designed' units, either in the form of isolated buildings related geometrically (Ledoux) or in the form of single physical units modelled on the Renaissance city or the Baroque palace.

In the actual, as opposed to the utopian, nineteenth century city of capitalist and imperial expansion, a similar movement toward coalescence into large units took place. At first this took the form of an increase in the number of recognisable building types. A late example of the latter is Dominech i Montaner's Hospital of St Paul in Barcelona, which asserts its symbolic presence in the city grid by its diagonal site layout. Others made use of the existing architectural language to which they gave new connotations (banks, hotels, the facades of railway stations, 'mansion flats'). But in both cases the new types had a representational intent: they were, in a genuine sense, new 'organs' of the city—secularised and democratised versions of the old theocratic or aristocratic institutions.

But this development gave way, during the first half of the twentieth century, to large units whose functions were no longer distinct from the anonymous and private functions of ancient cities and which took the form of buildings consisting of an addition of identical cells, primarily housing and offices. These developments were due to the progressive loss of viability (through inflation) of small-scale property and the corresponding rise of financial organisations able to invest on a large scale and reap the profits of such investment. Whether such organisations were public or private makes no difference to the principle involved; both were equally interested in the profitability of urban land.

There are notable exceptions to this tendency toward the parcelling out of the city into larger and larger units without a representational function. In both the Auditorium Building in Chicago and Rockefeller Center in New York, a large block of offices is combined with public functions (theatres, arcades, etc.) to create a new type of mixed-use building—a sort of microcosm of the city as a whole. Rockefeller Center is, in fact, an extreme case of a more general tendency in Chicago and Manhattan during their respective skyscraper booms, for large commercial enterprises to aim at a representational function. But though one might draw attention to even later examples, such as Place Bonaventure and Place Ville Marie in Montreal, the general tendency in this century has not been toward such quasi-representational types. It has been toward specialised blocks which, though they coarsen the grain of the city in the same way as representational buildings do and create discontinuity, they do not add to its stock of truly representational types.

IV

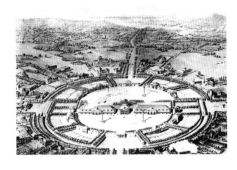

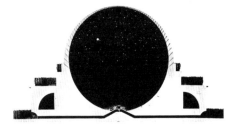

During the last two decades there have been numerous critiques of the modern city, and the coarsening of city fabric and loss of meaning in relation to the size and isolation of its elements are among the characteristics which have inspired them. Broadly, critical attacks on the modern city have been based on two models which I shall call the cybernetic and the formal, or the City as Process and the City as Form.

The cybernetic model consists either of radically disurbanist ideas (according to which developments in the media and the means of personalised transport make the city as such redundant) or ideas according to which the vitality of the city can be re-created by sufficiently subtle techniques of intervention, simulating the feedback mechanism found in biology and machinery. Christopher

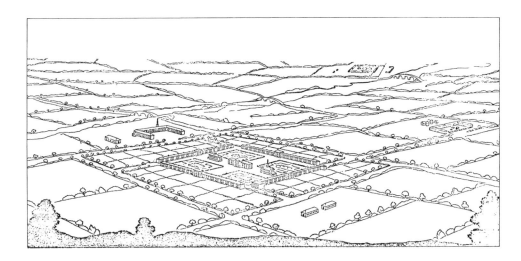

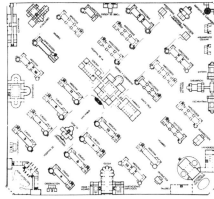

Alexander's paper "The City is Not a Tree" may be taken as an example of this school of thought.[3]

Disurbanists assume that the city exists purely for the sake of the products of contiguity. They ignore the fact that the physical contiguity itself and the phenomenal discontinuity of the global environment may have some meaning beyond that of the instrumentality with which it has always been associated in the past. They forget that, with the development of the specialised subsystems of the commercial state, there is a residue of human need which can no longer be seen as an epiphenomenon of the function of survival. The town or city may continue to satisfy a need after many of its original determinants have fallen away.

The weakness of the second kind of cybernetic model is, equally, that it does not account for the experience of the city on a phenomenal level. It remains on an abstract plane, and the principles it supports can function, whatever physical pattern the city might have.[4] Secretly, Alexander's model refers to a supposed pre-Renaissance or 'natural' city and cunningly suggests an abstract methodology by which this image can be achieved in modern Western society. Moreover, change, which is the basis of the cybernetic model, is regarded as permissive, rather than the result of conflict, and no distinction is made between arbitrary (and reversible) and motivated (and irreversible) change. A sort of millennium is postulated in which change has the maximum of possibility (because of feedback) and the minimum of meaning (because of the lack of any but trivial motivation).

The school of thought based on the idea of the City as Form also has two varieties. The first is represented by Kevin Lynch. In *The Image of the City* Lynch attempts to apply the findings of *Gestalt* psychology to problems of urban form. Although the book seems to spring from a picturesque and subjective viewpoint, it attempts to go beyond this and to set up a series of objective rules for city design. But although its approach seems preferable to that of the cybernetic

Opposite top: Galleria Vittorio Emmanuele II, Milan. Giuseppe Mengoni, 1865–1877.

Opposite middle: Ideal city of Chaux, Arc-et-Senans. Claude–Nicolas Ledoux, 1804. Perspective view, second project.

Opposite bottom: Project for a Cenotaph to Isaac Newton. Etienne–Louis Boullée, 1784. Section with the effect of night on the interior.

Top: Project for a phalanstery after Charles Fourier. Victor Considerant, 1834.

Bottom left: A village of harmony and cooperation. Robert Owen, 1817. Aerial view.

Bottom right: Hospital of St Paul, Barcelona. Domènech i Montaner, 1902–1912. Plan.

Rockefeller Center, New York.
Reinhard & Hofmeister; Corbett, Harrison,
& MacMurray; Hood & Fouilloux, 1931–1940.

type, insofar as it is based on a phenomenal awareness of the city, it fails to distinguish adequately, either at a morphological or historical level, among such radically different types as the Medieval, the Renaissance, and the modern city, seeking rather a level of abstraction which will embrace all three.

By restricting his systematic treatment to questions of psychological response, Lynch can only deal in an *ad hoc* way with the city itself, and in avoiding all typological analysis, he fails to isolate the characteristics which are peculiar to the modern city. Because he does not deal with the basic structure of the modern city, he is unable to demonstrate whether or not his prescriptions will, in fact, provide the minimum of legibility and coherence at which he aims—even if it is allowed that these criteria are in themselves adequate.

The second variety is represented both by Aldo Rossi and the "Rationalists", and by Colin Rowe, who, for the first time since the advent of modern architecture explicitly admit the syntagmata of classical architecture back into the modern

Auditorium Building, Chicago.
Adler and Sullivan, 1887–1889.

canon. In contrast to more 'functional' and processual theories of the city, these theories are clearly related to the City Beautiful Movement of Daniel Burnham. They talk of ends rather than means. Such an attitude obviously possesses *a prima facie* 'realism', since it allows for the division of the urban continuum into discrete blocks and a series of finite experiences, each of which can be designed according to definite aesthetic norms. All the other recent theories of the city have been vague when it has come to proposing specific solutions—a vagueness which is illustrated by the fact that every solution, however radical, is immediately seen to be inadequate in relation to the absolute criteria to which it aspires. The Rationalists' view, on the contrary, is concrete and accepts the brute fact that the city is made up of discrete parts and that these parts have to be consciously designed 'for now' and related to each other in a way that engages our aesthetic judgment. They go further and suggest that our knowledge of what is beautiful or ugly in the city is based on our memory of past forms of the city, since, without assuming continuity of cultural meaning, no aesthetic judgment is possible.[5]

These seem to be the two main streams of theory which treat the city as a formal entity. The first questions neither the symbolic and cultural role of the city nor its structure. Its terms of reference are largely psychological and perceptual. Nonetheless it is an improvement on the cybernetic model, since its discourse on the city is related to experience rather than to a positivistic and abstract utopia. At least it can do little harm. The second is more fundamentally critical of the lack of structure in the modern city and suggests an alternative structure based on the historical city. Whereas the protagonists of the City as Process believe that the aesthetic of the city has no independent existence but must derive from social criteria, the protagonists of the City as Form believe that urban aesthetics constitute a general 'science', grounded either in fundamental psychological laws or in meanings inherent in the typology of the traditional city.

V

The superblock is more (and less) than a building. It has implications of size and complexity but also of the lowering of architectural voltage, because, unlike the representational buildings of the past, it is unable to acquire the status of a metaphor.

Its lack of metaphorical charge is most noticeable in the office block and the housing block, its two characteristic twentieth century forms. Since the onset of the Modern Movement there has been hesitation as to whether these should become large buildings (the Beaux-Arts solution, and also that of Le Corbusier) or be elementalised into their component parts. Either way, they tend to stand in palpable isolation and to be differentiated from neighbouring superblocks, in the first case deliberately, and in the second simply because the elementalised block is the exception rather than the rule—in spite of the fact that in principle it can consume the whole city.

In the nineteenth century, residential superblocks (in Paris, Vienna, or Berlin) were still part of the anonymous structure of the city because they used a common 'language of building'—in other words, their constituent parts (windows, cornices, stringcourses, etc.) referred to the parts of architecture itself, rather than to the imagery of a particular type. In this way they receded into the background, indicating by default a private world which did not wish to flaunt itself in the public realm.

But with functionalist architecture, the building element as structural ornament disappears, and the signifying elements become the parts of the building defined by use. In Hertzberger's office buildings, for instance, an ideal volume of use is postulated and then extended by simple addition. The building dissolves, not discreetly behind an enigmatic and ambiguous public facade, but stridently into cubic elements piled one on top of the other.

In the same way certain housing blocks—at least those which share the same general philosophy as Safdie's Habitat—no longer hide their private repetitiveness behind a discreet order, whose forms proclaim the age-old presence of architecture, but seek an architectural language made up of the very housing cells which constitute their functional elements. Each house becomes a sign of itself and, in being separated out from its neighbours, merely succeeds in drawing attention to the biographies which play themselves out behind the facades. This attempt at individuality fails on two grounds. First, in asserting the individual, it only succeeds in exaggerating the mass. Secondly, it projects into the public realm (that is shared by all individuals as a collective possession) those signs of privacy which can never belong to it. It is in asymmetry that this privacy becomes aesthetically apparent. Asymmetry, one of the most fundamental doctrines of the Modern Movement, is bound by the rule that functions demand expression, and its presence announces the existence of all that is accidental and contingent in contrast to what is normative. This assertion of the contingent—which also celebrates stair towers, corridors, and ducts in the mistaken belief that these elements can 'unify' the ensemble of 'little houses'—is made with the hope of 'humanising' a large building. But far from doing this, it destroys any true mediation between the individual and the city as a whole, and reduces the city to an inhuman repetition of identical life-units.

This transformation of the housing block is closely related to the parallel development, outside the city, of suburbia. In suburbia the country villa, once the privilege of the few, becomes available to everyone; but this democratisation is only achieved at the cost of the radical devaluation of the villa type itself. The idea of the villa is kept alive by a progressively attenuated imagery, by means of which the illusion of civilised individuality is preserved, even though the very basis of its existence (privilege) has been destroyed.[6]

But if the ideal of suburbia is one of the sources of the architectural housing block, the image of the Medieval city is another. In the Medieval city the plots

Above: Habitat, Montreal. Moshe Safdie, 1967.

Opposite top: View of facades along a street in Bologna.

Opposite bottom: Suburban 'townhouses', USA, 1970s.

are small, and each house differs slightly from its neighbours. At the same time, unity is achieved through the existence of a universal architectural language. It therefore appears to provide a paradigm for those parts of the modern city reserved for housing—the more so as a policy of preservation allows a certain amount of 'infill' to take place and so perpetuates the illusion of 'organic' development. It is a powerful counter-image to the Renaissance principle of the city as a work of art, in which order is conceived as something that can only be achieved by the conscious effort of a single designer—an order based on hierarchy and subordination.[7]

In the Medieval street each house forms a metonymic unity but is different from its neighbour in the proportional relation of the parts making up this unity.[8] Clearly no information could be transmitted, either about the individual house or the group, unless the elements in the metonymic scheme formed a set. But whereas in the pre-industrial context the set is built into the culture, and only the manipulation of the set is a matter for the individual, in the modern context both the set and its manipulation are subject to individual choice.

In the pre-industrial set the rules of craft incorporated technical and significative norms simultaneously, whereas in the post-industrial set the rules of craft consist of technical norms only. The designer is simply provided with a range of technical possibilities, which he has to convert into a signifying system. Thus with each new project a new set has to be invented.

The most characteristic method of arriving at aesthetic norms in the modern economy is found in advertising and product design, in which the set is determined by a conventional repertoire modified by market research. The total cultural set has to be statistically deduced from a large number of apparently free choices—the reverse of a craft tradition in which the set is culturally determined. This procedure is used in architecture to a limited extent in the provision of houses on the free market, but it cannot be applied to the very large and capital-intensive entities with which we are concerned here. In such projects, the designer has to make an arbitrary choice, and for this he lacks the guidance of both a traditional, culturally determined set and a set determined by market research.[9]

The Modern Movement was aware of the unity of technique and language which existed in pre-industrial architecture and tried to create a similar unity between industrial building technique and a new system of signification. But industrial technology on its own was unable to provide any but the most generalised patterns of meaning in architecture; and for this reason it was forced (just as much as painting and music) to invent and define a new set of aesthetic rules. Thus it was faced with two incompatible tasks: to wrest from technology and function an architecture which would be organically connected with the modern economy and to create *de novo* an architecture depending on timeless aesthetic values. But, however inconsistent its aims may have been, modern architecture was right in thinking that a mere reproduction of the outward forms of traditional architecture, in an effort to re-establish architectural meaning, would not result in an authentic architecture. It would mean consigning to the whim of the individual designer everything which previously has been part of a common language.

This dilemma is at the root of the problems of the superblock as a vehicle for housing. The architect has either to rely on a cybernetic model of randomness (Safdie) or to invent a vocabulary which in some degree refers to the traditional language of architecture. In the first case the result achieves randomness but fails to provide the signifying set which alone could provide this randomness with meaning. In the second case the architect's choice of traditional elements, and the degree of literalness or generality with which he treats them, must always remain to some extent arbitrary.

A case in point is Ralph Erskine's Byker Wall housing project. Here the independent expression of certain architectural elements, such as balconies, windows, and porches, with discreet overtones of vernacular, has been combined with a contrived randomness (reminiscent perhaps of certain schemes by Caccia

Housing at Byker (Byker Wall), Newcastle
upon Tyne. Ralph Erskine, 1970–1974.

Dominiani in Milan in the 1950s, though more plastic and with a different attitude toward materials). This scheme is highly 'sensitive'; it appears to steer between the monotony of systems-built high-rise housing and the kitsch of projects like Port Grimeau. Here it should simply be pointed out that what sets out to provide an equivalent of the traditional ensemble, in which the basic set is culturally determined and individual choice is restricted to matters of detail, is, in fact, an entirely individual concept. As such it belongs to the tradition of "total design" which the superblock has inherited from the Renaissance via the transformations which took place during the eighteenth and nineteenth centuries.

The superblock, and with it the concepts of the "designed whole", is a fact of the modern capitalist state. It has evolved from the representational building and has gradually superseded the system according to which small plots were designed within a metonymic set. It is not simply a new type to be added to the repertoire of the city but a type of types, whose presence is rapidly destroying the traditional city.

1   Argan, Giulio Carlo, *The Renaissance City*, trans. Susan Edna Bassnett, New York: George Braziller Inc., 1969; It is important to note that, as Karl Popper has pointed out, this doctrine was instrumental as well as metaphysical; the development of modern science was due to the fact that a Platonic view of the world yielded insights that could be checked by observations and form the basis of predictions. See Popper, *Conjectures and Refutations: The Growth of Scientific Knowledge,* New York: Harper & Row, 1968.
2   Quoted and translated by Helen Rosenau, *Social Purpose in Architecture: Paris and London Compared, 1760–1800*, London: Studio Vista, 1970, p. 15. Original source Ph. Buonarotti, *Histoire de la conspiration pour l'egalite dite de Babeuf*, Paris, 1850, p. 146.
3   "A City is Not a Tree", *Architectural Forum* 122, April–May 1965, pp. 58–61.
4   Aldo van Eyck has rightly criticised Alexander's thesis, pointing out that his cybernetic model would operate just as well in a city which had hierarchical structure as one which had not, and that therefore the processes described by Alexander, while they might be necessary, are not sufficient. The mental image created by Alexander is one of perfect and subtle, continuous adaptation. As such it is an image on an operational level and ignores the teleology which has to be assumed for the operations to have any meaning. What is the idea *toward which* the city 'adapts' itself?
5   See Aldo Rossi, *L'architettura della città*, Padua: Marsilio Editori, 1966; English edition Cambridge, MA: MIT Press, 1982, and Colin Rowe and Fred Koetter, *Collage City*, Cambridge, MA: MIT Press, 1978.
6   This phenomenon is perhaps more characteristic of Anglo-Saxon countries than of others, though it seems to be spreading to cultures hitherto more urbanised.
7   In reality it is the 'unplanned' parts of the Renaissance city rather than the true Medieval city which provide this image. The characteristic streets are those which contain a certain number of merchants' houses, where surplus wealth has permitted a display of status—a fact which makes the use of this as a paradigm for low-cost housing even more absurd.
8   The word "metonymic" is used here in the sense of semantic and positional contiguity as defined by Roman Jakobson. See "Two Aspects of Language and Two Types of Aphasic Disturbances", *Studies in Child Language and Aphasia*, The Hague: Mouton & Co, 1971, or *Selected Writings,* vol. II, The Hague: Mouton & Co, 1971, pp. 239–259.
9   I am not concerned here with whether market research can provide anything more than a devalued and reduced version of a received tradition. I am concerned with it merely as a fact.

Centraal Beheer

First published *Architecture Plus*, vol. 2, no. 5, September/October 1974.

Alberti's statement that a building was a small city, and a city a large building has acquired a new, literal meaning in the twentieth century with the arrival of the superblock. Whether it is a large piece of real estate destined for mixed-use, or a large administrative unit under single occupation, the superblock radically alters the scale of the environment. Here is a new building type for which history provides no direct prototypes.

There seem to have been two basic solutions to this problem. On the one hand, the superblock has been based on a biological analogy according to which it consisted of partially independent organs arranged hierarchically under a central control. This was the method used by Le Corbusier, who more than any other Modern architect recognised the superblock as a typically Modern problem. Alternatively, the superblock has been considered as a self-regulating aggregate of relatively small parts, with any centralised control reduced to a minimum. Distorting Alberti's terms somewhat, it could be said that the first method turns the city into a building, while the second turns the building into a city.

During the early phase of the Modern Movement the first type of solution was generally adopted. Within the functionalist frame of reference—particularly that of the Corbusian theory of *objets-type*—the architectural programme was supposed to reflect the rational disposition of society; but since the Second World War, and especially in the last decade or so, there has been an increasing attempt to adopt the alternative solution, although its seeds have no doubt existed in the Modern Movement all along.

In the 1920s and 30s, it was believed that universal human needs could be established and that the precise functions of the various parts of a building could be defined in terms of these needs. The architects of the *Neue Sachlichkeit* believed that the only task of the architect lay in this analytical activity, but those who, like Le Corbusier, were endowed with a more complex mental machinery realised that beyond the satisfaction of 'objective' needs lay a vast area of metaphor and poetry which was available to all but which the architect, through his control of form, was especially suited to provide. The form-making role of the architect was therefore seen as directly increasing the wellbeing of the user through the mediation of artistic creation.

Both the functional determinism and the formal voluntarism of this attitude tend to be rejected by those who see buildings as potentially self-regulating systems. According to this theory it is the user who plays the active role in a building, while the architect's role is to provide the framework that allows the user to choose his own behaviour. The wellbeing of the user is the result of his own spontaneous activity and not of any forms imposed on his environment by the architect.

Talking of the Centraal Beheer, Herman Hertzberger makes the following statement:

> Architecture has never taken people very much into consideration. Pyramids, temples, cathedrals and palaces were implements for making an impression on them rather than offering them a more liberal life.... The pretension inherent in an office building that has a distinct form... must justify itself by improving the work situation of the people who work there or rather by offering them a helping hand to improve their own conditions by themselves.[1]

It is clear from this statement that Hertzberger believes in the second type of solution to the superblock, the solution that interprets the building as a small town. The designer should not try to establish behaviour patterns or particular formal hierarchies but should concentrate on providing the possibility of behaviour that is self-motivated.

The building itself confirms this general attitude. The plan consists of an aggregate of repeating cells of office accommodation nine metres square, open at their sides and separated from neighbouring cells by three metre wide voids lit from the roof and penetrating through the three storeys of the building. The cells are linked by bridges that prolong the implied circulation routes passing along the two axes of the cells. Each cell is supported by eight massive columns, occurring at third points on each side and serving further to insulate the circulation routes from the corner areas of the cells, which are reserved for office work.

There are four groups of such cells occupying the quadrants between a cruciform (or swastika-form) main circulation system on the diagonal of the overall square of the building, and in this system occur entrances, enquiry desks, coffee shops, escalators, elevators, and similar public functions. This public system does not break the pattern of cells but is created simply by joining the cells together and the voids between them, thus creating larger areas. The public areas are not cut off from the office cells any more than the cells are separated from each other.

Walking through the interconnected spaces of this building, enjoying enfilade diagonal views, sensing areas of relative quiet and relative movement, or looking into the voids flooded with daylight from above, one can believe it is indeed "a place where everyone would feel at home". This feeling seems to have been created by increasing the sense of total community while at the same time suggesting islands of semi-privacy with which individuals and groups can identify.

Although the building is occupied by a single firm (a large Amsterdam insurance company), the impression is of a number of different firms, because of the way the space is broken up by columns and voids and is subdivided subtly into different zones. The grey and large-pored surfaces of the building demand, and get, a good deal of soft, large, and brightly coloured bric-a-brac and indoor plants—although the extent to which these are the spontaneous acts of the employees or 'gifts' from a sensitive and tasteful management is not altogether clear.

The fundamental achievement of this building is that it puts into practice on a large scale a certain principle of publicly shared working space which has until now remained on the drawing boards—the principle that it is equally important to provide for an awareness of the whole building (in contrast to a building that is subdivided into self-contained office rooms) as to a sense of identity on the small scale (in contrast to the *Bürolandschaft* type of office plan).

Although this has not been achieved before on such a scale or with so much consistency and attention to detail, there are a number of partial prototypes for this building. In Frank Lloyd Wright's Larkin Building, open office spaces are arranged around a large central well that is lit from the roof. The ambiguity between inside and outside space occurs in numerous eighteenth and nineteenth century galleries throughout Europe, as does the contrast in scale between small cells and covered public spaces which prolong the street pattern of the city.

But the closest analogies are with Louis Kahn and Aldo van Eyck. In his Trenton Jewish Community Center, Kahn proposed an entirely novel way of distributing space in a large building. Colin Rowe, writing in *Oppositions 1*, has convincingly shown that this is a solution to the problem posed, but not solved, by Mies van der in the library project for the Illinois Institute of Technology. In the Mies building the weak rhythm provided by the slender, regularly spaced columns, implying a universal space, was denied by the necessity of compartmentalising the space into large self-contained 'rooms'. Kahn reintroduced the Renaissance principle according to which space is built up out of cells of space articulated by a 'strong' structure. The plaid pattern of "servant" and "served" spaces created an architectural order, while at the same time the functional spaces were allowed

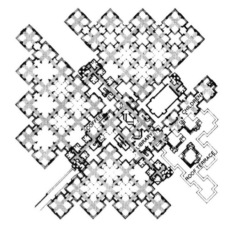

Top: Centraal Beheer, Apeldoorn, The Netherlands. Herman Hertzberger, 1972. First floor plan.

Bottom: Centraal Beheer. Exterior view.

to occupy a varying number of structural bays. Such a loose-fit, architecturally ordered scheme bears many resemblances to Hertzberger's project.

But the project also recalls the Children's Home by van Eyck in Amsterdam, in the way the building is made up of an accretion of identical cells clustering around or growing from a central stem. Hertzberger's achievement here is to have successfully carried out this idea in a multi-storey building, using roof lights not to provide working light but to create a refreshing sense of outside air penetrating into the heart of the building. Rather more remotely, perhaps, the building is also related to Montreal's Place Bonaventure and Place Ville Marie, in which the space of the city is annexed to a vast constructed and artificially serviced space. Finally, it was Le Corbusier himself who, by playing with the semantic ambiguities of 'house' and 'street' in a large structure, suggested a whole generation of plug-in schemes in which identical cells are inserted into a permanent megastructure.

The names of Le Corbusier and van Eyck remind us that Hertzberger's student hostel in Amsterdam was still strongly influenced by the Le Corbusier of the Unité and the Brazilian students' hostel in Paris. In the Amsterdam hostel the repetitive cellular nature of the students' rooms is completely dominated by the overall cube of the building, which is treated as a plastic unit in the manner of Le Corbusier.

Hertzberger's 'conversion' to van Eyck must have occurred in the 1960s during or after the completion of the hostel in 1965. Substantially the same scheme as the Centraal Beheer was submitted for the Valkenswaard Town Hall and Amsterdam City Hall competitions. Between the hostel and these two projects an entirely new attitude to composition has developed: a building is now seen as an elementarist composition of identical units. This change makes a consideration of the outside of the building essential.

However successful the interior of the building is, the exterior is much more problematic. One is forced to ask whether it is sufficient to make a building out of a single repeating unit and a single principle of organisation. The cellular spaces that are so successful inside, because of their modified transparency, immediately become an embarrassment when translated into the necessarily opaque surfaces of the outside. Furthermore, inside the building, one is never aware of more than a part of the space, and the repetition of structure and spaces is only vaguely sensed, while on the outside one becomes aware of the purely mechanical way the modular boxes are assembled. As in Safdie's Habitat, the movement of the surface is by means of increments that are always the same, always blatant, monotonous.

The questions of how one enters the building and how the building relates to its surroundings do not seem to have been considered as serious problems. The articulated surface, stepping back to form a truncated pyramid, seems to deny the possibility of entry and to make any frontalisation and space-making impossible. A clue to Hertzberger's attitude to the outside form of buildings may perhaps be found in one of the statements already quoted. He says that the buildings of the past were intent on "making an impression rather than offering a more liberal life". He seems here to align himself with those *grands simplificateurs* of the Modern Movement for whom architecture is simply the demonstration of some internal principle, of a 'system' that automatically ensures virtue in the same way that photosynthesis in a plant creates beauty. But there is no guarantee, in man-made objects, that a unitary principle similar to what can be deduced from the biochemistry of plant life will result in the wonderful variety found in nature. The puritanical fear of 'making an impression' may blind one to the fact that all buildings make an impression—Hertzberger's not least—and the problem is to decide what impression needs to be made, since our only contact with buildings is through the senses, and the laws of perception govern our responses to every three-dimensional object. The statement that "a building makes itself" (dear to both

Hertzberger and Kahn) may be an expression of belief, but it hardly corresponds to reality. Hertzberger's interior spaces are no less contrived because they are derived from a single repeating idea, and there is no law saying there should not be more than one governing formal idea in a building's conceptual order.

Perhaps the example of Le Corbusier might once more be invoked. In the Venice Hospital scheme he seems to have attempted to achieve precisely the type of integration between internal multiplicity and external calm that is so lacking in the Centraal Beheer. In the Hospital we find both an additive city-like schema in which identical units are repeated and a subtractive schema which allows the outside to be molded and articulated to respond to the space outside. It is true that the programme of the Hospital suggested a horizontal stratification of functions and that Le Corbusier used *pilotis* to gain access from underneath the spreading mass of the building. Therefore the solution is not entirely relevant to the problem of the office building. Nevertheless, its example shows that the problems of external form and of access are as important as those of the interior, and that, difficult as it may be to solve all these problems simultaneously, it is not impossible—once they have been admitted as problems and the complexities of the situation have been acknowledged.

1 Mellor, David, "Hertzberger, The Centraal Beheer Office Complex, Apeldoorn", *Architectural Design* 49, no. 2, 1974, pp. 108–117.

Plateau Beaubourg

First published in *Architectural Design*, vol. 47, no. 2, 1977.

"Culture", according to Raymond Williams, belongs to a group of words (together with "class", "industry", "democracy", and "art") which were either invented or given new meanings after the Industrial Revolution. But, although all modern states feel some degree of responsibility for the development of culture, the way this is implemented varies with the tradition of each individual country. In England the word carries faintly derisive or apologetic overtones (only to be taken seriously when linked to a folk hero like Shakespeare). In France, it seems, the very abstractness of the word invests it with irresistible authority, and while the French are evidently in the process of trying to liberalise their institutions along Scandinavian and Anglo-Saxon lines, it is the very existence of these traditions, enshrined in the habits of state patronage and in the academies, which has determined the concept of the Centre Pompidou.[1]

It is precisely this attempt to combine 'modernity' and traditional institutionalism, populism and gigantism, which makes both the programme and the architecture of the Centre Pompidou so problematic. In his published book on the Centre—a quasi-official apologia by one of its chief administrators—Claude Mollard makes a statement which brings this problem into focus. "Beaubourg", he says, "is the meeting of the tastes and preoccupations of a president and the aspirations, still latent, of the French people."[2]

Now it is quite acceptable that large projects should be initiated by the state. Living in a country where the government appears to suffer from almost total paralysis, we have cause to envy a people whose government is intellectually honest enough to admit the reality of political power and vigorous enough to act upon it. It is equally acceptable that the aspirations of ordinary citizens should be respected and encouraged. But to attribute to the people aspirations of which they are not yet conscious, and to justify government action on this assumption, is surely to indulge in double-talk of the most disingenuous kind.

The absurdity of the statement comes from the attempt to combine the principles of *laissez-faire* liberalism with those of a normative conservatism. It lies in holding simultaneously to the belief that, on the one hand, culture is an innate endowment of each individual and, on the other, that it represents a set of values that must be taught. The first proposition derives from Rousseau (partly through a misunderstanding) and is characteristic of the aspirations of liberal democracy; the second is the view which has generally been held by reforming conservatives ever since Edmund Burke.[3]

What is new in the Gaullist position is that the respect usual among conservatives for the traditional values of the 'organic' society has been replaced by an enthusiasm for the 'modern' and the avant-garde. This enthusiasm compounds the contradictions inherent in their attitude, since avant-gardism itself suffered from similar contradictions. On the one hand, it wished to abolish the academic (elitist) culture in the name of 'free creation' (the artistic equivalent of liberalism). On the other, it proposed a severe functionalism and a pure formalism which were unacceptable to the 'average man' because they excluded all those conventions and habits of feeling to which he is attached (and to which the commercialism of the liberal state attaches him more and more firmly).

Mollard asserts that the promoters of Beaubourg chose a 'functional' building—in contrast with what the protest movement, *Geste Architectural*, would have commissioned. The positivist tone of this statement makes it hardly distinguishable from the propaganda of the *Neue Sachlichkeit* architects and writers of the 1920s. It ignores the fact that, whatever their protestations, the architects of the 1920s were less concerned with creating a functional architecture than they were with creating the symbolism for a new social and cultural order. Once it is admitted that 'functionalism' is a system of representation and not a mere instrument, then it becomes a matter of legitimate discussion as to whether the values symbolised by this architecture are desirable or not. But such a discussion is cut short by the bland statement that architecture expresses nothing but its inherent usefulness. Any questioning of its forms can then be attributed to the fact that the questioner has not yet come to terms with the 'facts' of modern life.

Judging by Mollard's text, the architectural philosophy of the Beaubourg bureaucracy is based on the unmodified assertions of the avant-garde of the 1920s. He continually refers to the Bauhaus as the prototype for the kind of interdisciplinary artistic creation which Beaubourg is intended to encourage. Pierre Boulez is referred to as "the Gropius of music", presumably because he sees musical creation as an open-ended experiment based on the gradual disclosure of the 'laws of acoustics'—a movement of continual progress toward the ideal of a music deriving from natural laws. In a similar vein, Le Corbusier's "a house is a machine for living in" is quoted, with astonished approval, despite the fact that Le Corbusier himself severely qualified this statement as early as 1929.[4]

In fact, both Boulez and Le Corbusier are (or were), despite their adherence to expression theory, thoroughly immersed in the arts of the past—arts which were based, not directly on nature, but on human culture, and whose rules and conventions were the products of a certain social milieu. But these complexities and contradictions within the avant-garde itself are disregarded by the promoters of the Centre Pompidou. Instead, we are presented with a conception of functionalist and Expressionist art which is a rehash of the catchphrases of the 1920s, as if nothing at all had happened during the intervening 40 years. It is in these terms that the avant-garde is offered 'to the people' by the French establishment as providing for their 'still latent' aspirations. The complexity and diversity of the present situation in architecture, which is ignored by the Beaubourg establishment, was amply demonstrated by the variety among the entries for the competition itself. Yet the report of the competition jury made it sound as if the jury was still fighting the battles of the 1920s and was choosing between the 'truly modern' schemes and the academic ones. This was not so. Practically all the projects were, in a general sense, 'modern'. What the jury was, in fact, doing was making a choice between aspects of the Modern Movement which have become separated out into different streams.

Many of the projects interpreted the brief as something which could be classified and articulated into different elements and used this possibility to give meaning to the volumes and surfaces and to integrate the building into its surroundings— maintaining the roof line, picking up existing axes, breaking up the mass of the building by intersecting it with public arcades, and so on. The winning project was almost alone in ignoring all these problems, and by doing so it was able to present a scheme of brilliant simplicity and clarity. Instead of thinking of the building as consisting of separate spaces with varying degrees of fixity and flexibility, it proposed a solution in which the entire building was flexible and which consisted of a series of superimposed and uniform loft spaces. The structure, circulation, and service elements were then pulled to the outside surfaces and used to give interest to facades which otherwise would have been inexpressive.

But the uncompromising audacity of this solution was achieved at the expense of making the building into a vast self-sufficient block, inserted rather crudely into the city fabric, without regard for the existing scale of the surroundings. It is true that it was one of the few schemes to leave part of the site as a public open space. But perhaps because the scale of the new building is so different from that of the buildings on the other three sides, the space this creates seems residual.

What evidently appealed to the jury was the uncompromising way in which the building interpreted the Centre as a supermarket of culture and gave no spatial or plastic form to the various departments exhaustively specified in the brief. The building was to be a symbol for the hoped-for ultimate fusion between cultural disciplines and the assimilation of culture in the marketplace. If Baron Haussmann had asked for an umbrella to represent the market as a new type among the many existing types of public building, the jury of the Centre Pompidou chose an umbrella to symbolise the fact that culture as a whole was a marketplace and to incorporate this symbol in a unique and neutral building type into which, as into a box room, one could put the whole of that vague, unclassifiable baggage called "culture". The process was the opposite of what was intended in the eighteenth century. Instead of the multiplication of precisely defined organs of democratic life—Babeuf's "public stores… amphitheatres… circuses… aqueducts… bridges… archives… libraries"—all organs of culture were now to be reduced to a single entity, the prototype of which was the self-service store, the emblem of the liberal consumer society. Perhaps an even more potent image for the jury's concept of the cultural centre was the nineteenth century international exhibition, where the products of the world were displayed and where 'culture' was equated with 'information'.

Piano and Rogers' building belongs to a stream of the Modern Movement whose origins are more recent than the avant-garde of the 1920s. It derives in a fundamental sense from Mies van der Rohe's American phase, which was based on a reversal of the received notion of the Modern Movement that a building is an aggregate of linked or overlapping forms, each of which corresponds to a separate function. To Mies, modern functions were empirical and changing, while architecture was ideal and permanent, and his notion of the 'shed' was thus connected with neo-classicism. But there is an even closer affiliation to the notion of the elegant container associated with the work Eero Saarinen and Skidmore, Owings and Merrill and the Southern California Schools Development Programme directed by Ezra Ehrenkrantz, and through this to Charles Eames' Case Study House of 1949, in which a standardised technology provides the framework for aleatory gestures. Inherent in this development is the idea of the building as a flexible service mechanism which becomes a mere background to human activity.

The building as a beautifully designed container and as a servicing mechanism which recedes into the background when animated by people—these also seem to be the principles of the architecture of Piano and Rogers, and they are the qualities in their solution to the Centre Pompidou which were evidently admired by the jury.

I believe this concept of architecture as a servicing mechanism suffers from too reductivist an attitude. This is not to say that there are not many problems characteristic of the present day which suggest solutions of this type. But there is a tendency among those who pursue this concept to wish to apply it to a wide range of problems which are capable of being solved in other ways. Thus, in view of this tendency, and from the standpoint of the content of architecture, the concept suggests that the instruments of public life should be dismantled in the name of some vague apocalyptic vision of cultural fusion, just as paternalistic populism postpones spontaneous freedom in the name of the 'still latent' aspirations of the masses. From the point of view of the architecture itself, it suggests that architecture should not be conceived with any typology of spaces or human uses but that these functions should be handed over to the spontaneous forces of life.

This attitude assumes that architecture has no further task other than to perfect its own technology. It turns the problem of architecture as a representation of social values into a purely aesthetic one, since it assumes that the purpose of architecture is merely to accommodate any form of activity which may be required and has no positive attitude toward these activities. It creates institutions, while pretending that no institutionalisation of social life is necessary.

The Centre Pompidou represents this general philosophy, but to substantiate the criticism which is being made of it in these terms, a closer look at the building itself is necessary. Given its aims, are these aims fulfilled, and if not, is this owing to mistakes during detailed design, to accidental or uncontrollable factors, or to

more fundamental reasons connected with the general architectural philosophy which the building represents?

While it would clearly be presumptuous to try to infer from the building all the intentions of the architects and users, there are three words which recur with sufficient frequency in the jury's report and in Mollard's book to be used as an indication of the connotations the building is supposed to have. These words are "transparency", "flexibility", and "function". It would perhaps be useful to look at the building in terms of these three concepts.

Transparency

Transparency is connected with several ideas. It has been, of course, a widely acclaimed property of modern architecture in general, and is usually associated with the structural frame and the use of glass to create transparent planes. But it has been subject to various metaphoric interpretations during the course of the Modern Movement. In Expressionism it had strong spiritual and mystical overtones, and in De Stijl it was connected with the idea of an infinite abstract space. In the Centre Pompidou it is used with social connotations; the building is seen as an object which is accessible to everyone and can be appropriated by the public.

The quality of lightness and penetrability is a general feature of Piano/Rogers' architecture. The frame is generally expressed as a slender net and both external walls and internal partitions are seen as light and provisional. The competition drawings had exactly these qualities. The cube building as defined by the steel grid was seen merely as a sketch of the building's possibilities. The external surfaces of the building were set back behind the plane of the structure, and some of the bays of the grid were left open, giving the actual enclosed volume a random and, by implication, a provisional form. The surfaces of the enclosed volume were not indicated, and their solidity was further reduced by the use of an external staircase and by graphic display. All these devices gave the design a Constructivist quality, with strong overtones of the Vesnin brothers' Pravda building, in which a skeletal frame is animated by various moving elements and in which the transparency of the building reveals its internal mechanisms.

Some of this quality seems to have been lost in the actual building. In overcoming the technical problems of the glazed skin, the architects have had to

Centre Pompidou. Main facade elevation of winning competition scheme.

make the mullions much heavier than they appeared on the drawings, and this has reduced the transparency of the surface. The height of the building has been reduced, and the same accommodation has had to be fitted into a smaller volume; as a result, most of the open bays of the grid have been filled up.

The building in its formal and relatively massive form demands to be read in the round. Like most modern buildings, it is essentially a free-standing object, and it suffers from being hemmed in by the existing fabric of the city.

Flexibility

Flexibility is also an idea that belongs to the Modern Movement as a whole, but its interpretation as literal adaptability, as opposed to the idea of an object whose parts, though fixed, are freely related according to pragmatic requirements, is one of those separate streams into which modern architecture has developed in more recent years. The notion of literal adaptability presents problems when it is translated from the realm of the ideal into that of the real. The Beaubourg scheme demonstrates these problems in a dramatic way.

One of the essential properties of adaptability is that it can be realised without modifying the building's infrastructure, or destroying its intelligibility by the user. The philosophy behind the notion of flexibility is that the requirements of modern life are too complex and changeable to be determined at design stage.

In the case of the Centre Pompidou this principle of flexibility seems to have led to an over-schematic solution which does not take into account the size of the building. It seems to have been conceived on a much smaller scale, with the result that its elements are much bulkier than those originally imagined. It is difficult to envisage any function which would require an unimpeded 50 metre span with a height limitation of seven metres, three metres of which is taken up by the lattice beams. The absence of columns seems to be related to the original idea of adjustable floors. Now that they are of fixed and uniform height, the space feels too compressed, and this impression is accentuated by the deep lattices.

Another problem connected with the concept of the open, flexible floor plan is that it depends perceptually on all partitions and subdivisions being disconnected from the support structure. But however flexible the requirements may be in general, there are usually some functions which require complete and permanent separation. In the Centre Pompidou, complete openness has been achieved, except in one important case—that of the fire walls. Each floor is divided into two compartments by a wall across the building which extends from floor to ceiling. Conceptually this wall is a secondary and *ad hoc* element, but perceptually it belongs to the same category as the floor and ceiling planes. Consequently it appears as a powerful architectural element without architectural meaning.

A similar problem has occurred on the external wall on the east facade. This was originally intended to be transparent, and indeed the symmetry of the building, where a loft space is lined on each side with a 'servant' strip, demands that it should be so. The space relies for its clarity on both east and west surfaces being transparent. But the need to isolate the mechanical services which line this facade has resulted in the transparent wall being replaced by a solid one. At the same time, this wall underlines the fact that the conceptual parity between the two facades of the building is a fiction. According to the schematic plan, human circulation and the movement of mechanical systems belong to the same category—the one on the west facade and the other on the east. But they are radically different, not only on the level of meaning but also on the level of function.

Finally, the concept of the building as an open-planned flexible shed implies that many elements normally associated with the articulation of the building itself should become pieces of furniture which can be moved in accordance with the wishes of the users. But in practise, in a building containing several different

departments, the allocation of space to each one becomes a major logistic exercise and is the occasion for the invention of a new type of bureaucrat—the 'programmer'. Once these allocations have been made, there are powerful pressures to leave them unaltered, except in the case of extreme necessity, since any alteration of demarcation in one place has repercussions everywhere else. The introduction of an intermediary group of 'programmers' between the architect and the user makes it an open question whether a 'flexible space' is any more flexible in reality than spaces of a more conventional type.

Function

The word "function", when used in connection with architecture, has two senses. First, it simply means the way in which a building satisfies a set of pragmatically determined uses. Secondly, it means a certain architectural language, a language which represents a relation held to exist between human society and the mechanical

Top: Centre Pompidou. Interior view of the Musée National d'Art Moderne.

Bottom: Centre Pompidou. A typical interior showing the furniture system, designed by the Piano and Rogers team in conjunction with the manufacturers, which is used throughout the building.

and material basis of its culture. Any discussion of function often entails a constant oscillation between two different levels of logical thought. When buildings are described as "functional", the word is often used in the first sense but given the moral force of the second.

If we accept at face value the sense in which both the jury of the Beaubourg Competition and Claude Mollard describe the building as "functional", we would suppose them to mean a building which is 'sensible' and 'unostentatious'— indeed, the word "modest" is used several times in order to convey, presumably, the opposite of 'rhetorical' or 'gestural'—a building which avoids, in Mollard's words, "symbolic gestures which are more or less gratuitous".[5]

This is perhaps true in the sense that the architects have provided the clients with a number of open floors which they can subdivide at will. In terms of the various activities which go on in the building, the architecture has nothing whatever to say. But it does not follow from this that the building is 'modest' or 'non-rhetorical' in other respects. Given the enormous size of the building, and given the decision to make it with a series of uninterrupted loft spaces, it was inevitable, if it was not to be unbelievably boring (the oppression of non-rhetoric), that some large gestures would have to be made on the outside, and it is possible that as the design of the building progressed, it was realised that the scale of the structural members would be so vast that it would be impossible to maintain the delicate lightness of the original concept, and that something far more heroic would have to be asserted.

The elements of this heroism are the structural frame with its tubular columns, its expressively jointed, dynamically balanced gerberettes, and its 50 metre span lattice beams; the escalator climbing up the west facade, the *passerelles* at each floor, and the escape staircases inserted between these and the facade; and the mechanical service ducts and plant rooms (with their own secondary steel structure) which occupy the entire east facade. Given the initial concept, the development of all these elements has been carried out with logic, consistency, and an impeccable sense of style.

But in considering whether the 'symbolic gestures' are 'gratuitous' or not, we cannot just take them at their face value as an 'honest' expression of the material or function of the building. The Galerie des Machines and the Eiffel Tower were structural gestures but carried with them the idea of structural economy and minimal effort, whereas at Beaubourg the 'real' structural members are in places sheathed in stainless steel and thus appear both luxurious and larger than they actually are. Nor can the Centre Pompidou be equated with the work of the Constructivists, however strong the analogy may at first seem. For the Constructivists, the expression of structure and mechanical elements was connected with a social ideology and took its meaning from this. The Centre Pompidou seems to be more related to Archigram's work of the 60s and its meaning to be in the area of science fiction. This great machine of culture seems to have no ideological message: it presents an image of total mechanisation but makes no connection between this image and the other possible images of our culture.

Many of the criticisms made here of the building are detailed. But my purpose has been to show that even the most incidental faults derive from two fundamental decisions: that the building should be conceived of as a well-serviced shed and that its symbolism should be concerned with its mechanical support systems. The first has resulted in too schematic an interpretation of the brief, leaving the architect without any means of control over a host of unforeseen practical exigencies, and has relegated to other authorities formal decisions which properly belong to the architect. The second has resulted in a building which idealises process to the exclusion of any idea toward what this 'process' should be aimed. Both decisions presuppose that 'culture' is an absolute which cannot be mediated by any final form and that its achievement must be indefinitely postponed.

1. The simultaneous appearance of the Centre Pompidou and the (British) National Theatre neatly illustrates not only the different cultural preoccupations of the two countries but also the different time scale within which they work—15 years for the National Theatre, five years for the Centre Pompidou.
2. *L'enjeu du Centre Georges Pompidou*, Paris, 1976.
3. See Lovejoy, Arthur O, "The Supposed Primitivism of Rousseau", *Essays in the History of Ideas*, Baltimore: Johns Hopkins Press, 1948.
4. Le Corbusier, "In Defense of Architecture", trans, with a commentary by George Baird, *Oppositions*, October 1974, pp. 93–108.
5. Mollard, Claude, *Centre Georges Pompidou,* p. 154.

Opposite: Centre Pompidou. Service facade.

Above: Centre Pompidou. Service duct manifold model.

Frames to Framework

First published in *Encounter*, 1977.

Architectural literature seems to follow definite patterns. Most of the books produced at any one moment, whatever the apparent diversity of their subject matter, tend to reflect similar themes and obsessions. This phenomenon is certainly not restricted to architecture—it is true of all cultural discourse. But it is particularly true of architecture at the present moment, when the Modern Movement is passing through one of its recurrent crises—perhaps the most serious one since its beginning over half a century ago.

In reaction to the optimism and large-scale thinking of the 1960s (a period which itself claimed to have overcome the academicism into which the Modern Movement had declined), architects have retreated to a more cautious position. An attitude of mind is emerging which no longer conceives of architectural creation as an open-ended advance into a utopian future but rather as a process which takes place in the present. This 'present' includes much of what was previously thought to belong to a superseded past, and it may be that the power of architecture to communicate at all relies on its ability to understand and transform its own language.

Such a realisation cannot reproduce the eclecticism of the nineteenth century. The manner in which tradition can be acknowledged has itself changed, and it is the unprecedented nature of the present situation which is responsible for the divergence of views about the relation of architecture to history. The spectrum of opinion extends from vernacular semi-revival to a fresh look at the early phases of the Modern Movement itself. This diversity has been called "pluralism", but it is not eclecticism. Though certain factions may advocate a sort of eclecticism, the situation as a whole is not the same as that of the nineteenth century, when there was a universal belief in the connotational power of past styles.

The 1960s were characterised by two tendencies, both of which emphasised the 'process' of architectural production rather than its final achievement. The first was a tendency toward seeking the laws of architecture outside architecture itself—in mathematics, computer technology, systems analysis, or social analysis. The second was an enormous extension both of architecture's physical scale and of its imagery. The city was no longer thought to consist of individual buildings but conceived as a continuous and growing structure which dissolved the distinction between architecture and town planning, while its expressive power was thought to lie less in the conventional elements of architectural construction than in that of new technologies of mass consumption, space research, and—in the case of Archigram—the imagery of the Pop movement of the 60s.

This development has been chronicled in Reyner Banham's book *Megastructure: Urban Futures of the Recent Past*. Banham takes as his starting point Fumihiko Maki's definition of megastructure, 1964: "a large frame in which all the functions of a city or part of a city are housed"; or—in Banham's own words—"a permanent and dominating frame containing subordinate and transient accommodations".[1] He goes on to identify two further ingredients: different rates of obsolescence in the different scales of structure and the notions of flexibility, change, and feedback.

Banham traces the development of the movement in the work of several more or less self-contained groups: the Japanese Metabolists, the French Urbanisme Spatial group, the Italian Città-Territorio group, and the British Archigram. In discussing the (relatively few) projects where megastructural ideas have been realised, he stresses the Montreal Expo of 1967, which was not only suffused with the general mega-spirit but which commissioned such megastructural prototypes as Guntis Plesum's Theme Pavilion and Moshe Safdie's Habitat.

Though most architects know more or less what they mean by "megastructure", it becomes a somewhat slippery term as one tries to give it a precise definition, and in fact it is a fusion of several different trends. Banham has given it a wide definition—perhaps sometimes too wide. Projects such as the Chiesa Rossa scheme for Milan, 1961, and the Quartiere Direzionale scheme for Turin, 1963, are really no more than large-scale planning schemes in which self-contained blocks are linked by a network of transport and service routes.[2] They do not have (though in some ways they do adumbrate) the essential megastructural properties of continuity, modular growth, and evenness of texture, in which the old idea of the identity of form and function, symbolised in the *objet-type,* is superseded by the random and non-hierarchical slotting of all functions into the same framework. There is also a distinction, ignored by Banham, between true megastructures and large building complexes such as Denys Lasdun's University of East Anglia, in which a certain visual continuity conceals hierarchically arranged and static functional elements.

But many megastructures do have isolated blocks. How are they to be distinguished from more conventional schemes? This leads to a distinction between two basic types of megastructure: those in which the support structure is merely a sort of neutral grid, like the projects of Yona Friedman and Shadrach Woods' Free University of Berlin, and those in which the support structure is monumentalised, as with the Metabolists and Archigram. In these, the individual buildings are not *objets-type* but identical giant nodes, usually cylindrical. This type is often characterised by the selection of forms from a *catalogue imaginaire* of industrial ready-mades and involves their use on a new scale and for a new purpose. The common ancestor of this transformation and ambiguity of scale and meaning is the work of Le Corbusier, though with him it was controlled by formal composition, not present in megastructural design.

Banham rightly says that megastructural ideas were incipient in the Modern Movement from the outset. He is thorough in hunting down its antecedents, but there are some possible omissions. For instance, the concept of the infinite extension of an imaginary spatial grid, which belongs to both neo-Plasticism and Elementarism, and of which Frederick Kiesler's "Cité dans l'espace" at the Paris Exposition Internationale des Arts Decoratifs of 1925 was perhaps the definitive expression. Another source which Banham does not mention is Constructivism, with its semantic stress on the structural and material fabric of the building—on the rhetoric of process. The chemical factory by a student in Nikolai A Ladovsky's atelier, 1922, which features diagonal lattice enclosing huge cylindrical containers, seems to anticipate, on the level of expression, the entire Archigram oeuvre. But it would be only too easy to extend the provenance of the megastructure idea, since it belongs to the whole history of architecture. At an aesthetic level the super-imposition of two structural orders is a characteristic of post-Renaissance architecture; while at the level of social content, its development within the Modern Movement, especially in Le Corbusier, certainly owes something to the Fourierist tradition, if not specifically to the nineteenth century architect, Alessandro Antonelli, whose condominium apartments in Turin anticipated Nicholas Habraken's "support structure" thesis by half a century. But in spite of such arguable omissions, Banham's book is an important extension of his work as instant historian of the Modern Movement.

In this role he is bound to be overtaken by events, and the subtitle of the book testifies to the fact that he is conscious of recording a dead movement. He rationalises its demise in terms of his previously well-publicised scepticism about the role of the architect in modern society and sees the megastructure movement as a last desperate bid by architects for world power. But Banham's attitude toward architects has always been equivocal, and, to balance the account, there is a noticeable softening in his attitude to the "cultural baggage" which he so summarily dismissed in *Theory and Design in the First Machine Age.* This can be seen in his remarks concerning Patrick Hodgkinson's Brunswick Centre project (a very marginal megastructure): "Such professionalism and almost old-fashioned learning is not, in retrospect, to be despised. This is not the only building of its class that can be said to have been saved by old-time architectural skills in composition and design from the kind of cheerless chaos that infected so much of the less determined 'megastructure' housing of that period in England."[3] But he manages to include these caveats without giving the book an air of compromise or loss of faith. While cutting megastructures down to size, he still manages to convey the excitement that the movement generated in the 1960s.

Banham could, however, be criticised for too easily accepting the megastructuralists' own tendency to emphasise the iconographic aspects of architecture at the expense of its social or technical reality. He does make some passing criticisms of the frequent gap in megastructural schemes between technical feasibility and aesthetic image, but he does not attempt a thoroughgoing critique of these. He seems to accept the movement as a transitory fashion and fails to explain its rapid loss of impetus, or to demonstrate in what way its ideas might still be valid—even though its application might result in forms which were different from those of the 1960s.

The reaction against megastructures which has taken place in recent years is part of a more general reaction against the Modern Movement as a whole. This is exemplified in Brent C Brolin's book *The Failure of Modern Architecture,* which is a compendium of popular conceptions (and misconceptions) of the Modern Movement. Brolin's main theme is that the inspiration of the Modern Movement came largely from an outmoded nineteenth century positivism. He says, correctly, that while Modern architecture claimed to be offering 'functional' design, it was in fact a preference for a certain architectural style. But he does not give an adequate analysis of the intentions and meanings of this style. He criticises the Modern Movement for its puritanical attitude toward nineteenth century ornament, but he himself is equally puritanical about a style which represents and embodies a certain attitude toward modern society. Like many self-styled populists, he unintentionally allies himself with historical determinism and wants to replace the modern 'style' with a 'natural' and popular architecture, because he fails to see that all style is arbitrary and rule-governed.

Brolin's analysis of the nineteenth century takes little account of its ideological framework. He selects different aspects of nineteenth century capitalism and treats them sometimes as virtues (the love of ornament) and sometimes as sins (the maximum return on minimum investment), apparently without realising that these are two aspects of the same ethos. Many of Brolin's criticisms of modern architecture are justified if taken in isolation. But the total rejection of it as a homogeneous movement which he proposes would involve him in a much more radical view of its alternatives than he is prepared to accept. One such alternative seems to him to lie in the work of Robert Venturi, but Venturi's work fits quite comfortably into the framework of the Modern Movement, and the 'naïve observer' would probably find it difficult to distinguish it from the other products of modern architecture which it is supposed to contradict.

Radical critics of modern architecture may perhaps be divided into 'intellectual humanists' and 'grass-roots humanists'. The bracketing of these two together should not obscure the fact that intellectual humanists often have more in common with their functionalist adversaries than with their ostensible allies. This becomes clear if we compare their respective interpretations of the word "humanist"—in the first case, etymologically rooted in the Renaissance, and in the second case, floating vaguely in the liberal regions of twentieth century deism. This distinction is related to the more general conflict between classicism and romanticism, rationalism and pragmatism—a conflict which is nowadays often oversimplified into that between 'elitism' and 'populism'.

If Brolin could perhaps be called a "grass-roots humanist", Joseph Rykwert is a humanist with more claim to the term. His book *The Idea of a Town* is also, in a sense, an attack on some of the assumptions of modern architecture, but it is an attack at once more profound and more oblique than Brolin's. Whereas Brolin's idea of a "humane architecture" would be based on explicit, pragmatic "wants" and on an aesthetics of sensation, Rykwert would see it as having to fulfil man's ageless psychological needs—needs which are not immediately given, since all the conditions of modern life conspire to conceal them, just as in psychoanalytic theory the conscious, rationalising mind conceals the unconscious drives which underlie it. According to modern planning concepts, the town is purely economic and instrumental—it has no fixed dimensions and is usually thought of in terms of biological growth. But the town, as Rykwert says, "… is not really like a natural phenomenon…. If it is related to physiology at all, it is more like a dream than anything else."[4]

Rykwert's main thesis is that, in building houses and towns, men are re-enacting a ritual which derives from the fundamental and irrevocable split between nature and culture. This is not a new thesis—it is, for example, one of the main ideas of Mircea Eliade—but in this book it is supported by an unusual and fascinating wealth of anthropological material, drawn chiefly from the Mediterranean civilisations but also from the East and the tribal societies of Africa and America. According to Rykwert, what Etruscan and Roman towns shared with the whole ancient and "primitive" world were: "(1) the acting out, at the founding of any settlement, … of a dramatic show of the creation of the world; (2) the incarnation of that drama in the plan of the settlement, as well as in its social and religious institution; (3) the achieving of this second aim by the alignment of its axes with those of the universe; and finally (4) the rehearsal of the foundation cosmogony in regular festivals, and its commemorative embodiment in the monuments."[5] The essence of these acts, Rykwert says, "is to reconcile man to his fate through monument and ritual action".[6]

Underlying Rykwert's thesis is the notion that form always has symbolic meaning. Classical and post-classical interpretations of axial and orthogonal street layouts as practical recipes were always post-rationalisations of deeper layers of meaning revealed in religious and folk traditions. His point of view is antipathetic to the theory of cultural diffusion, and in discussing the adoption of such plans by the Etruscans, Rykwert says: "The orthogonal plan and the matter of orientation were too important in the life of a people to have been taken over arbitrarily…. They must in fact have had a context in the general world picture of the Etruscans into which they might fit."[7] Rykwert, of course, does not argue that practical considerations were not important; his point is that pragmatic and cosmological notions were unified in a total world view. Thus Hippodamus, who is credited (probably erroneously) with being the founder of the orthogonal city, was not just a chartered surveyor *avant la lettre* but a philosopher whose thought "does not separate out physical space, political space, urban space, but unifies them in one speculative exertion".[8] (JP Vernant, as quoted by Rykwert.)

Though some scholars, particularly British ones with empiricist leanings, will no doubt have their reservations about Rykwert's hypothesis, his view is supported by much recent philosophical and anthropological theory, and when it is a question of interpreting the ancient and primitive world and of redressing the balance of nineteenth century positivism, it seems completely convincing. But Rykwert's purpose is not just historical and descriptive. As an architect and a theorist he is concerned with using the findings of anthropology to build a prescriptive model which can be applied to the present day, and here his thesis is both more urgent and more problematic—though in justice to Rykwert it must be said that he acknowledges the immense difficulty of making a transition from the ancient to the modern world and makes no claims to having found a solution.

If we accept the Lévi-Straussian view that myths are empty structures of which the latest 'rational' explanation must be considered simply as a further elaboration (eg Marx or Freud), there seems almost no end to the social transformations that can legitimately 'stand in' for the original mythic content. But if, as with phenomenologists like Paul Ricoeur, we believe that the content of myths is archetypal (and Rykwert seems to incline to this view), we must interpret many aspects of modern social life as pathological and seek to recover a world of meaning which the modern world has distorted. As Rykwert points out, the modern city is an infinitely more complex physical and social mechanism than the ancient. This increase in mechanical complexity is balanced by a proportional loss of symbolic meaning both in the city as a whole and in its parts. Whereas in the ancient city the private fantasies of its inhabitants were hypostatised in its physical and social structure and in collective myths and rituals, today, whatever our perennial psychological needs, they do not find such collective and physical expression. The social realm is interpreted as the sum total of a number of private or family transactions. Can this situation be altered by manipulating the aesthetic and physical structure of the city, or is the structure itself the result of more profound social laws? Rykwert does not answer this question, nor does he say whether he considers it feasible or desirable to design entire cities according to new principles, or whether architecture can now play only an indirect, exemplary role in a 'virtual city' space.

The problem of the modern city revolves around two polar models, called by James Bird "disjointed incrementalism" and "goal orientation".[9] The megastructure idea is a projection of the first. It denies the need for the formal representation of the city as an idea and sees it as the sum total of an infinite number of individual 'freedoms'. The city emerges as a functional organisation which is self-regulating, needs no image of itself, and has no centre or limits. The idea of the city put forward by Rykwert is the exact opposite. The city is thought of as an intentional representation of man in the cosmos. It has a 'meaning', not so much in terms of its function as in terms of cosmology; it is discrete and has both centre and boundaries. (The megastructural city is not, of course, without an image, but its image is 'natural' and aesthetic. In the ancient city, the physical form was the structural analogue of certain concepts.) In *Centrality and Cities,* Bird tries to understand the relation between these two contradictory concepts and to reconcile them. As a geographer and a 'scientist' he is concerned with avoiding *a priori* judgments, but he is aware that, if science wants to understand the whole world, it must take into account human disposition and must therefore absorb the subjective. His approach depends a great deal on both Structuralism and Karl Popper's hypothetico-deductive model on the one hand and information theory and *Gestalt* psychology on the other—though he also has brief flirtations with Teilhard de Chardin and Arthur Koestler.

In these terms Bird sees 'centrality' as part of the fundamental structure of the human mind; it depends on the fact that meaning resides not in objects but in their relationship and in an ability to distinguish between dissimilar things. His final conclusion is that cities depend on a compromise between an order and centrality which is too obvious and a dispersion which is disquieting. In reading his book, with its scissors-and-paste assembly of innumerable authorities, one is led to the conclusion that it lacks a strong concept which could unify, at a higher level, the mass of data which he adduces, and which alone would justify his syncretic approach. Such a concept might, for instance, depend on a greater awareness of history, as a result of which it would become clear that the necessary compromise between order and disorder, confirmation and surprise, contains elements of eighteenth and nineteenth century picturesque theory—what Manfredo Tafuri has called the assimilation of the city with nature.[10] What appears to Bird as a fundamental human disposition may be a historical phenomenon, and its explanation would then depend on a theory of ideology. He does not, for instance, once mention the mnemonic function of cities—a function which is denied by the megastructural city, with its biological metaphors and its orientation toward an unknown future, but which is fundamental if we are to understand Rykwert's concept of myth and monument. The function of memory can be seen under two aspects, that of individual psychology and that of social transmission, and both are relevant to a discussion of buildings and towns.

A basic fact of existing cities, and one which still accounts for their 'readability', is the simultaneous existence and interpretation of different past styles. Ever since the end of the eighteenth century, and until the onset of the Modern Movement, eclecticism was the accepted way in which memory played its part in the city. The new and rapidly proliferating building types of the nineteenth century were able to be absorbed into the city as a representational system only by being annexed to one or another of the existing 'styles'. The concept of "style" and that of "type" were, therefore, the corollaries of an eclectic architecture.

The realisation that memory plays an essential part in the assignation of meaning to architecture has led some contemporary architects to a concept of "typology"—of the need for some kind of taxonomy by which the architectural system can be broken down into recognisable and memorisable parts. This has resulted in a new interest in the architectural theories of the early nineteenth century which tried to classify architecture into its 'types' or species, using the analogy of botany or zoology. On the face of it Nikolaus Pevsner's book *A History of Building Types* might seem to be a response to such an interest. But it is soon apparent that this is not the case. In his brief introduction Pevsner makes no attempt to establish a theoretical framework for his study. He puts forward no theory of types, nor does he relate his study of types to any historical tradition. He simply accepts typology as found in the nineteenth century and uses its methods to guide us through architectural history. This *ad hoc* procedure allows him to omit churches and houses from his book on the grounds that they have been adequately covered elsewhere, and thus makes impossible any systematic or comprehensive analysis of the relation of style to building type.

Professor Pevsner's method is similar to the one adopted in his survey of the English counties. But what was suitable for a guidebook is inappropriate for architectural history. We are presented with little more than a mass of historical information. Nonetheless, great care has been taken over the selection of plans and photographs, and these alone make the book a valuable record of the main post-Renaissance building types and their historical development.

Pevsner's only excursion into theory comes in the concluding chapter. The theory concerns eclecticism (which Pevsner always calls historicism—a word which, confusingly, has an opposite meaning in Hegelian exegesis). His tentative explanation of eclecticism is that "every building creates associations in the mind of the beholder, whether the architect wanted it or not".[11] This statement fails to distinguish between individual associations, and those which are conventional and collective. But Pevsner then goes on to ask the question: "What part does evocation play in the anti-period styles of the twentieth century? [...] We have to rely on direct evocation. But can we? Can we trust our own evocation as valid for others?"[12] This is an important question because it goes to the root conflict between the structuralist and semiological view of artistic meaning—held, for example, by EH Gombrich—and the expression theory of modern art and architecture, according to which a building 'expresses' its essence by the fact of its functionality. It is also important because it is the first time that Pevsner has acknowledged the problem of meaning in modern architecture.

Pevsner answers his own question in the affirmative and claims that universal meanings do lie in architectural forms *per se*, that "the International Modern... conveys clarity, precision, technological daring and a total denial of superfluity, but it also conveys neutrality".[13] Put in other terms, this last phrase means "the intentional meaning of a building is that it has no meaning". But for lack of meaning to be able to take on a positive signification, buildings displaying this quality have to be read against the mass of conventional buildings which formed their context (mental or physical). Similarly, those "aggressive" and "cyclopean" qualities which Pevsner disapproves of in the late work of Le Corbusier and his imitators only take on their full meaning within the context of the conventions set up in the early Modern Movement and in the earlier conventions of post-Renaissance architecture. To fix on one set of meanings and to attribute to them a sort of objective historical necessity is a dubious procedure. And by dealing with architectural history not as an evolutionary sequence of styles but as a panorama in which style and meaning are affixed, as a matter of convention, to certain building types. Pevsner seems to have taken the ground from under his own theory of direct and unambiguous expression.

But a demonstration of the weakness of the functionalist position adopted by Pevsner does not altogether dissolve the problem of the two aesthetic theories—one based on a social and contextual interpretation of art, the other on its natural expressiveness. The functionalists were trying to revive the certainties of the Renaissance and in that sense are close to Rykwert's archetypal scheme. Semiotics and structuralism, on the contrary, are the product of the disintegration of the Renaissance world which started in the seventeenth century and received its first formulations in the eighteenth century. The position seems similar to the conflict between Newtonian and Einsteinian physics. At the everyday level the former still operates, while its explanatory power has been taken over by the latter. Similarly, in architecture designers tend to work as if there were a natural bond between function and expression, form and meaning, while to understand the way architecture works on a historical scale, it is necessary to be a 'relativist' and to concede that the relation between form and meaning is conventional and arbitrary.

1   Banham, Reyner, *Megastructure: Urban Futures of the Recent Past*, New York: Harper & Row, Icon Editions, 1976, p. 9.
2   The Chiesa Rossa housing project was designed by Giorgio Bay at the Milan Polytechnic while the Quartiere Direzionale scheme was planned by Lodovico Quaroni and team.
3   Banham, pp. 188–189.
4   Rykwert, Joseph, *The Idea of a Town: The Anthropology of Urban Form in Rome, Italy and the Ancient World*, London: Faber & Faber, 1976, p. 24.
5   Rykwert, *The Idea of a Town*, p. 194.
6   Rykwert, *The Idea of a Town*, p. 195.
7   Rykwert, *The Idea of a Town*, p. 86.
8   Rykwert, *The Idea of a Town*, p. 87.
9   Bird, James, *Centrality and Cities*, London and Boston: Routledge & Kegan Paul, Ltd, 1977.
10 Tafuri, Manfredo, *Architecture and Utopia,* Barbara Luigia LaPenta trans, Cambridge, MA: MIT Press, 1976.
11 Nikolaus Pevsner, *A History of Building Types*, Princeton, NJ: Princeton University Press, 1976, p. 293.
12 Pevsner, *A History of Building Types*.
13 Pevsner, *A History of Building Types*.

Historicism and the Limits of Semiology

First published in *Encounter*, September 1972.

Any discussion of architecture considered as a system of signs must come to terms with the fact that semiology is derived from the study of language. Its validity, therefore, depends on the extent to which the signifying component of architecture and other non-linguistic systems is reducible to something which they have in common with language.

One of the confusing things about semiology is that, because of this basis in linguistics, it has tended to oscillate between the study of language and the study of aesthetics. The studies carried out in Moscow and Prague in the second decade of the twentieth century were concerned with literary criticism as much as with linguistics and were therefore normative in aim. Those of Ferdinand de Saussure, on the other hand, were concerned with language, and their aim was descriptive. What unites them, however, is something that might be called the empirical method. The Prague School studied texts, de Saussure studied the spoken language, and both tried to eliminate the normative, 'idealist' preconceptions that had dominated literary and linguistic studies in the nineteenth century. From this point of view, semiology can be thought of as coterminous with, and part of, the Modern Movement and therefore intimately bound up with the historicism which, at least in one interpretation, it tries to deny.

It might be interesting to investigate the relation between the Russian and Czech literary criticism of the early 1900s and similar formalistic studies that were carried out in the same period in the plastic arts and architecture in Russia and Germany. But here I shall deal more with the relation of architecture with post-Saussurian semiology—that is, with semiology based on what has come to be known as structural linguistics. I shall try to show the limitations of the linguistic analogy, particularly with regard to such Saussurian concepts as *synchrony* and *diachrony,* when it is applied to aesthetic systems such as architecture. This might clear the air and allow one to look at semiology as a critical tool rather than as an explanatory science. To some extent Roland Barthes has tried to do this, but unfortunately the influence of his *Elements of Semiology* has tended to obscure rather than clarify the relation between aesthetics and linguistics, and semiology is now in danger of becoming an academic study unrelated to practice. What one would hope is that the study of architecture as a sign system could provide a critical tool to bridge the gap between the long-winded trivialities of behaviouristic sociology and the formalism which seems to be its only alternative.

The study of language has taught us that we cannot regard the world as a series of facts each of which has its own symbol of representation. By isolating the synchronic aspect of language, de Saussure was able to demonstrate that it is only by operating within the structure of a given language that we gain access to the world of fact. The diachronic or historical study of language, whatever other uses it may have, is not able to reveal how people actually speak language and therefore how they represent the world and communicate about the world with each other. This point of view, which has the characteristic virtues of the empirical method, is based on the assumption that we can only discover the truth by taking observable entities as our object of study. De Saussure does not discuss the ontogenetic or phylogenetic process by which people come to speak; though important, for him these problems lie outside the realm of language. He merely points to the concrete facts of speech and deduces from them a theory of language. At the particular moment in time that he studies a language, he finds a total structure. It is because this structure already exists that the speaker is able to form concepts and to share these concepts within a society. Although de Saussure has to assume that the speaker is unconscious of the logic of the structure he uses, he does not have to assume that such a logic exists *a priori* as an ideal form. He eliminates this possibility by saying that the structure simply consists of oppositions or analogies between the elements of a code. From the analysis of an infinitely large system, a few basic rules of transformation can be deduced.

From our point of view, however, the interesting thing about de Saussure is that he postulated a general theory of semiotics, which would include the various expressive languages, and of which language itself was in a sense the paradigm. But he does not seem to have been very clear as to the relation in aesthetic systems between the arbitrary sign and the natural sign. He made a basic distinction between the index, which is causally related to what it indicates, and symbols and signs. Symbols were motivated (in other words, there was a metaphorical tie between symbols and what they signified), whereas signs were arbitrary and conventional. It seems that de Saussure was right in saying that the arbitrary quality of any sign system is necessary if it is to be socially available, because motivated sign systems (the sort of symbols CG Jung discusses, and the objects of our dreams) can be purely private. But while it may be true that the signs actually used in aesthetic systems are chosen arbitrarily from all the possible natural signs, this does not mean that signs themselves are arbitrary. And since aesthetic systems are socially available and can be distinguished from language as social phenomena (and not merely as intellectual constructs), their social function as symbols must be taken into account.

It is possible to show that aesthetic systems have properties which do not belong to language as defined by de Saussure. I will give a few examples:

1. In language, change only occurs in one part of the system at a time. In aesthetic systems, change often occurs in the whole system, eg, the change from Gothic to classical architecture, or from eclecticism to modern.
2. In language, change is always unintentional. In aesthetic systems, change is always intentional (though the intention may not be rationalised).
3. In language, the existence of precise perceptual degrees of difference in the phonic object is relatively unimportant, since it is sufficient for one word to be different from another for differences in meaning to adhere to those two words, or for analogies to exist between words to bring to mind associative meanings. In aesthetic systems, however, precise degrees of difference are important—the difference between the interval of a third and a fifth in music, for example. In music, the ability to distinguish degrees of difference is used to make a structure which is interesting in itself and to create meaning. In language, the ability to distinguish between different degrees of phonetic change is not used in this way, since in language the phonic object is absorbed by its meaning. What are interesting in language are the meanings that are attached to phonic objects, not those objects themselves.
4. De Saussure discusses language as being analogous to economic exchange: "It is not the metal of a piece of money that fixes its value." But in an aesthetic system using metal, it is precisely the intrinsic quality of the metal that is important (though, of course, the semantic properties attributed to this quality will vary from one culture to another).

By aesthetic systems, therefore, I mean systems whose sensible form is interesting in itself. In language, the indissoluble relationship between the signifier and the signified is a function of the arbitrary value of the signifier. In aesthetic systems, on the other hand, the meaning that can be attached to the sign is due to the fact that the sign is itself motivated and the signifier is invested with potential significance. This motivation may take the form of physiognomic properties, or of analogies between the form and the meaning (de Saussure quotes the example of the symbol of Justice carrying a pair of scales). Aesthetic systems in this sense include all the systems traditionally grouped under the fine arts and the applied arts—even though their only, or even their main, purpose may not be a signifying one.

These fundamental differences between language and art mean that in aesthetic systems the study of the diachronic dimension takes on a peculiar importance. Because the changes which occur in aesthetic systems are revolutionary and intentional, these changes are directly related to ideology, and ideology can only be understood in a historical context.

It is true that the historical changes that occur in language may themselves obey certain rules of transformation, and it may therefore be possible to study the dialectical interrelation between the synchronic and diachronic dimensions of language. This idea is suggested by Maurice Merleau-Ponty in his essay "The Phenomenology of Language", where he tries to forge a link between language 'as mine' and language as an object of study.[1] What he says is of crucial importance to the whole notion of structure applied to semiology and the human sciences. A structure is by definition a closed system, which is studied from a purely formal point of view. For example, when we study language synchronically, we are not concerned with the semantic element independent of the signifier. The 'value' represented by the signifier is taken for granted. It is an indissoluble part of the language we learn, which consists of phonic materials and their corresponding concepts as given.

On the other hand, in any of the non-linguistic sign systems which are in general use by society, the axioms which form the content of the structure under analysis are guides to conduct and have an immediate bearing on what we think ought to be the case in our social life. We are dealing with values that are ends in themselves and not a means to some other end. It is therefore impossible to avoid trying to get outside this system, and we have to take an attitude toward the values which the system assumes. If this is true in an ontological sense in the case of languages, as Merleau-Ponty suggested, it is even more so in the case of the semiological study of architecture, since this kind of study cannot be separated from criticism and the formation of value judgments.

The historical mutations in language itself are no doubt related to a historical evolution whose laws underlie a confused jumble of accidental facts. But they are not apparent to the user of the language, who does not have to create a metalanguage to explain the language he is using. Hence the need to study language 'as ours'—language as the system which exists at any one moment— and hence the distortions which result from studying language purely as a historical object and independently of its diacritical mode of operation, as was done in the nineteenth century.

On the contrary, in aesthetic languages, a metalanguage is a part of the process of creation, whether as a mythological underpinning of practice or as a critical apparatus by which practice can be judged. That is to say, the artist always operates according to procedures which he is conscious of in the form of a set of rules. These rules are normative in the sense that they reflect the attitudes, values, and ideology of a particular society. In Western civilisation, architecture, no less than the other arts, has been subject to a rapid process of change, and to understand architecture synchronically, in the present or at any other time, it is necessary to study it over a period sufficiently long to observe the changes to which it has been subjected. The period from the eighteenth century to the present is of particular importance in the field of diachronic studies, because it was during this period that historical change itself began to be seen as the field in which values had to be posited. Thus, while art continued to be subject to rules and norms, it began to be impossible to regard these norms as immutable. Throughout this period there is a growing tension between two opposing viewpoints. Both points of view tried to go beyond the obvious conventionality of architecture; but in the first case there was an attempt to find an *a priori* form of expression that lay behind the conventions, and in the second there was a rejection of the very idea of *a priori* values and an implicit rejection of aesthetics as anything but a support for ideology.

The first point of view was typical of the eighteenth century, when for the first time the systematic distinction was made between convention and natural law. In linguistics the grammarians made a distinction between speech and the laws of language which were accessible to introspective logic. The numerous inconsistencies and irregularities that appeared in speech were supposed to be the result of historical accidents which had obscured the original language. N Beauzée, in his *Grammaire Generate* of 1767, gives the following distinction between general grammar and particular grammar:

> General grammar is a science because its only object is the reasoned speculation about the immutable and general principles of language... particular grammar is an art because it envisages the practical application of the arbitrary and habitual institutions of a particular language to the general principles of language.[2]

The distinction which was made between the normative language and a particular language meant that the differences between languages at different times and places had no fundamental importance. Language was not, as it was to be for de Saussure, arbitrary in its very nature but only so to the extent that it had strayed from some supposed ideal norm.

In the study of history the eighteenth century distinguished in a similar way between the accidents of the historical process and the laws which underlay them. "Mankind", said David Hume, "are so much the same in all times and places that history informs us of nothing new or strange in this particular. Its chief use is only to discover the constant and universal principles of human nature."[3] Even Rousseau, concerned as he was to transform society completely, was unaware of anything that could be called process in history. In the famous opening sentence of *The Social Contract,* which begins, "Man is born free; and everywhere he is in chains", he goes on, "How did this change come about? *I do not know.* What can make it legitimate? That question I think I can answer." (My italics.)[4] Rousseau was not interested in the historical transformation that has led to society's present state. What interested him was applying to a future society the truths that had been lost in the ramifications of history—truths that possibly, he supposed, were understood in some remote golden age.

In architecture, the Baroque system was radically questioned. What had seemed to be laws suddenly appeared as mere convention. There was an attempt to reduce architecture to its functional and formal principles, and various formulae were developed to reconcile convention with the principles of reason. The Greco-Roman tradition was subjected to radical adaptation and dismemberment, though its fundamental grammar was retained for serious works of architecture.

All these examples indicate that the eighteenth century thought of progress as a *rappel à l'ordre.* If one only looked at the phenomenal world and sought council from one's own natural reason, one could arrive at ethical and aesthetic value judgments that were valid for all time. This led to the notion that there was no difference between the unbiased exercise of reason and the establishment of ideology.

In late eighteenth century German thought the whole attitude toward history and ideology changed: from Hegel onward history is seen, not as a random process, but as the very field which defines and limits reason. Two consequences follow from this. First, relativity enters into history. The different types of aesthetic language that exist in time and space are no longer seen as so many partial aspects of a universal norm but as the outcome of historical forces that produced them. In linguistics, philology replaces general grammar. The history of language is studied in order to find in it a principle of change and development. A hitherto exotic language, Sanskrit, is discovered to be related to the Romance and Teutonic languages through the postulation of a mother tongue common to them all. In architecture, the ideal Platonic model is no longer sought from the Bible or from the ancient Mediterranean cultures. A study of the age of faith justifies Gothic architecture as the reflection of the ideas and practices of its period.

The historical relativity is accompanied by a growing realisation that the nineteenth century possesses no architecture proper to its own age. Boullée had talked about the "character" that different buildings should have. But the deliberate choice of forms signifying particular ideas was not accompanied by a feeling of alienation from the language of classical forms itself. The different forms belonged to the lexicon of language and were part of a given synchronic structure similar to the synchronic structure of language.

These different forms were contained within a single ideology. In the nineteenth century, on the other hand, to choose a form was also to choose between ideologies. If the Gothic style was preferred, it signified that a certain ideology was also preferred; history was being used as a model, not to disclose a universal truth but to measure the ideology of a historical culture—that of the age of faith, in the example I have chosen—against the modern culture. Together with the revival of past styles, a feeling began to develop that, if Gothic was the characteristic style of the age of faith, if neo-classicism was the characteristic style of the Enlightenment, then the present age should have its own style, rooted in the technical progress that was its own characteristic sign. This growing feeling was the corollary of the fact that relativity was only one aspect of post-Hegelian epistemology. The other aspect was that history was seen as process. History progressed dialectically by transcending itself, each successive period absorbing the previous one and producing a new synthesis. Whether, as in Hegel, this process was seen as teleological—a movement toward the future incarnation of the Ideal that existed outside time—or, as in Marx, it was seen as dialectically working itself out in the class struggle seen according to the Darwinian model, need not concern us. What future? Once this idea was established, it was no longer possible to believe that a person in a particular period could, simply by introspection, discover the form of society, the language, and the aesthetic mode that was true for all time. No man could divest himself of his own social conditioning and speak *sub specie aeternitatis*. There were no fixed archetypes to which one could appeal. Instead of trying to discover such Platonic models, man's task was the empirical study of history. As Engels said, paraphrasing Hegel, "the world is not to be comprehended as a complex of ready-made things but as a complex of processes, in which the things apparently stable, … go through an uninterrupted change of coming into being and passing away".[5]

The complex group of philological, sociological, and aesthetic concepts that I have just described I shall call historicism. The word "historicist" is subject to so many interpretations that it is necessary to state clearly the sense in which I am using it here. In architectural history, Nikolaus Pevsner, for example, uses the word historicism as synonymous with eclecticism.[6] In my opinion this is misleading. It separates two notions which are different aspects of the same type of thought: eclecticism and the concept of the *Zeitgeist*. Eclecticism is the result of historical relativity. As soon as it is believed that aesthetic codes are the product of particular phases of history, they become laid out before us, as it were. We do not need to imitate them, and indeed we should not do so since we believe that their necessity is tied to their own period. But they can be used, because they have been studied in and for themselves, as so many equivalent languages. In the classical period one learned Latin and Greek because these were close to the normative language which one was trying to reconstitute. In the nineteenth century one learned Sanskrit because Sanskrit was simply another version of a more general group of languages, none of which had normative priority over another. A culture that was no longer instinctively limited to one type of architectural language, but still lacked a method for developing its own, would be bound to use its new-found historical erudition to search for models in the historical tradition. Creation is impossible in an intellectual void. Until the revulsion from all the existing models reached a certain intensity—until these models had been exhausted of all meaning—it was in accord with artistic tradition to revert to existing models. In a sense the past styles that the nineteenth century used were its own styles; the diachrony of knowledge had become the synchrony of 'my language'. The same process had, after all, though for different reasons, occurred in the fifteenth century, when architecture went back to the classical model and made it its own and when, in language too, Latin words were introduced into the literary vocabulary. The eclecticism of the nineteenth century was not a unique event in European culture. What were unique were the beginnings of disbelief in the past which the study of the past had generated. This disbelief was reinforced by the other aspect of historicism that I have mentioned, the theory of dialectical development and of history as an irreversible flow.

Two factors seem to have contributed to the overthrow of eclecticism toward the end of the nineteenth century. The first was the rejection of bourgeois culture by the artistic elite. This rejection was not accompanied by any explicit social or political critique. The second was Marxist dialectical materialism and the spread of Socialist ideas. The Modern Movement in all the arts can only be understood in relation to these two social factors.

Architecture had a special relation to them. The fact that architecture was one of the useful arts made it hover precariously between the infrastructure and the superstructure in Marxist theory. The operationalism that was at the basis of Marxist thought could be transferred literally to architecture, and function could become the theoretical foundation of a new architectural praxis. "It is no longer a question... of inventing interconnections... out of our brains, but of discovering them in the facts", Engels had said.[7] What could be more obvious than to consider the facts of statics, structure, new materials, new social programmes, and to make out of these facts a new architecture?

What is left out of this equation is the question as to whether an architecture so constituted will still act as a sign. And if it does, what sort of sign is it? Does it become a sign simply by being a fact—an *index* of its physical functions? Or is it a more complex sort of sign involving an idea about those functions and about the mental world of the society which it serves? But in asking these questions I am anticipating problems I shall raise later.

Some time before socialist-functionalist theory was established in architecture, a movement had been developing in all the arts and in aesthetic theory, which was, as I have said, based more on rejection of bourgeois art than on a systematic critique of social infrastructures. The effect of this on architecture can be shown in a particular example. In the projects of the students working under Otto Wagner in Vienna in the first decade of the twentieth century, all the styles familiar to us in the various arts as Symbolism, Expressionism, and Art Nouveau are displayed side by side.[8] What all these projects have in common is the disintegration and fragmentation of nineteenth century eclecticism and the attempt to create a new style. It is true that many of these projects refer to existing models of some sort—to Mediterranean, Scottish, or Alpine vernacular architecture, for example, though all these models lie outside the conventional framework of bourgeois architecture. But many of them, particularly those of Karl Maria Kerndle and Josef Hoffmann, do not use any existing architectural model but take over certain Art Nouveau decorative schemes and enlarge them to the scale of the building as a whole. These schemes are rectangular and crystalline and avoid the use of naturalistic motives. We cannot help seeing them as the precursors of the simplified and stereometric forms that were later to emerge in the functionalist architecture of the 1920s. These tendencies in design had their counterpart in theoretical writings on art—particularly those of Theodor Lipps and Wilhelm Worringer, who tried to establish a theory of artistic reception based on psychological constants.

Art, according to Worringer, reveals universal subjective dispositions.[9] If we understand these dispositions we will arrive at an art that does not use the styles as norms but judges particular manifestations of art according to the fundamental and ageless rules of style itself.

At the beginning of the twentieth century we therefore find two parallel, and in a sense contradictory, theories of architecture, both deriving from post-Hegelian historicism. The first is a theory of moral purpose and objective fact, the second a theory of aesthetics and subjective feeling. But both theories reject the past as a guide to the present and are reductive and essentialist in spirit. The architecture that emerged after the First World War synthesised these theories by establishing functionalism as the dominant strain and calling in the art theory of natural expression and psychological constants whenever functionalism was unable to provide a solution. In linguistic terms, it reduced the architectural sign to an index of function, on the one hand, and the purely natural sign on the other.

Whether we are looking at the social or artistic aspects of this movement, we can see that it had strong deterministic features. By invoking the spirit of the age, modern theorists were presenting the objects of historical and psychological study as facts which were outside the control of the thinking and willing subject and constituted a sort of social or emotional categorical imperative. One aspect of this imperative was that the buildings which would serve the new society were thought of as analogous to biological types established by the laws of evolution. As an element in the range of instruments necessary for society, architecture was seen as belonging to the infrastructure of the historical process. History itself, through the agency of an elite, was determining the characteristic morphology of the new architecture and investing it with a set of *objets-type*. This idea of *objet-type* was closely related to the norm or type that is found in the study of zoological species. However much, in the words of Engels, history can be seen as a Heraclitean flux, it is nonetheless the passing away and coming into being of *types* which enable us to measure its dialectical process from lower to higher forms.

In modern architecture this idea of the biological norm was conflated with the idea of psycho-physical constants. This was an appeal to a determinism of a different kind. For although it reduced the creating of forms to a psychological function beneath consciousness, it could hardly avoid doing this by referring to constant cultural values, and in this sense returned to something close to eighteenth century rationalism. In Le Corbusier these two concepts are clearly stated. On the one hand, the mathematician and the scientist discover the laws of causality; on the other, the artist discovers the laws of harmony between the materials that are given to him.[10]

If we apply the principles of structural linguistics to these phenomena, it is clear that the theories behind modern architecture were opposed to the concept of architecture as a language with a large amount of combinatory freedom or associative meaning. In the sense that architecture was held to be determined by the forces of history, its laws were fixed and there was no place for free play in the ordering of forms. In the other sense of an architecture reflecting universal psychological laws, this freedom was obscured by the old myth of normative beauty. If there was freedom, it could only exist as a sort of symbiosis between the artist and those natural laws which he discovered by intuition.

But the actual practice of the architects of the 1920s, particularly the Russian Constructivists and Le Corbusier, was far from obeying the rules that had been implied by the theory. In fact, their work was still to a large extent based on existing models, even though these models were not necessarily the major styles that had been copied in the nineteenth century. Not only were classical and romantic themes incorporated into the new work but concepts lying outside the field of architecture were transposed. Thus, engineering forms were displayed in the work of the Vesnin brothers in Russia. These forms were a 'first articulation' drawn from the visible world and were used, rhetorically, to show that architecture was a matter of construction and not of outworn architectural compositional and decorative schemes. In Le Corbusier the imagery of ships was used to provide a new model for an architectural language and also to establish across history connections, at a deeper level, with age-old human themes—the monastic life of the twelfth century, for instance. This does not mean that modern architecture reverted to a nineteenth century eclecticism. In the nineteenth century entire semiological schemes were taken over. Modern architecture took fragments of everyday life and fragments found in history. Modern architecture in this sense was essentially constitutive. It broke down the meaning systems into the smallest units that could carry meaning and recombined them, regardless of the entire systems from which they had been extracted.

To what extent does this bring modern architecture into conformity with the linguistic model? In linguistics, by observing how people speak, it is possible to determine laws without destroying freedom. Language exists prior to the individual. But the fact that he has to learn his language does not make him a slave. Indeed, if nature, through the mediation of society, did not present him with a pre-existent language, he would not be able to form concepts. He applies the rules of language instinctively, and these rules are simply rules of combination. There is no *a priori* limit to the concepts that he can form. But in language this freedom of combination is, as I have said, due to the arbitrary nature of the relation between the signifier and signified.

Even in everyday language there exists a number of complex units or syntagmata which it is obligatory to use. Clearly the more of these complex units there are, or the larger each unit is, the more the freedom of the speaker will be reduced. Now this is precisely what happens in poetry and literature: literary genres, styles, forms, and types of expression are simply inherited syntagmata. The reason they exist is to give rise to concepts which represent a value in themselves. In *language* the value of the sign is neutral. It is the purpose of *poetry* to turn neutral signs into expressive signs. But although the poet inherits these syntagmata, he is not obliged to use them. Precisely because he has at his disposal a type of language which represents values, he is able to revise these values. This is what Barthes means when he says that poetry is resistant to myth, while language is not. Language never gives full meanings to its concepts: they remain open-ended and ready for recombination. Poetry, on the other hand, being a second-order language, gives a precise emotive significance to its concepts. By dislocating the syntagmata that have been inherited and by arranging words in an order which is different from that of normal speech, it is able to make people aware of the banality and falsity of their concepts. As Barthes says, if myth wants to conquer poetry, it has to swallow it whole and serve it up as a content of its own system. This critical and dismantling activity of poetry results in what Barthes calls a "regressive semiological system".[11]

The same can be said about architecture. Architecture never appears as a neutral combinatory system. The 'phonemes' and 'morphemes' in architecture (and we can only use these terms approximately) are motivated and invested with potential meaning. What could be more motivated than function, structural method, or forms in space? If we are to be as rigorously empirical as de Saussure was about speech, we have to admit that architecture cannot usefully be reduced to a collection of arbitrary elements. Modern architecture tried to reduce its elements to what was essential but not by reducing them to arbitrary units as in linguistic analysis. In the study of language the reduction is purely formal and does not alter the way we speak. In architecture it is reformative and intended to reconstitute architectural meaning.

In this context semiology appears as a magician who reveals by empirical study the complexity and richness of synchronic systems. But it also appears as a possible prescriptive tool and a method of criticism. In this capacity it can easily fall prey to any of the prevailing philosophies of modern architecture, including the 'kit of parts' theory that is put forward by certain utopian proponents of systems. This is the result of a confusion which comes from applying the principles of linguistics too literally. This confusion has been demonstrated by Lévi-Strauss in the field of music, and what he says can be applied in general to architecture.[12] Serial music, he points out, eliminates the meaningful structures of the inherited musical language (the relation of tones to the tonic, for example). It therefore no longer operates with two levels of articulation—the one which the composer finds at his disposition and the other in which he is free to create new combinations and meanings. With the apparent absolute freedom which this gives the composer, however, he runs the danger of being rendered inarticulate, unless he is close enough to the existent language to refer to it obliquely or to give a demonstration of its essence by attempting to reduce it to the 'degree zero'. Igor Stravinsky and Anton Webern might be given as examples of these respective types of reference. The musical 'kit of parts' which later Serialists propose would only make sense if the language of music were completely natural, leading to a theory of spontaneous music.[13]

But it also implies that music is like natural language, because natural language is the only sign system where a kit of parts provides freedom of combination. But we know that this is only possible in language because the units have already had arbitrary meanings attached to them. Thus we arrive at a nonsense statement: a completely natural system and a completely arbitrary system are the same thing.

We tend to forget that in analysing language we do not attempt to change it. Structural linguistics is a descriptive, and perhaps explanatory, method. It is concerned with the formal structures underlying language, not with its meaning or value system.

There is a very good reason why semiology in the same way must remain at the formal and descriptive level, and we can see this if we look at structures in a more general sense. Jean Piaget defines a structure as a self-regulating whole with a set of transformational rules and points out that in the field of natural logic, such a structure is always open-ended.[14] Since Kurt Gödel it has been realised that no system of logic can contain its own explanations: a given system is always built upon axioms which are subject to further analysis. The *form* of one system becomes the *content* of the next higher system, and so on. This regress does not concern the mathematician or the physicist, since what matters to him is the self-consistency of the system he has chosen to work within. But it must concern the philosopher, the social scientist, and the designer—and any discussion that deals with the language-like systems in normal use by society. In these systems value judgments have to be made. If a value is relative, it must be relative to *something*, and this something must itself be a value.

Here we come to the root of the problem both of semiology and modern architecture. If a language of any sort is merely the arrangement of minimal structures, these structures must already be full of given meanings, as they are in language. This is the necessary condition of social communication.

1   "On the Phenomenology of Language", *Signs*, Evanston, IL: Northwestern University Press, 1964, pp. 84–97.
2   Quoted and translated from Chomsky, Noam, *Cartesian Linguistics: A Chapter in the History of Rationalist Thought*, New York: Harper & Row, 1966, p. 53.
3   Hume, David, *An Inquiry Concerning Human Understanding*, Indianapolis: Bobbs-Merrill Company Inc, 1955, p. 93.
4   Rousseau, Jean Jacques *The Social Contract,* trans. GDH Cole, New York: EP Dutton & Company, Inc., 1950, p. 3.
5   Engels, Friedrich, *Ludwig Feuerbach and the Outcome of Classical German Philosophy*, ed. CP Dutt, New York: International Publishers, 1935, p. 44.
6   "Modern Architecture and the Historian, or the Return of Historicism", *RIBA Journal*, no. 68, April 1961, pp. 230–237.
7   Engels, Friedrich, *Ludwig Feuerbach,* p. 59.
8   See Graf, Otto Antonia, *Die Vergessene Wagnerschule*, Vienna: Verlag Jugend & Volk, 1969.
9   Worringer, Wilhelm, *Abstraction and Empathy: A Contribution to the Psychology of Style,* New York: International Universities Press, 1953.
10 Le Corbusier, "In Defense of Architecture", *Oppositions 4*, October 1974, pp. 93–108.
11 Barthes, Roland, "Myth Today", *Mythologies,* trans Annette Lavers, New York: Hill and Wang, 1972, p. 133.
12 Lévi-Strauss, Claude, *The Raw and the Cooked: Introduction to a Science of Mythology: I*, trans John and Doreen Weightman, New York: Harper & Row, 1969.
13 This seems to be the point of view of certain semiologists, eg., Abraham Moles, *Information Theory and Esthetic Perception,* Urbana: University of Illinois Press, 1966.
14 Piaget, Jean, *Structuralism*, trans. and ed. Chaninah Maschler, New York: Basic Books, Inc., 1970.

Sign and Substance: Reflections on Complexity, Las Vegas and Oberlin

First published in *Oppositions 14*, Autumn 1978.

Sufficient attention has not been given to the change in Robert Venturi's thought between his publication of *Complexity and Contradiction in Architecture* in 1966 and his publication, with Denise Scott Brown and Steven Izenour, *of Learning from Las Vegas* in 1972. If one is to comment on Venturi and Rauch's more recent buildings, it is necessary first to examine this change of position, so that the buildings may be placed in the context of both the theory and the oeuvre as a whole. The change is not total. There are many ideas that are common to the two books; the alteration of viewpoint is often more one of emphasis than of the introduction of radically new concepts. Ideas which were secondary in the first book become guiding ideas in the second. But this shift of viewpoint is nonetheless significant, and it is reflected in the work.

The main purpose of *Complexity and Contradiction in Architecture* was to refute the Modern Movement idea that the functional organisation of a building obeyed a unitary logic which constituted its aesthetic meaning. In showing that many 'logics' were involved in the design of a building and that architectural design was a process of 'accommodation' rather than deduction, Venturi inaugurated a shift in modern architectural theory and helped to open up a new path for architectural design and discourse.

Complexity and Contradiction emphasises the semantic complexities of the architectural message, and its approach is empirical, relativistic, and anti-Platonic. Nonetheless the semantic dimension of architecture is presented as suprahistorical. Architectural meanings are seen as the result of the manipulation of forms whose exemplary qualities are independent of the historical conditions under which they were produced. But Venturi is not concerned with establishing the constitutive and unvarying principles which this view implies. That such principles are assumed to exist is clear: "You build an order up and then break it down, but break it from strength rather than from weakness.... Expediency without order, of course, means chaos."[1] But what this 'principle of order' consists of is not made clear. Is it an order which springs from laws of formal organisation, or does it rather lie in constructional logic and functional imperatives? "Though we no longer argue over the primacy of form or function... we cannot ignore their interdependence."[2] From this it is not clear whether what is at stake is the play of redundant, multiple connotations on simple functional norms or the play of contingent facts on basic formal laws. Does function provide the framework which is distorted by 'forms', or do 'forms' provide the framework which is distorted by function? Whichever might be the case, these underlying principles, which one must assume if 'complexity' and 'contradiction' are to have any meaning (since nothing can appear complex except in relation to something simple, and since in order to contradict something it must itself be non-contradictory), are not the subject of the book. Rather it is concerned with the innumerable ways in which disorder and ambiguity can enhance the meaning of architecture.

It would have been useful if Venturi had made a distinction between those types of ambiguity which are held to be inherent to all artistic works (the subject of William Empson's *Seven Types of Ambiguity)* and those types which vary according to historical conditions (eg, Mannerism). Since in the latter case the ambiguities and contradictions depend on the prior existence of a language or style, the two kinds of ambiguity are, as it were, superimposed on each other. But this would have involved looking at architecture historically, and not treating history as a mere reservoir of examples.

In addition to this fundamental distinction, Venturi ignores that between complexities which are intentional and those which are the result of accretion over time. The focus of the text oscillates between the effect of a building on the perceptions of the observer and the effect intended by the designer as if these were the same thing. The book is thus a plea for complexity in general without suggesting how different kinds of complexity are related to particular historical circumstances, and therefore how the examples might apply to particular circumstances of our own time. This lack of historical perspective allows Venturi to include his empyrean examples of modern architecture and to discuss them at the same level at which he discusses examples from the past. It would be logical to deduce from this that when he is quoting buildings of Le Corbusier, Aalto, Kahn, or Luigi Moretti as "good" examples of complexity and contradiction, he is implying that the "general" principles of architecture are just as applicable to an architecture based on the principles of the Modern Movement as they are to any other. And from this it would follow that the two principles are not in conflict, and that the failures of modern architecture are due to extrinsic factors—economic distortions, bad designers, etc..

But at other times in the text it is implied that it is precisely the principle of the Modern Movement which are wrong and which are incapable of engendering any but the most simplistic and diagrammatic forms. Are, then, Le Corbusier and Aalto exceptions which prove the rule, because they contradict the principles which they believe in? But is it not precisely in such a contradiction that architecture of the highest sort is held to lie? Venturi's inclusion of the modern masters and his quoting of Josef Albers, in defense of the essential ambiguity of all art, suggests that a modernism which holds to the theory of the *tabula rasa* is perfectly compatible with the principle of complexity and contradiction within his own definition of those terms.[3] Historical examples could then be seen as incorporating general principles or types, whose persistence did not depend on the memory of those figures in which they had been embodied previously. But Venturi's attitude to past forms does not take account of Quatremère de Quincy's distinction between the type and the model. He sees past styles as available for reuse, not literally, but as conventional elements whose continuing vitality depends on their being distorted, so that they can be seen in relation to the often contradictory needs of the present. There is, therefore, some inconsistency between his book and his practice. The book does not exclude the possibility that the general principles of the Modern Movement were sound and might still form the basis of a complex and subtle architecture, but the practice assumes that there is no way in which the general principles of architecture can be dissociated from stylistic traditions. If we are to have architecture at all, we must abandon any attempt to found it exclusively on some assumed set of conditions belonging to modern life. The language of architecture rests on a dialectic between memory of past cultural forms and the experiences of the present.

However, in spite of the irony which this view implies, there is, throughout the book, a strong sense that an architectural order analogous to that of the past is still possible. Architecture is "perceived as form *and* substance.... These oscillating relationships... are the source of ambiguity and tension characteristic to the medium of architecture."[4] In the projects of the 60s, though the figures of past architecture are put in inverted commas and distorted, there is an attempt to integrate them within an architectural system. The contradictions are thought of as being derived from an ambiguity between 'real' and 'virtual' structure, which is inherent in all architecture. Ornament and stylistic dress may not be directly deducible from the architectural programme, but neither are they independent of it. Order and disorder, symmetry and asymmetry, are an integral part of the solution. What is real and what is illusory are inextricably interwoven and depend on that suspension of disbelief which all art entails. One is presented with the idea of an architecture which is arcane, and which, though it is accommodating to the needs of the client, is ultimately addressed to those who understand and love architecture for itself.

In *Learning from Las Vegas* there are two chief ways in which this point of view is modified. First, populism, which is a mere undercurrent in *Complexity and Contradiction,* becomes a main theme. Those popular pressures which were seen as the 'forces of life' that in all periods give architecture its vitality are now isolated as peculiarly modern, petit bourgeois, and, above all, American. The basis for this populist tendency can be seen in Venturi, Scott Brown, and Izenour's study of Las Vegas and Levittown, but there is an ambivalence in the authors' interpretation of the way in which kitsch is to be translated into conscious architecture. On the one hand, there is the position, held consistently by Denise Scott Brown, that the role of the architect is to understand and interpret the wishes of the client. According to this view, the road to an architecture of meaning lies in making concrete the internalised value systems of the users. The role of the architect, as in the Middle Ages, is that of the 'technician' who knows how to translate these values into structure and ornament. But, on the other hand, we know that today it is usually not the architect who is the expert in these matters but the developer or the contractor. Even when an architect is called in to provide the 'architecture', he is expected to share the objectives and taste of the client and to act merely as his agent. Now, there might be, an argument in favour of this point of view if modern society were constructed on Medieval or even eighteenth century lines, and if there were a convergence of taste between society as a whole (or its dominant subculture) and the artist whose role was to interpret its values. But such a situation simply does not exist today.

In order to assume the role of 'servant' to society, the modern architect must submit to a self-denying ordinance and play a game of 'let's pretend'. It is hardly conceivable that Venturi and Scott Brown are not aware of this; that they are was demonstrated by Robert Venturi's intervention at the recent Beaux-Arts Colloquium at the Architectural Association in London. Taking up one of the recurrent themes of the colloquium—the famous proclamation by Victor Hugo, in the second edition *of Notre Dame de Paris,* that architecture would be killed by the book—Venturi showed a number of recent projects whose purpose appeared to be to celebrate the death of architecture. In these projects, neutral structures were ornamented with 'incorrect' orders and other incongruous details. Who but other architects 'in the know' were the object of these exercises? Unlike the music hall comedian, whose jokes are understood by his box-office audience, Venturi's wit seems to be aimed solely at his fellow architects. The semiological intention of these projects is clearly not to provide the client with what he wants (though an essential part of the joke is that they do so *faute de mieux),* but to draw attention to the absurdity of popular taste.

My purpose here is not to discuss whether this particular subversive game is worthwhile but to show that it is an equivocation to pretend that it can be defended on the basis of a 'sincere' relationship between client and architect.

The second way in which *Learning from Las Vegas* differs from *Complexity and Contradiction* is that the architectural act is no longer seen as aiming at an integral aesthetic object but at an object whose aesthetic unity is *a priori* impossible. Function and aesthetics, substance and meaning, are now seen as incompatible (though equally important) entities. Venturi, Scott Brown and Rauch seem to have arrived at this theoretical position as a result of practical experience, and this is recorded in a passage so crucial that it is worth quoting in full:

After the appearance of *Complexity and Contradiction in Architecture*, we began to realise that few of our firm's buildings were complex and contradictory, at least not in their purely architectural qualities of space and structure.... We had failed to fit into our buildings double-functioning or vestigial elements, circumstantial distortions, expedient devices, eventful exceptions, exceptional diagonals, things in things, crowded or contained intricacies, linings or layerings, residual spaces, redundant spaces, ambiguities, inflections, dualisms, difficult wholes, or the phenomena of both-and. There was little in our work of inclusion, inconsistency, compromise, accommodation, adaptation, superadjacency, equivalence, multiple focus, juxtaposition, or good *and* bad space.[5]

This list deals a death blow to *Complexity and Contradiction,* whose arguments it both condenses and parodies. It is hardly surprising that Venturi and Rauch had been unable to include all these qualities in their buildings, but the list acts primarily as a rhetorical device which makes the theory that follows it seem not only reasonable but inevitable by comparison. This theory is that of the "decorated shed", according to which the architect should abjure "architectural qualities of space and structure" and concentrate instead on "symbolic content".

In fact, the argument of *Complexity and Contradiction* had already included the idea of the decorated shed in a weak form, since it had established the merely indirect connection between the appearance of a building and its substance and had drawn attention to the arbitrary nature of the architectural sign. But the meaning of the decorative skin was still seen as referring obliquely to the structure behind it, as is shown by the remark, quoted above, to the effect that form and function are interdependent. Even in *Learning from Las Vegas* it is stated that the structural ornament of Renaissance architecture "reinforces rather than contradicts the substance of the structure and space", but this precedent is rejected (without explanation) in favour of a Medieval paradigm in which the frontispiece of a cathedral is "a billboard with a building behind it".[6] One may question whether this is an adequate description of an element which not only provides a triumphal entry to the nave but anticipates the themes of the interior and establishes its symbolic meanings. But in any case, if it is held that one of the inherent complexities of architecture lies in the tension between what is real and what is apparent, the complete separation of the signifying and substantial parts of a building which this view of the Gothic facade implies can only weaken its complexity and trivialise its message.

The idea of the decorated shed was a witty and devastating attack on the expressionism of Paul Rudolph and other architects of the 1960s and the idea that all buildings should be isolated *objets-type* whose form 'expresses' their content. But it did, by its very incisiveness, convey the false impression that the only alternative to the expressionistic 'duck' was a building whose meaning lies in its appliqué ornament. The notion of the decorated shed seems to owe something to the nineteenth century concept of 'ornamented structure', as opposed to the 'structural ornament' of the Renaissance. But the nineteenth century idea was more a counterblast to nineteenth century ducks than to Renaissance architecture—to structural forms which were reproduced whole in ignoble materials, rather than those represented in more noble materials. As Joseph Rykwert has pointed out, Pugin's idea of ornamented structure, which is referred to in *Learning from Las Vegas,* included the notion that the ornament should be related, plastically and iconographically, to the 'real' building, whose structural form was thought of as an integral part of its meaning.[7]

This idea of the decorated shed, although it is presented as a typical modern solution, has its most obvious application in programmes resulting in large undifferentiated spaces—such as supermarkets and places of mass

entertainment—whose purely commercial origins defy any attempt to assimilate them in any tradition of architectural complexity. There are a number of recently published buildings by Venturi, Scott Brown and Rauch which do not fall into this category; they are quite clearly ducks rather than decorated sheds, that is to say their external forms conform to a unified architectural image whose connotations overlap those of their use and interior arrangement and reinforce the meanings which have been associated with them—often rustic and vernacular connotations achieved by direct, if ironic, quotation either from a local tradition or from Art Nouveau and National Romanticism. These parodistic essays in an "eclecticism of taste" break with Venturi's earlier buildings, in which the historical references are at once more generalised and more fragmentary, and which refer less to vernacular romanticism than to the classical tradition, however compromised this tradition is made to seem.[8]

It might appear from these examples as if Venturi and Rauch were moving toward a picturesque theory of genre—of different styles appropriate for different types of programme—but this expectation is not confirmed by their extension to the Allen Memorial Art Museum at Oberlin because, although this is a 'cultural' building with a strong 'architectural' context, they have chosen to interpret it as a decorated shed, presumably to avoid any attempt to give the extension any of those 'high art' qualities which are exhibited in the original building. This suggests that the idea of the decorated shed is not restricted to a limited kind of commercial programme but is applicable to all cases except those in which an intimate, personalised, vernacular symbolism is thought to be appropriate. It is therefore precisely buildings of a public kind which are associated with the idea of a decorated shed—buildings in which there is a need to contend with the irreconcilable demands of economy and rational construction, on the one hand, and public symbolism, on the other. It is noticeable that whereas in the earlier projects public and private buildings were both thought of as vehicles for a complexity in which space and structure were an integral part of the symbolism, in the more recent projects these two categories are treated differently. Public commissions are either given typically 'modern' solutions with little symbolic

Above: Allen Memorial Art Museum addition, Oberlin, Ohio. Venturi and Rauch, 1976. The addition steps back in two blocks; the gallery is clad in granite and rose sandstone, and the laboratory/library/studio portion is clad in buff brick.

Opposite: Allen Memorial Art Museum. Site plan and first floor plan (bottom); second floor pan (top).

content, or they are sheds, from whose purely decorative symbolism the architects maintain an ironic detachment. In commissions of a more domestic kind one has the impression that the architects identify with the nostalgic sentiments of their clients and provide them with buildings whose interior organisation and external expression speak the same language and attempt to recover a unique 'atmosphere'. The vernacular details and comforting chintzes are the result of a certain complicity between architect and client, and if the architect still lays claim to irony, it is not strong enough to subvert the values which the client sees reflected and made possible in the building.

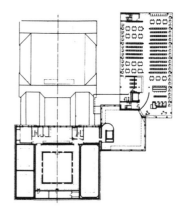

But the Oberlin extension is a public building, and its overall organisation is determined by the concept of the decorated shed. The problems of designing a new gallery and a teaching wing are considered to be 'modern' and 'functional'. At the same time there is no attempt at functional rhetoric. The 'functional' volumes are considered 'mute'. It is not their inherent structure or spatial disposition which provides their symbolic, cultural, or aesthetic dimensions. These must be provided by modifying the basic shell by means of design decisions of a second order. These seem to belong to four main categories:

1. *Surface ornament:* Examples include the checkerboard pattern (recalling Halsey Ricardo or Edwin Lutyens), picking up the colour and materials of the old building, though not its decorative scheme, and the blue and yellow roof fascia, suggesting the coloured rafters and soffit of the old roof, but in terms of modern stick-on decor.
2. *Treatment of external architectonic elements:* Examples are the projecting eaves of the flat roof, making reference to the eaves of the old building; the strip windows which echo its horizontal emphasis; and more particularly, perhaps, the second floor window at the back of the old building.
3. *Isolated symbolic elements:* Examples are the parodistic Ionic column and the fragment of white marble on the entrance bench. These could be called "external referents", since they refer either to a context beyond that of the building itself or to the cultural associations of the building (only marginally contributing to its aesthetic organisation).
4. *Spatial modifications:* These are the result of 'collisions' in the plan and produce splayed walls and other plastic modifications of the basic shed.

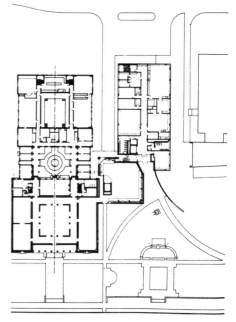

The building is not thought of, then, as a unified design in which the parts are capable of being consistently related to the whole, but as the result of a number of separate and conflicting demands. Frequently, the solution of two separate problems produces a conflict whose reconciliation seems to have suggested the solution of a third problem; for example, the decision to place the strip window immediately under the roof with no lintel and the need for a suspended ceiling for services and lighting in the gallery result in a coved splay, which reflects the daylight entering the gallery. But although this solution resolves the problem at a functional level, it deliberately leaves unresolved the problem of architectural meaning; the ceiling projects ambiguously without apparent means of support, its function as a suspended ceiling being contradicted by its sculptural termination.

This is one of many examples where the accommodation of conflicting demands gives rise to modifications of the basic shed. The treatment of mass and space offers several parallel cases. For example, the programme has been interpreted in terms of two 'sheds'. No attempt is made to relate these sheds artistically either to the old building or to each other. Instead, the new gallery butts unceremoniously up against the old gallery, rising above it and slicing its cornice about halfway along the flank wall. The teaching block is impacted into the new gallery, overlapping it rather than being articulated from it, so that at the point of junction each shed is subjected to mutually accommodating

compressions and distortions. Externally the effect of this compaction of the two volumes is to turn their external walls into a continuous stepped facade. But although the fenestration of this surface is manipulated to provide clues as to the different functions of the two blocks, the facade is not related to the spatial organisation of the volumes behind. It is here that the concept of the decorated shed makes itself felt. The play of contradiction and ambiguity on the facade does not penetrate into the building, whose spatial arrangement remains basically that of the two sheds stitched together. 'Interesting' incidents may be developed at their interface, but they do not spring from, or generate, any transformation of the initial spatial theme. In its concern for isolated incidents and effects, the extension at Oberlin demonstrates an inherent weakness of the concept of the decorated shed. No theory of meaning in architecture can make sense unless it seeks to establish a relation between the general concept of a building and its parts, or between its ornament and its structural and spatial scheme.

From this point of view the notion of the decorated shed seems to be the result of a misinterpretation of the architectural tradition. Compared to the sculptural extravaganza of modern expressionist architecture, traditional structures and the spaces they articulate often appear extremely simple. But they are not, for this reason, 'sheds' in the purely pragmatic sense in which Venturi uses the word. We find in them the subtle distillation of a long tradition in which the practical craft of building, the uses for which the building is intended, and a system of aesthetic representation are intimately connected. It is from this

interconnection that the richness of architecture—its complexities, ambiguities, and multiple meanings—has been developed. In reducing this complex tradition to two unrelated parts—the building of 'sheds' and the development of 'signs' on their surfaces—Venturi is proposing a reduction just as simplistic as that of the kind of modern architecture which he so effectively attacked in *Complexity and Contradiction.*

However, it would be a mistake to imagine that this 'misunderstanding' is unintentional. For the authors of *Learning from Las Vegas,* it seems any attempt to recover the unity of the architecture of the past is incompatible with the modern social world and presupposes an idealistic role for architecture which no longer exists. They thus reject both the Miesian solution, in which the shed is idealised into a temple, and that of the New York Five and the neo-rationalists, for instance, who, in their different ways, see architecture as an autonomous discourse. For Venturi, Scott Brown, and Izenour, there are no autonomous discourses, and architecture is embedded in a global ideology from which there is no escape.

According to this view, modern programmes, with the possible exception of houses where private nostalgia can still operate to create 'dream houses', do not have the ritualistic and ceremonial content which gave traditional architecture its symbolism. They are purely pragmatic. Spatial and structural organisation is a matter of common sense and empirical arrangement. If, for example, we had looked at Oberlin for spatial themes which were related to those of the

Opposite: Allen Memorial Art Museum, exterior view of roof and new gallery.

Above: Allen Memorial Art Museum. Junction between old and new buildings.

Allen Memorial Art Museum,
exterior view of junction between
old and new buildings.

original building (atria, central axes, single-loaded accommodation), or if we were shocked that the only means of access to the second floor library is by means of a fire stair tucked into a corner at the immediate point of entry, we would be attributing to client and users a sensibility which they do not possess, and ignoring the fact that, today, galleries and libraries, like offices and studios, are 'functional' spaces and do not have special meaning for society. The modern type is the loft building, not the uses which can be fitted into it, and there can therefore be no question of space and structure becoming representational.

The implications of the notion of the decorated shed are therefore far-reaching. They lead to the assertion that architectural meaning has become irretrievably separated from its substance. Architects are impotent in the face of a society whose values have made this split inevitable. It is not by the vision of an alternative architecture that these values can be criticised but only by the manipulation of its surface appearance, and then only by means of an equivocal irony in which these values are alternately condoned and 'exposed'. The architect, like the fool in Shakespeare, uses his subservient role to flatter the king and, at the same time, to tell him a few home truths.

The contradictions in the buildings of Venturi, Scott Brown and Rauch are not, like those of traditional architecture, subject to an overall aesthetic synthesis. They remain deliberately unresolved in a contentious dialectic of popular versus high; banal versus subtle; architecture as a mass media versus architect's architecture. They do not, as do other 'post-functionalist' buildings, attempt to define an alternative language to that of functionalism. They reveal, but do not overcome, the contradictions latent in the contemporary state of architecture, and this makes it difficult to find a basis for critical discussion of the work.

For these reasons I have done no more than attempt to interpret Venturi's point of view and reveal certain *internal* contradictions in his position; I have not attempted a definitive evaluation of his work.

1   Venturi, Robert, *Complexity and Contradiction in Architecture,* New York: The Museum of Modern Art, Doubleday & Co., 1966, pp. 46–47.
2   Venturi, *Complexity and Contradiction in Architecture*, p. 26.
3   See Tafuri, Manfredo, *Theories and History of Architecture,* New York: Harper & Row, 1980, pp. 213–214.
4   Venturi, *Complexity and Contradiction*, p. 29.
5   Venturi, Robert, Denise Scott Brown and Steven Izenour, *Learning from Las Vegas,* Cambridge, MA: MIT Press, 1972, p. 128.
6   Venturi, Scott Brown and Izenour, *Learning from Las Vegas*, p. 105.
7   "Ornament is no Crime", *Studio International,* vol. 190, October 1975, pp. 91–97.
8   For the definition of "eclecticism of taste" see Hitchcock, Henry Russell, *Modern Architecture: Romanticism and Reintegration,* New York: Hacker Art Books, 1970.

EH Gombrich and the Hegelian Tradition

First published in "Methodology of History", ed. D Porphyrios, *Architectural Design*, 1981.

In his essay *In Search of Cultural History,* EH Gombrich discusses the role of the art historian within the context of cultural studies and in doing so sets out some of the historiographic principles which form the basis of his work. Though he is primarily concerned with the history of painting, these principles apply, *mutatis mutandis,* to architecture, as a cultural phenomenon and as a system of aesthetic representation. It will be the intention of these notes to discuss some of these principles and their implications, using the chosen extract, as does Gombrich himself, as a methodological example.

The virtue of this passage is that, as a self-contained piece of historical analysis, it can be removed from its context without doing too much violence to Gombrich's thought. Gombrich's writings are unusually resistant to this kind of dismemberment because the ideas they contain unfold gradually, almost in spiral fashion, and it is often only after a rather long passage that his meaning is fully disclosed.

In Search of Cultural History, however, has a complexity all its own. This is due less to the wealth of illustrative material with which the argument is interlaced than to the historiographic problem to which he addresses himself. In elucidating this problem, Gombrich seems constantly to be struggling with and qualifying the premises from which he sets out. As these premises are basically Hegelian, his ideas are best approached by discussing his attitude toward Hegel.

In these notes I do not intend to question Gombrich's interpretation of Hegel's theory of history, or to inquire to what extent ideas imputed to Hegel might not apply in some degree to a whole tendency of German thought in the late eighteenth century, particularly to Herder and Humboldt. My purpose will be merely to investigate how Gombrich deals with what he sees as the Hegelian problem. The aspect of Hegel with which he is concerned is the theory according to which culture, in all its aspects, is a reflection of the stages through which human history passes in its continuous evolution from lower to higher states. Each stage has its peculiar spirit, which determines the nature of the cultural phenomena associated with it. If one possesses the key to the spirit of the age, one will be able to recognise it even in its smallest manifestation. And since, at any one stage, history can take one form and no other, every cultural phenomenon can be seen as absolutely necessary. What might appear as 'free' (ie. as inexplicable) would be an anomaly which could, in principle, be resolved by taking more phenomena into account.

According to Gombrich, it is this view which has provided art history with its main impetus in the search for an overall pattern of stylistic development.[1] But he also believes that its application has usually led historians to hasty and overly simple explanations which ignore the complexity of artistic and cultural facts. This view is consistent with Gombrich's approach to the interpretation of history, which, in general, follows Karl Popper's principle of falsifiability and is clearly incompatible with a theory of historical teleology. Yet, if the desire to find patterns is itself to be no more than a historical accident, the application of the principle of falsifiability to historical interpretation seems to present a problem. The only way to deal with Hegel's assumptions would be to regard them as 'hypotheses'. However, it would seem doubtful that they could be taken as hypotheses in the sense that Popper uses the word. A valid hypothesis is, according to Popper, one that can in principle be refuted. But no teleology of history could ever be refuted since it would never be possible to exhaust the facts which would be needed to falsify it. Hegel's theory of history is therefore not a hypothesis in the Popperian sense; it is an apodictic statement. As such it constitutes a belief, and like all beliefs it relies on exegesis to make it plausible. Since Gombrich explicitly rejects the exegetical method, it is difficult to see how the Hegelian assumptions behind art history can be other than an embarrassment.

Reading the earlier part of Gombrich's essay, one finds oneself constantly asking how it is possible for him to accept Hegel as a necessary source of modern art history and at the same time to reject the methodology which the Hegelian doctrine seems to demand. Or, to put the question in a slightly different form, how can one reconcile a point of view that simultaneously holds an assumption to be axiomatic and falsifiable? The application of the principle of falsifiability would seem either to reduce the assumption to a tautology (unity being predicated on the phrase 'the same period') or to make it meaningless.

Gombrich does not attack this problem head on. But, he does use arguments which suggest ways in which one might retain the essential Hegelian postulates without having to accept his historical teleology. His first argument lies in the distinction between 'periods' and 'movements'. It is implicit in Gombrich's view that movements are created by individuals, while periods are constructed after the event. According to Gombrich, Hegel attributed to periods the intentional properties which belong to movements. This criticism seems to be only partially successful, because he accepts that movements are not isolated and random events; they are accompanied by "badges, their outward signs, their style of behaviour, style of speech or dress"—in other words, that collective and block-like behaviour which enables one to recognise and isolate historical 'periods'. [2] We see from this that the original distinction between movements and periods is not so clear-cut as it seemed at first. If one's only access to movements was through the study of the actions and statements of the individuals who founded them, we would be no wiser than they as to the underlying significance of their actions, and history would reveal to us no new information; it would be a kind of biography—the sum total of innumerable psychological events. But history is the study of societies, and individuals within society exhibit collective behaviour which is often at variance with their explicit intentions. If we are not justified in extrapolating from individual psychology and in attributing to groups the psychological motives found in individuals, and if we cannot postulate a 'world historical spirit' which is somehow endowed with foresight, how are we to establish any coherent relationship between the explicit, individual, and atomic events which historical research uncovers? We must have some other principle on which to base a hypothesis which cannot be derived by induction from the events themselves.

Gombrich seems to accept Hegel's underlying assumption of a 'meaning' to history—his insistence that no event in history is isolated—but to reject the method by which Hegel tried to account for such a meaning.[3] He accepts Hegel's general concept of historical development and the need to study the actual events of history as if they were all part of a tapestry of meaning, rather than acknowledge or ignore them according to an *a priori* scheme. But he rejects Hegel's reintroduction of the *a priori* on the higher level at which all events must be shown to be the necessary effects of the 'will of history'. His historiography of culture thus seems to belong to the general trend of post-Hegelian historiography whose aim is, as Gombrich himself puts it, to "salvage the Hegelian assumptions without accepting Hegel's metaphysics".[4]

The twin concepts of 'period' and 'movement' open up a fissure in this metaphysical fabric, but they do not in themselves solve the problem of how one might reconcile Hegel's broad assumptions with a more 'scientific' and empirical approach. Gombrich's 'solution'—which seems to be central to his whole methodology—lies in another pair of opposed concepts: those of a symptom and syndrome.[5]

According to the *Oxford English Dictionary,* a symptom is a sign or token of the existence of something, while a syndrome is the concurrence of, or a set of concurrent, symptoms (of disease). If we attribute to periods the kind of consistency which belongs only to individual intention, we will look for a single cause underlying the events of a period. Visible events will be 'symptoms' of this hidden cause and will hold only instrumental interest or meaning in themselves. To this way of interpreting events, Gombrich opposes another. Instead of trying to explain everything in terms of 'hidden' causes, he proposes that we should observe the other events of the same kind which accompany the event being considered. This will provide the tool which is adequate for an explanation, and it has the advantage that it leaves the event which it seeks to explain intact. The event is no longer considered as a symptom and therefore reducible to another event at a lower level. It is one of a cluster of events which are not arranged hierarchically in a causal sequence but which nonetheless hang together to form a meaningful pattern—in other words they constitute a 'syndrome'.

In thus denying to the behaviour patterns of a period an absolute determination, and in giving them a certain autonomy, Gombrich is implying that they belong to a system of signification and that the relationship which holds between them is that of signs to other signs. The important thing about historical analysis is not to know how one event is caused by another but to know that one event will elicit a certain set of meanings whose references may be independent of any single determining factor. Thus, in the text which I have chosen to exemplify Gombrich's historical method, he says that we should not assume that, because in a particular case the collection of ideas summed up in the word 'romantic' may be accompanied by 'soft-focus' forms, it will necessarily be accompanied by these forms in all cases. 'Soft-focus' forms are not a symptom of the romantic attitude; both they and the romantic attitude belong to a syndrome whose elements will regroup themselves in different situations. It is clear from this that we cannot separate historiographic problems from a theory of signification. The view that all the cultural phenomena of a period are symptoms of the spirit of the age would imply that a work of art 'reflects' an idea and is capable of only one interpretation. Gombrich's notion of the work of art as part of a syndrome implies a different theory of signification according to which the relation of forms to their meanings is, in a certain sense, arbitrary. Meanings cannot be deduced from forms. These can only be deciphered if we know the social and artistic context within which they have been produced.

Forms do not have meaning in themselves; they are given meaning. Each set of forms can attract a number of different meanings, whose range is only limited by the extent to which form and meaning share certain structural properties. It is always possible to interpret any given set of forms in more than one way. Thus, in his criticism of Arnold Mauser's *The Social History of Art,* Gombrich paraphrases Hauser's interpretation of French classicism ("Rigid noblemen will like a rigid style and... agile merchants will be eager for novelty") and compares it to an alternative reading ("Blasé aristocrats love every new sensual stimuli while strict business men... want their art neat and solid") to show that both interpretations, though contradictory, are equally plausible.[6]

This attitude toward signification, though related explicitly in some of Gombrich's writings to information theory, has a certain resemblance to that of structural linguistics based on de Saussure. According to de Saussure, the linguistic sign is comprised of a signifier and a signified, and while these are arbitrarily related, they form an indissoluble unity. The signified cannot be thought of as having an independent existence prior to or outside language itself. The meaning of a linguistic unit relies, not on its correspondence with a pre-existent idea, but on its relation to the meanings of other linguistic units within the language. An understanding of how language works does not come from treating it as something which has degenerated from a 'pure' state, or is evolving toward a 'perfect' state, but from studying it as a synchronic system. When Gombrich says that cultural historians should "supplement the analysis of stylistic origins by an analysis of stylistic associations and responses", or that "continuity" studies should be supplemented by "contiguity" studies, he seems to be saying essentially the same thing, though without the implication that the synchronic analysis of cultural events could ever take the place of the diachronic studies.[7]

It is this tension between the diachronic and synchronic study of artistic works which creates the dialectical quality of Gombrich's thought—a thought that seeks to accommodate historical continuity and change, on the one hand, and a theory of signification independent of historical determination, on the other.

Art history in the modern sense becomes possible and necessary precisely at the moment when history is no longer seen, as it was in the classical period, as a more or less random accumulation of customs obscuring fixed norms. As soon as history is seen as disclosing different artistic periods, each possessing its own *raison d'être*, it becomes necessary to find a logic of historical change and a new theory of artistic meaning. Gombrich's view seems to be that Hegel's attempt to solve both these problems simultaneously by means of a teleological theory of history simply resulted in replacing the classical notion of absolute value before history by an absolute value at the end of history. Far from being a solution, this took away from the absolute all the specificity with which it had been endowed by classicism and replaced it by a vacuous notion of the 'idea', making it impossible to arrive at a theory of artistic meaning except by means of a crude *a priori* scheme. In spite of Hegel's acknowledgment that artistic phenomena have an essential autonomy, this theory is, in fact, incapable of explaining any artistic phenomenon at all in its richness and specificity.

Yet Hegel's scheme does seem to suggest a way in which its own limitations can be overcome. If artistic meaning can no longer be explained in terms of a fixed, external point of reference, partial explanations can at least be expected

Opposite: Friedrich Overbeck. *Italia and Germania*, 1828.

Above: Friedrich Overbeck. *Portrait of Franz Pforr*, 1810.

Left: JS Millet. *Men and Women Trussing Hay*, 1849–1850.

by taking into account as many of the complex conditioning factors of a work of art as possible. To do this it is necessary to assume at any one moment the existence of a system of values and to show that these values are a necessary condition of their alteration. Gombrich suggests an elementary model by which to gauge changes in artistic style—a Cartesian grid whose coordinates represent a set of images and a set of tasks respectively.[9] The image is always "necessary" (motivated) but becomes "sufficient" (meaningful) only when overlaid by the concrete social situation. In this way he implies that any non-historical system of aesthetics (eg. that of Rudolf Arnheim) would be misleading because it would attribute too much importance to the "natural" and "empty" sign. Here, he calls to mind the theory of "making and matching", which he elaborated in an earlier book in connection with the theory of representing "reality" in painting.[10]

In this model Gombrich is also proposing something different from the theory of structural linguistics. Whereas this seeks to disclose the permanent structures which make meaning possible, but leaves the meanings themselves to the unexplored regions of diachronic studies, Gombrich's scheme, in stressing the primacy of the image, makes meaning the core of the study of aesthetic signification. In terms of language, this would imply that it is not the relation between signifier and signified which is important in artistic works, but that between the signified and another signified—in other words, metaphor. This distinction is expressed by Thomas Aquinas (as quoted by Gombrich in another context):

> Any truth can be manifested in two ways: by things or by words.... The Scriptures contain a twofold truth. One lies in the things meant by the words used—that is the literal sense. The other in the way things become figures of other things, and in this consists the spiritual sense.[11]

For Gombrich the task of the cultural historian is not to 'explain away' the artistic phenomena which he studies. These phenomena contain 'truths' and values which are perennial, and part of the historian's task is to preserve these truths and values.[12] But they can no longer be taken for granted, and their preservation depends on a constant work of interpretation. Interpretation requires analysis

Above: Eugène Delacroix, *Christ on the Sea of Galilea*, 1853.

Opposie top: Jean-Auguste-Dominique Ingres, *Self-Portrait*, 1804.

Opposie bottom: Eugène Delacroix, *Self-Portrait*, circa 1837.

and the deconstruction of myth, the removal from the image of its original aura, and the 'explanation' of artistic works in terms of the infinitely complex web of meanings of which they are a part.

It may not be altogether outlandish to suggest that, in the delicate balance which Gombrich maintains between history as the accumulation of value and history as a continuous process of demythification, we can see an echo of the Hegelian project of reconciling idealistic dualism with a holistic metaphysics.

The problem which Gombrich tries to solve, and which faces all modern historiography, can also be seen, in more modern terms, as the conflict between the heritage of nineteenth century philology, with its positivistic bias, and the 'aesthetic revival' of the early twentieth century, which saw the individual work of art as the only valid object of art historical study. Gombrich wants to preserve the freedom of the artist, as the creator of unique works of art, against the tendency to 'explain' these works deterministically. To do this he leaves the door of analysis ajar by saying that the typological fixity of art is merely that which the artist finds at his disposal and which constitutes his ground of meaning. The artist and the art historian must start from this system of values. But they are able to alter these values and this constitutes their condition of freedom. In this way art as social communication (relative, arbitrary, and conventional) and art as the expression of transcendental value no longer present themselves as logically irreconcilable.

1   "No type of historian has a greater stake in this (Hegelian) approach than the historian of art. Indeed it might be claimed that a history, as opposed to a critical evaluation, of the art of the past only became possible in the light of this interpretation." Gombrich, EH, *In Search of Cultural History*, Oxford: Clarendon Press, 1969, p. 13.
2   Gombrich, *In Search of Cultural History*, p. 37.
3   On the dilemma caused by the breakdown of the Hegelian tradition, Gombrich writes: "No culture can be mapped out in its entirety, but no element of this culture can be understood in isolation", *In Search of Cultural History,* p. 41.
4   Gombrich, *In Search of Cultural History*, p. 25. In fact, the rivalry between empirical history and certain tendencies in the philosophy of history goes back to the beginning of the nineteenth century. It was already implicit in Wilhelm von Humboldt's seminal essay "On the Historian's Task" of 1821, in which he warned against the philosophical temptation to explain history in terms of final causes, and to see it as a teleological process. Although this was, presumably, a criticism of Enlightenment thought, it prefigured the anti-Hegelian position of such later historians as Leopold von Ranke. In this respect, Gombrich's anti-Hegelianism seems to belong to a well-established tradition within historicist thought.
5   Gombrich, *In Search of Cultural History*, p. 30.
6   Gombrich, EH, "The Social History of Art," *Meditations on a Hobby Horse and Other Essays on the Theory of Art,* 2nd ed., New York: Phaidon Publishers, Inc., 1971, p. 90.
7   Gombrich *In Search of Cultural History,* p. 38.
8   Gombrich, *In Search of Cultural History*, p. 43.
9   Gombrich, EH, *Symbolic Images: Studies in the Art of the Renaissance*, London: Phaidon Press Ltd., 1972, p. 8.
10 Gombrich, EH, *Art and Illusion: A Study in the Psychology of Pictorial Representation*, New York: Pantheon Books, Inc., 1960.
11 Quoted by Gombrich, *Symbolic Images*, pp. 13–14. Original source *St Thomas Aquinas, Quaestiones quodlibe-tales,* ed. P Mandonnet, Paris: 1926, VII, 14, p. 275.
12 "If we want to keep open our lines of communication which permit us to understand the greatest creations of mankind, we must study and teach the history of culture more deeply and more intensely than was necessary a generation ago." Gombrich, *In Search of Cultural History,* p. 45.

EH Gombrich:
"Symptoms and Syndromes" In Search of Cultural History

One may be interested in the manifold interactions between the various spheres of a culture and yet reject what I have called the 'exegetic method', the method, that is, that bases its interpretations on the detection of that kind of 'likeness' that leads the interpreter of the scriptures to link the passage of the Jews through the Red Sea with the Baptism of Christ. Hegel, it will be remembered, saw in the Egyptian sphinx an essential likeness with the position of Egyptian culture in which the Spirit began to emerge from animal nature, and carried the same metaphor through in his discussion of Egyptian religion and Egyptian hieroglyphics. The assumption is always that some essential structural similarity must be detected which permits the interpreter to subsume the various aspects of a culture under one formula. The art of van Eyck in Huizinga's persuasive morphology is not only to be connected with the theology and the literature of the time but it must be shown to share some of their fundamental characteristics. To criticise this assumption is not to deny the great ingenuity and learning expended by some cultural historians on the search for suggestive and memorable metaphorical descriptions. Nor is it to deny that such structural likenesses between various aspects of a period may be found to be interesting, as AO Lovejoy tried to demonstrate for eighteenth century Deism and classicism. But here as always any *a priori* assumption of such similarity can only spoil the interest of the search. Not only is there no iron law of such isomorphism, I even doubt whether we improve matters by replacing this kind of determinism with a probabilistic approach as has been proposed by WT Jones in his book on the Romantic Movement. The sub-title of this interesting book demands attention by promising a "new Method in Cultural Anthropology and History of Ideas"; it consists in drawing up such polarities as that between static and dynamic, or order and disorder, and examining certain periods for their bias towards one or the other end of these scales, a bias which would be expected to show up statistically at the periphery of the Hegelian wheel in art, science and political thought, though some of these spheres might be more recalcitrant to their expression than others. In the contrast between 'soft focus' and 'hard focus' the Romantic, he finds, will be likely to lean towards the first in metaphysics, in poetical imagery and in painting, a bias that must be symptomatic of Romantic mentality.

Such expectations, no doubt, accord well with commonsense psychology; but in fact no statistics are needed to show in this case that what looks plausible in this new method of salvaging Hegel still comes into conflict with historical fact. It so happens that it was romanticism which discovered the taste for the so-called 'primitives' in painting, which meant, at that time, the hard-edged, sharp-focused style of van Eyck or of the early Italians. If the first Romantic painters of Germany had one pet aversion it was the soft-focused bravura of their Baroque predecessors. Whatever their bias in metaphysics may have been, they saw in the smudged outline a symptom of artistic dishonesty and moral corruption. Their bias in the syndrome—to retain this useful term—was based on very different alternatives, alternatives peculiar to the problems of painting. Paradoxically, perhaps, they identified the hard and naïve with the other-worldly and the chaste. It was soft-focused naturalism that was symptomatic of the fall from grace.

We have met this bias before in the discussions among cultural historians of the symptomatic value of painting styles. It might not have assumed such importance if it had not been such a live issue in the very time and ambience of Hegel and of the young Burckhardt. This was, of course, the time when the trauma of the French Revolution aroused a new longing among certain circles for the lost paradise of Medieval culture. The German painters who became known as the Nazarenes regarded realism and sensuality as two inseparable sins and aimed at a linear style redolent of Fra Angelico and his Northern counterparts. They went to Rome where most of them converted to Roman Catholicism, they wore their hair long and walked about in velvet caps considered somehow to be *alt-deutsch*. Now here the style of these artists and their *Weltanschauung* was clearly and closely related, their mode of painting, like their costume, was really a badge, a manifesto of their dissociation from the nineteenth century. If you met a member of this circle you could almost infer from his attire what he would say and how he would paint except, of course, whether he would paint well or badly.

It is legitimate for the cultural historian to ask how such a syndrome arose which marks what we call a movement. It is possible to write the history of such a movement, to speculate about its beginnings and about the reason for its success or failure. It is equally necessary then to ask how firmly the style and the allegiance it once expressed remained correlated; how long, for instance, the anti-realistic mode of painting remained a badge of Roman Catholicism. In England the link between Catholicism and a love of Gothic is strong in Pugin, but was severed by Ruskin, while the Pre-Raphaelite Brotherhood even aimed at a certain naïve and sharp-focused realism.

Even here, though, the style expressed some kind of allegiance to the Age Faith. Judging by a passage from Bernard Shaw's first novel, this syndrome had dissolved by 1879 when it was written. In *Immaturity*, Shaw wittily described the interior decoration of a villa belonging to a patron of the arts, a salon with its walls of pale blue damask and its dadoes, "... painted with processions of pale maidens, picking flowers to pieces, reading books, looking ecstatically up, looking contemplatively down, played aborted guitars with an expressive curve of the neck and fingers... all on a ground of dead gold. People who disapproved of felt hats, tweed and velveteen clothes, long hair music on Sundays, pictures of the nude figure, literary women and avowal of agnosticism either dissembled or stayed away."

The syndrome, if Shaw was right, had changed from medievalism to aestheticism and a generalised nonconformism. Burne-Jones was now the badge of allegiance of a progressive creed.

The Beaux-Arts Plan: Viollet-le-Duc's Transformation of the Parisian *Hôtel Particulier*

First published in *Architectural Design Profiles* 17, vol. 48, nos. 11–12, 1978.

Professor Joseph Rykwert has, on several occasions, drawn attention to the epistemological break which took place when the classical tradition, as it had existed up until JPF Blondel, was subjected to the rationalistic critique of Jean-Nicolas-Louis Durand. With Durand, the foundations of a purely syntactic, as opposed to iconic, procedure are laid down, and the classical forms are reduced to a purely formal repertoire. There seems to be a contradiction between this syntactic approach and that of Durand's teacher, Boullée, who still believed in the metaphorical properties of classical form. But from another point of view Durand's theory can perhaps be seen as a logical extension of Boullée's, if we remember that for Boullée these metaphors spoke directly through the senses and were not dependent on allegorical conventions. Once the appeal of classical forms can be seen as directly psychological, the foundations are laid for an empirical investigation (of the kind that we find, for example, in Burke) and for eventual description and classification.[1]

Whatever the degree of dependence of Beaux-Arts practice on Durand, it is clear that both rely on the possibility of establishing certain rules of syntactic organisation or 'composition'. This notion of composition was opposed by the 'organic' wing of nineteenth century rationalism (represented most clearly and systematically by Eugene-Emmanuel Viollet-le-Duc) which was influential in the development of the twentieth century avant-garde. According to the organic theory, architectural forms should emerge from the application of correct principles and not from the manipulation of a repertoire of forms.

The idea of fixed forms which lies behind the idea of composition was in itself not new. It belonged to the ancient tradition and was related both to craft technique and the tradition of rhetoric. What could be said to be new in its interpretation in the late eighteenth century was the removal of these figures or tropes from the substratum of traditional practice and their subjection to systematic classification. It was the 'artificiality' of this process which was the basis, for example, of Louis Sullivan's objection to the notion of 'composition' when he wrote:

> Man invented a process called "composition": Nature has always brought forth organisations. Man, by means of physical power, mechanical resources, and mental ingenuity, may set things side by side; a composition will result, but not a great work of art.

The process of composition which Sullivan criticised involved the extreme development of certain codes which intervened between the conception of a work and its execution, and it is in the Beaux-Arts Prix de Rome projects that we see one such code, that of the plan, reaching its highest degree of articulation. The development of codes which intervene between conception and execution can perhaps be most clearly exemplified in the history of music. In ancient musical procedures (which still flourish in India), certain general rules are passed down from one generation to the next. These rules become elaborated as the result of successive inventions by individual executants. But with the development of musical notation, the production of music becomes split; there are now two 'executants', the one who 'composes' at his desk and the instrumentalist who interprets this composition. This division of labour involves certain sacrifices, but it makes possible a more complex musical structure, thanks to the availability of a visual code which aids memory and can be manipulated at leisure, outside the pressure of actual performance.

If I am here suggesting some sort of rough analogy between musical notation and the architectural plan, it is not to imply that they relate in exactly the same way to the musical or architectural product, nor that these codes had to wait until the eighteenth century to achieve some kind of 'destiny'. But it was nonetheless during this period that both music and architecture were 'imagined' with the greatest romantic intensity, and this 'imagining' would not have been possible without the availability of such codes and the more or less elaborate 'language' of forms which they embodied. It is surely no accident that the development of the symphony coincides approximately with the early development of the Beaux-Arts. Both cases involve rather complex and extended 'compositions' whose complexity was able to be controlled by the mediation of codes which represented and prefigured the intended object.

When we 'read' a Beaux-Arts plan, we seem to be carrying out three operations at the same time, or at any rate in quick succession. First, we interpret the marks on the page as a *Gestalt* pattern. Second, we translate this into an imagined two-dimensional space which we experience sequentially—following the direction of narrow, bounded spaces, halting at square spaces, interpreting rhythmically arranged points as transparent boundaries, and so on. Finally, we translate this into three-dimensional volumes.

From these interpretive steps we arrive at a coherent organisation which does not gain its meaning from any but the most generalised functional attributions. It is in this generalised 'programme' that one of the most striking analogies between the Beaux-Arts plan and the symphony lies. Both are characterised by a strong idealism and a certain degree of abstraction. Both are great set pieces. The symphony has no immediate social purpose or intended occasional use: it is intended for the concert hall, not the drawing room or the church. Yet in spite of this detachment from occasion, the symphony is a drama, and the ideas it gives rise to are related to 'human', everyday states of mind.

The Beaux-Arts programme has, of course, a precise social purpose, but it has some of the same generality of the symphonic programme and prefers subjects which can be assimilated to abstract ideas—monarchy, government, law, religion, exchange, etc.. These are the guiding ideas of the late eighteenth century and provide the programmatic repertoire for the early Prix de Rome.

After the 1830s the Beaux-Arts programmes became more particular and pragmatic. As capitalism provided architecture with new tasks, the grand abstractions of the eighteenth century began to be replaced by programmes whose moral and social meanings were weaker: a railway station, a casino, a private house for a rich banker. It may be that the 'ossification' which many commentators have noted in Beaux-Arts projects after the 1830s (David Van Zanten refers to this in his essay in "The Architecture of the Ecole des Beaux-Arts") is connected with the fact that forms developed in order to embody the ideas of the Enlightenment continued to be used after these ideas had begun to lose their meaning. It was a situation from which emerged, in the 1860s, two architects whose commitment to the new materialistic values of the Second Empire was equally strong but who interpreted them in different ways. With Charles Garnier, the Beaux-Arts plan is transformed into a vehicle for an architecture of ostentation and splendour. With Viollet-le-Duc it is rejected for the sake of 'functional' efficiency and the 'honest' expression of bourgeois values. This difference in interpretation can be seen if we compare their plans for the Paris Opèra. The logic and panache of Garnier's plan is instantaneously grasped. Viollet-le-Duc's plan lacks all immediate aesthetic qualities, and its virtues emerge only after a detailed study of its circulation and distribution.

An even more striking example of Viollet-le-Duc's rejection of Beaux-Arts planning methods can be seen in the plan for a Paris *hôtel* in the *Entretiens*.[2]

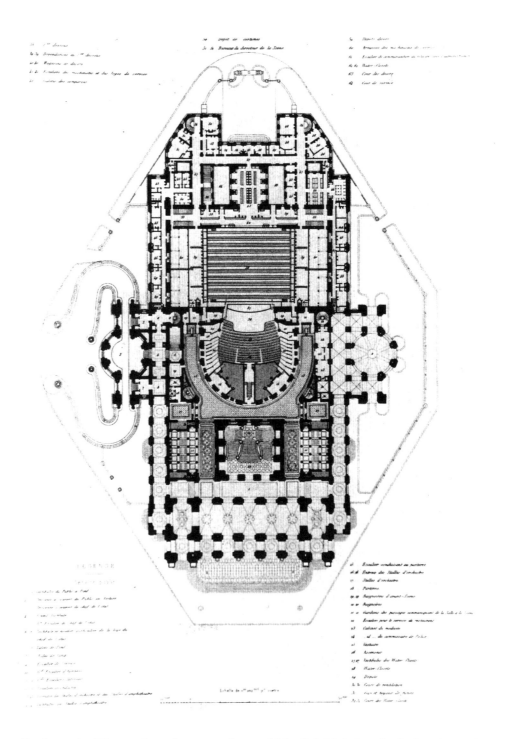

Opèra, Paris. Jean-Louis-Charles Garnier, 1862–1875. Plan.

In the typical Beaux-Arts plan a regular and 'ideal' field defines both the site and the extent of the building. All spaces within this field are formally controlled, and there are no residual spaces. Thus, if the plan is expressed in terms of figure/ground, the 'negative' spaces of the original diagram become 'positive' if this diagram is reversed. In this sense the space defined by the field can be said to be homologous.

The typical seventeenth century *hôtel* which Viollet-le-Duc illustrates, though it displays few of the formal complexities of the developed Beaux-Arts plan, shares with it this homologous quality. The open spaces of the *cour d'honneur* and the stables are treated like 'rooms', with the same simple boundary conditions as the internal spaces, so that the plan can be read as a Chinese box, with the large-scale

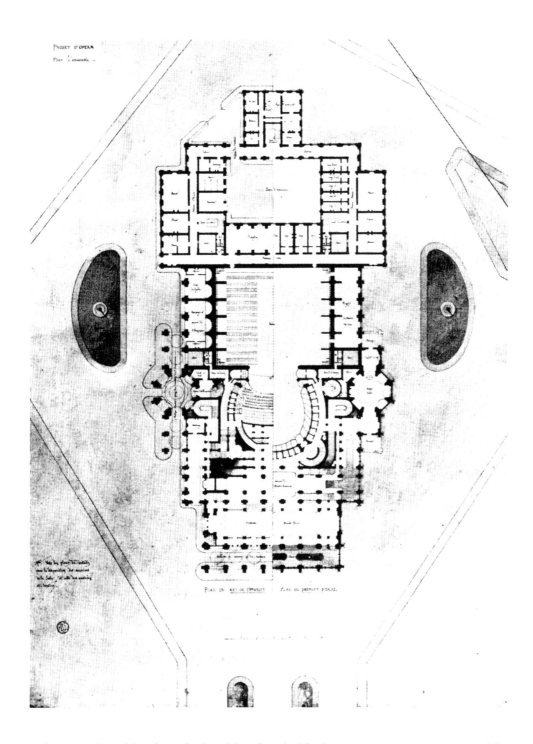

order—produced by the relationship of main blocks to open spaces—repeated in the small-scale relationship of the rooms within the blocks. There is no space left over 'within' the confines of the regular site.

In Viollet-le-Duc's alternative solution this unified spatial treatment is abandoned; the building becomes an object in an infinite spatial field which can never be read as anything but residual in relation to the building itself. It is true that Viollet-le-Duc retains the pattern by which a service wing and a block facing the road define the edges of the site, but this is purely vestigial, and the *corps de logis* detaches itself as an isolated pavilion, only tenuously connected to the service wing at the edge of the site. The model for this arrangement is obviously

Competition project for the Opèra, Paris.
Eugène-Emmanuel Viollet–le–Duc, 1861. Plan.

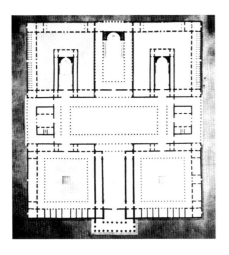

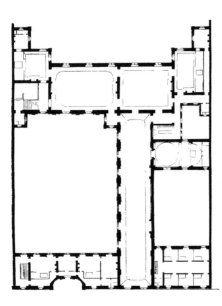

the suburban villa, which elsewhere in the text Viollet-le-Duc recommends as the ideal type of house for the new bourgeoisie.

Although Viollet-le-Duc adduces numerous practical arguments for the superiority of this new house type over the traditional one, they are not always convincing. Part of his motivation is ideological and cannot be justified on the rational basis which he is careful to establish. This 'irrational' component has to do with what he considers to be the correct 'image' of the bourgeois house—an image in which irregularity, complexity, and picturesque effect play a large part.

Thus, although the octagonal organisation of the *corps de logis* undoubtedly facilitates distribution by means of short *degagements,* there is no noticeable shortening of the circulation between the main apartments and the kitchens, and the *coeur d'honneur* and the *corps de logis* occupy a greater depth of site than in the seventeenth century house, thus reducing the area available for the garden. Again, despite Viollet-le-Duc's dislike of symmetry, his building is actually more symmetrical than the old one, with two identical apartments at the extremities of the ground floor plan and two identical master bedrooms on the first floor. Indeed, the symmetry is almost obsessional. Whereas in the older plan symmetries are local and the overall plan accommodates itself to the asymmetrical subdivisions of the plot, Viollet-le-Duc's plan, though developing the arms of the 'butterfly' unevenly, is rigidly symmetrical in its underlying structure.

In this single example we can observe a change which is much more profound than might be expected from Viollet-le-Duc's commonsense explanations. It demonstrates nothing less than a new attitude toward architectural space. Space is no longer an ideal field which is 'ordered' and totally humanised, as it was in the classical tradition taken over by the Beaux-Arts. Such a space is related to the homcotopic concept of Medieval and Renaissance cities and the creation of a man-made microcosm. With Viollet-le-Duc we see the abandonment of this in favour of a heterotopic space which consists of individual buildings unrelated—both conceptually and phenomenally—to their neighbours.

Viollet-le-Duc criticised the Beaux-Arts as a mindless repetition of worn out formulae, unsuited to the mores of the new dominant class. He was unable to see that the Beaux-Arts plan was the codified survival of a system of spatial organisation which symbolised a certain relation of man to the world. In his advocacy of pragmatic and instrumental planning he set in motion a development which reached its climax in the heterotopic space of the modern city and the exclusive concern of modern architecture for the individual *objet-type* set in an infinite and abstract space.

The 'butterfly' plan which he developed for his alternative hotel was enormously influential and reappears in the later phase of the Arts and Crafts Movement in England.[3] This type was also adopted for certain programmes by the architects of the Modern Movement, for example, the Zonnestraal Sanatorium at Hilversum by Johannes Duiker and Bernard Bijvoet, Aalto's Paimio Sanatorium, and High and Over by Connell, Ward and Lucas. But the butterfly plan was only a special case of a more general attitude, and it is possible to trace the typical Modern Movement notion of the plan developed from inside to outside, spreading out centrifugally from a single nucleus, to Viollet-le-Duc's rejection of the Beaux-Arts.

1   Burke, Edmund, *A Philosophical Enquiry into the Origin of Our Ideas of the Sublime and the Beautiful,* Notre Dame, Indiana: Notre Dame University Press, 1968.
2   Viollet-le-Duc, Eugene-Emmanuel, *Discourses on Architecture,* New York: Grove Press, 1959, pp. 264, 278, 280–281.
3   See Franklin, Jill, "Edwardian Butterfly Houses", *The Architectural Review*, no. 157, April 1975, pp. 220–225; and Saint, Andrew, *Richard Norman* Shaw, New Haven, CT: Yale University Press, 1976, p. 332. Saint says that Shaw's country house at Chesters, 1891–1893, was the origin of the butterfly plan, but Shaw must have been familiar with the *Entretiens,* and it is at least possible that he was influenced by Viollet-le-Duc's *hôtel* plan.

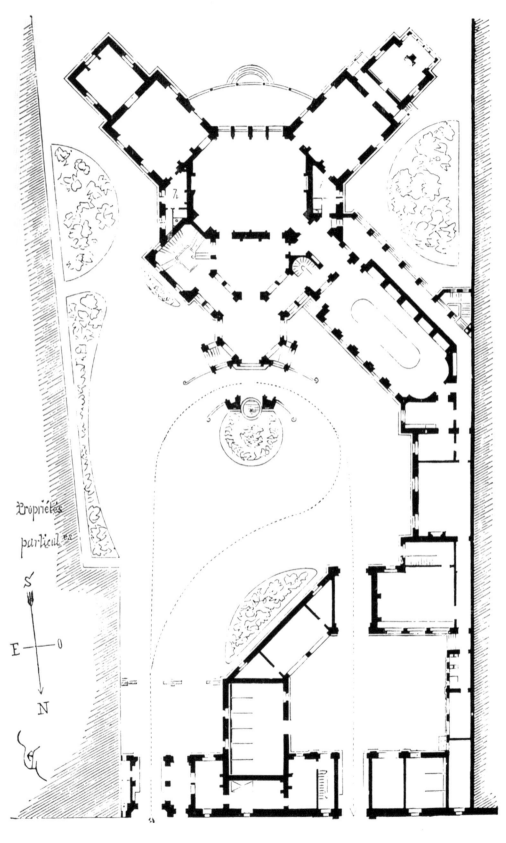

Propriétés
particul^{es}

Opposite top: Tribunal de Cassation, Premier Grand Prix. Henri Labrouste, 1824. Plan.

Opposite bottom: First floor plan of typical seventeenth century *hôtel particulier*.

Left: Viollet-le-Duc, *hôtel particulier* plan illustrated in the seventeenth *Entretien*, ground floor.

Form and Figure

First published in *Oppositions 12*, Spring 1978.

One of the symptoms of the reaction against functionalist doctrine has been a return to the use of stylistic elements borrowed from the past. This practice gains support from a variety of ideological positions (often mutually incompatible), and its forms are correspondingly varied. Later I will discuss two of these positions, associated with neo-realism and neo-rationalism respectively.[1] But my main purpose is to consider stylistic quotation as a single phenomenon and to examine it in relation both to the historical tradition and to modernism.

The use of stylistic elements of the past in contemporary buildings seems to be in direct contradiction to the principles of the Modern Movement. But this movement was never as monolithic as its chief apologists made out. In the 1920s and 1930s, we find many oblique references to the Beaux-Arts tradition and to vernacular buildings, particularly in the work of Le Corbusier. And since the Second World War there have been several tendencies which have disputed the functionalist and mechanistic tenets of the so-called International Style and have sought to recover, in one form or another, the 'architectural tradition'; one thinks of neo-classicism in America and Social Realism in Italy, both in the 1950s. But this recovery tended to be syntactic rather than iconic (classicising plans being combined with a typically modern spatial or elevational treatment), or it derived traditional forms (windows, ornament) from the 'natural' use of traditional materials, thus retaining its links with functionalist doctrine. These revisionist tendencies within the movement generally avoided literal quotations from the past and maintained one of the most persistent principles of Modern architecture—the prohibition of all direct stylistic reference.

This prohibition is altogether understandable within the context of the avant-garde since the second half of the nineteenth century—an avant-garde which set as its task the discovery of a 'language' which would be the product of its place in history. Eclecticism had introduced cultural relativism into architecture. The avant-garde sought a new definition of style which would reconcile the demands of 'nature' and 'reason' with the fact that culture was subject to historical evolution.

Discussion of avant-garde architecture has usually revolved around the relationship between form and function. Function has been held to give meaning to form, while form has been held to 'express' function. This proposition has formed the rational basis for architectural discourse within avant-garde theory, and even within academic theory, for 150 years or more. It is a proposition which assumes that the 'meaning' of architectural forms is the result of natural expression.

Here I want to look at avant-garde architecture from another point of view. What the theory of natural expression ignores is the importance throughout history of conventional meaning in architecture. Instead of seeing Modern architecture as the last step in an evolutionary process in which the natural relationship between form and function has been a constant, I think it would be useful to see the principle of natural expression as a break with an older tradition. If we look at the Modern Movement in this way, the fundamental dialectic no longer seems to be that between form and function but that between form and another entity, which I shall call figure. By form I mean a configuration that is held to have either a natural meaning or no meaning at all. By figure I mean a configuration whose meaning is given by culture, whether or not it is assumed that this meaning ultimately has a basis in nature.

Insofar as it has discussed the formal aspects of architecture, modern criticism has generally appealed to principles of form and set these in relation to function. The recent tendencies toward stylistic reference seem to be motivated by a need

to reintroduce the notion of figure into architecture and to see architectural configurations as already containing a set of cultural meanings.

The origins of what I call figure lie in the classical tradition of rhetoric. In fact, the word 'figure', together with the word 'trope', is quite precise as a technical term within classical poetics. I am using it here more loosely to apply to arts other than literature, but there is some justification for this, since in the Renaissance the theory of painting was to some extent explicitly based on that of classical rhetoric. We know that classical rhetoric, particularly in its literary mode, was preserved throughout the Middle Ages. Scholastic thought was both a fusion of, and a reconciliation between, the Judeo-Christian tradition and that of the ancients. In the Renaissance a further interpretation of these traditions was made in the light of a renewed study of classical literary sources.

According to the principle of rhetoric there is a distinction between what can be imagined and what can be thought. This distinction implies that a figure represents an idea. The purpose of this representation is persuasion. Figures representing ideas were thus organised didactically to persuade people to adopt the values of the good and the perfect for the benefit of either society or the soul. This concept also involves a distinction between figure and content. The figure gives an approximation, as faithfully as possible, of a content which remains ineffable. Thus, when we look at figures, we do not see truth itself but its reflections, or its emblems. These figures, or tropes, become to a certain extent fixed—they become conventional types. The social function of these types is to establish certain ideas in the mind of the spectator or listener and, ultimately, to reinforce and preserve an ideology.

The effectiveness of figures or tropes resides in their synthetic power. They draw together and crystallise a series of complex experiences, which are diffuse and imperceptible. The figure, therefore, is a condensation, the immediate effect of which is to suggest the richness and complexity of reality. In this way the spectator or listener is able to establish a relation between that which he sees or hears and his own experience. The use of the figure in Renaissance painting has been studied by Michael Baxandall.[2] Baxandall points out that in fifteenth century

Tommasco G Masaccio.
Saint Peter Raising the Son of Theophilus, 1428. Brancacci Chapel, Santa Maria de Carmine, Florence.

Gothic portal, Tours.

painting the figure was the image of a human gesture. The aim of such a gestural figure was both to arouse the emotions and to facilitate the memorisation of certain ideas. These images always showed general and non-individualised types, and "the narrative in which they took part was expressed in terms of massive and theatrical gestures". Alberti, in his treatise on painting, states that the movements of the soul are recognised in the movements of the body.[3] Thus the 'affections' (pain, joy, fear, shame, etc.) possess their equivalent gestures or postures.

I would suggest that there exists in architecture an equivalent to this gesture or figure in painting. Although architecture does not imitate the external world, it attaches itself to this world through our experience or our knowledge of buildings. All the brute facts of construction, all our perceptions of gravity, and all our disposition toward spatial enclosure are 'humanised' and become the signs of other things. In the architecture of the Middle Ages and the Renaissance we find a limited number of basic elements which are thus turned into signs: walls and their penetrations, columns, beams, arches, roofs, and so on. From among all the possible combinations of these different elements, each style chooses a certain repertoire and institutes a commentary on structural form.

The concept of figure which I am using is general and can be applied to both Gothic and Renaissance architecture, despite their fundamental differences. We recognise it equally in the aedicule, as isolated by John Summerson, and in the Vitruvian orders.[4] In both cases a figural composition is able to convey a complex set of ideas which are not inherent in the basic structural form from which it is derived and which refers to other ideas within the culture. In the case of the Vitruvian system, the different orders take on meaning through their mutual opposition (Doric/Corinthian) and their association with further oppositions (virility/delicacy), leading to their association with particular deities (which are themselves figural representations). Such systems are developed through the fixing of recognisable and—literally in the case of metaphor—memorisable entities. When a person imagines the function of a column or a roof, he sees in his mind's eye a particular column or roof and proceeds to make associations of meaning. In an analogous way, an entire building can become a metaphor, fixed by its typological content. Thus there exists a system of types, which correspond to the various genres of classical literature.

To some extent one can see that this metonymic, metaphoric, and typological procedure continued into the nineteenth century and even until today, if one thinks of popular architecture. It is a procedure which relies on the conventionality and typicality of forms and a set of meanings which have become fixed through social usage. But, this system tended gradually to degenerate during the eighteenth century. The original meanings attached to the orders and the typological catalogue became either vague or trivialised, and the underlying system of thought decomposed into a sort of diffuse memory. If thought still instinctively used the fixed classical figures and tropes, there was an uncertainty as to the precise role of the elements and their meaning within the *Weltanschauung*.

This degeneration in the system of figures descending from the Renaissance was tempered in the eighteenth century by the attempt to recover a sort of primitive experience of architecture. (The theory of the primitive hut proposed by Marc-Antoine Laugier has its adepts even today, whether in the behaviouristic theories of Christopher Alexander or among the neo-rationalists, for whom it remains a distillation of eighteenth century neo-classicism and is clothed with historical specificity). But perhaps the most radical modification of the classical system of architectural figures is found in the work of the 'visionary architects' of the French Revolution—Ledoux, Boullée, and Lequeu. These architects no longer believed that, as was the case in the Renaissance, the architectural figure corresponded to a hidden reality, revealed through Biblical or classical authority. Nonetheless, they continued to use the Greco-Roman repertoire, whose meanings were seen to be established by social custom. But although they operated within a conceptual

system inherited from the Renaissance according to which figures had metaphorical properties, they combined the traditional elements in a new way and were thus able to extend and modify classical meanings. The design of Lequeu called "Le Rendezvous de Bellevue" is an amalgam of quotations taken from different styles and organised according to 'picturesque' principles of composition. This building is a sort of *bricolage* made from figural fragments which are still recognisable whatever the degree of distortion. The case of Lequeu is perhaps different from that of Boullée or Ledoux because in his work classical composition seems often to be entirely abandoned. But even in an architecture based on picturesque principles, whose evident aim is to shock, the ability to provide this shock is dependent on the existence of traditional figures. One can, therefore, say of the work of all the visionary architects that it is not only an *architecture parlante* but also *une architecture qui parle de soi même*. It consciously manipulates an existing code, even though in the case of Lequeu it fragments this code. Emil Kaufmann and others have interpreted the work of Boullée, Ledoux, and Lequeu as being prophetic of the formal and abstract tendencies in the new architecture of the 1920s and 1930s, and in particular the work of Le Corbusier. I prefer to see it as presenting a parallel to the present day problem of the survival and reinterpretation of the figure of the rhetorical tradition.

At this point I would like to pass from a consideration of the notion of figure to that of form. The concept of pure form, of *Gestaltung,* posed as something external to style, probably comes from certain theoreticians of the late eighteenth century, such as Antoine Chrysostome Quatremère de Quincy, for whom the 'type' was an entity distinct from the 'model'. The model, for Quatremère, would be a concrete entity corresponding to a particular style, while the type implies a degree of abstraction and is beyond stylistic accident.

But the category of form in relation to architecture and the applied arts is not integrated into a theoretical system until the end of the nineteenth century. It is above all through Hermann Muthesius that we know this concept of form. Muthesius never defined precisely what he meant by this concept, but it is possible

to approach a definition by looking at the work of certain English designers of the late nineteenth century who influenced Muthesius, such as Christopher Dresser. These works are characterised by a degree of abstraction, a simplicity and purity of profile, and an absence of detail and ornament, all of which are typical of the late period of the Arts and Crafts Movement. It is also, possible to understand the relationship of form to architecture if we look at certain industrial structures illustrated by Muthesius in the Deutscher Werkbund *Jahrbuchs,* such as the North American grain silos.

The idea of form is equally present in the writings of certain aestheticians of the second half of the nineteenth century. Conrad Fiedler's theory of "pure visibility" and his assignment of a privileged position to perception among artistic activities is not unrelated to Heinrich Wolfflin's discussion of painting and architecture in terms of stylistic grammars or to Benedetto Croce's belief in art as a cognitive system independent of all discursive or associative operations.

It would seem probable that the idea of form has a neo-classical derivation. After the disappearance of the systems of thought which had descended from the Middle Ages and the Renaissance at the time of the 'scientific revolution' of the seventeenth century, architectural theory distinguished between "positive or natural beauty" and "arbitrary or customary beauty". For example, Christopher Wren declared that "positive beauty" in architecture depended on geometry, whereas all other beauties depended on custom.[5] This point of view persisted into the twentieth century, and we find, for instance, Jeanneret and Ozenfant asserting in the 1920s that the plastic arts are organised according to a primary quality defined by the elementary geometrical solids and that secondary qualities emerge by association of ideas.[6]

The notion of pure form had for its effect the reservation of a field of expression proper to each art. For this division of art into parallel departments music became the paradigm because the meanings of this art seemed to be articulated without any external reference. Non-figurative painting had the same property. If the specific field of music is tone and rhythm, that of the plastic arts is form and colour. The

Opposite left: The Natural Model: Laugier's primitve hut, 1753.

Opposite right: "Le Rendezvous de Bellevue", Jean-Jacques Lequeu, circa 1780.

Left: American grain storage, 1920.

Right: Christopher Dresser, Teapot, 1880.

objective of painting is not to describe or depict the objects of the external world but to reveal, through form, the laws which underlie the appearance of things. Literature shows a similar need—not only creative literature but also criticism. The Formalist criticism, which was developed in Moscow at the beginning of the 1920s and was based on Saussurian linguistics, put forward a theory according to which the object of criticism was situated exclusively in the interior of the text, and not in the subject treated by the text.

The rather vague notion of form which I have attempted to delineate by these few examples is a fundamental concept in the development of modern art. And although the special social, economic, and technological status of architecture had led it to emphasise function, this concept of pure form is no less important in the development of modern architecture than it is in the other arts.

We now have placed in their respective historical settings two apparently contradictory notions of the relation of forms to meaning in art and architecture. While the notion of figure includes conventional and associative meanings, that of form excludes them. While the notion of figure assumes that architecture is a language with a limited set of elements which already exist in their historical specificity, that of form holds that architectural forms can be reduced to an a-historical 'degree zero'; architecture as a historical phenomenon is not determined by what has existed before but by emergent social and technological facts operating on a number of constant physiological and psychological laws.

A further contradiction arises from this situation. On the one hand, the traditional figures of architecture are embedded in the imagination, and there continues to be a desire to repeat configurations which carry conventional meanings; on the other, the development of technology has created a separation between means and ends, between techniques and meaning, so that when figures are used they are not necessarily the logical result of the techniques employed. The recognition of technical necessity and the need for meaning are equally acknowledged, but they belong to different categories. The development of the notion of form was a response to this separation of means and ends and therefore sought the universal laws of aesthetics as independent of the extrinsic facts of technological or historical change. On the basis of these laws it would be possible, it was imagined, both to inoculate art against technology and to accept technology as a categorical imperative which no longer had the power to destroy meaning, because what was destroyed—the 'tradition'—was no longer to be considered as a constitutive element of meaning.

No attempt to return to figures, which are derived from the rhetorical tradition, or to respond to the popular tendency to see architectural forms in terms of meanings which are a part of their own history can ignore this evolution. We have seen that as early as the eighteenth century the rhetorical tradition was no longer something which could be taken for granted. On the one hand, Durand attempted to reduce it to a system of typological classifications, to turn it into an abstract system which could be manipulated independently of a living tradition. On the other, the newly rediscovered 'styles' could be applied to buildings to provide a whole series of subcultural meanings which no longer formed part of a coherent cosmology. This process of trivialisation of meaning continues today with the multiplication of kitsch objects, in which figures are reduced to cliches—to 'dead' metaphors. The figural cliché is the reverse side of the same coin that contains the notion of form and represents the 'instinctual' side of the same historical phenomenon—an instinct which is naturally exploited by the system of production. One of the chief arguments in favour of the return of the figure is that the market has recuperated a minimalist architecture based on the notion of pure form. The demands of economics and utility have shown that the 'principles' of modern architecture can be easily subverted. But it is equally true that this same urge has exploited, where this was profitable, what remains of the figural tradition.

The attempt to legitimatise this tradition and to give it back the authenticity which it lacks in the form of kitsch is not, therefore, a simple act of recovery. It

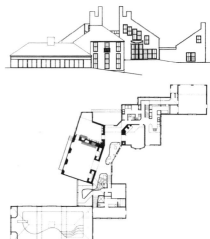

can be accomplished only in full consciousness of what it wants to supersede—not only abstract principles of form which have been unable to sustain meaning in architecture but also the world of kitsch which has only sustained meanings in an impoverished form.

We are dealing with a tradition which has come down to us in a fragmented condition. The process by which these pieces might be reassembled is far from clear, but we can see the attempt being made in different ways if we examine the work of two groups of architects who have attempted such a recovery of the figural tradition. The first group consists of a number of American architects of whom Charles Moore and Robert Venturi are perhaps the most representative. Moore uses what might be called 'figurative fragments' which are not organised into a coherent system. He does not, as did the eclectics of the early nineteenth century, attempt to reconstitute the figurative system of an entire building. Rather, he uses isolated and partial lexical figures, such as roofs, windows, and colonnades, and composes them in ways which are characteristically 'modern'—that is to say, according to a syntax which is functional and picturesque and a semantic which verges on the parodic. In both Moore and Venturi the figure tends to become isolated as a sign no longer restricted to the specific category of the architectural sign. Architecture is seen to belong to a more general sign system whose referents may or may not be architecture itself, according to local circumstances. The circumstantial nature of these signs is justified in terms of a liberal tradition which emphasises the uniqueness of the project and the taste of a particular client.

The second group consists of Aldo Rossi and the Italian neo-rationalists.

Rossi's work attempts to exclude all but the most general types and to avoid the circumstantial. Particular figures are used not because of the associations they arouse within a particular context or in relation to particular functions but because of their power to suggest archetypes—archetypes which are seen as belonging to the autonomous tradition of architecture itself. The 'ideal' nature of these signs belongs to an ideological framework which seeks to recover architecture as a collective experience.

But whatever their differences, both the neo-realists and the neo-rationalists refuse to reduce architecture to pure form. Both accept the figural tradition of architecture and its semantic connotations. How does this figural tradition reappear in their work? Certainly not as the total retrieval of a 'lost tradition' of rhetoric. Its recovery depends on a process in which fragments of an older language are reused. Moreover, the referents are not those of the original tradition, where they were a set of ideas belonging to the culture as a whole, of which the language of architecture was an integral part. What is being referred to is the architectural figure as such. What was once the form of a content is now the content itself. We are dealing with a sort of metalanguage—with an architecture which speaks of itself.

Left: House near New York. Charles W Moore with Richard B Oliver, 1976. South facade.

Right: House near New York. South elevation (top) and ground floor plan (bottom).

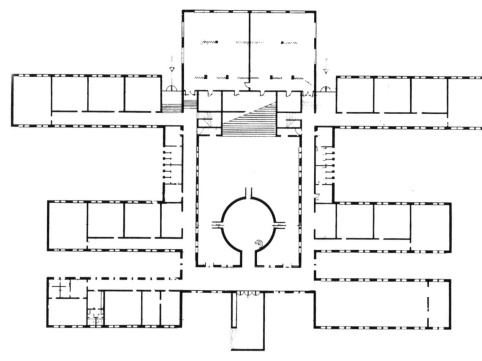

Left: Elementary School, Fagnano Olona. Aldo Rossi with G Braghieri and A Cantafora, 1972.

Right: Elementary School. Elevation of services block (top), plan of ground floor (bottom).

Opposite: Student Housing at Chieti. Aldo Rossi with G Braghieri and A Cantafora, 1976. Perspective.

Such an architecture is one in which 'fragments' of a tradition are re-appropriated. The fragmentary nature of the work of Moore and Venturi is self-evident. But it is not so clear in the case of Rossi because of his avowed intention to reconstruct an "entire" architecture. But that the term "fragment" can legitimately be applied to his work becomes clear when we see it in relation to technology. Precisely because of his claims to a sort of universality, this relation becomes critical. The works of Moore and Venturi make no such claims: they are produced within the pragmatic limits of any existing technology, and their commissions (small projects, mostly private houses) by nature avoid a conflict with 'advanced' technology. Rossi, on the other hand, in spite of the fact that in his writings he accepts the need to respond to technical evolution, implies in much of his work the avoidance of this imperative. What he seems to be saying is that the older techniques possessed more figural capacity. Historical figures were effective because they were pliable to a symbolic need which was a-historical. If we refer to a particular style, it is not just because the figures of this style have accumulated meanings in history which the memory retains (which would be pure associationalism) but because this style has unlocked a door to universal meanings. We can refer to it for the simple reason that the techniques by which it was achieved are still perfectly reasonable and practicable (even though they may not stretch our technical capacity to its limits). We must refer to it because any attempt to reach the 'degree zero' of figures (ie. to arrive at form) will automatically lead us back to the historical moments in which these universal meanings were made visible.

But when an entire architectural symbolism rests on the historical technology to which it was attached, it removes itself from certain characteristically modern means of production. It remains the vision of one man, possible to achieve in individual (and even very large) commissions because of the uneven development of building technology, but potentially thwarted where economy imposes its own pragmatic laws. What is 'rational' in society includes what is pragmatic. In the age of architectural rhetoric the demands of pragmatics were not in opposition to the demands of symbolic form; today they often are.

We must, therefore, see the return of the architectural figure as subject to the same laws of fragmentation which we see operating in all the other 'modern' arts—fragmentation in the works themselves, and also in terms of their social context. In excluding any reference to past styles, modern architecture took a similar position to that of 12-tone music in relation to the tonal system. But unlike music, modern architecture was polemically committed to the transformation of the 'real' world. If it has already abandoned this claim, it must accept a role similar to that of the other arts in relation to culture in general—a role in which 'possible' and 'virtual' worlds are created and in which the recovery of traditional meanings, through the use of the architectural figure, can never be integrated with a total system of representation, as it was in the rhetorical tradition.

1   I am using here the classification adopted by Mario Gandelsonas in "Neofunctionalism", *Oppositions 5*, Summer 1976, although the term "realist" is sufficiently vague to allow different interpretations, viz, that of Martin Steinmann and Bruno Reichlin, "Zum Problem der innerarchitektonischen Wirklichkeit", *Archithese,* no. 19, 1976, pp. 3–11. In his editorial for this issue Stanislaus von Moos draws attention to the disparity between these two definitions.
2   Baxandall, Michael, *Giotto and the Orators: Humanist Observers of Painting in Italy and the Discovery of Pictorial Composition, 1350–1450*, Oxford: Clarendon Press, 1971; and *Painting and Experience in Fifteenth Century Italy: A Primer in the Social History of Pictorial Style*, Oxford: Clarendon Press, 1972.
3   Alberti, Leone Battista, *On Painting,* New Haven, CT: Yale University Press, 1956.
4   Summerson, John, *Heavenly Mansions*, New York: WW Norton, 1963.
5   This assertion must be qualified; however, both Wrens' idea of geometry and Quatremère's of the 'type' were modifications of older symbolic traditions.
6   Jeanneret-Gris, Charles Edouard and Amedée Ozenfant, "Purisme", *l'Esprit Nouveau*, Paris 1920.

Notes 5 and 6 have been slightly altered from the original text in *Essays in Architectual Criticism*.

From *Bricolage* to Myth, or How to Put Humpty-Dumpty Together Again

First published in *Oppositions 12*, Spring 1978.

Criticism occupies the no-man's-land between enthusiasm and doubt, between poetic sympathy and analysis. Its purpose is not, except in rare cases, either to eulogise or condemn, and it can never grasp the essence of the work it discusses. It must try to get behind the work's apparent originality and expose its ideological framework without turning it into a mere tautology.

This applies particularly to the work of Michael Graves, with its appearance of being *sui generis* and its sensitivity to outside influences which it immediately absorbs into its own system. This essay, therefore, will attempt to discuss his work in terms of these broad contexts: the American tradition, the tradition of modern architecture, and the classical tradition. It is not suggested that a discussion of his work in these terms exhausts its meaning. It merely provides a rough-and-ready scaffold—a way of approaching the work obliquely.

Graves' work is so clearly related to the international Modern Movement that it is at first sight difficult to see in it any reference to purely American traditions. But some of the ways in which it differs (and differs profoundly) from European interpretations of the Modern Movement seem to be traceable to specifically American sources. Graves' apparent rejection of modern architecture as a social instrument—and his insistence that architecture communicates with individuals and not classes—does not operate in a social void. His work is made possible by social conditions, which are probably unique to the United States at the present moment (though they existed in Europe between 1890 and 1930). The chief of these is the existence of a type of client (whether institutional or private) who regards the architect not only as a technician who can solve functional problems, or satisfy a more or less pre-formulated and predictable set of desires, but also as an arbiter of taste. In this role he is called upon not only to decide matters of decorum; like the modern painter, he is expected to say something 'new', to propound a philosophy. No doubt this only applies to a minority of clients (and even these are probably often puzzled at the results), but their very existence explains how an architect as intensely 'private' as Michael Graves can insert himself within the institutionalised framework of society despite the absence of a clearly defined 'market'. If his work reflects a nostalgia for 'culture' which is characteristically American, and which, as Manfredo Tafuri has pointed out, can be traced back at least to the City Beautiful Movement, it depends on the existence of a type of client who has similar—though less well defined—aspirations.[1] In Europe the critique of a materialistic modern architecture has usually taken place under the banner of a betrayed populism. It is perhaps only in America that it could be launched in the name of intellectual culture. Certainly the importance in Graves' work of the French tradition—its assimilation, initially through the example of Le Corbusier, of the Beaux-Arts discipline of the plan, has its origins in a purely American tradition going back to Henry Hobson Richardson and Charles McKim.

But there also exists a technological condition peculiar to the United States which seems especially favourable to Graves' architecture and which is related to the social realm, insofar as it depends on the fact that most of his commissions are for private houses or additions. This is the balloon frame—a system of construction whose lightness and adaptability give the designer great freedom and allow him to treat structural matters in an *ad hoc* way. Without this form of construction an architectural language like that of Graves, which depends on a blurring of the distinction between what is real and what is virtual, and between structure and ornament, would hardly be conceivable. By using a system of construction which provides so few constraints, Graves is able to treat structure as a pure 'idea'. The regular grid, for example, which is such an important ingredient of his work, is relieved of those positivistic and utilitarian finalities which it had for Le Corbusier (eg. in the Maison Dom-ino). For Graves structure has become a pure metaphor, and he thus reverses the postulates of the Modern Movement in which the split between perception and calculation resulted in an emphasis on instrumentality.

The openness and transparency of Graves' houses are made possible by the use of the frame, while their complexity and ambiguity are made possible by the fact that the frame can be manipulated at will. These are qualities which his work shares with the Shingle Style, even more than with its Shavian counterpart, and seem characteristic of later nineteenth century American domestic architecture. In Europe the houses of the Modern Movement were relatively boxlike. The neo-Plasticist project of Theo van Doesburg and Mies van der Rohe were the exception, and it is these projects, as Vincent Scully has pointed out, which have such a striking resemblance to the houses of Frank Lloyd Wright, with their hovering planes and strung vertical accents. If the houses of Graves also have closer ties with neo-Plasticism than with the more typical houses of the European movement, it may be that, as in the case of Wright, there is a coincidence between

Fargo–Moorhead Cultural Center Bridge, Fargo, North Dakota, and Moorhead, Minnesota. Michael Graves, 1977–1978. South elevation.

Cubist spatial principles and an American tradition which, in its response to climate, its attitude toward nature, and its particular kind of sociability, creates an intermediate zone between the private realm of the house and the public realm of its environment. Not only the openness of the nineteenth century American house but also the proliferation of verandahs, porches, and bay windows, and the frequent placing of these on the diagonal suggest a parallel with the way Graves weaves secondary spaces in and out of the periphery of the cage, or superimposes a diagonal fragment on an otherwise orthogonal *parti*.

All this is perhaps to say no more than that the picturesque nineteenth century house is a precursor of a modern architecture which combines Cubist devices with an anecdotal and episodic elaboration of the programme. This should surprise us no more than similar connections in the other arts, for instance the fact that modern music took over from romantic music its rejection of classical symmetry and classical cadence.

In the context of contemporary American architecture, there are two figures with whom one is tempted to compare Graves. Among the architects of the New York Five, with whom Graves has become associated, it is Peter Eisenman with whom he seems to have the greatest affinity. In the mid-60s, when they worked together on a competition for a site located on the upper west side of Manhattan, they both shared the same influences—notably that of the Como School—and attempted to construct a new architectural language out of the basic vocabulary of the Modern Movement. But from the start they diverged— Eisenman toward a syntactic language of exclusion, Graves toward a language of allusion and metaphor. This semantic inclusiveness has led Graves to direct historical quotation, which now puts his work at the opposite pole from that of Eisenman. But in the work of both one finds an architecture in which the ideal completely dominates the pragmatic. It is true that Graves—in contrast to Eisenman—starts from the practical programme, the distribution of living spaces. But these quotidian considerations are merely a point of departure; they are immediately ritualised and turned into symbols—for example, the ritual of entry. With Eisenman the semantic dimension is conceptual and mathematical; with Graves it is sensuous and metaphysical.

Graves' later work might seem to bear some resemblance to (and even the imprint of) the work of Robert Venturi, with his parodistic use of traditional motifs. But this similarity is superficial. Graves shows no interest in what seems to be Venturi's chief concern: the problem of communication in modern democratic societies and of "architecture as mass medium". If Venturi wants to bridge the gap between "pop music and Vivaldi", Graves remains exclusively a 'serious' composer, for whom the possibility of communication is predicated on the existence—even in a fragmentary form—of a tradition of high architecture. This no doubt explains Venturi's preference for the romantic and populist overtones of vernacular architecture, as against that of Graves for the architecture of the classical and academic traditions.

Though the degree of dependence of Graves' work on American traditions is perhaps arguable, its affiliations with the Modern Movement are beyond dispute. The nostalgic quality of these affiliations has been stressed by other critics, but it should not be forgotten that Graves belongs to a generation for whom the Modern Movement still represented all that was vital and creative in architecture. To return to the 1920s and Le Corbusier was not an eclectic choice but a return to sources. What was new about this return was its rejection of functionalism and its claim that architecture had never exploited the formal and semantic possibilities of modernism as the other arts had. There was also the conviction that the 'new tradition' of avant-garde art constituted a historical development from which it was impossible to turn back.

It is certainly true that the development of the avant-garde marks a radical break with the form of artistic language which existed until the latter part of the nineteenth century. Traditionally, language was always thought of as describing something outside itself, in the 'real' world. The difference between natural language (considered as an instrument rather than a poetics) and artistic languages was merely that in the latter the form was an integral part of the message—the 'how' was as important as the 'what'. At whatever date we put the moment when the epistemological foundations of this 'rhetorical' world began to disintegrate, it was not until the end of the nineteenth century, and in the context of avant-garde art, that the content of a work began to become indistinguishable from its form. External reality was no longer seen as a *donnée* with its own preordained meanings but as a series of fragments, essentially enigmatic, whose meanings depended on how they were formally related or juxtaposed by the artist.

In modern architecture this process took the form of demolishing the traditional meanings associated with function. But these were replaced by another set of functional meanings, and architecture was still seen in terms of a functional programme which was translated, as directly as possible, into forms. In the work of both Graves and Eisenman, this linear relation between content and form has been rejected. Function has been absorbed into form. 'Functional' meanings still exist, but they no longer constitute a prior condition or derive their nourishment from a pragmatic level of operation. They are reconstructed on the basis of being a pure work of art with its own internally consistent laws.

By returning to the sources of modern architecture, Graves attempted to open up a seam which had never been fully exploited, as it had been in Cubist painting. In his work, the elements of *techné* and those of architecture (windows, walls, columns) are isolated and recombined in a way which allows new metonymic and metaphoric interpretations to be made. At the same time, rhythms, symmetries, perspectives, and diminutions are exploited in a way which suggests the need, in discussing his work, for a descriptive vocabulary such as existed in the Beaux-Arts tradition, and still exists in musical criticism, but which is generally lacking in modern architectural discourse.

Within this process no semantic distinction exists between functions and forms. They reinforce each other to produce meanings which extend in an unbroken chain from the most habitual and redundant to the most complex and information-laden. To respond to Michael Graves' architecture, it is essential to understand the 'reduction' which is involved in such a process, for it is this which makes his work specifically 'modern'. It involves the dismantling of the preconceptions which would allow one to have a ready-made idea of what a 'house' is and insists that the observer or user carry out a reconstruction of the object. Graves' elementarism is related both to the architecture of the Modern Movement and to modern art in general. It is tied to an elementarisation resulting from industrialisation and the disappearance of craft, and it strives for the condition of the *tabula rasa*, the primal statement.

The reconstruction of the object, made necessary by this process of analysis and reduction, involves the use of codes which are themselves meaningful and internally coherent. But what interests Graves is not the way in which these syntactically organised and semantically loaded elements already form a system whose meaning has been ideologically internalised. For him all the elements must be reduced to the same condition of "raw material". They have become dehistoricised and acquired "potentiality", and must be reconstructed consciously as a "structure". He is interested in how such a structure works perceptually as the product of conflicts and tensions in the psyche of the individual. He demonstrates the *process* by which meanings are generated, and this leads him to a language whose articulation depends on oppositions, fragmentation, and the visual pun.

In this process of reduction Graves does not attempt (as Peter Eisenman does) to strip the elements of their connotations. Columns, openings, spaces, all retain their qualities of body image and the meanings which have accumulated around them. Not only do the basic architectonic elements have meanings which relate to their functions, but their very isolation allows them to become metaphors. There is, indeed, a danger that these metaphors may remain private and incommunicable, and in his earlier work this danger is increased because of the reliance on relatively abstract forms. Where meanings are clear in his earlier work, they tend to be those which have already become established in modern architecture.

The most fundamental source of Graves' work (and it is this which links him with the other members of the so-called New York Five) is Le Corbusier. In Le Corbusier's work there is always a tension between the figurations and symmetries of the French classical tradition and the infinite improvisations which are demanded by modern life and which are made possible by the neutral grid. It is this tension which Graves exploits. But he superimposes on this Corbusian system—whose chief vehicle is the "free plan"—an open three-dimensional cage which was seldom used by Le Corbusier. The vertical planes of Graves' work are closely related to the work of Giuseppe Terragni—to such buildings as the Casa del Fascio and the Asile Infantile at Como, with their open structural cage, their delicate layering of structural planes, and their frequent absorption of the frame within the wall surface. The transparency of the cage enables Graves to provide an adumbration of the building's limits without destroying the flow of space between inside and outside. The dialectic between solid and planar elements and the structural grid becomes a basic architectural theme, not only in plan but as perceived in three dimensions, and dominates the whole plastic organisation in a way which it seldom does in the work of Le Corbusier.

Apart from these purely architectural sources, Graves' work is directly related to Cubist and Purist painting. His work as a painter is closer to his architecture than Le Corbusier's was to his. For Le Corbusier painting provided a lyrical outlet to some extent constrained by the logical and systematic researches of the architect, but Graves develops parallel themes in both painting and architecture, among which one finds the typically Cubist notion of a world built out of fragments, related to each other not according to the logic of the perceived world, but according to the laws of pictorial construction. His buildings are, as it were, projections into real three-dimensional space of a shallow pictorial space, and his spaces are frequently made up of planes which create an impression of Renaissance perspective or of successive planes of the Baroque theatre.

Although the dominance of the three-dimensional frame suggests, as in neo-Plasticism, the parity between all three dimensions, in Graves' work the plan is still thought of as possessing figural qualities which actually generate the vertical and spatial configurations, in the manner of Le Corbusier and the Beaux-Arts. It is in the development of the plan that the influence of his painting can be felt most strongly. The paintings suggest collages built up out of fragments which create diagonal fault lines or, as if with torn paper, trembling profiles suggestive of the edges of bodies. These elements reappear on his plans and create a nervous interplay of fragmentary planes, a web of countervailing spatial pressures inflected with slow curves or overlaid with diagonal figures.

Unlike the plans of Le Corbusier, with their muscular, vertebral sense of order, Graves' plans tend to be dispersed and episodic and often resemble, perhaps fortuitously, the plan of Pierre Chareau's Maison de Verre, with its multiple centres, complex spatial subdivisions, and gentle inflections. There is, in Graves' plans, a sense of almost endless elaboration and half-statement, every function being a clue for syntactic complexity or metaphorical qualification.

This elaboration is not arbitrary; it comes from an extreme sensitivity to context, and this is perhaps its chief difference from the tradition of the Modern Movement with its attempt to create architectural types of a new order in polemical contrast to the existing built environment. I have said that many of Graves' projects are additions. These additions draw attention to their difference from the existing

Above: Plan types. Le Corbusier and Pierre Jeanneret, 1910–1929.
© FLC / ADAGP, Paris and DACS, London 2009

Opposite: Hanselmann House, Fort Wayne, Indiana. Michael Graves, 1967. Axonometric.

buildings, but they do not ignore them. The old house is considered as a fragment which it is possible to extend and qualify in a way unforeseen in the original. In the Benacerraf House, for example, the wall separating the original house and the extension is removed, and the cage of the addition penetrates into the living spaces of the existing house to form a transparent veil which transforms the original space and overlays it with a new spatial meaning.

But sensitivity to context is equally apparent in completely new structures. The houses respond to the natural environment, which itself is modified by the building. The more typical houses of the Modern Movement tended to respond to the gross features of the environment (particularly orientation) by setting up elementary oppositions, for example, that between an open side which was fully glazed and a closed side which was solid. Graves uses this basic opposition as a compositional point, as can be seen in the Hanselmann House of 1965, where the theme open/closed is almost obsessively stated and is reinforced by a ritualistic frontalisation and a displacement of the front facade to form an additional plane of entry. But in other works, for instance the Snyderman House of 1969, the opposition closed/open is used with greater subtlety and is qualified by a number of conflicting contextual demands. The 'closed' surface is punctured by a variety of openings, and its function as a limiting plane is actually enhanced by its greater transparency. The way in which this and other diagrammatic expressions of opposition are modified in the design process is illustrated by comparing the sketches for the Snyderman House with the final design. In the early sketches the plan consists of two equal axes at right angles, the east–west axis being bounded on the west by a solid wall punctured by only one opening and on the east by an open surface with fragmentary obstructions. As the design progresses these ideas are retained but are overlaid with counterstatements. The west wall becomes a perforated screen. At the same time the east–west axis is strengthened by a *caesura* in the structural grid, while the north–south axis is suppressed. A diagonal is introduced by the erosion of the southeast corner and the skewing of the second floor accommodation—a diagonal which is reinforced by raising the south and east facades to three storeys. These moves suggest entry from the southeast corner and act in contrapuntal opposition to the plan's biaxial symmetry. The house is no longer a statement of simple oppositions but an overlay of several *different* oppositions, each element separately inviting contradictory interpretations.

Other ways in which Graves' buildings differ from more orthodox modern buildings can be seen by analysing the Gunwyn office conversion at Princeton of 1972. The elements used in this design are those which one might expect to find in a typical 'systems approach' building of the West Coast—tubular steel columns, exposed I-beams, standard lighting tracks, and office furniture. The basic imagery is industrial, efficient, smooth.

But there is another language superimposed on this. Whereas, according to functionalist practice, the systems should be logically independent, Graves (starting, as always, from Le Corbusier's poetic use of mechanical forms but going further into a world of free fantasy) deliberately overlaps them to produce ambiguities which gently subvert their primary and unequivocal meanings and give rise to less obvious correspondences.

The space of the office is complex, with various penetrations through three storeys. A hatch to the second floor office projects over one of these voids. Its wafer thin worktop is carried on a bracket attached to the column on the *opposite* side of the void, which thus reaches out to receive an unexpected but hardly onerous burden and at the same time provides the hatch with a frame which it has borrowed from the nearby tubular balustrade at floor level. Similar ambiguities are created when the glass brick wall to the office is prized open and an I-beam inserted to support its upper half. This I-beam, seen from alongside the office, appears as a jagged fragment mysteriously projecting from a column. Most of the columns are circular, but when they occur in a wall they turn into pilasters and merge

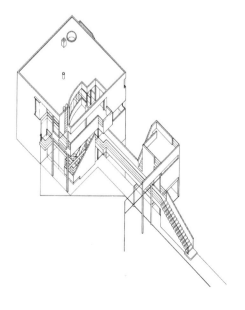

with the wall surface above. All these fragments and transpositions have a local, internal logic of their own. Their shock effect is a result of the way they undermine expected hierarchies. The fragments are differentiated by means of colour, for the most part brilliant, but intermixed with grass greens, sky blues and flesh pinks. Just as these colours suggest elements of nature, so does the metaphorical play of functional elements have anthropomorphic, and sometimes surreal, overtones relating mechanical functions to our own bodies and making us question reality.

Graves' buildings, in the phase of his work most directly influenced by the Modern Movement, consist of a large number of variations on a limited number of themes. The most persistent idea is that of the open frame defining a continuous space partially interrupted by planes and solids. Not only is horizontal space continuous but vertical penetrations occur at crucial points to create three-dimensional continuity. Through this space the frame is threaded, creating a dialectic between a rational *a priori* order and a circumstantial, sensuous, and complex plastic order. This is in essence the "free plan" of Le Corbusier, but developed with greater complexity in a repetition, transformation, and interweaving of formal themes reminiscent of musical structure. Tensions develop around the periphery of the building, and there is a maximum exploitation, by means of layered screenings and shallow recessions, of the plane of the facade— an intense moment of transition between the 'profane' world outside the house and the 'sacred' world inside.

Graves' work cannot be called "classical" in any strict sense. But his thought is permeated with a kind of eighteenth century deism and a belief that architecture is a perennial symbolic language, whose origins lie in nature and our response to nature. He finds support for these views in such modern writers as Geoffrey Scott and Mircea Eliade. The frequent use in his writings of the words "sacred" and "profane" shows that he regards architecture as a secular religion which is in some sense revelatory.

In his earlier work the symbolic images and metaphors are very generalised and are drawn from a repertoire of abstract forms chiefly derived from Le Corbusier and Terragni. This language is autonomous within an architectural tradition and operates through the use of certain graphic codes, the most important of which is the plan. But during the early 1970s Graves seems to have become dissatisfied with the expressive possibilities of this language and, above all, with the plan as an abstraction, and this dissatisfaction coincides with a radical change of style. The attitude behind it is expressed in the following programme notes for a student project: "The design of a guest house addition to an existing villa is given… to focus the students' attention on the perceptual elements of a building, the wall surfaces, and the spaces they describe…. The plan is seen as a conceptual tool, a two-dimensional diagram notational device, with limited capacity to express the perceptual elements which exist in three-dimensional space."[2]

Graves' buildings have always laid stress on these "perceptual elements"—especially on the function of the plane as a method of stratifying space, and as symbolic of the spaces which it defines or conceals. But in his earlier projects the solid and planar elements in themselves were reduced to the degree zero of expressiveness, in accordance with the functionalist precept of minimum interference with the industrial product as 'ready-made'. In his more recent work these elements have begun to be semantically elaborated. They are no longer the minimal ciphers which go to form a rich metonymy; they become overlaid with meanings belonging to the architectural tradition. Columns develop shafts and capitals; openings are qualified with architraves and pediments; wall surfaces become ornamented. A new dimension of purely architectural metaphor is added to the functionalist and natural metaphors of his earlier work.

It is possible that these ideas developed initially less from a process of deduction than from particular design problems. The use of figural elements seems, for example, to be connected with his habit of extracting the maximum of meaning from a given context. In the Claghorn House of 1974—which seems a pivotal work—the humble motif of a chair rail with bolection moldings is used as a way of linking the new to the old. This seems to have been suggested by the fact that the existing house had few spatial qualities but a strong nineteenth century flavour. This carrying through of motifs is similar to the use of the frame in the Benacerraf House. But here the process is reversed. Instead of the new extending its language back into the old, the thematics of the old are reused in the new. As if in sympathy with this, the outside of the addition has a heavily figural quality, with a broken pediment and a wall trellis, turning what would have been an inconsequential statement into one which is dense with parabolic meanings. At the same time, sombre colours echoing the period taste of the old house replace the clear colours of the earlier work.

At about the same time, architraves and other figural elements appear in Graves' paintings, and these underline the fact that the change to a figurative, ornamental architecture has not altered his method of composition with its dependence on collage. It is like the change from Analytical to Synthetic Cubism. Traditional figures are introduced as quotations and fragments, as were the functionalist motifs of the earlier work. Because these figures already exist in our memory, and because they are ornamental and not structural, they can be transposed, split up, inverted or distorted without losing their original meanings. The chief sources of this 'metalanguage' are Italian Mannerism, eighteenth century Romantic classicism, and the later Beaux-Arts. But in developing a language of ornament which is simple and allows for repetition, Graves has recourse to the language of Art Deco—that 'debased' style which tried to unite the more decorative aspects of Cubism with a remembered tradition of architectural ornament.

In Graves' earlier buildings the fundamental element is the frame or grid, creating a Cartesian field in which the planes and volumes locate themselves. It is impossible, in such a system, for the wall to develop any density; its function is simply to modulate space. In his more recent work the wall—or the wall

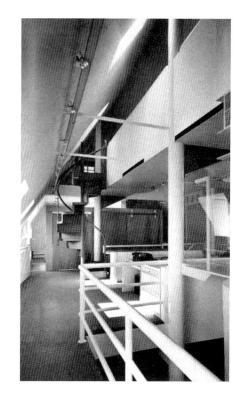

Opposite: Synderman House. South facade.

Above: Investment Office, Gunwyn Ventures, Princeton, New Jersey. Michael Graves, 1972. Second floor.

fragment—takes the place of the frame as the main organising element. Two consequences follow from this. First, the space is no longer continuous but is made up of discrete spatial figures bounded by walls or colonnades. The walls develop thickness, and the negative, solid spaces are read as *poché*. Figural space is seen as carved out of solid mass. During the preliminary stages of the design, the plan is allowed to suggest the spatial composition independently of its three-dimensional consequences; thus, in the Crooks House, the early sketches show no distinction between house walls and garden hedges; according to the code of the plan, they both define space in terms of void and solid, figure and *poché*. But this results in a metaphorical relationship between house and garden; the topiary defines internal spaces, whose 'ceiling' is the sky. We see here that ambiguity between fully enclosed space and semi-enclosed space which has always been a feature in Graves' buildings. The second consequence of the new importance given to the wall is that the shallow layering of space in the frontal plane of the building, which was previously created by parallel and separate planes suspended in the cage, is now flattened onto the wall surface itself. The wall becomes a bas-relief with layers of ornament which are built up or peeled away. Fragments of architectural motifs are assembled to create a balanced asymmetrical whole.

The massive architectural elements which occur on the facade are frequently distorted and transposed. Thus, in the studies for the Plocek House, several simultaneous interpretations of the same figures are invited. The main entry is monumentalised by the presence of two giant columns supporting a flat arch. But this monumentality is subverted by contradictions. The traditional flat arch with voussoirs is established but subjected to a figure-ground reversal by the removal of the keystone. The expected pyramidal composition is reversed; the centre is a void between the masses on either side, which become a 'split pair'. The voussoirs are read both in their normal sense, as radiating wedges on a flat plane, and as the receding lines of a *trompe l'oeil* perspective. The columns are structurally redundant in voussoir construction. Their role as pylons constricting and guarding the entrance is reinforced by the absence of capitals and the insertion of an architrave between them and the arch. Such transformations can be seen as an extension of the Mannerist permutation of a repertoire of figures, whereby two systems of meaning are superimposed, and their paradigmatic relations are stated explicitly in the same object, eg, in the 'Gibbs surround'.

In Graves' earlier work metonymic and metaphoric meanings had to be created by the relationship between elements which were themselves relatively mute. As soon as established architectural figures become the basic counters, relationships are established, not between irreducible forms but between the semantic contents existing in the figures. His buildings now become *bricolages* of recognisable figures complete with their historical connotations. For example, on the bridge of the Fargo-Moorhead Cultural Center project, there is an overt reference to Ledoux's barrel-shaped "House for the Surveyors of the River Loue" in the Saline de Chaux, and this image is conflated with a frozen waterfall reminiscent of the ornamental *urnes á congélation* on the main gate. But it is the way in which Ledoux has reduced the classical repertoire to pure geometrical figure which enables his forms to release primary and archetypal sensations. The historical reference by itself is not enough. Graves' work therefore depends on eighteenth century sensationalist theory, and not on pure historical associations.

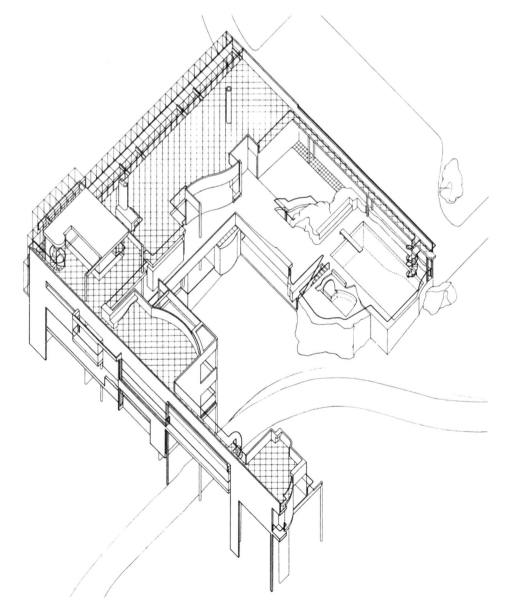

Opposite: Claghorn House, Princeton, New Jersey. Michael Graves, 1974. View of addition from the garden.

Left: Rockefeller House, Pocantico Hills, New York. Michael Graves, 1969. Axonometric.

Right: Urne à congélation, Porte de la Saline. Claude–Nicolas Ledoux, 1773–1779.

Perhaps the most important single aspect of Graves' work lies in the attitude toward nature which it reflects. There is, in his work, a continual dialectic between architecture as the product of reason, setting itself against nature, and architecture as a metaphor for nature. The drama of this dialectic is played out in the architecture itself. The open structure characteristic of his earlier work allows the virtual space of the building to be penetrated by outside space and frames the natural landscape. Thus defined by its structural elements, the building remains incomplete, as if arrested in the process of marking out a habitable space. References to the primitive act of building are filtered through the language of Cubism and advanced technology (itself a metaphor since the actual technology is mostly preindustrial). The round column, isolated against the sky, suggests the tree as primordial building material; free-form profiles either in plan or (as in the Benacerraf House) in elevation suggest the presence of nature within the man-made world of the building. There are references to a domesticated nature, as in the perforated steel beams with their suggestions of pergolas. An all-pervading nature is also evoked by the association of colours with the primary aspects of nature—sky, earth, water, and vegetation. The earlier buildings recall both conservatories and bowers or arbors, which protect man from nature by means of nature's own materials.

In the later work, Graves' classicist preferences are for garden structures (topiary, trellises) or for those architectural motifs which are associated with a mythologised nature—rustication, grottos, cascades, ruins. The fragmentation of the buildings suggests the presence of natural obstacles to conceptual completeness and the inability of man to establish order in the face of Time and Chance. One has the impression of an arcadia which is not only irretrievable but also somehow flawed.

These are the qualities which unite the two phases of Michael Graves' work, and which allow him to use the language of Cubism or of the classical tradition to re-create an architecture out of its primordial elements, to offer a new and intense interpretation of architecture itself and of man's cultural predicament in relation to nature.

Graves' work is a meditation on architecture. This is to say much more than it is concerned exclusively with the aesthetic. Such a concern is perfectly compatible with the problem of construction, which, in the case of a Le Corbusier or a Mies, is the *sine qua non* of aesthetic choice and is based on the (aesthetic) principle of economy of means. With Graves this problem is excluded; architectural meaning withdraws into the realm of 'pure visibility'; the substance of the building does not form a part of the ideal world imagined by the architect. Structure becomes a pure representation. The objective conditions of building and its subjective effect are now finally separated. Architecture is created and sustained in the psyche, and its legitimate boundaries are established by voluntary judgment acting on an imagination nourished by history.

The difference between these two systems of representation, and the different status which they attribute to the 'real,' can be seen if we compare two works by an engineer—Gustave Eiffel. The Tower and the Statue of Liberty represent. The two poles toward which structure gravitates at the end of the nineteenth century. In the first case, structure is the sufficient and necessary condition of meaning; in the second, the structure is purely 'enabling' and plays no part in the object as a sign. So long as one accepts the traditional distinction between sculpture and architecture the paradoxical relation between these two attitudes remains obscured. But it becomes apparent the moment one sees sculpture and architecture as two modes of representation, where meanings are derived either from the traditional subject of sculpture—the human form—or from architecture. Both the human form and its 'house' are perceived as cultural 'traces', not as natural and objective 'referents'. If architecture becomes the subject of representation, this representation necessarily includes the memory of the "problem" of structure.

Benacerraf House. Garden facade.

This system of representation is the exact opposite of the 'classical' process by which the ephemeral was translated into the durable, according to which durability as such was a value and materiality a symbol of the transcendental. With the instrumentalisation of structure, the mythic is rechanneled and, in the Modern Movement, takes up its abode in instrumentality itself. In the architecture of Michael Graves, the alternative route is taken. The myth becomes pure myth, recognised as such, and the architectural sign floats in the dematerialised world of *Gestalt*, and the dehistoricised world of memory and association.

1 "'European Graffiti.' Five x Five = Twenty-five", *Oppositions 5*, Summer 1976, p. 37.
2 Graves, Michael and Carol Constant, "The Swedish Connection", *Journal of Architectural Education*, September 1975.

PART II 1980–1989

Three Kinds of Historicism

First published in *Architectural Design* 53, 9/10, 1983.

The title of this essay is simply the starting point for an attempt to clarify the confusion that surrounds the word "historicism" in modern architectural criticism, and through this to throw some new light on the present situation in architecture in which a new consciousness of history has replaced the anti-historical bias of the early Modern Movement.

Dictionary definitions (and general usage) suggest that there are three interpretations of historicism: the theory that all socio-cultural phenomena are historically determined and that all truths are relative; a concern for the institutions and traditions of the past and the use of historical forms. The word historicism therefore can be applied to three quite separate objects: the first is a theory of history; the second, an attitude; the third, an artistic practice. There is no guarantee that the three have anything in common. I will investigate them to see how, if at all, they *are* related and then to see what light they throw on the phenomenon sometimes referred to as the *neo-avant-garde*.

The idea that values change and develop with historical time is by now so ingrained in common wisdom that it is difficult to imagine a different point of view. Yet the idea is, historically speaking, of fairly recent origin. It began to take shape in Europe as a whole in the seventeenth century, but was not given a constant philosophical or historiographic formulation until the rise of the Romantic Movement in Germany in the late eighteenth century. The word historicism, as it applies to our first definition, comes from the German word *historismus*. It used to be translated as historism, but, probably under the influence of Benedetto Croce, was changed to historicism—from the Italian *storicismo*—in the early years of this century.

In the German movement, historicism was connected with idealism and neo-Platonism. But the 'Idea' had connotations different from those associated with the classical thought of the seventeenth and eighteenth centuries. According to classical thought, cultural values derived from natural law. Indeed, the value of history for historians like David Hume and Montesquieu was that it provided evidence for the existence of this natural law. It was necessary, when studying history, to strip away the inessential and accidental and to expose the essential and universal. Through the study of history one learned with David Hume that "human nature was always and everywhere the same". It followed from this that what was of value in the cultural products of this human nature—art and architecture, for example—was equally fixed. Architecture, no less than painting, was an imitation of Nature through the intuition of her underlying laws. History, as the story of the contingent, merely had the effect of obscuring these laws. It is true that the rise of empirical science in the seventeenth century led certain theorists to question the immutable laws of architecture enshrined in the writings of Vitruvius (for instance Claude Perrault went so far as to say that the rules of proportion and the orders owed their authority to custom), but this was not a universally held view. The majority of architects and theorists of the seventeenth century still held the view that good architecture obeyed immutable natural laws. Even Laugier, writing at a time when the notion of taste had already undermined the classical certainties, claimed that Perrault was prompted by the spirit of contrariness and that the rules of architecture could be deduced from a few self-evident axioms based on our observation of nature. The best architecture was that which was close to Nature, and that which was closest to Nature could be found in the buildings of the Ancients—though sometimes even they had been mistaken, in which case archaeology had to be supplemented with reason.

The idealism of the neo-classical view of architecture was therefore absolutist and depended on a combination of authority, natural law and reason. Although in many ways the doctrines of neo-classicism differed from those of the Renaissance, the two held that the values of architecture referred to fixed laws, exemplified in Greco-Roman buildings.

This historicist view disputed the epistemology on which this view of architecture depended and gave an entirely different interpretation of the Ideal. According to historicism, the classical conception of a fixed and immutable ideal was, in fact, a false realism; it tried to apply to the works of man the same objective standards that it applied to the natural world as a whole. But man belonged to a different category from that of inorganic or organic nature. Man and his institutions could be studied only in relation to the context of their historical development. The individual and the social institutions he constructed were governed by a vital, genetic principle, not by fixed and eternal laws. Human reason was not a faithful reflection of abstract truths; it was the rationalisation of social customs and institutions, which had evolved slowly and which varied from place to place and from one time to another. The ideal was therefore an aim that emerged from historical experience and contingency. Although it might have been necessary to postulate an ideal that would be ultimately the same for all cultures, it could not be rationally grasped. We could give it only the names that belonged to the values of a local culture at its particular stage of development. Every culture therefore contained a mixture of truth and falsehood when measured against the ideal; equally, each culture could adhere only to its own notion of the true and the false, through values that were immanent in particular social and institutional forms.

In this view, society and its institutions were analogous to the individual. The individual can be defined only in terms unique to himself. Though he may be motivated by what he and his society see as objective norms of belief and conduct, his own essence cannot be reduced to these norms; it is constituted by the contingent factors of his birth and is subject to a unique development. The value of his life cannot be defined in a way that excludes his individuality. It is the same with societies, cultures and states; they develop according to organic laws which they have internalised in their structure. In them, truth cannot be separated from destiny.

Based on a new notion of history, this view found its chief expression in the field of historiography. The aim of the historian became to research into the past of a particular society for its own sake, not in order to confirm *a priori* principles and provide exemplars, as had been the case with the English and French historians of the eighteenth century. This new project was undertaken in the German speaking countries in reaction against the French rationalism that had dominated European thought for two centuries, and it coincided with the rise of German national consciousness. In the work of Leopold von Ranke, the first great historian of this school, the writing of history is characterised by two equally important tendencies: the objective and exhaustive examination of facts, and the attempt to penetrate the essential spirit of the country or period being studied. The dialectic between these two aims (which one might call the positivist and the idealist) had already been stated clearly by Wilhelm von Humboldt in his famous essay "On the Historian's Task" of 1821. According to von Humboldt, the events of history are given purpose and structure by a hidden spirit or idea, just as the idea or form is hidden in the infinitely variable forms of the visible world. It is the historian's task to reveal the idea beneath the empirical surface of historical events, just as it is the artist's task to reveal the ideal beneath the accidental appearance of bodies. At the same time, the idea can become apparent only through the detailed study of these events. Any imposition on history of an *a priori* purpose will inevitably distort *reality*, and it is this reality that is the object of historical study.

An ideal that emerges from particular historical events entails a relativising of cultures, aspects of the ideal to be revealed will differ from case to case; and this relativising of the historical view is obviously connected in some way with eclecticism in the practice of art and architecture. Yet eclecticism did not, in itself, result necessarily in a doctrine of relativism. It was the product of an interest in history which developed in the early eighteenth century—a phenomenon of the history of taste before it became connected with German historical theory. Indeed, returning to an architecture based on nature—a notion so foreign to the spirit of historicism—was itself one of the products of this new interest in, and attitude toward, history.

The attitude toward history during the eighteenth century was, in fundamental ways, different from that of the Renaissance. The Renaissance had a strong faith in its contemporary world. In returning to classical modes, it picked up the threads of a world that was more modern than recent Medieval culture. In the eighteenth century, on the contrary, the return to classicism was always accompanied by elements of poetic reverie, nostalgia, and a sense of irretrievable loss. Within the context of this type of historical consciousness, eclecticism took two forms which at first might seem incompatible. On the one hand, different styles could exist side by side, as when one finds a classical temple next to a Gothic ruin at Stowe. On the other hand, one style could come to stand for a dominant moral idea and be connected with an idea of social reform. This happens, for example, in the second half of the eighteenth century in France, when the desire to reform society initiates a return to austere classical forms, such as one finds in the architecture of Ledoux or the paintings of David. What is common to both forms of eclecticism is a strong feeling for the past, an awareness of the passage of historical time, and the ability of past styles to suggest certain poetic or moral ideas. The same motif can be the expression of private taste and the symbol of public morality. Robert Rosenblum gives the example of the Doric temple front forming the entrance to a cave, which was a folly in the garden of the banker Claude Bernard Saint-James before it became an emblem of revolution in a pageant at Lyon some years later.[1]

Eclecticism depends on the power of historical styles to become the emblems of ideas associated with the cultures that produced them. No doubt this relationship

Above: The Temple of Ancient Virtue at Stowe, near which stood a Gothic ruin.

Opposite top: Claude-Nicolas Ledoux, House of a Milliner 1773–1779. From *L'Architecture considérée sous le rapport de l'art, des moeurs et de la legislation*, 1804.

Opposite bottom: Jacques-Louis David, *Lictors Returning to Brutus the Bodies of His Sons,* 1789.

first made itself felt in the Renaissance, but by the late eighteenth century historical knowledge had vastly extended its range of cultural models. An interest in Gothic architecture and in the architecture of the orient existed alongside the classical tradition, which was itself augmented by the discovery of Greek architecture. The idea of a return to a strict and primitive classicism based on *a priori* principles and natural law was one aspect of a new situation giving rise to the new possibility of choice. Choice implies a standard of taste and a decision as to the correct norm—whether this norm is based on a relative scale or on an absolute standard.

Returning to our definition, we see that the "concern for the institutions of the past" and "the use of historical forms" belong to a broader category of historical phenomena than the historicist theory that "all socio-cultural phenomena are historically determined". It was not until the historicist theory was formulated that the idea of the relativism of culture values became an issue. The theory

made it impossible, in principle, to favour one style over another, since each style was organically related to a particular spatio-temporal culture and could not be judged except on its own terms. Yet historicist thought was not able to accept all that its theory implied. The historian Friedrich Meinecke pointed out that there were two ways in which historicism attempted to avoid the implications of relativism: by setting up one period as a paradigm and by what he called the "flight into the future".[2]

Representing a historical period as a paradigm would seem contrary to the principles of historicism and, in doing so, historical thought was clearly reverting to eclectic practice. But there was a difference: eclecticism had never severed completely its connections with the classical tradition. It had merely qualified this tradition with examples from other styles, either using these styles to give variety to classical themes or using them to purify the notion of classicism itself—as in the case of Gothic and Greek architecture. With romanticism and historicism, the break from classicism was complete. The style now set up as paradigmatic was Gothic, since Gothic represented not just a particular set of poetic associations, but a type of 'organic' society. Here we see a coincidence between positivism and historicism similar to that which I have noted already in Leopold von Ranke. For instance, in seeking the essence of Gothic architecture, Viollet-le-Duc reduced it to a set of instrumental principles that provided a dynamic model for contemporary practice.

The other method by which historicism tried to overcome relativism—the flight into the future—depended upon a different set of ideas. One of the essential notions of historicism was, as I have said, the idea of development. Not only were various cultures the result of geographical and temporal displacement, not only were cultures unique and irreducible to a single set of principles, but they were also subject to a law of growth and change. The notion of genetic development was essential. Without it, the various guises in which an ideal appeared in history would be entirely random and arbitrary, since there was no longer any absolute ideal against which to measure them. It was necessary to replace the notion of a fixed ideal with that of a *potential* ideal, which historical events were *leading up to*. Carried to its extreme, this view led to the idea of history as a teleological

process, in which all historical events were determined by final causes. History was now oriented toward an apocalyptic future and no longer toward a normative past. It was the philosophers of historicism, particularly Hegel, who stressed in this way the determinism of history, not the historians themselves. Indeed, von Ranke, (following von Humboldt) warned against the tendency of philosophy to schematise history by resorting to final causes. To him this was just as unacceptable as the classical notion of natural law because it denied what to the historians was the basis of historical development—the spiritual independence of the historical subject and the operation of free will in history.

Hegelian idealism, with its emphasis on historical teleology, replaced the will of the historical subject with the suprapersonal will of history itself. The ideal was not seen as informing the individual protagonists of history, as von Humboldt and von Ranke taught it; it constituted an implacable historical will, of which the historical subject was the unconscious agent.

The Hegelian notion of historical determinism, however much it was misunderstood, had a profound influence on the framework of thought characteristic

Opposite: Claude-Louis Chatelet, Le Rocher, Folie Saint-James Neuilly.

Above: Claude Couchet , *Design for a Revolutionary Pageant*, 1790.

of the artistic avant-garde in the late nineteenth century and early twentieth centuries.[3] Art and architecture could fulfil their historical destinies only by turning their backs on tradition. Only by looking toward the future could they be faithful to the spirit of history and give expression in their works to the spirit of their age. In architecture this meant the continual creation of new forms under the impulse of social and technological development, and the symbolic representation of society through these forms. Historians of the Modern Movement, such as Sigfried Giedion, Nikolaus Pevsner and Reyner Banham, have tended to emphasise this developmental aspect of the avant-garde.

But this mode of thought was not the only ingredient of the twentieth century avant-garde. First, there was what Philippe Junod, in his book *Transparence et opacité* has called "gnosiological idealism", whose principle theoretician was the nineteenth century philosopher Conrad Fiedler.[4] Growing out of the general atmosphere of the historicist tradition, this theory systematically sought to exclude from artistic creation the last traces of the idea of *imitation*. It rejected the notion that the work of art is a mirror in which one sees something else. Hegel himself was the principal victim of this radical idealism, since he held the view that the work of art was a reflection of an idea external to itself. The notion of the "opacity" of the work of art was developed further by the Russian formalists of the 1920s, and it became an essential component of avant-garde thinking.

Secondly, at the opposite extreme, there was in modernism the idea of natural law and a return to the basic principles of artistic form, which was close to the primitive neo-classicism of the Enlightenment. The tension between this and historicism is particularly noticeable in the writings and buildings of Le Corbusier.

It is not these two aspects of modernism that critics have attacked, but rather the idea of historical determinism. They have correctly pointed out that a blind faith in the future has the effect of handing over control of the architectural environment to market forces and their bureaucratic representatives. A movement that started as the symbolic representation of utopia has ended by becoming a tool of everyday economic practice. Critics have also shown (and equally correctly) that the systematic proscription of history as a source of architectural values cannot be sustained once the initial utopian impetus of modernism has been lost.

What these 'postmodernist' critics have been unable to establish is a theory of history that will give a firm basis for this newfound historical consciousness. Because their attack has been restricted mostly to two aspects of modernism—historical determinism and historical amnesia—all they have been able to propose is the reversal of these two ideas: history is not absolutely determined; the acceptance of tradition, *in some form*, is the condition of architectural meaning. These two propositions lack a systematic and legitimate basis of their own.

The fact that history cannot be considered as determined and teleological in any crude sense leaves open to question the relation between the historicity of all cultural production, on the other hand, and the cumulative and normative nature of cultural values on the other. We can hardly expect to return to a classical interpretation of history in which a universal natural law is an *a priori* against which one measures all cultural phenomena. One of the chief reasons why this would be inconceivable is that today we have a different relation to history from that of the eighteenth century. In the eighteenth century the dominant classes were well read in the classics and were able to interpret their culture in terms of classical culture, using it to provide examples and models for their conduct. We have seen that the notion of universal norms was a product of a lively and concrete sympathy for the historical past. Today, our knowledge of the past has increased vastly, but it is the province of specialists and is accompanied by ignorance and vagueness about history in our culture. The more our knowledge of the past becomes objective, the less the past can be applied in our own time. The use of the past to supply models for the present depends upon the ideological distortion of the past; and the whole effort of modern historiography is to eliminate these distortions.

In this sense, modern historiography is the direct descendant of historicism. As such, it is committed to a relativistic view of the past and resists the use of history to provide direct models.

On the other hand, it is equally difficult to imagine a culture that ignores the historical tradition altogether. The flight into the future, which characterised the phase of historicism that directly affected modernism, deliberately tried to instil a forgetfulness of history. In so doing, it brought to light what may be considered two weaknesses in nineteenth century historicist thought. First, it did not take account of cultural borrowing. In its concern to stress the uniqueness of each culture, it overlooked the extent to which all cultures, even the most 'indigenous', are based on the ideas and principles of other, pre-existent cultures. There has never been such a thing as an absolutely pure culture; to demonstrate this, one has only to mention the attraction that various proto-renaissances exerted on the Medieval world and the influence that the classical world never ceased to exert on European culture.

The second weakness of historicism (closely related to the first) is that it tended to suppress the role that the establishment of norms and types has always played in cultural development. It confused two things that are, in fact, unrelated: it confused the way in which cultures might be studied with the way in which cultures operate. While it might be fruitful to study history as if the culture under examination were a unique organism, it does not follow that it was such an organism in fact. How, for instance, could a historicist study a culture that believes in natural law, and in the principle of the imitation of the idea, without somehow contradicting his own method? To do this, historical analysis would have to reconcile two contradictory principles within itself. Paradoxical as this may seem, this is an important principle that must be faced. It suggests that our culture—and our architecture, as one of its manifestations—must make the same reconciliation. The uniqueness of our culture, which is the product of historical development, must be reconciled with the palpable fact that it operates within a historical context and contains within itself its own historical memory.

In what way can cultural memory manifest itself in architecture today? In my opinion it cannot do this by reverting to eclecticism, if by eclecticism we mean something belonging to eighteenth and nineteenth century culture. I have tried to show that in the eighteenth and nineteenth centuries eclecticism depended on the power of architectural style to become a sign or emblem for a certain set of ideas. But this depended on a knowledge of, and sympathetic identification with, the styles of the past and an ability to subject those styles to ideological distortions—distortions that were nonetheless predicated on a thorough knowledge of the styles themselves. Architecture is a form of knowledge by experience. But it is precisely this element of inward knowledge and experience that is lacking today. When we try to recover the past in architecture, we cross a chasm—the chasm of the late nineteenth and early twentieth centuries, during which the power of architectural styles to convey definite meanings disappeared entirely. Modern eclecticism is no longer ideologically active, as it was in the nineteenth century. When we revive the past now, we tend to express its most general and trivial connotations; it is merely the pastness of the past that is evoked. The phenomenon was already recognised 80 years ago by Aloïs Riegl, who drew attention to the two popular attitudes towards artistic works then prevalent: newness and oldness. As an emblem of 'pastness', modern historical recovery actually resists too accurate a memory of past styles; it is only in this way that it can become an item of cultural consumption. As modernism itself was recuperated by capitalism, so is postmodernism in all its guises. Modernism and postmodernism are two sides of the same coin. They are both essentially modern phenomena and are equally remote from the attitude toward history of the eighteenth and nineteenth century.

Given the fact that what we produce today is bound to be specifically modern, no matter how we incorporate the past into our work, we should look at that other tradition—the tradition of modernism—to see which of its elements inevitably persist in out attitude toward works of art and architecture. I have mentioned two aspects that are independent of the notion of historical determinism and the flight into the future: the opacity of the work of art and the search for primitive sources. Opacity denies that the work of art is merely a reflection or imitation of some model, whether the model is thought of as a Platonic form or as consisting of the 'real' world. In this sense it resists both idealism and naturalism. But it is not inconsistent with the idea of historical memory. By giving priority to the autonomy of artistic disciplines, it allows, even demands, the persistence of tradition as something that is internalised in these disciplines. The artistic tradition is one of those 'objective facts' that is transformed by the creative act.

It seems to me, therefore, that it is valid to approach the problem of tradition in architecture as the study of architecture as an autonomous discipline—a discipline which incorporates into itself a set of aesthetic norms that is the result of historical and cultural accumulation and which takes its meaning from this. But these aesthetic values can no longer be seen as constituting a closed system of rules or as representing a fixed and universal natural law. The notions of the opacity of the work of art and the search for basic principles do not presuppose that architecture is a closed system which has no contact with outside life, with the nonaesthetic. The aesthetic comes into being anew through the existence of a particular material situation, even if it is not wholly conditioned by this situation. Today's art historians tend toward the investigation of material conditions of artistic production of the past: today's architects should be equally aware of the transformation of the tradition brought about by these conditions.

What I have said implies that historicism, considered as the theory by which all sociocultural phenomena are historically determined, must still form the basis of our attitude toward history. But the slight of hand by which historicist idealism replaced the fixed ideal with an emergent idea can no longer be accepted. Such a unitary and mystical concept is bound to lead to systems of thought—both political and artistic—that presuppose what, in fact, remains to be proved: that any given historical system is an organic unity leading inevitably to the progress of mankind.

On the contrary, all system of thought, all ideological constructs, are in need of constant, conscious criticism; and the process of revision can come about only on the assumption that there is a higher and more universal standard against which to measure the existing system. History provides both the ideas that are in need of criticism and the material out of which this criticism is forged. An architecture that is constantly aware of its own history, but constantly critical of the seduction of history, is what we should aim for today.

1   Rosenblum, Robert, *Transformations in Late Eighteenth Century Art*, Princeton: Princeton University Press, 1967, p.127.
2   Meinecke, Friedrich, "Geschichte und Gegenwort" ("History in relation to the present"), 1933, in *Vom Geschichtlichen Sinn und vom Sinn der Geschichte*, 1939, pp. 14 ff; cited by Karl Hinrichs in Meinecke, Freidrich, *Historism: The Rise of a New Historical Outlook*, London: Routledge and Kegan Paul, 1972, p. li.
3   In *Introduction to the Philosophy of World History*, Hegel lays greater stress on the need for an empirical approach than is often supposed.
4   Junod, Philippe, *Transparence et opacité,* Lausanne: L'Age d'homme, 1976.

Rationalism: a Philosophical Concept in Architecture

First published in *Das Abenteuer der Ideen: Architektur und Philosophie seit der Industriellen Revolution*, ed. Claus Baldus, Berlin: Internationale Bauausstellung, 1987.

From Classical Rationalism to the Enlightenment:
The Search for Beauty

There is a common-sense view that divides mental activities into the scientific, depending on reason, and the artistic, depending on feeling or intuition. Such a simple dichotomy fails to take account of both the role that intuition plays in scientific thought and the role that the judgment-forming intellect plays in artistic creation. Nevertheless, the distinction contains an element of truth—less as a way of distinguishing between science and art than as a way of distinguishing between different aspects of the artistic process.

Of all the arts, architecture is the one in which it is least possible to exclude the idea of rationality. A building has to satisfy pragmatic and constructional criteria, which circumscribe, even if they do not determine, the field within which the imagination of the architect works. Therefore the degree to which architecture can be said to be rational depends less on the presence or absence of 'rational' criteria than on the importance attributed to these criteria within the total process of architectural design and within particular ideologies. The rational in architecture never exists in isolation. It is not an art historical category like neo-classicism. It is one side of a complex system that can be expressed only dialectically in terms of a series of more or less homologous oppositions: reason/feeling, order/disorder, necessity/freedom, universal/particular, and so on.

But having made this initial distinction, we are immediately faced with another. The definition of the "rational" in architecture has not remained constant throughout history. We are dealing not with a simple, static concept, but with one that has varied according to the constellation of ideas dominating particular historical phases. These changes of meaning are dependent on changes in ideology and cannot be considered independently of either economic or social factors or philosophical ideas.

As a preliminary step in the definition of architectural rationalism, it is necessary to note the sense in which the term is used in the history of philosophy. In philosophy the primary distinction is that between rationalism and empiricism, or reason and experience. While the opposition of reason/feeling cannot be reduced to these philosophical categories, there is nonetheless a relation between them. In both cases *reason* implies the intervention of rule or law between the direct experience of the world and any praxis or *techné* such as architecture. It is this notion—that architecture is the result of the application of general rules, established by the operation of reason—that may be taken as the most general definition of rationalism in architecture.

The conflict between rationalism and empiricism is one between two concepts of knowledge (or science), that define it as *a priori* or *a posteriori*. To the extent that knowledge is held to be *a priori,* empirical knowledge appears to be random, unfounded, and subject to contingency. To the extent that knowledge is held to be *a posteriori,* the terms are reversed and it is *a priori* knowledge that becomes unsure and dependent on authority, received ideas, or habit. The history of architectural theory during the last two hundred years has been the history of the conflict between these two concepts of architectural knowledge. But more than this; the dominance of one or the other has determined the role ascribed to those other mental processes that cannot be subsumed under the operation of reason or science. When discussing rationalism in architecture, therefore, we are discussing two sets of varying relationships: those that come from different concepts of knowledge itself, and those that come from the distinction between knowledge and intuition or feeling.

The rationalist philosophy of the seventeenth century, which we take here as represented by Descartes, Spinoza, and Leibnitz, absorbed within its system the traditional view that there are innate ideas and that 'science' is a fundamentally *a priori* enterprise based on these ideas. Innate ideas must be thought of as implanted by God, and, as such, they may be enshrined in a wisdom that has been revealed to mankind in the past and that constitutes valid authority. Knowledge gained by experience and induction has, ultimately, to be measured against this authority.

Cartesian rationalism did not abandon this tradition, but it inaugurated a search for clarity of concept, rigor of deduction, and intuitional certainty of basic principles. This is reflected in seventeenth century academic artistic theory, of which Nicolas Boileau-Despréaux's *L'art poetique,* Jean-Philippe Rameau's *Traitede l'armonie réduite à ses principes naturels,* and François Blondel's *Cours d'architecture* may be taken as examples.

The principles enunciated in these works were themselves based on an older body of ideas. When, in the late fifteenth century, architecture was first constituted as a separate branch of science, an important part of the knowledge forming this science depended on the authority of the ancients and the precepts found in the only surviving ancient architectural treatise, that of Vitruvius. At the same time, architectural theory began to be inscribed within a general artistic doctrine derived from Aristotle, Horace, and Cicero, on the one hand, and neo-Platonism on the other. The most important component of this doctrine was the idea that art was an imitation of nature, and that the art of the ancients, being derived from this law, was also worthy of imitation. Thus, nature was chiefly approachable through the authority of the ancients. This notion of authority is closely linked to the seventeenth century doctrine of *a priori* knowledge and innate ideas.

One of the sources of the concept of imitation can be found in Aristotle's *Physics.* He says:

> If a house were one of the things provided by nature, it would be the same as it is now when produced by art. And if natural phenomena were produced not only by nature but also by art, they would in this case come into being through art in the same way as they do in nature.... In short, art either completes the process that nature is unable to work out fully, or it imitates nature.[1]

Here we see two ideas which, to the modern mind, seem quite different, if not contradictory: the idea that architecture and other artefacts are extensions of nature's laws, and the idea that this entails a process of imitation or representation. In fact, throughout the eighteenth and nineteenth centuries there is a progressive separation between these two ideas and the concept of architecture becomes split between its constructive and 'scientific' and its representational and 'artistic' functions, *reason* being reserved for the former and *feeling,* or *sentiment,* for the latter.

Such a split, however, would have been inconceivable to the classical mind. Access to the truth and beauty was by way of laws that were already inscribed— however obscurely—in nature. Truth was the revelation of what already existed, and if it depended on revelation it must equally be based on truths already revealed to previous men. All truth was therefore a re-presentation. This view is still found in certain writers until the end of the eighteenth century. The English architect John Wood the Elder held that the science of architecture was its speculative or metaphysical part, while the *art* of architecture was the knowledge of its specific causes and its application to human uses.[2] It is the final cause that gives meaning to architecture, not the efficient cause or the solutions to specific problems. The distinction we find here between science and art is the opposite of the one generally made today; science for Wood belonged to the realm of metaphysics and the unchanging, and art to the realm of the practical and the contingent. Quatremère de Quincy is equally adamant that architecture should imitate the *idea* of nature. This imitation results in a building having a certain 'character', which may be of three kinds—essential, relative, and accidental—according to whether one is imitating nature in her more generic and timeless aspects or in her more specific and momentary aspects.[3] (The idea of character comes from the theory of genres in Aristotle's *Poetics*. but de Quincy turns it into something rather neo-Platonic).

But a new attitude was developing within the ethos of seventeenth century Rationalism, which emphasised the role that both empirical science and individual intelligence played in the discovery of truth and which tended to throw doubt on the status of *a priori* knowledge and innate ideas, as much as on the authority of the ancients or of the Bible. The quarrel between the 'ancients' and the 'moderns' gave rise to an increasingly critical dispute as to which architectural rules belonged to the realm of innate ideas and which belonged to the realm of empirical experience. The 'lawful' now become split between what was eternal and absolute and what was customary—the latter coming increasingly under the guidance of 'taste'.

This split is exemplified in both architectural and musical theory. In architecture, Claude Perrault attacked the classical doctrine of the orders, claiming that the rules of proportion were based solely on custom.[4] In music, there was disagreement between the followers of Gioseffo Zarlino, 1517–1590, who had insisted on the mathematical basis for acceptable chords, and those of Vincenzo Galilei, 1533–1591, who had said that what was beautiful could only be decided by the ear.

In the face of this problem, it became the aim of the eighteenth century to reconcile a rationalistic *a priorism* with taste or subjective judgment and to show that the constitution of the individual human being tends toward a harmony with Natural Law. As Charles-Etienne Briseaux said:

> Nature always acts with the same wisdom and in a uniform manner...
> from which it can be concluded that the pleasure of the ear and the eye
> consists of the perfection of harmonic concordance as being analogous to
> our own constitutions... and that this principle resides' not only in music
> but in all the productions of the arts.[5]

In Laugier's *Essai sur l'architecture* of 1753, the rules of good architecture are presented as self-evident to the uncorrupted mind and eye; *a priori* reason is confirmed by empirical experience and by sensation. In this way, untutored reason confirms the truth of the earliest architecture and no longer depends on the guidance of particular antique models. But reason and truth were still tied to the purification of the tradition, of which more or less imperfect models already existed. Just as it was the task of the painter or sculptor, in classical and neo-classical doctrine, to imitate the idea lying behind the imperfect appearances of nature, so it was the task of the architect to uncover the types lying concealed in the manifold, but imperfect, examples presented by the history of architecture. Architecture is treated exactly as if it were a natural phenomenon. Even Carlo Lodoli, whose functionalism, *avant la lettre*, has often been mistaken for a pure empiricism, adhered to a concept of architectural ornament in which there is a clear distinction between what is normative and typical and what is due to 'accidental' cultural differences.[6] The Enlightenment may have wanted to replace *l'esprit du système* by *l'espirit systèmatique,* in order to free practice from the domination of authority and received ideas, but its aim was still to discover the universal and unchanging laws underlying empirical experience. A building such as Soufflot's Sainte-Geneviève. Uniting "the noble decoration of the Greeks and the lightness of the Gothic Architects", and the rationalism of a Lodoli or a Laugier both pointed to the need to free architecture from the arbitrary and tasteless rules to which it had succumbed under the Baroque and bring it back to nature, whose laws were simple and eternal.[7]

This project was similar in many ways to the Grammarian's search for the universal and rational laws of language.[8] Architecture was also a rational 'language', subject to the variations of character demanded by climate, custom, and decorum, but capable, nevertheless, of being reduced by the exercise of reason to a universal system, whose laws even genius could not escape. The eighteenth century is marked by the opposition reason/caprice, reason alone being capable of discerning universal truths. But this *reason* is now in alliance with subjective experience; empirical experience is no longer set in opposition to a reason that has been implanted in us by God and that constitutes an unquestioned authority. It is used as a supplementary proof of the existence of Natural Law.

Utilitarian and Eclectic Rationalism:
The Search for Utility

With the growth of utilitarianism the structure of thought on which the alliance between rationalism and classicism depended became increasingly tenuous 'Scientific' reason became increasingly directed to instrumental efficacy rather than metaphysics. Efficient causes replaced final causes. There was now no theory that could withstand the growth of caprice and eclecticism, or the proliferation of what Quatremère called "accidental character". JNL Durand, though still working within the formal language of classicism, justified a rational architecture purely on the grounds of economics and utility.[9] The efforts of architects and theorists like Durand, Legrand, Thomas Hope, and Schinkel were now directed to an irenic eclecticism which would select, in a system of combinations and permutations, appropriate stylistic elements from the panorama of history or from buildings of a utilitarian nature. There were now as many "architectures" (the word is Legrand's) as there were times and peoples; classicism was reduced to a specific tradition (admittedly "our own") whose use was purely justified by convention. At the end of his book *Essai sur l'histoire générale de l'architecture* of 1800, Legrand puts the rhetorical question:

> Can we not arrive at the end [of a modern architecture] by borrowing from all the genres what each has of the reasonable and exquisite, so as to compose a modern style appropriate to the climate, customs, materials... and rules of decorum of each country, and which will be the happy result of our knowledge of the art of building among all the peoples?[10]

Thomas Hope expresses the same opinion:

> No one seems yet to have conceived the... wish... of only borrowing of every former style in architecture, whatever it might present of the useful an ornamental, of the scientific and tasteful... and then composing an architecture which... grown on our own soil, and in harmony with our own climate, institutions and habits... should truly deserve the appellation of "our own".[11]

But however much these sentiments might seem to anticipate the "organic society" of romanticism and the Gothic Revival, they still adhere to eighteenth century notions of decorum and to that conception of "mechanical composition" which, ever since 1800, had been virulently attacked by the German Romantics.[12]

Structural and Organic Rationalism:
The Search for Authenticity

From the second half of the eighteenth century onward the conceptual split between architecture as construction and architecture as representation had begun to undermine seriously the unitary doctrine of classicism. But a weak form of classical doctrine nonetheless persisted, in which it was possible to think of the use of different styles as permissible within the classical notions of character and decorum.

The development of a rationalism based on the logic of structure took place chiefly in France, where, as far back as the seventeenth century, architects had recognised in Gothic architecture a rational constructive principle. The structural rationalists of the late eighteenth century did not reject classicism; they sought to subject it to more stringent functional analysis in terms of the new science of the strength of materials and in terms of use.[13] This tradition continued well into the nineteenth century, even after the impact of Comtian positivism. The belief, characteristic of the positivists, that science provides us with the only valid knowledge and that facts are its only objects, was quite compatible with a form of idealism that promoted all that was not reducible to experimental science to a vaguely neo-classicism realm of "Beauty".

This view was expressed by Léonce Reynaud, a prominent teacher of classical/rationalist persuasion in the mid-nineteenth century:

> Although I believe that considerations of a scientific kind must enter into the study of the forms of our buildings, I am far from thinking that they cover everything. That which touches the intimate essence of art is felt, not explained.[14]

For Reynaud, classicism was a set of broadly defined formal principles onto which an architecture appropriate to a scientific age could be grafted. Certain historical forms had reached a sort of perfection through evolution and should not be disregarded (echoes of this notion will still be found in Le Corbusier). The categories which Reynaud divided architectural values—utility, order and simplicity, and character—were similar to those that had been suggested by Durand half a century earlier.

The last representative of this tradition, César Daly, founder of the *Revue générale d'architecture,* defined architectural rationalism as follows:

1. Architecture is ornamented structure.
2. Architectural forms require rational justification and must derive their laws from science.
3. The task of the rationalist school is to reconcile architecture with modern science and technology.
4. Once the alliance of architecture and reason is accomplished, the next step is the alliance of architecture and sentiment.[15]

Among practising architects, the same syncretism between modern technique and classicism is often apparent. For example, in the Bibliothèque Sainte-Geneviève, Henri Labrouste does not allow his interest in iron structure to interfere with his idea—derived from classical theory—about the correct external form of a public monument.

This debate, however, took a different form among the Gothic Revivalists. According to them, Gothic architecture was not a style that could be used eclectically, as a way of eliciting literary associations *within* the classical definition of "character"; it should be seen as an *alternative* tradition to that of classicism. The difference between the Gothic Revivalists and the classical eclectics was that for the former structure itself became the basis of architectural meaning. Ornament and "representation" were now thought of as emerging from the structure of a building, rather than as arbitrary clothing that could be added to it. It followed that, of the three kinds of character described by Quatremère, only the first—essential character—was kept.

The chief spokesman for this school of thought and possibly the most influential architectural writer of the nineteenth century was Viollet-le-Duc.[16] For him technique becomes the basis for an architecture that is rational in its very essence. He sees in Gothic architecture a constructional principle that should become the methodological paradigm of a future architecture. In spite of a pre-dominance of restorations in Viollet's oeuvre and his nostalgia for Medieval culture, his writings exhibit the same adherence to positivism as those of the opposing school of classical eclectics, and an even stronger belief in the open-ended progress of mankind, which, it was supposed, would follow in the wake of the Industrial Revolution. But for Viollet the history of architecture is a continuous technological development, which excludes the possibility of repeating the 'perfect' forms derived from antiquity. The morphology of architecture is no longer determined by a taxonomy of external and historical *forms,* but by a system of underlying *functions.* "That which is generally regarded as a matter of true art, namely symmetry, the apparent form, is quite a secondary consideration."[17]

This 'evolutionary' rationalism, which tied architecture to an implacable and objective historical destiny, was combined with a subjective moralism. The principles of Gothic architecture were both rational *and* moral. In a brilliant analysis of Viollet's writings, Philippe Junod shows that he is constantly fluctuating between an objective and a subjective viewpoint. On the one hand, reason is opposed to sentiment, logic to fantasy, system to instinct, in a way that allies him to a rationalist tradition extending, *mutatis mutandis,* from Descartes to Comte; on the other, sincerity, honesty, and truth are opposed to pretense, falsehood, and lies. In this circular argument, Viollet appeals to subjective feeling to justify the rational, and to the rational to justify subjective feeling.[18]

What are those 'laws' which enable Viollet to fluctuate with such apparent inconsistency between a negative and a positive evaluation of subjective sentiment? They are the Laws of Nature, imperative equally to the head and the heart, to the objective world and to feeling. In discussing the relation between the parts of a building and the whole, Viollet says, "Just as one sees the leaf of a plant, one deduces from it the entire planet: from the bone of an animal, the entire animal, so, in seeing a profile, one deduces the members of architecture. And from the members the entire monument."[19] There was nothing particularly new in this analogy; Denis Diderot had already suggested that zoology offered the artist a typical example of functional coherence.[20] But by the mid-nineteenth century the argument had deepened. Viollet (like Gottfried Semper) could now adduce the example of Cuvier's "functional" taxonomy of animal species; moreover, he was following in the footsteps of German romanticism. His organic analogy is not far from that expressed by AW Schlegel in his *Dramatic Lectures*:

> The form is mechanical when... it is imparted to a material merely as an accidental addition, without relation to its nature.... Organic form, on the other hand, is innate; it unfolds itself from within and acquires its definiteness simultaneously with the total development of the germ.... All genuine forms are organic, ie. determined by the content of the work of art. In a word, art is nothing but a significant exterior, the speaking physiognomy of everything... which bears witness to its hidden nature.[21]

Unless we recognise this romantic and 'organicist' aspect of Viollet, which is integral to his interpretation of Gothic, it is difficult to explain his influence on the twentieth century avant-garde, on Art Nouveau vitalism, and on architects of the Chicago school. Louis Sullivan's theory of an "organic" architecture (taken over by Frank Lloyd Wright) is derived partly from Viollet and partly from the German Romantics (presumably via Coleridge and the American transcendentalists), and it is clearly expressed in the statement: "It is the pervading law of all things, organic and inorganic, of all things human and superhuman, of all true manifestations of the head, the heart and the soil, that life is recognisable in its expression, that form always follows function. This is the law."[22]

It is evident that a strict line cannot be drawn, in the nineteenth century, between positivistic rationalism and a romantic organicism, with its emphasis of the moral imperative that underlies the need to conform to the laws of nature. But in this essay we cannot pursue that other thread that leads from Viollet-le-Duc through Art Nouveau to organicism and expressionism because it would lead us away from the main stream of the twentieth century avant-garde, in which the theory of organic form was assimilated to ideas of an analytical and mechanistic kind, embracing the machine, rather than opposing it.

Rationalism and the Twentieth Century Avant-garde: The Search for Transparency

It has often been argued that it was not until the twentieth century that positivism and the structural rationalism of the nineteenth century bore fruit. If the law of historical evolution and progress was to be demonstrated, architecture would have finally to sever its ties with past styles and draw its meaning and its language exclusively from the objective conditions of technique and programme.

It was not until the end of the nineteenth century that certain architects began to put these principles into operation. Among these, HP Berlage and Otto Wagner were outstanding in the way in which they were able to transform their stylistic inheritance (Gothic Revival and neo-classical, retrospectively) by the application of rational constructional principles. The two paradigmatic 'halls' of the early twentieth century, the Amsterdam Exchange and the Post Office Savings building in Vienna, both assimilate the nineteenth century exhibition or railway shed to socio-cultural programmes and embed them in an architecture, which, though recognisably traditional in overall form, tries to develop a new kind or ornament derived from construction.

However, although the craftsmanlike principles embodied in these buildings were incorporated into the doctrine of the twentieth century avant-garde, the rationalism of the Modern Movement cannot be understood in these terms alone. Twentieth century rationalism differs radically from that of the nineteenth century, and to understand this difference it is necessary to analyse it in terms of three concepts: *logical atomism*, *functionalism* and *formalism* which, while not absolutely new, now take an entirely new form.

Logical Atomism

Logic was stressed in positivistic thought, but we have seen that for Viollet-le-Duc: there was always a passage from logic, via technique, to subjective feeling and organic nature. Viollet had talked about the machine as a paradigm for architecture, but for him mechanisation did not imply any change in the relation between the components of architecture and the building as a whole. Iron could be substituted for wood or stone, but this substitution, though it entailed substantial formal transformations, depended on the fact that these materials had analogous properties and could still be 'worked' in a craftsman-like way. It was precisely such linking of 'logic' and 'technique' that enabled Viollet to see architecture as a continuous process of evolution, whose principles remained constant, even if their material embodiment changed.

A series of developments in aesthetic theory, in philosophy, in construction, and in production in the late nineteenth and early twentieth centuries intervened to alter quite radically this fundamentally traditional conception of architecture. There can be no question of assigning causes and effects; we will merely juxtapose certain parallel developments that have *prima facie* similarities.

The constructional and productive conditions of twentieth century architecture were laid down in the second half of the nineteenth century by engineers using cast and wrought iron in the construction of bridges, greenhouses, train stations, and market and exhibition structures. In all these constructions it was possible to develop pragmatic and analytical methods with the minimum of interference from architectural ideology. A crucial example is Paxton's Crystal Palace of 1851, where for the first time and within the ambit of a typically English pragmatism, division of labour and standardisation of tools and materials became an essential part of the design concept. In the tower that Gustave Eiffel built for the Paris exhibition of 1889, in addition to these productive procedures, empirico-mathematical methods of design are used to produce forms of novel transparency and dynamism. A further development of construction is found later in the bridges of Robert Maillart, in which a completely new concept of reinforced concrete planes is developed.

The first application on a substantial scale of these new kinds of empirical procedure to architecture was the introduction of the steel frame in multi-storey office buildings in Chicago in the 1880s. In the steel frame the elements of construction are determined more by the needs of the production process than by the sort of constructional "logic" which formed the basis of Viollet's philosophy. The frame introduces a generalised system that minimises differences precisely when Viollet would have maximised them; for example, the differences between supporting and supported elements, and their point of connection. The forms that result are closer to Cartesian abstraction than to the quasi-"organic" laws of material and the visual expression of these laws.

There are broad parallels between such pragmatic developments and certain contemporary developments in philosophy, notably Bertrand Russell's theories of *logical constructionism* and *logical atomism,* which he started to develop in about 1900. In his theory of logical constructionism, Russell tried to show that all entities which were problematic from the point of view of empirical experience and common sense could be reduced to (or "constructed" out of) simpler and non-problematic entities: "The supreme maxim in scientific philosophising is this: wherever possible logical constructions are to be substituted for inferred identities." The theory of logical atomism, which Russell developed slightly later, was an attempt to give metaphysical status to this purely epistemological principle by postulating an ideal, empirically-based, language which would correspond to the structure of reality.

• The world consists of elementary entities possessing only elementary properties and connected through elementary relations.
• Our scientific world view has to be composed analogically out of elementary propositions.

The paradox of this project is that in order to satisfy empirical truth requirements, the world has to be subjected to a purely formal analysis and divested of all immediacy of meaning. It attempts to reduce all mental operations to those appropriate for the physical sciences.

There is a strong parallel between this view and that of the founders of the Modern Movement in the second decade of the twentieth century, who similarly wished to break down the inherited figures of art and architecture into their irreducible elements. Whether these elements are thought of as "formal" (as with Kandinsky, Mondrian, and the de Stijl movement) or as "constructive" (as in the Russian avant-garde), they constitute a lexicon of irreducible entities connected to each other by means of elementary relations. As in Russell's "constructionism," totalities are replaced by simples, whose meaning is immanent and self-evident.

This elementarisation can certainly be thought of as an impoverishment of the meanings carried by cultural convention. But it should be stressed that this was not the interpretation given to it in avant-garde artistic circles, where, on the contrary, it was construed as a means of attaining more profound—because more primitive—meanings and of distancing the artist from a "degenerate" bourgeois conception of art.

These tendencies had started before the events we have been describing. They can be seen, for example, in Impressionist and Post-Impressionist painting, where the manifold of perception is analysed into, and reconstructed out of, atomic units. They can also be seen in German formalist, neo-Kantian aesthetics, from Herbart to Fiedler, in which a logic of artistic perception is developed.[23] Such developments must be considered as part of a "rationalist" programme, insofar as they seek to apply the methodology of science to the analysis of subjective experience. It is from the inheritors of this analytical tradition in painting—principally Cubism—that the architectural modernists of the 1920s drew much of their formal inspiration.

An even more direct connection with the philosophy of logical atomism, however, may perhaps be seen in the work of Adolf Loos, whose *Raumplan Analysen*, were begun around the turn of the century. Here the space of the house is built up out of atomic "rooms" each with its own specificity. A further example is the house that Ludwig Wittgenstein built for his sister in 1926 in collaboration with the architect Paul Engelmann. In this house all the elements are redefined in terms of elementary functions and seem to reflect Wittigenstein's picture theory of language given in the *Tractatus logico-philosophicus* (and developed under the influence of Russell), according to which there is a one-to-one relationship between sentences and things. This house belongs equally to the spirit of the 1920s avant-garde and to Wittgenstein's own philosophical preoccupations; nothing could express more clearly his dictum "The meaning is the use."

The insistence on "use value" in the architecture of Loos and Wittgenstein links the idea of logical atomism to the notion of "function".

Functionalism

The idea, fundamental to the Modern Movement, that there is an overriding causal relation between functions and forms in architecture is part of a tradition going back to Vitruvius. Until the end of the eighteenth century, as we have seen, this idea was closely united with the idea of imitation in the sense given by Aristotle. But in the first half of the nineteenth century, under the influence of romanticism and historicism, it became associated with the notion of genetic development. An *inner necessity* took the place of *analogy* as the generator of forms expressive of the programme or the structure of a building. This "inner necessity" was capable of either an idealist interpretation (an invisible spirit giving direction to material causality) or a "scientific" or materialist interpretation (based on efficient causes and empirical evidence).

By the end of the nineteenth century the sense in which the word "function" was used in different disciplines had lost much of its idealist content. In mathematics, for example, function is no longer a relation between a variable and a known, fixed object; it is a relation between two variables. According to Ernst Mach, the notion of function should replace that of cause. When science gathers various elements into one equation, each element becomes a *function* of the others, the dependence among elements becomes reciprocal, and the relation between cause and effect becomes reversible.[24]

Such a notion of function, with its implication of a system that is independent of external "values", is closely related to the functionalist anthropology of Bronislaw Malinowski. According to Malinowski's hypothesis, societies are to be seen as self-organising systems, and the *function* of an element is the part it plays in maintaining the system. As Malinowski said: "The functional view... insists upon the principle that in every type of civilisation, every custom, material object, idea and belief, fulfills some vital function... within the working Whole."[25] The circularity of this argument is evident; the system is defined as the sum of the facts, while the "fact" is defined as what is relevant to the system.

Something analogous to this view is found in the Idea of a "functional" architecture. According to this, there must be no interference, in the design or evaluation of a building, from preconceived notions about what "architecture" is. It should be defined solely in terms of elements interacting with each other *within* the (empirically founded) system, which, in turn can only be defined as the sum of these elements.

The leftists among the *Neue Sachlichkeit* architects present, in their theory, an extreme example of this kind of "functionalism". When Hannes Meyer defined architecture as *function x economics* he was trying to reduce architecture to an absolutely primitive system excluding all *a priori* "values".[26] But of course the nature of this system was already given by his own arbitrary restriction of the relevant facts: those, like structure, economy, and fundamental "need", which could be empirically tested by the "scientific" method. In a fully axiomaticised field of knowledge such as mathematics, such arbitrary limitations are justified, and indeed essential. But in an affective and ideological field like architecture, their rigid application can be explained only by hidden ideological motives.

The term *functional*, as used in modern architecture, was coloured by this arbitrary limitation as to what could be logically deduced or empirically verified. The results, instead of being understood as aspects of a purely formal operation, as they are in mathematics, were taken as objectively true descriptions of the real world.

A similar situation pertained to "functionalism" in anthropology, where the recording of empirically observable behaviour was considered to be the only way of arriving at truth statements about a particular society.

In the 1940s, in anthropology and somewhat later in architecture, a structuralist critique was developed, whose purpose was to demonstrate that there was no necessary correlation between forms and structures on the one hand and "functions" and "behaviour patterns" on the other. Forms, it was claimed, were independent of the empirical situations which lent them "meaning" at any one time or place.

Formalism

We can define formalism as that type of thought which stresses rule-governed relationships rather than relationships of cause and effect. According to this definition, formalism is related to a purely mathematical definition of function. It studies the structures of given fields independently of what exists outside those fields; it is concerned with the "how" of things, not with the "why". This seems to be the characteristic of late nineteenth century and early twentieth century thought in widely different disciplines—philosophy, mathematics, art and architecture.

I have already mentioned this approach in connection with nineteenth century German aesthetic theory. It can also be seen, somewhat later, in the history of art. Here a formalist approach restricts the object of study to the formal structure of works of art and avoids discussion of what these works have been held to "mean" at particular historical periods. In the same way, it looks for a logic of historical change in the specifically artistic problems that have faced artists at different times, rather than seeing them as the (undemonstrable) result of external historical events. Aloïs Riegl, and Heinrich Wölfflin were representative of this point of view. Both were strongly influenced by Conrad Fiedler's theory of "pure visibility" and all, in turn, influenced the intellectual atmosphere of the artistic avant-garde of the early twentieth century.

While one of the aims of formalist art history was to break the hold of normative classical aesthetics, these aims could only be achieved by establishing more general norms which would apply to all art, of whatever period. It thus tended toward the establishment of ahistorical laws, and in doing so resembled classical theory itself. Formalist art theory concentrated on the "how" of art because it rejected the kind of "why" explanations always given to justify a particular system of values (or a particular style). But classical doctrine also concentrated on the "how" (the rules of good poetry and of rhetoric, etc.) precisely because it *accepted*, without question, a particular system of values.

The formalist tendencies of the twentieth century avant-garde therefore contradicted the historicist interpretations of modern architecture given by Viollet-le-Duc and his followers. Instead of seeing architecture as continuously developing according to a historical law of technical and social evolution, they carry the implication that modern architecture is a radical break with history—that it has reached a threshold which enables it to give form to the eternal laws of aesthetics. In this way it can be seen as a type of classicism, but one which rejects the specific, historically determined forms of the classical style. This view was, nonetheless, closely connected to developments in constructional techniques, which were seen as freeing the architect from those technical constraints that had previously tied architectural aesthetics to particular times and particular craft traditions.

One of the first architects explicitly to connect an industrialised architecture to classicism was Hermann Muthesius, who saw in it the means of arriving at a typology of architectural forms corresponding to universal laws of aesthetic perception. The rationalisation of building in terms of factory production would recreate, at a more abstract level, the very artistic traditions and cultural values it had helped to destroy.

In the 1920s most of the avant-garde architects began to accept the replacement of craft by the machine as the price architecture had to pay if it was to tackle the urgent social tasks presented to it. But, although this involved a certain simplification of masses and the stressing of the typical over the individual, its incipient classicism was overshadowed by the elementarist and montage-like compositional principles that denied the formal hierarchies of the classical *system*. This was particularly true of the left-wing architects like Hannes Meyer, Ernst May, Mart Stam, and Hans Schmidt, among others.

There is, in the work of these architects, and especially in the city layouts by Ludwig Hilbersheimer, an extreme schematicism, which transposes diagrams resulting from purely analytical operations into objects of the real, perceptual world. This is a primitive kind of formalism which halts the process of abstraction midway, as it were, without allowing it to work toward an adequate image.

In the work of Le Corbusier and Mies van der Rohe, however, this schematic formalism was combined with more overt classical tendencies. Le Corbusier's classicism, in particular, was quite explicit and was based on a rather generalised acceptance of the French classical tradition. In the greater part of his work he was concerned with reconciling the classical idea of an *a priori* artistic order with the idea of continuous progress inherited from historicism and positivism. His drawing of the Dom-ino frame was a demonstration of the dialectical principle that was to inform all his later work. Here the concrete frame has all the certainty of the Cartesian *a priori*. Within this frame, the volumes and the equipment of the house can be independently arranged, according to practical needs. The organisation of these needs is supposed to follow an empirical necessity whose laws are as rigorous as those of the Platonic frame and its implied cubic envelope (though, in fact, it is precisely here that the invention of the architect/artist comes into play, with all its freedom of metaphorical allusion). The dialogue between the frame and its infill is made apparent by means of Cubist techniques of spatial simultaneity, themselves made possible by new constructional techniques.

Le Corbusier's architecture gives artistic expression to the conflict between the two traditions of rationalism we have traced: the *a priori* and the empirical. On the one hand we find those "clear and distinct ideas" which, translated from a Cartesian metaphysics into the sensuous objects of art, have been promoted by French classical theorists from Boileau to Durand. On the other, we find the empirical and scientistic ideas of positivism, which are expressed as the functional, the accidental, and the contingent.

A formalism tending equally toward the classical is found in both Scandinavian and Italian modernism. In Scandinavia it is present in the work of Gunnar Asplund and the early work of Alvar Aalto—in both cases due to the existence of a strong tradition of neo-classicism dating from the first decade of the twentieth century.

In Italy this tendency is inseparable from the cultural demands of Fascism and the attempt to reconcile progressivist ideals with tradition. The example of Le Corbusier's architecture and writings was probably the most important single influence on the Italian avant-garde of the 1930s (the self-styled "rationalists" of Gruppo 7). In his book *Vers une architecture*, published in 1923, Le Corbusier had equated the products of modern technology, such as automobiles, with the Parthenon—each being presented as the result of an evolutionary process terminating in a perfect "type" form. This image enabled the Italian architects to reconcile the dynamic and mechanistic aspects of Futurism with the classical tradition.

Antonio Sant'Elia, in his *Città Nuova* of 1914, had synthesised ideas from Henri Sauvage and the Wagnerschule to produce the sublime image of a congested and mechanised modern city. If we compare the images in this book with a work of the rationalists, such as the Casa de Fascio by Giuseppe Terragni, and certain works by Eduardo Persico and Gino Pollini, we see that Sant'Elia's romantic expressionism has given way to a calm and timeless classicism. This classicism, however, lacks the stylistic iconography characteristic of the Novecento architects Giovanni Muzio and Marcello Piacentini. It is reduced to an abstract "framework" of deliberate neutrality.

Postmodernism:
The Search for Meaning

The Modern Movement of the 1920s was marked by an evangelical fervor which lent it all the attributes of a religious movement. As in all religious movements, its adherents had to pass through a *conversion to* a state of mind in which the smallest and most mundane aspects of life were transformed. The rationalism of the twentieth century avant-garde was combined with a dogmatic and idealistic anti-rationalism that could, perhaps, only survive in a pure form for a very short time.

Already in the 1930s a process of "liberalisation" set in, which culminated in the 1950s. This liberalisation did not abandon the rationalist position as a foundation, but sought to "humanise" it. In the 1930s Le Corbusier began to introduce natural materials and vernacular elements into his work. JJP Oud, who had been associated with the De Stijl movement, reintroduced ornament into his buildings, and Alvar Aalto developed a style that explicitly allowed room for "irrational" and "psychological" factors. After the Second World War this process continued under the various rubrics of "neo-empircism", "brutalism" and "neo-realism". At the same time, particularly in the United States, technical development reached a stage at which it became possible to harness the rational/constructive aspect of modernism to the ideological needs of real estate development, thus undermining modernism's utopian foundations.

None of these tendencies questioned the basic premises of modernist rationalism. They saw modernism as capable of gradually reforming itself from within, so as to absorb those "humanistic" and pragmatic needs that had been excluded from its original programme.

A parallel development can perhaps be seen in developments with analytical philosophy. Wittgenstein's "language games", introduced in the *Philosophical Investigations*, the "ordinary language" philosophy of JL Austin, and Karl Popper's concept of the "open society", all, in various ways, relinquished the attempt to equate the processes of rational analysis with the real world.

In the mid-1960s, a new architectural discourse emerged, which, instead of trying to reform architecture from within a specifically modernist tradition, sought rather to define rationalism in terms of an autonomous tradition of architecture. This movement originated in the circle of young architects grouped around Ernesto Rogers, the editor of the magazine *Casabella*. The specific transformation to which rationalism had been subject in historical development were seen as secondary to, and dependent upon, a deeper tradition according to which what is "rational" in architecture is that which conserves architecture as a cultural discourse throughout history. These ideas were based on an analogy with structural linguistics, which had stressed the paradigmatic value of the typical and invariant structures underlying individual speech acts.

Although there is an evident historical connection between this view and the formalistic aspects of modernism, they differ in one crucial aspect. Modernist formalism had assumed that architecture could be reduced to forms which corresponded to the structure of the human mind, whereas the new formalism we are describing sees the invariant elements of architecture as derived from architecture itself, as a social and cultural reality.

The implication of this view is that we should look upon the history of architecture— or at any rate a large segment of it—as if it were a continuous instant in which thought and memory are coextensive. The model for such a view is Enlightenment thought, which looked on progress not as the unpredictable and open-ended development it was to become for positivism, but as the rational rearrangement and exploitation of existing material. According to such a view, the typological characteristics of a rational architecture are not those that are created by technology or by specifically modern forms of social behaviour, but those that persist through technological and social change and anchor us to a permanent image of man. There is return to an eighteenth century view of reason, as the faculty which is, itself, outside history.

The architects who exemplify these attitudes most clearly are Giorgio Grassi and Aldo Rossi. The former emphasises the more ontological and tectonic aspects of the rationalist tradition, while the latter stresses those subjective and poetic images to which it can give rise.[28] As part of a more general "postmodern" technology, this type of rationalism must be seen as a defensive reaction to the current social conditions of production and consumption. It is not an accident that in both cases this output is small and deliberately modest in scale. Its protagonists seem to be saying that we have reached a stage of social evolution in which the products of man's reason are increasingly divorced from the experience of making, constructing or imagining. Writing, in 1894, of the distance between modern scientific conceptual thought and our capacity to reduce the world to sensuous images of order, Paul Valéry gave vent to very similar thoughts:

Why is it that only a small part of the world can be so reduced? There is a moment when the figural becomes so complicated, or the event seems so new, that we must abandon the attempt to consider them as a whole, or to proceed with their translation into continuous values. At what point did our Euclids halt their apprehension of form?[29]

Nearly 100 years later the problem has become all the more glaring. Can we still use the word rationalism in architecture in the sense that it has always been used despite all its changes of meaning: as the attempt to provide the sensuous analogue, the emblematic presence, of that reason which was once supposed to permeate the universe?

1 Aristotle, *Physics*, 199a, pp. 15–19.
2 Wood the Elder, John, *The Origin of Building, or the Plagiarism of the Heathens Detected*, London, 1741.
3 de Quincy, Quatemère, "Caractère" in *Architecture*, Paris, 1788. Also "Caractère" in *Dictionnaire historique d'architecture*, Paris, 1832.
4 See Herrmann, Wolfgang, *The Theory of Claude Perrault*, London: A Zwemmer, 1962.
5 Briseaux, Charles-Etienne, *Traite du beau essential dans les arts*, Paris, 1752.
6 See Rykwert, Joseph, *The First Moderns*, Cambridge: MIT Press, 1980, chapter 8.
7 For this and other contemporary opinions about Sainte-Geneviève, see Middleton, RD, "The Abbé de Cordemoy and the Graeco Gothic Ideal", *Journal of the Warburg and Courtauld Institutes*, no. 25, 1962, p. 111.
8 The search, during the Enlightenment, for the laws of a universal grammar was founded on the work of the Port Royale Grammarians, Arnaud and Lancelot, whose *Grammaire générale et raisonnée* was published in 1660. The English grammarian James Harris, 1709–1780, defined universal grammar as "that grammar which, without regarding the several idioms of particular languages, only respects those principles that are essential to them all". The principle figures of this tradition were: Cézar Chesneau Dumarsais, 1676–1746; Nicolas Beauzée, 1717–1789; and Destutt de Tracey, 1754–1836.
9 Durand, JNL, "Introduction", *Precis des lecons d'architecture donnees a l'Ecole Royale Polytechnique*, Paris, 1819.
10 Legrand, Jacques-Guillaume, *Essai sur l'histoire générale de l'architecture*, Paris, 1800.
11 Hope, Thomas, *An Historical Essay on Architecture,* 3rd ed., 1840, vol. 1, p. 495; quoted in Watkin, D, *Thomas Hope and the Neo-Classical Idea*, 1968, p. 214.
12 The crucial document of romantic artistic doctrine is the review *Das Athenaeum*, 1798–1800, written mostly by Friedrich and August Wilhelm Schlegel. This doctrine was disseminated in France and England by Madame de Stäel, whose book *De l'Allemagne* was published in 1813.
13 See Collins, Peter, *Changing Ideals in Modern Architecture*, Montreal: McGill-Queen's University Press, 1967, chapter 19, "Rationalism".
14 Reynaud, Léonce, *Traité d'architecture*, Paris, 1860–1863, p. ix.
15 See Collins, *Changing Ideals*, chapter 19.
16 Viollet-le-Duc's principal theoretical statements are to be found in the *Dictionnaire raisonné d'architecture française, du XIe au XVIe siècle*, Paris, 1858–1868 and *Entretiens sur l'architecture*, Paris, 1863–1872.
17 Viollet-le-Duc, *Entretiens*, no. 10.
18 See Philippe Junod, "La terminologie esthétique de Viollet-le-Duc", in *Viollet-le-Duc, centenaire de la mort à Lausanne*, Lausanne, 1979, p. 57.
19 Viollet-le-Duc, "Style", in *Dictionnaire raisonné*.
20 See Junod, "La terminologie".
21 Schlegel, AW, *Uber Dramatische Kunst und Literatur*, 2nd ed, Heidelberg, 1817, III, p. 8; cited by Rene Wellek, *A History of Modern Criticism*, Cambridge, 1981, vol. 2, p. 148.
22 Sullivan, Louis, *Kindergarten Chats and Other Writings*, New York, 1979, p. 191.
23 The German formalist aesthetic philosophers were antagonistic to the classical theory of imitation. According to Johann Friedrich Herbart, 1776–1841, beauty is an irreducible sensation which "means" nothing beyond itself. Herbart's approach was developed in different ways, and in the different arts, by Wilhelm Unger, Robert Zimmerman, Eduard Hanslick, Conrad Fiedler, and others, up to the end of the nineteenth century.
24 Mach, Ernst, *Die Mechanik in ihrer Entwicklung*.
25 Malinowski, Bronislaw, "Anthropology" in *Encyclopaedia Britannica*, 13th ed., supplement 1, Chicago, 1926.
26 See Claude Schnaidt, *Hannes Meyer*, Zurich: Arthur Niggli, 1965, p. 23.
27 See Hermann Muthesius' "Proposition" in the *Proceedings of the Deutscher Werkbund Congress at Cologne*, 1914. In 1912 the English critic TE Hulme also made an analogy between classicism and the machine when attacking expressionist poetry. See Raymond Williams, *Culture and Society*, New York, 1958.
28 See Ignacio Sola-Morales, "Critical Discipline", *Oppositions 23*, Winter 1981. This is a sensitive study of the work and ideas of Giorgio Grassi. See also Aldo Rossi, *The Architecture of the City*, Cambridge: MIT Press, 1982, and *A Scientific Autobiography* Cambridge, MIT Press, 1981.
29 Valery, Paul, "Introduction à la méthode de Leonardo da Vinci", *La Nouvelle revue française*, August 15, 1895; trans. in James R Lawler, ed., *Paul Valery, An Anthology*, Princeton: Princeton University Press, 1976, p. 61.

Composition versus the Project

First published in *Casabella* 50, January/February 1986.

In the so-called 'Anglo-Saxon' countries the ideological conflict symbolised by the opposition *composizione/projettazione* is marked less by a word that acts as the antonym of *composition* than by the simple exclusion of the word from the critical vocabulary. In the post-war years this proscription was typical of an architectural climate that was moral, utilitarian, and pragmatic. Criticism in this period ignored the ambiguity of the relationship between the idea of composition and the artistic avant-gardes. This essay will address some of these ambiguities.

Perhaps the most familiar use of the word *composition* is in the context of music, where in the nineteenth century the word must have had progressive rather than retrogressive connotations. This development was theoretically grounded in neo-Kantian aesthetics and German formalism, in which, as a kind of extension of Lessing, painting, music, and the arts in general were to be studied empirically under the two headings of material means and psychological reception. Paradoxically, these investigations into the means and effects special to each of the arts led to music becoming the paradigm of all the arts. One possible reason for this was that in the nineteenth century campaign against traditional theories of imitation—or at least against the increasingly realistic interpretation of these theories—music was seen as the art least contaminated by an object of imitation. *Composition* came to mean a creative procedure in which the artist created "out of nothing" and arranged his material according to laws generated within the work itself. At the same time the example of music made it possible to rethink the relationship between form and content characteristic of classical theory. Form was no longer thought of as a means of expressing a certain idea, but as indissoluble from, and co-extensive with, the idea. *Composition* therefore was able to stand for an aesthetic of immanence in which art became an independent kind of knowledge of the world and was no longer, as it had been both in the Medieval and the classical traditions, the means by which certain "truths" or concepts were given rhetorical clothing.[1]

The extent to which this general formalist tradition entered into the theory and practice of the twentieth century architectural avant-garde was obscured by the doctrine of functionalism, which had the effect of re-activating an apparently more traditional view of the "content" of the work of architecture, in the guise of the "architectural programme".

If, however, we exclude certain extreme "functionalists", we have to admit that formalism was one of the strongest impulses behind architectural modernism.[2] But the relationship between architecture and formalism was somewhat different from that which existed in the other arts. More than they, architecture maintained a stubborn stylistic eclecticism throughout the nineteenth century. This seems to be due to the fact that in architecture reference to the tradition is by means of syntagmata, figures, or tropes of such relative size that they refuse to be re-absorbed into the texture of the work as a whole. In the other arts it was possible throughout the nineteenth century to maintain a connection with tradition while at the same time breaking with many traditional procedures. (One thinks for example of the loss of tonal centrality in the work of Robert Schumann.) What was left of the tradition was subtle enough not immediately to give the impression that it was a quotation or imitation of previous forms. In this sense architecture seems the most archaic of the arts. Until the Renaissance it was common in all the arts for new work to reiterate extensive passages of old work without any suggestion of what we would now call plagiarism. Architecture is the only art where this practice still exists.

At least in part, the purpose of functionalism was to try to exorcise those persistent forms whose semantic and expressive functions depended on the repetition of previous forms. To this extent, functionalism was an alibi for a system of forms that were to be innocent of stylistic contamination. The meaning of a building could now be transferred from its form to its content, cutting form adrift and leaving it free to develop its own immanent meanings.

This process depended on compositional procedures precisely to the extent that the architecture avoided the repetition of previous formal solutions and the meanings embedded in them. This is evident if we take the example of neo-Plasticism. Though Mondrian was a painter, he worked closely with architects, with whom he shared a certain body of doctrine. His writings contain a litany of terms like "dynamic equilibrium", "mutual relations", "balance", "movement", "constructive elements", "relations of position", "determinate and objective composition", all of which are part of an attempt to develop a vocabulary with which to describe formal relationships in space. Moholy-Nagy was another theorist who developed a compositional terminology. The following quotation from his *Von Material zu Architectur* not only demonstrates this, but also shows the connection between functionalism and formalism already mentioned:

> The elements necessary to the fulfillment of a building unit in a spatial creation that can become a spatial experience for us. The ordering of space in this case is not more than the most economical union of planning methods and human needs. The current programme plays an important role in this but does not entirely determine the type of space created.[3]

It is clear that function—determining relationships that *can* become a spatial (that is, formal) experience but that does not *entirely* determine the type of space created—is merely a mask for form. All the escape hatches are carefully left open to provide a retreat from too rigorous an interpretation of functional determinism.

Function, in this system of ideas, provides a rationale for compositional play. It also acts as a catalyst. The main difference between modernist and classical composition is that in the former there is a high degree of freedom in the relationships between the parts. It is not so much that the elements themselves are infinite. Moholy-Nagy's definition of space is "the relationship between the positions of bodies" suggests that, for him at least, the elements were given and finite ("found").[4] It was their possibilities of combination that were infinite, since the rules for these were topological (they were "kinds of" relationships). The rest was up to the free invention of the architect.

When we turn from theory to practice we find the same thing. Rietveld's house for Madame Schroeder is a carefully composed three-dimensional object. The play of lines and planes is not the result of constructional necessity, even though the memory of such necessity enters into their semantics. In the numerous projects that usually preceded Le Corbusier's final solutions (for example, The Palace of the Soviets or the Centrosoyus), one can sense the exhilaration with which the architect plays with all the permutations of relationship between the fixed elements.[5] Functional distribution is only one among many types of variable that have to be synthesised into the solution. It is the degree to which these kinds of design are free from fixed rules or combination and are active and dynamic in their free play of forms, not the presence or absence of composition as such, that differentiates them from academic composition.

Nevertheless, despite the obvious importance of composition in modernist practice and despite the fact that the idea of composition earned with it progressivist overtones of artistic formalism, the connotations of the word in avant-garde circles were overwhelmingly negative and were irrevocably connected with the academic tradition and the architecture of stylistic imitation represented by the Ecole des Beaux-Arts. Therefore it might be helpful to glance at the role composition played in this tradition.

For Quatremère de Quincy the word *composition* was associated with the decline in the great building enterprises of the past and the resulting proliferation of vast and unbuildable paper projects. As he remarked in his *Dictionnaire*:

> One must say that modern times, and above all the schools, have perhaps allowed too much architectural composition to enter the practical exercises of students. One might observe that this abuse is derived, in its own way, from the same cause that multiplied the discourses and compositions of the rhetoreticians in ancient Rome.[6]

But the word *composition* does not seem to have come into general use in the Ecole des Beaux-Arts until the mid-nineteenth century. Before this the word *disposition* was more common.[7] Its use seems to be connected with a cluster of phenomena, one of the most important of which is eclecticism. Composition becomes a means by which rules of design common to all styles can be established. Already in the case of Dubut and Durand the weakening of meanings carried by the classical figures made it both possible and necessary to reduce these figures to ciphers in a system of combinations. *Composition* in academic usage seems to presuppose a body of rules that are astylar. It is true that before the 1880s the stylistic tradition was never abandoned. But there is much evidence in nineteenth century architectural criticism that the styles seemed increasingly "inauthentic". The apparent vitality of stylistic eclecticism in the nineteenth century is matched only by the virulence with which it was attacked from all quarters. Within the context of this collapse of "stylistic conviction", both the French and the English depended increasingly on compositional formulae, whether these were more or less regular as in the Ecole de Beaux-Arts, or irregular and picturesque, as in the English Gothic Revival and Free Style.

The idea of composition was directly inherited by the twentieth century avant-garde from the academic tradition. Moreover, in both cases it seems to have derived its authority from the same cause, namely the lack of any culturally imposed rules of style. If this was indeed the case, it would not be the first time that a revolutionary movement borrowed the structures and institutions of the very regime that it sought to destroy.

One of the ways in which composition was assimilated by modernism is illustrated by the spate of books on composition that overtook architectural discourse, at least in the anglophone countries, in the first decades of the twentieth century. Probably none of these books are of any great intrinsic value, but they do show how avant-garde ideas and attitudes filtered down to the more conservative ranks of the profession and the role that composition played in this process. An interesting example is provided by two books by the English architect Howard Robertson, *The Principles of Architectural Composition* and *Modern Architectural Design*.[8] The impulse for these books came from the revival of classicism, which was such a general phenomenon in Europe and America in the early twentieth century. (The frequency with which the change from the Gothicising forms of National Romanticism and Art Nouveau to those of classicism was a prelude to modernism is demonstrated in the work of Peter Behrens, Karl Moser, Mies and Le Corbusier, among others.) The message of Robertson's first book is that there are fundamental rules of composition in architecture that are independent of styles. Styles have relative value: they depend on the revolutions of taste. The values of architecture, on the contrary, are permanent. Robertson studies these under such headings as unity, composition of masses, contrast, proportion in detail, scale, composition of the plan, and relation of the plan to elevation. Clearly those categories are based on the teaching of the Ecole des Beaux-Arts, where Robertson had studied. They also depend on classical theory insofar as they claim that the rules of architecture are transhistorical. Most of the examples are of traditional buildings; nevertheless, there are certain similarities between the arguments in the book and those in Le Corbusier's *Vers une architecture*.

In his second book Robertson enlarges on some of the themes found in the first. The significance of this second volume lies in the fact that most of the examples are 'modern', and the tone of the book is cautiously 'avant-garde'. The author wants to show that applying the universal principles of architecture does not preclude a 'new architecture' suitable for a new way of life. If there is nothing contradictory in this it is because the 'principles' are entirely astylar. Robertson's new architecture tends to be rather anodyne, and his argument entirely lacks Le Corbusier's dialectical power. But these two books clearly show the continuing role of composition in the transition from a classicising to a modernist position.

Given these palpable connections, where should we look for the origins of the violent antagonism of the twentieth century avant-garde to composition? If one of the sources of the modernism of the 1920s was the classical revival and the belief in the transhistorical values of architecture, another was the romantic movement, with its concern for the processes of generation, growth, and development. It is from this system of ideas that the avant-garde drew its suspicion of composition, and the notions of separate parts and forms that came with it.

Such ideas of finality go back far beyond the Ecole des Beaux-Arts; they reverberate through the whole of the classical tradition. *Composition* in its modern sense may be of fairly recent origin, but the set of ideas to which it owes its origin has its roots in antiquity. It concerns the notion of arranging the parts of architecture like elements in a syntax, and according to certain *a priori* rules, to form a whole. This general sense is exemplified in Alberti's artistic theory. In *Della Pittura*, Alberti uses the word *composizione* to mean "the properties with which the parts of the things seen are presented together in the picture" ("*ragione di dipingere con la quale le parti delle cose vedute si porgono insieme in pictura*").[9] The equivalent word in *De Re Aedificatoria* is *collatio*—one of three terms within the concept *concinnitas*, the other two being *numerus* and *finito*.[10] Naturally, for Alberti the word *collatio* does not mean exactly the same as our word *composition*. Classical theory between the sixteenth and eighteenth centuries was concerned with arranging the parts of an architectural body in a system of proportions. In François Blondel's *course,* 'compositon' refers to the application of musical proportion to the orders.[11] It is not until the eighteenth century that the problem of arranging or juxtaposing different bodies to form a whole begins to take precedence over the arrangement of parts within a single body. But both these kinds of composition depend equally on the idea of a whole being made out of parts that are, in some sense, already given, so that it is always possible to think of this whole as an aggregation, however much the parts may overlap to give a strong unitary reading.[12]

These ideas persist into the late eighteenth century, and not only in architecture. As Lionel Gossman has pointed out, the model of culture for the eighteenth century historian was that of "a mechanism of functionally interrelated parts, each of which could in principle be detached and studied on its own". According to this way of thinking, a type of organisation (such as chivalry) "could appear in different moments in history, in different guises, as part of similarly structured societies and to fulfill similar needs".[13] Here the idea of *composition* is extended to mean the combination of parts found in different historical or geographical contexts (somewhat recalling the Aristotelian doctrine of "scattered beauties").

This whole manner of thinking about art and about history was rejected by the Romantics. It was Novalis who gave one of the most succinct definitions of the aim of romanticism in the mimetic arts: "There is a symptomatic imitation and a genetic imitation. The only living one is the second."[14] As Tzvetan Todorov points out, this implies a shift of attention away from the relationship among forms (which is thought of as the imitation of Symptoms and connected to composition) to the process of production (genetic imitation).[15] In Schelling we find a similar idea: "works born of juxtaposition of forms… would still remain wholly without beauty since what must give the work of art as a whole its beauty can no longer be form but something above form, namely: the essence… the expression of the spirit that must dwell there".[16]

In the realm of architecture it was Gothic that most often exemplified these organicist ideas. The kind of eclecticism proposed by Legrand, Hope, and Raoul-Rochette—an eclecticism in which one would select the best parts from all styles and compose them into new wholes—was thought of by the adherents of the Gothic school as entailing "*les accouplements monstrueux*".[17] The unity of style which Gothicists like Viollet-le-Duc demanded was based on an analogy between architecture and organic nature. Viollet expressed this idea when he said that one should be able to deduce the form of an entire building from the observation of one of its parts. In such a synechdochic structure, it would be absurd to talk about composition. The final forms of architecture, as of nature, should be the result of a certain principle of structuration, from which the form would follow automatically without the intervention of the "composer" artist's conscious judgment. It was no more necessary to imagine the architect composing a building than it was to imagine God interfering with the events in the universe after the initial creative act, which would contain the seed of all that followed.[18]

Viollet is normally thought of as a rationalist, and the avant-garde of the 1920s has been seen as lying within this rational heritage in its promotion of an architecture based on the application of industrial production and mechanisation. But it is sometimes forgotten that Viollet-le-Duc, as for LeCorbusier, to name but two of the principal actors in this tradition, there was a strong analogy between mechanical and organic forms. This fusion of apparently contradictory ideas has a long history. MH Abrams has pointed out that in early nineteenth century theory there was often mutual infiltration between mechanistic and organic beliefs, with mechanists claiming that organisms were higher-order machines and organicists claiming that machines were rudimentary types of organisms.[19]

If, as I suggest, the idea of composition is intimately connected with the conflict between the classical and the romantic traditions, the concept that would best represent the antonym of composition would probably be impressed by the word *system*. In spite of the continued use of composition as a technique of design, there has been a persistent tendency within architectural modernism to gravitate toward a concept of the building as a system. No doubt this tendency ultimately owes a great deal to German transcendental idealism, to the notion that the art and architecture of any period should be a reflection of the *Zeitgeist* and that the element of "choice" that composition entails contradicts such a holistc view.

It would hardly be an exaggeration to say that the reaction against modernism in the last 15 years or so is a symptom of the rejection of the claims of this idealism, with its insistence on the indivisibility and inevitability of cultural and technical development. Seen in this perspective, the dichotomy represented by *composizione/projettazione* or *composition/system* still carries a great deal of ideological meaning. *Composition* has been variously interpreted throughout the history of criticism, and there are good reasons why it should be reinterpreted for today.

1   It should be stressed, however, that in the figure/concept dichotomy implied by classical doctrine, the concept is not so abstract nor the figure so dependent as the Romantics tended to assert.
2   An instance of this is the influence of Conrad Fiedler's ideas on the teaching course at the Bauhaus.
3   Moholy-Nagy, Lazlo, *Von Material zu Architektur*, Munich, 1929; in Banham, Reyner, *Theory and Design in the First Machine Age*, London: Architectural Press, 1960, p. 317.
4   Banham, *Theory and Design in the First Machine Age*.
5   This process is well documented in Cohen, Jean-Louis, "Le Corbusier and the Mystique of the USSR", *Oppositions 23*, Winter 1981, p. 85.
6   de Quincy, Quatremère, "Composition", in *Dictionnaire historique d'architecture*, Paris, 1832.
7   Van Zanten, David, "Architectural Composition at the Ecole des Beaux-Arts from Charles Percier to Charles Ganier", in *The Architecture of the Ecole des Beaux-Arts,* Arthur Drexler ed., New York: Museum of Modern Art, 1977, p. 112. Van Zanten gives *distribution* as a further precursor of the word *compositon,* but this had quite a different meaning; see de Quincy, Quatremère, "Distribution", in *Dictionnaire*.
8   Robertson, Howard, *The Principles of Architectural Composition*, London, 1924 and *Modern Architectural Design*, London, 1932.
9   Battista Alberti, Leon, *Della Pittura, II.*
10   Battista Alberti, Leon, *De Re Aedificatoria, IX, 5.*
11   Blondel, François, *Cours d'architecture enseigne dans l'academie royale d'architecture*, Paris, 1675–1683.
12   Paul Frankl's classic distinction between an additive Renaissance and a subtractive Baroque, while not absolutely wrong, requires qualification.
13   Gossman, Lionel, *Mediaevalism and the Ideologies of the Enlightenment,* Baltimore: Johns Hopkins University Press, 1968, p. 351.
14   *Novalis, Oeuvres Complètes*, 1975, Gueme, A ed., quoted in *Theories of the Symbol*, Tzvetan Todorov, Ithaca: Cornell University Press, 1984, p. 169.
15   Todorov, Tzvetan Todorov, *Theories of the Symbol*, Ithaca: Cornell University Press, 1984, p. 169.
16   Schelling, FWJ, *Sammtliche Werke,* Stuttgart and Augsburg, p. 302, quoted in *Theories of the Symbol,* Tzvetan Todorov Todorov, Ithaca: Cornell University Press, 1984, p. 169.
17   For the controversy between Raoul-Kochette on the one hand, and Lassuas, Viollet-le-Duc, and the *Annales archeologiques* on the other, see Pevsner, Nikolaus, *Some Architectural Writers of the Nineteenth Century*, Oxford: Clarendon Press, 1972, pp. 201–202.
18   A good idea of Viollet-le-Duc's organicism can be gained from the entry under Proportion in his *Dictionnaire Raisonne,* in which he makes the following criticism of Quatremère de Quincy:

> Quatremère's idea of proportion, as stated in his *Dictionnaire*, covers that of the fixed, necessary and always similar and reciprocal proportions between parts that have a determined end. The celebrated academician seems not to have grasped the fact that proportions in architecture do not imply fixed, constant relations... but... *variable* relations, with the purpose of obtaining a harmonic scale. Quatremère also seems to be mistaken when he adds: "... it is evident that all the creations of nature have their dimensions but all do not have proportions...". Here he confuses *dimensions* with *proportions* and if he had consulted a botanist, he would have learned that there exist in all vegetable forms relations of proportion based on a constant law of the whole to the part.

Viollet's argument, for all its obscurities, reveals the similarities as well as the differences between his ideas and those of Quatremère. While they both believed in the transcendental value of the unity between the whole and the parts of a building, they interpreted this concept differently. Quatremère believed that priority should be given to the final form of the whole, to which the parts and their functions were subordinate. For Viollet, on the contrary, the whole was immanent in every part from the very beginning. The whole was the result of, and dependent on, the parts.

Contemporary with Viollet-le-Duc's pronouncement, a parallel debate was taking place within the scientific community between the zoologists Geoffrey Saint-Hilaire and Georges Cuvier. Very broadly, Geoffrey maintained that there was a single plan of construction for all beings and that the various animal forms were imperfect replicas of a single morphological type—a concept that can be traced to the metaphysical doctrine of the great chain of beings. Cuvier, on the contrary, believed that the different animal forms could be explained by the adaptation to the conditions of existence.

This discussion was closely followed, not only by Gothicists like Viollet-le-Duc, but by a group of architects who favoured a reformed classicism, including Henri Labrouste and Léonce Reynaud. Cuvier's arguments provided both these groups with an intellectual framework within which to attack the academic classical tradition.

van Eck, Caroline, *Organicism in nineteenth century architecture*, Amsterdam, 1994, p. 216; Jacob, François, *The Logic of Life: a History of Heredity*, Princeton, Princeton University Press, 1973, p. 100ff.

19   Abrams, MH, *The Mirror and the Lamp,* Oxford: Oxford University Press, 1953, p. 186.

Vernacular Classicism

First published in *Architectural Design* 54, 5/6, 1984.

The theories of architecture put forward in a given period often consist of transformations and recombinations of earlier theories. Moreover, it sometimes happens that a later theory reverses an earlier one and that two concepts previously antithetical may become allies.

The phrase "vernacular classicism" seems to be an example of this type of transformation. To all appearances it is an oxymoron. Throughout the self-consciously classical periods—both Hellenistic and post-Renaissance—*classic* stands to *vernacular* as high art stands to low art, though the actual words were not used until after the Romantic Movement. In romanticism, ideas associated with the vernacular were given a value independent of the place they had held in the classical hierarchy of artistic styles. The "low mimetic" style became the model for art in general and was used to express the kinds of serious ideas previously reserved for the "high mimetic" style.[1] But in romantic thought, the meanings carried by the two terms remained antithetical.

The word *classical* or *classic* was not used generally in connection with architecture or the visual arts until after the German Romantic Movement, when the opposition classic/romantic was first coined.[2] Previously, when critics or historians wished to refer to the art of Greece or Rome, they usually spoke of the "antique". Nonetheless, in poetics the word *classical* was used as early as the

Serlio, Scena Comica. From *The Five Books of Architecture*, 1611.

second century AD, when the grammarian Aulus Gellius used it to distinguish between the *scriptor classicus* and the *scriptor proletarius*. The words *classicus* and *proletarius* were borrowed from Roman tax law; *classicus* referred to the first of the four social orders supposedly founded by Servius Tullius. In this metaphorical translation to literature, the *scriptor classicus* was he who wrote for the few, and the *scriptor proletarius* for the many.

The word *classicus* was revived in the Renaissance, first in Italy, then in France and England, when it meant either texts used for instruction in schools or standard Greek and Roman texts worthy of imitation by modern authors. In this context, *classical* had the connotation of 'highest class', and it entailed the stylistic transformation of the various vernaculars of post-Medieval Europe in conformity with Greek or Roman models. It need hardly be said that this is one of the senses in which the word is still used today, though its normative implications are no longer taken for granted.[3]

It seems quite legitimate to use *classical* in this sense to describe the architecture of antiquity as well as the literature. The connection was indeed made in the Renaissance and in the following three centuries during which classical theory dominated all aspects of European culture. The post-Renaissance period revived not only many of the artistic practices of the ancients, but also their artistic theory: that of Vitruvius in architecture and those of Aristotle's *Poetics* and Horace's *Art of Poetry* in literature and painting. It is chiefly from these sources that academic classicism derived such fundamental ideas as *imitation* and *decorum*.

Thus, both in a certain phase of antiquity itself and in the Renaissance, *classical* signified practices codified in a system of canonic rules which claimed superiority over all other practices, whether these were taken as 'grammatical' in a narrow sense, or more broadly 'artistic'. A similar process had taken place in India in about the fourth century BC, when the ancient language of the Vedas

Serlio, Scena Tragica. From *The Five Books of Architecture*, 1611.

185

was codified by the grammarians and was called Sanskrit (from the roots, *san,* together, and *Kr,* make).

The word *vernacular* is equally derived from social and economic concepts. *Verna* meant slave, and *vernacular* signified a person residing in the house of his master. Hence the later applied meaning—first to language and then to the arts—of local, indigenous, and lowly forms.

Within the context of European history, then, the word *vernacular* can be to apply to practices of *making* (linguistic, constructional, etc.) that are either anterior to or untouched by classical theory and practice. Such practices, continuing in parallel with those of 'high art', were recognised by classical theory and were placed by it at the lowest level of the artistic hierarchy (in Serlio's representation of Comedy, for example, where the *fabrique* consists of 'vernacular' buildings arranged without symmetry, in contrast to the classical symmetry of the noble style more appropriate for Tragedy).

After the breakup of the classical system at the end of the eighteenth century, however, these nonclassical vernacular forms of art began to be studied in and for themselves. They began to be thought of not as 'styles' within a larger system, but as forms of art possessing their own significance, challenging the universalist claims of the classical canon. Art and literary criticism, after the onset of romanticism and historicism, attempted to reverse the values of the classical and the nonclassical

Right: Leone Battista Alberti, San Andrea in Mantua, designed 1470.

Opposite: Strasbourg Cathedral.

(eg. to establish Medieval art as superior to classical art) or to relativise all systems according to some theory of historical development.

Eric Auerbach's seminal literary study *Mimesis*, 1946, is an outstanding example of the latter tradition. Auerbach distinguished between the typology of classical literature and that of various nonclassical texts, notably the Bible and Medieval literature. Whereas, according to Auerbach, classical literature was characterised by "an abundant display of connectives… a precise gradation of temporal, comparative and concessive hypotaxes… and participle construction", the Bible and the writings of the Medieval period had a tendency to "string different pictures together like beads" and to "divide the course of events into a mosaic of parcelled pictures".[4] He saw these and other related features as belonging to a specifically Christian tradition whose ideas could not have been expressed in terms of classical decorum, since they demanded a mixture of styles: the treating of noble subjects in an ignoble setting.

Whether or not it would be legitimate to identify this kind of paratactic literary structure with 'vernacular' art in general, it seems evident that Auerbach is describing a general nonclassical tradition which flourished in the early period of Christian culture and which owed a great deal to local traditions. Clearly there are problems in trying to apply this paradigm to *all* Medieval art. The Gothic cathedral, for instance, is by no means a 'vernacular' building. It is a codified representational system, and, as Panofsky showed, was organised with a logic that was analogous to scholastic thought. It can therefore be claimed that High Gothic art had many of the underlying characteristics of classicism. Indeed it was itself based on antique architecture, in the form in which it had survived the Dark Ages and as modified by northern vernacular habits. But Medieval 'imitation' of building allows for a greater degree of paratactic freedom than is permitted in the predominantly hypotactic structures of classical architecture. The acceptance of the unequal towers of Chartres and other cathedrals and the additive and pragmatic arrangement of monastic complexes are cases in point. In contrast to this, a classical building was conceived as a body whose parts, perfectly distinct in themselves, were related to each other in a coordinated and self-sufficient hierarchy, on the analogy of the human body. The concept of 'order' which this exemplifies, and which characterised classical thought, was summed up in the Pythagorean epigram "order and measure *(taxis* and *symmetria)* are pleasing, disorder and excess *(ataxis* and *asymmetria)* are ugly and baneful".[5] Whatever logic the Gothic cathedral may have possessed, it did not represent this kind of order. It may have been intended to lead the faithful to a vision of perfection, but it did not in itself constitute a bodily image of such perfection.

What appealed to the Romantics about Medieval art was its mixture of styles and its parataxis. As evidence of a liking for a mixture of styles we can quote Ruskin in *The Stones of Venice*. "Everything in nature", he says, "has good and evil in it, and artists, considered as searchers after truth are… to be divided into three great classes…. Those on the right perceive and pursue the good and leave the evil; those in the centre, *the greatest,* perceive and pursue the good and the evil together and the whole thing verily as it is; those on the left perceive and pursue the evil and leave the good." [My italics.][6] Ruskin's "three great classes" are, of course, the same as those mentioned by Aristotle in the *Poetics*; he simply inverts them. As for the Romantics' love of parataxis, we find it in both literary and architectural criticism. In one of his "Fragments", Nuvalis describes the ideal modern poetry thus: "Disconnected, incoherent narratives that nonetheless have associations, like *dreams*. Simply poems that are perfectly harmonious, but also without coherence or any meaning… which must be like pure fragments of the most disparate ideas."[7] A similar attraction for the irrational and incomprehensible is found in the young Goethe's remarks about Strasbourg Cathedral: "With what unlooked for emotions did the sight surprise me… a sensation of wholeness, greatness filled my soul, which, composed of a thousand harmonious details, I could

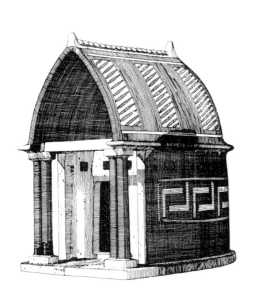

savour and enjoy, yet by no means understand or explain."[8] Friedrich Schlegel's descriptions of Gothic are couched in similar terms.

The notion of parataxis, or "laying things side by side" might seem, at first sight, incompatible with that other crucial concept of romantic aesthetics: organic wholeness. But for the Romantics the fragmentary and apparently disordered surface of a work of art, far from indicating a lack of organic unity, was in fact a sign of a more profound unity, which escaped analysis because it sprang from the depths of the artist's unconscious mind.

The 'primitivism' we find in the Enlightenment is very different from this romantic approach to vernacular architecture. The 'return' is not to a particular, idiosyncratic culture, based on local craft traditions; it is to the sources of architecture as a universal language obeying the necessities of natural law.

Neo-classicism looked back to a 'natural' architecture that must have existed before society became corrupted, or before architecture became fragmented into all those 'dialects' that historical research and travel had uncovered. The postulation of a common, primitive culture, which Laugier shares to some extent with Rousseau, does not involve the empirical discovery of an actual vernacular; it is an hypothesis based on what logically should have been the case, conflating the logical with the chronological.

We do not know a great deal about the pre-monumental architecture of ancient Greece, but what we do know leads us to believe that it had no relation to Laugier's primitive hut. Nor is it certain what the sources of Greek monumental architecture were.[9] Laugier was no more concerned with the real Mediterranean vernacular than was Rousseau with a historical primitive society. He was concerned with a distillation of classical doctrine. He was not seeking to return to the earliest hours of man, but to *the* pure sources of classical architecture. This process entailed, not the discovery of vernacular building, but the *re-vernacularisation* of classicism with which to substantiate a myth of origins.

Therefore, when we define *vernacular* in terms of the eighteenth century notion of the primitive, we are involved in an argument that is characteristically classical. The myth of origins, as recorded by Vitruvius, was an integral part of classical

Top left: Temple or house from Perachora, circa 750–725 BC.

Top right: The Market House, Tetbury, circa 1700.

doctrine and was necessary to the establishment of classicism as a universal system based on nature. But to 'understand' a particular belief in historical terms is not necessarily to subscribe to it. Today we can hardly fail to see the attempt of the eighteenth century to create an architectural ontology as having been bounded by eighteenth century epistemology. The belief in the essential being of architecture, and of its origins, is consistent with, and inextricable from, the ideas of the eighteenth century grammarians. Like language, architecture was held to be a universal form of knowledge, but one that was not thoroughly worked out. It had come about through the rough-and-ready ordering of our representations. The history and practise of both language and architecture presented the observer with the elements of truth; it was up to him to unravel the skein that had been wound up through the centuries without system, and to put its threads into the right order.[10] It is only in terms of such a linguistics that we can understand what the eighteenth century meant by ontological truth, and how it was applied in architectural discourse.

When, therefore, we use the expression "vernacular classicism", we are describing a process by which classicism, within the terms of its own theory of language, recreates its own origins, it is a movement backward within a closed *episteme*. In all attempts to discover an ontology of architecture within classicism (just as in all those cases where the classical system filtered down to local builders—from Italian farms to English market halls), we are likely to find traces of those elements of high style which originally belonged to a sophisticated and highly developed architecture of monuments—the very antithesis of vernacular building.

1   For a definition of high and low mimetic styles, see Frye, Northrop, *Anatomy of Criticism*, Princeton: Princeton University Press, 1971.
2   By Friedrich Schlegel; see Wellek, Rene, *History of Modern Criticism*, Cambridge: Cambridge University Press, 1981, vol. 2, p. 14.
3   Vestiges of the normative status of classical studies are curiously preserved in the Latin textbooks still used in schools in England. In them one still finds the general rules of grammar set out in the opening pages, as if the study of grammar and the study of Latin were one and the same thing. This example shows how the way of thinking engendered by classical texts (for example, in terms of the grammatical rules of language) has remained attached to the circumstances of its origin, and has superimposed itself on an indigenous and more empirical tradition. One learns grammar in connection with Latin, not in connection with one's own language, which is thought of as being "without rules".
4   Auerbach, Eric, "Roland against Ganelon" and "Adam and Eve" in *Mimesis*, Princeton: Princeton University Press, 1968.
5   Timpanaro-Cardini, *Pitagorici, Testimonianze e Frammenti*, Florence, 1958, p. 299; quoted in *Michelangelo and the Language of Art* , David Summers, Princeton: Princeton University Press, 1981, p. 314.
6   Ruskin, John, "The Nature of Gothic", in *The Stones of Venice*, London: George Alien, 1886, p. 187.
7   Novalis, *Oeuvres completes,* A Guerue ed., Paris, 1975; quoted in *Theories of the Symbol*, Tzvetan Todorov, Ithaca: Cornell University Press, 1982, p. 176.
8   Von Goethe, Wolfgang, "Von deutscher Baukunst", 1772. English translation in *Goethe on Art,* John Gage ed., London: Scolar Press, 1980, pp. 103–112.
9   Coulton, JJ, "The Problem of the Beginning", in *Greek Architects at Work,* London: Granada, 1982.
10 Foucault, Michel, "Speaking", in *The Order of Things*, New York: Pantheon, 1970.

A Way of Looking at the Present Situation

First published in *Casabella* 490, April 1983.

Changes in collective sensibility often establish themselves insidiously without the support of a coherent architectural theory. (I refer to a consensus within the architectural community, broadly defined, and not to any institutionalised consensus among the public or patronage, which, following its decline during the nineteenth century, has finally disappeared completely.)

It is possible, at the moment, to recognise a certain uniformity in the projects displayed in European magazines, exhibitions, and competitions, certain morphological and thematic regularities, which clearly differentiate this work from that produced a decade ago, or, more generally, from the work produced during the time (roughly 1946–1970) when the tenets of 'modern architecture' were applied without being fundamentally questioned. There are exceptions that are not easily explained, such as that in England, where it is still quite usual for exhibitions to consist largely of schemes inspired by a picturesque 'meccanoism'. But generally there has clearly been some (perhaps short-lived) compromise between the modernist tradition and new ideas based on a reassessment of the larger architectural tradition of classicism. This compromise usually avoids the literal quotation of those stylistic tropes handed down from the eclectic tradition, which were outlawed by the Modern Movement. For example, it still accepts the modernist rejection of ornament, or at least has reduced ornament to such devices as alternating material and colours, which remain tectonic, geometrical, and nonfigurative. But at the same time, it clearly makes a connection with the architectural tradition through such generalised themes as column, room, corridor, window, roof, and is concerned with notions of surface, limit, symmetry and difference, all of which bring into play the idea of the limits of architecture and open the possibility of architectural discourse as a critique rather than as a dogmatism. There is an awareness that, even in the avant-garde (or especially in the avant-garde), there was an element of transgression, creating a tension between a received tradition and new ideas, and that the meaning of avant-garde architecture lay precisely in the space between these two forces. Thus, this new sensibility seems to accept some of the reductionism of the Modern Movement. But in acknowledging that fundamental changes have occurred in the modern world, it assigns the origin of these changes to a period more remote from the present than

was believed in the modernist movement itself: to the late eighteenth century, when, for the first time, doubts arose as to the continuity of an 'organic' tradition and attempts were made to reform architecture on the principles of natural law and reason—both on the discovery of the true tradition and on a skepticism of tradition in general.

In attempting to give this phenomenon a theoretical framework, it would be wise to avoid redundant hypotheses—such as the one that holds that European culture took a wrong turn around 1800—hypotheses that take into account only the 'regressive' aspects of eighteenth century thought and ignore its 'progressive' aspects. (These two words are used in a descriptive, not prescriptive way.) Rather, we should seek a theory that does only as much as is necessary to explain the phenomenon. It might, for example, be argued that what we are witnessing is a reversal of the positions taken in the classical avant-garde of the 1920s.

There is, at the moment, a strong current of feeling that this avant-garde was somehow 'betrayed', that its utopian ideals have been distorted by its very success in the sphere of construction and real estate development. This betrayal is variously interpreted as a true betrayal (the extreme versions of this view, held by Claude Schnaidt and Anatole Kopp, among others, maintain that modernism was the true expression of an as yet unachieved socialism) or, as with Manfredo Tafuri, as the revelation of an underlying complicity between the Modern Movement and the capitalist system. According to Tafuri, the "materialism" of the Modern Movement was the final ideology of a political process that no longer had any use for philosophical idealism; the present absorption of modernism into the system is, therefore, less a betrayal than an exposure, in which what remained of the subversive in the original impulse has now been dissolved in an all-embracing system from which there is no escape.

Traces of these arguments can be seen in some recent pronouncements. (It is these that have to some extent instigated the present article.) OM Ungers says that "functionalism" vitiated the Modern Movement from the start. Vittorio Gregotti replies that it was not functionalism that was wrong, but a later "economic empiricism".[1] Perhaps a better term, which embraces both points of view, would be "Positivism". Positivism had its Utopian progressive component from the beginning. The point about Positivism, however, is not (pace Gregotti) whether or not it was Utopian, but the manner in which this utopianism was seen as functioning. In embracing a positivistic attitude, the Modern Movement applied to architecture the criteria of the physical sciences (and it was part of positivism that *all* aspects of culture could and should be so defined).

From one point of view, the 'experimentalism' in the Modern Movement had as its purpose the freeing of architecture from academic dogma. The theory of this Modern Movement never said that architecture was "nothing but" science

Opposite: Friedrich Weinbrenner, Koenigstrasse, Karlsruhe, 1808.

Left: Georgio Grassi, A Monestiroli, and R Raffaele Conti, Student housing at Chieti, 1978.

and technology. What it said was that its *main impulse* should be *openness* to technological and social reality. For this to happen it was necessary to reject *a priori* rules of architecture altogether. Insofar as there were rules to be applied to architecture, these should be the rules of scientific experiment.

We therefore see in modernism a positive and a negative charge, as it were. The rules of correct architecture were now implicit, not explicit. They were a court of appeal, whose purpose was to regulate the architectural system not to provide it with a constitution. This countervalency of the criteria of correct architecture varied between an explicit dialectic, as in Le Corbusier, and a suppressed and unacknowledged system of values, as in Hannes Meyer and ABC. But it was always there.

The contemporary situation seems to be one in which these charges have been reversed. Faced with the palpable inadequacy of a practice that refuses the formulation of architectural principles, and leaves them to work themselves out within the context of external criteria, it seeks these principles as a structure against which to solve empirical problems.

It is not a question of the autonomy of architecture—a meaningless phrase, since any principles of architecture are empty until embodied in an action, in the reality of a situation (using this word in literal and metaphorical senses—site, programme, technique).

Architecture itself, considered as a culturally defined concept, is merely a situation at a level deeper than immediate contingency. It is therefore neither necessary nor possible to establish it as a transcendental entity outside and beyond contingency, a Platonic idea somehow acting as the mold for that from which it borrows its forms in the first place. But this is not to deny architecture its ideality or to say that we no longer need to distinguish between matter and form. The ideality of architecture (or any art) lies in its ability to exemplify an *a priori* necessity that can never be given by any *particular* set of empirical conditions whatever.

This necessity was placed by positivism within the empirical. If the present situation may be said, in a certain sense, to be a reversal of this, it is because there is now a tendency to see the architectural tradition as that which gives architecture its constitution, while it is the world of empirical action that acts as the regulator.

1   Gregotti, Vittorio, "Common Enemies", in *Casabella* , September 1982, p. 10.

The Significance of Le Corbusier

First published in *The Le Corbusier Archive*, vol. 1, 1984.

Le Corbusier, more than any other architect of the Modern Movement, insisted that architecture was the product of the individual creative intelligence. The order it created was ideal, not pragmatic. If he said, "The house is a machine for living in", it was not so much to annex architecture to a branch of empirical science as to use the machine as a model for a work of art whose form and structure were determined by laws internal to itself. The laws which applied to technology were different from those which applied to architecture, the first being directed to the solution of practical problems, the second to the creation of states of mind. In both cases, however, the desired results could be obtained only by understanding the laws which controlled their production.

From this point of view Le Corbusier's famous statement can be interpreted as a metaphor for an aesthetic theory which underlay avant-garde art in general, and which had been anticipated in Conrad Fiedler's concept of the "opacity" of the work of art.[1] Le Corbusier and Ozenfant reformulated this theory in their discussion of Cubism: "In true Cubism there is something organic that passes from the interior to the exterior. Cubism was the first to want to make the picture an object, and not a species of panorama as in old painting."[2] But the analogy made by Le Corbusier between a building and a machine was more than a poetic metaphor; it was based on the assumption of an ontological identity between science and art. For the first time—so we can reconstruct the implicit argument—technology and architecture, reality and its representation, could be seen as converging. Technology, freed from the domination of brute and intractable matter by the application of scientific laws, was approaching the condition of immateriality. Its products no longer demonstrated the conflict between matter and spirit, as in the Renaissance; they adumbrated the dissolution of matter *into* spirit. Architecture, as an art, no longer had the task of creating meaning by means of signs attached to the surfaces of the buildings. The 'meaning' of architecture was now immanent in the pure forms the new technology made possible. Like a *poesis* in which words are identical to the ideas they represent, architecture had no more need of the mediating role of conventional and arbitrary signs; it would become its own sign. In this fundamental belief of 'functional' architecture we see both a reflection of modernist dogma in general and a special ingredient, connecting this dogma to progress and technology and bringing to the forefront redemptive and eschatological themes that were often merely recessive in the other arts. Architecture was to be not only the symbol but also the instrument of a new society.

But if the fusion of art and technology was at the basis of modern theory, in the case of Le Corbusier it was combined with a concept of architecture derived from an older tradition—that of classicism. According to this view, architectural value could be measured only against an absolute and timeless standard. The test of technology was not only that it released new energies but that it made possible a return to the fundamental and ahistorical principles of architecture, as exemplified in the great 'classical' periods—calm periods in which the means available were exactly equal to the ends desired.

The theory of architecture put forward in Le Corbusier's articles in *L'Esprit Nouveau* in the early 1920s was, in fact, an attempt to fuse two contradictory points of view—one stemming from the tradition of seventeenth century classical thought, and the other from German idealist historicism. According to the first, architectural value rests on eternal principles and natural law, and the various technical modifications to which it is historically subject are seen as irrelevant to its essence. According to the second, architectural value is relative to its position in history, and does not depend on any principles which can be established *a priori*.

In this case technology must appear as one of the essential parts of architecture, since no architectural value can be established independently of its empirical application at a particular time and place. Whereas the first qualifies the value of the exemplum with a belief in the universal power of reason, the second discards the exemplum and replaces it with immanent values that emerge from the historical reality in which they are embedded.

In Le Corbusier's *L'Esprit Nouveau* articles there is an unresolved conflict between these two points of view—a conflict in which the architect and engineer appear as protagonists playing varying roles. While the works of the engineer reflect the underlying mathematical order of the universe, the engineer is also seen representing the blind forces of history and as working toward the solution of practical problems. His works constitute the highest collective achievement of mankind and lead toward the rational organisation of society. On the other hand, it is precisely the fact that the engineer is not consciously concerned with values and is free from ideology that makes it impossible for him to replace the artist/architect, whose task is to satisfy a longing for images of the ideal. It is thus that Le Corbusier justifies the role of the artist/architect in an industrial society and establishes the work of architecture as simultaneously a work of technology and a work of art. Although the architect and the engineer employ different means and have different intentions, they are both working to the same historical ends; architecture cannot ignore technology, as it did in the nineteenth century. We therefore find in Le Corbusier a double assertion. On the one hand, he invokes historical destiny and demands a total commitment to technology and, ultimately, to the technocratic state. On the other, he clings to the idea of the architect as creative subject who transforms technology into art, material production into ideology.

Assessments of the value of Le Corbusier's architecture inevitably tend to oscillate between the two poles he himself set up, depending on whether attention is focused on his technocratic utopianism or on his buildings and projects as part of an avant-garde, yet autonomous, architectural tradition. It is possible—and legitimate—to see his architecture, as one sees twentieth century avant-garde painting, music, and literature, as the product of a relationship between the creative subject and an objective world, an objective world consisting both of an internalised artistic tradition and of external reality. This relationship is not based on any *a priori* definition of the ideal or on any confining notion of artistic form. To reject his work because it is thus predicated on creative freedom and because its reference to the tradition is oblique and reductive would be tantamount to rejecting the entire tradition of modernism. If, on the contrary, we accept the viewpoint of modernism, the part technology plays in the works of Le Corbusier appears as a means to artistic freedom, to the opening up of new worlds of aesthetic meaning. Its relation to social utopia is then 'weak' in the sense applicable to other avant-garde art forms. This explains the continued value placed on Le Corbusier's architectural aesthetic—a valuation that often exists alongside a total rejection of his view of a society dominated by technology and the quasi-fascist politics that this view entailed. Yet understandable—and even inevitable—as this double critical standard may be, it runs the risk of reducing the work of Le Corbusier to a species of 'chamber music' and of concentrating on individual works whose systematic relation to each other and whose social and political content can be conveniently ignored. But we would be missing the essential quality of Le Corbusier's work if we ignored the fact that each individual project was not only an object in its own right, but a fragment of a greater whole, taking its place in an entire system. Nor was this system 'artistic' in a narrow formalistic sense: it was based on a reinterpretation of the historical relationship between architecture and the social realm. However much our judgment of Le Corbusier's work tends toward this critical compartmentalisation, his work must first be seen as a whole, since its overall assumptions shed light on its smallest parts.

The dichotomy between engineering and architecture set forth in *L'Esprit Nouveau* is symptomatic of a dialectical tendency that runs through all Le

Corbusier's theory and practice, where a number of oppositions are either stated or implied: order/disorder; Platonic harmony/contingency; mind/organism; form/structure; symmetry/asymmetry. Though given a new urgency by the need to absorb the spirit of historicist idealism and accommodate the disruptive forces of technology, this dialectic belongs essentially to an eighteenth century tradition. It is totally absent in the theory and practice of the Dutch and German architects of the Modern Movement. (It is not by chance that Le Corbusier quoted Laugier in support of his ideas about urban planning.)

The relation between this recurring dialectic and the formal principles of his architecture can be seen most clearly if we compare the principles set out in the early chapters of *Vers une architecture,* collected from the articles in *L'Esprit Nouveau,* and his houses of the 1920s. The classicism inherent in Le Corbusier's conception of architecture is immediately apparent in his definition of the three parameters of design—volume, surface, plan. It is volume that establishes the primary experience of geometrical solids seen in light. It is, however, the surface bounding the volume which, properly speaking, constitutes architecture, since the surface must contain openings referring to the practical organisation of the building. There is thus a direct transition from pure geometrical form, which bypasses the traditional role of structure as symbolic representation as found, for example, in Auguste Perret. The structure, in Le Corbusier's system, is a concealed skeleton which simply provides a hidden and implicit order. The surface must be 'patterned', but in such a way as to preserve the unitary quality of the volume but without the order provided by a classical structural module. The pure cube and the regular grid provide a discipline within which the size, position, and degree of penetration of the voids can be determined by improvisation, following the suggestions of the plan.

In all these prescriptions there is a common dialectical theme. Freedom and improvisation, and technical determinism, are not presented as absolutes, as they are respectively in expressionist or *Sachlich* architecture. They are seen as only taking on meaning within an ordered and ideal framework, and in relation to a ground—whether this ground is seen to be established by the rational grid or the Platonic volume. Le Corbusier's formal syntax is therefore grounded on principles similar to those developed by *Gestalt* psychology and involves the establishment of the same controlled spatial field as exists in Cubist painting. Painting and architecture each transform a putative 'reality' into a virtual world whose reality is both phenomenal and tautological. In the houses at Garches and Poissy there is a constant ambiguity because the cube of the building is simultaneously established and denied, creating an aesthetic tension which the mind is always trying to resolve.

The analogy between Le Corbusier's houses and his own Purist painting is much more literal and figural than the analogy with Cubism as a whole. In both cases a Platonic regular frame defines a field in relation to which a number of objects are arranged—bottles, glasses, pipes in the painting; staircases, bathrooms, passages, closets in the houses. Both objects and spaces usually take the form of hollow containers whose curved convex surfaces project into, and interlock with, the neutral field. In considering this figural system, formal analysis must give way to an analysis of content and meaning. The arrangement of architectural volumes could have a direct analogy with only one kind of painting: *still life.* Not only are the objects of a still life susceptible to a high degree of abstraction without losing recognisability (an essential property of Cubism that distinguishes it from abstract painting), they also have a certain range of connotations which relates them to the contents of a house. As Meyer Shapiro has pointed out, the elements of a still life belong to a class of intimate, domestic, bourgeois objects whose meaning is derived, in the first instance, from their dependence on human action and purpose.[3] Moreover, the objects of a still life do not have a fixed spatial relationship to each other (unlike, say, the parts of a machine or the protagonists in an allegorical scene). They can be arranged at will, and therefore stand for the notion of the freedom of the artist. The freedom of arrangement of the objects given by technology which Le Corbusier insisted on is analogous to this, and relates him to a nineteenth century tradition that relieved the artist of responsibility for public statements and made him master of a private domain of sensibility. Allowing for the necessary change of scale, the solid volumes in Le Corbusier's 'Purist' houses— closets, bathrooms and so on— correspond to the objects in his paintings both in their flexibility of arrangement and their intimate functions and connotations. In the traditional *hôtel particulier,* of which the Corbusian houses are a kind of inversion, these humble and intimate spaces were concealed in the space between the principal rooms. In Le Corbusier's houses (in which there are no longer any domestic secrets), they become the main elements of plastic organisation. Interacting with the spatial field, and flooded with a neutral and uniform light, they suggest a domestic life of informal but bracing activity and of continuous aesthetic stimulation.

In his articles in *L'Esprit Nouveau* and in his houses of the 1920s, Le Corbusier may be said to have laid the foundations of his architectural aesthetic and to have projected a new style of private life. As in the case of a number of other architects of the Modern Movement, the private bourgeois residence was the experimental laboratory in which many of the basic ideas of a new architecture were developed. In recent years critical attention has tended to focus on this phase of formal exploration, but, if we look on Le Corbusier's influence within a larger time scale, we see that this was not always the case. In the period immediately after the Second World War, when the objective conditions of reconstruction and of welfare-state capitalism seemed momentarily to confirm Le Corbusier's conception of the architectural types of a new social order, his larger public buildings were the primary object of attention. Among these it is necessary to make a distinction between individual public buildings, designed as self-contained entities and appearing to establish a comprehensive typological repertoire, and mass housing and urbanism. In the 1920s Le Corbusier's research into the repeatable private dwelling (the "cell" from which, according to him, the whole of architecture should grow) and the city went hand-in-hand, underlining the extent to which "the housing problem" was seen as co-extensive with the problem of the modern city. If we exclude the office buildings forming the commercial core of the city, public buildings played no greater part in his urban plans than they did in the much less comprehensive plans of Ludwig Hilbersheimer, Walter Gropius, or Ernst May. Yet in the 1920s and early 1930s Le Corbusier designed a number of public buildings to be injected into an existing urban fabric—buildings whose relation to his ideal city plans remained ambiguous. Among the most significant of these projects were the Salvation Army Hostel and the Pavillon Suisse in Paris; the League of Nations building in Geneva; the Rentenanstalt office building in Zurich; the Centrosoyus building in Moscow. At least part of the fascination these projects held for architects and schools of architecture in the 1940s and 50s lay in the fact that they offered entirely new solutions to characteristically modern problems, while at the same time they could be assimilated to the compositional principles of the Ecole des Beaux-Arts. Their novelty lay in their exploitation of the freedom provided by modern construction and in their asymmetry and flexibility of articulation. But these new elements, which radically reinterpreted the traditional formal syntax of architecture, were subjected to a more or less traditional compositional procedure, and this seemed to give 'architecture' a new lease of life and to justify Le Corbusier's claim that the perennial values of architecture were compatible with the acceptance of the most innovative techniques and forms. A striking feature of these projects was their physical detachment from their immediate environment, but this quality was not likely to appear strange to architects who were familiar with Beaux-Arts projects of the turn of the century. Such projects were often characterised by programmatic complexity and public symbolism and were designed for imaginary sites with no context. They established a sort of *raison d'etre* for the 'architect-as-composer', operating on a *tabula rasa* where the nineteenth century equation "Function:Form" could be clearly asserted. Although most of these projects by Le Corbusier, unlike the Beaux-Arts projects, were, in fact, adapted to severe site constraints (and owed much of their brilliance to this fact), they were nonetheless thought of as complete entities, as *Gestalten,* breaking the continuity of the urban tissue (Salvation Army Hostel, Centrosoyus, Rentenanstalt) or placed as objects in a weakly defined field of other objects (Pavillon Suisse).[4]

The supple and active nature of these compositions is clearly linked to the notion of the machine, with its articulated parts—a feature still found in the machines of the 1920s, automobiles, airoplanes, and ships—and, as in such machines, the separate parts tend to have their own symmetrical, figural independence.

A further feature of many of these projects is the interpenetration of volumes, a kind of "simultaneity" made possible by raising the main volume on *piloti* and constituting a version of the "free plan" that allows the ground floor (reception, concierge, public rooms, etc.) to be developed on a different axis from that of the main floors, with their regular cellular subdivisions. As much as the houses of the 1920s, these projects conform systematically to the "Five Points"—*piloti*, roof terrace, free plan, free facade, and *fenêtre en longueur*—and exploit them in a number of ways.

Strong as may have been the influence of Le Corbusier's public buildings of the 1920s and early 1930s on architects of the immediate post-war period, however, his own post-war work shows a significant change in direction. The most striking evidence of this is the change from crystalline forms and precise detailing derived from the use of smooth rendered surfaces and steel and glass curtain walls, from which all suggestion of material substance has been abstracted, to the use of massive sculptural forms, tactile surfaces, and crude detailing associated with the use of raw concrete, brick, and wood. Although the immediate cause of this change was no doubt the shortage of steel in the post-war period in Europe, it also seems to have been the result of a change in attitude that was already manifest in his work in the 1930s. This can be inferred not only from the introduction into his paintings of the 1930s of "objects of poetic reaction"— organic *objets trouvés* and the female figure—but also from the use in his buildings of local materials—particularly in a series of houses he designed for rural settings (the Errazuriz house, designed but never built, for Chile, the de Mandrot house at Le Pradet, and the house at Mathes).

Le Corbusier's loss of faith in the application of industrial techniques to architecture dates from considerably before the war and seems to have been the result of his own failure to interest either the government or industrial management in the mass production of housing. It should be mentioned, however, that Le Corbusier's conception of standardisation and rationalisation had been significantly different from that of the German architects of the Modern Movement, as exemplified in the housing programme undertaken in Frankfurt under the direction of Ernst May. Whereas for May and his collaborators the problem was to arrive at the minimum apartment by the standardisation of dwellings as a series of fixed types, for Le Corbusier the problem was to standardise only certain elements with highly specific functions, falling under the category of "equipment", and leave the architect free to arrange these elements according to artistic principles and within an envelope that need not be fixed *a priori*. This entailed a sort of architect's "patent" on the entire design and subjected the pragmatic process of rationalisation to decisions on the part of the artist/architect, assimilating (as in his theory) the presumed rationality of the production process to an all-embracing artistic will. It is only in the light of Le Corbusier's notion of a dominant spiritual ideal that would give direction to the industrial process (carried out by the man of "mediocre destiny") that we can explain how it was possible for him to abandon, in the 1930s, an internationalist rationalism, imbued with Platonic meaning, for a renewed belief in the primacy of "the heart" over "the head" and a return to concepts in many ways similar to the vitalistic and regionalist ideas of his youth in La Chaux-de-Fonds. The change is clearly seen in his letter to Karel Teige of 1929, in which he refutes the deterministic ideas of the *Neue Sachlichkeit* architects of the political left.[5] (A close reading of *Vers une architecture,* however, shows that this change was perhaps more one of emphasis than of substance.) The shift in view must also be seen in relation to the new political climate in Europe, in which, under the influence of the economic depression, the internationalist optimism of the post-war years gave way to nationalist sentiment and authoritarian systems of government. In the early 1930s there was a general reaction against the avant-garde, especially in Russia and Germany, where it had established a foothold in government-sponsored projects, and a return to tradition, whether classical or vernacular. Both Le Corbusier's connection with French syndicalism (which, in its belief in direct action and its concept of cultural renewal, had close analogies with Fascism) and his interest in the development of regional and peripheral cultures date from this period. Not only did he turn his attention to urban projects for Rio de Janiero and Algiers, but, in these projects, he abandoned the geometrical approach of his earlier city plans in favour of an "organic" and "geographical" urbanism in which giant linear megastructures followed the natural contours of a primordial nature and which were set in relation to the horizon of mountains and sea (a theme renewed later in his design for the Capitol of Chandigarh). In Algiers this new concept of urban form was expressive of a romantic notion according to which North African and French traditions could be integrated, to create a new Mediterranean culture—an idea reminiscent of the Pan-Germanism of the National Socialists and implying a partition of the world into regions of "natural" culture. The city is still seen as the visual analogue of a technological organisation, but it now becomes an extension of nature and is experienced as a "distant" panorama, either from the vantage point of the individual dwelling or, in a more idealised form, from the air.[6]

"Reconstruction", under the aegis of the post-war welfare state, provided Le Corbusier for the first time with a symbolic and practical role that no longer depended on Utopian projection or authoritarian global intervention. Nevertheless his post-war work continued to develop many of the themes of the 1930s and 40s. In this work there is a new stress on the isolated building as a unique monument set in nature—no longer the artificially 'natural' nature of the early city plans, but a nature already humanised by cultivation and containing evidence of a vernacular building tradition. There is an attempt—at Cap Martin, Ronchamp, La Tourette, and the buildings at Chandigarh and Ahmedabad in India—to draw ideas from a generalised 'Mediterranean' tradition, from ancient or mythological typologies, or simply from the *genius loci.* The pure stereometric forms of a rationalised and Platonised technology give way to a greater lyricism—to sloping surfaces, Catalan vaults, and free plastic modeling. The concrete frame now becomes a kind of *charpenterie* suggesting those machines reproduced in the encyclopedia of which Roland Barthes says: "The wood which constitutes them keeps them subservient to a certain notion of *play;* these machines are (to us) like big toys."[7] Whereas in the 1920s Le Corbusier's interest in proportional systems had taken the form of an *a posteriori* checking of regular surfaces, after the war it became, with the publication of the Modulor, a numerical scale that could give Platonic validity to the smallest details and the most irregular forms. The attempt was to show (against all empirical evidence) that mass production and standardisation were compatible with the greatest artistic freedom, and, as such, it was merely an extension of the philosophy propounded in the 1920s. At the same time there is an increased interest in the mathematical regularity underlying organic forms, referring back to his studies of nature under the tutelage of L'Eplattenier at La Chaux-de-Fonds and to the neo-Platonism and symbolism of the 1890s.

The most characteristic post-war development was the almost universal adoption of the *brise-soleil,* which became the signature of Le Corbusier's late style, as *piloti* had been of his early work. The *brise-soleil* was a means of counteracting the vulnerability of the fully glazed facade to heat gain without having to return to the traditional hole-in-wall solid facade. In a manner wholly characteristic of Le Corbusier's dialectical logic, the ideal transparency of the external wall was not abandoned; its effects were counteracted by the addition of a new tectonic element. The *brise-soleil* was more than a technical device; it introduced a new architectural element in the form of a thick, permeable wall, whose depth and subdivisions gave the facade the modeling and aedicular expression that had been lost with the suppression of the window and the pilaster. It must therefore be seen as a step toward the recovery of a tradition of the monumental. It made it possible to transform the slab or the tower, as at Algiers or in the Chandigarh Secretariat, into a monumental form whose surface could be manipulated to create a hierarchy of scales, proportional both to the human being and to the building as a whole.

The *brise-soleil* thus contributed to the isolation of the individual building. Even in the area of housing, the development of the Unité d'habitation led to the monumentalisation of a type that had, in Le Corbusier's earlier urban projects, been seen as part of a continuum, or as the backdrop to vegetation. At the same time, the increased interest of Le Corbusier in the linear city is indicative not only of a continuation of the regionalist philosophy exhibited in the plans for Rio de Janiero and Algiers, but also of the postulation of an "invisible" infrastructure—now little more than the mental hypostasisation of the existing exchange routes of industrial capitalism—which allows for the piecemeal and *ad hoc* development of individual monumental buildings. The Unité d'habitation show a continued preoccupation with the pre-war theme of mass housing, but they also reflect a more pragmatic approach to the establishment and dissemination of modern architecture, in which the grip of economic rationalisation has been relaxed. The objective of collective living is now to be achieved by the creation of huge oneiric and symbolic objects.

The tendency toward monumentalisation in Le Corbusier's later work accentuates the conflict inherent in his work between architecture as a symbolic form and architecture as the anonymous expression of a collectivised society. The greater Le Corbusier's effort to 'humanise' the unit of mass housing or the bureaucratic slab, the more problematic became the equation between architecture and technology. In contemplating his work, we are forced to detach our experience of the building as an aesthetic object from our idea of the economic and industrial nexus of which it is a part.

The sense of unreality that this engenders is reinforced by another contradiction—that between architecture considered as the subversion and transformation of the tradition, and architecture as a common, "popular" practice based on technical norms. The adoption of norms was bound to lead to the formation of habits and conventions and to deny the iconoclastic and defamiliarising role that avant-garde architecture had assigned to itself. This process of familiarisation has, indeed, taken place over a large area of contemporary architectural production.

The ideological content of Le Corbusier's architecture has itself been subverted by the 'natural' development of capitalism and its 'recuperation' of the avant-garde. We must therefore see Le Corbusier's architecture as a historical phenomenon and disengage it from its original ideological context. Its subversiveness is part of its self-contained aesthetic and remains a constantly renewable experience, after the vision of a totally renewed society, of which it was originally a part, has receded from view. Le Corbusier's architecture belongs to a 'tradition of the new' which has now taken its place in our critical canon.

The split in our responses to the work of Le Corbusier no doubt owes something to the contradiction, apparent to the modern sensibility, between the abstract processes of modern life and the mythical power of art—a contradiction Le Corbusier was well aware of and tried to resolve by uniting architecture and engineering. Le Corbusier's monumental studies of Rio de Janeiro, Algiers, and Chandigarh (where a newly founded "liberal" state could offer him the same opportunities that a declining empire had offered Lutyens in New Delhi 40 years earlier) have something of the romantic and tragic grandeur of eighteenth century neo-classical fantasies and evoke the dream-like image of a technological world transformed into pure form. But the more purely aesthetic qualities of these unrealised or only partially successful projects of national symbolism are in most respects as great as they are in those other late works—Ronchamp, La Tourette—whose programmes no longer confront the problem of power, but rather retreat into a quietistic world where art and social existence are no longer in conflict.

Our ambivalence toward Le Corbusier reflects his own ambivalence toward the modern world and is the result of the uncertainties of our age. On the one hand, his concept of technocracy and his view of architecture as the means of moral and social engineering seem seriously flawed. On the other, the plastic power and metaphorical subtlety of his buildings—their originality and certainty of touch—cannot be denied. And yet his indisputable greatness as an architect can hardly be dissociated from the grandeur of his vision and the ruthless single-mindedness with which he pursued it. If in so many ways Le Corbusier was deluded, his delusion was that of the philosopher/architect for whom architecture, precisely because of the connection it implies between the ideal and the real, was the expression of the profoundest truths. He occupied one of those rare moments in history when it seemed that the vision of the artist and man of passion converged with a collective myth.

1   See Philippe Junod, *Transparence et Opacité*, Lausanne: L'Age d'homme, 1976.
2   Ozenfant, A, and CE Jeanneret, *La Peinture moderne,* Paris: Editions, 1927.
3   Shapiro, Meyer, "The Apples of Cézanne", in Shapiro, Meyer, *Modern Art, 19th and 20th Centuries*, New York: George Braziller, 1978.
4   It is true that Le Corbusier shows two of these buildings (the Salvation Army Hostel and the Centrosoyus) extended as part of a continuous urban tissue, similar in form to the *a redents* housing of the Ville Radieuse. But since they are smaller in scale and more differentiated than these, they have a purely analogous relationship to them. Moreover, their status as public buildings would seem to be compromised as soon as they are seen as part of a continuum. See "The Strategies of the *Grands Travaux*", this volume.
5   Le Corbusier, "In Defense of Architecture", trans George Baird et al, *Oppositions 4*, October 1974, pp. 93–108.
6   For a comprehensive study of Le Corbusier's various projects for Algiers, see McCleod, Mary, "Le Corbusier and Algiers", *Oppositions 19/20*, 1980.
7   Barthes, Roland, "The Plates of the Encyclopedia", in Barthes, Roland, *New Critical Essays,* New York: Hill and Wang, 1980.

Architecture and Engineering: Le Corbusier and the Paradox of Reason

First published in *Modulus*, 1980/1981.

In his book David to Delacroix Walter Friedlander distinguishes between two great currents in French painting, which he calls the rational and the irrational.[1] These categories, if we accept them, must apply in some measure to the other arts, including architecture. The rational current is moralising and didactic, and it belongs to the tradition of French classicism. It is tempting to see Le Corbusier as belonging to this didactic tradition and as bringing to the architectural avant-garde of the 1920s a peculiarly French combination of moralism, formalism, and classicism.[2]

Of all the architects of the Modern Movement, it is Le Corbusier who constructed its most elaborate theoretical underpinning. His architectural theory differs significantly from that of the other modern architects, in kind as well as degree. Whereas for Walter Gropius theory was instrumental and design its direct product, for Le Corbusier theory was justificatory. It seeks to justify architecture as an autonomous and normative discipline, and in this way belongs to the tradition of French architectural theory from Philibert de L'Orme to Ledoux.[3] His theoretical writings aimed to reconcile new phenomena resulting from modern industrial production with certain *a priori* architectural values. These values were seen as the conditions that made the practice of architecture intelligible.

Le Corbusier has often been called a positivist and has been criticised for trying to apply to the twentieth century a mental set belonging to the nineteenth century. Although he shared with the positivists their epistemological formalism, he did not share the priority they gave to the Fact.[4] As he says in *Vers une architecture*, "Architectural abstraction has the particular and magnificent property that, rooted in the brute fact it spiritualises it, because the brute fact is nothing but the materialisation, the symbol, of the possible Idea."[5]

Le Corbusier's formalism aimed at being theoretically systematic but it did not necessarily aim at the transformation of the real world. Yet it is easy to see why Le Corbusier has been called a positivist: he tenaciously clung to final solutions, as if he were asserting a direct, Bentham-like relation between form and function. This quality in Le Corbusier's work can be seen if we compare him with the Russian Constructivist theoreticians, who believed that theoretical systems and action on the material of the real world coincided. For them the empirical could always be used to criticise and modify artistic form, and such modifications would make these forms theoretically *more* correct. For Le Corbusier the empirical inhabits a different world from the ideal; there is never any possibility of a direct passage from Fact to Meaning. When he insisted on the inviolate quality of his designs, he was defending their ideal qualities and not their empirical ones. Indeed, he often clung to design solutions against all empirical evidence, as in the case of the Salvation Army Hostel, whose history has been documented by Brian Brace Taylor.[6]

Le Corbusier's architecture, its qualities as well as what may perhaps be considered its faults, comes directly from this dualistic philosophy. Nonetheless, he never satisfactorily reconciled his search for the timeless human values of architecture with his belief that modern technology and the structures of modern capitalism provided the means whereby these values could be re-established in a new form.

Le Corbusier's discourse attempted to synthesise, insofar as the problem of architecture was concerned, the contradictory world views current at the time of his intellectual formation. To understand these world views, and their resulting ideologies and contradictions, one must turn back to the architectural discourse of the seventeenth century, the moment when the Vitruvian tradition was first challenged. The form of this challenge is well known. In dividing architectural beauty into two kinds, *certain beauty* and *arbitrary beauty*, Claude Perrault introduced into architectural discourse the epistemological distinction between *a priori* and empirical knowledge, between the natural sign and the arbitrary sign, a distinction paralleled in contemporary philosophy and linguistic theory.[7] Perrault's definition could be interpreted in two ways: either as encouraging the search for natural causes of absolute beauty, which were no longer seen as derived from ancient authority, or as encouraging scepticism.

Perrault's theory exerted an influence on other architects, notably Christopher Wren. From Wren's notes, published in the *Parentalia*, one can see that Perrault's method was often used by subsequent theorists, not to justify custom and association as the basis of the architectural sign, but to find new sources of certainty which were accessible to reason. The empirical method discredited the old *a priori* certainties but created new ones in their place. A new set of phenomena hitherto thought of as secondary, particularly those in the field of optics, was now seen as subject to law and necessity and accessible to experiment and mathematical treatment. This conviction that taste and aesthetic judgment could be shown to rest on natural principles is characteristic of an important strand of eighteenth century thought. We recognise elements of this view in the thought of Le Corbusier.

By the end of the nineteenth century, however, this view had been modified and distorted by both positivism and historicism, which gave an entirely new emphasis to the problem of the law-like nature of man's experience: the first, by saying that knowledge finds its verification and ultimate meaning in action on the material world; the second, by trying to reconcile absolute truth with historical change and development. In Le Corbusier's thought these two impulses are overlaid by the idealism prevalent in the late nineteenth century, which was anti-positivist and anti-materialist and which somehow accepted the idealism of Hegel without the cultural relativism to which Hegel's system gave rise.[8]

In *The Education of Le Corbusier*, Paul Turner provides evidence that Le Corbusier was strongly influenced by Henry Provensal's book *L'art de Demain*, published in 1907.[9] According to Turner, this book stresses the accessibility of the Hegelian "Idea" to the intuitive grasp of the artist. This Idea does not seem identical to eighteenth century notions which held that truth and beauty are eternal because man is always and everywhere the same. Instead, it seems to assume an emergent Idea, which is capable for the first time of being realised because of the stage of historical development that man has reached. After a period of divergence, art and science had reached a point at which they once again could coalesce and become transparent to each other. Significantly, this philosophy is based on a certain notion of abstraction. Ideal beauty expressed mind and spirit rather than physical senses. Thus it is linked with science. Provensal's contention was that "Science, which begins by enfeebling sentiment, ends by strengthening it."[10]

This quality of abstraction has two interesting corollaries. First, architecture and music are considered the highest of the arts because both "resort to abstractions". (The idea of music as the paradigm for the arts was of course common at the end of the nineteenth century.) Second, architecture is said be concerned with cubic form, expressing directly the forms of mineral crystals which, alone among natural forms, are said to reveal nature's underlying mathematical structure. Architecture, says Provensal, is a matter of the composition of volumes, the juxtaposition of solid and void, of shade and light. "The artist", he says, "will find the elements of realisation of material where the plastic drama is crystallised under the beneficient action of light." Turner points out the obvious parallel between this and Le Corbusier's well-known formulation of architecture as "the learned, correct and magnificent play of volumes assembled in light".[11]

Turner's analysis of Provensal's text helps to solve a problem. Through it we are able to connect two ideas that have always seemed contradictory in Le Corbusier's thought: the idea of absolute and unchanging artistic values associated with eighteenth century classicism, and the idea of the spirit of the age, which stems from Hegel and the German historicist tradition. In Provensal's book, we find the combination of absolute values and the *avant-garde* idea of the 'new'. Hegel's grand cycle seems to have come to an end; the Spirit stands finally exposed, and once it has been revealed by an artistic elite, it will become accessible to all. This cyclical view of history, which invokes the idea of a return or repetition, is put forward explicitly by Le Corbusier in *Urbanisme*, when he discusses the ages of man.

Provensal's book no doubt helped form certain permanent traits of Le Corbusier's thought concerning the eternal and geometric nature of architecture, its relation to science at a fundamental level, and the idea of an imminent discovery, of an apocalyptic moment. Many other experiences, however, helped to crystallise Le Corbusier's conception of a new architecture, three of which seem to be of special importance. The first was the regionalist and artisanal doctrine Le Corbusier absorbed from his teacher at La Chaux-de-Fonds, L'Eplattenier.[12] This doctrine was derived from the Arts and Crafts Movement and Owen Jones' theories of ornament. L'Eplattenier taught that nature could be reduced to an underlying geometric structure. This notion was in many ways the antithesis of Provensal's ideas, since, instead of postulating an abstract Idea which could be represented directly, it saw the Idea as something revealed or disclosed in the concrete conditions of a particular time and place. It was part of a tradition that thought in terms of contingent rather than universal meaning and looked for a renewal of architecture through ornament and craftwork.

Le Corbusier was often tempted in his 20s by his vision of an artistic elite creating a popular art out of local conditions. But, at the same time, he was moving away from this vision, toward a more universalist view. Even when he travelled to Turkey and became absorbed in folk architecture, what most intrigued him was the way it could be reduced to a typology and seen as the basis of a universal language Writing later in *Urbanisme*, on the problem of architectural detail, he said;

> In the traditional architectural cities one finds habits of construction. Until the nineteenth century, a window, a door, were 'human' holes, elements to the human scale: the roofs were built according to procedures uniformly accepted and excellent. In Istanbul all houses were of wood, all roofs were of the same slope and the same tiles. All religious buildings were of stone.[13]

These traditional qualities are seen as embodying the principles with which to generate an entirely new architecture. There is also here, however, an element of nostalgia, and Le Corbusier never entirely abandoned the notion of an architecture incorporating craft techniques. In the 1930s, he was already combining such elements with the abstract terms of technology, much to the disapproval of the *Neue Sachlichkeit* purists.

The second experience was that of the architectural tradition. Among the protagonists of the Modern Movement a moralistic iconoclasm made it impossible to speak of tradition in any but the most general terms. To some extent Le Corbusier shared this attitude. But, sweeping as many of his judgements about architectural history were, they were nonetheless based on a close study of buildings and texts. For him, the tradition which had to be preserved and transformed was more than a set of moral precepts. It was, above all, a set of concrete examples, and the way he communicated this knowledge was by drawing.

Most of Le Corbusier's general precepts seem to have their origin in particular examples: Turkish houses, the monasteries of Mount Athos and Emo, the temple sites of India, Cambodia, and Chaldaea, Pompeian houses, the urban schemes of Louis XIV the studios and cafes of late nineteenth century Paris. This habit of mind

is not restricted to his interest in historical types, but marks his confrontation with the products of modern technology, the *objets-type* of modern civilisation. It is an essentially iconic procedure. The "Idea" is approached through the image. His mental wardrobe is full of objects ready to be used in a *bricolage*—objects which each seem to have been imprinted on his memory in a moment of epiphany.

Of the influences mentioned so far, that of Provensal and L'Eplattenier were concerned with theoretical principles. The final influence to be mentioned is the constructive principle exemplified in modern building technology. The sources of this influence lay outside the immediate experience of La Chaux-de-Fonds, in the industrially advanced countries, especially Germany and France.

We have seen that to some extent, the Hegelian idealism associated with Provensal's theories and the regionalism associated with L'Eplattenier were antagonistic to each other. It is also obvious that modern industry and technology were antagonistic to the revival of the crafts. Modern construction and the idealism of pure form both presuppose abstraction. Yet the abstraction of pure geometry differs from that of modern production techniques because the latter are concerned with the real, empirical world. Such an abstraction is the inheritor of nineteenth century positivism and instrumentalism, and to this extent is incompatible with the notion of ideal and absolute standards of beauty.

When Le Corbusier went to Germany, he was faced with modes of operation and a scale of production that were both abstract and instrumental. He admired the work of Behrens for AEG, and he found Muthesius' ideas sympathetic, insofar as they gave purity to spiritual over material values. (Muthesius had said that engineering buildings have aesthetic value *if* they embody formal principles, not *because* they embody these principles.)[14] But the utilitarian and materialistic nature of German culture did not seem to Le Corbusier to reflect this idea.[15]

Le Corbusier's response to Paris was different. In the principles of reinforced concrete developed by Auguste Perret he seems to have found an interpretation of constructional rationalism that was compatible with his idealism, One reason for this was the plastic nature of concrete and its malleability to the will of the designer. But in spite of the syntheses of classicism *à la* Behrens and Perret's rationalism that he achieved in the Villa Schwob, Le Corbusier was evidently still acutely aware of the conflict between an aesthetic idealism leaning toward the classical and an avant-gardism that wished to embrace the most modern tendencies. This conflict forms the subject of several extended passages in both *Vers une architecture* and *Urbanisme*, and they are worth analysing in some detail.

The first fundamental idea put forward in *Vers une architecture* is that by committing himself to the general principles of modern engineering, the architect will rediscover the sources of his own discipline. To demonstrate this Le Corbusier must first distinguish between engineering and architecture. The aim of the engineer is to provide what is *useful*. The aim of the architect is to arouse emotion. But since the engineer, through calculation, produces forms in harmony with the universe, and since the highest form of emotion aroused by architecture comes from its conformity with the selfsame universal laws, it follows that the engineer and the architect share a common foundation.[16] In this theory the difference between the engineer and the architect seems to lie in the degree of intentionality. Engineers make architecture, as it were, unintentionally. They make us feel harmony, but it is in the intentional manipulation of his feeling of harmony that the work of the architect lies. Thus, if in one sense the engineer and the architect start from the same foundation, in another sense architecture has its own basis, which lies in its ability to strike our senses by means of clear, simple forms. The engineer, proceeding by the route of knowledge, merely shows us the path of truth, whereas the architect makes this truth palpable.

This truth of the architect does not rest at brutal and obvious sensations. "Certain relations", Le Corbusier says, "are born which agitate our consciousness and put us in a state of joy (*jouissance*), when man makes use of memory, of

examination, of reasoning, of 'creation'."[17] By this statement Le Corbusier opens up architecture to an incalculable and infinite 'culture'. By implication, all the traditional values of architecture are invoked (since memory is involved).

But immediately, and without transition, he counters this idea by saying that our external world has been transformed as a result of the machine and that we have a new vision and a new social life.[18] We seem to see here an implied distinction between an internal, spiritual world that somehow remains constant in the face of an external world that has been completely transformed.

The dichotomy between engineering and architecture is taken up again in a later chapter. Here he says that when a thing responds to a need it satisfies "the whole of the first part of our mind"—that part in which the ultimate satisfaction of the spirit is not possible. This satisfaction belongs to architecture, through its attainment of "a state of Platonic grandeur, mathematical order, speculation, and the perception of harmony, through relationships which are moving".[19] The status of the useful in this architectural purpose is not made clear. One is left to deduce that concentration on the useful and the necessary purges the mind and frees it for Platonic contemplation. There is thus a moral imperative, an imperative of self-denial and asceticism, which seems to be the condition of aesthetic pleasure.

In discussing the aesthetic, Le Corbusier divides it into the sensuous and the intellectual. The sensuous is that aspect always enjoyed by simple peoples, and is expressed in decoration and colour. The intellectual is that aspect enjoyed by cultivated peoples, and is expressed in harmony and proportion. Each aspect is defined as "necessary superfluity".[20] But, immediately after this, he says that utility and economy provide satisfaction to the mind, whereas form (cubes, cylinders, etc.) provides satisfaction to the senses.[21] We therefore have a schema in which proportion and harmony belong to the mind in relation to decoration, but to the senses in relation to utility. The attribution of intellectual satisfaction to utility and to aesthetic form seems to suggest that he interprets "intellect"(*esprit*) in

Opposite: Le Corbusier, Istanbul, Turkey, travel sketch.

Above: Le Corbusier, Maison de Mme. De Mandrot, 1930–1931.

© FLC/ADAGP, Paris and DACS, London 2009

two diametrically opposed ways, one deriving from rationalism or positivism, the other from neo-Platonism.

In *Urbanisme* the theme of the engineer and the architect, reason and sentiment, is treated with greater breadth and at a more philosophical level. First, Le Corbusier propounds a theory of cultural evolution, based on general eighteenth century models from Rousseau to Hegel and resembling that of Vico in its cyclical implications. According to this scheme, the history of culture consists of three stages: that of the "human Animal", that of "the road to culture", and that of "the achievement of Equilibrium". In the first phase, man acts instinctively in accordance with universal law; in the second, acquisition of knowledge throws him into disequilibrium and awareness of his ignorance; and in the third, there is a new fusion of knowledge and universal law.[22]

The third stage is identified with classicism, in which, Le Corbusier says, we create "coldly and purely". Geometry and the right angle are the emblems of this stage. "The purpose of art", says Le Corbusier, "is to raise us above disorder and by this means to give us the spectacle of equilibrium."[23] There are three classical moments—Greece and Rome, the eighteenth century, and the modern world. Between these moments come periods of preparation, the Middle Ages and the nineteenth century, in which the acquisition of new knowledge throws the previous system into disequilibrium, but at the same time presages a new state of harmony.

Le Corbusier then discusses the role of intuition and sentiment (the sphere of the artist) within this cycle.[24] "Intuition", he says, "is the sum of acquired knowledge", which has been inscribed in the collective memory. "Sentiment" is an "emanation" of this inscribed knowledge. Thus, intuition and sentiment are not antagonistic to reason. They are, rather, reason under its instinctive, sensuous, and emotive aspects. Since, in the first instance, sentiment is dependent on reason, it is something that is "earned". It cannot be enjoyed cheaply, "it cannot be 'stolen'". This earned sentiment leads us beyond everyday experiences toward ideal form, toward style, toward culture. A sort of pyramid is implied, with pragmatic reason at the base and the concept of ideal form at the apex.

We have now, says Le Corbusier, arrived at the fateful moment in the historical cycle when our sentimental urges must be seen as identical to the rule of reason. The general, the typical, and the common appeal to us more than the individual and the exceptional. Sentiment no longer strives to be heroic: it recognises that the truly heroic is found in the apparently banal world of facts, disclosed by science.[25] This is true because the means at our disposal are now completely adequate to the ends desired. The state of equilibrium and calm thus attained are to be described as classical and are shared by all classical ages.

But at the same time, because we are wedded to outworn patterns of thought and response, this involves the complete upheaval of accepted ideas and the creation of something new.[26] Now, according to Le Corbusier's own reasoning, one would expect this situation of newness to produce a state of anxiety and strain; and one would expect classical equilibrium to be the outcome of gradual cultural acclimatisation. But this obvious contradiction is elided in Le Corbusier's text Instead, in the manner of Provensal's theory, the classical/eternal and the messianic/revolutionary are conflated.

Le Corbusier now looks at the conflict between the engineer and the architect from another angle. It is the nature of practical engineering to produce results that are provisional, whereas the work of art has a value that is perennial.[27]

Modern industrialism is the result of abstract reasoning, not of passion. It has no more need for "great men", only for "little men" with limited aims. "The work of reason", he says, "is cumulative and adds to itself little by little…. In our passions we are like a wine which is exported; we do not know at which table it will be served. The great works of humanity are elaborated more and more audaciously, and with a temerity which could bring down on us the anger of the gods."[28]

He adds: "The poet, on the other hand, judges and discerns the lasting quality of words. He is at the opposite pole from the calculators, and follows the undulating curve of the passions. Beyond the utilitarian he discerns the imperishable—man."[29]

But for Le Corbusier, this simple opposition between the man of science and the poet is very deceptive.[30] For if it is true that when we look at the world of the engineer we see a "melée of mediocre destinies", we also see "the rigour of works which move in a perfectly regulated way toward imposing realisations":

> Until now, the artefact was so precarious, so far from perfection... [But] a great revolution has intervened... which has overturned our equilibrium.... Suddenly we are armed with a fabulous apparatus which upsets our admirations and compromises our age-old hierarchies.... Reason? Passion? Two currents, two individuals who oppose one another. One looks behind, one ahead; one poet shines over the ruins, but the other may well be exterminated.[31]

The poet, therefore, must accept and celebrate the end products of that "man of mediocre destiny", the engineer.

But Le Corbusier still has doubts. If mechanical beauty were the result of pure reason, it would be perishable. In mechanical work, the most recent work is always the most beautiful. "Thus, beauty would be ephemeral and would soon fall into ridicule."[32] He asks himself whether the emotion produced by Eiffel's Gabarit Bridge will persist. "Here", he says, "reason does not suffice, and one has to suspend judgement. Here we see the mystery that surrounds the future of contemporary individual works.... When this passion of a man has passed, the works will continue to exist."[33] In other words, the work may survive its power to give rise to sensations of beauty and prove itself, in retrospect, to be lacking in those timeless qualities that constitute the true work of architecture.

Le Corbusier replies to this objection with a counter-argument. It would, he says, be a dangerous verdict if (realising this fact) we were to expect the engineer to put himself at the service of the man of passion; he would lose his *raison d'être*. Quite the contrary, it is the man of passion who must give way to the engineer:

> Individual passion only has the right to incarnate the collective phenomenon.
> The collective phenomenon is the state of soul of an epoch, conditioned

Gustave Eiffel, Gabarit Bridge.

in general as it is in the particular.... A general state of thinking is established... and the works of calculation... are carried by the general passion and enter into the measure of man.... In front of the works of calculation one is face to face with a phenomenon of high poetry; the individual is not responsible for it.... Man realises his potential.[34]

Here we see Le Corbusier resorting to the Hegelian world-spirit. Only if we attribute a kind of human will to this spirit do the words "passion", "sentiment", and "beauty" still have meaning.[35] But Le Corbusier does not explain how we are to reconcile this with the continued existence of the architect. If followed to its logical conclusion it would result in the disappearance of artistic production altogether. The artist/architect would no longer be needed for the task of idealisation. This task would be carried out unintentionally by the engineer, as the stand-in or proxy for the world-spirit. The ideological formation characteristic of the artist would be a thing of the past. At best, the artist/architect would become a sort of voyeur, passively echoing the dictates of history and abstract reason. Utopia would circulate continuously and weightlessly within reality.

But there is another idea suggested by this new interpretation of the artist. This is the Hegelian notion that the poet/philosopher is able to grasp the whole of history and see in it the operation of reason. This could be called the "overview" theory. It has implications for space as well as time. The pattern which the industrial order imprints on the earth, while fragmentary and alienating at ground level, can be seen to be meaningful from a sufficiently high altitude. The airplane is obviously a powerful symbol of this notion of overview, and it is not surprising that Le Corbusier talks so much about the view of buildings from the air.

Having considered the main problem dealt with in Le Corbusier's theory, one must now look at aspects of his theory covering the two specific areas of concern in his first works: urbanism and buildings. Although Le Corbusier's refusal to make any distinctions between architecture and town planning is theoretically correct, the difference in his application of theory to each field is so great that it seems legitimate to revert to the conventional distinction when considering the relation of his theory to his practice.

When Le Corbusier applies his theory to the city, he simply reverts to the unresolved duality between the engineer and the architect. The architect re-emerges in his pure ideological role. "The city", he says, "is profoundly anchored in the regions of calculation.... This will be essential for what is useful, and in consequence, perishable.... It remains for the city to last, for which other things than calculation are needed. This will be architecture, which is all that is beyond calculation."[36]

This simple dichotomy results in the setting side by side of the products of pragmatic reasoning and the establishment of pure form. The logic of the engineer results in a clear separation of functions, the total subjection of urban man to a process of abstract classification. In this way the Corbusian city is a kind of diagrammatic representation of the properties of the modern city as described by the nineteenth century German sociologist Georg Simmel. According to Simmel, all relations in the modern city are abstract and are reduced to quantity. The paradigm of this abstraction is money, the means by which the qualitative difference between objects is reduced to pure quantity.[37]

The abstract sociological implications of the Corbusian city are translated directly into their plastic equivalent—abstract geometrical form. Both on a sociological and an aesthetic level, there is a distance set up between everyday concrete existence and gratification. At the level of aesthetic response this distance is expressed in great ensembles seen in light.

This abstract and 'inhuman' aspect of the Corbusian city has often been remarked on. But we should remember Le Corbusier's own explanation of it. He saw it as an ideal, theoretical demonstration, not the plan for a real city.

Writing of the Ville Contemporaine in *Urbanisme*, he says:

Proceeding in the manner of an experimenter in his laboratory... I excluded all accidents, I gave myself an ideal terrain. The object was not to overcome the conditions of the pre-existent city, but to construct a theoretically watertight system, *to formulate the fundamental principles of modern urbanism. These principles*, if they are not contradicted, *can form the skeleton of the contemporary system of urbanism; they are the rule according to which the game can be played. After this, one looks at the special case—that is to say any case whatever—: Paris, London, New York, or some small provincial town.*[38] [my emphasis]

Similarly, describing the Plan Voisin for Paris, he says, "The plan does not claim to have found the final solution to the problems of the centre of Paris, but it may serve to raise the discussion to a level in keeping with the spirit of our age."[39] These disclaimers might be indicative of a certain scepticism. Although the logic is impeccable, he seems to say, the premise on which it is based might conceivably be contradicted, just as a scientific hypothesis can be refuted.

On the other hand, Le Corbusier's city is anything but a model in the scientific sense. It is a concrete image, fully worked out in all its details. Therefore one is forced to question the status of the general principles that the city illustrates. Is it scientific, neutral, and refutable, or is it artistic, ideological, and apodictic? Everything points to the latter interpretation. But if any further proof were needed, we might notice how Le Corbusier's concept of the city is firmly based on eighteenth century tradition.

Le Corbusier's connection with eighteenth century ideas and the way he differs from these is shown in the famous quotation from the Abbé Laugier which says that the city should display uniformity in the detail and a certain chaos in the whole. It is worthwhile to see what Laugier actually says about the city. His opening remarks are: "Most of our towns remain in a state of neglect, of confusion and disorder.... One builds new houses, but one does not change the bad distribution of streets.... Our towns are what they have been, a mass of houses put together without system, without economy, without design."[40]

This could almost be Le Corbusier himself speaking—Le Corbusier the rationalist, equating the efficient economic organisation of the city with its architectural order. But, curiously enough, it is Laugier's more purely aesthetic doctrine that Le Corbusier is interested in, although he seems to misinterpret it. What is Laugier's aesthetic doctrine? He says the city can be thought of as a forest or a park, where one finds:

... at the same time, order and *bizarrerie*, symmetry and variety; ... here a star, there a *patte-d'oie*; on one side spurs, on the other fans; further off parallels; everywhere open spaces of a different figure and design. The more choice, abundance, contrast, disorder in this composition, the more the park will have piquant and delicious beauties.... A park that was nothing but an assemblage of isolated and uniform squares, whose routes were only differentiated by number, would be very tedious and flat. In all things let us avoid an excess of regularity and symmetry.... Anyone who does not succeed in varying our pleasures never succeeds in pleasing us.

In a town the magnificence of the whole should be divided into:

... an infinity of beauties all of different details, where one hardly meets the same objects; where, walking from one end to the other, one finds in each quarter something new... where there is order but nonetheless a great confusion; where everything is an alignment but without monotony,

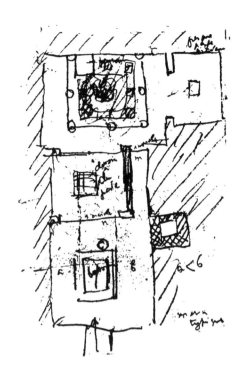

and where, from a multitude of regular parts, there results in the whole a certain idea of irregularity and chaos.[41]

Laugier presupposes classical order, regularity, alignment, and magnificence of form. His disorder is seen as a picturesque critique of this; it consists chiefly of the element of surprise. It is a matter of a "multitude of regular parts", that is to say, streets, squares, *pattes-d'oie*, stars, each of which is regular in itself, but all of which are different. Variety is created by using a wide repertoire of conventional urban forms.

Le Corbusier, on the contrary, conflates the notion of chaos, not with surprise, but with magnificence of effect, in blocks *à redents* composed to create plastic movement. Once the pattern is established, it is merely repeated.

At the same time, uniformity in the detail is given a different interpretation. It is not, as it seems to be in Laugier, a question of giving a number of set pieces their own regularity. It is a question of creating modular repetition of parts, in an attempt to recreate the linguistic order which he had noted in Istanbul, so that the eye will not be distracted from measuring the quality of the whole.[42]

For Laugier's city of surprise to work, one must presuppose a dense tissue, as in the metaphorical hunting forest which the city resembles. But in Le Corbusier there is no tissue, no foreground. Instead there is a literal forest or park across which one sees, at a distance, the great forms of housing blocks or office blocks. Is this distance not identical with the "overview" previously mentioned?

For Laugier the eighteenth century city is essentially undesignable. It consists of fragments of order. The mental idea of order no longer has its exact spatial equivalent, as it had in the Renaissance.[43] For Le Corbusier the capitalist city of the twentieth century is completely designable. But in designing it, he succeeds only in showing its monstrosity. There is no way in which the distance between the concrete and the abstract can be abridged. The Corbusian city remains as he saw it: "a theoretically rigorous system", a skeleton on which there is no flesh—and this in spite of its artistic manipulation, so different from the city of Hilbersheimer.

Le Corbusier's achievement lies rather in his creation of the fragments of the city. The only scale at which the concrete and the abstract can be reconnected is that of the individual building. If the dualism in Le Corbusier's thought produces an unresolved contradiction in his theory and a disembodied abstraction in his city, then in his buildings this dualism produces a dialectic in which aesthetic meaning is created. This dialectic consists of the interaction of pragmatic order (function) and ideal order (pure form).

Le Corbusier's theory now becomes a set of design principles, the most important of which are contained in the division of the building into volume, surface, and plan in his "Five Points of a New Architecture".[44]

Opposite left: House of the Tragic Poet, sketch of plan by Le Corbusier, 1911.

Opposite right: Le Corbusier, Villa Savoye, 1929–1931, architectural promenade.

Above: Le Corbusier, Villa Savoye, entry hall ramps.

© FLC/ADAGP, Paris and DACS, London 2009

In the notions of volume, surface, and plan the dialectical process is stated most clearly. Volume, the creation of pure geometrical solids, is the fundamental basis of architectural aesthetics. But we do not arrive at architecture, properly speaking, until this volume is penetrated and subdivided by elements of utility—specifically, with openings. These appear, phenomenally, as elements on the surface of the volume. The subdivisions, penetrations, etc., of this surface can either reinforce the basic volumes or destroy them. It is the architect's task to reinforce them.[45]

The plan is the means by which the three-dimensional volume is established. It seems, though Le Corbusier nowhere says this, that in spite of its rigorously diagrammatic qualities, the plan will reflect the three-dimensional form of the building. Since it is an iconic sign (in the Piercian sense) of the building, it will have strong iconic properties of its own. This is always true of Le Corbusier's plans. The simple dialectic is present in the plan as in the building as a whole. Thus, while the ideal order of the building implies a symmetrical and axial organisation of the plan and all its parts, utility demands that this ideal order be modified. Le Corbusier gives a paradigmatic example in the House of the Tragic Poet in Pompeii. He says of this plan:

> Everything is on axis but you cannot pass in a straight line. The axis is in the intentions, and the dignity given by the axis extends to humble things which the axis accommodates itself to. You get the impression that everything is ordered, but the sensation is rich. You notice then the comfortable breaking of the axis, which gives intensity to the volumes.[46]

Here it is clear that the pragmatic and utilitarian needs do not for Le Corbusier weaken the aesthetic meaning, but make it richer and more complex. We see therefore that Le Corbusier's ideas of both surface and plan reflect the same principles: a primary formal law brought into collision with utility, such that both interact within the complex whole of the work of architecture—a whole that includes both order and disorder.

The "Five Points" of a new architecture reinterpret the traditional elements of architecture in terms of this dialectic. First, the plan and the internal volumes are freed from the constraints of structure to take on configurations demanded by utility and convenience. At the same time, this freedom allows these volumes to take on anthropomorphic significance by means of visual metaphors in a way which is closely related to the objects represented in Purist paintings.[47] Third, the building is raised on *pilotis* and has a flat roof, and the facade (the surface) is projected forward from the structure. Any of these three moves helps to give the volume maximum isolation and purity.

There is a further consequence of the projection of the surface from the structure: the surface becomes a thin membrane—a pure surface. Indentations of this surface become explosive, since there is no inherent tendency of the surface itself to become modulated in any way (as, for instance, a masonry wall with pilasters and buttresses). These penetrations enable sculptural and anthropomorphic internal elements to be sensed simultaneously with the surface. Meaning (given by the elements derived from human life) and pure form exist in a state of constant interaction. This is seen in the attic opening in the centre of the entrance facade at Garches, when what is discreetly 'revealed' is both plastic and asymmetrical, anthropormorphic and chaotic.

The clearest demonstration of this aesthetic system is given by Le Corbusier in his diagrams showing the "Four Compositions". The first, Maison La Roche-Jeanneret, differs from the other three in not being "le prisme pur". It can be given order, Le Corbusier says, by classification and hierarchy. We can see this as being absorbed into any of the other three compositions.

Of the three pure prisms, the first represents the Villa Stein-de Monzie at Garches.[48] The second, the house in Tunis, is stated as being "trés facile". The cube is only suggested by the exposed Dom-ino-like frame, and the free volumes of the interior are generated from the centre and move toward the perimeter. In the third, Poissy, which clearly has paradigmatic value for Le Corbusier, the interior volumes are generated from the periphery and move toward the centre. The ideal cube is established, but the interior volumes are eaten away.

This brief analysis has only touched on Le Corbusier's architectural 'language' and has been restricted to a small body of early work, the period of *L'Esprit Nouveau* and Purism. Nonetheless, it has perhaps shown how his language and his theory were related. The aim has been to reveal some of the ideological roots of Le Corbusier's theory, the contradictions which arose from these, and some of the ways in which the theory was transformed into artistic practice, rather than to establish any fundamentally new thesis about Le Corbusier. Even so, we could generalise by saying that his theory and his practice were attempts to reconcile the traditions of rationalism and idealism, and that his theory is the culmination of a long dispute in which empirical science has progressively challenged the established claims of architecture.

In this historical process, the problem of architecture is part of a larger problem involving the whole notion of art. And if Le Corbusier seems to have been more successful in reconciling these contradictory claims in his buildings than in either his theory or his urban projects, it is probably because we can interpret these buildings as belonging to a modernist movement in the arts in general—a movement in which the work of art becomes increasingly solipsistic and self-referential.

Rather than trying to see Le Corbusier's buildings as an attempt to transform the real world it seems more fruitful to see them as constituting a reflexive system of order, in which contradictions are resolved at the level of metaphor. Whereas in his theory and in his urban projects the contradictions remain in the form of logical antithesis, in his buildings these contradictions interact. As in poetic metaphor, the elements of contradiction are resolved without losing their independence.

1   Friedlander, Walter, *David to Delacroix*, trans. Robert Goldwater, New York: Schocken Books, 1968.
2   Certain English art historians have recently attacked modernism in architecture because of its concern for morality; see, for example, David Watkin, *Morality and Architecture*. But they ignore the fact that the interaction of moral ideas with the idea of beauty is a characteristic of French classicism (and indeed also of Medieval and neo-Platonic aesthetics) and is by no means restricted to modern architecture. This interaction is, in fact, inseparable from any aesthetic theory that takes the tradition of rhetoric into account.
3   The word "autonomous" is not used here to imply a discipline divorced from contextual 'reality', but rather a discipline that constitutes a specific technique by which this reality is transformed.
4   By "formalism" I mean the idea that the logical and formal properties of the mind correspond in some way to the 'real' world. This can take a materialist or an idealist form, depending on whether priority is given to things or to ideas.
5   Le Corbusier, *Vers une architecture*, Paris: Editions Crès, 1923, p. 15.
6   Brace Taylor, Brian, *La Cité de Refuge di Le Corbusier 1929–1933*, Rome: Officina Edizione, 1979.
7   See Wolfgang Herrmann, *The Theory of Claude Perrault*, London: A Zwemmer, 1973.
8   The influence of Hegelian idealism, or some popular version of it, on the avant-garde of the early twentieth century is noted by Christopher Gray, in *Cubist Aesthetic Theories*, Baltimore: Johns Hopkins Press, 1953.
9   Turner, Paul Venable, *The Education of Le Corbusier*, New York and London: Garland Publishing, Inc., 1977. The first part of this essay is much indebted to Turner's study.
10   Turner, *The Education of Le Corbusier*, p. 18.
11   Turner, *The Education of Le Corbusier*, pp. 21–22. See Stanislaus von Moos, *Le Corbusier: Elements of a Synthesis*, Cambridge: MIT Press, 1979, p. 2.
12   See von Moos, *Le Corbusier: Elements of a Synthesis*, p. 2.
13   Le Corbusier, *Urbanisme*, Paris: Editions Crès, 1924, p. 66.
14   Turner, *The Education of Le Corbusier*, p. 77.
15   Turner, *The Education of Le Corbusier*, p. 76. Jeanneret's *Etude sur le mouvement d'art decorative en Allemagne,* however, shows that he was considerably more enthusiastic about German artistic developments when he visited that country in 1910 than the slightly anti-German tone of his later writings would lead one to believe. Moreover, it is clear that many of the key concepts in the *L'Esprit Nouveau* articles—including the distinction between architecture and engineering—owe

their inception to the *Deutscher Werkbund*, whose third annual conference in Berlin he attended. See Winifred Nerdinger, "*Standard et Type: Le Corbusier et Allemagne 1920–1927*" in *L'Esprit Nouveau: Le Corbusier et Industrie 1920–1925*, ed. Stanislaus von Moos, Strasbourg: Les Musees de la ville de Strasbourg, 1987; and Werner Oeschlin, "Influences, confluences et reniements" in *Le Corbusier: Une Encyclopedie*, ed. Jacques Lucan, Paris: Centre Georges Pompidou, 1987.

16 Le Corbusier, *Vers une architecture*, p.7.

17 Le Corbusier, *Vers une architecture*, p. 8.

18 Le Corbusier, *Vers une architecture*, p. 8.

19 Le Corbusier, *Vers une architecture*, p. 87.

20 Le Corbusier, *Vers une architecture*, p. 114.

21 Le Corbusier, *Vers une architecture*, p. 114.

22 Le Corbusier, *Urbanisme*, p. 34.

23 Le Corbusier, *Urbanisme*, p. 35.

24 Le Corbusier, *Urbanisme*, p. 33.

25 Le Corbusier, *Urbanisme*, p. 37.

26 Le Corbusier, *Urbanisme*, p. 37.

27 Le Corbusier, *Urbanisme*, p. 46.

28 Le Corbusier, *Urbanisme*, p. 44.

29 Le Corbusier, *Urbanisme*, p. 44.

30 Le Corbusier, *Urbanisme*, p. 44.

31 Le Corbusier, *Urbanisme*, p. 45.

32 Le Corbusier, *Urbanisme*, p. 46.

33 Le Corbusier, *Urbanisme*, p. 48.

34 Le Corbusier, *Urbanisme*, p, 49.

35 The finality that Le Corbusier attributes to technology is an extension of the Hegelian notion by which, as Lucio Colletti says, "material and effective causality... becomes a moment within ideal causality, ie. within finalism or teleology". See Lucio Colletti, *Marxism and Hegel*, London, 1973, p. 210.

36 Le Corbusier, *Urbanisme*, p. 50.

37 See Georg Simmel, "Die Grosstädte und das Geistesleben", 1903 trans. Kurt H Wolff, *The Sociology of Georg Simmel*, Glencoe, IL: The Free Press of Glencoe, 1950.

38 Le Corbusier, *Urbanisme*, p. 158.

39 Le Corbusier, *Urbanisme*, p. 273.

40 Laugier, P, *Essai sur l'architecture*, Paris, 1753. The actual quotation used by Le Corbusier comes in Laugier's later essay, *Observations sur l'architecture*, The Hague, 1765.

41 Laugier, *Essai sur l'architecture*.

42 Le Corbusier, *Urbanisme*, p. 67.

43 Pierre Patte's plan of Paris, in which he plots the results of a competition for monuments to Louis XV, may perhaps give some idea of Laugier's concept. Admittedly, this is a 'composite' plan, but the very idea of superimposing different fragments on the same plan is suggestive of Laugier's picturesque model. According to Herrmann, *Laugier and 18th Century French Theory*, London, 1961, Patte acknowledged his general indebtedness to Laugier.

44 Le Corbusier, *Vers une architecture*, "*les trois Rappels*"; Le Corbusier, *Oeuvre complète 1910–1929*, vol. 1, Zurich: Editions d'Architecture, 1964.

45 Le Corbusier, *Vers une architecture*, p. 25

46 Le Corbusier, *Vers une architecture*, p. 153.

47 For an interesting discussion of the anthropomorphism in Le Corbusier's abstract space of the grid, see Kurt Forster, "Antiquity and Modernity in the La Roche-Jeanneret Houses of 1923", *Oppositions 15/16*, 1980, pp. 131–153.

48 See Le Corbusier, *Précisions*, Paris: Edition Vincent Freal and Cie., 1960.

The Strategies of the
Grands Travaux

First published in *Le Corbusier: une Encyclopédie*, 1987.

Among the illustrations of the Centrosoyus and the Cité de Refuge in Le Corbusier's *Oeuvre complete* there are two showing the projects extended to adjacent sites to form complexes that assume the scale and texture of urban fragments. The Centrosoyus extension visualises a new administrative district with the Centrosoyus building as an organic part.[1] The extension of the Cité de Refuge proposes a *Cité d'Hospitalisation* linked to a new wing of the original building.

At first sight, there is nothing particularly surprising in these extensions, given Le Corbusier's tendency to treat each of his projects not only as the solution to a particular set of problems, but also as a prototypical element in a new urban totality. Yet the more we look at them, the more problematic they become. First, in being dissolved into the general urban texture and in thus losing their uniqueness, they seem to suffer a loss of representational power. Secondly, though the urban continuum they imply bears an obvious resemblance to such urban projects as the plan for the Porte de Sainte-Cloud of 1938, this resemblance seems purely formal.

Whether we interpret these two projects as administrative buildings or as 'social condensers' on the model of the Soviet avant-garde, it is difficult to imagine them constituting part of the linear continuum Le Corbusier reserved exclusively for housing in all his city plans. These extensions force a reinterpretation of the buildings according to which they become hybrids, hovering uncertainly between being *objets-type* and being part of an urban texture against which other *objets-type* might stand out as figures.

The ambiguity of these extensions invites an examination of the compositional principles of Le Corbusier's *grands travaux* of the inter-war years. The purpose is to discover how these principles were used to reconcile the disparate and often contradictory needs he had to satisfy in the buildings. These can be summarised as: (1) the need for the building to adapt to a specific site within a given urban context; (2) the need to create a building of symbolic presence; and (3) the need to establish the building as the representative of a type.

The main compositional principle of the four public buildings studied in this essay is 'elementarisation'. It distinguishes them from traditional schemes with closed courtyards, where the programmatic volumes are not distinct from each other. In Le Corbusier's *partis* for his *grands travaux,* each programme element is given its own form and is clearly articulated from its neighbour. The principal elements are linear bars (containing cellular accommodation) and centroidal masses (containing places of assembly). The linear bars are coupled to each other at right angles, to form open courts. The flexible jointing permits a large number of permutations in the overall plan, and Le Corbusier's early sketches show him trying out various possibilities.

This arrangement of articulated bars is first found in the Dom-ino housing projects of 1914, where they retain some of the picturesque qualities derived from the Garden City Movement and Camillo Sitte's *Der Stadtbau nach seinen kunstlerischen Grundsatzen*. In one particularly striking example, U- and L-shaped blocks create open rectangular spaces through which a country road meanders in contrapuntal movement. This counterpoint between static buildings and free circulation was to achieve its ultimate form in the block raised on *piloti*, which allowed the ground level to be developed independently of the upper levels. The articulated bars of Dom-ino were systematised as continuous bars of housing *a redents* in the Ville Contemporaine and the Plan Voisin. When Le Corbusier designed his major public

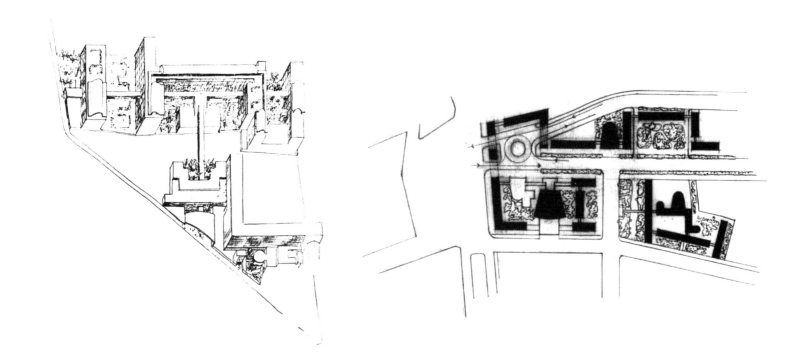

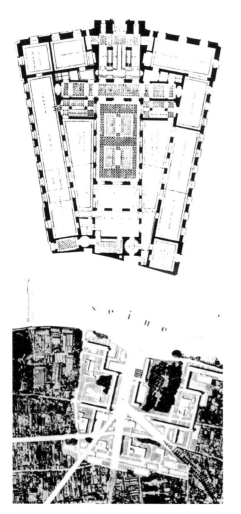

buildings in the late 1920s, he adapted this compositional procedure to the needs of multi-purpose buildings with their linear strings of offices or living cells.

There are strong analogies between this system of composition and the revolutionary changes in spatial organisation Le Corbusier had already worked out for houses and villas. In the houses, the solid *poche* between the rooms of traditional houses is replaced by a free-flowing space interrupted only by the convex, sculptural forms of specialised volumes—bathrooms, closets, and staircases. This complex 'hot' arrangement of spaces and volumes is set in contrast to the 'cool' Platonic geometry within which it is contained. Le Corbusier drew attention to the dialectic between outside and inside, pure geometry and free form, when, in describing the villa at Garches, he said: "On the exterior an architectural will is affirmed; on the inside all the functional needs are satisfied."[2]

A similar transformation occurs in the public buildings. But, whereas in the houses the ground for the play of volumes is the enveloping cube, pierced and hollowed out but never totally destroyed, in the public buildings the ground is formed by the linear bars, and the play of volumes now takes place externally. The public building is an open work of slender prisms defining the spatial limits of the ensemble, while at the same time implying its possible extension. All Le Corbusier's *grands travaux* of the late 1920s share these general formal characteristics.

Le Corbusier's city plans assume ideal sites, and in defending them he was careful to point out their intentionally schematic character.[3] The commissions for the public buildings of the late 1920s, on the contrary, required accommodation to local conditions. This was not, for Le Corbusier, a purely negative constraint. As the text of *Vers une architecture* makes clear, he had absorbed Auguste Choisy's theory of the picturesque, according to which the accidents of a given site play a constitutive role in the artistic organisation of architectural ensembles, resulting, as in the Acropolis in Athens, in compositions of balanced asymmetry that present the viewer with a *succession des tableaux*.[4] Even among Le Corbusier's houses, where the picturesque *promenade architectural* usually takes place within the constraints of the ideal cube, there are several whose external form is determined by the irregularities of their sites or by building regulations. The most celebrated

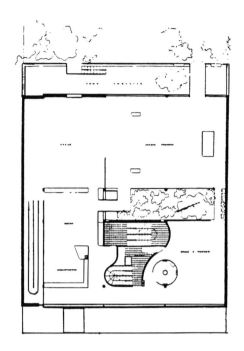

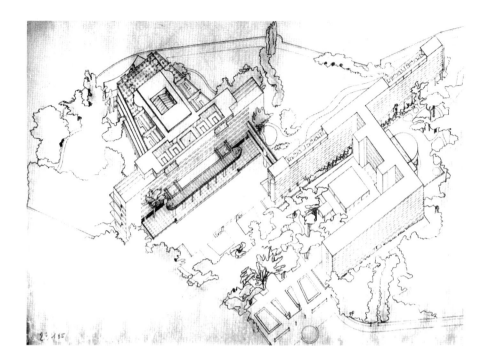

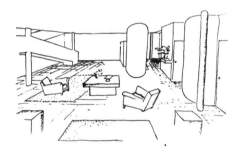

of these is the Maison La Roche-Jeanneret, which Le Corbusier described as "pyramidal"—the very word used by Choisy to describe that other irregular building, the Erechtheum. These houses remain, however, at least until the 1930s, the exception rather than the rule, whereas in the *grands travaux* picturesque grouping and asymmetry are normal.

For Le Corbusier, therefore, to be site specific required more than simply making a building conform to boundary lines and irregularly shaped sites. It entailed bringing into play a system of forms and masses related to a viewer occupying specific positions in space; in short, it was "composition", which means—in the sense given it by Choisy—the artistic resolution of unforeseen exigencies, not the application of *a priori* rules.

The Palais des Nations

The complex of the Palais des Nations consists of two blocks—the Assembly with its ancillary accommodation and the Secretariat—linked by a long bridge. The blocks are organised symmetrically about the two orthogonal axes, and the principal axis runs through the block containing the Assembly, which presents a long frontal surface to the visitor's line of approach.

Individually, each block belongs to the species of frontalised buildings reserved by Choisy for propylaea.[5] As a pair, however, they form a "balanced asymmetry" whose outline follows the shore of the lake and whose masses offer themselves as picturesque ensemblages partly screened by trees. The north side of the imagined symmetrical *parti* is missing. In the third edition of *Vers une architecture,* Le Corbusier appended a plan of the Palais showing an extension to the north, which may be an existing system of paths, its axis rotated by about ten degrees to conform to existing building and road alignments, so that even in its final form the building was not envisioned as perfectly symmetrical. The *parti* resembles certain sixteenth and seventeenth century projects in which long, narrow galleries are extended from older nuclei, such as the *Manica Lunga* of the Quirinale in Rome and the

Opposite top left: Le Corbusier, Project for a *Cité d'Hospitalisation*, extending to the rear of the Cité de Refuge, Paris, 1932. © FLC/ADAGP, Paris and DACS, London 2009

Opposite top right: Le Corbusier, Project for an extension to the neighbouring block of the Centrosoyus, Moscow, 1928. © FLC/ADAGP, Paris and DACS, London 2009

Opposite middle: Otto Wagner, *Bodenkreditanstalt*, (Land Credit Association), competition design, 1884, ground plan.

Opposite bottom: Le Corbusier, Plan for Porte de Saint-Cloud, 1938. © FLC/ADAGP, Paris and DACS, London 2009

Top left: Le Corbusier, Project for Villa Meyer, 1925, interior and plan. © FLC/ADAGP, Paris and DACS, London 2009

Top right: Le Corbusier, Palais des Nations, axonometric. © FLC/ADAGP, Paris and DACS, London 2009

Bottom: Le Corbusier, Lotissement Dom-ino, 1914, sketch showing aggregations of housing units. © FLC/ADAGP, Paris and DACS, London 2009

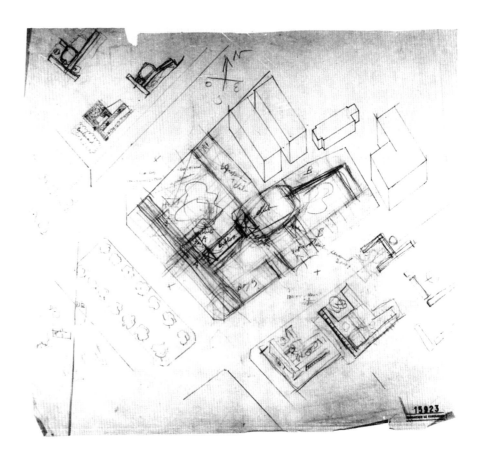

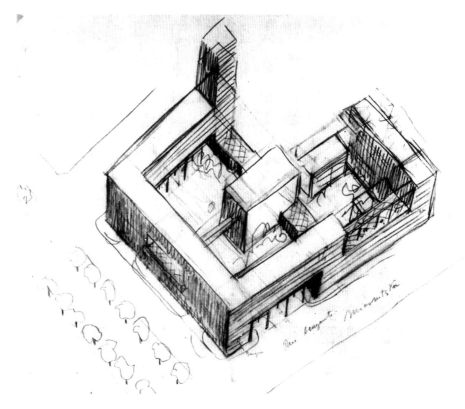

Top: Le Corbusier, Centrosoyus, sketch
for the first project.

Bottom: Le Corbusier, Centrosoyus, variation
on the first project.

Opposite: Le Corbusier, Centrosoyus, plan of
project as built, 1929.

© FLC/ADAGP, Paris and DACS, London 2009

Grande Galerie of the Louvre—especially the latter, with its initial development on only one side of the central axis and its slight shift of angle.

If we compare the arrangement of bars *a redents* in this plan with those in the Ville Contemporaine or the Plan Voisin, we see that whereas the urban blocks *a redents* are oriented in both directions, those at Geneva have one sided aspects, one facing the public realm of the entrance court, the other the private realm of the garden. In Le Corbusier's city plans the bars cut through a uniform and undifferentiated spatial continuum, while in the Geneva project the bars act as walls dividing the site into two phenomenally different kinds of space.

When talking of context, therefore, we refer not only to the physical context (rural or urban), but also the temporal, historical context. In the Palais des Nations, Le Corbusier has both adjusted the building to the exigencies of the site and restated a perennial tradition of architecture in terms of modern life. He seems to have wholeheartedly embraced the ceremonial, humanistic implications of the programme and to have attempted to give the building an appropriate character.

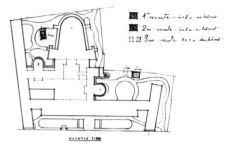

The Centrosoyus

Unlike the Palais des Nations, the Centrosoyus was assigned to an urban site and presented Le Corbusier with difficult contextual problems. The site was bounded by roads on its three regular sides, whereas the fourth side was formed by an irregular boundary cutting across the block. In his earliest solutions he rejected the articulated open system of bars he had used for the Palais de Nations and based his design on a simple perimeter courtyard block divided into quadrants, with the auditorium at the intersection of a cruciform system of circulation and with one quadrant omitted to avoid extending beyond the site boundary.[6] There are several extant variants of this early scheme, but in all of them the closed and regular quality of the plan is compensated for by irregular (and apparently somewhat arbitrary) elevational profiles and by wide penetrations at street level to gain access to the otherwise landlocked auditorium.

In these early solutions for the Centrosoyus, the short southwest side is the principal facade, on axis with the auditorium and facing the boulevard with its central reservation of trees. During the evolution of the design, the main facade migrated to the longer frontage facing Miasnitskaya Street. At the same time the courtyard arrangement was transformed and the scheme began to assume its final configuration of articulated bars forming an unequal H and providing the entrance facade with a shallow forecourt.

In these transformations we can see a persistent concern for maintaining the street alignments and for frontalised blocks, which it is necessary to penetrate in order to reach the 'private' interior space. At ground and first floor levels this interior space is always used for vast cloakrooms and foyers, which define a pattern of movement that is in counterpoint to the configuration of the blocks above. This contrapuntal movement became increasingly evident once the main bars were raised up on *piloti* and their configuration became more pliant.

One significant result of the H-shaped plan is that the tumultuous convex form of the auditorium and the horseshoe ramps becomes exposed to the northwest frontage, strongly implying public and private sides analogous to those of the Palais des Nations but seemingly inappropriate for the actual context of regular streets and blocks. At first, even after the courtyard scheme had been abandoned, the northwest frontage was symmetrically framed by two bars—one facing the boulevard, the other holding the auditorium—and the edge of the street was defined by a low colonnade. But when, in a final move, the auditorium was rotated 90 degrees so that its convex 'apse' faced the road, this contextual discipline was lost. The northwest facade became a 'back' relative to the formal, frontalised southwest and southeast facades and called for the kind of rural open space with distant views that would enable the building to be understood as

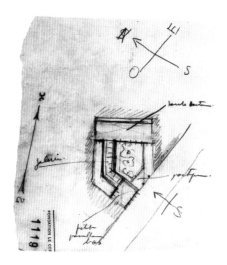

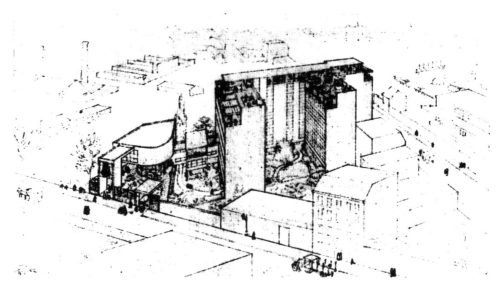

an object in space. Simultaneously, the overall plan became unambiguously diagonal and lost some of its earlier multivalency and complexity.

In the Centrosoyus one sees the unresolved tension, often found in the work of Le Corbusier, between the need for the building to form part of an existing urban framework, to form street edges, and to consist of frontalised facades and the need for it to exist as a freestanding object.

The Cité de Refuge

The site of the Cité de Refuge cuts across the centre of a triangular block formed by rue Cantagrel and rue de Chevaleret. In the *Oeuvre complete* it is described as follows:

> The site was extremely unfavourable: it provided a facade of only 17 metres to the south on rue Cantagrel and another of nine metres to the east on rue de Chevaleret: everything else was in the middle. If one had built directly on the street, according to custom, all the rooms would have overlooked courtyards and faced north.[7]

Although this passage sounds like special pleading, it is true that the site did not lend itself to a perimeter solution, even if one had been desired. What is open to question, however, is whether Le Corbusier's successive solutions did not, in fact, have recourse to a traditional typology other than that of the perimeter block. After all, this was a representational building and not a mere part of the urban tissue. Certainly, for Le Corbusier it had, above all, to represent modernity, but it was also called upon to symbolise a social and moral idea. In these circumstances one could reasonably expect the architect to turn to Parisian precedent in giving the building a symbolic presence and setting it off against its immediate surroundings. And, in fact, the *parti* of both the first and the final schemes have much in common with that of the Parisian *hôtel particulier*. The *corps de logis* is set back some distance from the street and consists of a block frontalised to the axis of approach and extending across the full width of the site. There is a portico *plomb sur la rue,* which acts as a sign of the building and also as a controlled point of entry to the site, which forms a relatively secluded private realm, walled off from the street.

Left: Le Corbusier, Cité de Refuge, early sketch.

Right: Le Corbusier, Cité de Refuge, bird's-eye view.

Opposite top: Le Corbusier, Cité de Refuge, final project, 1931, plan.

Opposite bottom: Le Corbusier, Cité de Refuge, view from rue Cantagrel.

© FLC/ADAGP, Paris and DACS, London 2009

Initially only the western half of the site was available. What appears to be one of the earliest sketches shows a cranked single-storey passage leading from the entry on rue Cantagrel to a six- or seven-storey dormitory block crossing the site from north to south. The east half of the site was developed by adding a second block parallel to the first and connecting them with a longitudinal block running west–east, extending to the rue Chevaleret boundary. At the change in direction of the entrance passage there was a rotunda containing the reception hall, which absorbed the axial rotation—a somewhat Beaux-Arts device. Over the rotunda a wedge-shaped lecture theatre was suspended. A *passarelle,* threading through a pavilion (the dispensary), connected the rotunda to the main building. In place of the *cour d'honneur* there was a sunken garden, which continued under the dormitory blocks.

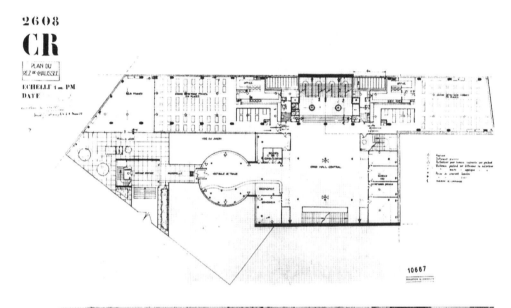

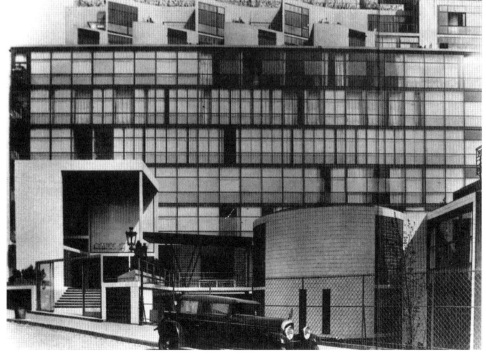

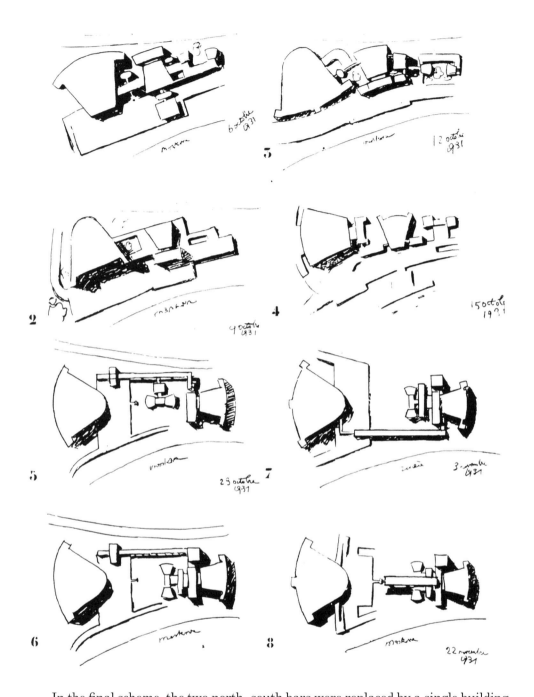

Top: Le Corbusier, Palais des Soviets, competition project, Moscow, 1931, successive variations of the design.

Bottom: Le Corbusier, Sketch of the forum at Pompeii.

© FLC/ADAGP, Paris and DACS, London 2009

In the final scheme, the two north–south bars were replaced by a single building running east–west along the northern boundary of the site. This new arrangement had a radical effect on the entry sequence, which now penetrated to the middle of the site before connecting to the main building at the point where the main stair and the wall separating men and women occurred. Le Corbusier, however, barely altered the elements of this sequence. He simply resited them so that they formed a series of small pavilions of various shapes running in front of and parallel to the main building, to which they were now connected by a protruding element containing the entrance foyer and lecture theatre.

From the start, therefore, Le Corbusier had visualised an elaborate *promenade architecturale* connecting the point of entry to the site with the main accommodation. Programmatically, the promenade consists of a series of initiatory acts, necessary before entering the inner sanctum of the building, and these acts are symbolised by

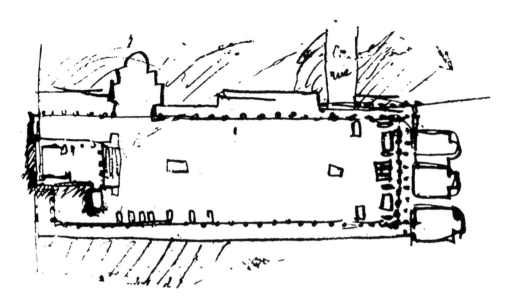

a series of architectural elements: portico, rotunda, *passarelle.* Yet it is important to note that this solution owes as much to the architectural demands of the site, and their formal implications, as it does to the practical and symbolic peculiarities of the programme. "This group of buildings", wrote Le Corbusier, "constitutes a kind of *hors d'oeuvre,* disposed in front of the great hostel building; this last serves, in fact, as ground to the very irregular group consisting of the portico and the social service spaces."[8] The reversal of *poché* space found in his houses is repeated on the outside; instead of a series of concave spaces carved out of the building, such as one might have found in a traditional Beaux-Arts scheme, we are presented with their convex negative—a small collection of architectural volumes. And now, instead of being disposed within the cube of the building, these objects are placed in front of it, and the table, as it were, on which they are displayed is tilted upward and becomes a vertical plane of reference. It seems impossible to separate the sensuous and intellectual pleasure derived from this arrangement of architectural forms from the site to which it owes its origin; as in the Palais de Nations and the Centrosoyus, the building is a response to accidental circumstances of the kind described by Choisy in his analysis of the Acropolis.

The Palais des Soviets

This project differs in its programmatic elements from the three we have discussed. The administrative content is very small, and the project consists mainly of a series of auditoria of different sizes. It also differs from them in its relation to the site. In the other projects the buildings are thought of as creating spatial boundaries. Long walls of offices or living cells form frontalised planes, the approach to which involves a more or less elaborate preparation. In all these projects there is at least the suggestion of a *cour d'honneur* and a *corps de logis,* and the centroidal masses of assembly spaces, and such, are presented as figures against the surface of a pure prism.

Despite the absence of accommodation suitable for such frontalised surfaces, the earliest solutions for the Palais des Soviets did provide an urban space—a huge 'forum' overlooking the Moscow river, against which the various auditoria are lined up, rather in the manner of the temples in the forum at Pompeii, of which Le Corbusier had published a sketch in *Vers une architecture.* This solution would presumably have required the equivalent of a portico to connect the irregular group of auditoria and unify them in a single grand gesture. In the second solution, Le Corbusier still provides an urban space facing the river but has moved the two main auditoria to the sides and defines the back of the space by a low range of offices raised on columns.

In the final scheme all attempts to create a specifically urban space are abandoned. The complex is now an object arranged along a spine, like a biological organism. The spaces it offers to the city are the pure epiphenomena of its own internal structure. The complex is symmetrical along the longitudinal axis only; on the other axis it consists of objects whose configuration is explosively centrifugal and asymmetrically balanced.[9]

The spine is purely formal because the range of offices, which in the second solution had formed a physical link between the two auditoria, is stopped halfway across the gap. Its end supports the acoustic reflector of the open-air assembly. The two auditoria only appear to be connected.

In thus interpreting the complex as a series of heterogeneous objects in space, Le Corbusier turned it into a Constructivist icon whose tumultuous silhouette complements that of the domes of Saint Basil and the Kremlin. The group of auditoria no longer have the backdrop required by the Cité de Refuge. They are isolated symbolic forms. The structural, acoustic, and circulatory demands of the complex are used to give expressive form to each element.

The desire to create a building of appropriate character led Le Corbusier to interpret the Palais des Nations in terms of what we might call "an architecture of humanism"; the same desire led him to make the Palais des Soviets into a symbol of mass culture and of the work of art in the age of the machine.

The Building versus the City

Our analysis shows that the need to adapt to the idiosyncrasies of particular sites made a positive contribution to the architectural quality of the *grands travaux* and cannot be considered as a mere obstacle to the achievement of a "new architecture". The arbitrary urban conditions with which Le Corbusier was faced played a catalytic role comparable to that of the "functions" in the internal arrangement of his houses.

In having to build in existing urban or rural contexts, no less than in having to give form and character to programmes with strongly idealist contents, Le Corbusier was also confronted with the architectural tradition. But these buildings are not a reflection of these factors alone. They reflect as well the tension between a traditional architecture and the types of a new and contentious architecture, and they thus call into question the urban contexts on which they depend.

When experienced as part of the urban fabric, these buildings do indeed stand out as types of a new architectural culture. That they can be read in this way is at least partly due to the extent to which they accommodate themselves to their context and in doing so expose both their similarity to, and difference from, traditional representational buildings.

When, however, Le Corbusier shows these buildings as extended, they immediately start to play a different role in the urban continuum. The use of flexible joints allows the bars to adapt to adjacent blocks *à redents* of the Ville Radieuse. A new urban pattern starts to emerge, tentacle-like, before the old one has ceased to exist. The original Centrosoyus and Cité de Refuge buildings are each absorbed into this new context. What had itself been experienced as a whole, with articulated parts that opened up the building to it surroundings but at the same time differentiated it from its neighbours now becomes part of a greater entity. Before, these buildings acted as the synecdochic fragments of an absent city; now they become part of the metonymic series of an actual city fragment.

However, this new urban fragment merely 'stands for' the new city and can never become part of it. Both extensions take the form of a web or a matrix. Only by denying their representational function could they assume the role of background buildings demanded of them. It is true that the articulation of their elements suggests their possible extension and allows them to become metamorphosed into small cities. From a purely formal point of view this seems to be an advantage; but from the point of view of architectural content or meaning, it is a serious disadvantage. For, while it enables Le Corbusier to make an apparently flawless demonstration of architecture in the process of becoming merged with the city, and of the consistency of a design strategy that makes a conversion possible, it also denies those very qualities of discreteness, difference and *lack* of continuity that would make it possible for these buildings to fulfil their larger signifying ambitions.

Perhaps this is merely reiterating what has been said many times, that the Corbusian city would be alienating and would lack the multivalency that his buildings possess in the highest degree. Yet an examination of the compositional principles of his large public buildings enables us to see this problem from a new angle. For the real difficulty with the transformation of the representational building into a fragment of urban tissue lies in Le Corbusier's application of the same principles of composition to both, despite the differences in their scale and purpose. Because the city blocks consisted of a system of articulations similar to that found in his larger public buildings, neither could act as satisfactory foil to the other.

In the Corbusian city it is only housing that can legitimately act as the background to the representational buildings. If an attempt is made to interpret in the same way the linear bars of cellular office space in his public buildings, the buildings start to disintegrate. All that is left as a possible representation of the public realm is that part of each structure that consists of places of public assembly. Only these can project, in their concentrated forms, the social meanings that the architecture of the city ought to provide. Yet, in the Corbusian scheme, it is only within the individual building that such a meaning can develop—that building whose abstract and neutral ranges of accommodation provide the necessary ground against which the dynamic figures generated by function can be displayed.

It is in this sense that the Corbusian city seems to lack any strategy by which representational buildings could continue to exist. The *grands travaux* of the late 1920s, with their original and seductive forms and their plentitude of meaning, thus seem to exist in an ambiguous and metaphorical world halfway between the existing city, of which they are a critique, and the city of the future, in which they would cease to exist.

1   See Cohen, Jean-Louis, "Le Corbusier and the Mystique of the USSR", *Oppositions 23*, Winter 1981, pp. 85–121.
2   Le Corbussier and Pierre Jeanneret, *Oeuvre complete 1910–1929*, Zurich: Editions Girsberger, 1935, p. 189.
3   See Le Corbusier, *Urbanisme*, Paris: Editions Crès, 1924, p. 158.
4   Choisy, Auguste, *L'Histoire de l'architecture*, Paris, 1899, *Architecture Grecque*; chapter 11, "La pittoresque dans l'art Grecque". In *Vers une architecure* Le Corbusier not only printed several engravings from the *Histoire* but also paraphrased much of its picturesque theory, particularly in the chapters "Troi rapelles à messieurs les architectes/III Le plan", and "Architecture/II L'illusion des plans". See also Banham, Reyner, *Theory and Design in the First Machine Age*, London: The Architectural Press, 1960, chapter 2.
5   Choisy, "La pittoresque dans l'art Grecque".
6   Desite Le Corbusier's tendency toward elementarism, the courtyard building is a recurrent type in his work. It occurs for the first time in the "Immeubles Villas" of 1922 (though these were dropped in his later city plans), and it formed the basis of two buildings in the Mundaneum project: the larger cloister surrounding the university and the exhibition buildings based on the theme "continents, nations, cities". In his later work the most outstanding example of this type is the monastery at Eveux, in which, as in the early schemes for the Centrosoyus, the interior of the court is opened to the outside at the lower levels and divided into quadrants.
7   Le Corbusier, *Oeuvre complète 1929–1934*, Zurich: Editions Girsberger, 1964, p. 98.
8   Le Corbusier, *Oeuvre complète 1929–1934*.
9   This uniaxiality is also a characteristic of the plan of the Ville Radieuse, which was initiated as a result of Le Corbusier's contacts with Moscow; see Cohen, "Le Corbusier and the Mystique of the USSR". The metaphor of biological structure and growth is similar in both cases.

Classicism and Ideology

First published in *Casabella* 489, March 1983.

The return to classical models by certain architects has raised the question of the meaning of styles and their capacity to imply political attitudes. It is rather like the problem of whether handwriting reveals the character of the writer. There has, however, usually been a normative handwriting, taught at school, against which to measure any individual variant. A similar double criterion has always bedevilled the problem of classicism in architecture: does the classical tradition have an ahistorical aesthetic value, or is it bounded by a specific history and therefore a specific set of inescapable political connotations?

The argument stems, ultimately, from the conflict between eighteenth century ideas of universal man and natural law, and nineteenth century historicism, which saw all cultural systems and their corresponding artefacts as relative to their position in history. But historicism did not result merely in cultural relativism; it entailed what one might call a "reversal of paradigms". Not only was classicism denied its ahistorical status, but, precisely because of its absolutist claims, it also acquired a new set of negative connotations, identifying it with class domination and authoritarian government. This negative view of classicism was one of the mainsprings of the nineteenth and twentieth century avant-garde, according to which architecture should not be bound to a set of stylistic rules, but should be a 'free' and 'spontaneous' reflection of life.

Formalism and structuralism have demonstrated that all cultural phenomena are rule-governed and that, therefore, the idea of a natural architecture is necessarily false. It seems inevitable that, sooner or later, this point of view would gravitate toward the one system of architecture that was explicitly based on rules—classicism.

At the same time, it would seem that such a return must be sceptical about classicism's own claim to be based on nature. Classicism, newly interpreted, would seem to gain its prestige more from its insistence that art is based on the mediation of convention and type than on the belief that a typology of forms has any ontological status in itself.

In fact, contemporary proponents of classicism, such as Leon Krier, tend to base their preference more on the self-evident beauty and humaneness of the classical tradition than on the cosmological beliefs of the sixteenth century.

Classicism has come to play a new role in which the passive admiration of the art of the eighteenth century, so characteristic of the twentieth century, has been converted into an active weapon against a putative naturalism that has no defences against the modern consumer society. If we remember the frequent recourse of the Modern Movement itself to eighteenth century models of order, proportion, and 'disornamentation', we cannot avoid seeing contemporary neo-classical trends as a closely related phenomenon, although no longer tied to the historicist notion of progress and conformity with the *Zeitgeist*. In both cases a minority culture attempts to destroy the hegemony of 'materialist' and philistine values. The first attempt failed because, obsessed with the analogy between Enlightenment rationalism and the rationalism of modern production, it was quickly co-opted by capitalist modes of production, distribution, and consumption. The second attempt, so the argument goes, is proof against such co-option because it is removed from all considerations of material progress. Thus, what has hitherto acted in the twentieth century as a countercultural ideal expressed in terms of passive consumption (monuments, concerts of eighteenth century music, exhibitions, background educational instruction) is now posited as an active mode of artistic practice.

Above: Bertram Goodhue, Nebraska State Capitol, Lincoln, Nebraska, 1920–1932.

Opposite: Albert Speer, German Pavilion for the International Exposition in Paris, 1937.

The very possibility of this reversal rests on the profound eclecticism of modern culture, in which different cultural paradigms exist side by side at different levels of discourse. Nothing could show more clearly the 'arbitrariness' of the aesthetic sign as it operates in the twentieth century.

Therefore, any attempt to link classicism with a particular political ideology or practice must itself appear as only one of a number of possible interpretations. An example of this is the connection of classical revivals to the totalitarian regimes of the first half of the twentieth century and the imputation of guilt by association. It can easily be shown that the preference of these regimes for classicism as the style for public buildings was only a special case of a more widespread cultural tendency shared alike by totalitarian and liberal regimes. Even if we admit that its use in the liberal democracies was often associated with imperialist dreams (The City Beautiful Movement, Lutyens' New Delhi), we can hardly deny that an admiration for (if not the practice of) classical art has been a feature of all those groups (even the most politically radical) that have tried to maintain 'cultural standards'. In this respect, advanced cultural thinking in the twentieth century is completely different from its equivalent in the mid-nineteenth century. The return to classical paradigms in architecture at the turn of the twentieth century, related to the neo-Kantian movement in philosophy and art history, was a complex event covering the whole political spectrum. It was equally capable of serving American, British, and Prussian commercial imperialism and the aspirations of social democracy in Scandinavia. It was linked equally to the rhetoric of 'statehood' and to the vernacular tradition.

The facts suggest that classicism cannot be identified objectively with any particular content or ideology, but that rather it is an architectural tradition capable of attracting a host of different and contradictory meanings within the same broad cultural environment.

All returns to classicism no doubt have one notion in common: the idea that it is impossible to create an architectural language *ex nihilo*. But there is another idea that every moment of neo-classicism shares, which is that there is a single, normative tradition in European architecture. Whatever immediate tactics may be its motivation, neo-classicism has always been a return to this normative tradition—a tradition that has once and for all established the boundaries of architecture as an art.

There seems to be two ways in which this idea has made its appearance in the twentieth century. It can assume that classicism is a figural tradition whose recovery involved the notion of imitation, even if one allows this imitation a certain amount of license. This is the sense in which we must interpret such varied phenomena as the Scandinavian neo-classicism of the 1920s and 30s, the classicism of the traditional Socialist and Fascist regimes, and that of certain contemporary architects, notably Leon Krier. The meaning of classicism here cannot be separated from the notion of its 'reproducability'. Alternatively, it can accept modern constructional techniques and programmes as in some sense determining, and interpret these in terms of classical principles. Here the meaning of classicism is either abstract and ahistorical, or, insofar as it refers to a figural classicism, it relies on ellipsis and irony (as with certain columns and pediments in Aldo Rossi's work, which remain detached and enigmatic, bursts of memory that refuse to be integrated as a synecdoche).

Indeed, it would seem that contemporary classicism can be measured by the extent to which the architect brings irony to the problem of relating the modern world to the values of the past.

Regionalism and Technology

First published in *Casabella* 491, May 1983.

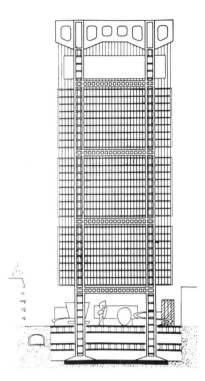

Recently there have been, once again, calls for a new regionalism in architecture. These vary (to take only two examples emanating from America) from Robert Stern's belief in the possibility of an American regionalism drawing on ethnic traditions, to the promotion of a "critical regionalism" in which what is celebrated would seem to be more the *loss* of authenticity than its recovery. But, like the regionalist philosophies which sprang up from within the ideology of modernism in the 1930s and 50s, the new regionalist doctrines are all based on the idea of a return to an artisanal architecture that somehow symbolises a cultural essence smothered by universal technology. This urge has a surprisingly old genealogy, going back to the Romantic Movement at the time of the French and Industrial revolutions. It suggests some sort of historical blockage in which the terms of the same debate keep on recurring without any substantial change. All regionalists seem to speak with the voices of the Schegel brothers and Pugin.

But there is another phenomenon which might equally be called "regionalism" that has nothing to do with any vernacular utopia or any critique of industrialism. This regionalism exists as part of the unconscious ideology underlying current practice and is connected with the actual political economic situation whose modalities are only indirectly related to any supposedly indigenous culture. It is the result of a complex interaction between modern international capitalism and various national traditions ingrained in institutions and attitudes. We should not expect to find, in this sort of regionalism, any differences of a fundamental kind, or complete survivals. Rather it manifests itself in the form of nuances. The materials of culture are similar in all cases, but each country tends to interpret these materials in a slightly different way. It is precisely because the ingredients of contemporary architecture are so similar all over the developed world that the slight differences of interpretation to which they are subjected in different countries are so interesting. Needless to say, the kind of regionalism I refer to has nothing to do with the old "regions of culture" attributed to ethnic characteristics, climate, language, and so on. Their areas of demarcation, on the contrary, are the most obvious and banal divisions of the modern political world, in which the nation-state is a reality. It is a regionalism based on politics. It seems curious that whenever regionalism is mentioned it is never these obvious regions of the political world that are referred to, but some imaginary entity, whose value is that it deflects attention from the most typical products of the twentieth century. If this phenomenon could be called Utopian, the new and existent regionalism is more like a pathology.

One of the ways in which it manifests itself is in differences of attitude toward the relationship between technology and 'architecture', where technology is taken as an external force acting on a cultural idea that has become professionally institutionalised. One of the most striking regional distinctions lies in the differences between American and European interpretations of this interaction. The American attitude toward technology has always been relaxed and pragmatic, whereas that of Europe has been idealistic and utopian. This contrast was underlined in a recent exhibition at the Museum of Modern Art in New York. The exhibit consisted of four skyscraper projects, three of which were American and one English. The American examples (by Philip Johnson, Cesar Pelli, and Gordon Bunshaft) were all concerned with the problems of external configuration and surface. The buildings were conceived as consisting of a given, maximised volume, wrapped with a skin. The main problems were whether there should be more than one tower, what configuration the tower

Above: Amancio Williams, Suspended Building for Offices, 1948.

Opposite: Norman Foster, Bank of Hong Kong, 1986, north elevation.

or towers should be given, and the treatment of the elevations. In recent American skyscrapers, design decisions have mostly been based on the idea of the volume as a parameter given by economics, the architectural problem lying in the nature of the surface enclosing this volume. No longer satisfied with the pure cube sheathed in a fully glazed curtain wall, architects have sought to give 'character' to skyscrapers either through the manipulation of the shape of the tower or through the ornamental treatment of the skin. From this general perspective, recent experiments by Cesar Pelli and Michael Graves belong to the same syndrome. The tower is a shed to be decorated, and this is possible because the technology of skyscraper design enforces a distinction between the skeleton of the building and its external surface. Indeed, in recent years, there have been several cases in which office towers have been completely resurfaced.

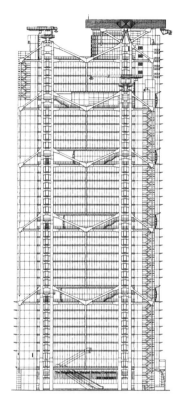

The English example, the Bank of Hong Kong by Norman Foster, was based on a completely different approach. It was conceived more as an expressive structure than as a sheathed cubic form. The roots of this connection lie within the international Modern Movement, and Foster's building must be seen as a descendent—conscious or unconscious—of the theoretical project for an office tower by Amancio Williams of 1948. In each case the building receives its visible expression from a tripartite division of mega-trusses from which several intermediate office floors are suspended. In Foster's building this concern for structural rhetoric seems to have resulted in an escalation of costs acceptable only for a building whose symbolic importance was as much national/political as commercial. This suggests a link between a certain kind of architecture and a certain kind of national consciousness.

In America the basic drive is commercial efficiency, accompanied by the need to show this as compatible with culture. The job of the architect is to transform a commercially viable building into a cultural icon, thus preserving the myth of free enterprise capitalism. In England, national pride is more closely connected with an engineering tradition dating from the nineteenth century—a tradition perhaps all the more compelling when seen from a period of national decline.

"Newness" and "Age-Value" in Aloïs Riegl

First published in *Oppositions 25*, Autumn 1982.

Aloïs Riegl's essay "The Modern Cult of Monuments: Its Character and Its Origin" sheds interesting light on the changing connotations of the words *modern* and *historical*.[1]

The categories Riegl uses in this essay took shape at the dawn of what has recently come to be called "modernism"—at a time when the artistic avant-garde of Vienna was calling for an art and architecture which would reflect modern life. Although his own purposes were limited to the theoretical and institutional problems associated with the preservation of artistic monuments, his remarks are clearly influenced by the historical context in which he lived and are, at the same time, sufficiently general for it to be possible to apply them to the contemporary situation in architecture.

Riegl distinguishes among three kinds of response to artistic works of the past. Such works may be interpreted as *intentional monuments,* as *unintentional monuments,* or simply as possessing *age-value.* He defines "age-value" as that which is "rooted purely in its value as memory... [which] springs from our appreciation of the time which has elapsed since [the work] was made and which has burdened it with traces of age". He continues:

> These monuments are nothing more than indispensable catalysts which trigger in the beholder a sense of the life cycle, of the emergence of the particular from the general and its gradual but inevitable dissolution back into the general. This immediate emotional effect depends on neither scholarly knowledge nor historical education.

He sets these categories in juxtaposition to two further concepts: that of the *Kunstwollen* (which attributes to works of the past its own artistic values) and something he variously calls "newness", "completeness", and "essential art-value" (which he defines as the essential quality of all new art of whatever period).

The notions of "age-value" and "newness" seem particularly apposite to the problems of contemporary architecture. Although Riegl attributes newness to all historical work when new, it is difficult to avoid the impression that he had in mind the ideas and work of contemporaries like Otto Wagner, and one is tempted to extend the concept to the Modern Movement which followed. The justification for this lies in his remark: "In our modern view, the new artefact requires flawless integrity of form and colour as well as of style... *the truly modern work must recall... earlier works as little as possible.*" [My italics.] Therefore there should be "newness value and the overwhelming aesthetic power it assumes whenever the circumstances are favourable".

Riegl himself establishes a sort of complementarity between this notion of "newness" and that of "age-value". He says that recognition of age-value depends on its contrast with new and modern artefacts:

> From man we expect accomplished artefacts as symbols of a necessary process of human production; on the other hand, from nature acting over time, we expect their disintegration as the symbol of an equally necessary passing.... What must be strictly avoided is interference with the action of nature's laws, be it the suppression of nature by man or the premature destruction of human creations by nature.

Therefore, although the two ideas are antithetical and must be kept rigidly separate, they are also complementary and dependent on each other. This idea corresponds closely to the ideas of the Modern Movement, in which the preservation of historical monuments sometimes went hand in hand with the destruction and rebuilding of the city (see Le Corbusier's 1936 Plan Voisin for the centre of Paris). Where historical works have here lost their meaning as part of the fabric of time and space and are preserved either as monuments or as emblems of a superseded past.

It is clear that the idea of "newness" does not have the same complementary relationship to the other two categories of historical awareness specified by Riegl—those pertaining to *intentional* and *unintentional* monuments, which, as Riegl points out, both depend on their commemorative value. In the first case historical awareness is the result of a point of view "which is still normative, authoritative, hence antique/medieval, and not historical in the modern sense, since it did not recognise development". There can therefore be no real distinction between the new and the old. In the second case, although there is consciousness of historical development, historical knowledge requires that the old be accurately reconstructed and be made to look as new as possible. In this historicist perspective the old takes on a surreal contemporaneity, historical time being, as it were, simultaneously affirmed and annulled, as in the reconstructions of Viollet-le-Duc.

The pair "newness" and "oldness" therefore belongs to a specifically modern sensibility to which Riegl was evidently acutely sensitive and whose future he vaguely anticipated. In terms of his own thought, one characteristic demand of age-value was that monuments should be allowed to grow old gracefully and exhibit the depredations of time, though in cases where the monument still has a practical or symbolic usefulness the idea of its "natural" decay could be made to include that equally "natural" arrest of decay which comes from continued use and repair. This point of view still saw something almost organic in the process by which the new superseded the old; it did not (and could not) anticipate the onslaught on the fabric of the past that was to characterise both the ideal city plans of the 1920s and 30s

Opposite left: Le Corbusier, Project for a business city in Paris, 1936, photomontage showing new and old sections of Paris. Le Corbusier's caption reads: "*Les nouvelles dimensions modernes et la mise en valeur des trésors historiques apportent une grace délicieuse.*"
© FLC/ADAGP, Paris and DACS, London 2009

Opposite right: Le Corbusier, Project for a business city in Paris, 1936.
© FLC/ADAGP, Paris and DACS, London 2009

Top: Tourists visiting the Colosseum in Rome, circa 1860.

Bottom: The Ramparts of Carcassonne before the restoration by Viollet-le-Duc, 1852.

and the actual urban planning of the mid-twentieth century, and which was to bring a new level of consciousness to the problem of the relation of the new to the old in architecture. Yet it is precisely here that Riegl's categories take on a new meaning. Although evidence of decay is no longer, as it was in Riegl's day, the most crucial element in our sense of age-value, it would seem that it is still the 'age' of historical buildings that constitutes their value today, rather than their qualities either as intentional or unintentional monuments. The past is valued for its 'pastness' and not because it provides models for a normative architecture or represents timeless architectural values (as it did from 1450 to roughly 1800), nor because it can be accurately reconstructed as evidence of the organic relationship between monuments and the societies that produced them (as was the case in the nineteenth century).

This can be demonstrated in two ways. First, the old is still defined, negatively, in relation to the new rather than in terms of positive qualities. The difference between 'postmodern' and 'modernist' points of view does not reside in any radical reassessment of our relationship to historical culture; it lies solely in the fact that, whereas according to the modernist ethos the sense of the new had positive value and an "overwhelming aesthetic power", it is now often denigrated as a symbol of reductivism. The complementarity of the new and the old still persists, but one of its terms is now missing.

Second, historical monuments no longer have that commemorative power which Riegl said was an essential feature of both intentional and unintentional monuments. Likewise, the aesthetic rules and the rules of propriety that were an integral part of their meaning no longer have any force. Contemporary eclecticism is based neither on a belief in the absolute norms of beauty, nor on the capacity of style to evoke definite sociocultural meanings.

It seems, therefore, that we are still in the period that Riegl defined as dominated by "age-value", even though the problems connected with this concept are no longer those that confronted Riegl himself.

1 Riegl, Aloïs , "The Modern Cult of Monuments: Its Character and Its Origin", trans., in *Oppositions 25*, p. 198.

Bull, Field, Volkman, Stockwell, Venetian Gardens development, Stockton, California,1974–1977.

Postmodern Critical Attitudes

First published in *Modernity and the Classical Tradition: Architectural Essays 1980–1987*, 1989.

The main purpose of cross-disciplinary discussions is not to blur the distinctions between the different arts, but to be able to define, and if necessary redefine, these distinctions with greater precision. It would be interesting, for example, to investigate the areas of agreement and disagreement between critics of architecture and critics of painting over a definition of postmodernism. Nonetheless there are certain factors common to present-day criticism in all the arts. The most important and at the same time most obvious of these is that we are no longer in the phase of modernism and the classical avant-garde.

In saying this I do not wish to imply that there was a monolithic critical position during this phase, even within a single discipline. But, if we look at the Modern Movement in architecture, we see that opinions, despite their mutual differences, had more in common with each other than any of them have with advanced critical opinion today. It is true that there exists an opinion that the expression "postmodern" is meaningless and that our period is continuous with modernism. But the existence of a strong and coherent movement *against* this idea is enough to distinguish our period from that of, say, the 1950s.

But to say that we live in a postmodern critical atmosphere is perhaps not to say a great deal, because so-called postmodernism contains, if possible, even more variations than did modernism itself.

I said that modernist criticism was far from monolithic. But, in fact, the critical statements of the architectural avant-garde during the 1920s and 30s show that there was considerable agreement. The leading ideas were even reiterated with a certain monotony. The heterogeneity belongs more to the artistic practice of different architects than to differences of opinion about what they were trying to do.

One of the leading ideas in the architectural Modern Movement was the doctrine of functionalism. Functionalism, it is true, was employed differently by different schools—the Dutch, German, Russian, and French—and by different architects. But not so differently as all that. Let us take the organic analogy as an example. It is usual to stress the difference between those critics and architects who used the analogy of organic form and growth and those who used the analogy of the machine. Wright versus Le Corbusier; Expressionism versus the *Neue Sachlichkeit*, and so on.

Yet both the organic and the mechanical analogies, which had been part of critical currency from the end of the eigtheenth century, depended on the fact that there was a certain slippery ambiguity in the terms. They tended to become each other. The same was true in modernism. There is no doubt that for Le Corbusier, for instance, the machine itself was a metaphor for nature. And, on the opposite side, what distinguished Wright or Hugo Häring from late nineteenth century Art Nouveau and allied them to the more rational wing of the Movement was precisely the notion of abstract form deriving from industrialisation.

So, if one were trying to sum up the classical avant-garde, one might say that it was concerned with the functional application of abstract form. But what exactly was meant by "function"? After all, function and utility had been important critical concepts since the late eighteenth century. How was modernism any different? A possible way of defining the difference would be to say that modernism removed from the idea of function all traces of propriety or decorum—anything in fact to do with social custom. It wished to create an architecture that was entirely motivated and natural, without contamination from the arbitrary forms that survived from history.

The Modernist Project, then, gave a privileged position to reason, abstraction, science, and technique; and it made two assumptions about modern society. The first was that the modern period must have its own unique cultural forms with as little contamination as possible from tradition, and the second was that society was like Locke's description of the mind; a *tabula rasa*. Human institutions and forms could be rationally created on the basis of known needs.

It is this positivistic and scientistic view of society and of culture, which was an integral part of modernism (at least in architecture), that postmodern criticism has made one of its main objects of attack. But it has done this in the name of at least two widely different models. I would like to call these—adapting Françoise Choay's useful terminology—the *progressivist* and the *culturalist* models.

For the progressivists, postmodernism is a transfiguration of modernism itself. It carries over many ideas associated with modernism—primarily the notion of a radical break with history—but transforms them. For the culturalists, on the contrary, postmodernism implies a complete disassociation from modernism and a reaction against it in favour of tradition.

I will take Jean-François Lyotard and his book *The Postmodern Condition: A Report on Knowledge* as representative of the progressivist position.[1] In so doing I am aware that Lyotard is not writing about architecture or even art, but about knowledge and science. But his interpretation of knowledge is so broad that his essay is essentially a critique of postmodern *culture,* and it is perfectly legitimate to extrapolate from his ideas to architecture so long as one remembers that such extrapolation is conjectural.

Lyotard's critique of modernism is made from a position which is as libertarian and anti-establishment as that of modernism itself. He is still concerned with the Enlightenment project of Freedom—the title of his essay, with its 'Encyclopedic' overtones, shows this—but he no longer believes that this can be achieved by the means that modernism and the Enlightenment shared: a concerted, rational 'programme' that would replace one set of controlling ideas with another (and therefore one set of controllers by another).

For him, the great meta-narratives that legitimised eighteenth and nineteenth century visions of society are no longer available. These meta-narratives were two in number: the first was the cognitive idea of spiritual and intellectual freedom, which was German in origin; the second was the practical idea of political freedom, which attained its principal expression in France. These two "master narratives" are no longer available, Lyotard claims, because technology—particularly information and communication technology—has irreversibly taken over all the positions of power. It cannot be frontally attacked, because it is, essentially, a success story, and it is judged purely on the basis of what it is good at: performance and efficiency and the maximising of output for a given energy expenditure. Though he does not say as much, Lyotard implies that modernism unknowingly aided this process through its conflation of science and technique and its belief in technique as a liberating force.

To the extent that he diagnoses post-industrial society in this way, Lyotard appears to agree largely with Niklas Luhmann and the German school of "*System theorie*" that in post-industrial society the *performativity of procedures* replaces the *normativity of laws*. But he strongly disagrees with Luhmann's apparently cynical and defeatist interpretation. He believes that we can prevent the system "taking over". He does not think this can be done in the manner of modernism, by frontal assault, because this would have to be based on technical control and would thus merely reinforce the very system it intended to undermine. But he believes that it can be done by action from within, because of certain in-built human factors that cannot be absorbed by the system. He makes use of a number of concepts to describe this power of resistance, this antibody within postmodern, post-industrial society. Three of these may be mentioned.

First, the idea of "narrative knowledge". Narrative knowledge distinguishes itself from scientific knowledge. It is prescriptive and not just descriptive. It is "knowing-how" rather than "knowing". Knowing how to live, how to listen, how to make. It includes value judgments about justice, happiness, and beauty. This kind of knowledge (which should perhaps be called "opinion") was the predominant kind of knowledge in the prescientific age. It is based on tradition and custom. It is, according to Lyotard, essential, and indeed still quite pervasive in everyday life.

Second, the idea of "language games". According to Lyotard there is a sort of incommensurability between different kinds of discourse, such that they cannot be reduced one to the other or to a common underlying type. Here he lumps together JL Austin and Ludwig Wittgenstein: the difference between denotative, performative, and prescriptive utterances (Austin), and between questions, promises, narrations (Wittgenstein).

Third, paralogy in science. Since scientific statements have to be tested according to certain agreed procedures, they differ from narrative statements, which are subject to no such constraint. However, science aims not at performative efficiency (as does technology) but at complexity, diversity, instability, and contradiction. The overall results of science are paralogical: they cannot be subsumed under a single logic or squared with each other. Science is always producing new statements.

It is evident that these concepts all tend toward the relative and the indeterminate. Knowledge is not *just* scientific knowledge. There are many language *games,* not just *language.* Science leads to multiplicity not to unicity. In a sense this view continues the breakdown of traditional certainties even further than modernism does. No global 'meaning' is necessary—just multiple meanings *(petits recits)*—which are immanent in the very interstices of existence.

What about the second type of postmodern criticism, the 'culturalist'? This is primarily concerned with validating specific traditional disciplines—such as architecture—rather than trying to provide an overall philosophy of art in post-industrial society. Therefore any example we may give will be more related to a specific practice than was the case with the progressivist view.

As we know, in architecture the culturalist view is marked by the claim that there are traditional values that are good independently of their place in history. But these traditional values are no longer the Platonic abstractions by which modernism provided itself with a genealogy (rejecting the father and going back to a shadowy and remote great-grandfather). They are nothing other than the devices and forms that the history of architecture has itself created. In other words, we must build on the experience of the past in order to create a contemporary architecture.

What varies in this kind of postmodern critical discourse is the extent to which the past is seen either as providing absolute models, or a set of general principles which have to be transformed if they are to be applicable to the modern world. There is nothing in postmodern criticism that can decide this point, and we find widely different interpretations of the idea of returning to the past. At one extreme we find someone like Robert Venturi, whose attitude toward tradition seems in some ways to be like that of Lyotard. Lyotard's emphasis on the indeterminate, the mixed, the pluralistic, and the fragmentary seems to echo the thesis of Venturi's *Complexity and Contradiction* and much of his architecture. At the other extreme we find an architect like Leon Krier, who treats the tradition of classicism as an absolute model even if he takes as much from neo-classicism as from Roman architecture.

In between these two extremes one finds a whole range of solution types in which classical forms are used fairly literally but are connected together in unfamiliar ways. Many architects are now using these traditional forms with a sense of parody or with a cartoon-like irreverence and an apparently unintentional vulgarity.

But different as they may be, they have one thing in common—they all reject the modernist prohibition against imitation. They all, to some extent, loosen the connection that historicist thought makes between artistic forms and the *Zeitgeist.* They all treat architecture as a discipline with its own internal tradition, which is at least partially independent of the change in technical, economic, and social conditions. In other words, they *de-historicise* architecture.

Perhaps, indeed, the greatest difference between this type of postmodernism and the first type is that the first type is fundamentally historicist. Instead of underemphasising the relevance of historical change, as culturalist postmodernism does, progressivist postmodernism emphasises it—emphasises the difference between our age and all those that preceded it. The historiographic model here seems to be that of Michel Foucault, with his notion of different periods and their different "epistomes", or of Thomas Kuhn, with his notion of changing "paradigms".

But here I would draw your attention to a curious reversal that seems to take place in the respective positions of progressivist and culturalist postmoderns in their relation to history. Lyotard would like to say that we are committed to a peculiar stage of cultural evolution which is different from anything that has gone before and which is intimately connected to the economic and technical developments of post-industrial society. He stresses this in his rejection of what he calls legitimation by the kind of meta-narrative characteristic of all traditional societies. But, as I have said, he also stresses the continued importance of narrative knowledge and the role of the *petit récit*. Is he not invoking an archaic and nostalgic image here? He says that, paradoxically, narrative knowledge, with its dependence on customary and traditional kinds of wisdom, has the effect of obliterating the past. It does so because, in the process of being re-enacted, the past *becomes* the present.

Translating this amnesiac model into architecture, one might imagine it applying to the Middle Ages, where a craft tradition internalised and transformed what had (remotely) been received from antiquity. One might also, perhaps, be able to apply it to the Renaissance, when a defunct tradition was revived and codified, but soon became second nature. It would, I think, be difficult to apply it to the end of the eighteenth century, when the past suddenly begins to seem very remote and is looked back to nostalgically, and more difficult to apply it to nineteenth century eclecticism and revivalism. Finally, it would be more difficult still to apply it to the present, when almost any more or less literal reference to the architectural tradition looks like a quotation.

As for the cultural postmodernists, we see a reciprocal reversal. Here the claim is that architecture is to an important extent free of historical determination. In returning to the past we are turning to eternal aesthetic values. Yet it is precisely the use of past forms that draws our attention to our remoteness from the time in which these forms were originally developed. We are reminded of the past *as the past*. The only way in which a building could make us feel that the values of architecture were eternal and not subject to historical change would be if its forms seemed "natural" to our way of life, in other words, "modern". But in this case we would have to be able to forget that these forms were specifically historical, as was no doubt possible in the Middle Ages and in the Renaissance. Historical time would have, once more, to become mythical time.

Finally, it might be interesting to compare the attitudes toward the 'new' in Lyotard and in culturalist postmodernism.

The new has been an ingredient of the avant-garde since the introduction of this term into critical discourse in the mid-nineteenth century. In truth, the argument goes back to the quarrel between the ancients and the moderns in the French academy in the seventeenth century. Then, of course, it arose in the field of science, but was applied by the Perrault brothers to architecture. "We can do better than the ancients." But in the nineteenth century avant-garde the new took on prophetic connotations: art was thought of as anticipating cultural freedom, chiefly through its ability to perceive and project reality.

In Lyotard the new is connected with science. In calling on the "players" in the "game" of scientific discourse to be ready to accept different "rules", he says, "the only legitimation that can make this kind of request admissible is that it will generate ideas, in other words, new statements". This belief in the new is even more extreme than it was in modernism, where statements were expected to be "true" and correspond to "reality" as well as be new.

It is probably not altogether fair to guess from Lyotard's view of science what might be his view of art. If narrative knowledge is the knowledge of custom, newness cannot be its most important property. (Absolute consistency is, after all, the last thing Lyotard is claiming.) Nonetheless there is a spirit in Lyotard which favours open endedness and risk, which has much in common with the classical avant-garde, and which is opposed to the conservative spirit of culturalist postmodernism.

Few culturalist postmodernists would deny that modern works are bound to be different from past works, if only because the artist or architect cannot be conscious of all the factors that are impinging on him. But they would nonetheless be likely to place the emphasis on what was *not* new in a design—on the element of tradition that was being transformed. It would seem, then, that in their attitudes both to the way historical memory operates in the present and to the concept of invention, progressivist and culturalist postmodernists have diametrically opposite views, however much they may agree about other matters.

It has been my purpose in this essay to try to elucidate a few of these differences, and, in so doing, to show that postmodernist criticism is very far from being monolithic. In my opinion not enough attention has been given to the fact that the same term is often used to refer to opposite ideas.

1   Lyotard, Jean-François, *The Postmodern Condition: A Report on Knowledge*, Minneapolis, MN: University of Minnesota Press, 1984.

Postmodernism and Structuralism: a Retrospective Glance

First published in *Assemblage 5*, February 1988.

The term "postmodern" seems, by turns, empty or tendentious. Probably the nearest we could get to an acceptable definition would be something along the lines of Andreas Huyssen's proposition: the movements in art and architecture that have taken the place of an exhausted High Modernism.[1] This definition implies that the unifying concepts of modernism have been replaced by a plurality of tendencies and that it would be foolish to expect a single guiding idea in postmodern practice. On the other hand, certain dominant tendencies can be discerned in each of the semi-autonomous institutions of contemporary culture, and this essay will investigate these within the field of architecture. This is not to say that in architecture we are confronted with a unique set of practices that have nothing in common with those of other disciplines. But before we can recognise the overlaps and transgressions that take place across the boundaries separating different fields, it is first necessary to establish provisional boundaries.

I will begin, therefore, by pointing to two characteristics of architecture that, it seems to me, differentiate it from the other arts and that help to explain the specific forms of postmodern practice that we find in architecture. The first way in which architecture differs from the other arts is that it is very expensive. With architecture so bound to the sources of finance and power, it is much more difficult for the architect than for other artists to operate within an apparently autonomous subculture or to retain that independence from bourgeois taste that has been the ambition of art since the early nineteenth century. To play an effective critical role, architecture has to ally itself with major economic tendencies claimed as progressive—as happened in the 1920s when 'modernisation' and technical advance were associated with social renewal and a utopian vision. The second way in which architecture differs from the other arts is that its mode of reception is one of distraction rather than contemplation. As Walter Benjamin pointed out in his essay "The Work of Art in the Age of Mechanical Reproduction", this distracted mode of reception—which led him to see architecture as a paradigm for those characteristically 'modern' arts, photography and cinema—is shaped by the establishment of habits.[2] Thus the power that initially seems to be invested in the architect is withdrawn from him, first, because he is a mere agent and, second, through a sort of indifference to architecture that results from its very ubiquity and usefulness. These factors have played a large part in the failure of the Modern Movement in architecture to live up to its own programme, based as it was on a somewhat fictitious view of the architect's prophetic and influential role in society.

The critique of modernism that developed in the late 1960s was overwhelmingly concerned with this failure. Modern architecture had promised no less than the complete renewal of the urban and rural environment. In this it differed from the avant-garde movements in the other arts, which could only promise a spiritual renewal. Of course, certain artistic movements—notably Dada and Surrealism—were closely connected with the political left; but only architecture offered a revolution in the actual social realm irrespective of whether or not its protagonists were on the political left (which, as it happens, many of them were). Only in the architectural avant-garde were the ideal world of art and the real world of empirical fact conflated without the presumptive need for political revolution.

Architecture founded its promise largely on the belief that technology could solve the practical and artistic problems of modern social existence.

Since the Modern Movement intended a global revolution, not merely of architectural taste, but of the urban environment, it is with the attack on the modernist city that we should begin our description of at least one strand of what is known as "postmodernism". Many factors contribute to the reaction against the modernist city. One is the view that it was essentially unbuildable except under those inherently rare political conditions that made possible a Brasilia or a Chandigarh—and that there the results were highly questionable from both a sociological and an aesthetic point of view. Another is that in existing cities, the piecemeal application of such modernist principles as zoning, highway construction, and the welcoming of skyscraper technology destroyed or rendered alien the central urban areas. A third is that the creation of large high-rise housing projects in the centre or on the periphery of the great cities obliterated all trace of the existing fabric and the community structure associated with it without providing a genuine alternative.

Thus we can observe two main phenomena: first, the fragmentary and piecemeal application of versions of the technological utopia of the 1920s as part either of welfare state politics or of capitalist growth; second, the appropriation of modernist techniques and imagery, originally utopian in intention, by business corporations and private interest pressure groups. In the first case the critique was sociological and psychological. In the second it was ideological: the very intention and meaning of the Modern Movement was seen as having been 'betrayed' and inverted, so that advanced building technology and its associated aesthetic, no longer the symbols of a new social order based on cooperation, became a means of enhancing the prestige of big business.

When we turn our attention from the city to the individual building we find that one of the strongest critiques was directed against the architectural version of Minimalism, closely tied to the doctrine of functionalism. As modern architecture was generally adopted after the war, adapting itself to the real tasks of building on a large scale, and being disseminated throughout the profession, its formal rules came to be applied in an increasingly perfunctory way. What could be called the proto-postmodern critique of modern architecture in the 1960s was largely based on the monotonous and boring quality of most modern buildings. Not only did these seem artistically incompetent, but they often failed as well to work at a technical and practical level. Even allowing for the naïve populism and philistinism of much of this criticism, we have to admit that it contained much truth. A good deal of professional arrogance was involved, and, for a short period, we had the curious spectacle of an entire professional body thinking of itself as an avant-garde. I believe that it is therefore important to understand that the anti-modernist reaction was, in fact, a reaction against a 'modern movement' that had become conservative, professionalised, and 'routinised'. It was not primarily directed against the seminal works of the 1920s or 1930s.

Also present, however, was a developing critique of modernist theory, especially the explicit doctrine of functionalism and the implicit doctrine of historicism. It has been correctly said that this critique was more often directed against the self-perpetuated mythology of modernism than against modern architecture itself—which was far from allowing itself to be restricted by the narrow concept of functionalism or the total rejection of history that was proclaimed by theory. But it is not so easy to separate the practice of modernism from its theory, and even if the criticism left certain modern works intact, it was high time to question a body of assumptions that had, by the mid-1960s, clearly become restricting and irrelevant.

Functionalism and Minimalism were closely bound together in architecture. This combination of ideas was not restricted to architecture—we can find a comparable system of ideas in the philosophy of Bertrand Russell and the anthropology of Bronislaw Malinowski, as well as, most apparently, in the music of Arnold

Schoenberg—but in architecture functionalism had an obvious commonsense application that it lacked elsewhere. Architecture, like music and the other arts, has traditionally depended on the arrangement or composition of a number of preformed rhetorical figures—what Charles Rosen, speaking of music but using an architectural metaphor, calls the use of "large blocks of prefabricated material". The new architecture of the 1920s sought to banish these tropes and formulae and to replace them with atomic elements that were considered formally and functionally irreducible. The meaning was to be derived from the formal and functional context of the work itself, supposedly independent of the stylistic cliches and rhetorical gestures handed down by the tradition.

One of the chief objects of the postmodern attack was this notion of a set of functions, tied to the particular work, but having a prior and external existence to it. The attack was not against the idea of a building having a purpose, but against the idea that the aesthetic form of the building should be utterly transparent to this purpose, defined by a set of more or less quantifiable functions. Such ideas had been questioned before, both by the enemies of modernism and by architects within the movement. But by the 1960s, just at the time that some architects had reduced the idea of functionalism to a would-be behaviouristic system, a weapon of attack against functionalism became available—a weapon that itself seemed to possess all the credentials of a positive science. This was Structuralism, as inaugurated by Ferdinand de Saussure and as developed variously by Roman Jakobson, Claude Lévi-Strauss, and Roland Barthes. According to this approach the ability of signs to convey meaning, within any sign system whatever, depends on an arbitrary and conventional structure of relationships within a particular system and not on the relation of signs to pre-existent or fixed referents in outside reality. The application of this linguistic model to architecture enabled 'function' to be seen as the false reification and naturalisation of a set of culturally determined values that might or might not be considered as part of the system of meaning constituted by a building.

The second object of attack was historical determinism. Modern architecture, as propounded by its main theorists and historians, depended on a theory of history established in the early nineteenth century that, in part, interpreted cultural development through the metaphor of organic development. In this it was closely connected to the aesthetic theory of romanticism and its use of the organic analogy to explain the structure of artistic form. According to an extreme historicist interpretation, the cultural practice of any one period could be understood only from its position on an evolutionary time scale and as part of a causal-temporal chain. This approach was as vulnerable as that of functionalism to a Structuralist critique. The counter model was again Saussure's linguistics, an explication in terms of structure replacing one advanced in terms of linear causality.

Cultural systems—the argument goes—like language itself, can be explained less as temporal processes than as spatial structures. The cultural meanings of a period are interrelated, and the meaning of any one word, or any single artistic form, depends on the existence of all the others. If we take a practice like architecture, we can see that, as in the case of language, history is present not as a process in which each phase negates a previous one, but as a series of traces that survive in current ways of looking at the world. An historical form can therefore be seen as raw material within the present practice of architecture—not as something that has been relegated to an external past.

The application of the linguistic model to the arts resulted in a certain confusion, for it could be interpreted in one of two ways: as a syntactics that was 'empty' or as a semantics that was 'full'. Neither of these interpretations contradicts the notion of the arbitrariness of the sign. Nor do they necessarily exclude each other, since one is concerned with the signifier and the other with the sign (signifier + signified) as its object of attention. But, I would argue, it is the second of these two interpretations that applies to architecture, a position best justified by Lévi-

Strauss in his discussion of a different field—that of music.[3] Lévi-Strauss bases his argument on the analogy of the double articulation of language. In music, meaning (that is, 'musical' meaning) is only imaginable if the sonic material has already been given a structure; new meanings can emerge only as modifications of an inherited structure. Now in music the basis for any such cultural structuration already exists in the natural degrees of dissonance. I would argue that a similar basis exists in architecture and that, therefore, architecture, like music, is both a natural and an arbitrary system.[4]

We can see from what I have said that structuralism was able to provide the rationale for an attack on two dogmas—functionalism and historical determinism— that were fundamental to the theory and practice of modernism. But Structuralism could provide only a general critical framework. To understand how a Structuralist critique might be applied to architecture requires a process of translation.

One means to such a translation is through the notion of type, which might explain how, within a system analogous to language, forms are generated in architecture. Just as language always pre-exists a group or individual speaker, the system of architecture preexists a particular period or architect. It is precisely through the persistence of earlier forms that the system can convey meaning. These forms, or *types,* interact with the tasks presented to architecture, in any moment in history, to form the entire system.

One of the many reasons why a typology of forms might have more impact on practice in architecture than in the other arts is the inherent reproducibility of architecture and its dependence on prototype. In the past, all the arts depended, to a greater or a lesser extent, on the faithful reproduction of prototypical elements. In classical artistic theory this use of prototypes was, so to speak, sublimated into the theory of mimesis, insofar as this applied to the imitation of models of classical art. The Romantic Movement condemned this concept as a denial of the absolute originality of each artwork; though the process was not destroyed, after romanticism it ceased to be a *de jure* practice and went underground. But in architecture the concept of reproducibility persisted. (It is curious that Benjamin does not mention this in his *Kunstwerk* essay.) Once an idea has been established in architecture it is repeated in countless examples. Though monuments are seldom repeated exactly, more humble buildings like houses are often identical. This is no doubt partly because such buildings are intended to satisfy basic and continuing human needs, and partly because to translate an idea into material form requires the mediation of a number of agents, which in turn demands a certain degree of standardisation.

All of which the Modern Movement understood. Both Hermann Muthesius and Le Corbusier made a connection between industrial production and an impersonal and normative classicism. The concepts of *Typisierung* and the *objet-type* were developed in the early days of the Modern Movement. But here the emphasis was on industrial production. The revival of the idea of type in the 1960s was certainly related to this aspect of modernism. But it differed from modernism in that it contained the notion of the repetition of certain morphologies in the history of architecture that appear to be independent of technical change. Giulio Carlo Argan, who revived this idea at a period of interest in Enlightenment architecture on the part of the *Casabella* group, based it on a rereading of the entry under "Type" in Quatremère de Quincy's *Dictionnaire historique d'architecture.* This notion of type has since become one of the recurrent ideas in the critical discourse of architecture.

In it we see an attempt to reinvest the form and body of a work of architecture with a dimension of meaning that depends on a kind of collective memory. The idea not only contests naïve functionalism and the tyranny of technology over form; it also sets up a new kind of necessity in the place of function and historical determinism. It sets limits to the imagination of the architect and binds him to something analogous to the concept of *langue* in Saussure—a received structure and a collective possession that must be presupposed before any significance can be attributed to the *parole* of the individual speaker.

But in the notion of type, both as established by Quatremère and as reinterpreted by Argan and the *Casabella* group, there is a distinction between type and model. The re-establishment of continuity between modern architecture and history was the drive behind the whole concept, and it was supposed that this could be achieved by establishing an architectural typology at a relatively abstract level. But it has not proved so easy to distinguish between the abstract and the concrete, and it has, in practice, been impossible to distinguish absolutely between type and model.

Rather than try to give an account of all the different tendencies that, during the last ten years or so, have produced various fusions between traditional modernism and historical reference, and between a strict idea of typology and a free eclecticism, I would prefer to concentrate on a single problem: one that involves the relationship between a recovery of the past in architecture and an attitude toward social reality. I will here be concerned with architecture as affirmation or criticism.

The problem of distinguishing between an affirmative and a critical postmodernism is immediately complicated by uncertainty as to what aspect of cultural production is being attacked and what reinforced. If we examine modernism and the avant-garde as a necessary precondition for the discussion of postmodernism, we see that it is already fraught with ambiguities and reversals in this matter. In the dialectic of *Gemeinschaft* and *Gesellschaft* we find the seeds of most of these later ambiguities.[5] According to the proponents of *Gemeinschaft,* life in industrialised society was abstract and alienating.[6] But this implied an opposite interpretation: a true modern culture could not be achieved until we overcame our resistance to abstraction and specialisation and were prepared to reject traditional values and their idealist underpinnings.

At the same time, the project of 'modernisation' stemming from the second interpretation of the *Gemeinschaft/Gesellschaft* opposition was itself imbued with an ideal content by architects like Muthesius and Le Corbusier. In a tendency related to the *rappel a l'ordre* in post-war Paris, the architecture of the machine age was seen as overcoming history to achieve a kind of transhistorical classicism. In an opposite movement, but still within this 'progressivist' frame of mind, certain *Neue Sachlichkeit* architects called for the abandonment of all artistic pretensions in an architecture that would be absolutely objective and transparent to social needs.

Already, therefore, we can see the formation of a set of oppositions that becomes increasingly important: high art versus popular art; 'modernisation' as the symbol of artistic purity versus 'modernisation' as the symbol of social renewal.

There was an analogous situation in painting: a distinction can be made between on the one hand, a true 'avant-garde' aiming at the subversion of the very concept of high art and, on the other, a 'modernism' continuous with the historical development of the high artistic tradition (a position advocated by both Clement Greenberg and Theodor Adorno). A case in point is the argument between Adorno and Benjamin over "The Work of Art in the Age of Mechanical Reproduction". Benjamin perceived the cinema, in positive terms, as a new mass culture; Adorno condemned all mass culture as a symptom of cultural decadence—a decadence that it was the purpose of modernist art to arrest. Adorno's aesthetic theory is a typical reversal of the character traits of *Gemeinschaft* and *Gesellschaft*. Now a *Gesellschaft*-like abstractionism was identified with the preservation of culture, preventing art from being swallowed up by the 'culture industry'. The autonomy of art, its aura, could only survive if the original conditions of its practice were abandoned.

If conflicts of this sort existed within modernism itself, those between the modernists and anti-modernists in the inter-war years were even more clear-cut. But they were cut along exactly the same cultural fault lines. In the 1930s, with the fading of post-war optimism in Russia and Western Europe and with the rise of Fascism, these conflicts became critical. The traditionalists surfaced in Germany, Italy, and Russia, promoting various forms of Social Realism. *Heimatstil* and state classicism in Germany, the projects of Marcello Piacentini in Mussolini's Rome, and the promotion of a 'bourgeois' realism in Russia were closely related. And the same tendencies existed at the time in the democratic countries—notably in the United States.

After the war, Social Realism continued in Russia; but in the West it was modernism that came to be associated with democracy and victory over Fascism. In Germany and France, despite their many differences, a monolithic and professionalised modernism developed that made any external criticism virtually impossible. It was mainly in Italy that an external critique developed, due in part to the ambiguous relation of modernism to Fascism, but also to the relative weakness of the institutional and financial structures, upon which large-scale housing and commercial development plans depended. This critique seems to have incorporated many influences, the chief of which was a new form of Social Realism—as found in the work of Ludovico Quaroni and Mario Ridolfi in Rome, whose housing projects borrowed formal elements from the vernacular tradition. In these tendencies we can perhaps discern the influence of Russian Social Realism and the artistic theories of Georg Lukács. At what point these various critical movements can be said to anticipate a 'postmodernism' is doubtful and probably not very important. But postmodern or not, the attitudes of the subsequent movement of neo-rationalism— as represented, for example, by Aldo Rossi—constituted an unambiguous and uncompromising rejection of the doctrine of functionalism and opened the door to association and memory and to historical quotation. The simultaneous acceptance of some of the typical solutions of the 1920s by Rossi and Giorgio Grassi was not based on an acceptance of modernist dogma. Instead, they added certain modernist inventions to a more general typological inventory of architecture. The turning points of architectural history, represented by the Enlightenment and the earliest years of the Modern Movement, were approached with renewed interest as periods that could still provide analogies and models for the present situation. For the first time we see the project of revising the Modern Movement from a perspective that is no longer inside the Modern Movement itself.

It is interesting to note that the most coherent critique of modernism in Europe— that of the Italians—came from architects who belonged to the political left and were concerned with the fundamentally social role of architecture. It is true that the neo-rationalists stressed the relative autonomy of architecture and that they no longer considered architecture as capable of generating a technical, social, or political revolution. But this negative attitude toward architecture's revolutionary potential was not due to any desire to preserve the political status quo. Rather, it arose out of a loss of faith in technology as a liberating force, in the idea of 'modernisation', and in the corresponding elements of a modernist architecture.

What I am suggesting is that in this branch of postmodernism resides a theory of the work of architecture that contradicts the conflation that Adorno and the Frankfurt School made between modernism and cultural resistance. This new theory goes back to the notion of *Gemeinschaft* in the sense that it is critical of the increasing routinisation and centralisation of modern capitalist culture and sees in the autonomous tradition of architecture one way of combating this culture. It seems clear that this position combines a rather conservative concern for certain cultural traditions with a critique of modern capitalism: the affirmation of particular architectural 'values' does not mean an endorsement of the existing political structure.

Indeed, it seems equally clear that the reintroduction of traditional stylistic elements and structures into contemporary architecture does not in itself 'mean' anything at all. It does not necessarily imply either an affirmation of genuine architectural values or a criticism of modern cultural tendencies. What if the big corporations, increasingly the patrons of large architectural projects, go along with this change of architectural image? What if they see it merely as a change of fashion that can be easily accommodated within state-of-the-art technology and budgetary constraints? This, of course, is precisely what has happened.

Architects who have been at the forefront of skyscraper development during the last 30 years have suddenly discovered that no economic (that is, functional) argument exists for a Minimalist architecture deriving its expressive power from abstract geometry or a sleek curtain wall. Within reasonable limits, it is economically feasible to complicate the profile of a tall building in a number of different ways, including some that vaguely recall classical compositions.

To understand the contradiction between these two different examples of postmodern practice, we must return to the notion of type. A typology of forms that seeks to make available the more invariant elements of the historical tradition cannot ignore the problem of the programme, however much it rejects function as the sole determinant of architecture. The use of historical forms implies some analogy—an analogy perhaps at the most general level—between the traditional uses associated with these forms and their present adaptation. Indeed, if, as the neo-rationalists claim, it is only through the manifestation of its autonomous codes that architecture can relate to social practice, this necessarily suggests, at some level, a homology between these codes and social practices.

If we look at the problem in this way we can see two poles limiting the use of historical motifs: at one pole, we find buildings whose purpose still bears some relation to a historically continuous *res publica,* or that are sited in dense, historically and artistically resonant urban contexts; at the other pole, we find new types without historical equivalence. The kind of postmodern practice associated with neo-rationalism often, though not invariably, fits into the first category. By contrast, the clearest examples of the second category are found in the forms of North America's predominant new building type, the corporate office building, whether low-spreading complexes in the countryside or towers in the city. Both programmatically and morphologically, this building type differs so greatly from any traditional type that when historical forms are applied to it, they operate in a kind of semantic void. These figures become merely the signs of 'culture'; a previous signifier and signified have been collapsed and served up again as a new sign. The substance of the type remains stubbornly modern, while the building's clothing serves to give it a false appearance of architectural complexity and cultural depth. Such an interpretation is naturally very useful to a corporation eager to convince the public that it plays a responsible role in the realm of culture. Of course architecture has always been used in this way to 'persuade', and whether such a rhetorical mode is acceptable or not is simply a question of one's position in a political spectrum. The problem that we encounter in the typical postmodern American office building is the lack of connection between the purpose of the building and the historical associations of its artistic form.

This situation seems to have been brought about by a cultural condition that is characteristically modern. During the last 250 years it has become increasingly possible to detach the aesthetic reception of works from the conditions of their creation. In his essay "The Modern System of the Arts", Paul Kristeller drew attention to the rise of amateur connoisseurship in the eighteenth century and the permanent shift this affected toward a receptionist theory of art.[7] The touchstone of artistic value was, he argued, no longer the artist or craftsman, but the spectator. This suggests a historically unique development since the eighteenth century; the "space of possibilities" of the artist and that of the spectator no longer coincide. The artist continues to be constrained by the technical and practical possibilities of his art, while the connoisseur is relatively free to adjust his threshold of perception to the art of different periods and different cultures.

This split between the artist and the spectator is an aspect of eclecticism seldom noticed. Eclecticism, which has usually been seen as something that exists equally for the artist and his audience, seems to be closely bound up with the increasing importance of connoisseurship. To take a counter example, a period such as the sixteenth century reveals a general convergence between the artistic preoccupations of the artist and those of the public. When it becomes possible for cultivated people to enjoy the works of a historically remote culture, the forms of these works are immediately absorbed into artistic practice. For instance, the discovery of gesso decoration in the Domus Aurea in Rome inspired Raphael and others to revive both the techniques and the forms of this genre.

The distance between the space of possibilities of the spectator and of the artist has continued to grow. Some contemporary designers assume that the artist has the same access to the past as the connoisseur. But there seems no reason why a 200 year trend in the opposite direction should suddenly be reversed. When artists go to museums, concert halls, or old cities, it is more in their capacity as connoisseurs than with the aim of learning how to operate a living tradition.

I began this paper with a claim for the importance of Structuralism in the critique of modernist architecture. I would like to end it by pointing to the inadequacy of Structuralism when the question is one of acting in a particular historical situation. Structuralism provides us with the field of possibilities that exists at any one moment; in doing so, it reintroduces the element of choice that was excluded by functionalism and historicism. But it remains silent about the motives for the choices that artists must continuously make—choices that, collectively, may determine the change from one set of paradigms to another.

No theory of architecture can ignore this problem. On the one hand, we must accept that there is no direct translation between function and form. Their relation is always mediated by custom and history. The architectural imagination should be free to choose from the entire cause of architectural forms without being constrained by *a priori* theories about the dictates of the spirit of the age. On the other hand, we should not think that this choice is unlimited. Architecture derives its meaning from the circumstances of its creation; and this implies that what is external to architecture—what can broadly be called its set of functions—is of vital importance. It is this that provides what Pierre Bourdieu has called the "motor". Structure and function are false opposites; they must be reconciled.

1   Huyssen, Andreas, "Mapping the Postmodern", *New German Critique*, no. 33, 1984, pp. 5–52.
2   Benjamin, Walter, "The Work of Art in the Age of Mechanical Reproduction", in *Illuminations,* trans. Harry Zohn, New York: Schocken Books, 1969, pp. 239–240.
3   Levi-Srauss, Claude, *Le Cru et le cuit*, Paris, 1964; English ed., *The Raw and the Cooked: Introduction to a Science of Mythology I,* trans. John and Doreen Weightman, New York: Harper & Row, 1969.
4   See Colquhoun, Alan, "Historicism and the Limits of Semiology", in this volume.
5   This typology originated with Ferdinand Tönnies, whose book *Gemeinschaft und Gesellschaft* of 1887 has had a lasting influence on sociological thought. *Gemeinschaft* and *Gesellschaft* are ideal types of association at the polar extremes of a continuum. In *Gemeinschaft*-like associations, relationships are spontaneous and affective and are ends in themselves. In *Gesellschaft*-like associations, on the contrary, relationships are the product of reason and calculation and are means to ends. The connection of this opposition, to that between historicism, with its concept of an organic society, and Enlightenment rationalism, with its belief in natural law, is obvious. The two types are not thought of as mutually exclusive and both are held to exist in varying proportions in all societies.
6   This point of view can be seen most clearly in the early phase of romanticism, for example, in AWN Pugin. The late nineteenth century German sociologists such as Tönnies and Georg Simmel were less prescriptive and more 'scientific' in their approach. Thus in his discussion of the modern city in his essay "*Die Grosstadte und das Geistesleben*" ("The Metropolis and Mental Life") of 1903, Simmel does not openly condemn the characteristic "abstract" and "nervous" quality of modern city life, despite his broad adherence to the school of *Lebensphilosophie*, trans. in Kurt H Wolff, ed., *The Sociology of Georg Simmel*, Glencoe, IL: Free Press of Glencoe, 1950.
7   Kristeller, Paul Oskar, "The Modern System of the Arts", in *The Renaissance and the Arts: Collected Works,* rev. ed., Princeton: Princeton University Press, 1980.

PART III 1989–2004

Reyner Banham: A Reading for the 1980s

First published in *Domus*, 1988.

Architectural historian and proselytiser of the avant-garde—"historian of the future" as he liked to call himself: do these professional roles not mark Reyner Banham as a successor to the two great historians of the early twentieth century, Sigfried Giedion and Nikolaus Pevsner? Certainly his attitudes and achievements were in many ways comparable to theirs (he wrote his PhD dissertation—later to be published under the title of *Theory and Design in the First Machine Age*—under Pevsner's supervision). As a second generation historian of the Modern Movement he set out, not to refute the canonic histories, but to undertake the more dispassionate investigation that greater distance in time made possible. Like Giedion and Pevsner, he believed that the revolution in architecture of the first two decades of the twentieth century had set the course for the architecture of the future.

But, unlike these historians, he was writing at a time when the precepts of the Modern Movement had been generally accepted by the architectural profession. That which had been a work of persuasion in the inter-war years had now become an actual programme of reconstruction. The tenor of any new history of the Movement was therefore bound to be different from that of earlier histories.

Heirs to a long tradition of idealist historiography stretching from Humboldt to Riegl, both Giedion and Pevsner had set out to provide the Modern Movement with a genealogy and to show its historical necessity. Though they both established various antecedents for the Movement, each had his preferred source. For Pevsner it was William Morris and the moral teachings of the Arts and Crafts Movement; for Giedion it was French Structural Rationalism. In *Theory and Design* Banham accepted both these hypotheses as to the origins of the Modern Movement. But he added a third: the academic tradition of the *Ecole des Beaux-Arts*. His list of "predisposing causes" thus, curiously, resembled a new version of the Vitruvian trilogy, with the academic traditions representing *Venustas*, long outlawed by nineteenth century 'progressive' theory.

Banham's demonstration of the extent to which modernist practice was influenced by academic aesthetic theory was impeccable, and it struck a mortal blow at Giedion's historical method, according to which the academic tradition did not qualify as one of the "constituent facts" of history. Banham's introduction of this tradition into a discourse on the Modern Movement was no doubt influenced by the attempt, then current in England, to reconcile modern architecture and the classical tradition, but he was far from accepting the views of critics like Colin Rowe, whose essay "The Mathematics of the Ideal Villa" of 1947 had postulated a link between Le Corbusier and Palladio. Instead, Banham adopted a highly nuanced position. Ostensibly, he used the evidence of academic influence to criticise the Modern Movement for failing to fulfil the hopes of the pre-war avant-garde, and for refusing to rise to the challenge of a continually changing technology. (Behind this critique lay the attack of a British Empiricist against continental Rationalism and Essentialism). But beyond this interpretation lay the implicit suggestion that the new in art must always be "contaminated" with the old (an equally empiricist perception). The rhetoric of *Theory and Design* was that of a scholarly investigation, and its double subversive message was partially concealed under a cloak of art historical respectability. But the stress put on Italian Futurism and (to a lesser extent) on Expressionism—thus breaking with Pevsner's definition of the "mainstream"—as well as the cruel confrontation of architecture with technology in the last chapter, betrayed the presence of a subtext trying to break the bonds of art historical conventionality and move into a radical critique of High Modernism. What was the basis of this critique? It can be best understood by reading the numerous articles that Banham wrote for *The Architectural Review*, *Industrial Design* and other less specialised journals such as *The New Statesman* and *New Society* in the 1950s and 60s. Many of these are more concerned with industrial design, film and the mass media than with architecture and they reflect the fact that Banham was a founder member of the Independent Group, and one of the early supporters of the English Pop Art movement. This movement, which was as much a revolt against the rigidities of English class society as it was an attack on the elitist values of High Modernism, looked to American products and advertising and the mass media for its artistic models. Banham's articles of the late 1950s reflect these enthusiasms. Many of them deliberately deal with ephemeral and 'low' subject matter (American cars, Sci-Fi movies, etc.) and attack the idea of the permanence of the work of art, encouraging forms of art that have an immediate power of communication and are quickly consumed and discarded. The products of the American "culture industry" are half ironically, half seriously extolled, while doubts about the compatibility of such products of capitalism and Banham's own socialist beliefs are knowingly acknowledged. In America, the Pop Art movement became the spearhead of an attack (in all the arts) on the kind of High Modernist orthodoxy represented, in painting, by Abstract Expressionism and the theories of Clement Greenberg. These movements, represented by artists such as Robert Rauschenberg, Jasper Johns and John Cage, found their spiritual ancestry in Marcel Duchamp and the Dadaists. Banham shared their views, and it is here that one can see the connection between many of the ideas put forward in *Theory and Design* and his more general views on modern culture. In an article which appeared in *The Architectural Review* he specifically connected popular art with technology, referring to a "pop architecture" that was a "branch of commerce".[1]

In spite of its affirmation of capitalist commercialism the Pop Art movement has, with some justification, been interpreted as an attempt to recover the iconoclastic and socially critical phase of the twentieth century avant-garde represented by Expressionism, Futurism, Dada and early Constructivism.[2] Like the majority of these movements it put in question the institution of art in modern society, and, in rejecting the High Modernist platform of Clement Greenberg, it was also rejecting the phase of modernism that had begun around 1923, which, under the labels of the *rappel a l'ordre* and the *Neue Sachlichkeit*, returned to more stable systems of order and representation. In architecture it was this constructive and disciplined movement that became synonymous with modernism as such, whether in the conservative, classicising forms of Le Corbusier and Mies van der Rohe, or in the materialist "functional" forms of Hannes Meyer and ABC. (In music this phase was represented, *mutatis mutandis*, by Schönberg).

It is against this background that one should see Banham's rejection of that 'mainstream' modernism that became the symbol or reconstruction after the Second World War and his search for *une architecture autre*.[3] In other words, the call for a technologically grounded architecture in *Theory and Design* cannot be separated from a general artistic and cultural critique with its roots in the avant-gardes of the years immediately preceding and during the First World War.

It was to record the signs of a true avant-garde architecture that Banham wrote his two later 'histories'—*The New Brutalism* and *Megastructures*. In each case he used his considerable historiographic and narrative skills to describe and promote contemporary movements, just as earlier he had written in support of the Pop Art movement.

These books may perhaps be seen as what Manfredo Tafuri has called "operative criticism"—that is to say, they are engaged in the construction of ideology rather than in its unmasking. As in *Theory and Design*, his criticism in these books oscillated between a discussion of these movements in terms which are well within the bounds of conventional professional discourse, and a much more radical tone; it is interesting to recall the harsh terms in which he rejected the 'compromises' of Peter and Alison Smithson.

In a short article it is only possible to give the briefest account of Banham's other important books. In *The Architecture of the Well Tempered Environment* he set out to give a brief history of the application to architecture of mechanical environmental controls. This book, which is unique in its attempt to break down the barriers between the disciplines of mechanical engineering and architecture, and which contains an extremely cogent criticism of Louis Kahn's Richards Laboratory in the University of Pennsylvania, ends on an even more millennialist note than *Theory and Design*, suggesting that, since the ultimate purpose of architecture is merely to provide a good physical environment, an architecture of the future may entirely dispense with the visible means of structural support that have been the theme of architectural aesthetics through the ages. It should be noted however that nine tenths of the book consisted of an historical narrative which depends on the existence of this traditional architecture and the way in which it is modified by technological change. Banham's way of looking at architecture in terms of the environment finds an even broader expression in his 'travel' books, *Los Angeles: The Architecture of Four Ecologies* and *Scenes in America Deserta*, the latter being his sole excursion into a purely literary genre. His last book, *A Concrete Atlantis*, reverts to his early art historical manner. The product of his years at Buffalo, it is a study of the early twentieth century American factories and grain silos which, through the illustrations in the *Deutsche Werkbund Jahrbücher*, and *L'Esprit Nouveau*, had such a strong influence on the European Modern Movement. The book is a kind of *codicil* to *Theory and Design*, especially where Banham shows that these American factories, which the Europeans had seen as the work of "noble savages", were in fact designed by sophisticated architects working in the Beaux-Arts tradition. As Janet Abrams points out however, this study remains purely formalistic and is not concerned with the social and ideological issues of which the short-lived 'daylight factory' of North America was the direct expression.[4]

In spite of the varieties and scope of Banham's writings, we must still return to *Theory and Design* and some of his earlier journalistic writings if we are to understand his ideas on design. Very schematically these can be reduced to two themes: the effect of the mass media on design, and the effect of technology on architecture. Both reflect his dominant concern with the impact of the machine on modern culture. There can be no doubt that, since the publication of *Theory and Design*, this impact has grown, as Banham predicted. It remains to consider whether it has had the kind of artistic and cultural consequences that he anticipated.

Like all historians who are concerned with projecting the future, Banham had to arbitrate between two equally important aspects of history: that which manifests itself as material cause, without which the future cannot exist, and that which manifests itself as individual freedom, without which it can have no purpose. What was the guarantee that the growth of the mass media would develop in the way Banham and the Pop Art movement hoped? In other words, did their idea coincide with "the forces of history", or were they, rather, the reaction to these "forces" of a group of artists who wanted to create works of art (in the traditional sense) out of a certain raw material, and whose work would therefore only affect a limited subculture? Banham's own historiography had done much to discredit the kind of crude determinism that underlay the theory and history of the Modern Movement, by showing the necessary over-determination of all artistic movements. Nonetheless, and contrary to the empirical precepts which he followed as an art historian, he continued to believe in a future which would be the expression of a general *Kunstwollen* in which the individual artist would be fully integrated in society, on the model of apparently 'organic' examples of Medieval history. In his faith in technology and the mass media his position echoes to some extent that of Walter Benjamin in his famous essay "The Work of Art in the Age of Mechanical Reproduction". It was a faith that dissimulated the fact that it was based on a moral preconception of how the mass media could be managed by an intellectual elite. Technology and the mass media were reified as quasi-natural phenomena with certain cultural consequences—consequences that were in fact assumed in the premise. But such an apocalyptic view was hardly compatible with Banham's enthusiasm for certain expressions of popular taste, which was based on their supplementary value and their redundancy—on the pure pleasure that they provided, and on the further pleasure, mixed with irony, resulting from their assimilation to the purpose of high art. This suggests not the application of technology and the mass media to society as it 'ought' to be (the moral dimension that Banham so often invokes) but rather the free play of semiosis within society as it is. Indeed, as if to confirm this, Banham often gives priority to the pleasures of style as against high flown moral intention. "It could still turn out", he writes in an article of 1966 on the subject of the *Archigram* magazine, "that the round cornered zoom styling of the movement's page layouts will have quite as much to do with the future architecture of democracy as any AA symposium on Decision Making".[5] Banham opened the eyes of many people to the fact that aesthetic forms were also semiological systems deeply embedded in social practices. Yet he never took the further step (taken, for example, by Roland Barthes in his *Mythologies*) of subjecting these forms to an ideology critique.

This postulation of an architecture of pleasure, freed from all puritanical restraint, seems to foreshadow the Robert Venturi of *Las Vegas* for whom the strip was "almost all right". It suggests that for Banham the value of technology lay in its communicative role, its power to multiply the occasions for a kind of distracted enjoyment on the part of a wide public. It also implies that a critique of High Modernism was not based so much on its dependence on a conservative academic tradition as on the 'purity' of its intentions, its high moral tone, and its presumption in telling the masses what is good for them. If we look at Banham's attitude to technology and the mass media in this way, we cannot avoid seeing his writings as among the harbingers of the postmodernism of the 1970s and 80s. For, once High Modernism's tone of aesthetic and moral purity is relaxed, how is it possible, logically, to refuse the consolations of social and artistic nostalgia, and of kitsch? In contrast to this populist and hedonistic view of "architecture in the age of mass media" Banham's writings recurrently reveal two other messages. The first is an extension of the chiliastic tradition of modernism, looking forward to *une architecture autre* that will be the totally transparent sign of a perfected and 'natural' society—in short, an invisible architecture. It is within the terms of this vision that he seems to couch his introduction to the work of Norman Foster. Noting the demise of modern architecture and its fragmentation into a multiplicity of tendencies, he finds consolation in the fact that the High-Tech style is one of these tendencies. What is no longer clear is whether this style is being presented as a step towards *une architecture autre*, or whether it is not rather the descendant of High Modernism with its claims to artistic inevitability and hegemony. In either case it is hardly compatible with the second idea that recurs in writings, according to which architecture is a system that draws its possibility of meaning not only from an extrinsic social context, but also from the work that it performs upon its own tradition. This idea is seldom stated explicitly, but is none the less present implicitly.

It is this idea, as well as that of an architecture of pleasure, that seems close to the 'postmodern condition'—a condition in which belief in a totalising and future oriented architecture has given way to an architecture that is multiple, improvisatory, circumstantial and auto-referential.

Far from tending towards a global and unitary solution, contemporary architecture is fractured with numerous approaches each of which claims to speak for architecture itself. Despite his belief in the irresistible force of technology, Banham himself, both as historian and as critic of culture, did much to open the way to this 'pluralism'—to an acceptance of an unrestrained world of forms and the denial of a totalising architecture. We are still experiencing the effect of the 'Pandora's Box' that Banham and others opened in their original attack on High Modernism.

1   Banham, Reyner, "Towards a pop architecture", *The Architectural Review,* July 1962 and in "Reyner Banham", *Design by Choice*, Penny Sparke ed., London: Academy Editions, 1981, p. 61.
2   See, for example, Huyssens, Andreas, "Mapping the Postmodern", *New German Critique*, no. 33, 1984, pp. 5–57 and in Huyssens, A, *After the Great Divide*, Bloomington, IN: Indiana University Press, 1986.
3   For Banham's definition of this term, see *The New Brutalism.*
4   Abrams, Janet, *Constructing the Corporate Image: a case study of the headquarters of the National Cash Registrar Company, Dayton, Ohio*, PhD dissertation in progress, 1988, Princeton University.
5   Banham, Reyner, "Zoom wave hits Architecture", *New Society* and in "Reyner Banham", *Design by Choice.*

The Le Corbusier Centenary

First published in *Journal of the Society of Architectural Historians*, 1990.

Anniversaries have become a standard part of modern artistic discourse. They are the occasion for exhibitions, for increasingly elaborate catalogues raisonnés and for the publication of monographs and biographies. The centenary of the birth of Le Corbusier was no exception. Exhibitions of his work, or of special aspects of it, took place in Paris, London, New York, Zurich, Strasbourg, Berlin, Geneva, and Madrid, to mention only the most important venues. These were mostly accompanied by catalogues containing scholarly articles. In addition, most of the major architectural journals in Europe ran special Le Corbusier issues, and a number of books on the architect (and two by him) were published or appeared for the first time in translation. The present review covers a selection of such books published in French or English during 1987.

Over the last 60 years the work of Le Corbusier has been the subject of two very different types of commentary. These might be called, respectively, myth-reinforcing or myth-destroying.

Although Le Corbusier became famous with the publication of *Vers une architecture* in 1923, the true inauguration of his myth dates from the publication in 1929 of the first volume of the *Oeuvre complète*. This and subsequent volumes canonised Le Corbusier as the most brilliant protagonist and publicist of the epic of the Modern Movement. Though published by Willi Boesinger, the *Oeuvre complète* was carefully supervised by Le Corbusier himself and owed its style in large measure to the techniques of representation developed by Ozenfant and Le Corbusier in their journal *L'Esprit Nouveau*, in which abruptly juxtaposed image and text contributed to an immediate visual effect. Everything in the *Oeuvre complète* was sensuous and concrete: no conscious mental effort was needed to translate idea into image. The rhetorical skill that made this possible was one of the chief qualities that distinguished Le Corbusier from other modern architects of his generation—both in his buildings and in his publications—and it was one of the most important factors contributing to Le Corbusier's place in the mythology of the Modern Movement. Whether the commentators on his work were sympathetic or antagonistic, they tended to measure themselves against the myth that he himself had created in the *Oeuvre complète*.

Around the time of his death in 1965 another sort of commentary started to develop—one that did not seek to diminish Le Corbusier as a historical figure, but which nonetheless tried to place him in an overall cultural context and to look at his work and ideas more dispassionately, seeing him as a figure who not only made history but was also made by it. If the critical biography by Stanislaus von Moos, *Le Corbusier: Elemente einer Synthese*, published in 1968, marked the first step of this more objective approach, its subsequent development was largely due to the opening of the Le Corbusier archives in Paris and La Chaux-de-Fonds after the architect's death, sources not available to von Moos when he was researching his book. One of the virtues of the centenary was that it marked a symbolic pause in the flow of scholarly publications on Le Corbusier that the opening of the archives had unloosed, enabling one to measure the extent to which Le Corbusier studies had evolved from the mythologies and demonologies of the 1950s.

Among the books reviewed here, two are recent translations of books by Le Corbusier: *Le voyage d'Orient* and *L'art décoratif d'aujourd'hui*. There is also one full-dress critical biography: William Curtis' *Le Corbusier: Ideas and Forms*. The remainder consist either of monographs on particular aspects of the work or collections of essays. Most of the latter occur in catalogues covering particular themes, but two of them cover Le Corbusier's entire oeuvre. The heterogeneity of this material, and the fact that several of the essays occur in more than one publication, has presented a methodological problem. This review attempts to solve this by grouping books and individual essays together under a certain number of thematic headings, rather than by dealing with each book separately.

Some preliminary remarks seem to be necessary on the two anthologies—*Le Corbusier: The Garland Essays* and *Le Corbusier, 1887–1965: une encyclopédie*. *The Garland Essays*, edited by H Allen Brooks, consist of essays originally included in the 32 volume *Le Corbusier Archive*, published by Garland Press between 1982 and 1985. This consists of photo reproductions of some 32,000 architectural drawings from Le Corbusier's office, which are now in the Fondation Le Corbusier in Paris. The essays are only loosely connected to the material in the *Le Corbusier Archive*, and since the circulation of the Archive is necessarily limited because of its bulk and cost, their publication in a separate book was both a logical and a welcome step. The essays range widely between the scholarly study, the broad survey, and the biographical reminiscence. Some of the essays are written from a critical standpoint, others attempt to recreate *con amore* the personality of Le Corbusier or to describe his methods of work. One of the most interesting essays belonging to the last category is that by Jannis Xenakis on the design process of the monastery of La Tourette.

Le Corbusier, 1887–1965: une encyclopédie, edited by Jacques Lucan, was the catalogue of the centenary exhibition at the Centre Pompidou in Paris, and it followed in the now well-established tradition of such catalogues in presenting the state of the art in Le Corbusier scholarship. The encyclopedic format was an ingenious way of covering a wide variety of material, though, unlike the case of a genuine encyclopedia, the reader still has to have recourse to a separate index. One or two of the entries are eccentric, but on the whole the book provides a rich matrix within which to place the historical figure of Le Corbusier. A disappointing number of entries are reprinted from earlier publications. To mention only a few, those by Manfredo Tafuri ("*Ville et mémoire*"), Timothy Benton ("*Loi Loncheur*") and Gilles Ragot ("*Exposition Internationale de Paris 1937*") have all appeared elsewhere. Mary McLeod has re-worked an article on Algiers that appeared in *Oppositions 18*, while new material from her as yet unpublished dissertation, such as that on *La Ferme Radieuse*, which does not receive an entry, has been overlooked ("Urbanism and Utopia: Le Corbusier from Regional Syndicalism to Vichy", Princeton, 1985).

Despite these shortcomings, the *Encyclopédie* is a major achievement.

Ideas and Forms

In *Le Corbusier: Ideas and Forms* William Curtis has produced a fluent and readable critical biography. As he already demonstrated in his book *Modern Architecture since 1900*, Curtis has a formidable skill in giving shape to complex and heterogeneous material. A great deal of new matter relating to Le Corbusier's life and work is included, and the smooth narrative structure of the book seems to echo the purposeful and heroic life of its subject. The book is divided into three parts. In the first Curtis deals with Le Corbusier's formation and early work. In the second he covers the crucial period between the wars when the architect found his life's purpose and designed his canonic buildings. In the final section Curtis covers the period after the Second World War when Le Corbusier's concept of the "machine age" was modified by cultural nostalgia and by a kind of cosmic symbolism.

As in his earlier book, Curtis dispenses with footnotes and replaces them with a bibliography and notes related to page numbers, a procedure that makes it virtually impossible to check his sources. In a book that necessarily depends almost entirely on secondary sources this is a serious disadvantage.

In his preface Curtis stresses the need for a new synthesis in Le Corbusier studies: "Many fine fragments of scholarship are lying about, waiting to be integrated into a new general structure." But he goes on, "Many different books could be written around someone as complex and wide-ranging as Le Corbusier. This one... is concerned above all with the ways in which the architect compressed many levels of meaning into his individual buildings, treating them as symbolic emblems... of a larger world-view" (page 7). Indeed, much of the book is taken up with analysis of the forms of Le Corbusier's buildings in terms of their iconography and symbolism. In his attributions of iconographic sources Curtis is not always sound. For example, the "classical ruin" shown in a sketch that Le Corbusier sent to Madame Meyer is not a "Mediterranean reverie" or "a Roman memory of the trip of 1911", but simply a view of Bélanger's Folie Saint-James as it would have appeared from the new house (page 76). Nevertheless, it is probably at this symbolic level that the book is most suggestive. Curtis is skeptical about many of the claims that Le Corbusier made for his own work. But he gives the impression that once the absurd millennialist pretensions have been disposed of in the name of good old English common sense, we are left with the pure gold of a timeless architecture. Curtis thus upholds one aspect of the mythology of the Modern Movement propagated by men like Giedion and Le Corbusier himself—the belief that the essence of a timeless architecture had been discovered.

Acceptance of this view, combined with simultaneous rejection of arguments based on the *Zeitgeist*, leads Curtis to separate aspects that were always present at the same time in Le Corbusier: the moral, existential side, embedded in a moment of history, and the formal-symbolic side, laying claim to transcendental value. In discussing the Unité d'habitation at Marseilles, which was posited on a relation between social and aesthetic realms, Curtis retreats into purely formal treatment.

Curtis' treatment of Chandigarh is equally one-sided. Although he is critical of the commercial centre ("a bleak no-man's land flanked by deadpan rows of *pilotis* and brutally proportioned balconies") and of the attempt to apply the precepts of the Athens Charter to Indian society, he is chiefly concerned with the Capitol complex, its symbolic form and its historical resonances. "The Chandigarh monuments idealise cherished notions of law and government with deep roots: they span the centuries by fusing modern and ancient myths in symbolic forms of prodigious authenticity. Although recent in fabrication they possess a timelessness that will insure them a major place in the stock of cultural memories." There is no doubt an element of truth behind these orotund phrases, but it is surely the historian's task to reveal the contradictions between myth and reality when he finds them, rather than provide us with happy endings.

Curtis' book often gives the impression that the author has miraculous access to Le Corbusier's mind. "By the time of *Vers une architecture*...", he tells us, "the architect was ready to spell out the forms he felt appropriate to the machine age." And again, "Beyond individual buildings it was Le Corbusier's intention to create the generic elements of an authentic modern architecture...." The way Curtis continually slides from this kind of teleology to a more critical mode makes it often difficult to judge his true critical position. On the whole, however, Curtis' criticisms of Le Corbusier are delivered *sotto voce*, so as not to disturb his subject's heroic stature, and at the end of the book it is the myth of a modern architecture purged of its modernity that wins the day. "As he slips further into history, his modernity matters less and less: it is the timeless levels in his art which have most to give to the future."

Formation and Early Work

At the end of *L'art décoratif d'aujourd'hui*, and excluded from the synoptic argument at the beginning of the book, there is a postscript entitled "Confession".

This, together with a brief autobiographical excursus in Volume I of the *Oeuvre complète*, was the only time (until he was quite old) that Le Corbusier referred to his pre-1914 career, almost all traces of which he systematically excluded from the *Oeuvre complète*. This portrait of the artist as a young man is presented as having happened "once upon a time", outside the historical frame defining the persona that is Le Corbusier, created in 1920. It describes the stumblings of a perceptive and passionate autodidact; but it is also the story of a double renunciation—that of European culture up until the First World War, and that of his own youth.

The reconstruction and interpretation of this lost period of Le Corbusier's earlier incarnation is one of the major achievements of post-archival Corbusian scholarship and it owes a great deal to the work of H Allen Brooks. In "Le Corbusier's formative years at La Chaux-de-Fonds" in *Le Corbusier: The Garland Essays* Brooks outlines Jeanneret's life until he left for Paris definitively in 1917 at the age of 30, tracing his development from his school training in the Symbolist tradition of the Decorative Arts Movement to his visits to Paris and Germany and his change of allegiance to the rationalism of Auguste Perret and the neo-classicism of Peter Behrens.

The houses designed by Jeanneret in and around La Chaux-de-Fonds during this period fall into three distinct categories: the National Romantic houses of 1905–1907, designed in collaboration with René Chapallaz; the two Behrens-like neo-classical houses of 1912; and the Villa Schwob of 1916, a transitional work of great originality which nonetheless shows the influence of both Perret and Behrens. These houses are the subject of the Academy Edition monograph, *Le Corbusier: Early Works of Charles-Edouard Jeanneret-Gris*. The main contributor to this monograph is Geoffrey Baker, who has provided a thorough documentation of each house (plus the Scala cinema of 1916) including formal analyses, descriptive drawings (site plans, floor plans, sections, elevations and axonometrics) and exterior and interior colour photographs of very high quality. All this information is new and provides an invaluable resource. Baker has paid much attention to the siting of the houses, showing in telling bird's-eye views how the first three houses, together with the house of Jeanneret's teacher L'Eplattenier, were grouped to form one of those cultural colonies in a rural setting so dear to the Art Nouveau Movement. When discussing the neo-classical houses, Baker notes the "acropolis-like" approach to the Jeanneret villa. But one wonders if this analogy would have occurred to the author had it not been for the passages in *L'Esprit Nouveau* which are based on Choisy's analysis of the acropolis in his *Histoire de l'architecture*—a book that Jeanneret did not read until 1913 (see Jacques Lucan, "Acropole", *Le Corbusier: une encyclopédie*, page 21). Baker also fails to do justice to the influence on Jeanneret of the German neo-classical Revival, or of Alexandre Cingria-Vaneyre's vision of a Mediterraneanised Suisse Romande.

The book suffers from organisational problems. Not only is there a good deal of repetition, each house being described two or three times, but the whole structure of the book is ambiguous, Baker's major contribution being sandwiched between an anonymous foreword and two essays by Jacques Gubler, originally published in 1981. These essays, although relegated to the back of the book and in spite of their age, provide essential background information about the town of La Chaux-de-Fonds, which had been rebuilt in the 1790s according to the principles of "a broadly *Ponts et chaussées*-style urbanism" and had become the watchmaking centre of the world, and about the clients for the houses (local magnates with progressive tastes, analogous to the entrepreneurs of Art Nouveau Barcelona). Gubler should surely have been invited to write an updated introduction which could then have been followed by Baker's essentially formal analyses.

Shortly before he built his two neo-classical houses, Jeanneret's views about modern artistic culture had been profoundly shaken. This change is reflected in the journal he wrote recording his travels in Eastern Europe, Turkey, and Greece in 1911. This has now been published in English translation by Ivan Zaknic under the title *Journey to the East*. The journal has a checkered publication history. Part of it was serialised in the La Chaux-de-Fonds newspaper *La Feuille d'avis* in 1911. After two unsuccessful attempts at publication in 1912 and 1914, Le Corbusier published excerpts in *L'almanach d'architecture moderne* in 1925 under the title "*Camet de route 1910*" [sic]. Finally it was published in full as *Le voyage d'Orient*. This is the book that Zaknic has now translated.

The tone of the journal alternates between optimism and a Spenglerian pessimism. Beneath its eager and colourful descriptions of places and people, two main themes emerge. The first is that art is the reflection of a collective culture and is the work of history. Jeanneret no longer looks for inspiration, as he had in his journey to Italy in 1907, in the decorative work of the Medieval artist/craftsman; he seeks it in the anonymous and typical forms of entire cultures. The second theme is the contrast between the 'soft' folk culture of Turkey and the 'hard' classical culture of Greece and the Acropolis. He is saddened by "the catastrophe that will inevitably ruin Stamboul: the advent of modern times" (page 160). In contrast to this 'feminine' Istanbul, "the Parthenon, a terrible machine, grinds [crushes] and dominates... a sovereign cube facing the sea" (page 212). "It is a prophetic art from which one cannot escape. As insentient as an immense and unalterable truth" (page 236). The whole of the future for Le Corbusier seems to be contained in this sentence.

Zaknic's book suffers from a comparison with Giuliano Gresleri's *Il viaggio in oriente*, which was published in 1984. Both books contain Jeanneret's text and a selection of his sketches. But while Zaknic's introduction is little more than a formality, Gresleri's provides a detailed cultural background that gives depth and meaning to Jeanneret's text. Gresleri also includes Jeanneret's letters to his parents and to his intellectual mentor, William Ritter, as well as a selection of the photographs he took on the tour. Zaknic discounts these on the grounds of Le Corbusier's later preference for sketching as a way of imprinting visual experience on the memory, but the photographs have considerable interest as an essential Part of the mixed-media documentation of the journey.

In spite of their occasional infelicities of translation Zaknic and Nicole Pertuiset have performed a useful service in producing this book. It is a great pity, however, that MIT Press did not commission a translation of Gresleri's book while they were about it.

Gresleri is also represented in *Le Corbusier: une encyclopédie* where, in his article "*Antiquité*", he traces the conversion to classicism that was to be the motivation of Jeanneret's journey to the East. He shows how this conversion was the result of exposure to "ideological" tendencies then current in Europe, chiefly through his contact with William Ritter and the books of Cingria-Vaneyre in 1910. He characterises Le Corbusier's subsequent lifelong obsession with the Parthenon as the idea of "the eternal return of architecture, in moments of crisis, towards a place where all uncertainty is abolished".

Jeanneret's 1911 tour was also preceded by a stay of several months in Germany for the purpose of researching his book *Etude sur le movement d'art decoratif en Allemagne*. This stay, in which Jeanneret's new-found classical leanings were reinforced, is the subject of another article in *Le Corbusier: une encyclopédie*: Werner Oechslin's "Influences, confluences et reniements". Oechslin does not repeat the detailed information about Jeanneret's German visit given by Gresleri in his introduction to *Il viaggio in oriente*. Rather he is concerned with vindicating the German influences on Jeanneret that were later suppressed by Le Corbusier. Whereas Gresleri emphasises the influence on Jeanneret of French writers such as Elie Faure and Pierre Gusman (particularly in connection with his attitudes to Greek and Roman architecture), Oechslin stresses the influence of idealist tendencies represented by Alois Riegl's theory of the *Kunstwollen*, which, he claims, forms the kernel of the aesthetic doctrine of *Vers une architecture*. It seems probable in fact that Jeanneret's theories developed in response to common European tendencies, which took different forms according to whether they attached themselves to French positivist or German idealist traditions, to both of which Jeanneret was exposed.

Oechslin's main point is that the German visit of 1910–1911 was crucial to the formation of ideas that were later to be crystallised in the *L'Esprit Nouveau* articles. Jeanneret was present at the Werkbund Congress in June 1910. Oechslin quotes a remark made by Karl Ernst Osthaus at this congress, which clearly adumbrates the idea of the free plan: "Another possibility created by concrete is the establishment, in buildings of several storeys, of plans of upper floors being independent of plans of lower floors… I see absolutely no reason why we should hold on to the old rigidity of construction if the advantages for habitability of a house result in the displacement of partitions."

Among the many other influences cited by Oechslin, one of the most important was Werner Hegemann's exhibition of urbanism in Berlin in 1910. It was this that was largely responsible for modifying the Sittesque views upon which Jeanneret had based his unpublished essay *La construction des villes*, and which, anomalously, continued to inform his urban designs right up to the war. Oechslin even hazards the guess that it was at this exhibition that Jeanneret first encountered Pierre Patte's plan for Paris, and that this may have impelled him to study French eighteenth century planning at the Bibliotheque Nationale in 1915. Oechslin discusses the influence that Peter Behrens exerted on the villas of 1912 and on the use of *tracés regulateurs*. He might also have mentioned the close parallels between Heinrich Tessenow's ideas about asymmetry in house planning, put forward in his book *Hausbau und Dergleichen*, and those of Le Corbusier on Pompeian houses expressed in *L'Esprit Nouveau*. However, in assessing the extent of German influence on Jeanneret, one must bear in mind that, as Gresleri has shown, Jeanneret's turn to classicism was due to his contacts with intellectual literary circles in Neuchâtel, as well as to his connection with William Ritter in Munich.

The opinions that Jeanneret expressed on German applied art in his *Etude* were by no means all favourable, and it is possible that Oechslin exaggerates the extent of his *volte face* on Germany after the war. Nonetheless, it is clear that in his anti-German articles in *L'Esprit Nouveau*, Le Corbusier deliberately suppressed his debt to the German architects of the *Deutsche Werkbund* circle with whom he had contact in 1910–1911.

L'Esprit Nouveau

The journal *L'Esprit Nouveau* consisted of 28 numbers published in Paris between October 1920 and January 1925. It was founded by the Dada poet Paul Dermée in association with Amedée Ozenfant and Le Corbusier. Dermée ceased to be an editor in December 1920. Starting life as *Revue d'esthetique internationale*, it acquired in January 1921 the more ambitious title of *Revue internationale illustrée de l'activité contemporaine* and its articles covered every aspect of culture from the visual arts to sports. Among its most important (and famous) contributions was a series of articles by Le Corbusier on architecture, urbanism, and the decorative arts, later published in book form. Two of the books, *Vers une architecture* and *Urbanisme*, were translated almost immediately into English; *L'art décoratif d'aujourd'hui* had to wait until 1987. Part of the reason for this delay may be that the term "decorative arts" has weaker connotations in English than in French, where it is related to a system of classification belonging to the Beaux-Arts. In fact, the book forms an essential part of a trilogy dealing with the applied arts from the smallest to the largest scale. As James Dunnett (who has provided a very adequate translation) points out in his brief introduction, the book is primarily concerned with what today would be called "design".

As is the case with all of Le Corbusier's writings, the book is addressed to a wide audience and the style is dogmatic, energetic, and vivid, with simple expressions serving as shorthand for often quite complex philosophical ideas. Because it is a collection of separate articles, it does not contain a systematic thread of ideas. It aims to persuade by the force of its verbal and visual imagery. Its main idea, following a long nineteenth century reformist tradition, is that the term "decorative" is an anachronism in the world of machine production. The artistic quality of objects of everyday life is not denied, but it is held to be incompatible with ornament that has been 'added' to a pre-existent object. Instead, the beauty of an object is an immanent property of its form, which is derived from either function or geometry. At the same time Le Corbusier distinguishes between the object of use and the work of art. The object of use has only one purpose: to be useful. It releases energy for more spiritual pursuits, including the contemplation of works of art.

Le Corbusier never resolves the apparent contradiction between two concepts of art put forward in this book—one based on the intentional work of 'fine art', the other on the unconscious adaptation of useful objects to function. From one point of view, it seems that he wants to reserve for the work of art the whole spiritual dimension of life; from another, humble objects seem also to be endowed with transcendent aesthetic qualities. When he comes to insert architecture into his system, we find that it occupies an ambiguous place between the useful object and the work of art. Architecture is a "spiritual expression in material form… a construct of the mind (*système de l'esprit*) giving material form to its consciousness of the age".

The theory of architecture and applied arts put forward in *The Decorative Art of Today* formed part of a cultural programme that can only be grasped by looking at *L'Esprit Nouveau* as a whole. This is the task that Stanislaus von Moos has set himself in his catalogue for the centenary exhibition on *L'Esprit Nouveau* mounted successively in Zurich, Berlin, Strasbourg, and Paris, and published in its French version under the title *L'Esprit Nouveau: Le Corbusier et industrie*.

The nucleus of the book is a selection of images from the pages of *L'Esprit Nouveau* accompanied by a catalogue raisonné. No less than 17 researchers were recruited for this task, and the result is the most comprehensive and informative account of *L'Esprit Nouveau* to date. The selection is divided into four sections: architecture and urbanism; art and art theory; music, theatre and sport; and industrial products. In this way the full range of subjects covered by the journal is presented in a coherent form and looked at in detail from a variety of perspectives. What comes out clearly is the connection between the cultural theory of *L'Esprit Nouveau* and the *Rappel a l'ordre* movement that dominated French artistic circles in the years immediately after the First World War (this was already stressed by Françoise Levaillant in her article "*Norme et forme a travers l'Esprit Nouveau*" in *Le Retour d l'ordre*, Paris, 1975). But equally striking is the extent of Ozenfant and Le Corbusier's debt to Dada and Surrealist visual techniques of estrangement, in spite of their classicising and positivistic stance and their explicit antagonism to Dada.

The book also contains 11 essays on various aspects of Le Corbusier's work during the period of *L'Esprit Nouveau*. One of the most interesting of these is an article by von Moos himself, entitled "*Dans l'antichambre du machine age*". In this he discusses Le Corbusier's reaction to industrialisation, advertising, and the media. Von Moos takes as his point of departure Walter Benjamin's 1934 essay, "The Author as Producer". Using a distinction made by Benjamin, von Moos claims that Le Corbusier was trying to change the role of the architect within the relations of production of architecture, rather than being content to reflect modernity on an aesthetic level. Both in his attempt to intervene in the production of urban housing and in his use of the media in *L'Esprit Nouveau* he was, according to von Moos, going outside the traditional role of the architect. Though Le Corbusier can hardly be said to have had the same ends in view as those promoted by Benjamin in "The Work of Art in the Age of Mechanical Reproduction", it is certainly true that Le Corbusier's use of modern techniques of mass communication was fundamental to *L'Esprit Nouveau*. Not only did he use advertising material to finance the journal, but he also used it as copy, promoting the idea of anonymous design (Roneo metal doors, for example) and thus making the advertiser an accomplice in his own architectural strategy. Von Moos points out how foreign these tactics were to the Bauhaus with its belief in the need to infuse the products of industry with spiritual value. Perhaps these two attitudes relate, respectively, to a French positivist tradition going back to Saint Simon and to German nineteenth century idealism.

In her article *"L'Esprit Nouveau: architecture et publicite"* in *Le Corbusier: une encyclopédie*, Beatriz Colomina also discusses "the blurring of the limits between publicity and content" in *L'Esprit Nouveau*, making an even stronger claim than von Moos for the importance of Le Corbusier's role as manipulator of advertising and the media. The emphasis both authors place on this aspect of Le Corbusier's work raises questions as to his attitude toward what was later to be called consumerism, for, as Mary McLeod and Joan Ockman have pointed out, Le Corbusier in another context expressed a profound antipathy for advertising ("Some Comments on Reproduction with Reference to Colomina and Hays", in Beatriz Colomina, editor, *Architectureproduction*, New York, 1988, page 227).

The Villas

Tim Benton's *The Villas of Le Corbusier, 1920–1930* consists of monographs of 14 houses (including one apartment, the Beistegui) designed or built by Le Corbusier and Pierre Jeanneret in the 1920s (originally published as *Le Corbusier: villas*, Paris, 1984). These are grouped in four chapters entitled "The World of Purism", "The Architectural Promenade", "Complex Programs", and "Classic Houses". These titles should be taken with a grain of salt, since all the projects belong to the world of Purism and most of them exhibit the architectural promenade in one form or another.

In addition to an introduction, the book has an annex containing summaries of the main facts for each house, synoptic tables of dates and craftsmen, and a catalogue of drawings as numbered by the Fondation. The book is not a complete study of the houses of the period, since it excludes the Citrohen-type houses, the Villa Baiseaux in Tunis, and the house that Le Corbusier built for his parents on Lac Léman. A few errors have crept into this English edition of the book, including "symbolic" as a translation of the French "Symbiose".

The text deals exhaustively with the history of each project, providing information on sites, costs, contractual arrangements, relations between client and architect, and design development. Ever since Garland published the drawings in the Fondation Le Corbusier, it has been apparent that most of the projects that came out of Le Corbusier and Jeanneret's office were the result of a long and agonising process of trial and error, in which many alternatives were tried out. To those nurtured on the *Oeuvre complète* this was rather shocking, as if a number of immaculate conceptions had turned out to be the result of miscegenation. What Benton has been able to do is to relate these transformations (in the case of the villas) to the contingent circumstances and to suggest a chronological sequence.

As Benton makes clear, the process of development changed with different projects. Sometimes, as in the Villa Stein-de Monzie, the early ideas are full of picturesque incidents which are gradually tamed and subordinated to the grid and the cube. At the same time, an opposite process takes place in which contaminations occur between parts that had previously been schematically discrete. Benton draws attention to the fact that Le Corbusier's solutions often contain traces of earlier stages of development. For example, in the Villa Stein-de Monzie the tripartite plan shows vestiges of the original programme according to which the house was to be divided into two apartments sharing certain common facilities. The effect of the transformations, in which cost considerations often work in alliance with classicising tendencies, is an increase in spatial complexity and dramatic tension within an apparently simpler overall form.

The development of the Villa Savoye is quite different. There are a few preliminary sketches, which Benton illustrates in a separate essay ("The Villa Savoye and the Architect's Practice", in *Le Corbusier: The Garland Essays*). One of these shows a car ramp penetrating the house at second floor level. Another shows a flat, rather Miesian cube seen diagonally from below in the manner of a *Wagnerschule* drawing (comparison with drawing number 31-044 indicates that this is a drawing of the Villa Savoye and not merely an idea that was later taken up for the villa, as Benton seems to suggest). But the first extant set of drawings for the Villa Savoye shows the final idea fully worked out. After this, a series of weird alternatives followed in an attempt to reduce costs, only to end in a return to a shrunken version of the original design.

Benton's exposition both here and elsewhere in the book is often hard to follow. To grasp all the steps in the process of transformation it is necessary to refer continually to the Garland set or the *Oeuvre complète* because of the lack of adequate illustrations in the present book. In the case of the Villa Savoye, these difficulties are compounded by the fact that the plans specially drawn to illustrate the main stages of development are printed at different scales (presumably in the interest of a neat page design); and in some cases the plans are wrongly oriented relative to each other. On the evidence presented, it is difficult to understand why the famous "rogue" solution of 26 November 1928, which incidentally bears a certain resemblance to an early scheme for the Villa Stein, should have been cheaper than the original scheme. In fact its overall dimensions were considerably less, as can be seen in Max Risselada, *Raumplan versus Plan Libre*.

Among the various questions taken up by Benton in his introduction is the role played by Le Corbusier in the office in the 1920s. Benton's researches have led him to the conclusion that it was often that of a "disturber of order", and that his interventions often took the form of the addition of "symbolic and resonant" forms to "dry" solutions. This is an intriguing idea, if only because it ties in with Le Corbusier's early Ruskinian training as designer/decorator, but it must be balanced by the fact that Le Corbusier had an opposite tendency to schematicism. We should probably also see this 'disturbing' role as being due to a desire to infuse the buildings with the signs of vital and spontaneous energy. This Dionysian side is one of the revelations of the drawings in the Fondation, which show how awkward some of his first ideas were in their search for new solutions with functional-organic analogies.

Benton also discusses the problem of the relation between mass housing and the one-off villa. For the author there is a continuous passage from one to the other since the villas grew out of typologies developed for houses in series and in turn acted as test beds for larger urbanistic ideas. Other critics (including Richard Ingersoll in his review of this book in *Design Book Review* 14, 1988, pages 19–33) take a sociological position similar to that of Le Corbusier's *Neue Sachlichkeit* critics of the period, accusing him of bad sociology in using, for instance, the artist's studio as a model for mass housing. Both points of view are valid, but they should be seen against a broader background of cultural criticism. Le Corbusier saw mass production less as a means to solving a social need than as the way the modern age would achieve a wholly new collective culture—one that nonetheless would be analogous to the great, unified cultures of the past.

Benton's book is a major scholarly achievement. Discussion of Le Corbusier's houses has usually been at a formal level, but this type of analysis is criticised by Monique Eleb-Vidal in her essay entitled "*Hôtel particulier*" in *Le Corbusier: une encyclopédie*. Eleb-Vidal shows that many of Le Corbusier's planning methods were based on a particularly French tradition of *convenance* going back to the early seventeenth century and culminating with Jacques-François Blondel in the eighteenth century. Starting from Le Corbusier's discussion of the bedroom and its dependencies in his book *Précisions*, Eleb-Vidal shows that he used the freedom gained by the structural frame to reformulate a traditional concern for complex differentiation of functions within the *appartement* or *cellule* of the bedroom suite. In this way Eleb-Vidal has introduced into Corbusian studies a welcome concern for the relation of forms to their social functions.

Geneva

Early in 1927 Le Corbusier and Jeanneret submitted their designs for the League of Nations competition, their first project for a major public building. A few months later the Belgian lawyer Paul Otlet published his brochure on the Mundaneum, which included plans by Le Corbusier and Jeanneret. These two abortive projects are the main subjects of *Le Corbusier à Genève*, the catalogue of an exhibition held in Geneva in the centenary year.

The League of Nations building is the subject of two essays. The first, by Inès Lamunière and Patrick Daventhary, provides an acute analysis of the functional and formal organisation of the building and reconstructs the design development from drawings in the archives. The second, by Richard Guincerot, gives a detailed history of the competition, demolishing a few myths in the process. We learn that the jury premiated nine designs (one for each member of the jury). A surprising number of choices fell along national lines, Le Corbusier being chosen by the avant-garde Swiss architect Karl Moser, who was also responsible for awarding a second mention to Hannes Meyer. The final choice was made by a committee of five diplomats. Le Corbusier tried unsuccessfully to sue the winner for plagiarism—the ultimate gesture in a series of frantic moves aimed at obtaining the commission.

As Catherine Courtiau points out in her comprehensive essay, "*La Cité Internationale*", Paul Otlet's project for the Mundaneum, the centre of a proposed "world city" on the shores of Lac Léman close to the site of the League of Nations, had its origins in the spirit of internationalism that developed in the late nineteenth century and that was revived after the disaster of the First World War. Otlet had already prompted an earlier world centre in Belgium, designed on City Beautiful lines by Andersen and Hébrard in 1910. Otlet asked Le Corbusier and Jeanneret to prepare plans for the Mundaneum in 1927. Their design, in which geometry and number play a symbolic role, corresponds closely to the mixture of positivism and mysticism in Otlet's thought, with its Fourieresque utopianism and its connection with freemasonry.

The core of the project was an international museum, to be divided into three sections: historical (time), scientific or international (objects), and geographic or national (place). The Ziggurat that Le Corbusier designed for the museum is analysed by Giuliano Cresleri in his essay "*Le Mundaneum, lecture du projet*". It is also discussed by Dario Matteoni in the entry "Mundaneum" in *Le Corbusier: une encyclopédie*. Both authors draw attention to the fact that in legendary ziggurats the movement is an ascent from earth to heaven while in the International Museum the visitor descends along an ever broadening spiral to an indeterminate present. The contradictions of this "secular" symbolism were attacked by Karel Teige who, in the Czech magazine *Stavba*, accused Le Corbusier of mystification in his attempt to apply a transcendental symbolism to modern life. Two other sets of projects are discussed in *Le Corbusier à Genève*. The first is Le Corbusier's various plans for housing in Geneva, culminating in a study of the only project built, the Immeuble Clarté, from the point of view of prefabrication and dry construction. The second project is the *petite maison* that Le Corbusier built in 1924 for his parents near Vevey on Lac Léman. This is the subject of two essays, one by Adolph Stiller giving a constructional history of the building, the other by Bruno Reichlin using the house as a vehicle for a discussion of the famous controversy between August Perret and his erstwhile pupil, Le Corbusier, over the relative merits of the *fenêtre en longueur* and the classical window. (This excellent article originally appeared in *Daedalus 13*, 1984, in English and German.)

The City of Refuge

As Kenneth Frampton points out in his introduction, Brian Brace Taylor's book on *The City of Refuge* was the first study of one of Le Corbusier's major public buildings from the perspective of a social and technical critique. We have since had Jean Louis Cohen's somewhat less tendentious study of the Centrosoyus, but Taylor's monograph remains a milestone in the historiography of modern architecture and its publication in English is long overdue. Taylor sets out his aims as follows: "A critical analysis of the Cité de Refuge is instructive for a number of reasons...: first of all its socio-economic and political significance as an architectural type; then its production as a physical object..., finally, the role of Le Corbusier as architect, particularly his way of operating in concrete reality."

Influenced by Michel Foucault's books on the institutionalisation of the socially marginalised, Taylor defines the Cité de Refuge typologically as a "heterotopia"— that is, a self-contained place set apart from normal social space. The models for such a type include monasteries, socialist utopias like Fourier's Phalanstere, and established institutions such as prisons and lunatic asylums. Taylor connects the Cité de Refuge and its parent organisation, the Salvation Army, with negative rather than positive aspects of seclusion and implies through this a whole critique of modernism, especially that of Le Corbusier, with its fixation on the *objet-type* fulfilling a specialised and often insidiously authoritarian social function.

Like von Moos, Taylor aims at demystifying the legend of Le Corbusier, but he comes to the opposite conclusions. Whereas for von Moos Le Corbusier's use of the media in his writings places him in the ranks of an avant-garde that sought to subvert the traditional concept of the architect, for Taylor Le Corbusier continued to operate as the artist/architect who was ignorant of the new technologies he was advocating. Though he does not say as much, Taylor implies that Le Corbusier belonged to a tradition of mimesis, according to which architecture primarily fulfils an ideological and representational rather than a practical function. Taylor's reconstruction of the building process reveals a gap between Le Corbusier's aspirations to modernity and his ability to translate these into reality. It could be argued that such a gap between the ideal and the real is the inevitable result of a utopian view that ascribes normative value to technology and, as such, is built into the Modern Movement. Curtis, in *Le Corbusier: Ideas and Forms*, tries to solve this dilemma by emphasising the ideal dimension of architecture, assimilating technical and social aspiration to a transcendental aesthetics. Taylor takes the opposite course. To him Le Corbusier's architecture, since it claims to be scientific, must be judged by the pragmatic criteria of science. By that criteria, the Cité de Refuge obviously failed in a number of ways, and Taylor shows the widening gap that developed during the design and building process between the client's and user's perception of the building and that of the architect, and the architect's increasing megalomania and decreasing grasp of reality. Taylor's view has broader implications than the merely pragmatic, suggesting that what a building is is not just what the architect intends, but its whole history from inception and use to final decay.

Whatever truth there may be in this view, the fact remains that the Cité de Refuge has become sufficiently important as a cultural icon for a historian like Taylor to devote a monograph to it. And just as there is an undertow of social and technical criticism in Curtis' book, so there is an undertow of aesthetic praise in

Taylor's. Taylor does not explore the relation between the aesthetic qualities of the building and its technical and social failures.

Taylor may perhaps be blamed for not trying to resolve the contradictions of his own critique, but his book remains a valuable study, important precisely to the extent that it refuses the totalising view that modern architecture had of itself and that its critics and historians frequently sought to perpetuate.

Le Corbusier and the USSR

In October 1928 Le Corbusier visited Moscow to present his winning design for the Centrosoyus. Between then and 1932 he made two more visits to Russia and completed his designs for the Palace of the Soviets. These four years of intense involvement with Russia and their subsequent repercussions are the subject of Jean-Louis Cohen's book, *La mystique de l'URSS*. In the opening chapter Cohen places his book in the context of Corbusian studies: "Today the layers of documentation are beginning to reveal their potential, while a whole set of mental reservations have arisen which allow us to deal with the most contradictory aspects of the life and work of Le Corbusier and to make out the contours of his personality." It is this cautious critical approach that informs Cohen's valuable book.

Much of the material was published in *Oppositions 23* under the title "Le Corbusier and the Mystique of the USSR", but the present book is far greater in scope, providing complete accounts of the Centrosoyus and the Palace of the Soviets, together with a thorough treatment of their cultural and political context and their critical reception in Russia. In addition, Cohen discusses the articles on Constructivism in *L'Esprit Nouveau*, the relationship between Le Corbusier's theory and the theories of the Russian avant-garde, and Le Corbusier's involvement with the projects for the Ville Vert holiday town near Moscow and with the "Disurbanist" controversy, out of which grew his initial formulation of the Ville Radieuse.

The story of the relationship between the Russian avant-garde after the Revolution and the Western European avant-gardes has yet to be fully explored. The attitude of the Russians was extremely ambivalent. On the one hand, the architects and artists of the avant-garde must have felt a sense of continuity with their pre-revolutionary past, which the Revolution seemed to confirm and give additional meaning to. From this point of view it was natural that they would want to renew contacts with the West as soon as the political situation allowed. At both a technical and an artistic level, the Russian architects had a need for such a renewal. On the other hand, the Revolution had given Russian architects a sense of social purpose and a distrust for the cultural institutions of the West.

As for the Western avant-garde, it saw Russia as the country in which the principles of cultural modernism were most likely to succeed, whether or not it associated the artistic avant-garde with social revolution. Le Corbusier's own relationship with the Russian avant-garde was not based on any fundamental sympathy with communism. In this he differed from many members of the German avant-garde. As Cohen points out, Le Corbusier drew much of his authority in Russia from his connection with the Parisian artistic and intellectual milieu, rather than from his social or political views.

It is against this confused background that Jean-Louis Cohen depicts the love affair between Le Corbusier and the Russian avant-garde—a love affair based on almost total mutual misunderstanding. The attitude toward Le Corbusier on the part of the Russians differed considerably and reflected the different degrees of politicisation within the Russian avant-garde itself. Alexander Vesnin and Moisei Ginzburg were staunch supporters of Le Corbusier. The latter's book *Style and Epoch* was closely modelled on *Vers une architecture* and laid great stress on ahistorical classical values. On the other hand, El Lissitzky, in alliance with the *Neue Sachlichkeit* movement, attacked Le Corbusier for his aestheticism and mystifications, as did Karel Teige (who is the subject of a separate article by Jean-Louis Cohen in *Le Corbusier: une encylopédie*).

Cohen's account of the critical reception of Le Corbusier in the 1930s in Russia is of great interest. In the 1920s, despite certain critical voices, Le Corbusier was generally regarded as an unchallenged master. After the debacle of the Palace of the Soviets competition, the tone becomes much more critical. What is perhaps surprising, given the increasingly ideological terms of the architectural debate, is the moderation and subtlety of much of the criticism. The intelligence of the critic David Arkin's articles on Le Corbusier is particularly striking. Whereas in the late 1920s Le Corbusier's critics accused him of being too artistic, those of the 30s found him too technological and functional. But there was a common factor: both criticised him for aestheticising technology and for ignoring social issues. To some extent these criticisms were also directed in the 1930s at the Constructivists within the USSR who were sometimes referred to as "nihilists of the left" in the growing atmosphere of Socialist Realism. But it was Le Corbusier, with his "a-political" technocratic ideas, who was the chief object of socialist attack in both Russia and France.

Cohen's book, with its thorough documentation of the ideological debates pivoting round Le Corbusier in the late 1920s and 30s in Russia, gives a new dimension to Le Corbusier's international role. It also raises questions about the relation between architecture and politics that are still relevant today.

Le Corbusier and Adolf Loos

The relationship between the work of Le Corbusier and Adolf Loos is the subject of *Raumplan versus Plan Libre*, edited by Max Risselada. The book is, in fact, the catalogue of a sumptuous travelling exhibition of architectural models prepared in 1987 by the School of Architecture at the Delft University of Technology, Holland.

In his introduction Risselada traces the history behind the exhibition: first, the revival of interest in Loos in the 1960s and second, the formal analysis of Le Corbusier's Purist period houses, initiated by Colin Rowe and Robert Slutsky in the late 1950s. At the formal level, as Risselada points out, there is an obvious basis for comparison; both architects treat the house as a spatio-temporal "architectural promenade", and both tend to compress a complex sequence of spaces within a regular hexahedron. But whereas with Loos the vertical surfaces are continuous and the horizontal surfaces discontinuous (providing rooms on different levels and of differing heights), with Le Corbusier the opposite is the case, the floors remaining constant (though sometimes voided) and the walls on each floor adapting themselves freely to different functions (the free plan). Loos' Raumplan is probably derived from English freestyle houses, and examples can be found in Great Britain as early as the 1860s of houses where each room is on a different level.

Risselada links these diverse spatio-structural systems to a much more fundamental difference, that between space-making and mass-making architecture: "On the one hand spaces in which the entire body can dwell—all the senses being involved; on the other hand spaces where there is perhaps only room for the roaming eye." This distinction, which in fact is based on an idea put forward by Loos in his essay "The Principle of Cladding", seems to be the difference between an art that accepts the complexity of the lifeworld and an art that seeks to order this world according to *a priori* principles. It is easy to see how the houses of Loos and Le Corbusier might correspond to these two types. The floor plan of a house by Loos has no iconic value in itself, whereas a plan by Le Corbusier is a visual icon of the "idea" of the building. Both architects dissolve the traditional house, but whereas with Loos the house can only be understood sequentially and empirically, with Le Corbusier it is understood instantaneously as a mental image.

Unfortunately, Risselada does not allow himself enough space to develop this interesting comparison. The formal analyses that follow are useful in themselves (especially van den Beek's study of Loos' houses with its analytical diagrams showing the way the spatial sequences might actually be experienced), but they do not succeed in bringing the houses of the two architects under a single set of critical criteria, and we are left with two systems of ideas, excellently described, but completely unconnected with each other.

Where a fruitful comparison between the two architects does occur is in the essay "Le Corbusier and Loos" by Stanislaus von Moos. This is the product of von Moos' research into the journal *L'Esprit Nouveau* and the essay is also included in the book *L'Esprit Nouveau: Le Corbusier et l'industrie*. In this essay von Moos explores the similarities and differences between the two architects' theoretical positions as opposed to their differences of practice. As he correctly states, both architects held to a Darwinist theory of design, involving the use of "ready-mades" (von Moos here extends, perhaps rather dubiously, Marcel Duchamp's concept) and rejecting the concept of the *Gesamtkunstwerke* which had been taken over from Richard Wagner by the Art Nouveau Movement and the Viennese Secession. Von Moos is careful to explain that Le Corbusier's condemnation of the Secession (1908) predates his knowledge of Adolf Loos' writings by five years. And, in fact, his rejection of the Secession takes a different form from that of Loos, leading to his acceptance (for a few years) of the neo-classical revival propagated by Paul Mebes and Peter Behrens. In spite of the classical tendencies he shared with Le Corbusier, Loos never embraced this movement, though he came close to it during his brief "reorientation" toward the classical vernacular in the early 1920s.

The more fundamental differences between the two architects emerged in the 1920s when Le Corbusier abandoned the traditional concept of a craft-based architecture in favour of an architecture based on machine production, a step that Loos never took, in spite of his insistence on the reality of a new 'folk' culture of anonymous industrial design. Von Moos makes it clear that Loos' persistent craft approach led him to retain traditional notions of *bienséance* and *convenance*. He held (with Karl Kraus) that there was a difference between the Urn and the Chamberpot, and that "only a small part of architecture belongs to art: the tomb and the monument". For Le Corbusier, on the contrary, all architecture belonged to art. The move from the craft tradition to abstract design associated with mechanical production had the effect for him of moving architectural design even more firmly into the territory of the conceptualising architect. Acting as Hegel's observer/philosopher, and at the same time reinventing Kantian aesthetics, the Corbusian architect becomes aware of the transcendental meaning of the anonymous forms created by calculation. For Le Corbusier, architecture, once freed from the material shackles of craft by the machine, becomes a pure creation of the mind and therefore an expression of the highest spiritual values. For Loos, this role was reserved for the great work of art, with its intensity of private experience, or the monument, with its dependence on social convention.

It is a striking, though perhaps not altogether surprising, fact that the majority of the books reviewed here deal either with Le Corbusier's formative years before the First World War or with the work of the "heroic" period of the 1920s and early 1930s. The extent of scholarly and critical interest in the early and middle period work suggests a decline in the critical fortunes of work of the post-war period. This seems to be consistent with a change in attitude to the Modern Movement as a whole that has occurred in the last two decades. A decreasing number of critics see the present as an unproblematic evolution from the early Modern Movement —as its coming of age. The modernism that is of interest now is that which looked (often with horror) at the break with history that the twentieth century had inaugurated, rather than the modernism that later sought to reconcile the modern world with a timeless humanism.

The decline in Le Corbusier as a role model for this kind of reconciliation has not resulted in any decline of critical interest in the work of Le Corbusier the innovator. Quite the contrary. Le Corbusier's ideas and works have increasingly come to be seen as paradigmatic of the great cultural and artistic changes that have taken place since the turn of the century. The hooks that appeared in his centenary year fulfil a need to penetrate deeper into the period in which these changes were first perceived and interpreted, in order to understand better our own cultural predicament.

The Nineteenth Century Terminus Station as Cultural Artefact

First published in *Casabella*, 624, June, 1995.

> Architecture is always dream and function; expression of a utopia
> and instrument of a convenience... use never does anything but
> shelter meaning.
>
> Roland Barthes

Of all the tangible results of the Industrial Revolution the railway station was surely the most subversive. Factories and their working populations were increasingly segregated from the bourgeois city dweller, exhibition halls were temporary, arcades penetrated the secret interstices of the city block without affecting its visible structure. The railway station, alone, introduced an industrial space containing large pieces of machinery into the city, and the tracks which led to it cut a swath through the outer city fabric, opening up to the traveler disturbing views of a normally hidden chaos. Not only did the railway station alter the physical form of the city, it also introduced a new kind of social space in which the masses of people were thrown together while at the same time each person was enclosed in his or her private drama—a new kind of covered street like an arcade, but vaster and more specialised.

From its earliest examples the railway station consisted of two disproportionate halves; an enormous covered hall over the tracks, and a reception building abutting it. The reception building became the mediator between the city, to which it was assimilated, and the shed, whose mysterious rituals it concealed from view. It was the reception building, in its function of propylaeum that chiefly exercised the imagination of the nineteenth century architect. The dichotomy inherent in the programme focused the debate that reverberated through the nineteenth century; should new building types, such as stations, adjust themselves to the existing rules of monumental architecture, or should they be accepted as a new 'language' of iron and glass? Progressive architects sang the praises of the new materials and their poetic possibilities, but when it came to constructing a new building like a station, even Léonce Reynaud, architect and engineer of the first Gare du Nord, who saw iron as "*le plus bienfaisante peut-être de toutes les inventions de l'epoque*", did not feel compelled to substitute iron for stone.[1] Coming after the Modern Movement of the 1920s we tend to see this nineteenth century debate in black and white terms, but in fact, when nineteenth century architects like César Daly and Léonce Reynaud spoke as moderns, they spoke from within a tradition of architecture which seemed as immutable as all the other conditions of their lives.

The two countries chiefly involved in the early development of the railway station and in fixing its typology were England and France. With the invention of the steam engine England had taken the lead in industrial development in the first decades of the nineteenth century. By 1830 there were 15,000 steam engines in commission in Great Britain compared to 3,000 in France, the next most industrialised country. With the application of steam power to transport, made possible by the invention of metal tracks, British railway engineering became the model for continental Europe. In the early 1830s the Saint-Simonien engineer Eugène Flachet, visited England to study the railway system.[2] English entrepreneurs, engineers and financiers played an important role in the development of new industries on the continent, including the railway systems. Teams of skilled artisans from England were even employed on the construction of railways in France.

Between 1830 and 1845 England provided the prototypes for station design in Europe and North America, but after 1845 France started to take the lead in both the conceptualisation and the design of railway stations. The dominance of the French in railway station design after 1845 cannot be attributed to the extensiveness of the French network. By 1850 the networks in Great Britain and Belgium were virtually complete, and in Germany they were well advanced, while in France the major part of the network was still in the planning stage. French dominance in the field was due to other factors, among which were the continuing influence of the Ecole des Beaux-Arts and the systematic approach of both government policy-makers and designers. In spite of the relative backwardness of the French railway network, the construction of terminus stations in Paris in the 1850s and 60s was slightly ahead of that in London. During this period, in professional journals, both countries reported fairly extensively on each other's development.[3]

In spite of fundamental similarities on the level of technology and ideology, there were considerable differences of approach in the unfolding construction of the railway network and the design of railway stations in the two countries. In this comparison, the French appear as positive and encoded, the English as negative and un-coded. The differences are best seen in the context of three levels of culture of increasing specificity:

1. The different political practices; *dirigiste* in France, *laissez faire* in Britain.
2. The utopian component in the early development of industrial capitalism in France in contrast to the pragmatic approach of the British.
3. Differences at the level of architectural theory and practice.

To speak first of the political context; the French railway system, despite pressure for nationalisation from the left, remained in private hands. Nonetheless, the state determined strategic development, and the network expanded on the basis of collaboration between the public and private sectors. In England, on the contrary, the whole development was left to market forces, leading to a scramble for contracts and a multiplicity of competing projects. In 1846 no less than 1,263 projects for new lines were put before Parliament.[4] According to a paper read to the Institute of Civil Engineers in London in 1858, the existence of government planning in France led to lower construction costs and a higher return on investment than in England, where devotion to the principal of free competition may have produced some benefits to the user, but had ruinous results for the shareholder.[5] According to another British commentator, the functional arrangements of stations in France was generally perceived to be superior to that of English stations, due to greater initial expenditure, the allocation of larger sites, the architectural training of engineers, and the closer connection between engineers and the working and management of the lines.[6]

In France, unlike in England, there was continuity between the utopian trends of the Enlightenment and the early nineteenth century ideas of progress. Utopian movements such as the Fourierists and the Saint-Simoniens constituted important political, commercial and professional pressure groups. César Daly, editor of the *Revue Générale de l'architecture et des travaux publics* (founded in 1840) was a Fourierist, and the *Revue Générale* acted simultaneously as a channel for socially progressive ideas and as a source of technical and architectural information. It was the Saint-Simoniens, however, who provided much of the motive force and expertise (financial, managerial and technical) in the development of industry and public works, including the railway and canal systems, that began to get under way with the July monarchy in 1830, and reached a climax under the Second Empire.

The Saint-Simoniens were involved with the new railway system both as entrepreneurs and as engineers.[7] Their most immediate impact on the design

Top: John Foster (architect), George Stephenson (engineer), Crown Street Station, Liverpool, 1829–1830.

Bottom: François Duquesnay, Gare de l'Est, Paris, 1847–1852.

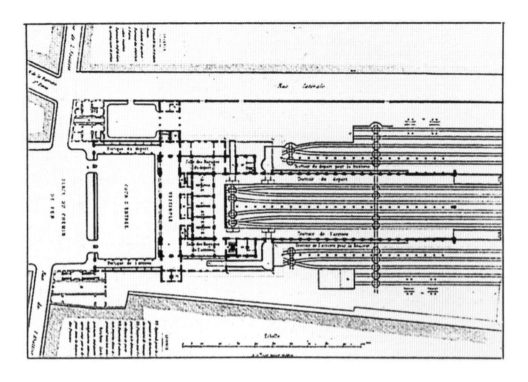

of stations was on the train shed structure, but they also had a more general influence on the development of new architectural types, particularly in the case of market buildings. Baltard's revised solution for les Halles, after the first pavilion had been demolished on the orders of Napoleon III, was based both on Eugène Flachat's unsuccessful entry to the les Halles competition and on his design for the shed roof of the Gare Saint Lazare of 1851.[8] There was no group in England corresponding to the Saint-Simoniens, combining social vision with entrepreneurial and technical expertise. The Utilitarians never wielded as much political influence in England as did the Saint-Simoniens in France, and their major achievement, the founding of University College, London, remained a somewhat isolated example of intervention at a politico-cultural level.

The building of stations in the large French cities was affected not only by *l'esprit systèmatique* that the Saint-Simoniens applied to the railway system as a whole, but also by the concept of the city as a discrete political and formal entity. In his book *Architectes et ingénieurs au siècle des lumières*, Antoine Picon contrasts the rational city of the eighteenth century which "*reste confinée à l'intérieur du périmètre régulier de ses boulevards*", with the 'unlimited' city of the nineteenth century which "*oscilla... entre la reconquête de son centre au moyen des séquences d'équipement et l'extension indéfinie de sa périphérie*".[9] But, even though it involved radically new types of building, this 'reconquest of the centre' remained within the mental horizon of the eighteenth century city, and the new stations of the 1850s and 60s were conceived of as urban monuments adding to the collection of such monuments already in existence. In London, on the contrary, no such concept of the city existed, and the station was thought of more as an instrument of utility than as a monument.

Within strictly architectural discourse we find the same divergence. Whereas in England the picturesque movement and theories of association had radically undermined the older classical tradition, in France such ideas had been absorbed into this tradition. Notions such as *convenance* and *caractère* which had been subject to extension and modification by JF Blondel in the later eighteenth century, still formed the basis of architectural esthetics. 'Convenance' referred equally to the useful and the beautiful, to reason and taste.[10] There was no theoretical limit to

Above: Léonce Reynaud, Gare du Nord I, Paris.

Opposite top: Lewis Cubitt, King's Cross Station, London, 1851–1852.

Opposite bottom: King's Cross Station, plan.

the new types that could be introduced into the architectural repertoire. In the early nineteenth century in France, the idea of the connection between beauty and utility formed part of a still active classical doctrine, whereas in England, for example in the case of Pugin, the idea of beauty became associated with both an anti-classical and anti-industrial utopia, leaving new building types such as railway stations without the support of a theory.

The synthetic character of the idea of *convenance* also led in France to a close connection between architects and engineers. Although the founding of the Ecole des Pons et Chaussées in 1775 and the Ecole Polytechnique in 1795 had reduced the area of competence of the architect, the new schools maintained close connections with the Ecole des Beaux-Arts and engineers were required to receive architectural training. When the progressives within the academy triumphed over the strict neo-classical doctrine of Quatremére de Quincy in 1830, this did not signal the end of the classical tradition, but rather its liberalisation, in line with the liberalism of the new political regime. The close connection between the architectural profession and political power encouraged conservative and conciliatory attitudes in architecture.

These attitudes informed the early design of railway stations in France. The practical arrangements of stations were understood as being as much the concern of architects as were their artistic and representational aspects. It was thought that the station should have its own character, which would be intimately connected with its morphology. In his articles on stations in the *Revue Générale* César Daly dealt equally with the problems of distribution and expression. In 1846 and again in 1859 he sketched a typology of terminus stations, listing all the possible

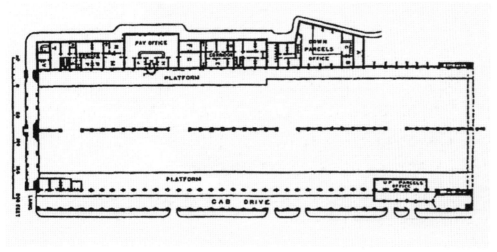

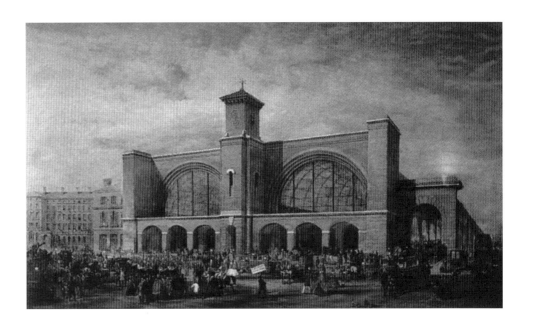

arrangements, with their advantages and disadvantages. [11] He was particularly concerned with the position of the reception building relative to the train shed. Side buildings (continuing the earliest English practice in which there were only two tracks) were more convenient for the passenger, who was not obliged to walk the whole length of the platform to reach his compartment, but the head building had the dual advantage of providing a clearer entrance to the station and a more monumental facade. This problem solved itself, as the century progressed, in favour of the head building, when the multiplication of arrival and departure tracks made the side station obsolete. But in the earlier stations some sort of compromise was usually adopted.

In his 1846 article Daly placed the railway station firmly in line of succession to the tradition of public buildings: "*Nous sommes arrivés à une époque qui demande encore plus de marchés publics, d'usines, d'entrepôts, de gares et de stations de chemin de fer que d'arcs de triomphe et de temples élevés à la gloire....*"[12] In another passage he underscores his conception of the station as belonging to architecture as an art: "*... le programme d'une station de chemin de fer peut offrir quelque chose de la netteté indispensable à la production d'une oeuvre d'art*".[13] Besides Daly, several other writers analysed the problem of the railway station. In his *Traité d'architecture* of 1850 Léonce Reynaud, apart from repeating Daly's analysis of distribution, stressed the need for a body of doctrine covering the new type, which, however, he thought was not yet possible. All stations up to the time of writing appeared to him unsatisfactory, being either "too provisional or too academic", and he warned against striving for monumentality, recommending the use of iron for its symbolic potential.[14] Auguste Perdonnet and Pierre Chabat also wrote treaties on the railway station.[15] Perdonnet, like Daly, connects stations to the monumental tradition, saying that, like theatres, temples and churches, railway stations have a distinctive architecture of their own.

Though English and French progressive architects in the early nineteenth century were in fairly close contact with each other and shared many points of doctrine, there were differences in the embedded traditions of the two countries and these were reflected in differences in approach towards station design. In England the station as a whole was not theorised; instead architecture is seen as providing decoration for an engineering structure. Even an engineer like RJ Hood, who deplored the fact that English, unlike French, engineers received no architectural training, could say that "engineers should rely on architects only for elevations

Above: King's Cross Station, London.

Opposite: JI Hittorf (architect), Léonce Reynaud (engineer) Gare du Nord II, Paris, 1861–1864.

and decorations of railway stations".[17] The plans of English stations show that they were made by engineers who were ignorant of that relation between utility and beauty, the pragmatic and the ideal, that was part of the classical tradition and informed the French approach. This can clearly be seen if we compare the plans of say, Paddington, King's Cross or St Pancras stations to those of the Gare de l'Est or of the first and second Gare du Nord. The French plans show an order, hierarchy and symmetry that is lacking in the English plans, which are arranged purely from a pragmatic point of view.

There were two closely related theoretical problems facing the station architects and engineers in France. The first was the need to reconcile distributional requirements with those of monumentality. The second challenge was to reconcile the two components of the station—the reception building and the train shed. The doctrine that the character of a building depended on the expression of its function demanded that the train shed should be the principal element of the composition. At least until the 1860s this element was thought of in terms of the traditional typology of large public halls, such as Roman baths and Medieval churches. Both these analogies were *topoi* of the nineteenth century—and not only in France.

These problems of reconciliation received their first canonic solution in the Gare de l'Est, 1847–1852, by François Duquesney. The main facade of this station is developed on successive planes. On the first plane, an arcaded entrance foyer extends over the whole facade, which is flanked by two pavilions. On the second plane, the pediment and thermal window of the train shed appears over the foyer, recessive but dominant, framed by the two pavilions. Along each side, an arcaded entrance is similarly contained between pavilions, stressing the closure of the entire composition.

In the second Gare du Nord, 1861–1864, by Jaques-Ignace Hittorf with the aid of enginner Léonce Reynaud, there is the same insistence on the expression of the train shed, but now the whole composition is brought forward to a single plane and consists of an elongated and elaborately articulated and pedimented screen.

The only London station that is in any way comparable to these Parisian stations is that of King's Cross, 1851–1852, by Lewis Cubitt. This structure has certain features in common with the Gare de l'Est. The facade has two thermal windows (compared to the single window in the Gare de l'Est) corresponding to the double vaults of the train shed behind. The analogy between King's Cross and the Gare de l'Est was not lost on contemporary critics. For James Fergusson King's Cross was "entirely truthful", but he considered the Gare de l'Est superior, saying that "from a higher degree of ornamentation it becomes really an object of architectural art and one perfectly appropriate to its purpose without too many imitative features borrowed from any particular style".[18] The terms in which Fergusson discusses these stations are, in fact, French; Cubitt's building is based on a different tradition—that of the stripped classicism of English Palladianism. Many English public buildings of this kind were illustrated in the pages of the *Revue Générale* and make a strong contrast to French (and indeed continental) architecture. (For precisely the reason that Fergusson criticised it, modernist critics of the 1930s considered King's Cross to be one of the precursors of 'Modern architecture'.) While the Gare de l'Est is decorated according to an appropriate iconographic scheme, King's Cross consists of

severe undecorated surfaces of London stock brick, whose thickness is expressed by stepped reveals in the arches, in the manner of John Soane. Its monumental quality derives entirely from its proportions and the solidity of its masses, while the Gare de l'Est is more 'elegant', its surfaces flatter and supplemented by ornament.

The contrast between these two stations can also be seen in their relative systems of distribution. The plans of the Gare de l'Est (like the Gare du Nord) are organised symmetrically with important ranges of rooms along both sides of the sheds. In contrast, the plan of King's Cross is asymmetrical and appears to be organised quite casually. This effect is due partly to circumstance: in English stations, unlike those on the continent, there was no *octroi* levied on arriving passengers, and therefore no need for any service building on the arrival side.

Except in the case of King's Cross no architects in England felt the need to give the station monumentality or character by announcing the entrance or the volume of the train shed on the main facade. The typical London station of the 1850s and 1860s was masked by a huge hotel building. Such buildings were rare in Paris, only appearing, later, in the second Gare Saint Lazare, 1887, and the Gare d'Orsay, 1889. Perdonnet remarked on the fact that station hotels were rare in Paris because, in spite of the fact that stations were supposed to be important public monuments, their precincts had, by the 1860s, developed a "bad reputation".[19]

The culmination of the hotel/station combination was reached at St Pancras, 1863. At this station both the train shed and the hotel were *tours de force*. The train shed, by the engineers WH Barlow and RM Ordish, was unrivalled in span until 1889. The hotel, by Gilbert Scott, was an enormous Gothic extravaganza. Perhaps more than any other station St Pancras represent the unbridgeable gap that existed in the mentality of nineteenth century Europe between material and cultural life—a gap summed up by Scott himself when he said that his design for the hotel was "possibly too good for is purpose". St Pancras also epitomises the refusal of England to grant the railway station the status of a representational public building or to consider it as possessing architectural unity.

Yet the ambitions of the French architects to reconcile technology with art in the terminal railway station, on the basis of an elastic and irenic classicism, was itself frustrated by technical and social change. In the 1870s, following the 'second Industrial Revolution', it was in Germany that the next stage in station development took place. A satisfactory way of expressing the character of the station as a type by means of displaying the train shed gable became virtually impossible with the development of multiple tracks and the need for huge lateral concourses, as for example, in the stations in Frankfurt, 1879–1888, and Leipzig, 1907–1915. The Stazione Centrale in Milan, 1913–1930, is a late example of this type. The facades of these late nineteenth and early twentieth century stations were expressed in a neo-baroque or neo-classical language and in heavy masonry construction.

In spite of this development, many French stations continued to emphasise iron and glass construction—a tendency possibly connected with the parallel development of exhibition structures, in which iron technology carried distinctly nationalistic implications. French engineers built extensively in Eastern Europe. In Gustave Eiffel's design for the West Bahnhof in Budapest, and in certain Prix de Rome designs of the 1870s, the step which had been recommended by Reynaud and Daly in the 1850s, was finally taken: the main facade was represented entirely in iron and glass, with stonework restricted to end pylons.

At the end of the nineteenth century it is the concourse that takes the place of the train shed as the chief symbolic space of the terminus station, while, in North America, especially in multi-level stations, this role is played by the ticket hall. At the same time, electrification makes it possible to dispense with the train shed vault. What we witness here is one of those massive 'paradigm shifts' that seem to occur as the result of a number of simultaneous and seemingly unrelated factors. Economics and function alone are not able to explain either the appearance or the disappearance of the train shed; already in the 1850s engineers where complaining that the train shed vault was extravagant.[20] We must assume that there were strong symbolic and ideological motives behind the ferro-vitreous shed structures of the nineteenth century. Nor was the disappearance of the shed vault due to the relaxation of the need for monumentality, since the reinforced concrete concourses of stations such as Leipzig and Karlsrule were highly monumental. A new architecturally symbolic paradigm of mass and surface as opposed to line and transparency comes into play. The meaning of the station retreats from the phenomenon of contact between people and machinery, which no longer holds the imagination.

While architects of the mid-nineteenth century were generally obsessed with the problem of reconciling the railway station with the tradition of urban monuments, there existed a parallel consciousness of the station—something one might call its 'phenomenology'—which only coincided with the intentions of the architects at certain points. One might say, if one were to differentiate between production and reception, that while both architect and public were affected by the same phenomenon—the absolute newness of the railway station and its power to create cultural and psychological shock—they reacted to this shock in opposite ways. While the architects were concerned with naturalising the railway shed, and cushioning its shock effect, the more articulate of the non-architects—the writers and painters—were interested in precisely what was new and shocking about it.

What had the power to shock in the station was the huge evanescent space of the train shed with its iron and glass roof. It was a space that had no definite closure, or rather, one that was simultaneously closed and open. It was generally thought of in the nineteenth century as 'industrial space' in contrast to 'architectural space'. Such spaces were not unique in the nineteenth century, but in the railway station the disturbing industrial quality common to them all was increased by the presence of steam engines in close contact with people, and the violent stimulation of the senses which resulted.

The structure of the train shed was solely the work of engineers, and this was true even when, as in France, there was a close collaboration between engineer and architect. At least when the architect and engineer were one and the same person, as in the case of Léonce Reynaud, one might have expected the two discourses to merge. Yet, in his architectural treatise, Reynaud remains silent on the subject of the design of the train shed roof.[21] The trusses and arches with their endless permutations and improvement were the result of experiment and calculation, but it would be a mistake to underestimate the role that intuition and aesthetic judgment played in their design, or the degree of awareness on the part of the engineers of their symbolic importance. The structure of the shed

Opposite: WP Frith, *The Railway Station*, 1863.

Above: Gustave Eiffel, West Station, Budapest, 1874–1877.

vault was just as much a 'cultural' artefact as the 'architecture' that clothed it, but one of a different order. Such cultural factors are apparent in the different lines of development of the shed roof in England and France. On the whole the English preferred the form of the arch while the French, following the pioneer designs of Antoine Polonceau, preferred the truss, as in the second Gare du Nord and the Gare Saint Lazare of 1851. (There are, however, exceptions to this rule, notably the magnificent arched vault of the Gare de l'Est.) It is possible that the predominance in France of the truss roof is connected with the preference of French station architects for triangular pediments.

The reception buildings were related in scale and treatment to the familiar urban fabric, and they formed a transitional zone mediating between the city and the industrial space of the shed. Even though, in French stations, the shed was normally represented on the facade, the passengers experienced a greater barrier when moving literally between the city and the train shed than was the case in England. There was a practical reason for this. Whereas in England there was free access to the platforms, in France travellers had to remain in the waiting rooms until the arrival of their train (a fact still noted with disgust in the English Beadeker for Paris of 1894). Perdonnet recognised the superiority of the English system, seeing it as a symptom of advanced industrialisation; "... this is truly a grand and beautiful spectacle which gives a good idea of this power and liberalism of the companies that have given their country those magnificent instruments. The travelers who can freely enter the station at all hours, familiarise themselves with machines by studying them. By admiring them, they lose their fear of them, and thus the railways become popular."[22]

In his book *The Railway Journey*, Wolfgang Schivelbusch discusses the adjustment of the passenger to the shock of rail travel in the early nineteenth century in terms of Freud's concept of the "stimulus shield". Historicising Freud on the basis of certain remarks by Walter Benjamin, he suggests that modern man develops a protective mechanism for interiorising the stimuli that come to him from an industrialised environment, just as, in George Simmel's analysis, the city dweller protects himself from the stimuli of the modern city by adopting a blasé attitude.[23] Extending this analogy, Schivelbusch suggests that the reception

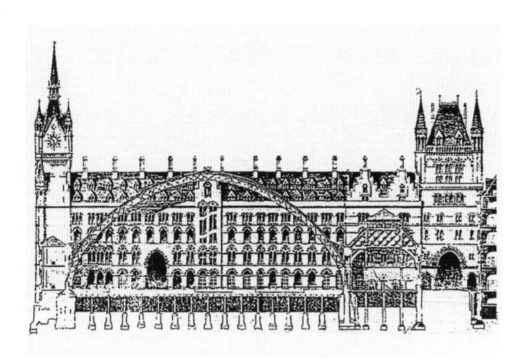

building of the railway station, by screening out the stimuli of the train shed, acted as a kind of stimulus shield. But perhaps it could be said that the shed itself, by reifying the space of the machine, also acted as a stimulus shield. However this may be, the strange contrast between the enclosed spaces of the reception building and the open space of the train shed has been a continuous source of inspiration for artists and writers, and has entered the language of dreams.

Between 1860 and the 1920s the railway station is the frequent subject of painters and is continually being reinterpreted according to new cultural paradigms. For WH Frith or Karl Karger the station is the site of a genre scene in the manner of Balzac or Dickens. With Manet and Monet the station and the people in it became optical events, snapshots of modern bourgeois life and of visual and atmospheric stimulation. For the Futurists the station stands for the violent motion of machine civilisation, while in a De Chirico or a Delvaux it is the site of the uncanny. In each case the station stands for all that is new, stimulating, disturbing, or alienating in modern life.

It is the same with the representation of the station in literature. Of all nineteenth century critics it was Emile Zola who most vividly recorded the progressivist view of the new metal and glass structures appearing in Paris. In *Le Ventre de Paris*, 1873, he describes Les Halles, which "… appeared like a steam engine, a furnace intended for the consumption of a whole people, a huge stomach of metal, bolted, riveted, made of wood, glass and cast iron, elegant and powerful like a machine". Claude Lantier, the hero of *L'oeuvre*, 1880, expresses a view of the new architecture of train sheds that echoes the belief in progress of the Saint-Simoniens of the 1830s:

If there ever was a century in which architecture should have a style of its own, it was the century about to begin. Down with Greek temples, there was no use for them in modern society! Down with Gothic cathedrals—belief in legends was dead! Down with the Renaissance… it would never house modern democracy! What was wanted was an architectural formula to fit that democracy… something big and strong and simple, the sort of thing that was already asserting itself in railway stations and market halls, the solid elegance of metal girders.[24]

Opposite: Claude Monet, *La Gare Saint-Lazare*, 1877.

Above: Sir George Gilbert Scott (architect), WH Barlow and RM Ordish (engineers), St Pancras Station, London, 1868–1876.

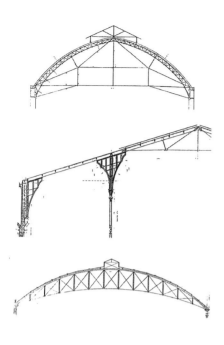

But by 1896, in a mood that brings to mind the urban sociology of George Simmel and the retreat into the subjectivism of Art Nouveau, Zola had changed his mind: "modern society is racked without end by a nervous irritability. We are sick and tired of progress, industry and science."[25]

When, just after the First World War, Marcel Proust published, in *A l'hombre des jeunes filles en fleurs*, what must be the last and the greatest literary description of the railway station, the automobile had already become the rival of the railway as a mode of travel. In the process of bringing back to consciousness the narrator's departure for Balbec in the 1880s, Proust transforms the railway station from an instrument of modernity into an inner experience, an archetype and a symbol of death. This passage is interwoven with a reflection on museums, and, according to Adorno, the associative link between the two subjects is precisely the painting of the Gare Saint Lazare by Monet that used to hang in the Jeu de Paume.[26]

Today one would make this journey by car, believing in this way to render it more agreeable… but in fact the specific pleasure of travelling is not that it makes it possible to alight en route and to stop whenever one is tired; it is to make the difference between departure and arrival not as insensible but as profound as possible, to experience it in its totality, intact, exactly as it was in our thoughts when our imagination carried us from the place where we lived to the heart of the place where we desired to be, in a single leap that seemed to us less miraculous because it covered a certain distance than because it united two distinct and individual beings, carried us from one name to another name, and encapsulated the mysterious operation accomplished in those special places, railway stations, which are not as it were part of the town in which they are found but contain its essence and at the same time, by means of a written sign, bear its name.

Unfortunately these wonderful places called stations, from which one departs for a far-off place, are also tragic places, for if the miracle is accomplished thanks to which these countries which had not yet existed except in our thoughts become those in which we actually live, for this very reason one has to give up the idea of leaving the station waiting room and returning immediately to the familiar room where one was a moment ago. One has to abandon all hope of sleeping again in one's home, once one has decided to penetrate the pestiferous cavern through which one gains access to the mystery, like that of Saint Lazare where I went to find the train to Balbec, and which deployed above the disemboweled city one of those bleak and boundless skies, pregnant with the menace of immanent drama, like certain skies, of an almost Parisian modernity, by Mantegna or Veronese, and under which what can only be accomplished is some terrible and solemn act such as a departure by train or the elevation of the cross.

1   Reynaud, Léonce, *Traité d'architecture*, Paris, 1850 (second edition, 1863), vol. 2, chapter X, "Gares de chemin de fer".
2   Marrey, Bernard, "Saint-Simoniens, Fourieristes et architecture", p. 75, in *Archives d'architecture moderne*, no. 20, 1981, pp. 74–99.
3   Particularly in *The Builder* and in the *Revue générale de l'architecture et des travaux publics*.
4   *The Builder*, vol. 33, 1875, p. 223.
5   *The Builder*, vol. 16, 1858, p. 60.
6   *The Builder*, vol. 16, 1858, p. 340.
7   Marrey, "Saint-Simoniens", pp. 75–80.
8   Marrey, "Saint-Simoniens", p. 78
9   Picon, Antoine, *Architects et ingénieurs au siècle des lumières*, p. 230.
10 Picon, *Architects et ingénieurs au siècle des lumières*, p. 86.
11 *Revue générale de l'architecture*, no. 6, 1846, and no. 17, 1859.
12 *Revue générale de l'architecture*, no. 6, 1846.
13 *Revue générale de l'architecture*, no. 17, 1859.
14 Reynaud, *Traité d'architecture*, "Gares de chemin de fer".

15 Perdonnet, Auguste, *Traité elementaire de chemin de fer*, 1856, and Nouveau Portefeuille, 1857–1860. Pierre Chabat, *Batiments de chemin de fer*, 1862–1966.
16 Perdonnet, *Traité elementaire*, p. 492, quoted in Carrol LV Meeks; *The Railroad Station, an architectural history*, Yale University Press, 1956, p. 42.
17 *The Builder*, no. 16, 1858, p. 340.
18 Quoted in Pevsner, Nikolaus, *Some architectural writers of the nineteenth century*, Oxford, 1972, p. 246; and Carrol LV Meeks, *The Railroad Station*, p. 65.
19 See Shivelbusch, Wolfgang, *The Railway Journey: The Industrialisation of Time and Space in the 19th Century*, p. 172.
20 *The Builder*, vol. 16, p. 340.
21 Reynaud, *Traité d'architecture*.
22 Perdonnet, *Traité elementaire…*, first edition, vol. 2, p. 30, quoted in Wolfgang Schivelbusch, *The Railway Journey*, p. 176.
23 Simmel, Georg, "The metropolis and mental life", in *The Sociology of Georg Simmel*, ed. Kurt Wolff, Glencoe, IL, 1950.
24 Quoted in Silverman, Deborah, *Art Nouveau in fin-de-siècle France: Politics, Psychology and Style*, University of California Press, 1989, p. 7.
25 Quoted in Silverman, *Art Nouveau in fin-de-siècle France*, p.7.
26 Adorno, Theodor W, "Valery Proust Museum", in *Prisms*, Cambridge, MA: MIT Press, 1967.

Opposite top: Section of the cupola of the shelter of the carriages, Gare de l'Est, Paris.

Opposite middle: Half-section of the truss, Gare du Nord II, Paris.

Opposite bottom: EA Cowper (engineer), New Street Station, Birmingham, 1854.

Above: Hauptbahnhof, Karlsruhe, 1907–1913.

Regionalism 1

First published in *Postcolonial Spaces*, 1992.

Ever since the late eighteenth century one of the main directions of architectural criticism has been that of regionalism. According to this approach, architecture should be firmly based on specific regional practices based on climate, geography, local materials, and local cultural traditions. It has been tacitly assumed that such a foundation is necessary for the development of an authentic modern architecture. I want to subject this idea itself to criticism and to consider the notion of regionalism so defined in relation to the conditions of late capitalism.

I would like first to put the concept of regionalism into its historical context. Let me begin, therefore, by looking at the historical period nearest to us, the avant-garde of the early twentieth century. The twentieth century avant-garde can always be viewed from one of two perspectives: either as having inherited the principles of the Enlightenment, or as emerging from the tradition of the Enlightenment's great enemy, romanticism. One can hardly avoid noticing the presence of these contradictory strands: on the one hand the promotion of rationalism, universalism, and identity; on the other a recurrent enthusiasm for nominalism, empiricism, intuition, and difference. These contradictions came into the open during the famous debate between Hermann Muthesius and Henry Van de Velde at the Deutsche Werkbund Conference at Cologne in 1914, when Van de Velde maintained a Ruskinian belief in the virtues of the artist/craftsman and a betrayed Medieval tradition.

At first glance it would appear that the former stand—universalism and rationalism—was triumphant in the Modern Movement of the 1920s. The elementariness of de Stijl, the *rappel l'ordre* of Le Corbusier, and the *Neue Sachlichkeit* in Germany and Switzerland were all basically rationalistic. But, as has often been pointed out, the situation was in reality a good deal more complicated. Regionalism was only one side of the Modern Movement. For example, when the paradigm of Schinkelesque classicism emerged in the first decade of the twentieth century, it not only laid claim to universal values but took over and transformed the regionalist philosophy of the Art Nouveau movement that it replaced. One example of this phenomenon is when classicism and "Mediterraneanism" were adopted by the cultural nationalists of *Suisse romande*.[1] This fact was influential in forming the mature ideology of Le Corbusier, in whose work reference to the Mediterranean vernacular (cubic form, white walls, etc.) was just as prominent as the idea of industrial standardisation. These tendencies became increasingly important in Le Corbusier's work in the 1930s when, under the influence of anarcho-syndicalism, he began to think in terms of separate vernacular regional traditions, and even proposed a Europe divided into 'natural' regions, including a Mediterranean region.[2] But Le Corbusier was only one case among many, though certainly the most articulate. Mediterraneanism was, I believe, deeply embedded in the whole Modern Movement from 1905 onwards. As for regionalism, one only has to look at the introductions to the successive editions of Sigfried Giedion's *Space, Time and Architecture*, first published in 1940 and revised in five editions until 1968, to realise the extent to which regionalist ideas increasingly permeated modernist theory in the post-war period. For example, Alvar Aalto's work was added in the second edition.

So there is a case for saying that the 1920s was not just the simple triumph of rationalism that it often seems. Instead, it should perhaps be seen as the stage on which a deep conflict of ideologies was still being enacted. What was the nature of this conflict? To answer this question it is necessary to go back to the eighteenth century and the beginnings of romanticism and historicism. It was then that

Europeans started to notice the existence of ancient cultures that were neither antique nor Biblical. At the same time they began to be interested in their own pasts—in the vernaculars that had existed before the revival of antiquity in the Renaissance. One of the most significant results of this process was the creation of an alternative model for humanistic culture, one that made a sharp distinction between the study of nature and human history. Both Johann Gottfried Herder and Giambattista Vico independently claimed that the two studies demanded totally different methods, scientific in the one case and hermeneutic in the other.

This doctrine had a powerful effect in the German speaking countries because it coincided with the revolt against the hegemony of French culture. But it also affected France and England. Elaborate genealogies were invented to support the new sentiment of nationhood. The English traced their ancestry to the Anglo-Saxons, or, even more remotely, the Celts, who, in their Scottish Highland incarnation, arrived complete with a fictitious poet, Ossian. In Germany, the Goths were supposed to have invented Gothic architecture on German soil until it was proved (by an Englishman) that this event had taken place on the Isle de France. I will return to this "invention of tradition", as it has been called by the historian Eric Hobsbawm, when I come to mention the National Romanticism of the late nineteenth century.[3]

More important for an understanding of the origins of the doctrine of regionalism are the theories that were developed later in the nineteenth century, again mostly in Germany, concerning the problem of the rationalisation of social life under industrial capitalism. This process was perhaps given its most powerful formulation by Max Weber when he coined two expressions that are still by-words for our present situation: the "disenchantment" of the world due to individualisation and secularisation, and the "iron cage" of capitalism in which the modern world is imprisoned.

Among the concepts that German post-Romantic theory used, two are of particular interest, if only because they reduce the problem to simple binary oppositions. The first is the distinction between *Zivilization* and *Kultur*. As Norbert Elias has shown, this distinction goes back to the early nineteenth century and was the direct result of the German revolt against French cultural dominance. *Zivilization* meant aristocratic materialism and superficiality, as opposed to the less brilliant but more profound *Kultur*.[4] The idea of this distinction spread to other countries with the dissemination of romanticism. In England Samuel Taylor Coleridge adopted the word "culture" with its German connotations. The concept was absorbed by John Ruskin and William Morris, whose Medievalism, became the cornerstone of the Arts and Crafts Movement. In France itself, a school of historiography influenced by Chateaubriand held the view that the Frankish invasions of the fifth century were the true origins of modern French culture, rather than the institutions founded by the Gallo-Romans.[5] In the late nineteenth century the idea of *Zivilization* received the slightly different connotation of modern technological society, in opposition to pre-industrial human values. But, both in the earlier and later senses, *Zivilization* represented the international and universal as against the instinctual, autochthonous, and particular. We find approximately the same set of ideas in Giedion's *Space, Time and Architecture* when be writes about the split in modern life between feeling and intellect—a conflict that he hoped to dissolve by arguing that science and modern art were in reality dealing with the same phenomena but from different perspectives.

The distinction between *Zivilization* and *Kultur* is a fruitful way of looking at the widespread nationalist movements of the 1890s, which in so many ways repeated the impulse of the earlier romantic movement. Just as the Germans had done around 1800, so a number of groups distanced themselves from the countries by which they had been politically or culturally dominated: the Irish from the English, the Catalonians from the Castillians, the Finns from the Russians and the Swedes.[6] In Finland, for example, the Finnish language was officially adopted, an ancestral aural literature was 'reconstructed', and an eclectic architecture representing 'Finnishness' was put together from various stylistic sources, some indigenous, some external (for example, one of its main sources was the English Arts and Crafts Movement).[7] Such a representation of national 'essence' was largely fictional, but it had a clear ideological function: the legitimisation of a nation-state in terms of a regional culture, and in this it was successful.

The notion of *Kultur* was also taken up, in spirit if not in name, by chauvinistic movements in the late nineteenth and early twentieth centuries. Maurice Barrès wrote in 1902:

> There is in France a state morality... Kantianism. This claims to regulate universal man, without taking individual differences into account. It tends to form young persons from Lorraine, Province, Brittany, and Paris in terms of an abstract, ideal man, who is everywhere the same, whereas the need will be for men rooted solidly in our soil, in our history.[8]

In Germany the idea was adopted by the National Socialists in the 1920s, taking up the ideas of Houston Stewart Chamberlain, who had used the distinction *Zivilization/Kultur* to promote the concept of racial purity.[9] In so doing they recruited several architects of the Heimatschutz persuasion, such as Paul Schulze-Naumburg, whose ideas were derived from the Arts and Crafts Movement.

The second concept I want to discuss is the distinction between *Gesellschaft* and *Gemeinschaft*—a distinction made by Ferdinand Tönnies in his book of that title of 1887.[10] According to Tönnies these two words represent two types of human association. *Gesellschaft*-like associations are the result of rational deliberation, whereas *Gemeinschaft*-like associations are those that have developed organically. Again, we find the same opposition as in the case of *Zivilization* and *Kultur*, one term based on the idea of a natural law independent of historical or geographical contingency, the other implying rootedness in the soil. Examples of the former are bureaucracies, factories, and corporations, in which social relations are rational means to a desired end. Examples of the latter are the family, friendship groups, clans, and religious sects—all groupings in which social relations are ends in themselves.

The doctrine of regionalism belongs to the *Kultur* and *Gemeinschaft* side of these oppositions. The problem I would like to address is this: given the radically changed circumstances of the modern world, does this cluster of concepts still make sense, and, if so, in what way will its concept of culture—above all in its architectural manifestations—differ from those of its earlier incarnations: romanticism. Art Nouveau, and the early twentieth century avant-garde?

Obviously, the anxieties that were experienced in these periods have not simply evaporated. Many still feel disquiet at the increasingly abstract and homogenised world of modern post-industrial society. But it is questionable whether these doubts can any longer be expressed adequately in terms of the oppositions I have outlined. Clearly, the doctrine of regionalism is based on an ideal social model—one might call it the "essentialist model". According to this model, all societies contain a core, or essence, that must be discovered and preserved. One aspect of this essence lies in local geography, climate, and customs, involving the use and transformation of local, 'natural' materials. This is the aspect that has most often been invoked in connection with architecture.

The first thing to note about this model is that it was formulated in the late eighteenth century precisely at the moment when the phenomena that it described seemed to be threatened and about to disappear. This is hardly surprising. The elements of society that operate without friction are invisible. It is only when imbalances and frictions begin to occur that it becomes possible to see them. So, from the start, the concept of a regional architecture was not exactly what it seemed. It was more an object of desire than one objective fact. The architecture of regionalism put forward by the romantics was not that "authentic thing" of which it had formed a mental image, but only its representation. The question as to whether such an authentic thing ever existed is an idle one, so long as our only access to it is by means of its later conceptualisation. Nevertheless, the theory of regionalism adopted by the Modern Movement insisted on the need of such an architecture to be "authentic". Thus, what had to be eliminated were the very practices of the Romantics themselves, by which *Gemeinschaft*-like societies had been invoked by mimicking their forms. It was not by such means that the essence of regional architectures could be recovered, but rather by discovering the causal relations that existed between forms and their environment. But if what I have said is correct this would be a hopeless task, even if we restricted ourselves to the regionalisms of romanticism. What would be discovered after the outer layer of mimetic forms had been removed would simply be a deeper level of mimesis. The use of local materials, sensitivity to context, scale, and so on would all be so many ways of representing 'the idea' of an authentic, regional architecture. The search for absolute authenticity that the doctrine of regionalism implies is likely to create an oversimplified picture of a complex cultural situation.

Fear of such an oversimplified approach seems to have lain behind one of the more sophisticated recent theories of regionalism. By qualifying the old term "regionalism" with the new term "critical", Alexander Tzonis and Liane Lefaivre have tried to pre-empt any imputation of regressive nostalgia. According to them, the word "critical", in this context, means two things. First it means "resistance against the appropriation of a way of life and a bond of human relations by alien economic and power interests".[11] If we take away the mildly Marxian overtones of this statement what is left corresponds exactly to the notions of *Kultur* and *Gemeinschaft* that I have outlined above. It represents an attempt to preserve a regional essence that is seen to be in mortal danger and to uphold the qualities of *Kultur* against the incursions of a universalising and rationalising *Zivilization*. But any doctrine of regionalism has always implied such an intention, so that, taken in this sense, the word "critical" would seem to add nothing of substance to the concept. The second meaning Tzonis and Lefaivre give to the word critical is to create resistance against the merely nostalgic return of the past by removing regional elements from their natural contexts so as to defamiliarise them and create an effect of estrangement. This seems to be based on the Russian Formalist theory of "making strange".

These two meanings do not seem to have anything to do with each other. What is being presented as a single idea, "critical regionalism", is in fact two separate ideas. But the problem goes deeper, because the second interpretation of critical actually appears to contradict the first. It draws attention to the fact that the postulated organic world of regional artefacts no longer exists. Far from resisting the appropriations of rationalisation, it confirms them by suggesting that all that remains of an original, unitary body of regional architecture are shards, fragments, bits, and pieces that have been torn from their original context. Taking this view, any attempt to retrieve the original contents in all their original wholeness would result only in a sort of kitsch. The only possible attitude towards regionalism and the values of *Kultur* and *Gemeinschaft* would therefore be one of irony.

Behind the doctrine of a regionalism based on the old virtues of an organic (and therefore unconscious) social and artistic unity, lies the doctrine of a sophisticated manneristic art that consciously juxtaposes incongruous elements to produce unstable combinations. This being so, perhaps we should stop using the word regionalisms and look for other ways of conceptualising the problems to which the word is supposed to respond.

In saying this I am not saying that there are no longer any regions with their characteristic climates and customs. What I want to say is that regionality is only one among many concepts of architectural representation and that to give it special importance is to follow a well-trodden critical tradition that no longer has the relevance that it had in the past. It is true that many interesting contemporary designs refer to local materials, typologies, and morphologies. But in doing so their architects are not trying to express the essence of particular regions, but are using local features as motifs in a compositional process in order to produce original, unique, and context-relevant architectural ideas.

Take, for example, a recent building by the Swiss architects Jacques Herzog and Pierre de Meuron. In their small house in Italy there is play between local dry stone walling (standing for the rural) and a 'rational' concrete frame such that wall and frame are related in unexpected ways. It is impossible to read this building as a synthesis. Rather it is a sort of endless text. What we find here cannot be called "regionalism". Instead it is a work that makes subtle comments on a number of architectural codes, including the *fenêtre en longueur*, the cube, the frame, and the 'organicity' of natural materials. One is not quite sure whether what is being suggested is tectonic solidity or theatricality, closure, or openness. In contemplating the building the mind tends to oscillate between a number of hypotheses, none of which are completely confirmed or denied.

Another example is the housing recently built in The Hague, The Netherlands, by Alvaro Siza. Here Siza imitates—but rather indirectly—certain features of Dutch vernacular classicism, such as its entry system, window proportions, and materials. Can this be called regionalism? If so, whose regionalism? But is not the question an absurdity? The one fact that could be called "regional" is its ownership. If one wants to use the word "regional" in such a context one must see it as a second-order system, filtered through the eclectic sensibility of a particular architect. It is the result of a voluntaristic interpretation of urbanistic values, one that takes into account existing urban forms as an artistic context; it is certainly not a confirmation of a living local tradition. The architectural codes that were once tied to the customs of autonomous cultural regions have long ago been liberated from this dependence. It is a matter of free choice, localism and traditionalism can therefore be seen as universal potentials always lurking on the reverse face of modernisation and rationalisation.

One of the intentions of a regionalist approach is the preservation of 'difference'. But difference, which used to be insured by the coexistence of watertight and autonomous regions of culture, now depends largely on two other phenomena: individualism and the nation-state. As regards individualism, the architect, as the agent through which the work of architecture is realised, is himself the product of modern rationalisation and division of labour. Designs that emphasise local architecture are no more privileged today than other ways of adapting architecture to the conditions of modernity. The combination of these various ways is the result of the choices of individual architects who are operating from within multiple codes.

With respect to the nation-state, in spite of the world-wide and almost instantaneous dissemination of technologies and codes, which results in an underlying similarity of the architecture in all Western and most Eastern countries at any one moment, it is usually possible to distinguish between the more typical products of individual countries. In this sense, the nation-state is the modern "region"—a region in which culture is coextensive with political power. But this culture is of a different kind from that of the regions of the pre-industrial world. We may not quite agree with Ernst Renan when, in a lecture at the Sorbonne in 1882, he denied that national boundaries were dictated by language, race, religion, or any other "natural" factor.[12] But at least we can admit the truth of his statement that what creates a nation is a will towards political unity rather than any pre-existent set of customs. These two functions may be coextensive but they do not have to be. The need for placing regions that often differ from each other under a single political umbrella comes from the needs of the modern industrial economy. As Ernest Gellner has pointed out, the reasons for the rise of the nation-state were the opposite of those underlying regional differentiation. Differences between regions were part of the structure of the agrarian world. The needs of industrial society, on the contrary, demand a high degree of uniformity and the flattening out of local differences.[13]

Perhaps it will be argued that this is not true universally. Recent events in the ex-Yugoslavia and the ex-USSR have shown that old regional identities are still very much alive. But it is difficult to assess the status of regionalism in these cases, since it is obvious that ethnic emotions are being fanned for political reasons—that is, reasons connected with the formation of modern nation-states and the control of political power. The conflict in the ex-Yugoslavia cannot be attributed to profound differences in regional cultures but rather to residues of previous conflicts between the Habsburg, Ottoman, and Russian empires. As far as architecture and everyday artefacts are concerned, the cultures of the combatants are identical. The person who stands for the satanic 'other' is not marked by any specific cultural differences. Indeed one of the striking aspects of the television coverage of the war is that it is taking place in the familiar and banal context of badly built modern blocks of apartments and supermarkets—contexts common to the entire modern world.

A more plausible exception may be made of the so-called "developing world"—especially that part of the 'third world' consisting of ancient cultures, such as the Indian and the Islamic. In these countries, it will be argued, nationhood does sometimes coincide with living cultural traditions—traditions that are in conflict with modernisation. But however much we hope that crucial aspects of these traditions may turn out to be conformable with modernisation, we have to admit that the modern technologies and cultural paradigms that increasingly predominate in the urban centres of these countries also affect the rural areas. In these societies different historical times exist together, and under these circumstances it is already difficult to speak of 'authentic' local traditions in a cultural field such as architecture. It may be desirable to satisfy the demand for traditional forms with their socially embedded, allegorical meanings, even though the artistic and craftsman-like traditions that originally supported them have begun to atrophy, due to prolonged contact with the West. But these are matters of strategy rather than of essence.

With these questions we come to the core of the problem. What is the relation between cultural patterns and technologies? The problem is, to some extent, obscured in the West, because industrialisation evolved out of local cultural traditions, and adaptation to a post-industrialised culture is already quite far advanced. The problem is glaring, however, in the East and in Africa because of the friction between two worlds and two times: the agrarian and the industrial. Are cultural patterns absolutely dependent on an industrial base, or can they maintain a certain independence? Is an industrialised culture irrevocably Eurocentric?

But these questions take me too far from my theme, and I would like to end by looking again at the problem from the point of view of the technologically advanced countries, and at the same time to sum up my observations on the concept of regionalism, as it concerns these countries. Modern post-industrial culture is more uniform than traditional cultures because the means of production and dissemination are standardised and ubiquitous. But this uniformity seems to be compensated for by a flexibility that comes from the nature of modern techniques of communication, making it possible to move rapidly between codes and to vary messages to an unprecedented extent. This greater freedom, this ability of industrial society to tolerate difference within itself, however, does not follow the same laws that accounted for differences within traditional societies. In these societies, codes within a given cultural region were completely rigid. It was precisely this rigidity that accounted for the differences between different regions. In modern societies these regional differences are largely obliterated. Instead, there exist large, uniform, highly centralised cultural/political entities, within which differences of an unpredictable, unstable, and apparently random kind tend to develop.

The concept of regionality depends on it being possible to correlate cultural codes with geographical regions. It is based on traditional systems of communication in which climate, geography, craft traditions, and religions were absolutely determining. These determinants are rapidly disappearing and in large parts of the world no longer exist. That being the case, how is "value" established? Whereas in earlier times value belonged to the world of necessity, it now belongs to the world of freedom that Immanuel Kant foretold at the end of the eighteenth century. Modern society is polyvalent—that is to say, its codes are generated randomly from within a universal system of rationalisation that, in itself, claims to be "value free".

Clearly this way of generating meaning and difference in modern technological society has serious consequences for architecture, whose codes have always been even less amenable to individual and random manipulation than the other 'arts' and more dependent on impersonal and imperative typologies and techniques. In the pre-industrialised world these technologies—summed up in the Greek word *techne*—were connected with myths relating to the earth and the cosmos. In modern society "technique" is irreversibly disconnected from the phenomenal world of the visible, tangible experience upon which such myths were built. In the modern media the process of means-end abstraction has resulted in the rerouting of artistic codes from the stable to the apparently random. To speak more accurately, they have been rerouted from the public to the private realm. Such a process of "privatisation" has been suggested by Michel de Certeau, for whom modern technocratic life has not so much destroyed the myths and narratives characteristic of agrarian societies, as it has confined them to the family and the individual, where they reappear as fragments of an older narration.[13]

This, then, is the problem of architecture in the postmodern world: it seems no longer possible to envisage an architecture that has the stable, public meanings that it had when it was connected with the soil and with the regions. How should we define the kinds of architecture that are taking its place?

1   Gresleri, Guiliano, "*Vers une Architecture Classique*", *Le Corbusier: Une Encyclopedic*, ed. Jacques Lacan, Paris: Centre Georges Pompidou, 1987.
2   McLeod, Mary, "Le Corbusier in Algiers", *Oppositions 19/20*, Winter/Spring, 1980, p. 55.
3   Hobsbawm, Eric and Terence Ranger, *The Invention of Tradition*, Cambridge: Cambridge University Press, 1983.
4   Elias, Norbert, *History of Manners*, Oxford: Blackwell, 1994.
5   Thorn, Martin, "Tribes within Nations: the ancient Germans and the history of modern France", *Nation and Narration*, ed. Homi K Bhabha, London: Routledge, 1991, pp. 25–26.
6   Though the Irish revolt started much earlier, its cultural manifestations belong to the 1890s.
7   As had already happened in the Balkans earlier in the century.
8   Barrès, Maurice, as cited in Thorn, "Tribes within Nations", pp. 38–39.
9   Stewart Chamberlain, Houston, *Die Grundlagen des neunzehnten Jahrhunderts*, Munich, 1900. trans. into English as *Foundations of the Nineteenth Century*, New York, 1910.
10 Tönnies, Ferdinand, *Gemeinschaft und Gesellschaft*, Leipzig, 1887.
11 Tzonis, Alexander, and Liane Lefaivre, "The Grid and the Pathway: An Introduction to the Work of Dimitris and Susana Antonakakis", *Architecture in Greece*, no. 15, Athens, 1981.
12 Gellner, Ernest, *Nations and Nationalism*, Oxford; Basil: Blackwell, 1983.
13 de Certeau, Michel, *The Practice of Everyday Life*, Berkeley, CA: University of California Press, 1984.

Regionalism 2

First published in *Casabella,* January/February 1996.

I. Regionalism, Romanticism, Historicism

The discourse of regionalism belongs to the larger collection of ideas normally known as historicism, according to which cultural values, including those of architecture, are not *a priori*, unchanging, and universal but depend on particular, local, and inherited practices. This concept carries with it the apparently paradoxical assumption that one culture is able to "understand" another, thus reintroducing, at another level, the universalism that it has just thrown out. Regionalism also implies the belief that regional cultures are autochthonous and spring from the folk rather than from standards imposed by social and intellectual elites. Generally speaking, supporters of regionalism have been concerned with anonymous, vernacular architecture (though there are exceptions, as when classic traditions are identified with particular nation-states, to be discussed later).

Regionalism has always been implicated in a metaphysics of difference, rejecting all attempts to generalise cultural values into systems based on the concept of natural law or other such universalising theories.

The idea that culture is particular and hereditary rather than universal and rational sprang from anti-Enlightenment tendencies within eighteenth century thought, exemplified—though in different ways—by Herder and Vico. Later historicists were to see history as an evolving system, but for Herder and Vico history was a decline from a golden age, and this idealisation of the past was to be shared by the various regionalist movements of the nineteenth and twentieth centuries.

Historicism and romanticism led the attack on the classical system of the arts that had dominated Europe since the Renaissance. The Enlightenment had already disputed the mythical substructure of classical thought but it had left in place many of its concepts, including that of imitation. In romantic theory, imitation ceases to be the representation of external forms and becomes the revelation of an inner, organic, and indivisible structure. In a corresponding movement, historicism forbids the artist the freedom to combine, mechanically, as it were, different historical forms as if they were lying ready-to-hand in the same historical space. But the nineteenth century, in its obsession with the past, never freed itself from the classical tradition of imitation. The problem of how to recover eternal architectural values without imitating the forms in which they were embodied was apparently insoluble. Thus, there were two traditions leading to regionalism, one stemming from classicism and the other from romanticism; one figural and combinatory, the other functional and holistic.

II. Regionalism and Eclecticism

At first sight eclecticism would appear to be the antithesis of regionalism, with its doctrine of authenticity. Yet if we accept the proposition that regionalism was heir to two separate traditions and that its proponents have always had difficulty in relinquishing stylistic imitation, we must admit that the two concepts are dialectically related. Within eclecticism the criteria of choice are still the classical ones of propriety and character. Just as, in the classical tradition, the different orders were the appropriate metaphorical representation of certain ideas, so, in eighteenth century eclecticism, different styles produced certain associations. In both cases, architecture was seen as capable of creating specific moods in the observer.

In the classical tradition it was accepted that this was achieved by artifice, in other words by deception, (the *vraisemblable)*. Although this idea began to be challenged in the late eighteenth century, nineteenth century eclecticism still followed it implicitly. The romantic attack on the classical tradition was, on the contrary, based on the belief that the 'idea' could be symbolised without the mediation of secondary images. Translated into the terms of regionalism, this implied that the genius of the folk had a subtle body that persisted through changes in external form. This simultaneous appeal to the *Zeitgeist* and to the past depended on the possibility of the resurrection and transformation of an essence—an idea that could take hold only when history came to be seen as evolutionary and apocalyptic and the idea of a fixed golden age had lost its power.

III. Regionalism and Nationalism

Regionalism owed much of its influence to the growing power of the centralised nation-state. The relation between them was two-fold; on the one hand, peoples whose cultural identity had been suppressed used the concept of the *Volk* to legitimise claims to unification or independence: on the other, nation-states themselves sometimes idealised their own folk traditions. Germany in the early nineteenth century and France in the late nineteenth century are the main examples. It is often hard to distinguish between these two types. German romanticism, which was searching for a common cultural and political identity, was exported to France and England, both of which already had such an identity, and all three nations claimed a similarly reconstructed Medieval world as their own.

The phenomenon of international cultural traditions being used to reinforce the self-image of individual nation-states occurred again in the early twentieth century, when both Germany and France appropriated aspects of the classical tradition.

The romantic idea of the *Volk* and the positivist idea of material progress (and its corollary, liberal politics) were in contention with each other throughout the nineteenth century. In the 1890s there was a renewed burst of interest in folk myths, and this found expression in the movements of reform of the crafts as well as in the Art Nouveau Movement. These tendencies were simultaneously progressive and regressive. Enthusiasm for primitive, naif, and popular art prompted the rejection of classicism and the search for new forms. But they also encouraged a return to tradition and the condemnation of industrialism. In Belgium and Catalonia the Art Nouveau Movement emphasised modernity and novelty and became the emblem of a new industrial bourgeoisie. In Finland, on the other hand, it played a more mystical role, conjuring up remote folk origins, even if it represented these in the current idioms of the Arts and Crafts Movement, just as in the music of Jean Sibelius we find late romantic forms being used to convey the primitive essence of the Finnish landscape.

In Germany and France, too, conservatism existed alongside experimentalism. Julius Langbehn's best-selling book *Rembrandt the Educator,* 1890, claimed *völkisch* origins for a common Germanic *Kultur.* In France, Charles Maurras and Maurice Barrès promoted regional diversity and rejected a republicanism that had suppressed regional traditions in the name of an abstract, universal principle. This ideology was accompanied by a regionalist movement in architecture, equivalent to the *Heimatschutz* movement in Germany.

IV. Regionalism and the 1920s Avant-gardes

The pages of *L'Esprit Nouveau* testify to the antagonism of Le Corbusier to the eclectic regionalism that dominated popular architectural taste in post-war France. Le Corbusier was merely the most persuasive of those in Europe as a whole who opposed eclecticism with the ideal of universal modernism based on the abstract forms of modern painting and the industrialisation of the building industry.

Unlike Mies van der Rohe, who was still designing Biedermeier villas for wealthy clients as late as 1926, Le Corbusier had renounced his pre-war, Behrens-inspired neo-classicism. But he nevertheless claimed to be working within the French classical tradition—a claim that was in harmony with post-war French nationalist sentiment and critical opinion. It is not only in the context of post-war France that we find this *rappel à l'ordre*—this connection between modernism and classicism (a connection that had, in fact, already been made in *Werkbund* circles before the war). In Scandinavia the modernism of the 1930s grew directly out of the neo-classicism of the 1920s, as can be seen in the early work of Asplund and Aalto. In Germany, critics supporting the *Neue Sachlichkeit* movement in painting recognised its kinship with the French post-war neo-classicism of painters like Picasso. If we slightly extend the meaning of "classical", we can add to this list the Dutch *de Stijl* movement, which promoted a rationalism that was opposed to the idea of an organic architecture springing from the soil. But in spite of the predominantly rationalist spirit of the post-war avant-garde, *völkisch* and anti-rationalist ideas lay just below the surface. The "organic" or "functionalist" school in Germany, and the post-1929 work of Aalto (so enthusiastically championed by Giedion in the later editions of *Space, Time and Architecture),* proposed a regional modernism based on concrete local conditions and specific programmes.

Even before the First World War, as I have already suggested, classicism had been seen as an essential ingredient of regionalist architecture in France. It is therefore not altogether surprising to find Le Corbusier, in 1928, writing a book *(Une Maison—Un Palais)* in which a fisherman's hut is seen as the humble forerunner of 'high classicism', thus separating classicism from its aristocratic and elitist connotations. We seem to be dealing here with an abstract notion of classicism which, with its emphasis on ethnography, is conformable to romantic theory. From the late 1920s Le Corbusier's interest in vernacular and regional building increased. Disillusioned, like many French intellectuals of the period, with parliamentary democracy, he became involved with the proto-Fascist neo-Syndicalist movement, with its combination of populist regionalism and authoritarian technocracy. Unlike the governments of Germany and the USSR, which outlawed modernism and returned to eclecticism, Le Corbusier and the neo-Syndicalists conflated regionalism with modernism, believing that art and technology were inseparable and that modern architecture would become popular.

The belief that popular customs and regional traditions could be reconciled with modern technology remained the mainspring of Le Corbusier's work for the rest of his life. Already in 1929 he had stated the problem with characteristic lucidity:

L'Architecture est le résultat de l'état d'esprit d'une époque. Nous sommes en face d'un évènement de la pensée contemporaine; évènement international… les techniques, les problèmes posés, comme les moyens scientifiques de réalisation, sont universels. Pourtant, les régions ne se confondront pas, car les conditions climatiques, géographiques, topographiques, les courants des races et mille choses aujourd'hui encore profondes, guideront toujours la solution vers des formes conditionnées.

[Architecture is the result of the state of mind of its time. We are facing an event in contemporary thought; an international event, which we didn't realise ten years ago; the techniques, the problems raised, like the scientific means to solve them, are universal. Nevertheless, there will be no confusion of regions; for climatic, geographic, topographic conditions, the currents of race and thousands of things still today unknown, will always guide solutions toward forms conditioned by them.][1]

This statement can be taken as more or less representative of a post-1930s architectural avant-garde that sought a modernism that would be determined simultaneously by modern technology and by the perennial architectural values inscribed in regional materials and customs.

V. Regionalism and Late Capitalism

The statement by Le Corbusier quoted above makes several assumptions, the most important of which are:

1. Modern architecture is (should be?) conditioned by a universal technology.
2. Modern architecture is (should be?) conditioned by local customs, climates, etc..

Despite (or because of) the clarity of the statement, it presents two determinants as independent absolutes whose relation to each other remains a total mystery. What it ignores is the possibility that universal technology and local custom are intimately connected, so that a change in one necessarily produces a change in the other. The idea that they are somehow independent of each other seems to be derived from the Saint-Simonean notion that technical decisions made by specialists who "know what they are doing" merely provide the optimum conditions for the peoples' enjoyment of unchanging needs and desires. But under the conditions of late capitalism desires and needs do not remain constant. They are affected by the changing technologies which make them possible. This is precisely the difference between the modern and the pre-industrial world. But in revenge, if, in this way, desires seem to become fluid, the gross economic conditions that create this fluidity become increasingly universal, abstract, and interdependent. Once the economy as a whole is commercialised the 'natural' (ie. stable) relation between the individual and the social group ceases to exist, as sociologists like Georg Simmel and Max Weber pointed out many years ago. When subsistence farming gives way to cash crop farming (as has happened in Europe and is even now happening in, for example, India), the old symbiotic relation between culture and nature disappears. In Western Europe, manual, rural economies co-existed for a long time with industrialisation and this gave some plausibility to the regionalist argument. But in late capitalism the arm of technology extends into the remotest regions, even in the so-called "developing" countries which have no choice but to modernise.

The relationship between industrialisation and traditional cultures and techniques is not one in which they become organically fused with one another, as Le Corbusier implied, but one of hybridisation, where different cultural paradigms, detached from their original contexts, co-exist in an impure and unstable form. As an example of this in the area of urbanism, one can cite the co-existence of different economies in a city like Chandigarh, where an 'unofficial' economy of recycling has become necessary to facilitate the circulation of goods to the lowest social strata. (In Le Corbusier's plan such a theoretically impossible situation was not allowed for.) But this is the first stage of a process in which age-old habits become transformed and contaminated with international cultural paradigms spread by modern systems of communication. Local customs do not disappear completely; they become 're-territorialised'. Virtual cultures of choice take the place of cultures born of economic necessity. Dubrovnik becomes Disney World.

In conclusion, it is worth mentioning a third assumption in Le Corbusier's statement according to which society is conceptualised as an end-game situation. Culture is seen as having achieved a state of harmony and balance. An imagined and ideal state of organic unity is presented as a situation immediately attainable—an instant Utopia. In this situation of tautological illusion all 'solutions' become self-fulfilling prophecies. This is true both of the claim that there is a "spirit of the époque" and of the belief in the persistence of regional cultures. But the real situation is not one of cultural stasis and fulfillment, but of indeterminacy and change, in which a complex, interlocking global economy creates new forms out of old cultures as it goes along—forms whose precise and determinate nature cannot be foretold with any accuracy. Architecture will certainly, when the economic conditions allow, continue to imagine ideal socio-cultural forms, but its influence over social reality will be limited.

1   *Precisions: On the Present State of Architecture and City Planning*, trans. Edith S Aujame, Cambridge, MA: MIT Press, 1991, p. 218.

Axonometry, Ancient and the Modern

First published in *Alberto Sartoris: Torino*, 1992.

In the final paragraph of his essay "Perspective as Symbolic Form", Erwin Panofsky opposes perspective to another practice, which he sees as having dominated artistic representation in the ancient and oriental worlds, and as having, in a certain sense, reappeared with modernism (which he calls "Expressionism").[1] Panofsky does not specify this practice, but he does supply its protagonists with arguments against perspective. According to the ancients, perspective stands condemned because, to use Plato's words, it does not show the "true size" of things, and puts appearance above reality. According to the moderns, perspective fails because of its narrow rationalism. Although these criticisms seem at first sight to contradict each other, Panofsky has no difficulty in showing that the contradiction is only apparent. It makes little difference whether perspective is seen as betraying truth in its objective or subjective form, since in both cases what is involved is an unacceptable *schematisation of empirical experience*.[2]

The system at which Panofsky surely hints is what is now called "parallel or orthographic projection", particularly that branch of it known as "axonometry"—using this word broadly to include "oblique projection" in general. In this essay, I will use Panofksy's argument as the starting point for a discussion of the connection between the ancient or 'archaic' use of axonometry and its 'recovery' by the avant-garde of the 1920s, borrowing from previous research, particularly that of Bruno Reichlin, Yve-Alain Bois and Massimo Scolari.[3] In the period between the 'rediscovery' of perspective in the fifteenth century and the rise of modernism in the twentieth century—the whole period of 'modern history' in fact—parallel projection became restricted to the mathematical and technical sphere. Its increasingly instrumental role and its technical applications were obviously important factors in its adoption by an avant-garde dedicated to the concepts of modernity; but, if this might tempt us to attribute to axonometry a predominantly instrumental role in modern architecture, we still have to explain why it was hardly ever used in architectural representations in the nineteenth and early twentieth centuries. We are forced to acknowledge that its role in architecture, as in painting, was largely metaphorical, whether the metaphors were drawn from an aestheticised science, or from the world of metaphysical ideas. The question is: what is the connection between these two symbolic modes—between, on the one hand, a discourse that consciously uses archaic forms and metaphysical terms of reference, and on the other hand, the impulse towards the mechanical world of modern technology and science. Are we, here also, dealing with a contradiction that is more apparent than real?

Ancient Empirical Axonometry

The empirical use of axonometry is anterior to its theorisation. To describe its use in archaic art, it is not necessary, or even correct, to invoke the concept of 'projection'. What we mean by axonometry in the archaic context is the creation of a 'picture' of the three-dimensional world on a two-dimensional surface, such that there is no reduction of the size of objects as they recede from the observer. In the case of regular objects such as buildings and furniture, the lines bordering receding planes do not converge to a point but remain parallel, as they do in the 'real' object. Such a system does not describe objects as we actually *see* them, with the accuracy of perspective (though perspective is itself a schematisation of our experience), but it is closer than perspective to the way we form a mental image of objects, since their dimensions remain constant with distance; it is closer to our 'haptic' or 'muscular-tactile' apperceptions—those non-visual apperceptions that contribute to the synthetic representation of reality.[4] The conventions involved in archaic art are often called 'conceptual'. This is no more true of archaic art than it is of perspective. The exclusive use of 'conceptual' for pre-perspective representation leads to the fallacy that it is 'intellectual' and 'abstract', when in fact it is essentially concrete and intuitive. In some ancient art (Buddhist cave painting in India, Pompeian and Christian Medieval painting) empirical axonometry is often combined quite casually with rudimentary perspective. In this sense, therefore, perspective must be seen to be just as archaic as parallel projection. But precisely because of its unsystematic use, such perspective does not disturb the surface of the picture, and tunnel-like recession is avoided. In archaic painting, spatial depth is not measured by the size of objects, but by their position within the vertical field. The oblique plays an important role in this system, simultaneously representing depth, and belonging to the organisation of the surface *qua* surface, as in Chinese and Persian paintings. Although an observer is postulated in relation to the object, usually looking down upon it, he is placed at an indeterminant distance and does not occupy a singular position in relation to the scene depicted. The observer is an ideal observer.

The Metaphysics of Vision

If—rather than concerning ourselves with these empirical practices, we search for the earliest theorisations of representation—we are led beyond representation itself to optics and the projection of shadows. In ancient Greece, there are two competing theories of vision: that of Euclid, according to which rays emanate from the eye in a visual pyramid (extramission), and that of Leucippus (later modified by Democritus) according to which the images of things emanate from things themselves (intromission). There is possibly a connection between this pair of hypotheses and the experiments attributed to Apollonius in which shadows were used to project the celestial sphere onto a plane—'orthographic' or 'stereographic', depending on whether the source of light was the sun or a candle placed near to the sphere.[5] It is not too far-fetched to suggest a connection between this experiment and systems of representation, since it was a topos of early theory that the origins of painting lay in tracing the outlines of the shadow cast by a figure on the wall.[6] One only has, in imagination, to move the plane of representation to a position *between* the source of light and the object, to arrive at the two systems of projection that have competed with each other throughout history: that in which the rays converge, and are predicated on the human eye (or candle) and that in which the rays are parallel and are predicated on the eye of God (or the sun).

Roman painting tended towards the first hypothesis. In it we find a naturalism in which aerial and geometrical perspective exist alongside axonometry. Although at Pompeii we find many paintings which experiment with 'phenomenological' versions of perspective, involving the roving eye and multiple vanishing points, it seems probable that the theory of the single vanishing point existed in antiquity.[7]

Scolari shows that both Plotinus' aesthetic doctrine and that of the early Middle Ages were fundamentally hostile to the naturalistic view of the world implied by Roman perspective. He cites André Grabar who, in a famous essay, demonstrated the extent to which Plotinus' theory of vision influenced Medieval art.[8] The suppression of pictorial depth, the avoidance of foreshortening, the existence, in some cases, of reverse foreshortening, the delineation of a high degree of detail—all of these traits were consistent with a certain state of mind in the viewer. In this state of mind, in which beauty is supposed to be contemplated

Mosaic, Istanbul, circa 1320.

with the inner eye, the viewer loses all consciousness of self and is projected, as it were, into the object viewed and becomes similar to it. Objects lose their density and become transparent. The viewer's experience is more that of touching than of thinking. No explicit mention is made by Grabar of the use of axonometric, but it is implied by Plotinus' explicit rejection of perspective and his denial of any role to the empirical subject.

The early Medieval theory of vision came from Plato via Plotinus. It was the Arabs who, in the tenth century, initiated a renewed study of Greek optics as a whole. The first important text, Al-Kindi's *De Aspectibus*, was critical of Euclid's *Optica* on many points but accepted his theory of extramission. Among his arguments there is one based on the association (derived from Lucretius and the Atomists) between intromission and 'true' or coherent forms, and between extramission and accidental forms 'distorted' due to relative position. This suggests that while Arab theory implied a general connection between optics and systems of representation, it had little connection with Islamic artistic practice, which was based on axonometry and therefore committed to the representation of 'true' forms.

Alhazen's *De Aspectibus* or *Perspectiva* refuted the theory of extramission, but retained Euclid's visual pyramid and made it compatible with a theory of intromission that was no longer bound up with the idea of coherent form. His work must therefore be seen as a step towards linear perspective, albeit an unconscious one.

The thirteenth century revival of optics in Europe, associated with the names of Grosseteste, Roger Bacon, Pecham and Witelo, consisted of the reconciliation of Arab and Greek optical theory with a metaphysics of light derived from neo-Platonism. It is not possible to say, as it is in the case of Plotinus, that the optical theory of the thirteenth century has a coherent attitude toward artistic representation. In some ways it looked back to neo-Platonism, in other ways it prepared the way for the 'desacralisation' of optics and for the development of linear perspective. Indeed, much of the thirteenth century optics passed into the Renaissance more or less unchanged.[9]

The Schematisation of the Empirical and the Instrumentalisation of Axonometry

Medieval optics never became completely separated from metaphysics and dogmatics. It was the same with representation, the purpose of which was not to investigate what appeared to the individual subject but what existed *a priori*, in objective reality. In the Renaissance a new validity was given to the immediate données of subjective experience and to the representation of appearances. Beauty was held to result from the imitation (literal or idealised) of what was seen by the outer eye, not from the reproduction of what was seen by the inner eye.

This change is shown in the representation of architectural settings. After the late fifteenth century, these began to be represented in accordance with the rules of perspective as codified by Alberti and Piero della Francesca. But following the very impulse toward the investigation of the empirical that lay behind this application of perspective, an entire science of projection began to develop, which included parallel projection as well as perspective—a development that would not reach its climax until the late eighteenth century.[10]

A clear distinction began to be made between the representation of architecture as a *mis-en-scène* for human action in paintings, and the representation of architecture as a means to its conceptualisation and construction. In his letter to Pope Leo X of 1519, Raffael recommended that architectural drawings should be rigorously descriptive, in accordance with Vitruvius' two categories: *orthographia* (elevation) and *ichnographia* (plan), to which he added a third: the section. Vitruvius had also listed a third type: *scenographia* (perspective) but this was rejected because it only provided false information. The advantage of such drawings was that they provided the kind of precise information necessary to construct a building. Their disadvantage was that they provided this information in an analytic form that was difficult to interpret, and that did not provide a synthetic image. The only kind of drawing that could provide such an image and still present the building in terms of its true dimensions was the axonometric. Thus, the kind of objective 'truth' that had been demanded for representation in general by the neo-Platonists was now demanded from drawings whose sole purpose was pragmatic and instrumental. In both cases, what was needed was an 'image' that could be grasped instantaneously and did not require the intervention of discursive reasoning.

There are many examples of axonometric drawings being used for this purpose in the Renaissance. Leonardo da Vinci's "cavalier perspectives" of centralised churches and fortifications are the most famous. These are seen from a bird's eye position, which is also true of Peruzzi's beautiful cut-away views—especially that of his project for St Peter's, though this is in reality a perspective drawing with a very remote vanishing point. Machinery (which at this time was barely distinguishable from the building that housed and supported it) is often represented in the same way. An exception to this bird's-eye view can be found in the drawings of cornices in the *Codex Coner* (attributed to the School of Bramante) where the objects are presented from below in order to be able to see the carving on the soffits, anticipating the 'worm's-eye view' axonometric drawings of Choisy in the late nineteenth century.[11]

One of the most important applications of axonometry was in the representation of fortifications. It is here also, within a literature of war which developed as a specialised genre in the sixteenth century, that we find a theory of axonometry which explicitly sets it apart from perspective. Scolari cites several sixteenth and seventeenth century treatises on military axonometry, including GB Bellici's *Nuova invention di fabbricar fortezze* of 1598, in which the author justifies the use of axonometry because "we need to see the thing whole, distinct, clear: one can find truth precisely with compasses", and in which he claims that axonometry is superior to perspective because "one single view does not serve, since the whole has to be shown".[12] This quotation shows the extent to which the vocabulary of neo-Platonic aesthetics was adapted to the realm of pragmatics. The 'truth' which the drawing is supposed to reveal has shed its metaphysical connotations, but it is 'truth' nonetheless, and is a form of cognition.

The debate about Euclid's and Democritus' theories of vision, with their rival aesthetic implications, was resolved in the course of the sixteenth and seventeenth centuries by dividing the field of representation into two discrete parts. Mimesis in general became absorbed by perspective, while parallel projection and axonometry were preferred wherever the criterion of value was descriptive accuracy. Only in the nineteenth century with the development of non-Euclidian geometry by Lobachevsky, Gauss and Riemann would mathematics, by its own actions, be forced out of its specialised role and offer a challenge to the common sense view of the world that perspective had come to stand for. At this point—the moment of the avant-garde—assumptions of the 'naturalness' of perspective were questioned and positions were adopted that had something in common with Medieval aesthetics. The first moves in this direction can be seen in retrospect to have been taken by Gérard Desargues with the invention of projective geometry. The notion that parallel lines meet at infinity ceased to appear as a scandal as soon as what had been conceptualised as discrete realities became seen as moments along a continuum. Desargues, who worked in both pure and applied geometry, made improvements in gnomics (underlining, once again, the intimate connections between techniques of projection and the theory of shadows) and in stereotomy. These developments reached their culmination with the invention of descriptive geometry by Gaspard Monge in the late eighteenth century. With Monge the jumble of craft rules which had survived from the Middle Ages (eg. in stereotomy

Opposite: Etching from *The Different Artificial Machines*, Agostino Ramelli, Paris, 1588.

Above: Drawing from the *Codex Coner*, circa 1515.

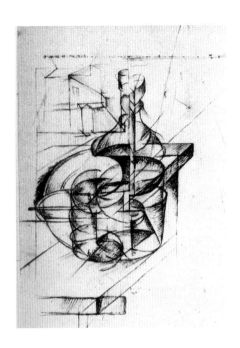

Bottle, Table and Houses, Umberto Boccioni, 1912–1913.

and carpentry), and which had been partially rationalised by Desargues, were finally generalised into a system which allowed for any three-dimensional problem to be solved on paper in terms of projections and traces. Monge's purpose was to put under unified intellectual control the new technologies emerging with the Industrial Revolution, and he had a more pragmatic counterpart in England in William Farish, who 'reinvented' isometric projection as a method of explaining to students the general principles of machinery.[13]

As Bois points out, the ground had been prepared for the introduction of axonometry by the avant-garde by the fact that axonometry began to be taught in schools of engineering in the late nineteenth century.[14] At the same time the writings of Viollet-le-Duc had led to a new aesthetic value being placed by architects on engineering, in direct confrontation with classical Beaux-Arts teaching. The 'worm's-eye view' axonometrics used by Auguste Choisy in his *Histoire de l'architecture* must be seen as part of this movement. By means of this drawing technique Choisy was able to demonstrate that the history of architecture and that of construction were co-terminous. His axonometrics was intended to show, in a synthetic image, the organic connection between the plan of a building and its structural evolution in three-dimensional space.

Axonometry and Modernism

The idea for which Viollet provided the ground and Choisy the technique, that the representation of architecture should not only provide a superficial and contingent picture of a building, but should disclose its inner structure, was undoubtedly one of the primary motives behind the use of axonometry by avant-garde architects. This attitude developed within the historical tradition that has been described, according to which a certain kind of drawing—parallel projection in all its forms—was reserved for technical representations. But it gave this tradition a new meaning. A technique which shows how an object works, becomes, with modernism, not merely a useful tool for the construction of something, but an example and a metaphor for the idea of construction itself. The work of art is now seen, not as the outward form of beauty (*schein*) but as a kind of 'working drawing' of reality. It is in this way that the axonometric drawing, as used by the architectural avant-garde, becomes a part of that which it is supposed to be describing, and is always needed to supplement the 'real' object and complete its meaning. In a certain sense, it no longer needs the object. What had been a means has become an end.

But it would be a mistake if, in drawing attention to this epistemological and 'intellectual' role of representation, we ignored the presence in the avant-garde of an equally strong anti-intellectual drive—that is to say, the impulse to provide an instantaneous, sensuous and non-discursive understanding of the world. This impulse was no doubt first felt in its modern form in romanticism, with the replacement of the allegory by the symbol, of the mirror by the lamp, but it has a more remote paradigm in neo-Platonism. The peculiarity and paradox of modernism was that it sought to achieve this non-discursive knowledge through the discursive concepts of science and technology.

Axonometrics can be found in some Cubist paintings, especially those of Juan Gris, where the diagonal plays a part in connecting depth to the surface. It also occasionally appears in Futurism, notably and strikingly in Boccioni's *Bottle, Table, Houses* in which a ghostly axonometric skeleton supports an image in which normally solid objects have become transparent and in which the invisible forces connecting them are revealed. This drawing illustrates perfectly the idea that Lissitzky attributed to the Futurists—that the observer should no longer exist outside the object, but partake of its space. The parallel between this idea and neo-Platonic aesthetics does not need to be underlined.

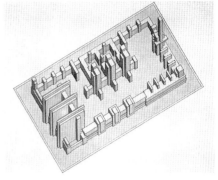

With the partial exception of Mies van der Rohe and Le Corbusier, axonometric projection was extensively used by avant-garde architects, and it would certainly be interesting to examine its role in the work of architects as different from each other as Hannes Meyer and Giuseppi Terragni. But it is in the work of three other figures that we see the greatest contribution to the use of axonometry in the avant-garde: Alberto Sartoris, Theo van Doesberg and El Lissitzky. Of the three, Sartoris was the only architect by profession and his drawings are the most 'architectural' and the least apparently concerned with problems of reflexivity and with metaphysical ideas. But with Sartoris no less than with the others, axonometry becomes an art form in its own right, intrinsically bound up with the 'content' of the objects it is describing.

Sartoris' formation belonged to the tradition of draftsmanship in which the draftsman became, in a certain sense, the paradigmatic artist/technician of architecture. This process represents a displacement of the ancient traditions of *technè*, creating a new role for the 'hand' of the architect in a world of mechanical reproduction—a role which 'imitates' the very thing that has disenfranchised it. At the same time ornament ceases to be made by handicraft, it is 'drawn', and, in the process, becomes strictly geometrical and subject to the law of the set square and T-square. Some of Sartoris' drawings of the early 1920s show how this concept of ornament, in which the traditional difference between 'form' and 'ornament' seems to be annulled, can be particularly well visualised by means of an axonometric drawing—indeed, hardly in any other way. It is as if the representational technique itself has suggested and generated the plastic language of the building. A different, but analogous, 'cubic' architecture, with its repeating forms in diminishing scale, can be seen in the maquettes of Malevich's *Arkitectons*, some of which he also represents in axonometric drawings. In both cases ornament has been abstracted into forms which are simply smaller three-dimensional versions of the overall form of the building.

Left: Leonardo da Vinci, Perspective drawing of a centralised church.

Right: Alberto Sartoris, Urban plan for the city university of Turin, 1927.

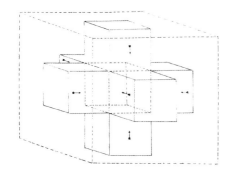

In Sartoris' work of the late 1920s this type of architecture, which still betrayed aspects of secessionist ornamentalism, is replaced by another, in which the form *becomes* the ornament, and all non-functional (non-iconic) elements are eliminated. This can be seen if we compare the final version of the *Padiglione alla mostra di Torino* of 1928 with the *Casa-Atelier per il pittore Salladin Van Berchem* of 1930. In the former, abstract 'scale-giving' elements are still attached to a simpler cubic volume, imitating traditional ornament, but lacking its meanings. In the latter, the cube of the building has been blown apart, and the functionally distinct volumes provide, in themselves and in their articulation, the play of differences necessary to generate meaning. But in viewing such a building 'in reality' the total meaning would only be revealed piecemeal, over time. An axonometric drawing allows this meaning to be registered instantaneously. By representing the building in such a way that all its dimensions can be perceived in one *coup d'oeil*, time is transformed into space.

The revolution that occurred in Sartoris' architectural ideas around 1927 was probably due to the example of van Doesburg's and van Esteren's axonometric drawings and maquettes of an 'artist's house', exhibited in Paris in 1923, one of the most powerful sets of images produced by the whole avant-garde. Contrary to usual belief, this was not van Doesburg's first excursion into axonometry; an earlier drawing (of 1922) shows a house broken down into cubes, just as the 'artist's house' will be further broken down into planes.

In Doesburg's axonometric drawings the object has been reduced to a system of planes, and has lost its impenetrable solidity. The eye can penetrate into its interstices; it has become part of space rather than something *in* space. The drawings exploit the spatial ambiguities of axonometric, and van Doesburg somehow saw them as a representation of the fourth dimension: "In a future period of the development of modern architecture the plan will disappear... thanks to non-Euclidian calculations in four dimensions."[15] The belief that there is a visual equivalent to the concept of *n*-dimensional space—a concept derived from analytical geometry which results from operating with four or more equations—seems like a simple category mistake. If so, it was a fairly common one among avant-garde writers and artists in the years immediately preceding the First World War.

In 1925, van Doesburg made axonometric studies of the 'Tesseract' or hypercube. This seems to have been based on a book by HP Manning of 1914 in which there is an illustration of "eight cubes which can be folded out to form a hypercube". It seems likely that this image, in turn, was derived not only from Charles Howard Hinton's book of 1906, *The Fourth Dimension*, but also from drawings of the 'glass box' which, around 1910, was used in the USA to illustrate the principle of 'third angle projection' as used in technical drawing. The unfolded views of this image can be reassembled into a D^3 cube, and in his book Manning proceeds, by analogy, to reassemble D^3 cubes into a D^4 hypercube.[16]

In the paintings of El Lissitzky, axonometry systematically replaces perspective. This substitution is all the more striking through its being made by placing recognisable architectonic forms in an infinite, gravity-less, illusionistic space (derived from Malevich) which sets up definite expectations of perspective. He even tries to enhance the feeling of disorientation and disembodiment in these paintings by sometimes giving each object its own axis of recession. As Bois points out, this procedure seems to weaken the vertiginous properties inherent in axonometric projection itself.[17] In fact, the spatial ambiguity of axonometry, which is such an important aspect of its use by the avant-garde, is more apparent in the representations of the Proun room shown at the *Grosse Berliner Kunstausellung* in 1923, where, as in van Doesburg's counter constructions, what would in reality be a temporal experience is transferred into an instantaneous spatial image.

El Lissitzky was sceptical about the possibility of giving sensuous form to the fourth dimension. He wrote, of non-Euclidian space: "Our senses are incapable of visualising these spaces, as opposed to mathematics which by its very nature

Outline representation of a *Tesseract*,
Theo van Doesburg, 1925.

operates independently of our senses... we can change the form of our physical space, but not its structure, ie its three-dimensionality."[18] But this avoidance of the 'category mistake' made by van Doesburg still allowed El Lissitzky to claim that modern art, by making use of the concepts of modern science, could symbolise irrational or imaginary space. El Lissetzky, in fact, wanted to retain the utopian aspect of modernism—but it was a materialist utopia, firmly based on technique, which rejected the mysticism which had entered the Russian avant-garde largely through the writings of Ouspensky.[19]

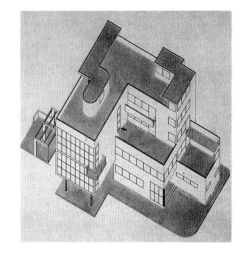

Within the historical avant-garde, science and mathematics operated metaphorically at two levels: at the level of the object as 'machine organism', and at the level of a metaphysics springing from developments in mathematics which, starting with Desargues in the seventeenth century, had threatened the common sense view of the world which science itself, with its schematisation of empirical evidence, had inaugurated in the first place. Nineteenth century science and mathematics opened up a world of paradox and unreason, remote from everyday assumptions and conventions, all the more awesome as its success in the 'real' world was confirmed. At this level, in renouncing concepts and practices which earlier science had established and legitimised and which common-sense had affirmed—notably perspective with its supposed 'naturalness'—modern artists and architects explored a realm of metaphysics reminiscent of that associated with systems of representation and theories of vision that had existed in the pre-modern world. At both these levels of metaphor, axonometry played a crucial part, by making possible that fusion of vision and cognition, of intuition and understanding which had characterised 'archaic' and Medieval aesthetics.

Did the recovery of axonometry, with its combination of modern science and archaic metaphysics, constitute a 'symbolic form', equivalent to that great system which Panofsky isolated in his essay? It certainly seems reasonable to assert that such a 'symbolic form' existed universally in the pre-modern world. But it would be wrong to suggest that we are dealing with the same phenomenon in the twentieth century.

Axonometry in the pre-modern societies, and perspective in modern society, were both systems of representation that corresponded to total ways of looking at the world and they had their equivalents in the other cultural forms of their time. The use of axonometry by the historical avant-garde cannot claim the same status. Far from being replaced by axonometry, perspective (and the subjective point of view that it represents) is just as persuasive as it has ever been, and dominates advertising, the electronic and photographic media and computer aided design. Axonometry represents a counter culture, but both it and the cluster of ideas that belong to it, though in some sense they continue to be relevant to today's neo-avant-garde, depend on the continued dominance of that very 'perspectival' view of the world which they put in question.

Top: Studio for the painter Saladin van Berchem, Alberto Sartoris, lithograph, 1930.

Bottom: Counter Construction, Theo van Doesburg, 1923.

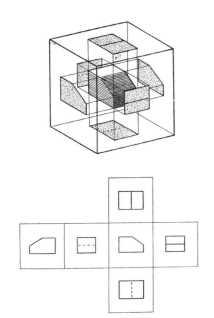

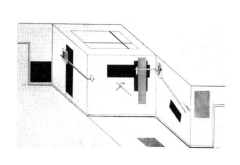

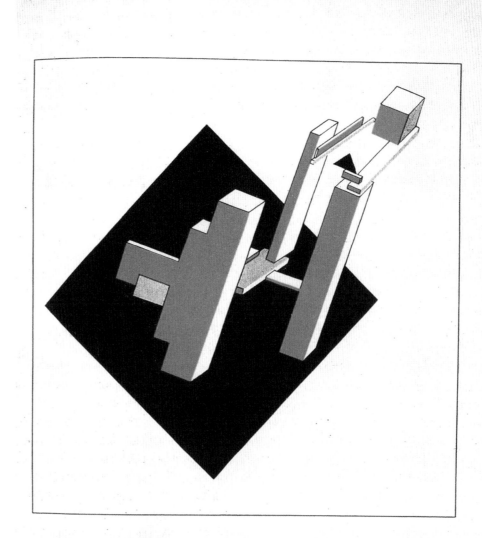

Top left: Outline representation of the "glass case" used to teach the projection of third angles in the engineering schools of America, circa 1914.

Bottom left: Rooms of Proun, El Lissitzky, Grosse Berliner Kunstausstellung, 1923.

Right: Lithograph, El Lissitzky, 1920.

1 Panofsky, Erwin, *Die Perspective Als Symbolische Form*, 1924–1925.

2 Panofsky, *Die Perspective Als Symbolische Form*.

3 Reichlin, Bruno, "Axonometry as project", *Lotus International*, no. 22; Bois, Yves-Alain, "Metamorphosis of Axonometry", *Daidalos* no. 1, 1981; and "Lissitzky, Malevich and the Question of Space", Gallerie Chauvelin, *Suprematisme*, pp. 29–46; Massimo Scolari, "Elements for a History of Axonometry", *Architectural Design*, 55 5/6.

4 The term "Muscular Tactile" is used by William Ivins Jr. to describe the general characteristics of Greek art; *Art and Geometry. A Study of Space Intuitions*, New York, 1964. The word "haptic" was used by Aloïs Riegl to describe the early phase of artistic practice in the general evolution of art from the haptic (or tactile) to the optic. For a discussion of 'primitive' representation as found in early societies and in children, see Rudolf Arnheim, *Art and Visual Perception*, London, 1967.

5 See PJ Booker, *A History of Engineering Drawing*, London, 1963, chapter 1.

6 See Oeschslin, Werner, "Geometry and Line. The Vitruvian Science of Architectural Drawing", *Daidalos*, no. 1, pp. 25–35.

7 See John White, *The Birth and Rebirth of Pictorial Space*, London, 1967, pp. 250–255. White gives a convincing argument in support of the view that Vitruvius' brief and obscure remarks concerning perspective (*De Architectura*, Book I, Chapter 2, and Book VII, Preface) refer to the concept of the single vanishing point.

8 Grabar, André, "Plotin et les origins de l'esthetique medievale", *Cahiers Archeologiques*, no. 1, 1945. Scolari discusses this essay at some length, but does not emphasise the connection between neo-Platonic aesthetics and modernism.

9 See Scolari, Massimo and David Lindberg, *Theories of Vision from Al-Kindi to Kepler*, Chicago, 1976.

10 In terms of a *systematic* definition, axonometry is part of descriptive geometry, ie it is a method of projection enabling a three-dimensional object (say, a cube) to be represented on a flat surface. It shares with orthographic projection (plan, elevation, section) the fact that the centre of projection is at infinity, and the radii are at 90 degrees to the picture plane. It differs from it in that the radii are oblique to the object. The representation of a cube by its XYZ axes provides a 'secondary geometry' by which to construct an axonometric without projection.

Axonometry is a generic term, and there are different kinds of axonometric drawings. One distinction is based on the relative scales of the three axes. In an *iso-metric* all axes are to the same scale and there is no foreshortening (the only kind of projection which yields this is that in which the radii are parallel to the diagonal of the cube, producing the 'isometric cube' inscribed in a hexagon). In a *di-metric* and a *tri-metric*, two and three axes are of different scales respectively.

Another distinction is that between drawings in which all surfaces are oblique to the picture plane and those in which one surface is parallel to it: 'oblique projection' in the case of one of the elevations, 'planometric projection' in the case of the plan. Architects have tended to prefer planometric projection, because of the traditional importance assumed by the plan in the conceptualising of a building.

11 See Lotz, Wolfgang, *Studies in Italian Renaissance Architecture*, pp. 11–17 and pp. 181–186. Lotz describes these drawings, however, as "perspectives".

12 Massimo Scolari.

13 PJ Booker draws attention to the different attitudes towards technical drawing in France and in the Anglophone countries. Whereas in America, and to a lesser extent in England, the approach was purely pragmatic, in France it was theoretical—a difference which reflects the philosophical distinction between empiricism and rationalism. Monge's doctrine and the rationalist philosophy that it represented was disseminated throughout the continent of Europe by Napoleon's conquests, whereas it was only sporadically applied in England and America.

14 Bois, "Metamorphosis in Axonometry".

15 Theo Van Doeburg, "L'Evolution de l'architecture moderne en Hollande", *Architecture vivante*, Autumn and Winter 1925, p. 18.

16 See Dalrymple Henderson, Linda, *The Fourth Dimension and Non-Euclidean Geometry in Modern Art*, chapters 1 and 5. See also, Booker, chapter 14.

17 Bois, "Lissitzky, Malevich and Questions of Space".

18 El Lissitzky, "K und Pangeometrie", in *Europa Almanach*, Potsdam, 1925.

19 See Henderson, chapters 1 and 6.

Criticism and Self-criticism
in German Modernism

First published in *Moderne Architektur in Deutschland*, 1900–1960, 1994.

I

Reforming or revolutionary artistic movements were common to most of the major industrialised countries between the last decades of the nineteenth century and the onset of totalitarian regimes in the early 1930s. But architectural modernism and the debates surrounding it took a unique form in Germany—a form at once idiosyncratic and exemplary. This was inevitable, given the intense philosophical discussions that had taken place during the later nineteenth century in Germany concerning the implications of industrial capitalism, invoking an already well-established distinction between *Kultur* and *Zivilisation*. The notion of *Kultur* had been borrowed by the French and English Romantics, but in those countries the debate was cushioned by relatively stable institutional structures and did not strongly influence national policy (though in England it produced the influential Arts and Crafts Movement with its critique of artistic standards in conditions of industrial manufacture).[1] In Germany, however, owing to its recent unification, its relatively archaic political institutions, and the demographic instability caused by extremely rapid industrialisation, *Kultur* and *Zivilisation* became the *mots-clef* for a broad social and political movement of national renewal. The more purely artistic aspects of modernism in Germany, and the intense debates which they generated, can therefore be fully understood only as part of a more extensive debate concerned with national identity in the context of the rapidly disappearing values of pre-industrial society. It was precisely these values which, ever since the release of Germany from the hegemony of French culture after the Napoleonic wars, had seemed to many to represent all that was quintessentially German, in contrast to the rationalism and materialism of the Western countries, with their roots in the Enlightenment. Yet Germany herself had become industrialised, and because industrialisation in that country had come into collision with feudal structures its effects had been even more destructive of traditional values than they had been in France and England, where modernisation had taken place more gradually. Modernism in Germany was part of the general problem of *Modernisation*, affecting every aspect of social and cultural life, and we find the same terms of reference being adopted by both conservatives and progressives. Many of the nostalgic, folk-based ideas of nationalists like Paul de Lagarde and Julius Langbehn penetrated the avant-garde, while at the other extreme a positive evaluation of modernity and the machine was shared by modernists and many right wing thinkers.[2] It is against this confused background that we must interpret the passionate discussions that took place in Germany in the first three decades of the twentieth century, not only between modernists and traditionalists but also within modernism itself.

II

Between 1900 and 1914 there were two main strands within modernism, which were in fundamental conflict with each other. The first was the tradition of Arts and Crafts and *Jugendstil* Movements, which, though dedicated to new forms, were permeated with a nostalgia for pre-industrialised patterns of life. The second was the drive towards modernisation and the acceptance of all the implications of machine production. Although both ideologies were concerned with the relation between art and life, each had a different view of what this relation should be. To use Ferdinand Tönnies' famous distinction, the Arts and Crafts tradition staked the survival of art on the preservation of *Gemeinschaft* type social relations and a direct, personal and intuitive connection between the artist and the material to be transformed, while for those who saw the machine as inevitably superseding handicraft it was essential to reconcile art with *Gesellschaft*-type organisations and a mediated, impersonal and intellectual relation between artist and material.[3] It is important to stress that the problem of the abstract nature of machine production was taken up in connection not only with the decorative or applied arts, but also with art and architecture in general. It became a matter of deciding the extent of the similarities and differences between two processes of conceptualisation, artistic and scientific. Critical opinion tended to be polarised between those for whom abstract conceptualisation meant materialism and those for whom it was the essential means by which matter is transformed into Form and Idea. Hence two different views of the Enlightenment developed, one in which it was seen as having been the precursor of a materialistic positivism and the other in which it appeared to usher in the rule of reason and freedom.

III

The main forum for a positive view of the machine in connection with applied art was the Werkbund. Formed in 1907, the Werkbund was modelled on the English Arts and Crafts Society, but it also had German antecedents such as the Vereinigte Werkstätten and the Dresdner Werkstätten which, though modelled on the English 'Guilds', had already come to terms with the machine. Another antecedent was the Dürerbund, founded in 1902 by Ferdinand Avenarius to advise the government, the public and business on aesthetic matters. Avenarius was also a founder member of the Werkbund.[4] Though a concern for handicraft was still stressed by many members of the Werkbund, and could be justified by the fact that modern production techniques had by no means eliminated all manual operations, the chief emphasis among the designer members of the Werkbund was on the need to understand the characteristics of modern materials and machine techniques.

Although the aims of the society were essentially practical and political (improvement of quality and the creation of an export market), they also had a theoretical dimension. Already at the first Werkbund congress of 1908, the sculptor Rudolf Bosselt promoted the idea that aesthetics were independent of material quality and that abstract *Gestaltung* was more important than material and construction.[5] In saying this he was clearly implying that the role of the artist in forming a concept of the work was equally important in both handiwork and machine work, and, in this sense, the notion of *Gestalt* took a position 'above' the dispute over the precedence of handicraft or machine production. Peter Behrens put forward a similar theory claiming that the sources of modern architecture lay in classicism, not in Gothic, as had been maintained by the Arts and Crafts and *Jugendstil* Movements (to which he himself had belonged only a year or two earlier). According to Behrens, modern architecture should be based on "proportionality and order".[6] Since industrialisation, in substantially eliminating the artisan, had also eliminated ornament, the aesthetic effect of modern buildings should depend solely on the disposition of their masses, whose smooth surfaces and regular rhythms were appropriate to an age of speed.[7] (Similar ideas had already been put forward in Austria by Otto Wagner.)

The implication that form took precedent over material and technique, though it contradicted the theories of the followers of Gottfried Semper, had a long history in nineteenth century German aesthetic theory, beginning with the psychological approach to aesthetics of Herbart and Zimmermann.[8] But its immediate source, as was acknowledged by Behrens himself, lay in the neo-Kantian theories of Conrad Fiedler, Adolf Hilderbrand and Hans von Marées, according to which the content and idea of a work of art consisted exclusively in its visual formal organisation.[9] "The content of the work of art", Fiedler had said, "is nothing but the formation (*Gestaltung*) itself."[10] This idea also influenced late nineteenth century art historians such as Alöis Riegl and Heinrich Wölfflin. The former's concept of the *Kuntswollen* was at least in part derived from the theories of Fiedler. It is through such 'critical historians', as well as through the direct influence of Peter Behrens, that formalist theory was to become an important subtext of the post-war *Neue Sachlichkeit* movement.

IV

The change in critical thought and practice from Gothic to classical paradigms that we see in Behrens was not confined to Germany. In the 1890s an equivalent change in public taste took place in England and America—a change that was reflected in the work of Edwin Lutyens and McKim Mead and White. In France, in the first decade of the twentieth century, Auguste Perret reinterpreted Viollet-le-Duc's rationalism in terms of classicism, while in the field of interior design the 'coloristes' replaced the Art Nouveau *Gesamtkunstwerk* with matching neo-classical ensembles.[11] This movement had strong affinities with the work and ideas of Adolf Loos in Vienna. These facts are mentioned not to try to establish direct causal connections between the various phenomena (though in the case of France there does seem to have been direct German influence), but merely to counteract any impression that events in Germany took place within a cultural vacuum.[12] In Germany, the problem of whether to follow Medieval or classical models was an aspect of the more general dichotomy between *Kultur* and *Zivilisation*.

In a fundamental way this conflict was also the basis of the dispute between Muthesius and Van de Velde at the 1914 Werkbund congress in Cologne, in which Van de Velde attacked Muthesius' concept of *Typisierung*. But in this case the polemic was more immediately concerned with artistic politics than with aesthetic theories. Van de Velde's attack on Muthesius was not based on a narrow defense of handicraft, since, although he was suspicious of industry, he had always acknowledged the importance of the machine in modern design.[13] It was, rather, a rejection of what he saw as the attempt by Muthesius to bureaucratise art in the interest of the State, with a consequent loss of freedom for the artist. Van de Velde did not deny the tendency of every artistic tradition to establish its own standards of quality; what he did deny was that the *a priori* imposition of such types, under the protective mask of the theory of classical order and anonymity, would ever lead to a higher quality of design.[14] Le Corbusier, who accepted Muthesius' classical thesis, but linked it to a theory of the Darwinian evolution of forms, was later to accuse Gropius of enforcing just such *a priori* limitations at the Bauhaus. But, in fact, Gropius supported Van de Velde in the Cologne dispute and was equally opposed to Muthesius' attempt to limit the freedom of the designer. This fact reinforces the view of Marcel Franciscono that Gropius' involvement with Expressionism when director of the Arbeitsrat für Kunst in 1919 was not so complete a break with his pre-war ideas as is often supposed.[15]

V

The debates so far discussed belonged to critical positions which either privileged the applied arts (Van de Velde) or which drew conclusions from aesthetic theory or architecture, seen as a discipline with its own formal and tectonic traditions (Behrens). But in 1911, on the European stage, a series of radical and closely interrelated developments took place in painting which would have a wide-ranging effect on architecture and provide it with a new formal vocabulary outside its own traditions, and a new way of thinking of the machine in relation to architectural aesthetics. Cubism, Futurism and Expressionism were all characterised by a rejection of imitation and a denial of the solidity or finality of forms, and, as such, can be seen as a fulfilment of Fiedler's theory of pure visibility, which has been given a neo-classical interpretation by Behrens. According to one closely argued view, the word "expressionism" was originally coined in France to describe Fauvism and especially the painting of Matisse (nature filtered through a subjective vision), but it quickly came to designate German modernist art in general.[16] A contemporary German dictionary refers to expressionism as "that direction of present-day art which strives to express the inner experience instead of impressions from the outer world… it is always influenced by the material of the art (colour, line, surface, sound, rhythm) and always works with them, awakening or increasing feelings but not imitating nature".[17] The word was first used in German literary criticism in 1911, by Otto zur Linde, as a label for the Charon group of poets who were opposed to impressionism (*Ausdruckskunst* versus *Einsdruckskunst*).[18] According to the art critic Wilhelm Hausenstein, writing in 1919, Expressionism had two poles: the metaphysical and the formal.[19] Adopting these categories, it is clear that, from a formal point of view, Expressionism was part of an evolution within specific genres, while 'metaphysically' it had far broader implications, and aimed at dissolving the barriers between the genres and between art and life.

Before the war, the Expressionist painters had been involved in a running battle with the Wilhelmine art establishment.[20] Immediately after the war, their anti-establishment ideas were converted, for a brief moment, into a programme of political action, spurred by the hope that political revolution in Germany would make it possible to put an end to the capitalist art market, dismantle the imperial art institutions, and create a new proletarian art public.[21] Much of the pre-war architecture that later came to be called "Expressionist" was closer to the spirit of Jugendstil than to the Expressionist movement in painting. In 1918 and 1919, however, a new solidarity developed between architects and painters in the context of the Arbeitsrat für Kunst and the Novembergruppe, which were modelled on the groups being formed at the same time by revolutionary workers and soldiers. The term "expressionist" was used at this time to describe not only the new painting, but also the Cubist and Expressionist inspired architectural drawings produced by architects and other members of the Arbeitsrat.[22] The architects Bruno Taut and Walter Gropius and the architectural critic Adolf Behne were the leading figures in the Arbeitsrat für Kunst. These groups were, in a sense, rivals of the Werkbund, which was perceived by the radicals to be an instrument of imperialism and commercial interests—a point of view to which, however, Taut, Gropius and Behne had subscribed even before the war.[23] None the less, in spite of the critical attitude of the radical architects towards the Werkbund, they continued to be members and were able to influence its policies from within. The radical architects were in conflict with both the pre-war ideas of the Werkbund and the 'revolutionary conservatives'. On the one hand, they subscribed to the idea of the unity between art and the *Volk* and were opposed to art being dominated by capitalist values; on the other hand, they also opposed the views of revolutionary conservatives like Karl Scheffler, who proposed the dismantling of industrial production in favour of a national reversion to handicraft.[24]

For a short time the conservatives and their allies amongst the older generations of Art and Crafts architects gained control of the Werkbund, but eventually—in 1923—the Werkbund broke with the Arbeitsgemeinschaft für Handwerkskulter and other conservative groups such as the Bund Heimatschutz.[25] By this time the Expressionist movement had disintegrated and the Werkbund had become identified with the new progressive movement: the *Neues Bauen*. The Werkbund journal, *Die Form*, which had run for a few issues in 1922, resumed publication in 1925.[26] Its main concern was now with architecture and urbanism rather than with the applied arts. In this it followed a general post-war trend in Europe, which emphasised architecture as metaphor and instrument of reconstruction, especially in the realm of housing.[27]

VI

The political role of the Expressionists was highly ambiguous. Joan Weinstein has shown how precarious the movement's claim to revolutionary status was in the light of its *de facto* co-option in 1919 by both the capitalist art market and the SPD.[28] Criticism of the government's artistic policy by leftwing Expressionists like Adolf Behne did not prevent increasing accusations from the left—particularly by the Dadaists—that the Expressionists had sold out to the Weimar establishment.

In a well known essay written in 1934, Georg Lukács launched a retrospective attack on Expressionism, maintaining that the fragmentary and nihilistic nature of Expressionism was a reflection of bourgeois decadence, and not, as the Expressionists themselves claimed, a critique of bourgeois values.[29] This accusation of Expressionist bad faith was made from a standpoint of Socialist Realism—a position not shared by all Marxists. In 1938, for example, Ernst Bloch sharply contested Lukács' essay, accusing him of having failed to liberate himself from classical systems, and defending Expressionism as a genuine reflection of utopian ideals.[30] Bloch saw the nihilistic aspect of Expressionism as a necessary part of the transition from the old world to the new.

VII

The mood of the avant-garde in Europe after the war was one favouring collectivism, realism, reconstruction and modernisation, in contrast to the anarchistic utopianism of the pre-war movements. This is true whether we are looking at the conservative modernism of the *Rappel à l'ordre* or the movement associated with the journal *Valori Plastici* in France and Italy, respectively, the radical Constructivism and Productivism in the USSR, or the bitter, sardonic realism of the *Neue Sachlichkeit* painters in Germany. It is the *Neue Sachlichkeit*, in so far as it applies to both painting and architecture, which concerns us here. The term was first used by Gustav Hartlaub in 1923 or 1924 to describe the 'post-Expressionist' paintings that he was arranging to exhibit in 1925 in the Kunsthalle, Mannheim. Hartlaub wanted to demonstrate the existence of a universal post-war trend towards realism, and his original plan had been to include neo-classicists from France, like Picasso, alongside German 'magic-realists'.[31] The term *Neue Sachlichkeit* was also sometimes used to describe the architecture of the *Neues Bauen* movement.[32]

The concept of *Sachlichkeit* had been common in architectural criticism before the war. It had been introduced by Muthesius (who probably took it from Alfred Lichtwark), to describe sober, unornamented design, and it became very popular around 1902.[33] There was thus a certain continuity between pre-war and post-war ideas, and many of the concepts used by the Werkbund between 1907 and 1914 were 'reactivated', after the interregnum of Expressionism. Yet there were fundamental differences between Behren's idealist wish to 'spiritualise' and dignify the machine in terms of timeless classical principles, and the spirit of the *Neues Bauen*. Some of these differences can be attributed to the influence of Expressionism itself, particularly the tendency towards abstraction, the rejection of all traditional stereotypes, the 'overvaluation' of architecture and the belief in its power to transform social reality. But others were more like an extension of pre-war ideas: the acceptance of 'Amerikanismus' and Taylorism, and the

Gestaltung of rational organisation. Above all, the 'object' was reconstituted, albeit in accordance with a new model: the machine.

VIII

In his book *Post-Expressionism: Magic Realism* of 1925, the critic Franz Roh compared Expressionist and *Neue Sachlichkeit* paintings in the following terms:

> The expressionist generation had rightly opposed [Impressionism] with a man of ethical norms... the utopian who disdains mere connoisseurship of a life already lived.... The most recent artist corresponds to a third type. He does not abandon any of the constructive goal-directedness, but he does know how to combine it with an intensified down-to-earth quality, a savouring of what exists, as well as with objects to be intensified. This is neither the 'empirical political' and Machiavellian, nor the un-political, exclusively moral philosopher, but the ethical *homo politicus*, with equal emphasis on both concepts. The new situation... will be the narrow path bordered by the abysses typical of the left and the right.[34]

This perfectly exemplifies the cautious and 'realistic' policies of the Weimar Republic, and provides an excellent framework within which to discuss the architectural controversies of the 1920s. Roh's book also contains a table setting out the oppositions between Expressionism and the *Neue Sachlichkeit*, the following selection from which would seem to apply equally to painting and architecture:

Expressionism	Post-Expressionism
Ecstatic objects	Sober objects
Extravagant	Severe, puritanical
Warm	Cool, even cold
Like unfinished stone	Like polished metal
Rich in diagonals, tilting, often pointed	Usually at right angles, parallel to the frame
Contesting the limits of the frame	Respecting the frame
Primitive	Cultivated.

IX

The continuities and discontinuities between pre-war and post-war ideas of the avant-garde, and between Expressionism and *Neue Sachlichkeit*, can be studied in the critical writings of Adolf Behne, who had begun to play an important role in formulating the ideology of the avant-garde when he was associated with the Arbeitsrat für Kunst. At this time he was an ardent supporter of Expressionism, sharing its belief that socialism would engender a truly popular and spontaneous art and architecture, breaking with every tradition. In the essay "*Ruf zum Bauen*" of 1920 Behne made a passionate plea for a visionary architecture rather than an architecture concerned with immediate practical problems.[35] The essay is heavily millennialist in tone, consciously drawing on the ideas of Paul Scheerbart's *Glas Arkitektur*, and arguing that architecture should have a determining role in the creation of a new society. Although he denies that he is an Expressionist—"it is building itself that will free us from problems and from all the 'isms' there are"—he denigrates the practical and technical aspects of buildings in favour of an architecture of 'fantasy'. Perhaps, rather than lingering over this apparent contradiction, we should see the article as a confirmation of the continuities between expressionism and the new *Neues Bauen*. And, indeed, there is another idea in the article which suggests that the metamorphosis that took place in Behne's thinking when he espoused the *Neues Bauen* a year or so later was not so complete as it seems, and that, as with Gropius, the changes of allegiance from Expressionism the *Neues Bauen* primarily marked a change of form, and was only partly a change of substance. The idea in question is the following: "What is small must derive from what is great, from the whole."

This is a concept that reappears and is developed in much greater detail in the essay "*Kunst, Handwerk, Technik*" of 1922.[36] Ostensibly a rebuttal of Expressionist philosophy, this essay starts with a denial of the opposition to *Technik* which had been axiomatic for both the Arts and Crafts Movement and Expressionism. The division of labour that is characteristic of machine work is now seen as superior to *Handwerk*. The difference between *Handwerk* and *Technik* is merely that *Technik* tends toward a greater degree of intellectualisation. Craft work, far from privileging imperfections and idiosyncrasies, as Ruskin had taught, had always aimed at the greatest possible precision. Therefore, to the extent that machine work achieves greater precision it is superior to craft work. Division of labour, with its abolition of the personal, is an improvement on the old 'organic' relation between the individual craftsman and his task, because it is the result of a higher consciousness. The worker loses his personality, but in exchange receives a membership card to a greater whole. His work, because it is part of a supra-personal unity, becomes spiritualised and dematerialised. At the same time social life becomes collectivised, and the means to this collectivisation is the machine. We are now in a period of transition, leading from a position in which the worker is a mere cog in a machine, to one in which he will understand the totality of which he is a part. At this point he will no longer need to identify himself with his 'calling'. The relationship between man and God is also different. Instead of being reified and personalised, but impotent, God becomes diffuse, but all-powerful. The disappearance of craft work will not destroy art. There is a fundamental difference between art and craft. The unity of hand work is organic, while the unity of art is constructed out of discrete parts, and depends on the separation of disciplines and the furthest possible development of each. We should no longer look on Gothic and the Medieval *Gesamtkunstwerk* as the models for artistic unity. The work of art, considered as an organisation of parts, is a *Gesellschaft*. Art is similar to technology; in both, the dominant role is played by the conceptualising intellect. Behne quotes Lu Märten as saying that, as daily life becomes shaped into pure, honest, functional forms, art will be reabsorbed into life and lose its independent identity.[37]

The theory of the *Neues Bauen* summarised here contains many of the ideas being put forward at the same time, though with a different emphasis in each case, by van Doesburg, El Lissitzky and Le Corbusier. It embraces the *Gesellschaft*-type of organisation typical of industrialised societies and rejects the *Gemeinschaft* characteristics of pre-industrial societies as outdated and inferior. It associates architecture with art rather than with the applied arts. It sees both art and architecture as governed by the concept of *Gestaltung* and as created in the mind of the artist. Its aesthetic assumptions are based on the theories of Fiedler and Riegl (though, in fact, many of these ideas had also been claimed for Expressionism by Wilhelm Worringer).[38] It postulates an elective affinity between art and technology, and thus goes further than Behrens and Muthesius in incorporating the machine into architectural aesthetics. But it does not simply oppose *Technik* to *Handwerk*, and embrace the former at the expense of the latter. It transforms the idea of *Technik*, bringing it over to the opposite camp. Industrial production is no longer seen as alienating man from community, from the whole, but as connecting him with a greater whole. The community that the 'new man' is invited to join exists in a sphere closer to the Godhead, and is illuminated by an intellectual light reminiscent of neo-Platonic cosmology. It is in this sense that the quasi-religious and the utopian ideas of Expressionism, far from being condemned in the name of a pragmatic realism, have been absorbed and redefined. Both Expressionism and the *Neues Bauen* depended on totalising theories based on a Cartesian separation of spirit and matter, subject and object; the difference between them is that, in the case of the *Neues Bauen*, the spirit has been able to descend to earth because the earth (in the form of the machine) has been dematerialised by the intellect of man. It can now be seen how, in 'Bauen', Behne could have combined such apparently incompatible ideas with a good conscience. The previously cited sentence should now be given in full:

> What is small must derive from what is great, from the whole; otherwise it is trivial. The whole cannot be obtained through the parts; the whole embraces the parts. Our aim is the whole. Our castles in the air are built on firmer foundations than the hasty day-to-day work which seems so down-to-earth. In reality it is not rooted in the earth at all, but planted out in little subdivided plots and parcels of land. Our castles in the air stand on the earth, on the stars, on the firmament, on the whole.[39]

X

The *Neues Bauen* was not a seamless system. In spite of its acceptance of the new technology, it had absorbed, without fully digesting, the conflict between *Kultur* and *Zivilisation* that had dominated the pre-war avant-garde. One example of this has already been mentioned: the transfer by Behne of Taylorism onto the side of *Kultur*. Continuing to use Behne as a touchstone for contemporary theory, we find other traces of *Kultur* and *Lebensphilosophie* which seem to be in conflict with the rationalist aspect of the *Neues Bauen* movement. In his book *Die Moderne Zweckbau*, of 1926, Behne reintroduces the theme of the 'organic': "Rectangular space, the straight line, is not functional but mechanistic. If I proceed consistently from biological function, orthogonal space is senseless because its four corners are dead space, useless. If I demarcated that portion of a room that is actually used I would arrive at a curve. The ebb and flow of organic life does not know the right angle or the straight line."[40] In this statement the difference between the organic and the mechanistic, the dissolution of which had been the cornerstone of the argument in "*Kunst, Handwerk, Technik*", is reinstated. Behne now seems to associate himself with the 'organicists' and 'functionalists', like Hugo Häring and Hans Scharoun, who rejected the 'right-angle' school, seeking to express, by their curvilinear and irrational, non-Euclidean forms, the spaces generated by 'natural' human associations and movements.[41] There was a distinct line of descent connecting the work of these architects and the fantastical architectural projects of 1918 and 1919, and indeed Sigfried Giedion, when he dismissed expressionism as beneath consideration in *Space, Time and Architecture*, made no distinction between them: "Men who were later to do grimly serious work in housing developments abandoned themselves to a romantic mysticism, dreamed of fairy castles on the peak of Monte Rosa. Others built concrete towers as flaccid as jellyfish."[42] During the 1920s there was an ongoing disagreement, within the *Neues Bauen*, between the 'functionalists' and the 'rationalists'. Theo van Doesburg criticised the functionalists for their rigid determinism, defending a rationalist approach on the grounds that an orthogonal, regular architecture provided neutral grids which allowed for unpredictable change.[43]

Given the enthusiasm with which Behne had championed an abstract rationalism in "*Kunst, Handwerk, Technik*" it is perhaps surprising to find him taking up arms in support of the functionalists. But there are many indications that he constantly oscillated between two opposite conceptions of 'the whole' constituting modernity—one derived from the tradition of *Lebensphilosophie*, with its underlying concept of the organic, the other based on the kind of mystical rationalism characteristic of van Doesburg and El Lissitzky.

IX

This inner conflict is also evident in Behne's criticism of examples of the *Neues Bauen*, particularly the public housing that was its most important manifestation. In an article he wrote for *Die Form* in 1930 on the Dammerstock Karlsruhe settlement by Otto Haesler, Behne starts by protesting that his criticisms should not be taken as a condemnation of the general direction of modernist housing, nor should they be confused with the usual criticism of such projects by reactionary conservatives.[44] The rest of the article, however, is a crushing attack on the project, which he accuses of being both scientistic and formalistic. In a housing project, he says, the architect should attempt to create a balance between a complex set of different requirements. He should not, as Haesler has done, approach the problem as if it can be solved logically, as in a scientific experiment. This will lead to a kind of formulism in which the architect imposes his own rules on the inhabitant and denies him the freedom to live as he chooses. In this architectural dictatorship the inhabitant becomes an 'abstract dweller'. "Dammersock's method becomes the dictatorial method—the method of 'either-or' rather than the 'and'", which is how the inhabitant thinks.[45] The architect, in using this approach, becomes more hygienic than the hygienist. "Medical research has shown that the inhabitants of houses that are considered to be unhygienic are healthier than the inhabitants of hygienic houses." Hygienic considerations are never clearly defined or consistent. In true hygiene, balance depends on many factors, and this should also be so in architecture. Behne also attacks the impoverished urbanism of the Zeilenbau settlements. Row-houses can only become urban when they are integrated with the city. Despite Behne's careful disclaimer, the article was interpreted by the ABC architect Hans Schmidt as an attack on the *Neues Bauen*.[46] Schmidt misunderstood Behne's article, attributing the faults of Dimmerstock to too little aesthetic consistency rather than too much. In his reply to Schmidt, Behne summarised his own position thus: "We have a lot of work ahead of us: the anchorage of the new architecture in the common masses, and the transformation of a passive system into one of consumer product and demand, even if by this process a few precious stones are knocked off the crown of aesthetics."[47]

What seems to emerge in Behne's article is an existential tone that differs from the totalising spirit of both the Expressionists and the *Neue Sachlichkeit* utopias characteristic of the texts previously discussed. To be sure, the new tone has something in common with Expressionist ideas, particularly its vitalistic belief in a popular will and its rejection of formalism and schematism, but the introduction of a radical indeterminism in the relation between form and function and the emphasis on daily life seem to be new. It is possible that this apparent change is merely the result of the circumstances of the Dammerstock article, in which Behne is not trying to expound a theoretical system but is responding to architecture at a very concrete level. This problem could only be resolved by a closer analysis of Behne's whole *oeuvre*.

XII

Behne's fluctuating thought can be complemented and illuminated by turning to the writings of Siegfried Kracauer. Kracauer was trained as an architect and practiced for ten years before turning to literature and cultural criticism. His ideas, though seldom mentioned in the context of the architectural debates of the 1920s, are intensely relevant to them precisely in proportion to their concern for what is peripheral to normal architectural discourse. Kracauer's early ideas were strongly influenced by Georg Simmel, and present a generally negative view of the cultural effects of capitalist rationality, sharing many of the ideas of Expressionism. But in his essays "Cult of Distraction: On Berlin's Picture Palaces" and "Mass Ornament" his attitude toward rationalism becomes, if not wholly positive, at least complex and qualified.[48] Kracauer's new interest in mass culture emerges in the opening sentence of "Mass Ornament", where he writes that the surface manifestations of an epoch provide a better insight into the historical process than the judgments a period makes about itself. One such surface manifestation is the spectacle of the Tiller Girls, whose coordinated movements exactly mimic the factory production line. This should not be condemned, but rather welcomed as a new, popular kind of ornament, superior to the exhausted forms of 'high art'. In an argument that puts reason in opposition to nature, Kracauer claims that the abstract processes which are a part of capitalism can ultimately liberate humanity from enslavement to nature. In the essay "The Cult of Distraction" Kracauer cites the cinema as a further example of a mechanised system of representation which, with its superficial images and its distracted mode of reception, is able to inoculate the masses against the naturalisation process of capitalism. The lack of culture in modern mass society can be compensated for "only in terms of the same surface sphere which imposed the lack in the first place".[49] But, for Kracuer, to praise the Tiller Girls and the cinema is not to be satisfied with the abstract processes they exemplify. They are merely the first, necessary steps in the transformation of society and unification of ornament and life. Capitalism is reason, but obscured reason. Its fault is not that it rationalises too much, but that it rationalises too little. The rationalisation stops half-way, becoming frozen in a formalism. It is incapable of applying itself to the empirical. We should not try to impede the development of abstract reason by seeking to return to the old mythological concreteness. We should seek a new concreteness by allowing reason to penetrate the empirical world of lived experience. Kracauer's concept of rational abstraction resembles Behne's acceptance of the division of labour. But, while for Behne the individual is supposed to reconnect to reality through an intellectual understanding of his position in a 'higher' unity, for Kracauer this can only be accomplished at the level of the concrete. Kracauer thus distances himself radically from both Expressionist nostalgia and the machine-worship of the *Neue Sachlichkeit*.

XIII

Though conservative thought in the 1920s is usually seen as looking back regretfully to a mythical German *Gemeinschaft*, in fact, as Jeffrey Herf has shown, many conservative thinkers saw the machine as an instrument in the revitalisation of traditional values.[50] In the novels of Ernst Jünger we find an aestheticisation of the machine in the context of modern warfare, in which a symbiotic, quasi-natural relationship is posited between the machine and the heroic individual. Modern industrial society is seen as providing the conditions for the individual to immerse himself in the crowd and to take part in a system of transcendental meaning.[51] The problem of the relation between technology and *Kultur* was also the subject of debate among engineers.[52] A prevalent point of view was that the enemy of *Kultur* was not technology itself, but *Amerikanismus* and the money economy. Carl Weihe, editor between 1921 and 1934 of the journal *Technik und Kultur*, denied that the governing principle of technology was abstract reason. Rather, technology was "an infusion of spirit into labour power".[53] In developing his ideas, Weihe relied on Shopenhauer's distinction between visualising thought and conceptualising thought (a distinction also found in both Wittgenstein and Heidegger).[54] In a teleological outlook resembling that of Aristotle, Weihe saw technology as an extension of nature, and grounded in final causes. It was this that distinguished it from capitalist commercialism. The market only throws up ephemeral forms, whereas the engineer makes permanent forms, for the creation of which he must have a mental image of the *Gestalt* of the objects to be created.[55] These views were opposite to those of Kracauer, for whom the aestheticisation and reification of the machine was a process that needed to be countered by the critical and solvent power of conceptual reason. Weihe's anti-capitalist rhetoric, as Herf points out, reflected a desire to return to a pre-capitalist, feudal concept of 'service', as opposed to work done for profit.[56] The similarity between these ideas and those of the avant-garde architects should be noted, particularly Le Corbusier. In both Weihe's ideas and those of the *Neue Bauen*, the artistic properties of *Kultur*—passion, intuition and other 'anti-bourgeois' values—are projected onto the machine, which expressionists and conservatives alike had relegated to the sphere of *Zivilisation*, the same conjuring trick as that which Behne had performed when he transferred the division of labour from the side of *Zivilisation* to the side of *Kultur* in his "*Kunst, Handwerk, Technik*" essay. In both the reactionary modernism of the engineers studied by Herf and the progressive modernism of the *Neue Sachlichkeit* architects, art and technology are seen as the result of *Gestaltung* formed in the mind of the creator. Art and technology are equated.

XIV

Some tentative generalisations seem justified on the basis of this brief and fragmentary study of criticism and self-criticism in German modernism:

- The period 1900 to 1933 must be studied as a whole. The questions raised and the solutions proposed in the post-war period can be fully understood only if they are seen in relation to pre-war debates.

- In the discourse of German modernism there are frequent oblique references to the nineteenth century German philosophical traditions, and the ideas of Kant, Hegel, Schopenhauer, Dilthey, Marx and Nietzsche can be sensed below the surface of arguments even when they are not explicitly mentioned. The same theories are often used for opposite reasons, and the cultural left and right often base their arguments on the same premises. There seems, notably, to have been a sort of revival of left and right Hegelianism.

- The basic problem faced by the period as a whole was that of tradition versus modernity. Progressives were often as concerned for the preservation of Volkisch values as were the conservatives. Conversely, conservatives were often as concerned as were progressives to show that modern technology belonged to the world of Kultur and thus did not constitute a threat to traditional values.

- What Max Webber called "the ethic of ultimate ends, as opposed to the ethic of responsibility", when referring to the revolutionary conservatives, can also be attributed to the modernists. In either case there is a tendency to aestheticise both politics and technology. It is this which accounts for a much-noted phenomenon: the frequent similarities between the ideas of the avant-garde and those of Facism.

- In the 1920s there is tension between formalists and empiricists. Form (*Gestalt*) is used as an idea to combat the short-term materialism and pragmatism of capitalism. But a kind of pragmatism is also used to combat the aesthetic and scientific formalism of the *Neues Bauen* architects. This can be seen in the existential attitude of critics of the *Neues Bauen* like Behne (sometimes) and Kracauer (always), who retained the faith in popular opinion and the spontaneity of the masses which was characteristic of the Expressionist movement, but who combined this with an acceptance of technological abstraction and a belief in the Enlightenment.

1 The word 'culture' in English normally has a less specific meaning than in German. In this essay it is sometimes use in this vaguer sense.

2 Stern, Fritz, *The Politics of Cultural Despair*, Berkeley, CA, 1961, p. 175.

3 Tönnies, Ferdinand, *Gemeinschaft und Gesellschaft*, Leipzig, 1887.

4 Stern, p. 174. Joan Campbell, *The German Werkbund*, Princeton, NJ, 1978, pp. 24–25.

5 Fanciscono, Marcel, *Walter Gropius and the Creation of the Bauhaus in Weimar*, Urbana, IL, 1971.

6 Franciscono, *Walter Gropius and the Creation of the Bauhaus in Weimar,* p. 30.

7 Franciscono, *Walter Gropius and the Creation of the Bauhaus in Weimar,* p. 31.

8 It was largely owing to the views published by Alöis Riegl that Semper became identified with a materialist philosophy of architecture. In fact Riegl attributed this philosophy more to Semper's followers than to Riegl himself. See Alöis Riegl, *Stilfragen*, "Introduction", English trans.: *The Problems of Style*, Princeton, NJ, 1992; Mundt, Ernst K, "Three Aspects of Aesthetic Theory", *Journal of Aesthetics and Art Criticism*, xvii, no. 3, March 1959.

9 Mundt, "Three Aspects of Aesthetic Theory".

10 Fiedler, Conrad, *Uber die Beurteilung von Werkern der Bildenden Kunst*, quoted in Peter Selz, *German Expressionist Painting*, Berkeley, CA, 1957, p. 5.

11 Troy, Nancy, *Modernism and the Decorative Arts in France: Art Nouveau to Le Corbusier*, New Haven, 1991, pp. 67–78.

12 Troy, *Modernism and the Decorative Arts in France,* pp. 72–73.

13 Franciscono, *Walter Gropius and the Creation of the Bauhaus in Weimar,* p. 35.

14 Campbell, *The German Werkbund*, pp. 62–63.

15 Franciscono, *Walter Gropius and the Creation of the Bauhaus in Weimar,* pp. 71–87.

16 Gordon, Donald, "On the Origin of the word Expressionism", *Journal of the Warburg and Courtauld Institutes*, 29, 1966, pp. 368–385. The French origin of the term "expressionism" has been challenged by Geoffrey Perkins, *Contemporary Theory of Expressionism*, Bern and Frankfurt, 1974. See Gordon, Donald, *Expressionism: Art and Idea*, New Haven, 1987, p. 238, note 13. See also Richard Brinkmann, *Exressionismus: Internationale Forschung zu einen interntionalen Phanomen*, Stuttgart, 1980, cited in Gordon.

17 *Lexicon Brockhaus*, 1926 edition.

18 Bithel, Jethro, *Modern German Literature*, London 1939, p. 359, note 1.

19 Hausenstein, Wilhelm, "Art of This Moment", in *Der Neue Merkur*, 1919, quoted in *German Expressionism: Documents from the end of the Wilhelmine Empire to the Rise of National Socialism*, ed. Rose-Carol Washton Long, New York, 1993, p. 382.

20 Weinstein, Joan, "The November Revolution and the Institutionalization of Expressionism in Berlin", 1988, in *Twentieth Century Art Theory: Urbanism, Politics and Mass Culture*, ed. Richard Hertz and Norman Klein, NJ: Prentice Hall, 1990.

21 Weinstein, "The November Revolution and the Institutionalization of Expressionism in Berlin".

22 Weinstein, "The November Revolution and the Institutionalization of Expressionism in Berlin".

23 Campbell, *The German Werkbund*, p. 123.

24 Campbell, *The German Werkbund*, pp. 126–130.

25 Campbell, *The German Werkbund*, p. 169.

26 Campbell, *The German Werkbund*, pp. 142–143 and 172.

27 For the importance of architecture as a metaphor of reconstruction in post-war France, see Kenneth Silver, *Esprit de Corps: The Art of the Parisian Avant-Garde and the First World War 1914–1925*, Princeton, NJ, 1989, pp. 323–325.

28 Weinstein, "The November Revolution and the Institutionalization of Expressionism in Berlin".

29 Lukács, Georg, "Expressionism: Its Significance and Decline", in *International Literature*, no. 1, 1934, pp. 153–173.

30 Bloch, Ernst, "Diskussionen über Espressionismus", *Das Wort 3*, no. 6, June 1938, pp. 103–112, quoted in Long, pp. 323–325.

31 Wieland, Schmied, "Neue Sachlichkeit and the German Realism of the Twenties", London: Arts Council, 1978, p. 9.

32 For an opinion on the different connotations of *Neue Sachlichkeit*, as applied to painting and architecture, see Fritz Schmalenbach, "The Term 'Neue Sachlichkeit'", in *Art Bulletin*, no. 22, September, 1940, pp. 161–165.

33 Franciscono, *Walter Gropius and the Creation of the Bauhaus in Weimar,* p. 28, note 37.

34 Roh, Franz, *Nach-Expressionismus, Magische Realismus: Probleme der Neuesten Europäischen Malerei*, Leipzig, 1925, quoted in Long, pp. 299–305.

35 Behne, Adolf, "Ruf zum Bauen", introduction to an illustrated book on architecture published by the *Arbeitsrat für Kunst* in 1920.

36 Behne, Adolf, "Kunst, Handwerk, Technik", in *Die Neue Rundschau*, 33, no. 10, 1922, pp. 1021–1037.

37 Märten, Lu, "Die Diktatur der Machine", in *Das Neue Reich*, Ostwald; Remer, Berlin, vol. 1–2, 1920.

38 Worringer, Wilhelm, *Abstraction and Empathy: A Contribution to the Psychology of Style,* London, 1948.

39 Behne, "Ruf zum Bauen".

40 Behne, Adolf, *Der Moderne Zweckbau*, Munich, 1926, p. 42, quoted in Rosmarie Haag Bletter, "Expressionism and the New Objectivity", *Art Journal*, Summer 1983.

41 The term "functionalism" is often given the same meaning as *Neues Bauen* and *Neue Sachlichkeit*. But in the mid-1920s it had a connotation that was closer to what is now normally called

"organicism", in opposition to "rationalism". Functionalist forms emphasised difference and uniqueness, whereas rationalist forms emphasised identity and generality.

42 Giedion, Sigfried, *Space, Time and Architecture*, Cambridge, MA, 1962, p. 242, quoted in Franciscono, p. 8.

43 Van Doesburg, *On European Architecture: Complete Essays from Het Bouwbedrijt, 1924–1931*, 1990, pp. 88–94.

44 Behne, Adolf, "Dammerstock", in *Die Form*, 1930, p. 6.

45 This terminology is the same as that used by Robert Venturi in *Complexity and Contradiction*, New York, 1966.

46 Schmidt, Hans, "Zum Zeilenbau der Dammerstock Siedlung", in *Die Form*, 1930, p. 14.

47 Behne, Adolf, "Dammerstock-Schlusswort", in *Die Form*, 1930, p. 18.

48 Kracauer, Siegfried, "Das Ornament der Masse", 1927, English trans. "Mass Ornament", *New German Critique*, no 5, Spring 1975, pp. 67–76: Kracauer, Siegfried, "Kult der Zerstreuung", English trans. "The Cult of Distraction", *New German Critique*, no. 40, Winter 1987, pp. 91–96.

49 Kracauer, "Kult der Zerstreuung" ("Cult of Distraction").

50 Herf, Jeffrey, *Reactionary Modernists: Technology, Culture and Politics in Weimar and the Third Reich*, Cambridge, 1984.

51 Herf, chapter 4, "Ernst Jünger's Magic Realism", pp. 70–108.

52 Herf, chapter 7, "Engineers as Idealogues", pp. 152–188.

54 Weihe, Carl, *Technik und Kultur*, p. 28, quoted in Herf, p. 175.

54 Herf, pp. 175–176.

55 Herf, pp. 176 and 178.

56 Herf, p. 171.

Architectural Manifestos of the 1960s in America

First published in *Faces*, 1993/1994. Revised 2008.

In the United States, as in Europe, the 60s were a period of rapid change after the stagnation of the 50s, and what makes them worth revisiting is that many of the problems which obtained then continue to face us today. The two 'manifestos' I propose to consider helped define the cultural movement of the 60s. They are Robert Venturi's book *Complexity and Contradiction in Architecture* published in 1967, on one hand, and the essay by Colin Rowe and Robert Slutsky, "Transparency, Literal and Phenomenal", first published in *Perspecta* in 1963, on the other. Both texts directly attacked the modernist tradition as it had been handed down, with various alterations, from the 30s to the 50s. Their authors agreed on some points, but disagreed radically on others, as I will attempt to describe.

There were, of course, other important cultural and artistic trends in the 60s which I will have to leave aside in this account. I am thinking here of Jane Jacobs' critique of modernist planning in her book *The Death and Life of Great American Cities*, of Buckminster Fuller's technological utopianism, of Marshall McLuhan's writings on the media, of Pop Art. All these trends similarly had a bearing on the architectural debate, but I must mention them only in passing because I have deliberately chosen today to confine myself to two theorists whose ideas were firmly focused on architecture as a clearly distinct entity.

But, I am going to talk about Venturi and Rowe in relation to two other people, two 'twins'. Although there is undoubtedly something arbitrary about this twinning, it will allow me to place Venturi and Rowe in the context of a wider debate. Venturi's twin will be Louis Kahn, and Rowe's, Peter Eisenman. Kahn and Venturi knew one another at the University of Pennsylvania, and the latter openly acknowledged his debt to his older colleague. Eisenman's intellectual debt to Colin Rowe has similarly been clearly established historically, however much the former may subsequently have distanced himself from the latter.

The situation in the 50s

Before I embark on my main theme, I must say a few words about the state of architecture in the 50s in America.

For all the fact that America's 'modern-ness' had provided a model for the Modernist Movement in Europe in the 20s, when the movement spread to America in the early 30s it arrived stripped of its utopian and social dimension. Hitchcock and Johnson's book *The International Style*, published in 1932 to mark the famous exhibition they organised at the Museum of Modern Art in New York, approached the Modernist Movement from an essentially aesthetic and stylistic angle. True, there were already socially based architectural ideas circulating in the States, notably in connection with the New Deal and the theories on urban planning of Lewis Mumford and Clarence Stein. But on the whole modernism was taken up across the Atlantic at an aesthetic rather than a social or planning level, which goes a long way to explaining the kind of modernism which grew up in America after the Second World War. This American brand of modernism accommodated itself happily to both a middle class lifestyle and the needs of large corporations, and while modernist architecture was the dominant style in the United States in the post-war period, it was not accompanied, as it had been in the Europe of the 1920s, by any of the social measures associated with the welfare state.

The greatest influence on American architecture in the 50s was without doubt Mies van der Rohe. Following his emigration to Chicago in the late 30s, his work had taken a markedly neo-classical turn. Mies had developed a prototype based on a central core which he applied to every project almost without exception, and which differed sharply from the more articulated designs which came out of his work in Germany before the war. In the United States designs featuring one or more symmetrically arranged buildings became very frequent in the 50s. While these buildings bore a clear relationship with those of Mies in terms of design, they were palpably un-Miesian in their architectural ornamentation. Although this type of neo-classicism was widespread, some architects were revisiting other modernist styles like Expressionism. But, there too, forms were treated in a decorative, superficial way, as is manifest in the buildings of Johnson, Johansen, Stone, Yamasaki and many other well-known architects of the period.

Louis Kahn

It was against this rather depressing backdrop that the ideas and work of Louis Kahn and Robert Venturi took shape. Although Kahn's approach shows some similarities to the prevailing post-war neo-classical tendency, he subjected this to a radical critique which marked on the one hand a return to a sort of primitive modernism, but also on the other, a partial rejection of modernism. Kahn is a modernist in his idealism and his essentialism, in his belief in the power of architecture to transcend everyday life and to create the symbols of an ideal world. But he is anti-modernist in his rejection of the idea of modernity. Kahn's ideal world does not connect the particular present with a utopian future, as Le Corbusier's did, for example. It harks backs to an eternal truth of architecture, transcending history.

In Kahn's hands, the Miesian building becomes *archetypal*—a square room defined by a solid structure of masonry. His buildings articulate a hierarchy of spaces of the same order. They orchestrate space without being slavishly shaped by the functions they serve. Kahn termed a scheme like this a "form", in the sense of the symbolic representation of an idea. A "project" for him was the process by which this fundamental idea was adjusted to accommodate particular planning and practical requirements. However this accommodation was achieved, the fundamental Platonic form remained paramount. Incidental or unexpected elements were for their part treated as exceptional and above all as subordinate.

Complexity and Contradiction

In his book *Complexity and Contradiction in Architecture* Robert Venturi puts forward an argument which, like Kahn's, amounts to a critique of certain aspects of modernist doctrine. But his attitude to modernism is the opposite of Kahn's. While Kahn wanted to establish an architecture on the same absolutist foundation as modernism, Venturi is in search of an architecture which is stripped of such metaphysical structure. What he rejects is the all-encompassing, even dogmatic, aspect of modernism. By contrast, he totally accepts the very aspect Kahn rejected—its empiricism.

Venturi's commitment to an empirical approach which accommodates problems must not be mistaken, however, for some sort of positivist creed where science and technology are concerned. On the contrary, Venturi's empirical approach is above all pragmatic, an architecture of compromise, conflict, and an absence of resolution. For him this situation is an inevitable consequence of competing practical requirements and more generally of a tension between the real and the ideal. Venturi, like Kahn, is an idealist, but a *weak* idealist. If there is one rhetorical device which encapsulates his work, it is the oxymoron.

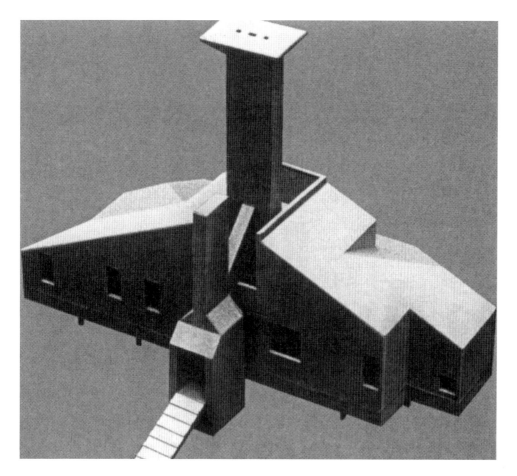

In sharp contrast to the modernist tendency to disregard all historical antecedent, Robert Venturi illustrates *Complexity and Contradiction* with copious examples of traditional architecture. In this he shows his links to the Beaux-Arts tradition, which survived far longer in the United States than in most of Europe, and in which he was trained, but he steers clear of the definitive examples which litter classical histories of architecture. Instead he concentrates on buildings or parts of buildings which strike him as exceptional, remarkable, because they exhibit ambiguity and paradox rather than classical harmony.

One of the most significant antitheses in the book, but which remains largely implicit, is that between history and modernity. Venturi's concept of history is very different from Kahn's. For Kahn, history gives an external appearance to forms which are essentially *a-historical*. Underlying historical forms there are primary, original ideas. In Venturi's eyes, by contrast, history supplies types not archetypes. It was a theory which he did not articulate until his second book, *Learning from Las Vegas*, published in 1971 and written in collaboration with Denise Scott-Brown, but the idea of types runs right through *Complexity and Contradiction*, as well and informs his earliest buildings. For Venturi a type is an element, such as a roof or a window, which derives its meaning not so much from its function but rather from its familiar character. A type is a *conventional* iconic form which lends a building meaning. Venturi's attack on modernism hinges on the emphasis he places on generating meaning through habitual associations and connotations which go beyond simple function. Where modernism tolerates similarities between new and old forms only when these are the product of a common logic, Venturi believes that such similarities must be present for architectural thinking to take place. But he also highlights the

Opposite top and bottom: Goldenberg House, Rydal, Louis Kahn, model and plan, 1959.

Left: Beach House, Robert Venturi, model, 1959.

Right top and bottom: Vanna Venturi House, Chestnut Hill, Robert Venturi, facade and entrance plan, 1962–1964.

problematic nature of making reference in the modern world to historical types and the impossibility of doing so without reference to anything else. The types he uses in his architecture—individual elements such as roofs and windows—together make up a vocabulary but lack a resolved, defining syntax. Laden with irony, these elements have a borrowed, fragile quality, like parts in a collage.

If we compare Venturi's use of elements such as windows with Kahn's, we find both similarities and differences. Kahn, like a true modernist, wanted to reinvent the window, just as he wanted to reinvent the wall of which the window was an integral part. Where Le Corbusier, however, endeavoured to rethink the entire question of windows in the light of modern technology, Kahn sought to rediscover the subtleties of lighting to be found in traditional windows, in which structural constraints are inseparable from lighting constraints. Kahn's windows were both rudimentary and highly refined at the same time.

Venturi, on the other hand, had no desire to reinvent the window, whether it was using modern techniques or enduring prototypes. He thought of windows as belonging to a set of types. A window had to be recognisable in its 'windowness'. But there are nevertheless similarities between Kahn and Venturi as far as windows are concerned, and it could be argued that, by re-establishing the traditional window as a formal element in a solid wall, the former in a sense opened the way forward for the latter.

Venturi's approach to individual elements cannot be completely separated from his attitude to the overall design. As I have said, when Kahn was obliged to accommodate the unexpected and to adapt to particular circumstances, he did it without destroying the pure geometry intrinsic to his design. In contrast, for Venturi, particular circumstances are not something to accept grudgingly, but provide the very basis of the design. This does not mean that there is not a geometric structure in Venturi's designs. The exteriors are generally simple and geometrically unified in shape, as is the case in a number of his earliest houses. This means the roof can adopt a familiar pointed protective form, associated with the job it does of shielding the inside from outside forces. But inside these regular envelopes, the designs are complex and irregular, giving rhetorical emphasis to the functional requirements of the interiors. Venturi's designs conjure up buildings whose ordered spaces are lived in physically, and at close range, in contrast to those of Le Corbusier, which, albeit often highly complex, come across primarily as visual symbols of an intellectual kind.

Venturi's *ad hoc* treatment of interior plans is at odds with the more unified design of his facades. He articulated this contradiction later in *Learning from Las Vegas* when he coined the term "the decorated shed". The facade is viewed as an eloquent surface which gives meaning to a building whose interior organisation is considered simply in terms of utility: contrary to both modernist and traditional theory, there is no organic relationship between the facade and the interior plan.

Finally, I would like to point out the many links that can be found between such architectural thinking and the ideas of *Pop Art* which was in its heyday in the early 60s. Just as Pop Art did in the realm of painting, Robert Venturi ranked 'low art' above 'high art'. He too saw signs and advertising as legitimate elements of the urban environment. It is possible to see his work as part of a much wider, immanent 'post-modern' movement, which rejected the formalist theory of modernism propounded by the American art historian Clement Greenberg, and enthusiastically welcomed all the consumer society had on offer and the rapid development of mass media.

Transparency Literal and the Phenomenal

Like Venturi's book, Rowe and Slutsky's essay represents a critique of certain aspects of modernist practice and theory. The two texts agree about the millennarian leanings of modernism, which both condemn. But they differ when it comes to the aspects of modernist doctrine worth keeping. In contrast to Venturi, Rowe rejects any idea that functionality should be taken into account. He does not deny, of course, that architecture has a useful end. But he sees this as contributing to the meaning of a building in a vague, general way, rather than a central one. He wants to link modern architecture more closely to modernism in general, and to modern painting in particular. For him the essence of modernism lies in the *absorption* of 'content' into 'form', in other words in the fact that art has given up seeking to imitate external reality. Considered in this light, the modernist 'functionalist aesthetic' is a throwback to naturalism because it assumes a literal imitation of technological reality. Rowe and Slutsky begin their essay, therefore, by looking at Cubism in both its Synthetic and Analytic phases, which they argue is a representation of a virtual, subjective or phenomenal space. Cubism presupposes that our perception of the world relies on an interpretative faculty of the brain without which our sense impressions would remain chaotic. This interpretative faculty allows artists to exploit representations that highlight the problematic nature of 'reality', to create ambiguous spatial relationships which the brain is compelled to resolve.

This is an idea that has at least one of its sources in a specific tradition: the idealist-formalist aesthetic theory of Adolf Hildebrand. In his book of 1893, The Problem of Form in Painting and Sculpture, Hildebrand insists on the quasi Kantian thesis that we interpose our own mental concepts between ourselves and the world. He distinguishes between "apparent" form (Erscheinungsform) and "real" form (Dasseinform). The sculptor's task is to make the real form of the object apparent to the observer. The book had an enormous influence, especially on the art historians Alois Rigel and Heinrich Wolfflin. Riegl's categories of "haptic" and "optic" spring from the distinction Hildebrand made between close and distant vision. Hildebrand saw his categories as applying to architecture as well as sculpture and Wolfflin did not fail to adapt certain aspects of Hildebrand's theory to an examination of the visual properties of architecture. Consequently, in transposing Hidlebrand's concept of spatial depth to both painting and architecture, Rowe and Slutsky were simply following existing precedents—though they do not acknowledge the fact.

According to Hildebrand, we tend to "read" a sculpture as if it were bisected by a succession of planes. From a viewer's point of view, a sculpture in the round is similar to a sculpture in relief. Rowe and Slutsky apply this line of reasoning to architecture. To back up their argument they analyse the two buildings by Le Corbusier: the Villa Stein at Garches and the competition project for the Palais des Nations. In both cases they employ a process of reduction to show that the buildings should be perceived as a succession of planes related frontally to the observer. Like Husserl in his phenomenological process of reduction, Rowe and Slutsky wish to make us suspend our habitual perception of these buildings. Even when they picture an observer in motion, as they do in their analysis of the Palais des Nations, they imagine him perceiving the building not in a haphazard way, but in a visually orchestrated and controlled way.

Although clearly related to Hildebrand, Rowe and Slutsky depart from him on a key point. Hildebrand, in structuring depth in terms of imaginary planes, aims at clarifying the observer's perception of depth. For Rowe and Slutsky, on the other hand, what the architect or artist must get the observer to experience is not clarity but ambiguity. Due to the replacement of clarity by ambiguity a radical difference opens up between Hildebrand's concept of virtual space and that of Rowe and Slutsky. It might be thought that the emergence of modern architecture, with its emphasis in light and transparent materials, was a sort of realistic confirmation of Hildebrand's concept of imaginary planes. But Rowe and Slutsky—using the analogy of analytical Cubism—reject any argument that would rely on such actual ethereality. They distinguish sharply between the

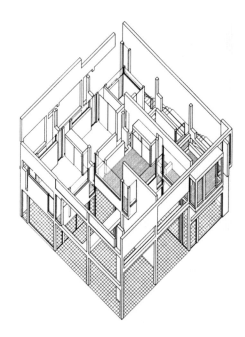

Opposite top: Bauhaus Dessau, Walter Gropius, 1926.

Opposite bottom: Villa Stein, Garches, Le Corbusier, 1927.

Top and bottom: House II, Harwick, Vermont, Peter Eisenman, 1969–1970.

literal transparency of the curtain wall in the Bauhaus building at Dessau and the implied or virtual transparency of the Villa Stein with its opaque surfaces. For them, the façade of a modern building should act as the first of several opaque planes and their imaginary extensions that together summarise—on a sensuous and intuitive level—the building's spatial organisation.

Before going on to consider Peter Eisenman's appropriation and critique of Rowe and Slutsky's ideas, it will be necessary to return briefly to Robert Venturi. One of the ways in which Ventury differs from orthodox modernist theory is that he sees historical contingency playing a relatively weak part in the construction of meaning. He agrees with modernism that the meaning of a building derives in part from external factors such as programme, function and relation to site. But for him the meanings attached to such functions extend to the traces they retain of historical memory. For Ventura, the memory of a thing is an important part of its total meaning. In this it operates like a language.

This differentiates him from Rowe and Slutsky, who are largely concerned with form and discount the contribution memory makes to architectural meaning. This might lead one to suppose that the ideas of Rowe and Slutsky lie outside language altogether. But if we take into account the theory of structural linguistics as defined by de Saussure, we will see that this is by no means the case. According to this theory, language is a system of signs each of which consists of both a syntactic and a semantic part. Therefore, to the extent that architecture is analogous to language, there are grounds for saying that it has a formal syntax equivalent to that of language. From this perspective, Rowe and Slutsky's concept of form must be considered to be linguistic, though unlike Venturi, they are interested only in its syntactic and not at all in its semantic aspect.

But at this point, there is a complication. For the relation between form and meaning in language is arbitrary and conventional, whereas, in their invocation of phenomenology, Rowe and Slutsky imply that artistic forms have inherent meaning and, furthermore, that these are anterior to language. This entails a doubling of meaning. Behind the "meaning" of the immediate form, there lies another transcendent, ideal or symbolic meaning which has to be decoded by an equally transcendent subject. It is at this moment that Peter Eisenman enters the scene. For Eisenman, the problem of Rowe and Slutsky's formal reductivism was not that it "bracketed out" functional considerations, but that it involved a reading of the architectural object that oscillated between the real object as perceived and a purely imaginary entity lying behind the object—its "ideal" structure. In a series of house projects between the 1960s and 1980s, Eisenman tried to eliminate all such imaginary entities. In adopting Rowe and Slutsky's radical formalism, he turned it into something even more reductive and "abstract". He tried to make his houses strictly analogous to syntactical structure in language in which formal differences are emphasised but carry with them no inherent meanings. In the few exceptions to this principle of exclusion, only the most ineradicable of conventions, such as staircases, doors etc. are retained. The earliest of these houses resemble the work of the "minimalist" sculptors like Donald Judd and Robert Morris.

In this brief overview of the ideas of Venturi and Rowe and Slutsky, and their alto-egos Lois Kahn and Peter Eisenman, I am only too aware that I have only been able to scratch the surface of their ideas. Re-reading their writings today is a rewarding experience—an exhilarating reminder of the intense formalist and structuralist architectural debates of the 1960s.

Lost Illusions

Previously unpublished. Written 2002.

Since the inception of modernism there have been fundamental, but often unacknowledged, changes in the cultural and political conditions determining the relationship of modern architecture to society. These changes have invalidated many of the assumptions that lay behind the ideology of the Modern Movement.

In the early years of the twentieth century, avant-gardists believed that a change in architectural style was inextricably bound up with a change in society. Capitalism and industrialism had brought unprecedented progress in material conditions but at the same time it had destabilised traditional social relations. Modernist artists and architects believed a change in art itself would trigger a change in society as a whole, the effect of which would be to reintegrate art with social life. The vague belief that a reformed architecture would be the agency by which a social utopia could be achieved was the main driving force behind the early Modern Movement.

This set of beliefs was based on contradictory reactions on the part of the architectural avant-gardes to the rapid process of industrialisation that had taken place in the second half of the nineteenth century. On the one hand, they fervently embraced modernity, believing that architecture had to adapt itself to technological change and in the process completely revolutionise its aesthetic principles. On the other hand, they feared the process of social and cultural destabilisation that had resulted from industrial capitalism. Their programme was simultaneously innovative and conservative.

A positive reaction to modernity is encouraged by the development of the arts and sciences since the break up of feudalism in the late Middle Ages. Under feudalism, the organisation of what the French call "*les arts et metiers*" had been entirely subordinated to the church. With the rise of capitalism and the urban bourgeoisie in the late Middle Ages, art became progressively more independent of religious authority and there was a slow but continuous movement toward autonomy in both art and technology. Although the arts remained under court patronage until the late eighteenth century, the artwork itself was increasingly seen as the product of individual genius. At the end of the nineteenth century, after a century of industrial development, the concept of artistic autonomy— of *Art pour l'Art*—was promoted by the aesthetic movement, in the belief that it was only by establishing the complete autonomy of art that artistic values could be maintained in a social context dominated by the pursuit of commercial profit. Innovation and progress were the direct result of a new valorisation of the individual.

At the same time, in complete opposition to the progressive liberation of the artist from social control, there was a movement within the avant-gardes that sought a return to pre-capitalist forms of social organisation. One of the causes of the decline in cultural values since the Industrial Revolution was seen to have been the introduction of the division of labour. We have seen that this perception triggered the aesthetic movement and the idea of the autonomy of art, but it also created the opposite desire to return to pre-capitalist forms of social cohesion and 'community' in which the arts had supposedly been integrated into the social fabric. This impulse was motivated by a nostalgia for the cultural unity of pre-industrial society—a unity which, it was thought, had been destroyed by capitalism and machine production.

The various progressive movements in architecture and the industrial arts from the 1890s until the Second World War were deeply embroiled in this contradiction between the inevitability and desirability of technological advance on the one hand, and the recovery of the organic unity of pre-capitalist societies on the other. Let me give a few examples.

The Arts and Crafts Movement and the closely affiliated Art Nouveau and *Jugendstil* movements, following the theories of William Morris, had attempted to revive the crafts on the model of the Medieval guilds. Around the turn of the century a counter-movement emerged which rejected the Medievalising spirit of these movements. This counter-movement became the dominant ideology of the *Deutsche Werkbund* under the leadership of architects Hermann Muthesius and Peter Behrens. These architects realised that the industrial arts had to become mechanised. Far from returning to handwork and ornament, the useful objects of the future would need to be *sahlich* and simple. From now on, aesthetic value would be found not in the hand forming of materials, but in Form itself, or *Gestalt*—as conceptualised by the artist-intellectual rather than the artist-craftsman. At the same time, the fantasy of the individual artist would have to be curbed in the interest of normative and repeatable standards.

But this abandonment of the handicrafts in favour of machine production by the *Deutsche Werkbund* did not alter the belief in reformers in the need to re-establish the lost unity of the pre-capitalist world. For Muthesius the uncontrolled market place of capitalism was responsible for the catastrophic decline in the artistic quality of modern consumer products during the nineteenth century. In order to redeem the industrial arts it would be necessary to eliminate the uncertainties of the market as well as the middleman who controlled it. He proposed that the production of consumer objects should be placed in the hands of a few large corporations. These firms would be obliged to employ artists, who would thus regain control of the design process which they had lost with the advent of machine production and the division of labour. The corporations would act rather like the Medieval craftsmens' guilds, monopolising the market and controlling public taste. We see here an attempt by Muthesius to uncouple technology from capitalism.

Muthesius based his idea of a modern architecture on the "type" or standard. He associated the type with modern production methods, but he also saw it as related to a perennial classical tradition. Only through typification, and I quote, "can architecture recover that universal significance which was characteristic of it in times of harmonious culture". But there was a problem with Muthesius' conflation of these two ideas. When it appears in tradition, the standardisation of forms aims at a certain aesthetic result. When applied to modern mass production, however, standardisation serves merely to facilitate repetition and to coordinate the different phases of production that have been separated by the division of labour. No telos or specific end is envisaged other than that of increased efficiency of production. We can further illustrate the distinction between these two senses of type by looking at the work of a later modernist: Le Corbusier. In the 1940s, Le Corbusier tried to reconcile artistic quality and industrial efficiency by introducing the *Modulor*. This is usually seen as a proportional system, but in fact it was addressed specifically to the problem of mass production, and to harness the industrial process to his concept of platonic beauty, much as Muthesius had attempted to do when he put the artist in control of the factory floor. Le Corbusier realised that without any such conscious intervention on the part of the artist, modular coordination was simply a way of using mass production to satisfy a large and variable market, and to operate in the market as efficiently as possible.

A similar attempt to control the market was proposed by Bruno Taut, after the short-lived Communist Revolution of 1918 in Germany. In an open letter to the Socialist government, he wrote that art and life must form a unity. The aim of art must be the fusion of arts under the wing of a great architecture. As a result of this, the artist would be "the modeller of the new sensibilities of the *Volk*, responsible for the visible structure of the new state. He must control the form-giving process from the statue right down to the coin and the postage stamp." Taut's totalitarian visions, like those of Muthesius, implied an authoritarian alternative to the existing liberal politics associated with modern industrial development, and a return to a totalising pre-capitalist vision of society. Taut was not so explicit about the need for technology as Muthesius was. But he never condemned it and he clearly believed that it was compatible with the administrative measures necessary to retrieve the lost unity of artistic culture.

The same was true of Le Corbusier in the 1930s, when he became involved with the French neo-Syndicalist movement. This movement attacked the inefficient parliamentary system of modern liberal democracies, and proposed its replacement by a government of technocrats who would be able to implement a national economic plan. The plan would take into account the needs of the regions and cater for the emotional needs of ordinary people. "Abstract man" would be replaced by *l'homme réal*—a man belonging to the community and to the soil. Though this movement was different from both the classical model of Muthesius and the Volkisch model of Taut, it was nonetheless equally based on a rejection of current democratic notions of society in favour of a return to organically unified society that supposedly existed before the rise of capitalism. It wanted simultaneously to regress to an earlier phase of social organisation and at the same time to maintain the greatest possible development of technology.

To recapitulate: architectural aspirations towards a unified modern culture were characterised by a critique of capitalism on the one hand and on the other by a desire for the continuation of technical development. The idea of continuous technical and artistic innovation—which the artistic avant-gardes shared with the capitalist system itself, and which presupposed the autonomy of art and technology—was incongruously combined with a desire to return to the state of normalcy that had been characteristic of pre-capitalist societies and which alone, it was thought, would satisfy the deep and unchanging needs of the people.

This idea was in fact based on a simple but false analogy. Because each historical period seemed, in retrospect, to constitute a cultural totality, it was assumed that the modern age must exhibit a unity in every way analogous to this. This assumption was false on two grounds. First, the fact that each past period seems to us to constitute a unified whole does not mean that this unity was apparent to people living at the time. Conversely, although the events of our own time may seem heterogeneous to us, they may well seem unified to future generations. Secondly, and rather more importantly, history does not provide any proof whatever that our own period cannot, in fact, differ from previous periods in (seemingly) crucial ways. It may well be that the conditions of modernity preclude the further repetition of certain aspects of the past that we would like to continue. The fact that we can, in the present, still enjoy the cultural products of the past does not in itself guarantee their survival as practices.

Today it seems impossible to believe, as was often believed by progressives in the first half of the twentieth century, that the modern age can replicate the sort of unity that appears to have characterised pre-industrial societies. Since the Second World War it has been possible to believe that democratic governments, in the form of welfare states, could achieve a unified egalitarian society. But even if such a belief could be justified, such social ambitions do not necessarily entail the idea of a unified, normative artistic culture. It seems very unlikely that we can presuppose a common system of codes that binds artistic and social institutions together, as existed in the past. It is precisely the absence of common codes that characterises modern society, which is disunited, fragmentary and subject to continuous changes of fashion. The arts and architecture are more than ever characterised by the concept of the individual genius and artistic autonomy. At the same time, art is connected with the media and the world of fashion, and is thus antagonistic to the notion of fixed, uniform aesthetic standards. It strives continuously for the new and spectacular. There is no sign that the 'general public' is any nearer than it ever was in arriving at a consensus in the matter of architectural styles, or to accepting a single notion of what is the 'modern', or even the need to be 'modern' at all. In suggesting that such a 'pluralism' is an inevitable consequence of late capitalism, I am not implying that capitalism is a totalising, closed system which necessarily resists any attempt of conscious modification by political means. What I am suggesting is that no political modification is likely to effect a wholesale and uniform transformation of cultural forms of the kind that was hoped for by modernists.

Esprit de Corps

First published in *Design Review*, no. 26, nd.

The First World War is often perceived as having merely accelerated revolutionary changes in the artistic practises inaugurated by Symbolism, Expressionism, Cubism, and Futurism. This view of modernism's continuity—with a full flowering after the war—has been particularly stressed in architectural historiography. According to most of the historians of the Modern Movement, a stabilised and coherent modern architecture only emerged in the early 1920s. But infact, around the time of the First World War, there was a fundamental change of direction in the avant-garde—including that of architecture—introducing conservative and classicising tendencies which set themselves in opposition to what were seen as the anarchistic and nihilistic tendencies of the pre-war movements.

This change is brilliantly described by Kenneth Silver in his book *Esprit de Corps*. Silver's ostensible subject is the change that overcame the Parisian avant-garde painters under the pressure of war-time patriotism and the effect of this in the immediate post-war years. This provides the author with a naturally circumscribed and highly dramatic theme. But the latent content of the book is much broader and is concerned with important aspects of the post-war avant-garde in Europe as a whole.

In his opening chapter Silver sets the scene by describing the philistinism and chauvinism which, fanned by conservative writers like Leon Daudet and Charles Maurras, imposed its views on the whole nation. The fear of Germany that these sentiments reveal was the result of the rapid rise of Germany as a military power after the Franco-Prussian war of 1871, and the subsequent infiltration of German goods into the French market, threatening the dominance of French craftsmanship and taste. The German threat was interpreted in strangely contradictory ways. On the one hand a degenerate German Romanticism (represented chiefly by Richard Wagner) was seen as undermining the French classical tradition; on the other, Germany's greater capacity for collective work and superior organisation threatened an increasingly slack and frivolous France. Germany—at once more degenerate and more virile than France—was cast in the alternating roles of feminine temptress and masculine bully. All modernist art, including Pointillism, Cubism and Futurism, was considered to be of German origin and its corrupting influence to be the work of German-Jewish art dealers. The perception of modern art being German was not restricted to France, however; the German art dealer Wilhelm Uhde was to claim, in 1928, that Picasso owed a debt to German (presumably Expressionist) culture.

The first part of the book deals with the reactions of progressive artists and intellectuals to these infantile, officially promoted views. The pressures of social conformity are common to all countries in war-time, but these must have been especially great in a country like France where the ties between culture and the state have always been strong. It is hardly surprising that many within these groups yielded to the collective paranoia, seeing themselves as intellectual warriors fighting in the common cause. The critic Clement Janins struck the right tone in the catalogue for the triennial exhibition of French art in Paris in 1916: "The painter has seized his brushes, the sculptor his rough sketches, the ceramicist his wheel and his glaze… all have set hearts beating in agreement with the hearts of heroes."

Although the two main progressive journals, Jean Cocteau's *Le Mot* and Amédée Ozenfant's *L'Elan*, poked fun at such reactionary critics, their own defense of the avant-garde was expressed in an admonitory and reformist tone. In his essay *"Quand le symbolisme fut mort"*, Paul Dermée wrote that after a period of exuberance, art must concern itself with "organisation, arrangement and science". Charles Sarolea called for an "*esprit nouveau*" (apparently the first appearance of a term usually attributed to Apollinaire) of "solid good sense inherited from the classics". Music was not exempt from the general spirit of revisionism; in 1917 Cocteau issued a call-to-order to French composers: "You can't get lost in the Debussy mist as you can in the Wagnerian fog, but you can catch cold there." (In his last compositions Debussy did indeed revert to neo-classical forms). The Cubist painters also reacted to the war-time atmosphere. Gino Severini and Robert Delauney both turned against Cubism, while Juan Gris, although he never abandoned Cubism, fused it with naturalism and traditional subjects. Picasso who responded to public taste with greater detachment and irony, introduced the theme of *Commedia del'Arte* in his curtain design for Diaghilev's ballet *Parade*, and began a series of works in the style of Ingres (though his first work in this manner predated the outbreak of war by a few weeks).

No doubt this reversion to traditional forms was closely connected—as Silver claims—to the chauvinistic atmosphere generated by the war. Yet there was another factor tending in the same direction that Silver ignores. This was the general return to classical models in architecture and the decorative arts in both Germany and France some ten years before the war. This movement was initiated around 1905 in Germany, when Paul Mebes and Peter Behrens led a revival of Biedermeier and Schinkelesque neo-classicism, and it found an echo in France with Auguste Peret's Theatre des Champs Elysees.

This building was attacked by many French critics for introducing an alien German form of abstract classicism, but the French reaction to the German neo-classical movement was not always so negative. In 1910 the Salon d'Automne mounted an exhibition of the work of a group of Munich interior decorators the French reaction to which was extremely positive. In her book *Modernism and the Decorative Arts in France*, 1991, Nancy Troy shows that already in the first decade of the century, French designers, like their German counterparts, were reacting against Art Nouveau, rejecting the concept of "total design" and designing ensembles in the Empire, Directoire and Louis Philippe styles. The principles behind these so-called "*Coloristes*" (with whom Charles Edouard Jeanneret—soon to become Le Corbusier—was closely associated during his early visits to Paris) were in many ways similar to those which Adolf Loos was promoting in Vienna at the same time.

Another example of the general pre-war turn to classicism is the work of the Swiss choreographer Emile Jaques Dalcroze, whose famous school of dance at Hellerau was built in a neo-classical style by the German architect Heinrich Tessenow, with neo-Grec stage sets by Adolf Appia. According to Silver, Dalcroze's "eurythmics" serve as an example of post-war French classicism. Yet the school was founded in 1911 and involved the collaboration of German, Swiss and French artists.

Silver shows how French war-time conservative ideology persisted in the immediate post-war years. The period before the classical revival was perceived as having been individualistic and lacking in a sense of community. Progressive painters as well as those on the artistic and political right now extolled the French classical tradition and denigrated the Romantic tradition running from Rousseau to Bergson. Silver analyses the post-war work of the pre-war avant-garde. He distinguishes between two kinds of post-war artists—those who turned their backs on Cubism (either in a terminal rejection as with Delaunay, La Fresnaye and Severini or reducing it to one of several possible manners as with Picasso), and those who continued with Cubism, classicising it in various ways (as with Braque, Picasso, Gris and Leger). The only important painter who escapes this classification is Matisse, but Silver subjects the pre- and post-war work of this artist to minute scrutiny, showing how it also responded to artistic fashion. He also mentions parallel tendencies in the other arts—including, Paul Valery's *Epolinos* and Stravinsky's *Pulchinello*.

In post-war criticism there was a signincant re-evaluation of the pre-war avant-garde. Cubism, according to Cocteau, was "a classicism after the romanticism of the Fauves". Cézanne was subject to a confusing set of critical reversals. Some, like Emile Bernard, who had claimed Cézanne for classicism even before the war, now condemned him for being a naturalist and offered Puvis de Chavannes' idealised pastorals as sounder classical models. Others, like Gris, praised Cézanne precisely for his classicism, contradicting the predominant pre-war view that he had practised a "penetrating" naturalism that "plunges into profound reality, growing luminous as it forces the unknowable into retreat", (Metzinger and Gleize, 1912).

Among the painters who continued to practise a modified Cubism, Silver discusses Leger, comparing *La Ville* of 1919 with *Le Grand Dejeuner* of 1921, quoting the painter's own opinion about the transformation from analysis to classical synthesis represented by these two paintings. For Leger there had to be a balance: "The romantic pushes towards the left—an excess of subjectivity (a warm state). His opposite pushes towards the right—an excess of objectivity (a cold state)." A balance between these two states would achieve a socially orientated art that communicated with ordinary people. Another aspect of Leger's work brought out by Silver is his interest in the theatre as a collective art—one in which mechanism figured as prominently as human actors (a notion that links Leger to the Berlin theatre and the Soviet avant-garde). One of the main concepts developed during the war was, indeed, the notion of the social collective and the need to heal the split that had developed between art and everyday life. The same idea is expressed in Silver's book which posits classicism as an antidote to the individualism that had condemned the artist to the margins of society. He proposed a new "Academy—not, obviously, the old école, re-plastered... but an edifice, a brand new monument having, as generating principles, the eternal laws of construction".

With this cluster of metaphors, Severini broaches a theme that Silver mentions on several occasions: architecture seen as a paradigm for the arts—an idea with a long provenance. In the context of this book, it emerges not only as a reference for the literal need for reconstruction after the war, but also as a metaphor for an art that is restrained, objective and socially responsible. The question of architecture's perceived paradigmatic role in the consolidation of a post-war classicism is raised again in Silver's last chapter as part of a discussion of Le Corbusier's *Pavillon de l'Esprit Nouveau*, exhibited at the *Exposition Internationale des Arts Decoratifs et Industrial Modernes* in Paris in 1925. One of the main purposes of the exhibition was to reassert the pre-eminence of the French artisanal tradition, challenged by Germany before the war. The emphasis of the French section of the exposition was on individual objects of luxury. The sole dissenting voice was that of Le Corbusier whose Pavillon was based on an internationalist and progressivist programme of mass production and mass consumption. As an architectural demonstration of Purist aesthetics, the Pavillon emphasised the universal condition of modernity rather than any specifically French set of values; its architectural language belonged to the emerging international Modern Movement. It was closely related to the De Stijl group in Holland and the Bauhaus in Germany.

As Silver shows, this international spirit was compromised by a rhetoric that still reflected patriotic, anti-German sentiments often barely distinguishable from the chauvinism of *L'Action Francaise* and the far right. These articles are Silver's last examples of a French avant-garde coloured by war-time conservatism, completing the picture of a wholesale retreat of the French avant-garde from a pre-war position of revolutionary dynamism to one of conservative nationalism.

Convincing as it is in many ways, this interpretation castes some doubt on Silver's treatment of the European avant-garde as a whole. He tends to attribute to French war-time trauma many changes in style and ideology that were in fact the result of links, between France and Europe as a whole—particularly with Germany—in the period immediately before and immediately after the war. The parallelism between the classicising architectures of Peter Behrens and Auguste Peret has already been mentioned. We might add a similar parallelism between Hermann Muthesius, 1910, and Le Corbusier, 1911, both of whom associated the new spirit of classicism with a technologically advanced modern architecture. The turn to classicism in French painting after the war also had strong parallels with events in Weimar Germany, with the dethronement of Expressionism by the *Neue Sachlichkeit*. So strong was the perceived relation between the French and German movements at the time that the *Neue Sachlichkeit* exposition in Mannheim in 1923 was originally intended to include neo-classical paintings by French painters, including Picasso.

Not only was neo-classicism a Europe-wide movement, but the formal spirit of neo-classicism was capable of giving expression to contradictory political views. In France the set of concepts that underlay the *Rappel à l'Ordre* of the 1920s—concepts such as 'reconstruction', 'organisation' and 'collectivism'—could be subject to both a left- and a right-wing interpretation. This ambiguity can also be seen in the Soviet avant-garde, which could include both the 'formalists' seeking the permanent laws of aesthetics independent of any social component, and the 'objective', socially oriented Constructivists. The tendency towards 'totalisation' that Silver points to when discussing post-war aesthetic theory in France was present in all the avant-garde movements in the rest of Europe, whether on the right or left. It was part of the taste for final solutions that ran through the avant-garde in the post-war years, distinguishing it from the nihilistic, experimental and analytical pre-war movements.

The occasional one-sidedness of Silvers' interpretations is the product of the very historical frame that makes his book so successful in its own terms. It would clearly be unfair to blame him for not having written a different book. In setting out to tell a story that has hitherto been neglected—the story of the relations between the Parisian avant-garde and war-time French society—Kenneth Silver must be congratulated. He has produced an informative and elegant book.

Notes on Public Policy and City Planning in Europe since 1840

Previously unpublished. Written 2003.

When we use the tem "public policy" in connection with building we tend to think of two different but connected problems: housing and urbanism. These two categories emerged in the 1830s and resulted from the application of the machine to agricultural and industrial production and the consequent migration of the workers from the country to the city. As a result of these developments, a degree of state control was used to curb the engine of *laissez-faire* urban change.

Among the changes that the Industrial Revolution had on the city, two stand out. On the one hand the population of the city began to increase rapidly, creating the new problem of a continuously expanding 'city without limits'. On the other hand the social classes began to be spatially separated. The working class was concentrated near factories in existing cities or new settlements, or was forced out of the city to the suburbs by the rising cost of land. The new middle classes also moved out to the suburbs but in the opposite direction, up-wind of the factories and the working class areas. These two effects resulted in a new zoning pattern in which housing was separate from the rest of the city. But it also inaugurated a new discipline: City Planning, and an attempt to recover the organic unity of the traditional city.

If, as I have suggested, we should consider *laissez-faire* and the instruments of state control as being two sides of the same coin, it can be of no surprise that England—the first country to suffer the effects of the industrialisation process, and with a government deeply antagonistic to state interference in the market—should also have been the first to pass legislation on housing. And it is perhaps no more surprising that in France, where industrialisation followed hard upon that of England, but with a less catastrophic redistribution of population, we find the Saint-Simonians first proposing a proactive state, and then providing most of the entrepreneurs involved in laying down the French technical infrastructure.

Early Housing Legislation

The core of English housing legislation in the nineteenth century consisted of the two Public Health Acts of 1848 and 1875. This legislation was narrowly pragmatic, concerned with setting minimum hygienic and constructional standards, and it was largely triggered by the fear of cholera. English housing legislation became a model for the continent, but the results in the country of origin were depressing: endless back-to-back two-storey row houses along mean streets without trees, public spaces, or even shops. The problem was: how to satisfy the new demand for housing at a minimal standard, while guaranteeing a profit for the builder.

The first time architects were employed in the supply of workers' housing was in the building of model, 'company' towns by philanthropic or simply far-sighted industrialists, in which the state played no part. We find these in Belgium, France and Germany, as well as in England. The first company housing to appear in Europe was at Bois du Lac, Belgium, in 1838. England followed with Saltaire, near Bradford, in 1850, the first workers' settlement to be based on some conception of community life, though the house plans and layouts hardly varied from standard builder's practice.

In France, the pioneer company housing was the *Cité Ouvrière* at Mulhouse, Alsace, of 1853. Here, a new house type was introduced, the so-called four-in-a-bloc unit, derived from a model four-house unit that had been built by the architect Henry Roberts at the Great Exhibition in Hyde Park in 1851. In Germany the first example was the rapidly industrialising Ruhr valley, in which the four-in-a-block type was also used.

City Planning

Parallel with this company housing in newly urbanised areas there were developments in city planning. In England the problem of the city as such did not initially arise. It is true that, with the slum clearance acts of 1875 and 1885, renovation of the existing fabric in the centres of English cities began. But this did not amount to a policy for city expansion; it merely replaced slums with more hygienic housing.

On the continent, however, from the 1850s onwards, great attention was given to the problem of controlling the growth of cities. The main concern was in adapting the city to the needs of the new bourgeois economy. In Paris, Louis Napoleon and Baron Haussman cut wide boulevards lined with trees and apartment buildings through the seventeenth century fabric, turning it into an efficient bourgeois city. In the Ringstrasse in Vienna, the city walls were demolished and replaced by middle class housing, public buildings and parks. In Barcelona, the Medieval city was extended by Cerdà by means of an extensive regular grid of apartment buildings. In all these cases the initiative came from the central or municipal government using various techniques for raising capital. In London, between the 1840s and the 1870s there was also a huge expansion of middle class housing. In the richest suburbs, Belgravia and Kensington, regular tree-lined avenues lined with six-storey houses were built. Unlike similar projects on the continent, this was a purely private development carried out by a few aristocratic landowners. This fact explains its disjunction from the rest of the city but also its internal aesthetic unity, comparable in some ways to the extensions in Paris, Barcelona or Vienna with their greater degree of state or municipal intervention.

In Germany, after the unification of this country in 1870, there was also extensive legislation to control urban growth. And between 1880 and 1910 there were numerous competitions for the extension of cities like Cologne, Munich and Berlin, taking their cue from Paris and Vienna. Until the 1880s these developments in housing and in city planning took place within the parameters of an optimistic liberalism, using the rational, geometric road patterns inherited from the classical/baroque tradition. But in the 1880s a reaction set in against the prevailing spirit of rationalism and with it a new concept of city planning emerged.

One of the first signs of this new ideology was a book published in 1889 by the Austrian planner Camillo Sitte, entitled *City Planning According to Artistic Principles*. Sitte believed that the beauty of cities lay precisely in the improvised irregularities that resulted from successive historic accretions. Modern planners destroyed this meaningful pattern when they attempted to apply to the city the principles of scientific logic and regularity.

The Garden City Movement

The source of Sitte's ideas lay in the critique of Enlightenment rationalism that had been mounted by the Romantic Movement. The next important development in urbanism, the Garden City Movement, had the same roots. Ebenezer Howard, whose influential book, *Garden Cities of Tomorrow* launched the movement, was inspired by William Morris' utopian socialism and, more immediately, by Edward Bellamy's *Looking Backward*, which proposed a sort of Saint-Simonian state capitalism. Howard conceived garden cities as self-supporting towns surrounded by countryside and limited in size, which would progressively replace the large cities of industrial capitalism.

Howard's idea was converted into reality by the architect Raymond Unwin. At Letchworth, near London, Unwin dropped the idea of the self-supporting city, turning the garden city into a garden suburb. In this less revolutionary form it was to have a world-wide influence. Unwin's designs were based on the vernacular style of Phillip Webb, but it was Camillo Sitte's *Der Städtebau* that provided him with a theory of urban aesthetics.

The Garden City idea spread rapidly in Europe. In 1903, the Société des Cités Jardins was formed in France. The movement was supported by many French urbanists, notably by Georges Benoit-Lévy, and, in the context of an efficient French administrative apparatus, was adopted by official planning offices. But it was not until the 1920s that 16 such 'Garden Cities' were built on the outskirts of Paris. (These have since been completely engulfed by suburbia.)

The German Garden City movement was founded in 1902. It became identified with a widespread middle class reaction against liberal materialism and sought a return to the community values of the pre-industrial small town. The German movement grafted Schiller's concept of education through art onto Morris' utopian socialism, in the belief that good architecture would educate the masses in democracy and civic virtue. Two Garden Cities were built before the First World War—Hellerau, near Dresden in 1908, and Falkenberg, near Berlin, begun in 1912 and completed after the war. Hellerau, founded by the industrialist Karl Schmidt, was not a 'company town' in the normal sense, but an experimental self-governing community. The German movement, in spite of its genuinely utopian inspiration and its practical successes, was soon overtaken by the reactionary tide of *Volkisch* nationalism that swept over the country in the years leading up to the First World War.

It is hardly surprising that Ebenezer Howard's anti-city ideas should have originated in England, where free-for-all capitalism made the control of the city appear impossible. As I have indicated, the experience of the continent had been somewhat different. In France and Austria, and, after 1870, in Germany, highly centralised bureaucracies had developed limited techniques for controlling city growth, in the spirit of what Max Weber would later call "capitalist rationalisation", working within the framework of *laissez-faire* liberalism.

Between 1880 and 1930, however, this tradition of urban planning was radicalised. Not only in the countries in which techniques of urban planning had already been established, but also in England and America, those havens of *laissez-faire*, a new collectivist ideology emerged, and governments of all political colours began to play a role in the planning process. This movement was still ostensibly positivist in tone, but this concealed nostalgia for the pre-capitalist city. The debate on the city broadened, embracing the regionalist implications of the Garden City Movement. This change in professional and political attitudes can be exemplified by developments in England. The London County Council was established in 1888, and immediately set up an architects' department responsible for new housing developments. In 1909 a Housing and Town Planning Act was passed, and in the following year an International Town Planning Conference took place in London in which the most important city planners from the USA and Europe took part. These events marked a few years of world-wide optimism about the possibilities of world peace and social reform. Urban planners believed that, through a combination of rational planning and aesthetic norms, it would be possible once again to create cities of organic unity and social equilibrium.

Housing, Planning, and the Modernist Avant-garde

Almost simultaneously with the spread of the idea of urban planning, a new architectural ideology began to take root, that of avant-garde modernism. This movement, in the birth of which the Deutsche Werkbund played a dominant role, was predicated on the belief that the inexorable rise of modern technology had invalidated all attempts to base modern architecture on historical paradigms, such as those that had been applied by nineteenth century city planners like Josef Stübben, Camillo Sitte and Unwin. As Françoise Choay has shown, the idea that modern technology would revolutionise the city had been anticipated by Cerdà in the 1850s. But the idea now appeared in the form of a new aesthetic theory—one that was closely bound up with the rise of modernist art and the avant-gardist concepts of the *Zeigeist* and the *tabula rasa*. The new concept was to prove difficult to reconcile with an urbanism, which, in spite of its social utopianism, was still thought of in terms of typological continuity between new extensions of the city and the existing urban structure. The tension between these two contradictory formal ideas can be seen in the urban and housing projects that were inaugurated by Social Democratic governments in the 1920s. Taking the examples of Vienna, Weimar Germany and Holland, we see that each achieved its housing reforms on the basis of different and sometimes inconsistent concepts of the typological and stylistic relation between the new housing and the existing city.

In Vienna, with its Communist dominated Social Democratic government, the new housing consisted of very large perimeter blocks embedded in the centre of the city. The architectural typology of these blocks was relatively conservative, but their monumental scale made them stand out from the tradition of the city fabric as symbolic bastions of working class power, a fact taken advantage of by the workers in the short-lived Communist uprising in Vienna after the First World War.

In Weimar Germany, city governments were empowered to set up planning offices to execute large public housing programmes. These projects, which were mostly directed by avant-garde architects, consisted mainly of *Seidlungen* on the edges of cities. The traditional perimeter block and its post-war Viennese variant were rejected by many municipalities and replaced by regularly spaced linear blocks separated by communal gardens. A closed plan was replaced by an open plan, thus returning to an earlier spirit of rationalism. The new *Siedlungen* were intended as a critique of the existing city—above all the notorious *Mietkasernen*. But they did not go beyond their limited brief to suggest an urban alternative. They were suburban enclaves, distinct from—but still parasitically dependent on—the old city which they rejected.

In Holland, legislation giving the government power to expropriate land for social purposes was passed as early as 1890. Unlike in Germany, the new housing in Holland was seen as an integral part of the city structure. Well-known progressive architects were employed as chief planning officers, beginning with Berlage, who made extension plans for Amsterdam, The Hague and Purmerend between 1900 and 1911. Berlage was followed, after the First World War, by Dudok in Hilversum. JJP Oud in Rotterdam and Van Eesteren in Amsterdam. The city extensions which these architects presided over were based on the principal of typological continuity, and were within the tradition of urbanism that had grown up in the late nineteenth century. But Oud, after having built several housing schemes based on a perimeter block plan—such as Tusschendyken in Rotterdam, 1918–1921—began, in 1929, to experiment with modernist types that were against the grain of this tradition. These made important contributions to the modernist movement, but they represented a sharp break with the principle of continuity that Oud himself, as City Planner, had previously espoused.

The Post-Second World War Welfare State

After the Second World War, various kinds of Welfare State were introduced in Western Europe. The UK presents—at least in terms of its own tradition—the most radical example. Following legislation already introduced in the 1930s, and far-reaching proposals by the war-time coalition government, the post-war Labour government nationalised essential industries and services, and set up a national health service. In city planning, the recommendations of the Barlow Report of 1940 and Patrick Abercrombie's Greater London Plan of 1944 were adopted under the Town Planning Act of 1946. Strongly influenced by the regionalist ideas of Ebenezer Howard and Patrick Geddes, Abercrombie's plan proposed a halt to any further expansion of London and instituted a programme of regional dispersion in the form of self-sufficient new towns, to provide homes for people displaced by the redevelopment of the bombed out parts of the East End in central London. The English new towns became, for a time, planning models in Scandinavia and Italy, though the inadequacy of their small-town concept of social life and leisure soon became apparent. This regional policy was not accompanied by a coherent plan for the existing city. The LCC and the London boroughs implemented a programme of piecemeal replacement of bombed or dilapidated housing stock, made possible by new laws of municipal expropriation, but without any clear overall urban policy. The result was the fragmentary development consisting of a mixture of two-storey houses and Swedish-type high-rise point blocks. Thus, London's traditional fragmentary structure was sustained and even reinforced.

In France, the tradition of strong central government and the privileged national position allotted to Paris in the national economy, resulted in more coordinated and systematic approach to the post-war planning and housing in the French capital than in London, though it took longer to get off the ground. There has always been a clearer distinction between the city and the suburbs in Paris than in London, a distinction that was reinforced by the building of the ring road—the so-called *periferique*—as a symbolic boundary, replacing the real, defensive boundary. Within this boundary, development has been under strict control. In 1948, a policy of Grands Ensembles was launched to absorb the massive influx into the city, and this resulted in concentrations of high-rise slabs on rather large sites—the opposite of the fragmented English approach. However, the same degree of investment and planning was not applied to the suburbs, which are as chaotic as those of London. In 1965, as the result of a new policy of descentralisation, a national plan was put into effect for the creation of New Towns, 20 years after those of England. According to Tafuri, if French planning in this period had a defect, it was the tendency to create rigid laws to which innumerable exceptions then had to be made—exactly the opposite of English planning legislation, whose strengths (and weaknesses) lay in its very vagueness and flexibility.

Since the 1970s the European Welfare States have become modified under financial and economic pressure, and public building programmes have been progressively privatised or semi-privatised. Planning as a discipline has become increasingly abstracted from visible and symbolic forms—in other words from architecture, especially in the UK. Given these developments of late capitalism, how are we to assess the future of public housing policy? Faced with the failure of 150 years of urban planning to substantially alter the physiognomy of cities or to stem the tide of demographic and technical change, it is tempting to see the whole project of modern city planning as having been a colossal failure. This view would seem to be confirmed if we look at the evolution of the present day city from a global perspective. To take two random examples from the West: first, the original problem of migration from the country to the city within each state has been transformed into the problem of migration from developing to developed countries. Secondly, it becomes increasingly clear that the modern city must now be considered as co-extensive with whole regions—indeed, in small countries like Belgium, Holland and Switzerland, as co-extensive with the entire national territory. If we turn our attention from the West to the developing world, we see that in recent years cities have expanded with an unprecedented rapidity, under cultural conditions quite different from those originally faced in the West. In this situation, previous Western models are often useless.

But the failure of planning seems less catastrophic if we look at it with less utopian eyes—if we think of it as a series of attempts to manage the problems of the modern city as they arose: to make limited improvements, adding to the palimpsest of the existing city, but without ever transforming it as a whole, or trying to block the transformational momentum of late capitalism.

Looked at it this way, it might be said that the failure of modern planning is the failure of a mirage. The mirage was to ascribe to the modern age of technology a fixed totality or *Gestaltung* characteristic of pre-capitalist cultures. Especially since the onset of modernism, the chaos of the modern city has been opposed by a number of utopias. In the manner of all utopias, the city has been presented (in opposition to the real city, its 'other') as having an ideal order and stability, wrapped in a myth of past organicity and a logic of scientific rationality. Rather, we should see conflict and change as the normal condition of the cities of the late capitalist world. The main thing to realise is that planning must take place in a context of continuous technological and social change and in accordance with local conditions—a process which cannot be reversed but can, up to a point, be guided. This modifies the concept of planning, but it does not invalidate it. Perhaps planning can be imagined as a classic feedback problem of regulation, which, in human societies, means conscious foresight and adjustment.

References:

Bullock, Nicholas, and James Read, *The Movement for housing reform in Germany and France 1840–1914*, Cambridge University Press, 1985.

Choay, Françoise, *Le règle et le modèle: sur la théorie de l'architecture et de l'urbanisme*, Paris, 1980.

Collins, G and Ch C Collins, *Camillo Sitte: the Birth of Modern City Planning*, New York, 1986.

Dehaene, Michiel, *A Descriptive Tradition in Urbanism*: *Patrick Abercrombie and the Legacy of Geddesian Survey*, Leuven: Katholieke Universiteit, 2002.

Evenson, Norma, *Paris: a Century of Change, 1878–1978*, Yale, 1979.

Sebastian Marot ed., *Le Visiteur: ville, territoire, paysage, architecture*, Autumn 2000, Paris: Societe francaise des architects.

Sutcliffe, Anthony, ed., *The Rise of Modern Urban Planning, 1800–1914*, New York, 1980.

Manfredo, Tafuri, and Francesco Dal Co, *Modern Architecture*, London, 1980.

Teige, Karel, *The Minimum Dwelling*, Cambridge, MA: MIT Press, 2002.

Changing Museum

Given as a lecture at the Thyssen-Bornemisza Gallery, Madrid. Published in *Festschrift für Stanislaus von Moos*, Zürich, 2005.

"Museum" and "gallery"—these two words are often used interchangeably. Yet their modern use still reflects, if only faintly, their different etymologies. The word 'museum' originally meant the place where antiquities and objects of natural history were stored or displayed. The word "gallery", on the contrary, had a purely architectural meaning—that of a long covered space open on one side. In the late sixteenth century, the word began to be associated with a particular use—the display of works of art. More recently, a new gloss has been superimposed on these earlier meanings: the museum as a place that houses public art collections as opposed to the gallery, the site where works of art are offered for sale.

The changing meanings of these two terms overlap, but do not coincide. The one is concerned with objects considered to have unchanging cultural, even 'cult' value, the other with works of art in their relation to the world of social interaction and exchange. These different emphases point to a situation that has existed ever since the work of art has lost its exclusive ties with religious and aristocratic power. At this point, the work of art began to be severed from its architectural support and started its gradual transformation into an autonomous object. This split resulted in ambiguity as to the relation between the architectural container and the art it contained. For example, in the 1820s, a famous argument took place between Aloïs Hirt and Karl Friedrich Schinkel over the Altes Museum in Berlin, Schinkel called for the unity of architecture and art under the leadership of the former and the historian Hirt asserting that "art objects are not there for the museum; the museum is there for the objects".[1] The problem of the relation between the art object and its architectural frame re-emerged several times in the nineteenth century—from Lenoir's Musée National des Monuments Français in Paris, to the Pergamon-Museum in Berlin, where the question was that of authentic presentation of the object in relation to its supposed original context. Theodor W Adorno pointed to another aspect of the problem in his essay "Valéry Proust Museum", in which he reflected on the different reactions of Paul Valéry and Marcel Proust to the exhibiting of works in the abstract space of the modern museum.[2] For Valéry, to exhibit the work of art in a museum was to tear it from its living context and to deny its historical essence. For Proust, on the contrary, it was precisely the abstract context of the museum that ensured the work's immortality, opening it up to reinterpretation by successive generations of viewers.

Whatever their differences, Proust and Valéry both saw the work of art as concealing/revealing an ideal core of meaning. This idealist view was also fundamental to the modernist convention of the museum space as a white cube—the internal concave equivalent of its purist external envelope. Under modernism, the white surface—famously eulogised by Le Corbusier in his "Law of Ripolin"—was seen as the best background to the painting as a self-contained object.[3] The painting became an autonomous object within the museum space, just as the building, conceived as an 'object-type', was an autonomous object within the larger environment, its meaning entirely contained within its own form. The French architect Urban Cassan expressed this idea in 1930 when he said, "[Modern buildings], precisely because they are building types (*édifices-type*) must, through the true expression of their purpose and the harmony of their forms, be intrinsically beautiful."[4]

Although the white cube has survived today (if only by default), the philosophy on which it was implicitly based, ie. of the work of art as an autonomous object,

has fared less well, having been under attack for at least 50 years. Although this development has been the subject of much critical writing both in art and architecture, the two discourses have seldom been connected. It is only with the recent increase of museum building that the problem of the relation between a museum building and its artistic contents has resurfaced.

This paper will approach some aspects of the problem and attempt to reconnect the museum to its programmatic ground, or at least to enquire into what kinds of relationship may be said to hold between the two. It will be organised around three broad architectural categories. These categories are not 'types', nor are they intended to cover the whole range of contemporary museum design. They represent what appear to be three important and discrete, if often overlapping, tendencies in contemporary museum production, which can be summarised as:

The white cube (and its cognate, the object-type).
The Museum as found space.
The Museum as a work of art.

The White Cube

While most museums continue to display objects in white cubic spaces, few still reflect the broader notion of object-type. One notable exception is the Beyeler Collection in Basel by Renzo Piano, which is a remarkable consistent example of the object type.

The gallery plan is generated by a structural grid, in which some spaces are filled and some are left void to create a labyrinth of interconnecting white rooms. All external walls are opaque except those at the ends of the building, which are fully glazed, providing views into the garden (and into the gallery from the garden). The most characteristic feature of the building is the system of filtered day-lighting, which extends uniformly over the gallery ceiling. The appearance of this lighting system on the outside in the form of a saw-tooth roof profile gives the building much of its character. The building stands as a single pavilion and seems to fulfil perfectly Cassan's criteria for the object-type, which reveals its own function.

One further feature deserves attention: the division of the space into separate rooms. This is not uncommon in recent museums. Indeed it seems to have become something of a norm and is probably asked for by curators, at least in those galleries that consist of orthodox modernist collections. This compartmentalisation of the museum space breaks with the modernist concept of continuous, flowing space, as in Le Corbusier's Mundaneum museum or Frank Lloyd Wright's Guggenheim Museum in New York. In the Beyeler museum building, the effect of compartmentalisation is to some extent neutralised by the continuous nature of the roof light, which reasserts the museum's underlying spatial homogeneity. But in many museums of the 1980s (at the height of a classicising 'postmodernism') systems for roof lighting were used precisely to emphasise the uniqueness of each room—for instance in Isozaki's Museum of Modern Art in Los Angeles, in Venturi's Sainsbury Wing at the National Gallery and Stirling's Tate Gallery extension, both in London. An even greater insistence on the uniqueness of each individual room can be seen in Rafael Moneo's Museum of Modern Art in Stockholm where each room is emphasised externally as well as internally by a pyramidal roof with a lantern at its apex.

The Museum as Found Space

This paper is not concerned with the conversion of Palazzi or other monuments into the museums, which is so common in Italy and Spain. Rather, it is concerned with the adaptation for museum use of redundant nineteenth century industrial spaces—a practice that has increased exponentially in the last two or three decades. At one extreme, we find the kind of loft spaces characteristic of Soho in Manhattan and similar places in other cities, which display temporary exhibitions of works of art for sale. At the other extreme, there are the large industrial structures that have been used either to re-house or extend national collections or to provide space for changing exhibitions or mixed media events.

Although such converted spaces are usually a response to the demand for galleries in city-centre locations, they often conceal a deeper motivation: the ideological transformation of the programme of the museum itself. The abandoned industrial building provides not just a convenient and affordable space but also a specific type of space—one whose 'neutrality' is quite different from that of the white cube and depends on what one might describe as its state of innocence and its lack of artistic intention. Typically, the space consists of undivided, often top-lit sheds with exposed metal roof structures and widely spaced concrete or steel columns that allow complete flexibility of distribution. The Temporary Contemporary Museum in Los Angeles by Frank O Gehry, 1983, and the 'Magasin' gallery in Grenoble by Patrick Bouchain, 1985, are examples of this kind of space. This involves a subtle change in the relationship between the work of art and its environment, and a change from the contemplative attention of the viewer to one that is more relaxed but at the same time more engaged. These 'non-designed' industrial interiors are characterised by a material roughness that is—even when painted white—very different from the abstract and ideal nature of the white cube.

This spatial property would seem to be connected with the critique of the art object as autonomous that originally appeared as a strand of modernist theory, according to which the art object should become re-absorbed into the class of ordinary objects, as in Futurism, De Stijl, and Constructivism.

The same concept re-emerged in a different form at the end of the Second World War with the publication to Maurice Merleau-Ponty's book *Phénomenologie de la Perception*.[5] After its eventual translation into English 18 years later, it began to exert an influence on American Minimalist sculptors such as Richard Serra and Donald Judd.[6]

Opposite: Renzo Piano, Beyeler Collection, Basel 1992–1997. Interior.

Above: Patrick Bouchain, Le Magasin, Grenoble 1985, Interior.

A fundamental premise of Merleau-Ponty's book is the idea that the world is presented to the subject as a sequence of partial views in time. "The system of experience", he wrote, "is not arrayed before me as if I were God, it is lived by me from a certain point of view. I am not the spectator, I am involved."[7] The minimalists inferred from this the work of art should consist of nothing but the presentation of a simple perception or sequence of perceptions. It should be a single integrated object, not a composition of separate parts, and it should not assume any inner meaning beyond that given by this immediate perception. The corollary of this idea was that the viewing subject could not be thought of as being autonomous in a Cartesian sense. He is involved with the object of his perception.

How do these ideas fit with the work of Serra and Judd? Firstly, the fact that they are sculptors is important. While painting is abstracted from the immediate space of the viewer by its two-dimensionality, sculpture, being literally three-dimensional, is part of that space. It was precisely this *prima facie* assimilation of sculpture to the 'real' space occupied by the viewer that interested Minimalists of the 1960s like Robert Morris, Richard Serra, and Donald Judd in their attack on the High Modernist ideology of the autonomous work of art. In *Circuit*, 1972 by Serra, the object has become an arrangement of rectangular planes whose interest lies in the spaces they create. The space of the room is modified in such a way that the viewer is enticed to move bodily to the voided centre and explore the newly created space in its relation to the given boundaries of the room. Although Serra's contempt for the architect's white cube is well documented, he seems happy to accept it as a raw material to be controlled and modified. He treats every existing space, whether in a museum, a city, or in nature as a found space to be modified. It is interesting to contemplate the utterly destabilising effect Serra's work would have if placed in one of the calm and immaculate rooms of the Fondation Beyeler.

The affiliation with phenomenology in the work of Judd is perhaps less obvious than that of Serra. Judd has none of Serra's interest in the signs of basic technological processes. His objects show no traces of having been 'worked' or smelted. For Judd the artist's vision is not a *tabula rasa* but is part of a common cultural world already inscribed within social codes. It is through these codes that he finds a reductive, mass produced materiality in which all the signs of hand-work have been eliminated along with the last vestiges of artistic choice. His box-like, shiny and candy-coloured objects could almost be found in a supermarket. Much of this seems alien to Merleau-Ponty, though it should not be forgotten that Merleau-Ponty himself, towards the end of his life, struggled to incorporate Lévi-Strauss' Structuralist theory, according to which socially determined structures constitute an irreducible component of all phenomenal experience.

Judd had a definite idea of how his objects should be exhibited: "Almost all art for the last 30 years" he wrote, "has been shown in white plastered galleries vaguely derived from modern architecture [...]. This is an uncontested convention, not one demanded by the artist. It is a particular appearance, not a fact of nature. This is art seen in a commercial situation, not as it should be seen. The artwork should no longer be disembodied spatially and temporally as in most museums. The space around my work is crucial to it; as much thought has gone into the installation as the piece itself."[8]

To prove his point, Judd established a permanent collection of his work at Marfa, Texas, displaying it in converted aircraft sheds that are ostentatiously utilitarian and 'undesigned'. They are almost like 'facts of nature'. The sculptures rest directly on the floor or are attached to wall like enigmatic pieces of furniture or fittings from which all functionality has been drained. Convincing as these installations are in establishing a new continuity between the work of art and its environment, Judd's statements are not without inconsistencies. For example, the way he talks of 'facts of nature' and exhibits his work in a remote desert region suggest romantic, Thoreauesque affiliations that seem to contradict his typically anti-idealist stance.

Judd's museum spaces at Marfa are early cases of the museum as industrial found space but the sculptor was essentially concerned with the reception of his work by the private viewer, albeit a viewer no longer thought of as a transcendent subject. The museums that will now be discussed are, on the contrary, all concerned with the relation to the artwork of something like a collective mass subject, difficult as this concept is to pin down. The prototype of this type of museum space is undoubtedly the Centre Pompidou with its open loft spaces. But the Pompidou was a new building and its architects had to make a decision about style. The structure was represented as an open framework with strong industrial association, rhetorically animated with the 'natural signs' of mass movement. On the whole, contemporary architects, in using existing industrial buildings, tend to minimise their commitment to such public statements.

Three found-space museums will be discussed. In the first, the Tate Modern in London, Herzog & de Meuron have converted an enormous electrical power station dating from the 1930s into a museum to house temporary modernist exhibitions and the Tate Gallery's own collection of modern art. The original structure is a high basilica hall bisected by a row of widely spread giant steel stanchions. In Herzog & de Meuron's solution, one half of this dual space is tightly packed with the museum galleries and their supporting services (administration, bookshop, restaurant, etc.), while the other half has been left completely empty. This simple and seemingly rather banal distribution has the advantage of preserving the structural and spatial integrity of the original building. But it would also seem to have certain disadvantages. Compressing all the galleries within one half of the building has limited their size and has made any spatial flexibility virtually impossible. This is less of a problem in the case of the permanent collection, which is not very large, than in the case of the temporary exhibitions, which are the museum's chief strength. The voided half of the building, however, has turned out to be highly successful. The exposed steel structure preserves the tough quality of found industrial space, whilst

Opposite: Richard Serra, *Circuit*, 1972.

Above: Donald Judd, Marfa Gallery.

the lofty, top-lit hall itself serves simultaneously as a public forum and a site for large and spectacular installations. But in spite of these advantages, the resulting museum seems to be something of a political compromise between the didactic requirements of a conventional modern art collection and the desire for a new, sublime kind of popular space. This unresolved dichotomy of purpose is undoubtedly the result of the architect's decision to divide the building into two incommensurate halves.

In the second example—the Musée d'Orsay in Paris—the problem is not duality, which in the Tate Modern has at least the quality of being open and dynamic, but its static division into three. The rather *pompier*-like tripartite symmetry of the original *fin-de-siècle* railway terminal has been used by Gae Aulenti to emphasise the conservative connotation of a national collection. Not only this, in placing a purely rhetorical arrangement of 'forgotten' salon sculpture along the central axis, the architect has banished the painting galleries in the side isles and has created intractable problems of distribution and circulation.

In the third example—the Palais de Tokyo in Paris—the approach is exactly the opposite of that of the Musée d'Orsay.[9] Instead of 'remonumentalising' an industrial building as Gae Aulenti has done, the architects have 'demonumentalised' a monument. The Palais de Tokyo occupies the west wing of a museum sited between Avenue du President Wilson and the Seine. The building dates from the International Expositions of 1937 and was designed by the architects Dondel and Aubert, to provide a permanent home for two collections of modern art, one belonging to the nation, the other belonging to the city. It consists of two pavilions joined by a colonnade. The east wing of the building still contains the city collection, known as the Musée d'Art Moderne de la Ville de Paris, but the national collection in the west wing was moved to the Centre Pompidou in 1974. Since then the Ministry of Culture has rented out the vacant structure to various short-term uses, the most recent of which—a *Palais du Cinema*—was aborted when the process of stripping the Art Déco interior was about 90 per cent completed.

The present installation under the sobriquet "*Site de création contemporaine*" is scheduled to be replaced in 2005. It was devised by the art critic Nicolas Bourriaud and executed by architect Anne Lacaton and Philippe Vassal. Its main purpose is to house temporary exhibitions by young, unknown artists. The decision of the curator and the architects to leave the space exactly as they have found it was not only based on economics (though this surely must have been a consideration in an installation that was to be scrapped in three years); it was also a demonstration of the theory—pronounced by Bourriaud in his recent book *Esthétique rationale*—that the essence of art lies solely in the creation of relations between people, the forms of art themselves having no intrinsic value. Bourriaud's book makes no reference whatever to architecture and it is clear that for him architecture plays no constitutive role in establishing these conditions of artistic sociability. Yet, in fact, the partially dismantled space of the museum is marked everywhere by traces of the original *parti*. The found space, though it has a factory-like and provisional bareness about it, does not read as a disused factory but as what it actually is: a disused museum. This seems to challenge the iconoclastic pretensions of the architects. In claiming to naturalise the museum and transform it into a building site, the architects evidently never anticipated the extent to which the contingencies of the original Art Déco plan—its spatial idiosyncrasies and complexities—would affect the present installation.

The Museum as a Work of Art

In parallel with the museum as found space there has emerged its dialectical opposite—the museum as a work of art. Like the museum as found space, this

phenomenon has its socio-economic causes, ie., the increased reliance of state-run museums on private funding and the apparently inexhaustible public demand for museums (and not only art museums). In both cases, museum authorities stand to gain financially by creating 'landmark' buildings. The role of such buildings is to stand out from their urban surroundings. In classical Modernism, if new buildings conflicted with their urban context, it was because they claimed to set the tone for a future context (Le Corbusier's competition entry for the Palais de Tokyo is a convenient case in point).[10] Today, 'landmark' buildings stand in narcissistic isolation and refer to nothing but themselves.

One of the clearest examples of the museum as a work of art is Frank Gehry's Guggenheim Museum in Bilbao.[11] It will be discussed here under a number of sub-headings.

Gehry and the Use of the Computer

The Guggenheim Bilbao—together with the Disney Concert Hall in Los Angeles—is the culmination of a process of change in Gehry's style that began in the early 1980s.[12] Most of Gehry's commissions before that had been on a rather small scale and their programmes had been broken up into loose assemblages of simple architectural entities, often with subtle references to the local Los Angeles vernacular. With the Aerospace Museum of 1982 the architect faced the problem of adapting this additive architectural language to a large and complex public building that could not literally be broken up into separate pavilions. In order to avoid the impression of a huge monolith, he began to break up the facade of the building into shallow non-orthogonal facets, a process that eventually led to the more radical three-dimensional fragmentation of the Guggenheim Bilbao and Disney Concert Hall. Other architects were also experimenting with non-Euclidean geometries during these years. But in the Guggenheim, Gehry

Opposite top: Gai Aulenti, Musée d'Orsay, Paris. Interior.

Opposite bottom: Herzog & de Meuron, Tate Modern, London 1998–2000. Interior.

Above: Dondel and Aubert, Palais de Tokyo, Paris, 1937.

341

carried the process to its logical extreme by virtually dissolving large sections of the building into freeform sculptural fragments, a development made practicable by the systematic application of digital technology.

The computer programme CATIA used for the Guggenheim was developed by the French aerospace industry. Its role in the Guggenheim was very specific. It is concerned with the economics of constructing irregular surfaces, not with the generation of structural forms. The programme provides the contractor with information, enabling him to translate almost any surface into the scale of architecture and to do it quickly and cheaply enough to make it economically viable. In a sense, it does for irrational surfaces what Gaspard Monge's 'descriptive geometry' did for Euclidean surfaces in the early years of the Industrial Revolution.

The ability of the computer to locate every point on a carved surface does away with the need for rational comprehension on the part of the designer in conceiving, or the observer in perceiving, a building. Thanks to the computer, pure empiricism has no longer any practical need for the mediating grasp of the intellect. The maximum of an empirical nominalism coexists with the maximum of abstraction. The space between nominalism and abstraction is left void. The mind no longer needs to understand itself. After a long evolutionary detour, human thought returns to its primitive instinctual roots.

Empirical Structure

The structure of the Guggenheim has an empirical, not a rational logic. All it has to do is work. In this, Gehry's work differs from that of, for example, Calatrava, which, though equally 'expressionist', is always derived from the principles of rational construction. The structural system used by Gehry is that of the American balloon frame transformed into a closely spaced steel skeleton to which purlins are fixed to support the external membrane. In this sequence the outer profile (designed by the architect) determines the supporting structure (designed by the engineer). This sort of structure is analogous to that of an object such the Statue of Liberty, a giant anthropomorphic outer form supported on an *ad-hoc* skeleton. In the case of the Guggenheim (as indeed in the case of the Statue of Liberty) this structure is sometimes made visible from the inside, demystifying for the observer, in a frisson of surprise, the miracle of the exterior.

Relation of Outside to Inside

One of the most striking things about the Guggenheim Bilbao is the lack of visible connection between the outer forms and the interior volumes of the building. The visual logic of the one is different from the functional logic of the other. In one of his interviews, Gehry himself has insisted on the separation between the pragmatic organisation of his buildings and the imaginative creation of their external forms: "Solving all the functional problems is an intellectual exercise. That is a different part of my brain [from the creative part]. It is not less important, just different."[13] This is a laid-back snub to the old-style organicist "form follows function" argument (but who believes that anymore?). What is new is the bland switch to the other equally positivist extreme. In Le Corbusier there was also a split between practical interior arrangement and external Platonic form, but these were dialectically mediated. In Gehry there is no trace of dialectic; the separation is absolute, grounded on physiology— "a different part of my brain". The contemporary architect who is closest to Gehry in this empirical logic is Robert Venturi with his decorated shed.

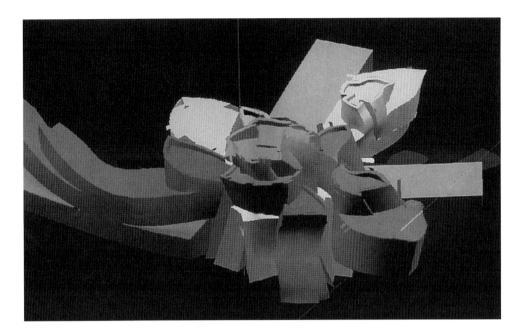
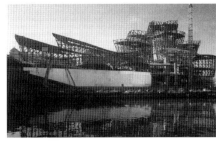

The Plan

The plan of the Guggenheim is somewhat rudimentary and consists of a central core from which a number of volumes radiate like the petals of a flower. These volumes consist of two different types—large free form galleries and conventional parallelepipeds containing sequences of small galleries and the administrative offices. This contrast between free-form volumes and parallelepipeds is a favourite theme in Gehry's later work, though the photographs usually concentrate on the free forms and seldom include the parallelepipeds. On plan, the galleries look like semi-independent organs or polyps stuck on to the core of the central multi-storey lobby. Each has its own economy of shape and size and is capable of growing to an enormous size, as in the case of the largest of the galleries, which reaches out to the road viaduct, crossing the site as if by some obscure magnetic attraction. This ad-hoc assembly is held together visually by the simplest of pyramidal compositions. The public enters directly into the central core, through the wedge of space between the two largest parallelepipeds. When one circulates between the galleries, it is impossible to move directly from gallery to gallery; one has to pass through the central core and start all over again. The core acts rather like the information centre in an airport or railway station. The plan is quite static; there is no overall *promenade architecturale*. The disconnection between the different galleries seems to be appropriate for parallel temporary exhibitions, which are historically or stylistically unrelated to each other and constitute a sort of supermarket of modern art.

The Building Considered as a Frame for Art

Most people seem to regard the Guggenheim Bilbao as a large sculpture and are impressed by its sensuous beauty and especially by its titanium surface, which caresses the eye with a sort of sumptuous, velvety dullness. There seems no reason to disagree with this consensus. But we should also be aware of its various, sometimes rather odd implications.

We usually, perhaps subliminally, imagine a building as in some sense 'framing' the activity that it contains. The idea of the building as a frame seems to be

Left: Frank O Gehry, Guggenheim Museum, Bilbao. Rendering.

Right top: Frank O Gehry, Guggenheim Museum, Bilbao.

Right bottom: Frank O Gehry, Guggenheim Museum, Bilbao 1997.

Sol Le Witt, Installations
Guggenheim Museum, 1998.

implied in the brief remarks in Kant's *Critique of Judgement*, where the *parerga* (this means accessories or trimmings, and Kant uses it in the sense of both frame and ornament) are spoken of in connection with works of art in general (including architecture) and are said to be supplementary to the work itself (the *ergon*, plural *erga*).[14] In a museum, the 'framed' activity is precisely that of displaying works of art. What happens if such a 'frame' starts claiming the status of a work of art in its own right? That which was different and supplementary suddenly becomes identical with what it contains. Something strange like this happens in the case of Gehry's Guggenheim, where the 'normal' protocols differentiating the genres of architecture and fine art are abandoned in favour of forms that are widely interpreted as sculptural. The problem of the transgression of legitimate boundaries of the genre has, of course, arisen before in architectural history, notably in the case of Borromini. If we raise it here, are we not reverting to a perennial neo-classical defensiveness? Or are we perhaps witnessing a state of unravelment altogether more radical than anything in past history—a rejection of the notion of 'boundary' as such? Yet, as we have seen, the contrast between rectangular order and 'un-form' is part of Gehry's own architectural vocabulary.

There is, however, a certain homology between the Guggenheim Museum and the art displayed within it. If we again take the Minimalist sculptors as an example, Gehry's building seems to share certain aspects of their phenomenological approach, that is the idea that there should be nothing more there than meets the eye, and a preference for paratactic formal structures as well as an emphasis on materiality and surface effects. Gehry's irregular and dynamically shaped galleries seem, indeed, to be eminently suitable sites for context specific works such as the temporary mural that Sol Le Witt installed in the gallery in 1998.

Yet we should not ignore certain differences between Gehry's approach and that of the Minimalists. These differences probably have much to do with the fact that architecture and sculpture have different relations of scale to the human body. The calligraphic and gestural forms of Gehry's architecture would probably be rather uninteresting, if reduced to the normal scale of sculpture. With their reliance on an idealist concept of artistic inspiration and spontaneity they might even seem old fashioned compared to the work of sculptors like Morris, Serra or Judd.

I began this paper by referring to the different meanings of 'museum' and 'gallery'. The museum, I suggested, is connected with the maintenance of permanent values, while the gallery partakes of the changing values of the market place. But I failed to mention one obvious point. These differences were complementary. The market value of the work tended to be stabilised by the canons established in the museum, while the museum itself was continuously revising its values in response to the art market. A kind of balance existed between the two.

This relatively stable relation between the museum and the gallery has not survived late capitalism and mass society. There is no longer a commonly held notion of the value of works of art outside a specialised an idiotically inflated art market. That being the case, it would seem that the museum has lost much of its *raison d'être*. Why, then, does the public flock to it in ever greater numbers? It must surely be because it constitutes a *new* public—one shaped by universal education, leisure and, above all, by the information media. This public is not part of the art market. Nor is it a minority that seeks from the museum confirmation of its consecrated values. It is a fundamentally new phenomenon and one that awaits definition. The three kinds of contemporary museum/gallery that I have discussed seem, in their heterogeneity, to be the product of the modern museum's thoroughly ambiguous cultural status.

1   Crimp, Douglas "The End of Art and the Origin of the Museum", *Art Journal*, 46, 1987, p. 263, cited in Can Bilsel, SM, *Architecture in the Museum*, Princeton University, unpublished PhD thesis, 2003.
2   Adorno, Theodor W, "Valéry Proust Museum", *Prisms*, Cambridge MA: MIT Press, 1967, pp. 173–187.
3   Corbusier/Jeanneret, Charles-Edouard, *L'art decorative d'aujourd'hui*, Paris, 1925; English edition: *The Decorative Art of Today*, London, The Architectural Press, 1987, pp. 185–192.
4   Cassan, Urban, "Hommes, Maisons, Paysages" Paris, 1930, cited in *Le Temps des Gares*, exhibition catalogue Centre Georges Pompidou, Paris, 1978, p. 54.
5   Merleau-Ponty, Maurice, *Phenomenologie de la Perception*, Paris, 1944; English edition: *Phenomenology of Perception*, London, 1962
6   Krauss, Rosalind E, *Passages in Modern Sculpture* and *The Originality of the Avant Garde and other Modernist Myths*, Cambridge MA: MIT Press, 1981, pp. 239–240 and pp. 267–270; Potts, Alex, *The Sculptural Imagination*, New Haven, CT: Yale University Press, 2000, pp. 207–234.
7   Merleau-Ponty, *Phenomenologie de la Perception*, p. 304.
8   Donald Judd, quoted in Potts, *The Sculptural Imagination*, p. 308.
9   Didelon, Valéry, "Economie de l'architecture: à-propos de la rénovation du Palais de Tokyo", in *Le Visiteur 6, Les Editions de l'Imprimeur* no. 9, Paris, Autumn 2002, pp. 6–19.
10 See Le Corbusier et Jeanneret, Pierre, *Oeuvre Complete*, vol. 3, 1934–1938; Bill, Max (ed.), *Les editions d'Architecture*, Zurich, Artemis, 1947, pp. 82–89.
11 See van Bruggen, Coosje & Gehry, Frank O, *Guggenheim Museum, Bilbao*, New York, Solomon R Guggenheim Foundation 1997–1998.
12 See Quaderni, Mirko Zandini ed., "Frank O Gehry: America come contesto", *Lotus 20*, Milan: Electa, 1994.
13 cited in van Bruggen, *Guggenheim Museum, Bilbao*.
14 Kant, Immanuel, "Analytic of the Beautiful", *Critique of Judgement*, para. 14, 2nd edition. "What we call ornaments (*parerga*) ie. those things that do not belong to the complete representation of the object but only externally as complements, and which augment the satisfaction of taste, do so only by their form; as, for example, the frames of pictures, the draperies of statues, or the colonnades of palaces."

Index

© 2009 Black Dog Publishing Limited, London, UK and the authors.
All rights reserved.

Designed by Matthew Pull at Black Dog Publishing.

Black Dog Publishing Limited
10A Acton Street
London WC1X 9NG
United Kingdom

T + 44 (0) 207 713 5097
F + 44 (0) 207 713 8682

info@blackdogonline.com
www.blackdogonline.com

ISBN: 978 1 906155 20 9
British Library Cataloguing-in-Publication Data.
A CIP record for this book is available from the British Library.

Black Dog Publishing Limited, London, UK, is an environmentally
responsible company. *Collected Essays in Architectural Criticism*
is printed on Sappi Magno Satin, an FSC certified paper.

All rights reserved. No part of this publication may be reproduced, stored
in a retrieval system, or transmitted, in any form or by any means, electronic,
mechanical, photocopying, recording, or otherwise, without prior permission
of the publisher.

Unless otherwise credited images are reproduced from original sources supplied
by the author. The publisher would like to thank Kenneth Frampton, Michael
Graves, Herman Hertzberger, and Robert and Denise Venturi for permission
to reproduce material used in this publication.

Every effort has been made to trace the copyright holders, but if any have
been inadvertently overlooked the necessary arrangements will be made
at the first opportunity.

architecture art design
fashion history photography
theory and things

www.blackdogonline.com